Land Transactions and Finance

BLACK LETTER OUTLINES

Land Transactions and Finance

by Grant S. Nelson
Professor of Law
University of California, Los Angeles

Dale A. Whitman
Professor of Law
University of Missouri-Columbia

FOURTH EDITION

THOMSON
WEST

Mat #40188263

COPYRIGHT © 1983, 1988 WEST PUBLISHING CO.
COPYRIGHT © 1998 WEST GROUP
© 2004 West, a Thomson business
   610 Opperman Drive
   P.O. Box 64526
   St. Paul, MN 55164–05261
   800–328–9352

ISBN 0–314–15043–9

 PRINTED ON 10% POST CONSUMER RECYCLED PAPER

Summary of Contents

APPENDICES

App.

*

Table of Contents

APPENDICES

*

Capsule Summary

■ I. CONTRACTS FOR THE SALE OF LAND

Most real estate transfers are preceded by contracts of sale. Some period of time, typically thirty to ninety days, transpires between the contract's execution and the "closing" or transfer of title. Contracts of this type are often termed "earnest money contracts."

A. THE STATUTE OF FRAUDS

1. Requirement of Writing

The Statute requires that the contract "or some memorandum or note thereof" be in writing. Some cases dispense with the requirement if the party resisting enforcement of the contract admits its existence.

2. Multiple Pieces of Paper

The writing may be shown by more than one piece of paper, so long as all of the essential elements are present in the papers considered together.

3. Consequences of a Lack of Writing

If there is no sufficient writing, neither party can enforce the contract, either at law for damages or in equity for specific performance. However, the contract is not void (by the majority view) and it may be the basis for an action for rescission and restitution.

4. Elements Which the Writing Must Contain

In general, the following elements are necessary: (1) the names of the parties or some other identification of them; (2) an identification of the land; and (3) words indicating an intent to sell the land. The price need not be mentioned if the parties did not agree on one; the court will assume that a reasonable price was intended. If the price was agreed to, most recent cases require it to be included in the writing. The date of closing need not be included even if the parties agreed to a date. If no date was agreed to, the court will assume that a reasonable time after the contract signing was intended.

5. The Signature

Most American statutes require the writing to have been signed by "the party to be charged"—that is, the person who is resisting its enforcement in the lawsuit.

B. RESCISSION AND MODIFICATION

1. Oral Rescission

The courts nearly always enforce oral rescissions, on the ground that the parties' action has not created (but rather, has eliminated) a contract for the sale of land, and hence, does not fall within the statute.

2. Oral Modifications

If a new contract, as orally modified, would fall within the Statute of Frauds, courts conclude that the new contract cannot be enforced; the old contract (if supported by a writing) is still in effect.

3. Enforcing Oral Modifications by Estoppel

If a party detrimentally relies upon an oral modification, the other party may be estopped from enforcing the original contract terms.

C. THE PART PERFORMANCE DOCTRINE

Part performance is a judicially-created exception to the Statute of Frauds, and permits courts to enforce a contract in equity even though there is no sufficient writing to satisfy the Statute.

1. Acts of Part Performance

Three types of acts (all by the purchaser) are generally recognized by the courts: (1) payment of all or a substantial part of the purchase price; (2) taking possession of the property; and (3) making substantial improvements on the land. Most courts require a combination of at least two of the acts listed above, and a few courts require all three. A number of recent cases have accepted acts of reliance on the contract other than these three.

2. Rationales for Part Performance

a. The Evidentiary Rationale

Courts following this theory regard part performance as a substitute for the evidence which a writing would provide, and thus see the acts as justifying enforcement of the contract. Cases taking this approach usually say that the acts of part performance must be "unequivocally referable" to the contract—that is that they cannot be explained on any ground other than the existence of a contract.

b. Estoppel

Courts which use this approach to part performance focus on the unfairness to the party who claims that a contract exists but who cannot enforce it because of a lack of a writing.

c. Mixing the Two Theories

Some courts seem to invoke both an evidentiary and an estoppel theory of part performance, without clearly electing one approach or the other.

d. Which Party Can Use Part Performance

Courts using an evidentiary approach sometimes permit either party to use the purchaser's acts as evidence of the existence of a contract. Courts which follow the estoppel theory, on the other hand, generally hold that only a purchaser can use the purchaser's acts of part performance to overcome the lack of a writing.

e.   Enforcement in Equity Only

The general rule is that the part performance doctrine is unavailable in an action at law.

D.   REMEDIES FOR BREACH OF A REAL ESTATE CONTRACT

1.   Damages

The general measure of "loss of bargain" (expectation) damages is the difference between the contract price and the market value of the land on the date of the breach.

a.   Events Occurring After the Breach

In general, changes in value of the real estate which occur after the date of breach are irrelevant.

b.   Good Faith Failure of Title

About half of the American courts limit the purchaser to rescission and restitution, and refuse to grant the purchaser loss-of-bargain damages, if the seller's breach is a result of a title failure which was not a product of the seller's bad faith.

c.   Special Damage Recovery

In addition to loss-of-bargain damages, a non-breaching party may recover additional damages of several types if the necessary facts can be shown. These types include: (1) expenditures in reliance on the contract, such as title search and survey costs; (2) lost profits; and (3) increased interest expense. If the land is subject to a title defect or is smaller in area than represented, the purchaser may decide to proceed with the sale anyway, and may then claim damages to compensate for the discrepancy or shortage.

2.   Liquidated Damages and Retention of Deposit

In the great majority of land contracts, the purchaser makes an earnest money deposit of funds with the seller or seller's real estate broker.

a. **Liquidated Damages or Forfeiture?**

Courts usually purport to decide whether the retention of the deposit would be a valid liquidation of damages or an invalid penalty or forfeiture. The majority of cases focus on whether the earnest money amount constituted a reasonable estimate of the probable actual damages. Amount up to 10% of the price are routinely upheld.

b. **Preclusion of Other Remedies**

Most cases hold that the presence of a liquidated damages clause bars recovery of actual damages unless the contract specifically provides to the contrary. Such a clause normally will not bar specific performance unless the clause makes it very clear that retention of the deposit was regarded by the parties as the seller's only remedy.

c. **Election of Remedies**

Courts commonly require the seller to elect to retain or return the deposit within a short time after the breach has occurred: if the deposit is not returned, they may well conclude that the seller is barred from seeking other remedies.

3. **Specific Performance**

Either the vendor or purchaser may generally obtain an order for specific performance compelling the other party to complete the contract.

a. **Rationale—Property Unique**

Specific performance is generally justified on the ground that real property is unique, and that the remedy at law (damages) is thus always inadequate. While this reasoning is sensible when a *purchaser* seeks specific performance, some courts are becoming less inclined to permit a *seller* to utilize this rationale for specific relief, especially if the seller is a developer holding a large number of similar parcels or units for sale.

b. **Circumstances Under Which Specific Performance is Unavailable**

Specific performance will not be ordered by a court where: (1) the seller lacks title; (2) the contract itself excludes specific performance as a remedy; (3) the property was purchased simply for resale (split of authority).

c.   **Fairness and Vagueness**

Courts frequently impose a higher standard of contract specificity when asked to specifically enforce a contract than when asked to award damages. Moreover, it is widely held that a contract ought not to be specifically enforced if enforcement would be unjust or unfair. The injustice need not rise to level of fraud or deception, but may simply be overreaching or harsh dealing.

d.   **Damages in Addition to Specific Performance**

Where a long time has elapsed since the originally agreed closing date, this delay may have well cost the plaintiff significant amounts of money. Consequently, a court will often award damages in addition to entering a decree of specific performance.

4.   **Vendor's Lien**

Equity courts recognize an implied lien, similar to a mortgage, in favor of the vendor for the unpaid portion of the purchase price on land. While this lien has little practical value to the vendor prior to the transfer of title, it is of greater significance once legal title has been transferred to the vendee. Even here, however, because the vendor usually obtains some more specific security device, such as a mortgage or deed of trust, reliance on the vendor's lien is still relatively uncommon. Since the lien is equitable in nature, it will generally be unenforceable if the land has been acquired by a bona fide purchaser for value.

5.   **Restitution**

The term restitution indicates that a party to a contract has received from the other party something which the latter paid in or contributed at some prior stage in the contract's life. Restitution occurs most commonly in connection with rescission of the contract.

a.   **Relationship to Rescission**

One meaning of the term "rescission" is a voluntary agreement between the parties under which they agree to "unwind" the contract with each returning to the other whatever has been paid or contributed and with no further obligation on either to perform. A second meaning is that rescission is an order of a court which places the parties back in the positions which they held before the contract was entered into. The latter is a judicial remedy available for contract breach.

b. Restitution is a Mutual Remedy

One who seeks and obtains restitution must also be willing to give restitution to the other party.

6. Vendee's Lien

When a purchaser properly demands restitution, the courts recognize an equitable lien in the purchaser's favor to aid in recovery of restitutionary damages. This lien must be foreclosed judicially, and cannot be asserted against a bona fide purchaser.

E. TIME OF PERFORMANCE

If time has not been made "of the essence", even a party who tenders a late performance may still enforce the contract so long as he or she is not unreasonably late. If time is deemed to be of the essence, a late tender of performance by one party is a material breach, and fully excuses the other from performing. However, even if time is of the essence, courts often find waivers of strict performance from oral or written statements or from the surrounding circumstances.

F. CONDITIONS IN REALTY SALES CONTRACTS

A condition may be entirely outside the control of the parties, or it may depend on some action by one of the parties. In the latter situation, courts frequently infer a duty on the party who must take action to use good faith efforts to make the condition occur.

1. Precedent and Concurrent Conditions

A condition precedent is one which must occur before a party has a duty of performance. A concurrent condition is one which is expected to occur simultaneously with the party's performance.

2. Waiver of Conditions

If a condition is for the sole benefit of one party, that party may waive it and proceed to enforce the contract.

3. Concurrent Conditions and Tender

The "closing" of the contract usually involves the delivery of a deed by the seller and the payment of the purchase money by the buyer. These performances are usually regarded as concurrent conditions, so that neither party is obligated to perform unless and until the other party has tendered his or her own performance.

4. Circumstances Excusing Tender

Tender is unnecessary when: (a) the opposing party has clearly repudiated the contract; (b) other circumstances make it obvious that the opposing party is unwilling to perform; (c) the opposing party's evasive conduct has made a tender difficult or impossible; or (d) the opposing party's performance has become impossible.

G. QUALITY OF TITLE

Unless the parties agree to the contrary, the law will infer in every sales contract a covenant that the vendor's title must be "marketable."

1. Marketable Title

A marketable title need not be a perfect title, but rather one that is free from all reasonable risks of attack and would be acceptable to a reasonable purchaser.

2. Types of Title Defects

Almost any defect which may prevent the vendor from transferring a fee simple absolute title can impair marketability.

a. Flaws in the Chain of Ownership

A title may be unmarketable, for example, because some conveyance in the chain of title is forged, undelivered, obtained by fraud or duress, or executed by a minor.

b. **Encumbrances**

Encumbrances that may make title unmarketable include outstanding leases, restrictive covenants, mortgages, easements, party wall agreements, options, contracts of sale, and various types of liens.

c. **Actions Depriving the Vendor of Title**

A vendor may have lost his or her interest, for example, to an adverse possessor or to the government by eminent domain.

d. **Other Matters Making Title Unmarketable**

Other types of defects not usually thought to relate to title as such have nevertheless been treated by some courts as rendering title unmarketable. They include encroachments by improvements on the subject property on a neighboring parcel or vice versa, and existing violations of zoning ordinances.

3. **Timing of Marketable Title**

The title need not be marketable until the date fixed for transfer of legal title. Some recent cases, however, have given the purchaser the right of rescission prior to closing if it appeared very unlikely that the vendor could cure the title defects.

4. **Merger**

Once a deed has been delivered and accepted, the contract's covenants of title are said to be "merged into the deed" and can no longer be the basis of legal action.

5. **Relation of Title Covenants to the Deed**

The fact that a contract contains covenants of title does not dictate the type of deed which may be used. Thus a contract clause stating that title will be marketable does not mean that a warranty deed must be delivered. Normally the contract will state what type of deed is to be used and, if no statement is made, the courts will usually look to local practice and custom.

H. EQUITABLE CONVERSION

1. **Origin of the Doctrine**

English equity courts began treating the real estate contract, during its executory period, as if it had already been performed for some purposes. As a consequence, under the doctrine of Equitable Conversion, the vendor's interest is deemed to be personal property and the purchaser's interest is considered real estate, even though no closing has yet occurred. Most American states follow this doctrine.

2. **Characterization Upon the Death of Party**

   a. **Death of the Vendor**

   If the vendor dies, the "bare" legal title descends to the vendor's heirs or devisees, but they hold it subject to a duty to convey to the purchaser. The proceeds of sale, however, ultimately are turned over to the legatees or next of kin—the recipients of the vendor's personal property. In intestate succession situations, the heirs and next of kin are usually the same persons. But if the vendor left a will, the application of equitable conversion means that the legatees, and not the devisees, will receive the contract purchase price. In some circumstances, however, the equitable conversion result has been modified or rejected by statute or judicial decision.

   b. **Death of the Purchaser**

   The right to acquire the land under the contract passes as realty to the purchaser's heirs or devisees. Many courts apply the principle of "exoneration" which requires the purchase price to be paid out of the personal property assets of the estate, thus reducing the amount received by legatees or next of kin.

3. **Claims of Judgment Creditors**

   In most states, a statute provides that a judgment becomes a lien upon the defendant's real property in the county where the judgment is docketed. When the judgment is against the purchaser, the great majority of states apply equitable conversion and subject the purchaser's interest to the judgment lien. When the judgment is against the vendor, there is a fairly even split of authority, with a slight majority permitting the lien to attach (since the vendor still has legal title), while the minority apply equitable conversion and treat the vendor's interest as personal property to which no lien attaches.

4. **Risk of Loss**

   Under equitable conversion, the purchaser is regarded as the owner of the property during the executory period of the contract, and therefore bears the risk of casualty loss (e.g., fire). If a loss occurs during the executory period, the purchaser must nonetheless pay the full purchase price. Some courts have also applied equitable conversion to non-casualty losses in value, such as a zoning change or the filing of an eminent domain action. There has been considerable criticism of the use of equitable conversion in this context. A sizeable minority of states have modified or rejected equitable conversion in the context of risk of loss.

5. Impact of Casualty Insurance

a. Vendor Insured, Risk on Purchaser

In this situation courts generally permit the vendor to enforce the contract only if he or she is willing to abate the price to the extent of any insurance recovery. This gives the purchaser the benefit of the insurance indirectly.

b. Purchaser Insured, Risk on Vendor

A purchaser may attempt to collect the insurance proceeds and at the same time avoid his or her contract of purchase. Many cases allow the insurer to avoid paying the claim on the ground that the purchaser has no loss and, therefore there is nothing for the insurer to indemnify. Where the insurance company has already paid the claim, several states have adopted the argument that the insurance was intended for vendor's benefit as well even though the vendor was not named as an insured in the policy.

6. Time of Conversion

Equitable conversion, where applicable, does not occur until there is a fully formed and enforceable contract of sale. On the other hand, if the contract is enforceable at the critical time (the loss, death of a party, etc.), it does not matter if the contract is later rescinded or abandoned. While there is considerable dicta in the cases that no conversion occurs until all conditions of the contract have been fulfilled, this is often disregarded in practice and a conversion found despite the presence of unfulfilled conditions.

■ II. CONVEYANCES AND TITLES

A. THE DEED

In early English history, a transferor of land met with the transferee on or within sight of the land itself, and handed over a twig or clod while reciting to witnesses that the transfer was being made. This was referred to as "feoffment with livery of seisin."

1. Early Antecedents of the Deed

a. The Grant

Even in very early times, non-possessory interests and non-freehold interests were transferred by a written instrument under seal.

b. The Lease and Release

Under this process a common law conveyor would first grant a lease to the conveyee of short duration and then, immediately thereafter, would transfer his or her reversion to the conveyee by means of a second grant, termed a release.

c. The Bargain and Sale Deed

If a contract for the sale of land did not indicate that further payment was to be made, the English courts interpreted the Statute of Uses as placing legal (and not merely equitable) title in the purchaser. This form became known as the "bargain and sale deed."

d. The Covenant to Stand Seized

If a land owner made a promise to hold the land for the use of another person to whom he was related by blood or marriage, the English courts applied the Statute of Uses to treat the equitable title in the hands of the conveyee as a legal title.

2. Writing Required

In modern law, the Statute of Frauds requires a conveyance to be in writing, so livery of seisin is no longer a valid means of transferring title.

3. **Elements of a Deed**

Deeds must contain much the same information as contracts of sale: identification of the parties, description of the land, some words indicating a present intent to convey, and the grantor's signature. No consideration need be given or recited, although recitation of consideration is very common.

   a. **Grantee's Name in Blank**

   While normally a deed with no grantee's name is void, many courts uphold such deeds once the person to whom the deed is delivered has inserted his or her name.

   b. **Non-Existent Grantee**

   If the grantee does not exist, the deed is void.

4. **Construction of Deeds**

   a. **Extrinsic Evidence**

   While many old cases state that extrinsic evidence can be considered only if ambiguity in the language of a deed is "latent" rather than "patent," many modern courts now admit extrinsic evidence whether the ambiguity is latent or patent.

   b. **Easement or Possessory Interest**

   Courts often have difficulty determining whether language which describes and conveys a highway or railroad right-of-way is a possessory estate or only an easement.

   c. **Reservations and Exceptions**

   A reservation is language which creates in the grantor a new interest in the land which did not exist independently before he made the deed. An exception is the retention by the grantor of some interest which existed previously, such as a certain physical part of the land.

5. **Defects in Deeds**

   a. **Reformation**

   If a deed does not accurately reflect the intention of one of the parties, equity will reform it if the other party was also under a mistake or was guilty of fraud, other inequitable conduct, or even silence in the face of knowledge of the error.

b. The Void–Voidable Distinction

A void deed will be set aside even as against a subsequent BFP, while a merely voidable deed will not.

c. Defects Rendering Deed Void

Forgery, lack of delivery, and fraud in the execution almost always render a deed void.

d. Defects Rendering a Deed Voidable

Defects which make a deed only voidable include fraud in the inducement, insanity, lack of capacity, duress, undue influence, mistake, and breach of fiduciary duty.

6. Land Descriptions

a. Metes and Bounds

A metes and bounds description is one which individually describes every line which is part of the parcel's boundaries.

b. The Government Survey System

This system was adopted by Congress in 1785, and most land outside the original colonies has been surveyed under it. It divides the surface into townships (each 36 square miles, 6 miles on a side) and each township into 36 sections (each one square mile).

c. The Plat

A plat is a map which meets certain standards of format and accuracy, is legally approved by some government agency, and is filed as a permanent record in the local recording office.

d. Monuments

Land descriptions commonly use references to monuments, such as streets, trees, rivers, or walls which have a certain width. Title normally passes to the monument's center line.

e. Accretion and Reliction

A river or stream which is the boundary of land may shift its location gradually over time. If this occurs slowly by accretion or reliction, the additional land becomes the property of the abutting owner. If the change in the stream's location is by avulsion (a rapid change), the boundaries of the abutting owners are not affected.

f.   Priorities in Interpretation

Sometimes a description contains conflicting information about a boundary line. The usual priorities in interpreting a deed are as follows: 1. natural monuments; 2. artificial monuments and marked and surveyed lines; 3. adjacent tracts or boundaries; 4. courses or directions; 5. distances; 6. area or quantity.

B.   DELIVERY, ACCEPTANCE, AND ESCROW OF DEEDS

1.   Delivery and Intent

Delivery does not necessarily require the manual handing over of the deed to the grantee. The critical question is whether the grantor has done some act with intent to make the deed *presently* operative.

2.   Deeds as Will Substitutes

Often, a grantor will attempt to use a deed as the equivalent of a will, attempting to reserve the right to revoke it until death. Such deeds are frequently invalidated because the grantor lacks an intent to make an *immediate* transfer.

3.   Conditional Deliveries

The majority view is that the grantor may not impose oral condition upon the delivery of a deed; such conditions are ignored and the delivery is considered absolute.

4.   Deeds Conveying Future Interests

A deed conveying a future interest can be made conditional upon the happening of a future event if the terms constituting the condition are spelled out in the deed itself.

5. Acceptance

Delivery is not complete unless the grantor accepts the deed.

6. Escrows

In a general sense, an escrow is the entire arrangement under which an instrument such as a deed is deposited with some custodian with instructions that it should be delivered to another party (such as the grantee) on the occurrence of some future condition.

a. Relation Back

When the conditions of an escrow are fulfilled and the deed is delivered to the grantee by the escrow agent, the delivery "relates back" to the time the deed was handed to the custodian.

b. Unauthorized Delivery by Escrow Agent

If an escrow agent delivers the deed to the grantee even though some conditions are unsatisfied, the delivery is ineffective and no title passes to the grantee.

c. Death Escrows

Where the escrow is made conditional upon the grantor's death, the delivery out of escrow will relate back (and thereby be valid despite the grantor's intervening incompetence, for example) even though there is no underlying contract. Moreover, the courts often say that the delivery of the deed to the escrow agent passes immediate title to a future interest to the grantee.

d. Duties of Escrow Agents

The escrow agent owes a duty of reasonable care and skill to both grantor and grantee and is a fiduciary in the narrow sense that he or she must carry out the escrow instructions with complete fidelity and accuracy.

7. Estoppel by Deed

Most modern cases hold that a grantor who delivers a deed while having no title, but who subsequently obtains a valid title to land, will be estopped to deny that the title belongs to the grantee.

a. Type of Deed

The estoppel doctrine works only if the deed given by the grantor contains some representation about the quality of the title being conveyed.

b. Preclusion of Other Remedies

The grantee who does not want the title to inure to him or her has the option to pursue an action for damages for breach of a covenant of title in the deed.

c. Rights of BFP's

Suppose that, after receiving the title, the grantor makes a second deed to a bona fide purchaser. In a jurisdiction which indexes its public records by the name of the party, the first deed is quite difficult for the second grantee to find, since the second grantee must search in the grantor index for years earlier than the year in which the grantor obtained title. Consequently, the majority of courts considering the question have treated the first deed as unrecorded, so that the subsequent grantee may treat it as void under the recording acts. This reasoning is inapplicable in a tract-index jurisdiction.

C. PRACTICAL LOCATION OF BOUNDARIES

1. Boundaries by Agreement

Parties may fix their boundary by an explicit (though oral) agreement if they are uncertain or unaware of the correct location or a dispute as to the true location exists between them. They must mark their agreed line on the ground.

2. Boundaries by Acquiescence

Adjacent owners may make a marked line their boundary by long-term recognition and acceptance of it. Generally speaking, silence by one party in the face of the other's action (as by erecting a fence) is sufficient acquiescence. Courts often require the acquiescence to continue for the adverse possession period.

3. Boundaries by Estoppel

If one owner misrepresents to the other the location of a boundary between them, and if the second relies on those representations and takes detrimental action, the party who represented the line's location is estopped to deny its accuracy, and the boundary is shifted accordingly.

4. Boundary by Common Grantor

When a grantor erroneously marks a line on ground described by lot numbers and sells parcels by reference to that line, purchasers must regard the line as binding notwithstanding its incorrect location.

D. DEDICATION

1. Acts of Dedication

An offer to dedicate may be found from a variety of actions, such as an oral statement by the owner or the filing of a map or plat in which certain areas are marked and dedicated to the public.

2. Type of Interest Dedicated

The dedicating party can specify the interest being transferred. In the absence of such an explicit statement, courts will determine the party's probable intent.

3. Acceptance

Acceptance can be found from local government's taking over of maintenance or construction of improvements on the land, from approval of a plat which shows areas marked for public use, or by long or substantial public use of the land.

E. COVENANTS OF TITLE

While a "quitclaim" deed expressly refutes the existence of all covenants of title, a "warranty" deed contains certain covenants concerning the quality of the title it conveys.

1. **Distinctions Between Contract and Deed Covenants**

   Several important difference exist between the implied covenant of marketable title in contracts of sale and those in deeds. First, the deed covenants take effect only when the deed is delivered, and at that point the contract's covenants are "merged into the deed." Second, the deed covenants are violated only by an actual defect of title, not a mere risk or doubt about title quality. Third, the only remedy for violation of a deed covenant is damages, while contract covenants may also give rise to rescission or specific performance with partial abatement of the price.

2. **Present Covenants**

   Three of the traditional title covenants are termed "present" because they are violated, if at all, only at the moment the deed containing them is delivered. The present covenants are as follows:

   a. Covenant of Seisin

   b. Right to Convey

   c. Covenant Against Encumbrances

3. **Future Covenants**

   These covenants are considered violated only when the grantee or a successor grantee is "evicted" or disturbed in his possession by the person claiming the outstanding interest. The future covenants are as follows:

   a. Warranty and Quiet Enjoyment

   b. Further Assurances

4. **What is an Eviction?**

   The future covenants are breached only by an eviction. An eviction is an assertion of a claim to the land by a person with paramount (better) title than the grantee's; it need not necessarily involve physical interference with the grantee's possession

5. **Damages**

   In most states the party who makes a title covenant cannot be held liable in damages for more than the amount he or she received when the land was sold.

6. Additional Elements of Damage

The grantee is generally allowed to recover interest on the award of damages. Attorneys' fees and court costs in litigating the title with a third party are also allowed if the third party's claim of a paramount interest is determined to be valid.

F. THE RECORDING SYSTEM

All American states operate recording systems which assist the public in determining who has title to any given parcel of land. For the most part, these systems do not involve the government in making any affirmative representations about the title.

1. Limitations of the Recording System

The recording system sometimes yields erroneous results to title searchers. There are at least four reasons for this. First, the recorded instruments themselves may in fact be unenforceable. Second, certain interests need not be recorded in order to be effective against subsequent parties dealing with the land. Third, because title searchers often limit their search to the last fifty or sixty years, there is some risk that an earlier document may have created a title defect. Finally, the title searcher may simply make a clerical error or mistake of judgment.

2. Basic Operation

Recording acts protect subsequent purchasers against *prior* unrecorded interests. The statutes take three distinct approaches:

a. "Notice" Type Statutes

A subsequent taker prevails against a prior unrecorded claimant if the former takes without notice of the latter's claim and pays value.

b. "Race" Type Statutes

A subsequent taker prevails against a prior unrecorded claimant if the former records before the latter.

c. **"Notice–Race" Type Statutes**

A subsequent taker prevails against a prior unrecorded claimant if the former takes without notice, pays value and records first.

3. **Interests and Conveyances Outside the Recording Acts**

A variety of interests and conveyances are not covered by the recording acts, and cannot be divested by a failure to record them. Interests which are commonly considered outside the recording acts include short-term leases, unfiled mechanics' liens (which, if eventually filed, relate back to the date the work was commenced), and the dower or curtesy claims of undisclosed spouses. In addition, records of some types of conveyances such as by will, intestate succession and takings by eminent domain are usually maintained in offices other than the usual recording office. Finally, certain interests created without a document, such as those created by adverse possession or by prescription, cannot (and need not) be recorded.

4. **Payment of Value**

Nearly all recording acts (except the pure "race" statutes) protect subsequent transferees only if they take without notice and pay value.

a. **Judgment Creditors**

Most cases hold that the judgment creditor has not paid value and thus will not be protected as against a prior unrecorded conveyance by the judgment defendant.

b. **Security for Preexisting Debt**

The great majority of cases hold that a lender that takes a mortgage or other interest in land to secure what was a previously unsecured debt has given no value unless the lender also makes some further concession, such as promising to forbear bringing suit, at the time the mortgage is received.

c. **Conveyance in Satisfaction of Preexisting Debt**

While the cases are divided, the better view is that when a debtor transfers land to a creditor in satisfaction of a preexisting unsecured debt, value has been paid, since the creditor's claim against the debtor is discharged.

5. **Taking Without Notice**

To be a bona fide purchaser, one must take without notice of the prior unrecorded conveyance. The three main types of notice are: actual knowledge; constructive notice of facts which would be learned from a view of the property; and constructive notice of information found in the public records.

a. **Quitclaim Deed**

Older authority holds that one who takes by quitclaim deed cannot be a bona fide purchaser. The majority of modern cases reject this rule.

b. **Unrecorded Documents in the Chain of Title**

A purchaser is generally held to notice of the contents of documents in his or her own chain of title, even if they are not recorded.

c. **The Shelter Principle**

Once a bona fide purchaser has perfected his or her title through the operation of the recording acts, the purchaser can pass that perfected status along to future grantees even if they do not qualify as BFPs.

d. **Purchases in Installments**

A purchaser who is paying for the land in installments may get notice of a prior unrecorded conveyance after making some payments but before making others. Courts attempt to protect the purchaser "pro tanto", giving him or her protection to the extent of the payments made while in good faith.

6. **Indexes to the Records**

a. **Name Indexes**

In every state two sets of index books are maintained, one of them alphabetically by the last names of grantors and the other alphabetically by the last names of grantees.

b. **Tract Indexes**

In about a half a dozen states, a page or set of pages in the index book is devoted to listing all documents which affect a particular tract of land, such as a quarter section or a block in a subdivision.

c. **Content of the Index Books**

Index books give the names of the parties, the date of the instrument and the date of its recording, and the book and page number in the "deed books" where the full document itself can be found.

7. **Search Methods**

In a tract index system, the searcher simply runs his or her eye down the appropriate column on the relevant page in the index book, makes note of all documents which affect the land being searched, and then reads those documents. In a name index system, the search is much more complex and consists of three steps: (1) identifying the "chain of title" by use of the grantee index; (2) identifying any "adverse" conveyances by use of the grantor index; and (3) reading all of the documents thus identified. Whether a name or tract index system is used, the searcher must also check various sources outside the recorder's office such as the bankruptcy court, local trial court docket, tax and assessment lien records, and perhaps various local government offices.

8. **Improper Indexing**

If a document is improperly indexed or not indexed at all, the majority of cases treat the document as recorded despite the misindexing. The trend of recent cases is to reverse this view, and to regard the document as unrecorded.

9. **Chain of Title Problems**

Certain types of adverse conveyances are difficult or impossible to find in a name index recording system, even though they are in fact copied into the deed books and are accurately indexed. There are four general types of such problems:

a. The Wild Deed

b. The Late–Recorded Deed

c. The Early–Recorded Deed

d. The Deed Which Conveys One Parcel and Encumbers Another.

G. MARKETABLE TITLE ACTS

Normally it is risky for a searcher not to examine title all the way back to a sovereign's conveyance. Marketable title acts attempt to limit the period of search by cutting off the legal effect of documents recorded prior to the "root of title."

1. The Root of Title

A root of title is usually defined by the acts as a deed in the chain of title recorded earlier than some fixed number of years (say, 20 to 40 years) before the search being made.

2. Effect of the Acts

In general, the acts provide that no interest created prior to the root of title will affect the title.

3. Exceptions

Interests that are not cut off by the usual marketable title act include claims of the United States Government, rights of state and local governments, visible easements, utility and railroad easements, mineral rights, etc.

H.   TORRENS TITLE REGISTRATION

In about ten states there is an alternative to the conventional recording system known as a "Torrens" or title registration system. This system involves the issuance of certificates of title by the local government, similar to those used for motor vehicles.

1. Initial Registration

Entrance into the Torrens system is voluntary, and it is not widely used except in a few locations, such as Minneapolis–St. Paul, Minnesota, Hawaii, Cook County, Illinois, and some areas of Massachusetts.

2. Transfers Under the System

A transfer of land, or the creation of a lien or encumbrance against it, is not binding until registered upon the certificate. When the fee title is transferred a new certificate is issued.

3. Indemnity Fund

To compensate persons whose interests are cut off by an error of the registrar, a fund is created through the collection of payments from all persons registering or transferring their titles.

4.   Problems With the System

The title registration system has been vigorously opposed by title insurance companies and many title lawyers. Its growth has been slow, and indemnity funds have often been considered inadequate. Several states have repealed their registration statutes, or have discontinued accepting new registrations, during the past two decades.

I.   TITLE INSURANCE

A title insurance policy is the insurance company's promise to indemnify the insured party if the title to land is not in the condition stated on the face of the policy, and if the insured suffers a loss as a result. Two main types of policies are issued, insuring owners and mortgagees respectively.

1.   Exceptions and Exclusions

The title policy will contain a schedule of exceptions which lists the encumbrances or other title matters which have been disclosed in the insurance company search, and which are therefore not insured against. In addition the policies typically contain a number of standard exclusions for such matters as zoning and other police power regulations, rights of eminent domain, matters which a survey would disclose, rights of parties in possession, and unfiled mechanics' liens.

2.   Effective Date

The title company is not liable for events which may occur after the effective date of the policy. The company's liability is also limited to the face amount of the policy.

3.   Protection of Insured as a Warrantor

If an insured resells the property and is later sued on the warranty contained in a warranty deed, the title policy will usually continue to protect the insured and will indemnify him for any judgment which he is required to pay, assuming that the title defect in question existed at the time the title policy was issued.

4. Tort Liability

Several recent cases have held title insurers liable on tort rather than contract theories. The tort theory can give rise to punitive damages and can supersede exceptions to coverage listed in the policy.

■ III. INTRODUCTION TO THE LAW OF REAL ESTATE FINANCE

A. IMPACT OF ENGLISH HISTORY

1. The Common Law Mortgage

The English common law mortgage of the 14th and 15th centuries was a conveyance of a fee simple estate to the lender, subject to the condition subsequent that if the borrower repaid the mortgage debt on the due date (law day) the borrower would have the right to re-enter and terminate the lender's estate.

2. The Intervention of Equity Courts: The Equity of Redemption

By the 17th Century, as a result of intervention by equity courts, the mortgagor routinely was able, as a matter of right, to redeem the land by payment of the mortgage debt so long as tender was made within a reasonable time after the law day. This right to "pay late" became known then and is referred to today as the mortgagor's "equity of redemption."

3. The Equitable Remedy of Foreclosure

Equity developed the mortgagee's right to foreclosure. Under this remedy, if the mortgagor did not pay within a time period specified by the court, the mortgagor's redemption right was forever barred. Because no sale of the land was involved, this type of foreclosure was called "strict foreclosure."

B. THE AMERICAN DEVELOPMENT

American courts recognize the mortgagor's equity of redemption and today refuse to enforce any attempt to clog that redemption right.

1. **Foreclosure by Sale**

    Foreclosure in the United States is almost always by public sale.

2. **Statutory Redemption**

    In many states, the mortgagor has, as a matter of legislative grace, the right to redeem after the foreclosure sale for various periods of time, as short as a few months in some jurisdictions to as long as eighteen months in others. Statutory redemption is usually available only after a valid foreclosure has occurred.

3. **The Title, Lien and Intermediate Theories of Mortgage Law**

    Under the title theory, the mortgagee has the legal title and thus the right to possession of the mortgaged real estate until the mortgage debt is satisfied. Under the lien theory, the mortgagor retains both the legal and equitable title, and thus, the right to possession to the foreclosed land, until a valid foreclosure has taken place. The intermediate theory, in effect in a few states, gives the right to possession to the mortgagor until default and to the mortgagee thereafter.

4. **The Deed of Trust as a Mortgage Variant**

    Under a deed of trust, a trustor (the mortgagor) conveys Blackacre to a trustee (sometimes a corporation, but often the lender's attorney, employee, or officer,) to be held as security for the payment of a debt by the trustor to the beneficiary (mortgagee). The deed of trust is essentially a mortgage with a power of sale, and is governed by traditional substantive mortgage principles. Unlike the deed of trust, certain land financing devices are viewed as *mortgage substitutes* rather than mortgage variants. They are utilized in large measure to avoid the impact of many pro-mortgagor substantive mortgage law principles.

C. SOME BASIC MORTGAGE LAW PRINCIPLES

1. **The Long Term Installment Mortgage and the Acceleration Clause**

    Since the 1930s most mortgages have been amortized or repaid in equal installments over a substantial number of years. However, sellers of real estate who provide financing to their buyers sometimes use "balloon" mortgages. Usually these mortgages involve short terms, perhaps three to five years, during which borrowers usually make interest payments only or some minimal payments on principal. The entire principal comes due or "balloons" at the end of the period. In virtually all mortgages, an acceleration clause enables the mortgagee, in the event of the mortgagor's default, to declare the entire principal balance immediately due and payable.

2. Some Basic Mortgage Priority Principles

The purchaser at a foreclosure sale of a senior mortgage will acquire a title that is free and clear of all mortgages or other liens or interests subordinate to the mortgage being foreclosed. A corollary of this principle is that the purchaser at the foreclosure sale of a junior lien takes title subject to any liens or other interests senior to the mortgage being foreclosed. Consequently, a purchaser at a foreclosure sale of such a mortgage should be willing to pay, at most, an amount that equals the fair market value of the land free and clear of liens, less the amount of any senior liens thereon.

■ IV.   THE USE OF MORTGAGE SUBSTITUTES

A.   THE RULE AGAINST CLOGGING THE EQUITY OF REDEMPTION

Mortgage law is generally perceived to be "pro-mortgagor". This perception is especially strengthened by the rule prohibiting clogs of the mortgagor's equity of redemption. This doctrine renders unenforceable and void any agreement by the mortgagor that is part of the original mortgage transaction and that purports to cut off or modify that equity of redemption. As a result, lenders utilize a variety of mortgage substitutes they hope will avoid mortgage law consequences.

B.   THE ABSOLUTE DEED

Lenders commonly utilize as a security device an absolute deed from the borrower to the lender that does not contain defeasance language.

1. **The Absolute Deed Unaccompanied by a Collateral Writing: Extrinsic Evidence**

Parol evidence is admissible to establish that an absolute deed was intended to be a security device, and hence that the borrower has an equity of redemption. A few states, however, require that the party seeking to establish an absolute deed as a mortgage prove that defeasance language was omitted because of ignorance, mistake, fraud, or undue advantage.

a. **Burden of Proof**

Most states hold that mortgage intent must be established by clear and convincing evidence.

b. **Parol Evidence Rule Inapplicable**

The parol evidence rule is generally inapplicable to the absolute deed situation, on the theory that the absolute deed was not intended to embody the complete agreement of the parties and that the oral agreement simply supplements the deed concerning a matter about which the deed does not deal.

c. **Statute of Frauds Not a Bar**

The Statute of Frauds is not violated because a judicial determination that an absolute deed is a mortgage is not deemed to create in or transfer to the grantor an interest in land.

d. **Factors That Establish an Absolute Deed as a Mortgage**

Factors that are important include:

1. Presence of debt.

2. Actual statements of the parties.

3. Disparity between the amount received by the grantor and the fair market value of the land conveyed.

4. Possession.

5. Payment of real estate taxes.

6. Improvements by grantor.

7. Nature of the parties.

2. The Absolute Deed With Collateral Written Instrument

If the collateral writing contains language of defeasance or a promise to reconvey upon payment of money acknowledged to be a debt and the two instruments were executed as part of a single transaction, the transaction will be treated as a mortgage.

a. Use of Parol Evidence

The parol evidence rule is inapplicable to bar parol evidence because such evidence is not utilized to diminish or vary the writings, but rather to establish that the documents were part of a single mortgage transaction.

b. Timing of the Two Writings

The two writings need not be executed simultaneously in order for both to be treated as part of a single mortgage transaction.

c. Nature of the Collateral Writing

While there is some authority to the contrary, the collateral writing need not satisfy the same formalities followed in executing the absolute deed.

C. THE CONDITIONAL SALE

These transactions include the use of an absolute deed together with a second written document, which professes expressly to be an instrument such as a contract or option to resell to the grantor the land described in the deed. The two most common types of this transaction include: (1) A sale and conveyance of the land by grantor to grantee with an option in grantor to repurchase it. (2) A sale and conveyance by grantor to grantee and a lease by grantee to grantor with an option in grantor to repurchase.

1. Reasons for Use

The conditional sale is motivated by the lender-grantee's desire to avoid the consequences of mortgage or usury law or to obtain capital gains tax treatment of what otherwise would be considered interest income subject to taxation as ordinary income.

2. Use of Extrinsic Evidence

Extrinsic evidence is admissible to establish that a conditional sale is a mortgage. While some courts require clear and convincing evidence of mortgage intent, others hold that a mere preponderance of evidence of such intent will suffice.

3. Factors Establishing a Conditional Sale as a Mortgage

The factors enumerated in connection with utilizing extrinsic evidence establishing an absolute deed to be a mortgage are also important in the conditional sale setting.

D. TWO PROBLEMS COMMON TO ABSOLUTE DEED AND CONDITIONAL SALE TRANSACTIONS

1. Use of Specific Language Negating a Mortgage Transaction

When other credible evidence supports a finding that the parties intended to create a mortgage transaction, a court will not be bound by specific contract or deed language negating such an intent.

2. Application of the Same Burden of Proof to Grantor and Grantee

While there is authority that the burden of proof is the same for grantee as well as grantor, persuasive arguments exist that a heavier burden should apply to a grantee who seeks to establish the transaction as a mortgage.

E. THE INSTALLMENT LAND CONTRACT

This mortgage substitute is the economic equivalent of a seller purchase-money mortgage. It is also known as a "contract for deed" or "long term land contract." The vendor retains legal title until the contract is fully paid and usually relies on a forfeiture clause in the event of vendee default.

1. Distinguished from Earnest Money Contracts

An earnest money contract is an executory contract for the sale of land that governs the buyer and seller during the period from the date of the bargain to the date of the closing. At the latter date, the seller usually delivers a deed to buyer and mortgages or security agreements, if any, are executed. The installment land contract, on the other hand, takes the place of such mortgages or security agreements.

2. The Forfeiture Remedy

Almost all installment land contracts provide that time is of the essence and that when a vendee defaults, the vendor has the option to declare the contract terminated, to retain possession of the premises and to retain all previous payments as liquidated damages.

3. Other Remedies for Vendee Breach

Notwithstanding pervasive reliance on the forfeiture remedy, a vendor occasionally opts for certain contract remedies.

a. Specific Performance for the Price

Under this remedy, the vendor tenders title to the land and the vendee is ordered to pay the remainder of the contract price. Many courts require, as a condition precedent, that the contract contain an acceleration clause (allowing vendor to declare the entire debt due and payable upon vendee breach).

b. Specific Performance for the Installments Due

This remedy gives the vendor the amount of past due installments plus interest. It will only be used where the absence of an acceleration clause makes specific performance for the remainder of the contract price unavailable.

c. Foreclosure of the Vendee's Rights

This remedy, where permitted, allows the vendor to treat the installment land contract as a mortgage and results in a judicial sale of the land.

d. Strict Foreclosure

Under this remedy, the court will grant a fixed period of time during which the vendee must redeem by paying the balance of the contract price. If the vendee fails to do so, title to the land is confirmed in the vendor.

e. **Suit for Damages**

This remedy allows the vendor to receive damages measured by the differences between the contract price and the fair market value of the land as of the date of vendee's breach. Because of the election of remedies doctrine, it is probably only available where the vendee has abandoned the land.

4. **Comments on the Forfeiture Remedy**

While the forfeiture clause may occasionally be enforced, few if any jurisdictions will automatically enforce such a provision.

5. **Legislative Limitation on Forfeiture**

At least a dozen states have statutes that limit the harshness of the forfeiture remedy. Such statutes tend to accomplish at least two results. First, statutory grace periods similar to the statutory rights sometimes given to defaulting mortgagors are afforded to installment land contract vendees. Second, the presence of such statutes tends to institutionalize or formalize the forfeiture concept.

6. **Judicial Limitations on Forfeiture**

a. **Waiver by Vendor as an Excuse for Delinquency**

Some courts hold that a past pattern of vendor acceptance of late payments constitutes a waiver of time provisions of the contract. Where waiver is found, a vendee will be permitted to tender the balance due on the contract or, in some instances, be able to reinstate the contract by the payment of arrearages.

b. **Recognition of an Equity of Redemption**

Some courts have held that a vendee in default should have the right, within a reasonable time, to pay the balance on the contract, or in a few instances, the arrearages, before losing the land. Some courts view this right as unconditional, while others limit it to situations where the vendee has paid a substantial amount on the contract. This vendee right represents the functional equivalent of the mortgagor's equity of redemption.

c. **Restitution**

Where the courts do not yet recognize a vendee's equity of redemption or where a vendee is unable or unwilling to redeem, courts may grant forfeiture, but require that the vendor refund payments made by the vendee on the contract to the extent they exceed the vendor's actual damages.

d. Foreclosure as a Mortgage

Some state courts and the Restatement treat installment land contracts as mortgages, at least in those situations where the vendee has made more than nominal payments on the contract.

7. Election of Remedies

Once forfeiture has been effectuated, the vendor normally is barred from recovery of the mortgage equivalent of a deficiency judgment.

8. Mortgaging the Vendee's Interest

As a vendee pays off an installment land contract and/or inflation increases the value of the land, the vendee's interest often becomes an important source of security for borrowing by the vendee.

a. Mortgageability

Most states hold that a vendee's interest is mortgageable.

b. Rights of the Vendee's Mortgagee to Notice

A majority of cases hold that the vendor cannot declare a forfeiture without first providing to the vendee's mortgagee who has recorded its mortgage notice of intention to invoke forfeiture and an opportunity to protect itself. A minority approach limits the duty to notify to those situations where the vendor has actual knowledge of the mortgage on the vendee's interest.

9. Rights of Judgment Creditors of the Vendee

Most states hold that the vendee's interest is real estate for purposes of state judgment lien statutes. This result is achieved either by applying equitable conversion or by statutory interpretation.

10. Mortgaging the Vendor's Interest

The vendor's interest is mortgageable. Under Revised UCC Article 9, promulgated in 2000, a lender to a vendor generally validly perfects a security interest in the vendor's interest by filing a financing statement in the appropriate office. There may also still be good reasons to record an assignment in the real estate records.

11. Rights of Judgment Creditors of the Vendor

Notwithstanding the equitable conversion doctrine, courts usually treat the vendor's interest in an installment land contract as "real estate" for purposes of judgment lien statutes.

F. THE NEGATIVE COVENANT AS A MORTGAGE SUBSTITUTE

A lender will sometimes require the borrower to execute a promise not to encumber or transfer, so long as the loan remains unpaid, certain of the borrower's real estate. The question is whether the negative covenant constitutes an equitable mortgage on that real estate.

1. Reasons for Use

Many lenders believe the negative covenant will, in the event of a borrower's default, give them the option of proceeding against the borrower either as a secured or as an unsecured creditor.

2. Judicial Treatment

Most courts hold that, in the absence of other intent to create a mortgage, the negative covenant does not create an equitable mortgage or security interest in favor of the lender.

■ V. RIGHTS AND DUTIES PRIOR TO FORECLOSURE

A. THEORIES OF TITLE AND THE RIGHT TO POSSESSION

Three theories of mortgage law exist in the United States—the title, lien and intermediate theories.

1. Title Theory

Under this theory, legal "title" is in the mortgagee until the mortgage has either been satisfied or foreclosed. The mortgagee has the right to possession and thus, the right to rents and profits from the mortgaged real estate until the mortgage debt is paid or foreclosure occurs.

2. The Lien Theory

The majority of states take the position that the mortgagee acquires only a lien on the mortgaged premises and that legal and equitable title remain in the mortgagor until a valid foreclosure takes place. Most lien theory states will enforce mortgage language that confers the right to possession on the mortgagee if the mortgagor defaults.

3. The Intermediate Theory

Under this approach, the lien theory is applied until default and the title theory thereafter. In other words, a mortgagee has the right to possession and to collect rents and profits after the mortgagor defaults.

4. The Mortgagee in Possession

There are certain situations where even strict lien theory states will allow a mortgagee to remain in possession of the mortgaged real estate until the mortgage has been satisfied or the mortgage validly foreclosed. This can be the case where the mortgagor "lets" the mortgagee take possession or where possession has been acquired by virtue of an invalid foreclosure sale or where the mortgagor has abandoned the premises.

5. Duties of the Mortgagee in Possession

The mortgagee has the duty to manage the property in a reasonably prudent manner so as to keep it in a good state of preservation and to apply the rents, after deducting therefrom valid expenses, to reduce the mortgage debt.

6. The Assignment of Rents Clause

The vast majority of states, whether lien or title, enforce an assignment of rents clause contained in the mortgage or executed contemporaneously therewith. Jurisdictions differ substantially, however, at to when the assignment is "effective" between the parties and "perfected" as against third parties. Moreover, the requirements for actually collecting (foreclosing upon) the rents vary significantly from state to state.

B. THE APPOINTMENT OF A RECEIVER

An equitable receivership entails the judicial appointment of a third person to take possession of the mortgaged property to preserve it and to collect rents.

1. Reasons for Use

Mortgagees often prefer not to take on the relatively strict accounting responsibilities and other obligations incident to being a mortgagee in possession. Moreover, a receivership will often be favored over simply enforcing an assignment of rents clause because the latter remedy is of little value if the mortgaged property is unrented or partially rented.

2. Standard for Appointment

In most states, whether title or lien, the mortgagee must, at a bare minimum, establish that the mortgage is in default, the security is inadequate, and the mortgagor has committed waste. Sometimes it is stated that courts require the establishment of some "distinct equitable ground, such as danger of loss, waste, destruction or serious impairment of the property to warrant the appointment of a receiver."

3. Impact of Other Factors on Appointment

a. Receivership and Assignment of Rents Clauses

In many states, neither the presence of a mortgage clause authorizing the appointment of a receiver on default nor an assignment of rents clause enhance the chances of appointment. In other states, one or both of the clauses may be considered a relevant factor and may favorably influence a court to appoint a receiver. Under the Restatement the presence of either clause mandates the appointment of a receiver so long as there is a default in the mortgage obligation.

b. Statutory Provisions

Some statutes authorize the appointment of a receiver as a matter of right where the mortgage contains a receivership clause. Others tie the appointment to the existence of a rents and profits clause.

4. Ex Parte Receiverships

Several jurisdictions appoint receivers by *ex parte* order. This entails the appointment of a receiver, usually pending judicial foreclosure, without affording notice or an opportunity for a hearing to the mortgagor or other interested parties. Constitutional attacks thus far have proven unsuccessful because courts conclude that the mortgagor's right to a hearing after appointment suffices for constitutional purposes or that the mortgagor has waived his due process rights by previously agreeing in the mortgage to the ex parte appointment of a receiver.

C. WASTE

Waste is an act of the mortgagor or a third party that harms the real estate as security. It is in the nature of a tort, and liability does not depend on the presence of mortgage language.

1. What Constitutes Waste?

Waste includes physical damage to the land or improvements, failure of the mortgagor to make reasonably necessary repairs, failure to pay property taxes, failure to comply with mortgage covenants dealing with the property's physical condition, and failure to remit rents when a valid mortgage on the rents has been enforced.

2. Remedies for Waste

There are three remedies for waste by the mortgagor: damages, an injunction, and foreclosure of the mortgage. If the waste is committed by a third party, foreclosure is not available. Recovery of damages is limited by the following principles:

a. Loan Balance

Damages may never exceed the balance owing on the mortgage debt, and the mortgagee must apply any damage recovery against the debt.

b. Amount of Waste

Recovery may not exceed the actual amount of the waste, as measured either by the loss of value of the property or by the cost of repair.

c. **Impairment of Security**

Damages may not exceed the amount by which the lender's security has been impaired by the waste. There is widespread disagreement as to how to measure the impairment of the security. The best view, adopted by the Restatement, is that the lender should recover enough to restore the loan-to-value ratio to its scheduled level. If the loan has already been foreclosed at the time damages are sought, the loan-to-value ratio has become irrelevant, and the lender can simply recover up to its deficiency (limited, of course, by the amount of the waste itself).

3. **Waste by Successors of the Mortgagor**

Subsequent owners of the real estate are liable for any waste they commit, even if they did not assume the mortgage.

4. **Waste by Persons With No Interest in the Real Estate**

Third parties are liable for waste if they damage the real estate or improvements. The only remedies available to the mortgagee against them are damages and an injunction. They are liable, by the majority view, only if they had actual knowledge of the mortgage when they committed the harm. The impairment of security test is not applicable in actions against third parties.

D. MORTGAGEE LIABILITY FOR ENVIRONMENTAL CONTAMINATION

Even though a mortgagee is normally not liable to third parties, private or governmental, for the physical condition of the mortgaged premises or injuries that occur on it, there is some potential for liability under the federal Comprehensive Environmental Response, Compensation, and Liability Act ("CERCLA") and state counterparts.

1. **An Overview of CERCLA**

CERCLA imposes broad liability on "owners and operators" of hazardous waste sites. The liability, when imposed, is "strict" and "joint and several."

2. **The Mortgagee and CERCLA**

The mortgagee is concerned about CERCLA in at least two respects. First, when does pre-foreclosure oversight of a mortgagor's operations by the mortgagee represent impermissible "participation in management" that will render it liable as an "owner and operator?" Second, when a mortgagee acquires ownership through foreclosure or a deed in lieu, will it be liable as an "owner" of the premises?

3. The 1992 EPA Lender Liability Regulation

Largely in response to the foregoing concerns, the EPA in 1992 promulgated a regulation that largely answered the foregoing two questions against mortgagee liability. The Regulation, however, was invalidated by judicial decision in 1994.

4. 1996 Congressional Amendments to CERCLA

Mortgagees finally obtained their desired protection from CERCLA liability in 1996 when Congress enacted the Asset Conservation, Lender Liability, and Deposit Insurance Protection Act of 1996. The 1996 statute put the seal of approval on the previous judicially-invalidated regulation. As a result, mortgagees may safely engage in a broad degree of monitoring and supervision of mortgagor's activities without incurring liability for "participating in management." Similarly, mortgagees may acquire title by foreclosure or deed in lieu without becoming liable for hazardous waste cleanup, so long as they seek to sell the property in a commercially reasonable manner and time period. Note that state statutes often impose liability similar to that under CERCLA, and that the 1996 statute does not insulate lenders against state liability.

E.   INSURANCE PROCEEDS AND REAL ESTATE TAXES

Insurance policies on mortgaged real estate will specifically insure both mortgagor and mortgagee "as their interests may appear." Two types of such policies are the "loss payable policy" and the "standard mortgage policy."

1. The Loss Payable Policy

Under this rarely used policy, the mortgagee is the mere appointee of the mortgagor to receive payment and its right to recover is completely dependent upon the right of the mortgagor. If a mortgagor is barred from recovery, so too will be the mortgagee.

2. **The Standard Mortgage Policy**

Under this type of policy, the mortgagee's right of recovery cannot be defeated by any act or failure to act by the mortgagor, even though it would defeat the latter's right of recovery. This type of policy is much more widely used today than the loss payable policy.

3. **Restoration of the Premises**

Today most commonly used mortgage forms specifically provide for the disposition of the insurance proceeds after a casualty loss. In the absence of specific language, however, a majority of courts permit the mortgagee to utilize the proceeds to prepay the mortgage debt. Such recovery is not conditional on the mortgagee being able to establish that application of the proceeds to restoration would impair mortgage security. There is minority authority that, absent impairment of mortgage security, the mortgagor has the option to use the insurance proceeds to rebuild, even though mortgage language affirmatively gives the mortgagee the choice of prepayment or rebuilding.

4. **Mortgagee Purchase at Foreclosure Sale—Effect on Insurance Proceeds**

Where a mortgagee is a foreclosure purchaser for the amount of the mortgage debt, either before or after a casualty loss, it can affect the mortgagee's right to the insurance proceeds payable as a result of that loss.

a. **Loss Payable Policy**

Cases uniformly prohibit the mortgagee from recovering on the policy.

b. **Standard Mortgage Policy**

If the loss occurs after the foreclosure sale, the mortgagee is permitted to recover. Where the foreclosure follows the loss, and the mortgagee purchased the property at foreclosure for the amount of the debt, most courts prohibit mortgagee recovery.

5. **Interest on Escrow or Reserve Accounts for Insurance and Taxes**

Absent a statutory or regulatory mandate, most courts have refused to require mortgagees to account for income earned by the mortgagee on escrows or reserves for taxes and insurance.

a.   **Judicial Challenges**

While plaintiffs were initially successful during the 1970's using class action challenges asserting the right to interest on escrowed funds, this trend was short-lived because mortgage forms were modified and courts by the late 1970's began to refuse to require the payment of interest to borrowers.

b.   **Statutory and Other Regulation of Escrow and Reserve Deposits**

Numerous state statutes require mortgagees to pay interest to residential mortgagors on escrowed funds. Currently no federal law or regulation requires mortgagees to pay interest on escrow accounts.

6.   **Escrow Accounting Under RESPA**

The federal Real Estate Settlement Procedures Act (RESPA) allows lenders on home loans to collect monthly no more than 1/12 of the annual taxes, insurance, and other items being escrowed. It also allows lenders to maintain a "cushion" in the account of no more than 1/6 of the annual amounts of these items. Under HUD regulations, the "cushion" must be calculated on an "aggregate" basis (that is, taking all of the items into account). This means that the escrow account, at its lowest point in the annual cycle, should decline to 1/6 of the total annual taxes, insurance, etc.

■ VI.   TRANSFER BY THE MORTGAGOR

A.   TRANSFERABILITY OF THE MORTGAGOR'S INTEREST

1.   In General

A mortgagor's interest or "equity" normally is freely transferable. Absent agreement by the mortgagee, however, the mortgagor cannot escape personal liability on the mortgage debt by the transfer of his or her interest to a purchaser-grantee.

2. Transfer "Subject To" the Mortgage

When a transfer is made simply "subject-to" an existing mortgage, the grantee does not become personally liable to either the mortgagee or the mortgagor-grantor.

3. Assumption Transfers

When a grantee-purchaser "assumes" an existing mortgage, she becomes personally liable to pay off the mortgage debt.

4. Assumption Transfers—How Created

Normally, the assumption agreement is contained in the deed to the assuming grantee. That language usually will state that grantee "assumes and agrees to pay" the described mortgage "according to its terms." In the absence of such specific language, however, courts usually will permit the use of extrinsic evidence—other writings and oral statements—to show that an assumption was intended.

5. The Implied Assumption Problem

Some states hold that where, in addition to a conveyance "subject to" the mortgage, the full value of the land is agreed on as the purchase price and the purchaser deducts the mortgage amount from it, the purchaser becomes personally liable. In such states purchaser personal liability can be avoided by including in the deed, after the words "subject to," a statement that the mortgage is not being assumed by the grantee.

6. Rights of Grantor Against Non–Assuming Grantee

While the grantor-mortgagor has no personal claim against a non-assuming grantee, when the mortgage debt becomes due, the mortgagor may pay it and become subrogated to the rights of the mortgagee against the real estate.

7. Rights of Grantor Against Assuming Grantee

In addition to the rights described in Subsection 6, above, the mortgagor also has personal rights against an assuming grantee based on the assumption contract. When the grantee fails to pay the mortgage debt according to its terms, the mortgagor has the right to pay the mortgage debt and then sue the grantee for reimbursement. In addition, the mortgagor may, without paying the debt, apply for a court order compelling the grantee to pay it under the doctrine of exoneration.

8. **Mortgagee's Rights Against Assuming Grantees**

The two most significant theories that support the mortgagee's right to recover from an assuming grantee personally are described below.

a. **The Third Party Beneficiary Theory**

The mortgagee is deemed to be a third party beneficiary of the assumption contract between the mortgagor and the grantee.

b. **The Subrogation–Derivative Theory**

The mortgagee has right to be subrogated to the mortgagor's rights against an assuming grantee. Since the mortgagor has a right to recover from an assuming grantee personally upon the breach of an assumption agreement, the mortgagee has the same right.

9. **Mortgagee Rights Against Successive Grantees**

When mortgaged real estate has an unbroken chain of assuming grantee-owners, each of them becomes and remains liable to the mortgagee until the mortgage debt is paid.

10. **Break in the Chain of Assumptions**

Courts differ as to whether a mortgagee can hold an assuming grantee liable when any earlier grantee in the chain of ownership failed to assume the mortgage debt.

a. **The Third Party Beneficiary Theory**

Some courts require, as a condition precedent to mortgagee achieving creditor beneficiary status, that there be promisee liability—in other words, that G–2's grantor actually be personally liable to the mortgagee. Where this rule applies, once there is a break in the chain, no further grantee can be held personally liable. Under the Restatement (Third) of Property (Mortgages), however, that any transferee who assumes is liable "whether or not the transferor is personally liable."

b. **The Subrogation–Derivative Theory**

Under this approach, the mortgagee can reach a subsequent assuming grantee because it has the right to stand in the mortgagor's and subsequent grantee-debtor's shoes. Once a non-assuming grantee intervenes, thereafter there will be no grantee-debtor to whom the mortgagee can be subrogated.

11. Grantee's Assertion of Mortgagor's Defenses Against the Mortgagee

The general rule is that an assuming or subject to grantee cannot utilize any defenses the mortgagor may have against the mortgagee.

12. Release of the Mortgagor Upon a Transfer of the Real Estate

Normally the mortgagor remains liable on the mortgage debt after transferring the real estate. However, it is possible that the mortgagee will give an express release of liability to the mortgagor. Indeed, there is an argument that under an OTS regulation issued pursuant to Section 341 of the Garn Act, the mortgagee *must* give a release if it approves an assumption by the new owner under a due-on-sale clause. In addition, under FHA loans the mortgagor is automatically released from liability 5 years after making the transfer if the loan is not then in default.

13. Discharge of the Mortgagor After Transfer of the Real Estate: The Suretyship Defenses

Agreements between grantee and mortgagee that extend or modify the mortgage debt or release the grantee can often have the unforeseen effect of releasing the mortgagor's personal liability on the mortgage debt. This result stems from viewing the parties as being in a suretyship relationship.

a. Release of the Assuming Grantee

The cases generally hold that if the mortgagee releases the assuming grantee, the mortgagor is automatically released as well.

b. Release or Impairment of Security by the Mortgagee

If all of the security is released, the better view is that the mortgagor is discharged from liability to the extent of the value of the property released. However, many cases discharge the mortgagor completely. If only part of the security is released or impaired, the better view is that the mortgagee is discharged to the extent that the security becomes inadequate to cover the debt. Again, many cases give a complete discharge.

c. Modification of the Obligation by the Mortgagee

The majority of cases give the mortgagor a complete discharge, no matter what the nature of the modification. However, the better view, as represented by the Restatement (Third) of Suretyship and Guaranty § 41, is that the discharge is only to the extent that the modification would otherwise damage the mortgagor. (Many types of modifications are actually *favorable* to the mortgagor, and under this view would cause no discharge at all.)

d. Extension of Time to Pay by Mortgagee

The majority of cases discharge the mortgagor completely if the mortgagee gives the grantee an extension of time. (If the grantee did not assume, the discharge is only to the extent of the land's value.) The better view, adopted by the Restatement (Third) of Suretyship and Guaranty § 40(b), is that the mortgagor is discharged only to the extent that he or she would otherwise be damaged by the extension.

14. Methods of Avoiding the Suretyship Defenses

There are several methods by which the mortgagee may prevent the suretyship defenses discussed above from arising.

a. Mortgagor's Consent to Mortgagee's Action

If the mortgagor consents to the release, modification, or extension by the mortgagee, the mortgagor will not be discharged. The consent may be given in the original mortgage, or it may be given before, at the time of, or after the release, modification, or extension.

b. A "Preservation of Recourse" Clause in the Release or Extension Agreement

Under the Restatement § 38, a mortgagee that grants a release of liability or a time extension to a grantee may insert a "preservation of recourse" clause. This clause, in effect, warns the grantee that the release or extension is not binding on the mortgagor, and that the mortgagor may still enforce the obligation against the grantee according to its original terms. Using such a clause does not guarantee that the mortgagor won't be discharged, but it makes a discharge less likely, since by preserving the mortgagor's full recourse against the grantee, it makes it less probable that the grantee will suffer damage as a result of the release or extension.

B. RESTRICTIONS ON TRANSFER—THE DUE–ON–CLAUSES

The due-on-sale clause gives the mortgagee the option of declaring the entire mortgage debt due and payable if the mortgagor transfers the mortgaged real estate without the consent of the mortgagee. The due-on-encumbrance clause gives the mortgagee the same right to accelerate if the mortgaged real estate is further encumbered without the mortgagee's consent.

1. Purpose of the Due–On–Clauses

Mortgagees utilize the due-on-sale clause for two purposes: (1) to protect against a new grantee who may endanger the mortgage security or who is a greater credit risk than the mortgagor; and (2) to enable the mortgagee to recall lower than current market interest rate fixed rate loans. The due-on-encumbrance clause is used primarily to protect the mortgagee against the risk of junior lien financing that increases mortgagor debt burden and reduces his stake in the mortgaged real estate.

2. Judicial Approaches to Due–On–Sale Clauses

Most courts traditionally concluded that due-on-sale clauses represent, at most, indirect restraints on alienation.

a. The Tendency Toward Automatic Enforcement Approach

This majority approach favored automatic enforcement of due-on-sale clauses, or at least the cases in this category support a strong presumption in favor of their validity. These cases recognize the validity of protecting the mortgagee against the vagaries of the interest market.

b. Valid Only to Protect Security Approach

This minority approach held that while due-on-sale clauses can be reasonable in individual cases, the burden is on the mortgagee to justify their use in such cases. As a practical matter, the mortgagee had the burden to establish either impairment of security or an increased risk of default and foreclosure. This approach has been largely overruled by the Garn–St. Germain Act, discussed below.

3. Policy Arguments Concerning Enforcement

a. Buyers of Real Estate

Those who favor limited or no enforcement of due-on-sale clauses argue that countless home buyers may be driven from the market during periods of rising interest rates unless they are able to purchase by assuming existing lower than market interest rate mortgages.

b. Sellers of Real Estate

Sellers argue that enforcement of due-on-sale clauses force them either to reduce the price of their homes significantly to enable buyers to qualify for institutional high interest rate financing or to do the same thing indirectly by financing part of the purchase price themselves at lower than market interest rates.

c. Mortgage Lenders

While several arguments buttress this group's position, two are probably more significant than others. First, lenders stress that because a large portion of their mortgage portfolios consists of older, lower yielding mortgages, they have difficulty in paying the higher short term rates demanded by depositors. Second, they argue that if due-on-sale clauses are not enforced, an inordinate interest rate advantage may be afforded to relatively affluent buyers over those who are less affluent.

4. The Garn–St. Germain Act

This Act was effective October 15, 1982 and broadly preempts state law that restricts the enforcement of due-on clauses. Consequently, such clauses are generally made enforceable.

a. Lenders Covered

Every lender, whether institutional or individual, is covered by the Act.

b. Loans Covered

Every loan secured by a lien on real property is covered by the Act. Included within this definition are loans secured by a leasehold or subleasehold.

c. Types of Transfer Restrictions Covered

The Act preempts state law with respect to due-on clauses that "authorize a lender, at its option, to declare due and payable sums secured by the lender's security instrument if all or any part of the property, or an interest therein * * * is sold or transferred without lender's prior written consent."

d. **Time of Transfer**

A transfer is covered by the Act if it occurred after October 15, 1982.

e. **Transfers in Which Due–On Enforcement is Prohibited**

The Act enumerates eight situations in which due-on clauses may not be enforced. These generally involve "involuntary", intra-family, divorce or probate transfers. These exceptions to enforcement apply only if the mortgaged real estate contains "less than five dwelling units."

f. **The Exemption for Window Period Loans**

States that restricted due-on enforcement prior to October 15, 1982 are known as "window-period" states. In those states enforcement of the Act was deferred until October 15, 1985. State law continued to govern during that period.

g. **Estoppel**

In certain relatively rare circumstances, a mortgagee may, under state case law, be held estopped to assert, or to have waived, its rights under an otherwise enforceable due-on clause. This defense is probably not preempted by the Act.

h. **Release of Original Mortgagor**

When a mortgagee consents to a transfer and the grantee assumes the original mortgage, the Act relieves the original mortgagor of liability on the mortgage debt.

5. **Concealment of the Transfer**

Parties commonly attempt to avoid the due-on problem by concealing the transfer from the mortgagee. As a practical matter, however, mortgagees often learn of these transactions through a variety of means.

a. **Effect of Failure to Record Transfer**

Failure to record the transfer, depending upon the jurisdiction, can leave the purchaser's title vulnerable to mortgages and other liens that are subsequently created by or arise against the mortgagor-grantor.

b.   Duty to Notify the Mortgagee of Transfer

To the extent that a duty to notify the mortgagee of the proposed transfer is implicit in a due-on-sale clause, the mortgagee will be able to recover from the mortgagor and his grantee, the difference between the interest rate specified in the mortgage and the market rate at the time of the transfer.

c.   Ethical Problems

There are significant ethical implications in counseling a client to conceal a transfer or in arranging the details of the transaction. Both the Model Code of Professional Responsibility (1969) and the Model Rules of Professional Conduct (1983) prohibit the lawyer from informing the lender of the transfer. It is unclear whether the Code or the Rules prohibit a lawyer from advising and assisting in a concealment transaction.

6.   Restrictions on Transfer in Installment Land Contracts

Installment land contract vendors have traditionally included provisions prohibiting assignment by the vendee without the vendor's consent. There is a growing tendency today to regard them as unreasonable restraints on alienation unless the vendor establishes that enforcement is reasonable under the circumstances of the individual case. Regulations under the Garn Act make such "no-transfer" provisions enforceable, but not for the purpose of invoking forfeiture.

■ VII.   TRANSFER BY THE MORTGAGEE

A.   NATURE OF THE MORTGAGEE'S INTEREST

1.   The Two–Fold Nature of the Mortgagee's Interests

A real estate mortgagee owns the personal obligation owed by the mortgagor (usually represented by a promissory note) and an interest in the real estate that is the security for that obligation (usually represented by a mortgage or deed of trust).

2. Primary Importance of the Obligation

The mortgage security follows the obligation. Whoever is the transferee of the obligation automatically obtains the benefit of the security interest in the land.

3. Governing Law

The transfer of the mortgagee's interest is governed by the law of contracts and real property. Where a negotiable promissory note is involved, Article 3 of the UCC governs transfers. If a security interests in the note and mortgage is created, Article 9 of the UCC governs priorities, perfection, and realization on the security interest.

B. RIGHTS AND OBLIGATIONS ASSIGNEE VIS À VIS THE MORTGAGOR

1. Qualifying as a Holder in Due Course (HDC)

Holder in due course status can be achieved by satisfying three requirements: (1) the promissory note itself must be negotiable; (2) the process by which the note is transferred must constitute a proper negotiation; and (3) the transferee must be in "due course"—that is, must take in good faith, for value, and without notice that the note is overdue, has been dishonored, or is subject to any defense or claim to it on the part of any person.

a. Negotiability

To be negotiable, a promissory note must contain an unconditional promise to pay a fixed amount of money on demand or at a definite time. It must be payable to "bearer" or to the "order" of the payee, and may not (with certain exceptions) contain any other undertaking or instruction in addition to the payment of money. The "fixed amount" requirement is satisfied even if the note provides for interest, whether fixed or adjustable rate. The note may include an undertaking to give maintain, or protect the collateral.

b. Negotiation

To constitute a proper negotiation, a promissory note must be transferred by endorsement. In addition, the assignee must acquire physical possession of the note.

2. The Rights of an Assignee Who is a HDC

a. Personal Defenses

The HDC takes free of "personal" defenses. These include: failure or lack of consideration, breach of warranty, unconscionability and most types of fraud.

b. "Real" Defenses

A HDC takes subject to "real" defenses. These include: (a) infancy, to the extent that it is a defense to a simple contract; (b) duress, lack of legal capacity, or illegality that nullifies the maker's obligation; (c) such misrepresentation as has induced the party to sign the instrument with neither knowledge nor reasonable opportunity to obtain knowledge of its character or its essential terms; and (d) discharge in insolvency proceedings.

3. Non–HDC Status

a. The Patent–Latent Equity Distinction

If the defense to enforcement of the note and mortgage can be asserted by the maker-mortgagor, it is referred to as a patent equity. If the defense is capable of being raised by someone other than the maker-mortgagor, it is called a latent equity.

b. Raising Patent Equities Against Transferee

Patent equities may be raised against an assignee of a mortgagee to the same extent that they could have been raised against the original mortgagee.

c. Estoppel Certificates

An assignee of a note and mortgage who believes that HDC status may be lacking often insists on an estoppel certificate from maker-mortgagor. In this document the maker-mortgagor certifies that the note is valid and that it is not subject to defenses by the maker-mortgagor. Since such certificates are signed only by the maker-mortgagor, they only protect the assignee against patent equities.

d. Raising Latent Equities Against the Maker–Mortgagor

Under the UCC a non-HDC is subject to "simple contract" defenses under state contract law. Most of the state cases hold that an assignee of a contract who pays value and has no notice of latent equities takes free of them. By contrast, the assignee is subject to any patent equities. However, this is not unreasonable, since the assignee can insist on an estoppel certificate as a means on disclosing patent equities.

4. **Limitations on the Holder in Due Course Doctrine**

In the past two decades, courts, legislatures and regulatory bodies have imposed substantial limitations on the HDC doctrine in a wide variety of consumer lending contexts.

a. **The Close Connectedness Concept**

Some courts hold that holder in due course status may be denied to an assignee of a negotiable note who is too closely connected to the original holder.

b. **Legislation and Other Regulation**

The UCCC, which has been enacted in a 1968 or 1974 version in at least fifteen states, in general abolishes HDC status for many assignees of vendor home improvement mortgages (usually junior liens) and a limited number of first mortgages as well.

Under a "trade regulation rule" adopted by the Federal Trade Commission in 1975 and titled "Preservation of Consumer's Claims and Defenses," it is an unfair trade practice for a provider of goods and services to finance a sale without including in the debt instrument specific ten point type-bold face language that makes the holder subject to the maker's claims and defenses.

Under the Uniform Land Transactions Act, a debtor, as a general principle, may, absent a waiver, assert against an assignee of a note and mortgage all claims and defenses that arise prior to the debtor's receipt of written notice of assignment.

5. **Payment to Assignor as a Defense**

a. **Negotiable Notes**

After a negotiable note has been delivered to another person for the purpose of transferring the right of enforcement to that person, payment to the original payee or to anyone other than the person in possession or his agent does not constitute a valid payment of the mortgage debt. This is so even if the payor does not know that the note has been transferred.

b. Nonnegotiable Notes

Even if the note is non-negotiable, there is substantial case authority for the same result—that payment (and particularly a final payoff) to anyone other than the possessor of the note is ineffective. However, the better rule is that an assignee of a nonnegotiable note takes it subject to all payments made before the maker receives notice of the assignment.

c. Suggested Alternative Rule

It seems clear that the law with respect to negotiable notes should be changed so as to make payment to the mortgagee binding if made before notice of the assignment is provided to the mortgagor. The present law is out of touch with common expectations and commercial practice.

6. Other Payment and Recording Act Problems

a. Mortgagor's Transferee vs. Assignee of Mortgage

If the original mortgagor transfers the land to a grantee after the assignment of the mortgage has been recorded, further payment by the grantee to the original mortgagor will not be credited on the mortgage debt, whether the debt is a negotiable note or not. The recording of the assignment will constitute constructive notice of the assignment to the grantee.

b. Wrongful Satisfaction of the Mortgage by the Original Mortgagee

Assume a negotiable note and mortgage are assigned to a HDC, who fails to record the assignment. Then the original mortgagee (1) wrongfully records a satisfaction of the mortgage of record and (2) the mortgagor conveys to a grantee who is a bona fide purchaser for value. The grantee is entitled to rely on the recorded satisfaction, and will take the land free and clear of the mortgage debt.

c. Wrongful Satisfaction by a Trustee Under a Deed of Trust

Potential subsequent grantees are entitled to assume that when the trustee reconveys the land to the mortgagor, she is acting in accordance with the note holder's instructions. Even if the note and mortgage have been assigned, the trustee's reconveyance will bind the assignee.

C. ASSIGNMENT OF THE MORTGAGE FOR SECURITY PURPOSES

Mortgagees often obtain loans by pledging their notes and mortgages as security. In essence what results is a mortgage on a note and mortgage.

1. Application of Article 9 of the UCC to Such Assignments

It is clear that UCC Article 9 governs pledges of (security interests in) notes and mortgages. To the extent that Article 9 is applicable, "perfection" of the pledgee-lender's interest is necessary to protect the lender against subsequent parties who claim an interest in such notes and mortgages. Revised Article 9 provides two methods of perfection.

a. UCC–1 Filing

The pledgee may perfect by filing a UCC–1 financing statement with the office of the Secretary of State. It was believed by the drafters that this method will be effective against the "strong-arm" powers of the mortgagee-pledgor's trustee in bankruptcy.

b. Taking Possession

Instead of filing a financing statement, the pledgee may perfect by taking physical possession of the promissory note.

c. Which Method is Better?

Article 9 provides that a pledgee who perfects by taking possession of the note will have priority over an earlier pledgee who perfecting by filing a financing statement, unless the later pledgee had actual knowledge of the former. Hence, pledgees should employ filing as a method of perfection only if they are confident that the mortgagee-pledgor will not attempt to "double-pledge" the note. If a pledgee is not certain of this, the safe approach is to take possession (which will make a "double-pledging" of the note impossible).

2.   **The Significance of Applying Article 9 of the UCC to Mortgage Note Assignments**

Under Revised Article 9, perfection of a security interest in the note (by either method described above) will automatically perfect the security interest in the mortgage as well.

3.   **Recording an Assignment**

It is not necessary for the pledgee of the note to record a security assignment of the mortgage in the real property records in order to perfect. Moreover, if the mortgagee-pledgor defaults on the debt secured by the security assignment, Revised Article 9 permits the pledgee to record in the real property records a "transfer statement," reciting the existence of the pledge, the pledgor's default, and the fact that the pledgee has realized on the security assignment.

D.   PARTICIPATIONS

A common transaction that is part of the secondary mortgage market is the sale of fractional or "participation" interests in one or more mortgage loans held by the originating lender.

1.   **Rights of the Participants After Default**

Where one or more loans go into default, as among the participants, almost all courts, in the absence of a contrary agreement, grant a pro-rata priority. As between the lead lender and the participants, under the better view, priority is also pro-rata. In the absence of a specific priority agreement or a guarantee of payment by the lead, participants have no special priority vis à vis the lead lender.

2.   **Lead Lender Misconduct**

To avoid problems caused by lead lender misconduct, participants can insist that the notes be marked so as to provide notice to non-participant third parties that they are subject to participants' rights. An alternate and better approach is to place the notes in the hands of a third-party trustee with appropriate instructions dealing with the trustee's authority to release them.

3.   Lead Lender Bankruptcy

When a lead lender goes into bankruptcy, its general creditors or trustee in bankruptcy may claim that the participation arrangement was insufficient to transfer ownership of the notes to the participants and that they therefore remain part of the bankrupt lead lender's estate. Two arguments are used to support this position:

a.   Loan of Money by Participants to Lead Lender

Under this theory, the participation really amounts to a loan of money by the participants to the lead lender with the notes and mortgages constituting loan security. In order for the participants to be secured creditors, the perfection of a UCC Article 9 security interest in them, a recording of an assignment in the real estate records, or both would be necessary.

b.   Assignment of Mortgage Loan Proceeds

Under this theory, the participants do not receive property interests in the notes themselves, but rather only assignments of the loan proceeds. Only the lead lender, as assignor, has the right to enforce the mortgage notes and thus the participants have no ownership interests.

These arguments can be effectively rebutted if the documents make clear that a sale, not a loan, is intended, and if the payments to which the participants are entitled are simply pro-rata pass-throughs of the payments made by the mortgagor on the underlying mortgage loan.

■ VIII.   DISCHARGE OF THE DEBT AND MORTGAGE: BY PAYMENT OR OTHERWISE

A.   PREPAYMENT OF THE MORTGAGE DEBT

1.   At Common Law

There is no common law right to prepay a mortgage debt. The Restatement (Third) of Property (Mortgages) § 6.2 and several recent cases reverse this result, allowing free prepayment unless the mortgage documents restrict or prohibit it.

2. Prohibitions on Prepayment

A clause in a mortgage prohibiting prepayment for some period of time, or even for the entire term of the loan, is valid and enforceable.

3. Prepayment Fees

Many mortgages permit prepayment, but exact a charge or "prepayment fee" for the privilege of doing so.

4. Reasons for Using Prepayment Fees

Prepayment fees are utilized for two reasons: (1) to compensate lenders for fixed costs that otherwise cannot be recaptured at the inception of loans or over their amortization; and (2) to discourage borrowers from refinancing during periods of declining interest rates.

5. Judicial Treatment of Prepayment Penalties

Several arguments have been employed by borrowers seeking to avoid prepayment fees, but the fees have virtually always been upheld in the state courts.

a. The Usury Argument

Prepayment fees are not usurious because they represent a charge for returning money and not interest for the right to use it.

b. Restraint on Alienation

Prepayment penalties are not unreasonable restraints on alienation. However, a combination of a prohibition on prepayment with a prohibition on sale of the real estate subject to the mortgage constitutes an invalid restraint on alienation.

c. Liquidated Damages v. Penalty Analysis

A few state courts have recognized that a prepayment fee is a type of liquidated damage clause. However, these courts have nearly always found that the fees in question were reasonable advance estimates of probable damages, and not invalid penalties.

6. Acceleration by Mortgagee After Mortgagor Default

Most of the cases hold that a prepayment charge may not be collected where acceleration and foreclosure occurs as a result of an honest inability to pay.

However, a few recent cases allow enforcement of the fee if the mortgage documents specifically provided for it in the context of default and acceleration.

7. Other Involuntary Prepayments

Courts have usually refused to permit the collection of a prepayment fee if the payment was "involuntary," as for example, in the case of casualty loss or the exercise of the condemnation power. Here, again, there is recent authority upholding the fee if the documents specifically impose it in the case of an "involuntary" prepayment.

8. Prepayment Charges Incident to Due–On Enforcement

Prepayment charges will generally be unenforceable where prepayment is triggered by actual or threatened due-on enforcement. A regulation of the OTS specifically prohibits collection of the fee if a due-on-sale clause is enforced in a mortgage on an owner-occupied home.

9. Prepayment Fees in Bankruptcy

When a real estate borrower is in bankruptcy, and makes a prepayment, the issue is usually whether the prepayment fee is recognized as a secured claim of the lender by the bankruptcy court. Under Bankruptcy Code § 506(b), such fees are secured claims only if they are "reasonable." Unlike the state courts, the bankruptcy courts have been quite aggressive in finding excessively large fees to be unreasonable and hence unsecured.

10. Statutory and Regulatory Limitations

a. State Legislation

While statutes are not uniform, they commonly limit the exaction of prepayment charges in residential real estate loan transactions to one to three percent of the principal balance, depending upon the number of years the loan has been outstanding.

b. Office of Thrift Supervision

Currently, OTS regulations provided that "subject to the terms of the loan contract," a federally-chartered savings and loan association may "impose a fee for any prepayment of a loan." This regulation is preemptive of contrary state law, and allows federal thrift institutions to collect prepayment fees even when other financial institutions are not permitted to do so.

c. Comptroller of the Currency

The Comptroller does not have a specific regulation concerning validity of prepayment fees charged by national banks. However, the Comptroller has taken the position that prepayment fees are "interest," and thus are chargeable nationwide by a national bank if its home state allows them.

d. Fannie Mae and Freddie Mac

The Fannie Mae–Freddie Mac single-family home loan form permits prepayment without fee. However, the Fannie Mae–Freddie Mac multi-family form imposes a prepayment fee, computed by use of a "yield maintenance" formula.

B. LATE PAYMENT CHARGES AND DEFAULT INTEREST

1. Judicial Approaches to Late Payment Charges and Default Interest

a. Liquidated Damages vs. Penalty Analysis

A late payment charge or a provision for increased interest upon default will be regarded as an invalid penalty if the charge is not reasonably related to the mortgagee's actual damages caused by the default. Fees calculated as a percentage of the loan balance are more likely to be struck down than those based on a percentage of the delinquent installment. Generally, late fees up to 5% or 6% of the delinquent installment, and default interest increases of 5% to 6% above the regular interest rate, have been upheld without difficulty.

b. Late Payments as Usury

Most courts refuse to characterize late payments as interest for usury purposes because the mortgagor has it in his or her power to avoid the penalty by paying the debt. Default interest is much more likely to be held subject to the usury statutes.

c. **Late Fees and Default Interest in Bankruptcy**

In bankruptcy, the issue is usually whether the fee or increased interest is a secured claim. The answer is governed by Bankruptcy Code § 506(b), which requires such fees to be "reasonable." The bankruptcy courts have been aggressive in striking down excessive fees and default interest rates.

2. **Legislative and Regulatory Impact**

a. **State Regulation**

A growing number of states regulate late payment charges by statute. Almost all such statutes have in common a requirement that late charges be calculated as a percentage of the late installment rather than of the principal balance of the loan. They may also impose a ceiling on late fees, such as the lesser of a fixed dollar amount (say, $5 to $10) or a percentage of the installment. On the other hand, default interest is seldom regulated (except, of course, by usury statutes).

b. **The Uniform Consumer Credit Code**

Under the UCCC, late fees are limited to the lesser of $5 or 5% of the late installment; the limitation applies only if the loan interest rate is 12% or more, and the loan is for personal, family, household or agricultural purposes.

c. **Federal Regulation**

In the case of FHA and VA loans, there is a 15 day grace period, and the penalty is limited to 4% of the late installment. Fannie Mae requires as to non-federally insured or guaranteed mortgages a late charge of 4% of the late installment after a 15 day grace period. Freddie Mac permits, but does not require, the collection of a maximum 5% late charge after a 15 day grace period.

All federally-regulated lenders are prohibited from charging a late fee when the only delinquency is the borrower's failure to pay a previously-assessed late fee. Federal thrift institutions are authorized by OTS to charge any late fees their contracts permit; any limitations under state law are preempted. However, they may not impose a charge more than one time for the same late installment. Each payment received must be applied to the longest outstanding installment due. The thrift institution may not deduct late charges from regular installment payments, but must collect them separately.

C.   PAYMENT AND REDEMPTION

1.   Payment by One Who is Primarily Responsible for the Obligation

When a mortgage debt is paid in full by one who is primarily responsible for payment, the mortgage is extinguished.

a.   Who is Primarily Responsible?

Those primarily responsible include the mortgagor and any subsequent grantees of the real estate, whether they assumed the mortgage debt or not.

b.   When can Payment be Made?

Payment may be made only when payment is due (either by the terms of the loan or by virtue of an acceleration), or prior to that time if the mortgagee is willing to accept it or applicable prepayment principles permit it.

c.   Payment Must be in Full

Redemption occurs only when the debt is paid in full (including all valid fees, charges, and accrued interest), unless the mortgagee is willing to accept a lesser amount in lieu of full payment.

d.   The Payor's Right to a Written Discharge

When a redemption is made by one who is primarily responsible, the mortgagee has a duty to provide a recordable written satisfaction or release. If the mortgagee refuses, a court will order execution of such a document.

e.   Agreement Not to Extinguish the Mortgage

In some instances (e.g., "home equity" or line-of-credit loans) the parties may agree that the mortgage will not be extinguished even though the balance of the loan debt is paid down to zero. Such agreements are enforceable.

2. Payment by One Who is Not Primarily Responsible for the Obligation.

When payment in full is made by one who is not primarily responsible for the mortgage debt, the mortgage is not extinguished, but is deemed assigned to the payor under the principle of subrogation.

a. What Payors are not Primarily Responsible?

Those not primarily responsible include holders of junior liens and other junior interests in the real estate, such as subordinate tenants. They also include cotenants, life tenants, and other similar interest holders, to the extent that someone else has a duty to reimburse them for part of the payment they have made.

b. When Can Payment be Made?

Those who are not responsible can pay only when the debt is due by its terms or has been accelerated. They cannot prepay even if the mortgagee is willing to accept prepayment.

c. The Payor's Right to a Written Assignment

The payor is entitled to a written assignment evidencing his or her subrogation right, and may obtain a court order compelling it if the mortgagee refuses to give it.

3. Payment by a Refinancing Lender

Assume a borrower has two mortgages on the property, and wishes to refinance the senior loan in order to get a lower interest rate. The borrower arranges a loan with a new lender in the amount necessary to pay off the senior mortgage loan. The new lender obtains a title examination, but the title examiner negligently fails to report the existence of the second mortgage. The new lender then pays off the old senior mortgage, which is discharged. However, the former second mortgagee now asserts that it is in first priority position, and that the new mortgage is subordinate to it. To avoid this conclusion, the new lender argues that it has the priority of the old senior loan that it paid, under the doctrine of subrogation. There are three views as to whether subrogation should be allowed.

a. New Lender Held to Constructive Notice

Under this minority view, if the second mortgage is recorded, the refinancing lender is held to have had notice of it, and therefore cannot make an equitable claim of subrogation. As a practical matter, this view nearly always results in denial of subrogation.

b.   New Lender Subrogated Unless it had Actual Notice

Under this view, probably the majority view, the refinancing lender can have subrogation unless it had actual notice of the second mortgage.

c.   New Lender May Have Subrogation Even if it had Actual Notice.

Under this view, also a minority, the refinancing lender can have subrogation even if it had actual notice of the second mortgage, provided that it can establish that it had a reasonable expectation of gaining first priority.

d.   Use of Actual Assignment

The refinancing lender can avoid this argument, and can always be assured of maintaining first priority position, by obtaining an actual written assignment of the mortgage from the senior lender who is being paid off.

e.   Different Terms in Refinancing Mortgage

If the terms of the refinancing mortgage are more burdensome that the terms of the senior mortgage that was paid off, the courts should and will deny subrogation to the extent of any harm or damage that the intervening mortgagee would suffer as a result of the changed terms.

4.   Tender as the Equivalent of Payment

A tender of the payment—that is, a present offer to pay immediately in full, coupled with present ability to do so—has the same effect as an actual payment: it extinguishes the mortgage or assigns it (as the case may be, depending on whether the payor was or was not primarily responsible). It also stops the running of interest.

a.   Tender Must be Unconditional

To have the above effect, the tender must be unconditional. However, a condition that the mortgagee give a document of discharge or assignment is permitted, since that is the mortgagee's duty in any event.

b. **Tender Must be Kept Good**

To be effective, the tender must be kept good. This means the payor must continue to be ready, willing, and able to pay at all times.

D. MORTGAGES SECURING NON–MONETARY OBLIGATIONS

An obligation must be capable of being reduced to a money equivalent to be validly secured by a mortgage.

E. MERGER, DEED IN LIEU OF FORECLOSURE AND RELATED PROBLEMS

1. An Introduction to Merger

The basic merger theory holds that when a mortgagee's interest and fee title coincide and meet in the same person, the lesser estate, the mortgage, merges into the fee title and is extinguished. The merger theory can be utilized either as a defense to an action on a mortgage debt or as an argument that the mortgage no longer exists.

2. Mortgagee Foreclosure Purchase Where Mortgagee Owns Both Junior and Senior Mortgages: Merger and Destruction of Debt

a. **Mortgagee Purchase at Junior Sale**

Where a holder of both junior and senior mortgages forecloses the *junior* mortgage and purchases at the foreclosure sale, many courts hold that the foreclosure purchase destroys the mortgagee's right to sue the mortgagor personally on the first mortgage debt.

b. **Mortgagee Purchase at Senior Sale**

Where the mortgagee purchases at the *senior* sale, the general rule is that such a purchase does not destroy the mortgagee's ability later to collect on the junior mortgage debt.

3.   The Merger Doctrine and Mortgage Extinguishment: The Deed in Lieu of Foreclosure

It is a common practice for a mortgagee to take a conveyance of the fee from the mortgagor in satisfaction of the mortgage debt and as a substitute for foreclosure.

a.   The Merger Problem

If, subsequent to the original mortgage, the mortgagor has imposed another lien on the mortgaged land, the deed in lieu, unlike a foreclosure, will not cut off that junior lien. More important, the junior lienor may well argue that since both the fee title and the mortgage have merged in the mortgagee, the mortgage has been destroyed. Most courts avoid the latter result, however, by applying the presumption that the mortgagee, the person in whom the mortgage and fee interest were merged, intended a result most favorable to him or her—namely, that the mortgage continues to exist.

b.   Avoidance of the Merger Problem

The mortgagee should conduct a thorough title search before taking a deed in lieu to determine whether intervening liens exist. If such intervening interests are discovered, the only prudent alternative is to go through an actual foreclosure.

4.   Other Difficulties With the Deed in Lieu

It can be argued that the deed in lieu is really an absolute deed disguised as a mortgage. Moreover, it is vulnerable to the traditional principle that equity can set aside transactions that are unfair and unconscionable.

■ IX.   FORECLOSURE

A.   DETERMINING THE FORECLOSURE AMOUNT: PROBLEMS OF ACCELERATION

Virtually all mortgages today include acceleration clauses, which, in the event of mortgagor's default, give the mortgagee the right to declare the entire debt due and payable.

1. **Notice as a Condition Precedent**

    Notice to the mortgagor is not necessarily required for a valid acceleration. However, the mortgagee must perform some affirmative, overt act evidencing its intention to actuate the acceleration clause. Tender by the mortgagor of the arrearages prior to the occurrence of that affirmative act destroys the right to accelerate as to that default.

2. **Judicial Limits on Acceleration**

    a. **Waiver**

        Acceleration has been defeated in situations where there has been a consistent prior pattern of acceptance of late payments by the mortgagee.

    b. **Hardship as a Ground for Defeating Acceleration**

        The majority of courts hold that a mortgagor will not be relieved from the enforcement of an acceleration clause for a default occurring because of his or her negligence, inadvertence, mistake or by accident unless the mortgagee is guilty of fraud, bad faith, or other conduct that would render enforcement of the acceleration clause unconscionable. However, a significant number of decisions protect a mortgagor from acceleration where the default arises as a result of accident or a mistake while acting in good faith, or unusual circumstances beyond mortgagor's control.

3. **Statutory and Regulatory Limitations**

    a. **State Statutes**

        Many states have enacted "arrearages" legislation permitting the mortgagor to defeat acceleration by tendering, within a specific time period, the amount that would have been due in the absence of default and acceleration.

    b. **Federal Agency Guidelines**

        FHA and VA guidelines extend the time which must elapse between default and foreclosure and require the mortgagee to permit reinstatement by payment of arrearages.

    c. **Fannie Mae–Freddie Mac Standard Form Provisions**

        The Fannie Mae–Freddie Mace 1–to–4–family residential mortgage form requires detailed mailed notice and a 30 day grace period as a condition precedent to acceleration. It also affords the mortgagee the right to defeat acceleration until five days prior to foreclosure by payment of arrearages and reasonable attorneys' fees.

4. The Absence of an Acceleration Clause

The failure to provide an acceleration clause in a mortgage leaves the mortgagee with two undesirable options.

a. Property Capable of Physical Division

Where the mortgaged real estate is capable of physical division a court can order a foreclosure sale of only so much property as will be needed to satisfy the unpaid installment.

b. Property Incapable of Physical Division

In this situation, a court can order: (1) all of the property sold free and clear of the mortgage lien or, (2) all of the property sold to satisfy the unpaid installment, but subject to the remaining balance of the mortgage debt.

5. Marshaling

When a mortgage covers two or more parcels of land, the marshaling concept requires the foreclosing court to direct that the parcels be foreclosed in an order which will minimize the potentially harmful effect on third parties.

a. The "Two Funds" Rule

If some of the mortgaged parcels are also subject to junior mortgages or liens, while the others are not, marshaling requires that the parcels which have no junior liens be foreclosed first, thus reducing the possibility that the junior lienors will be wiped out unnecessarily.

b. The Inverse Order of Alienation Rule

If the mortgaged parcels have been sold to several purchasers who have not assumed the obligation to pay the mortgage, marshaling requires that the parcels be sold at foreclosure in the inverse order of their transfer by the mortgagor; i.e., the last to be sold by the mortgagor will be foreclosed first.

c. **No Prejudice to Senior Mortgagee**

Neither the "inverse order" rule nor the "two funds" rule will be applied where doing so would prejudice the rights of the senior mortgagee.

B. METHODS OF FORECLOSURE

1. Major Methods

a. **Judicial Foreclosure**

This form of foreclosure is the most widely available in the United States. Because it is a judicial proceeding, it entails the normal incidents of litigation: service of process on all persons who are necessary parties; formal pleadings; and a judicial trial.

b. **Power of Sale Foreclosure**

This method is non-judicial and is speedier than judicial foreclosure. In order to qualify for this type of foreclosure, the mortgage must contain a power of sale. Only slightly more than half of the states recognize this type of foreclosure, and in most of them it is available only if the mortgage is in the form of a deed of trust.

2. Minor Methods

Less commonly used foreclosure methods in this country include: (1) Judicial Strict Foreclosure; (2) Entry Without Process; (3) Action at Law for A Writ of Entry; and (4) Scire Facias.

C. JUDICIAL FORECLOSURE

1. Use in Power of Sale States

Judicial foreclosure is sometimes used in power of sale states, even though it is slower and more costly. Reasons for use of judicial foreclosure include: (1)

the mortgage form did not contain a power of sale; (2) judicial intervention is necessary to correct other defects in the mortgage; (3) the mortgage is in the form of an absolute deed; or (4) where there are other liens on the mortgaged real estate and priority is uncertain.

2.   The Necessary–Proper Party Distinction

a.   The Purpose of Foreclosure

Foreclosure should terminate the rights of all parties whose interest in the land are "subject to" or "subordinate" to the mortgage being foreclosed. The more basic and descriptive purpose of foreclosure, however, is to give the purchaser at the foreclosure sale the same title that the mortgagor had when the mortgage being foreclosed was executed.

b.   Necessary Parties

A party is "necessary" if failure to join him or her in the action will not accomplish the purposes of foreclosure described above. All persons with interests junior to the mortgage being foreclosed are "necessary" parties.

c.   Proper Parties

It is occasionally important to join as parties certain unconsenting persons and bind them even though they do not qualify as necessary parties. To the extent that this can be accomplished, such persons can be considered "proper" parties.

3.   The Senior Lienholder as a Party

Normally a senior lienholder may not be made a party without its consent. Nevertheless, it may be made a party where the foreclosing mortgagee is seeking to ascertain the amount or terms of the senior lien or where the priority status of the supposedly senior lien is unclear.

4.   The Lessee as a Party

If a lease is senior to the mortgage being foreclosed, the lease is unaffected by the foreclosure. If the lease is junior, joinder of the lessee in the foreclosure proceedings terminates the lease and lessee's obligations under it.

5. The Omitted Party Problem

Generally, parties with junior interests who are omitted from a judicial foreclosure are unaffected by the foreclosure proceeding; their interests continue to exist, and they have the rights described below. (Of course, a junior interest holder who failed to record his or her interest may be cut off by the usual operation of the recording acts.)

a. The Omitted Owner

If the owner of the equity of redemption is omitted from a judicial foreclosure proceeding, the proceeding is ineffective as to the owner, and his or her right to redeem is unaffected. Such a person can redeem the land by paying the mortgage debt to the foreclosure sale purchaser, since the latter has acquired the rights of the foreclosing mortgagee.

b. The Omitted Junior Lienor and the Foreclosure Sale Purchaser

The Junior Lienor's Remedies. The omitted junior lienor may foreclose its mortgage subject to the first mortgage (which is considered "revived" for this purpose), or it may "redeem" by paying the foreclosure purchaser the amount of the first mortgage debt.

The Foreclosure Sale Purchaser's Remedies. First, the foreclosure purchaser, as an assignee of the rights of the senior mortgagee, may reforeclose the senior mortgage. Second, the purchaser, standing in the shoes of the foreclosed mortgagor, may "redeem" from the holder of the omitted junior lien by paying the junior lienor the amount of its debt. Third, in certain limited circumstances, the sale purchaser may obtain strict foreclosure against the junior lienor, in effect cutting off the junior lien without going through another foreclosure.

Junior Lienor v. Foreclosure Sale Purchaser. If both the omitted junior lienor and the foreclosure sale purchaser attempt to "redeem" from each other, the latter will prevail.

c. Omitted Parties: Statutory Redemption vs. Equitable Redemption

The equitable right to redeem accrues at mortgage maturity and ends when there is a valid foreclosure. Statutory redemption, however, begins only after a valid foreclosure has taken place. Thus, because the foreclosure was invalid as to them, an omitted owner or junior lienor must utilize equitable and not statutory redemption.

D. POWER OF SALE FORECLOSURE

1. Effect of Power of Sale Foreclosure

If the mortgagee complies with statutory requirements, power of sale foreclosure normally accomplishes the identical purposes achieved by judicial foreclosure.

2. Stability of Power of Sale Titles

In spite of its substantial advantages in terms of cost and time, power of sale foreclosure produces titles that are somewhat more subject to later attack than those produced by judicial foreclosure.

3. Classification of Power of Sale Foreclosure Defects

Where power of sale foreclosure defects are so serious as to render a foreclosure void, the purchaser at the sale and subsequent grantees acquire nothing. On the other hand, some foreclosure defects are so inconsequential as to have no impact on the validity of the sale. Between the two foregoing extremes are defects that render the sale voidable. If the sale is voidable, legal title passes to the foreclosure purchaser, but the equitable right of redemption or "equitable title" does not. Such equitable rights, however, can be cut off if the land gets into the hands of a bona fide purchaser.

4. Who is a Bona Fide Purchaser?

A foreclosure sale purchaser will be treated as a BFP, and thus take free of voidable defects, if value has been paid and if (a) she has no actual knowledge of the defects; (b) she is not placed on reasonable notice from recorded instruments; and (c) the defects are not such that a reasonable person attending the sale exercising reasonable care would have discovered them. A subsequent grantee who acquires the land from the foreclosure purchaser will be treated as a BFP, and thus take free of voidable defects, if value has been paid and (a) she had no actual knowledge of the defects and (b) she was not placed on reasonable notice of the defects from recorded instruments. A purchasing mortgagee will not be treated as a BFP.

5. Specific Defects

Often one power of sale defect alone may be insufficient to affect the validity of a foreclosure, but the cumulative impact of that defect operating in conjunction with others enhances the chances of a successful attack on the foreclosure. The following are some of the more commonly raised grounds for setting aside a power of sale foreclosure:

a.   Inadequacy of Foreclosure Sale Price

b.   Improper Time of Sale

c.   Improper Place of Sale

d.   Sale Improperly Held by Parcel or Bulk

e.   Chilled Bidding

f.   Purchase by the Mortgagee or Beneficiary

6.   Nature of the Trustee's Duties Under a Deed of Trust

Because a trustee under a deed of trust represents parties whose interests are often antithetical, courts do not purport to apply normal trust law standards to such trustees. Hence it is important to focus on specific questions that have arisen concerning the trustee's role.

a.   Mortgagee (Beneficiary) Purchase at Trustee's Sale

So long as a trustee is not employed by or otherwise closely associated with the mortgagee, it is permissible for the mortgagee to purchase at the sale.

b.   Trustee Purchase at Sale

A trustee, at least without the express consent of the mortgagor, may not purchase the premises for his own account.

c.   Trustee and Employee or Part–Owner of Mortgagee

Some courts hold that where the connection between the trustee and mortgagee is substantial, purchase by the mortgagee is really an indirect purchase by the trustee and thus voidable. An alternative judicial approach followed by a few courts holds that where, for example, the trustee is an important officer of the mortgagee, the deed of trust, in effect, becomes a mortgage and the law of mortgages rather than of trust deeds applies. Such a sale to the mortgagee is voidable because the mortgagee is treated as if it had purchased at its own sale.

d. Trustee Duty to Ascertain Whether Foreclosure is Justified

Absent unusual circumstances known to the trustee, he may, upon receiving a request for foreclosure from the mortgagee, proceed upon that advice without making any affirmative investigation of the facts of the default.

e. Trustee Duty to Disclose Title or Property Defects to Sale Purchasers

Normally the trustee is under no duty to make representations or to answer questions. However, if questions are asked and the trustee undertakes to answer, then such answers must be full and accurate. Nothing may then be concealed.

f. The "Commercially Reasonable" Standard

A few courts have borrowed the "commercial reasonableness" standard from Article § 9–504 of the UCC and applied it to power of sale real estate foreclosures. At least for purposes of permitting a deficiency judgment, they require that the foreclosure sale have been on commercially reasonable terms.

g. The Impact of Presumption Statutes

Several states have statutes that provide that recitals of statutory compliance contained in a trustee's deed are prima facie evidence of such compliance. Some statutes also provide that such recitals establish conclusive evidence of compliance as to bona fide purchasers.

h. Failure to Provide Notice to Junior Interests—Should a Judicial Foreclosure Analogy Apply?

If a power of sale statute requires notice to the holders of junior interests (and most such statutes do not), then logically the result of the foreclosing mortgagee's failure to provide that notice would be identical to omitting a junior interest holder in a judicial foreclosure, as discussed above. Whether this result will actually be reached by the courts in power of sale states, however, is largely undecided. The question is complicated by the existence of the statutes establishing a presumption of validity for power of sale foreclosures, as discussed above.

7. Remedies for Defective Power of Sale Foreclosure

a. Injunction Against Sale

The injunction suit is the remedy commonly used by a mortgagor or other injured party to prevent an improper foreclosure sale from occurring when it has not yet been consummated. Some courts require that the mortgagor tender the mortgage debt as a condition precedent to injunctive relief.

b. **The Suit to Set Aside the Sale**

This remedy, employed after the sale has occurred, may be based not only the substantive grounds that would have justified an injunction suit, but also to raise defects that were inherent in the foreclosure process itself. Tender is more frequently viewed as a condition precedent to this sort of suit than it is in a suit for an injunction. Moreover, if the defect merely renders the sale voidable, this remedy is unavailable against a BFP.

c. **Damages for Wrongful Foreclosure**

This remedy can be utilized by a mortgagor or junior lienor who can not bring a suit to set aside the sale because the land has been acquired by a BFP. The mortgagor's damages are measured as the difference between the fair market value of the real estate and the aggregate amount of liens as of the date of the defective foreclosure sale. For the junior lienor claimant, the measure is the difference between the fair market value of the mortgaged real estate and the value of senior liens thereon as of the date of the wrongful foreclosure. The majority of courts allow a mortgagor to sue for damages even though a suit to set aside would also be available.

E. POWER OF SALE FORECLOSURE—CONSTITUTIONALITY

1. Constitutional Notice Requirements

Assuming that power of sale legislation constitutes state or federal action for purposes of the due process clauses of the 14th and 5th amendments, such legislation violates due process to the extent that it does not require at least mailed notice to those parties who, in a judicial foreclosure, would be characterized as necessary parties.

2. Constitutional Hearing Requirements

Assuming that state or federal action is present, power of sale legislation violates the hearing requirements of due process to the extent that it does not require a hearing at which interested parties can challenge both the legal right to foreclosure and the propriety of the decision to do so. There is some authority that where the foreclosing mortgagee is the United States government, federal agency rules, regulations or practice that mandate an internal agency hearing may satisfy procedural due process requirements even though the state power of sale statute that is used by that agency otherwise fails to meet hearing requirements.

3. Enforceability of Waiver Provisions

While the foregoing constitutional defects are theoretically capable of being waived in the mortgage itself or in a separate agreement, a waiver must be very clearly expressed and specifically bargained for. Hence, most waiver attempts will be either constitutionally unsound or, for practical purposes, unworkable.

4. The State Action—Federal Action Problem

Power of sale legislation can be unconstitutional only if, for purposes of the 14th amendment, "significant state involvement" exists or, in the case of the 5th amendment, sufficient "federal action" is established.

a. Power of Sale and "State Action"

State action litigation has focused on five theories: "direct" state action; the "encouragement" theory; the governmental function theory; the judicial enforcement theory; and the "pervasiveness" theory. While the United States Supreme Court has not yet decided the state action question in the power of sale context, its decisions in related areas and the opinions of other courts directly dealing with power of sale foreclosure, make it increasingly unlikely that state action can be found on any of the foregoing theories.

b. Power of Sale and the Government as the Foreclosing Entity

Where a direct instrumentality of the state or federal government is the foreclosing mortgagee, courts cannot avoid the notice and hearing defects inherent in power of sale foreclosure. In such cases, it is not the power of sale legislation, but rather the foreclosing mortgagee itself that supplies the requisite governmental action under the 5th or 14th amendment. The FmHA, the VA, and the FHA will probably each be considered direct instrumentalities of the United States. On the other hand there is authority that GNMA will not be considered the federal government for purposes of the 5th Amendment. Moreover, quasi-governmental entities such as Fannie Mae and the Freddie Mac will probably not be considered to be acting as the federal government for foreclosure purposes. If the foreclosing entity is a non-governmental entity, the presence of federal subsidies or federal regulation will not trigger a finding of federal action.

F. THE UNIFORM NONJUDICIAL FORECLOSURE ACT

1. Methods of Foreclosure

The Act provides for three methods of foreclosure: (1) the auction sale; (2) negotiated sale and (3) by appraisal.

2. Notice Provisions

The Act uses a "two notice" system. The foreclosing creditor must give both a "notice of default" and a "notice of foreclosure."

3. Due Process Concerns

The Act provides for mailed or personal service notice to those whose interests are put at risk by foreclosure. Residential debtors have a right to an informal meeting with a representative of the mortgagee to present reasons why the foreclosure should not go forward.

4. Redemption

The Act recognizes equitable redemption before foreclosure, but does not permit statutory redemption.

5. Deficiency Liability

Debtors under the Act are subject to deficiency judgments except for residential debtors who act in "good faith." Any deficiency judgment under the Act is limited by the "fair market value" concept.

6. Protections for Residential Debtors

The Act gives residential debtors a variety of protections that do not benefit other debtors.

G.   DISPOSITION OF FORECLOSURE SURPLUS

1.   Common Law Rule

When a mortgage foreclosure surplus occurs, the liens and other interests terminated by the foreclosure attach to the surplus in the order of priority they enjoyed prior to the foreclosure. The foreclosed mortgagor's claim to the surplus is junior to all valid liens terminated by the foreclosure.

2.   Effect of Statutes

Statutes in some jurisdictions specifically codify the common law approach described above. On the other hand, statutes often award the surplus to the "mortgagor, his heirs, successors and assigns" and make no mention of junior lienholders. Such statutes should be, and generally are, construed in favor of junior lienors by interpreting the word "assigns" to include the junior lienholders as assignees.

3.   Mortgage Form Language

Even if the mortgage documents purport to award surplus to the "mortgagor, heirs and assigns," and make no reference to junior lienors, courts will nonetheless give priority in the surplus to junior lienors over the mortgagor.

4.   Claims of Those Senior to Foreclosed Mortgagee

Only one whose interest in the foreclosed real estate was terminated may share in the surplus; hence, persons with interests senior to the foreclosed mortgage may not do so.

5.   Junior Liens Not Yet in Default

Most courts allow junior interests whose liens are not yet in default to share immediately in a senior foreclosure surplus.

H.   REACQUISITION OF TITLE BY HOLDER OF THE EQUITY OF REDEMPTION AND RELATED ISSUES

1.   Foreclosure Purchase by Mortgagor or Other Equity Holder

Under the prevailing view, a mortgagor or other holder of the equity of redemption who purchases the mortgaged real estate at a foreclosure sale acquires title subject to any lien or other interest that previously was junior to the foreclosed mortgage

2. **Foreclosure Purchase by Holder of Junior Interest: Impact on Other Junior Interests**

A holder of a junior interest who purchases real estate at the foreclosure sale of any senior lien on that real estate acquires title free and clear of the interest of the holder of the equity of redemption and of any interest that previously was junior to the foreclosed mortgage.

I. STATUTORY REDEMPTION

1. **Purpose of Statutory Redemption**

The four legislative goals underlying statutory redemption are: (1) to allow the mortgagor an additional time period to obtain refinancing; (2) to permit a financially hard-pressed mortgagor additional use of the real estate; (3) to encourage those who bid at the foreclosure sale to offer a fair price; and (4) where junior lienors are allowed to redeem, to allow them to protect their security that would be otherwise lost.

2. **Criticisms of Statutory Redemption**

It has been argued that statutory redemption: (1) discourages prompt payment of the mortgage debt; (2) retards third party bidding and (3) encourages the mortgagor to "milk" the property and to avoid necessary maintenance.

3. **The Operation of Typical Statutes**

    a. **Strict Priority Approach**

    After the foreclosure sale, the mortgagor generally has a six to twelve month period to redeem by payment of the foreclosure sale price plus a statutory rate of interest to the sale purchaser. If the mortgagor redeems there can be no further redemption. If the mortgagor fails to redeem within the specified period, then junior lienholders each have a five day period, in order of their pre-foreclosure priority, to redeem by paying the sale purchaser the foreclosure sale price plus the amount of the lien of any lienor who has redeemed in a previous five day period.

b. The Scramble Method

Under this method there is no exclusive redemption period for the mortgagor. Rather, redemption may be made from the purchaser by both mortgagors or junior lienholders, although if redemption is ever made by the mortgagor, redemption ends. As between junior lienholders, each may redeem at any time irrespective of their priority. However, priority is relevant in determining how much the redeeming lienor must pay.

4. Redemption by Mortgagor: Revival of Liens

If the mortgagor redeems, the majority view is that all liens existing prior to the foreclosure sale are revived, including, to the extent of any deficiency, the lien under which the real estate was sold. Some courts reach this result as to junior liens, but not as to a deficiency lien. Others hold that while other junior liens are revived if redemption is by the original debtor-mortgagor, they are not if it is by a subsequent grantee.

5. Redemption by Junior Lienor: Revival of Liens

Redemption by a junior lienor gives the latter the same title the foreclosure sale purchaser would have obtained had there been no redemption. Thus, there is no revival of junior liens.

J. ANTI–DEFICIENCY LEGISLATION

1. The One Action Rule

Under this rule, in effect in California and five or six other states, a mortgagee must bring a foreclosure action prior to seeking to hold the mortgagor personally liable on the mortgage debt. In other words, an initial action on the debt is not permitted. The rule is sometime called a "security first" rule.

2. Fair Value Legislation

This type of legislation defines the deficiency as the difference between the mortgage debt and the "fair value" of the foreclosed real estate. Its purpose is to avoid penalizing the mortgagor with a larger deficiency judgment if the property sells at foreclosure for a sub-market price.

3. Prohibition of Deficiency Judgments and Power of Sale Foreclosure

Several states, such as California, prohibit deficiency judgments after power of sale foreclosure.

4. Prohibition of Deficiency Judgments in Foreclosure of Purchase Money Mortgages

Several states prohibit deficiency judgments in a variety of situations involving purchase money mortgages. In some states the prohibition bars only deficiency judgments in favor of vendor-mortgagees, while in others the bar applies to third party lenders as well as vendors. A few states interpret such legislation to prohibit a pre-foreclosure action against the mortgagor on the debt, as well as a deficiency judgment after foreclosure.

5. Deficiency Judgments and Installment Land Contracts

a. The Election of Remedies Problem

Even in the absence of anti-deficiency legislation, the election of remedies doctrine bars an installment land contract vendor from first invoking forfeiture and then seeking to recover the difference between the balance owing on the contract price and what the land is worth.

b. Vendor Proceeding as a Foreclosing Mortgagee

To the extent that a vendor has the option of treating an installment land contract as a mortgage and elects to do so, she can, in the absence of anti-deficiency legislation, obtain a deficiency judgment for the difference between the contract price and the foreclosure sale price. The election of remedies doctrine is not applied when a judicial foreclosure is employed. Whether anti-deficiency legislation will bar a deficiency judgment against a vendee will depend on whether such legislation is construed to encompass installment land contracts.

K. SERVICEMEMBERS CIVIL RELIEF ACT

The Servicemembers Civil Relief Act (Act) provides certain protections to service-person mortgagors with respect to mortgages on real estate executed prior to entrance on active duty. (Citations are to 50 U.S.C.A. App. §§ 501–596.)

1.   **Statutes of Limitation**

Section 526 generally tolls all statutes of limitation that otherwise would run against a service person. This section has been held specifically applicable to statutory redemption periods after foreclosure.

2.   **Section 525 Stay**

Under section 525, during military service or within 90 days thereafter, a serviceperson-debtor is authorized to petition a court to stay any civil action or proceeding.

3.   **Installment Land Contracts**

Section 532 makes it a criminal offense to exercise any right or option such as termination of the contract, repossession of the land or rescission, except by judicial action, with respect to most contracts executed prior to vendee's entry into the military.

4.   **Mortgages and Deeds of Trust**

Section 533 provides that after default in a mortgage loan executed prior to the mortgagor's entrance into military service, the mortgagee can not sell, foreclose, or seize the mortgaged real estate during the period of service plus 90 days thereafter without a court order.

5.   **Section 527 Limitation on Mortgage Interest Rates**

Section 527 limits interest to 6 percent during military service on obligations incurred before entering service, even though a higher rate was originally agreed upon. The interest rate is automatically reduced unless the mortgagee establishes that military service has no material effect on the ability to pay in excess of 6 percent.

6.   **Waiver of Rights by Serviceperson–Mortgagor**

A serviceperson-mortgagor may waive the Act's protections if the waiver is "made pursuant to a written agreement of the parties that is executed during or after the servicemember's period of military service."

L. BANKRUPTCY

1. Classification of Bankruptcy Proceedings

There are four types of bankruptcy proceedings: Chapter 7 ("straight bankruptcy"); Chapter 11 (business reorganization); Chapter 12 (family farmers); and Chapter 13 (wage-earners).

2. The Automatic Stay

All foreclosure proceedings, whether judicial or power of sale, are automatically stayed by the filing of any bankruptcy proceeding.

3. Straight Bankruptcy

Straight bankruptcy entails the liquidation of the debtor's non-exempt assets to satisfy his or her creditors according to the priority and the amount of their claims. Such a proceeding ultimately discharges the debtor of most pre-bankruptcy debts. Whether the automatic stay with respect to any particular mortgagee will be lifted depends upon whether the debtor-mortgagor has "equity" in the mortgaged real estate.

4. The Trustee's Avoidance Powers

The Code affords the trustee an impressive arsenal of weapons to attack vulnerable real estate security.

a. Section 558

This section gives the trustee the benefit of any defense available to the debtor.

b. Section 544(A)(3)

This section affords the trustee, irrespective of actual knowledge on her part, the status of a bona fide purchaser of real property from the debtor who has perfected under state law.

c. Section 551

Under this provision, a trustee who uses her powers under the Code to avoid a senior lien becomes subrogated to the rights of the senior lienor up to the amount of the senior debt.

d. **Section 548**

Under this provision, transfers made by the debtor within one year of bankruptcy may be set aside by the trustee if they were made with the intent to hinder, delay or defraud any creditor to whom the debtor was or became indebted. In addition, this provision allows the trustee to set aside certain "constructively fraudulent" transfers made by the debtor.

e. **Section 547**

To the extent that a mortgage is granted by an insolvent mortgagor within 90 days of bankruptcy, and it would enable the creditor to realize more on its claim than it otherwise would receive in a straight bankruptcy liquidation, it constitutes a voidable preference.

5. **The Chapter 11 Reorganization**

Chapter 11 proceedings provide for the reorganization of corporate and other business debtors. Such plans can often provide for the deferral or stretching out of payments on secured debts, and in some instances, a reduction in principal as well as interest on such debts.

a. **Relief From Stay**

The filing of a Chapter 11 petition, like the filing of other bankruptcy proceedings, stays any pending or future state foreclosure proceedings. Under section 362 of the Code, the bankruptcy court may "terminate, annul, modify or condition such stay (1) for cause, including the lack of adequate protection of an interest in property of such [mortgagee]; or (2) with respect to a stay of an act against property, if (A) the [mortgagor] does not have an equity in the property; and (B) such property is not necessary to an effective reorganization."

b. **Which Stay Relief is Preferred?**

Generally, mortgagees seem to prefer Ground Number 2 over Ground Number 1. Perhaps the reason lies in the fact that if the court finds both a lack of equity and that the property is unnecessary to an effective reorganization, it will invariably dissolve the stay because, by definition, there is no reason for the court to retain control over it. On the other hand, a finding of inadequate protection alone may simply result in a decree ordering additional protection for the mortgagee or some modification, rather than dissolution, of the stay.

c.   **Stay Relief Where Debtor is a "Single Asset Real Estate" Mortgagor**

Section 362 (d)(3), enacted as part of the Bankruptcy Reform Act of 1994, makes it easier for the mortgagee to obtain stay relief where the mortgage is on "single asset real estate."

6.   **Chapter 13 "Wage Earner" Plans**

This type of proceeding is aimed at the rehabilitation of the debtor by the extension and reduction of both unsecured and certain secured claims. The Chapter 13 plan to some extent is to the salaried person or wage earner what Chapter 11 is to the corporate or similar business entity. Real estate mortgagees can be made part of the plan against their consent, and may have their claims modified as long as the plan affords them certain statutorily mandated protections. While mortgages on the debtor's principal residence may not be modified without the mortgagee's consent, courts, under the *Taddeo* case, will keep the stay against foreclosure in effect so long as pre-petition arrearages are in the process of being cured, current payments are being made, and the plan itself is not in default. Most home mortgages may not be "bifurcated"—a form of impermissible modification

7.   **Family Farmer Bankruptcy Act of 1986 (Chapter 12)**

Chapter 12, in large measure, extends Chapter 13 protections to the family farmer, and the substance and structure of the two chapters are very similar. In general, Chapter 12 affords important powers to the farmer-debtor, including the ability to (1) reduce secured indebtedness to the current value of the underlying security; (2) repay the reduced amount over an extended period of time; and (3) satisfy unsecured claims—including those that become unsecured by the foregoing "write-down" of the security—by paying to the plan only the farmer's "disposable income". When the plan is completed successfully, the farmer will be discharged of his or her unsecured indebtedness.

8.   **Setting Aside Pre–Bankruptcy Foreclosures**

Until 1994, federal courts frequently used § 548 of the Code to set aside pre-bankruptcy foreclosures as fraudulent conveyances, but that argument is no longer available. In addition, to a much more limited extent, such foreclosures have been successfully attacked as voidable preferences.

a.   **The Foreclosure Sale as a Fraudulent Conveyance**

Under the *Durrett* decision, a foreclosure sale that yielded less than 70 percent of the property's fair market value was a voidable fraudulent conveyance if the sale occurred while the debtor was insolvent (or became so as a result of the foreclosure sale) and within one year prior to the commencement of bankruptcy proceedings. However, this approach was rejected by the United States Supreme Court in 1994. As a result, section 548 of the Code now provides no ground for invalidating noncollusive state foreclosure sales based on inadequacy of the price, so long as all other requirements of state foreclosure law have been satisfied.

b. The Installment Land Contract as a Fraudulent Conveyance

The *Durrett* approach may remain a viable basis for invalidating certain installment land contract forfeitures.

c. The Foreclosure Sale as a Preference

At least two bankruptcy courts and two federal district courts have held that a foreclosure purchase by the mortgagee can be a voidable preference if it satisfies the 6–part preference test under section 547 of the Code. However, the Court of Appeals for the Ninth Circuit has rejected this use of section 547, as have one or two other courts.

9. Right to Rents During Pendency of a Bankruptcy Proceeding

Whether rents accruing during bankruptcy will be available to the trustee or debtor in possession, on the one hand, or the mortgagee holding an assignment of rents, on the other, is governed both by state assignment of rents law and provisions of the Bankruptcy Reform Act of 1994.

10. Installment Land Contracts in Bankruptcy

Section 365(a) of the Bankruptcy Code authorizes the trustee to "assume or reject" any "executory contract" of the debtor. Sometimes this provision will affect the rights and obligations of parties to installment land contracts.

a. Vendor Bankruptcy

When the vendee is in possession, the vendor's bankruptcy trustee's right to reject the contract is subject to the vendee's right under section 365(i) of the Code to obtain legal title by completing the payments provided for under the contract.

b. Vendee Bankruptcy

If the installment land contract is deemed an "executory contract" for purposes of section 365(a) of the Code, then section 365(b) provides that if the debtor has defaulted under the contract, the trustee, at the time of assumption, must cure the default, compensate the vendor for any loss resulting from the default, and provide adequate assurance of future performance of the contractual obligations. If this is not possible, it will have the effect of forcing rejection of the contract and the vendee will lose the land. On the other hand, if the installment land contract is characterized as a mortgage or security interest, the vendor will be afforded the status of a mortgagee, and he or she will be entitled only to the contract balance and not to the land.

■ X. SOME PRIORITY PROBLEMS

A. PURCHASE MONEY MORTGAGES

1. The Purchase Money Mortgage Priority Rule

A purchase money mortgage, whether of the vendor or third party type, executed at the same time as the deed of purchase, or as part of one transaction, is presumed to be senior to any other claim or lien attaching to the land through the buyer-mortgagor.

2. Recording Act Problems

While the purchase money mortgage will normally gain priority over *prior* liens and interests arising through the buyer, if the mortgage is not recorded it may lose priority to liens or interests that arise *subsequent* to the purchase money mortgage.

3. The Vendor's Purchase Money Mortgage Preference

When there is a priority dispute between a vendor's purchase money mortgagee and a purchase money mortgage held by a third party, and that dispute can not be resolved by the recording act or express agreement between the parties, preference is generally given to the vendor.

B. AFTER–ACQUIRED PROPERTY CLAUSES

1. General Validity

A mortgage that contains an after-acquired property clause purports not only to mortgage the real estate it specifically describes, but also any real estate that mortgagor subsequently acquires. As between the mortgagor and mortgagee, such clauses generally create an equitable lien on the subsequently acquired real estate. Some jurisdictions limit the coverage of the clause to subsequently acquired real estate that is functionally related to the real estate described in the original mortgage.

2. Pre–Existing and Purchase Money Liens

The equitable lien that attaches to mortgagor's subsequently acquired real estate as a result of an after-acquired property clause is junior to pre-existing liens thereon and to purchase money mortgages created in the process of its acquisition.

3. Relationship to Accession

An after-acquired property clause is utilized to ensure that the mortgagee acquires a lien on any parcels of land subsequently acquired by the mortgagor. Such a clause is not necessary to cover improvements on the originally mortgaged land; they are subjected to the mortgage because of the doctrine of accession and the law of fixtures.

4. Recording Act Problems

Even though an after-acquired property clause may be effective to create a lien on real estate subsequently acquired by the mortgagor, recording act problems make it difficult for the beneficiary of the clause to obtain priority over other parties that acquire interests in that real estate from or through the mortgagor.

C. REPLACEMENT, REFINANCING AND MODIFICATION OF SENIOR MORTGAGEES: EFFECT ON JUNIOR LIENORS

1. Replacement or Refinancing by Original Mortgagee

Where a senior mortgagee discharges its mortgage of record, and, as part of the same transaction, takes and records a new mortgage, it retains the predecessor's priority as against an intervening lienor except to the extent that: (1) any change in the terms of the mortgage or the obligation it secures is materially prejudicial to the intervening lienor or (2) the senior mortgagee intends to subordinate its mortgage to the intervening lien.

2. Replacement or Refinancing by New Mortgagee

Under the doctrine of equitable subrogation, where a senior mortgagee releases its mortgage of record, and, as part of the same transaction, a new mortgagee takes and records a new mortgage, the new mortgagee retains the predecessor's priority as against an intervening lienor except to the extent that: (1) any change in the terms of the new mortgage or the obligation it secures is materially prejudicial to the intervening lienor or (2) the new mortgagee intends to subordinate its mortgage to the intervening lien.

3. Modification of Senior Mortgage: Impact on Junior Lienors

Where the parties modify a senior mortgage or the obligation it secures, the mortgage as modified retains its priority as against an intervening lienor except to the extent that the modification materially prejudices that lienor.

D. FIXTURES

1. Section 9–313 of the Uniform Commercial Code

Fixtures are dealt with in one of two versions of Section 9–313. One or two states may adhere to the original 1962 version of 9–313 (1962 Code) but virtually all jurisdictions have adopted a 1972 amended version of Section 9–313 (1972 Code). All references hereafter are to the 1972 Code.

2. What is a Fixture?

The Code delineates three categories of goods: "(1) those which retain their chattel characteristics entirely and are not part of the real estate; (2) ordinary building materials which have become an integral part of the real estate and cannot retain their chattel characteristics for purposes of finance; and (3) an intermediate class which becomes real estate for certain purposes but as to which chattel security may be preserved." 1972 Code Comment 3.

3. The Problem of Where to File

If a creditor obtaining a security interest in a fixture desires protection against real estate mortgagees, he or she must make a "fixture filing" in the office where a mortgage on the real estate would be recorded. If the property turns out to be a fixture, filing in the real estate records automatically protects the creditor against other personal property claimants as well. If the only protection sought is against personal property claimants, a filing in the standard personal property files suffices.

4. Priority Rules Under the UCC

a. Prior Real Estate Mortgage

The chattel mortgagee will prevail as to a fixture if (1) it is a purchase money mortgage and (2) a fixture filing is made either before it was affixed to the real estate or within ten days thereafter. Where the chattel mortgagee is not a purchase money lender, the real estate mortgagee will prevail.

b. Subsequent Real Estate Mortgage

The chattel mortgagee will have priority if, prior to the recording of the real estate mortgage, the goods (1) became fixtures and (2) the mortgage was perfected by a fixture filing.

5. Construction Mortgages

Where goods become fixtures during the construction process, the construction mortgagee has priority as to all advances made under the mortgage to finance the acquisition of and construction on the land.

6. Remedies to Enforce Priority

Where the real estate mortgagee has priority over a fixture mortgagee, the latter is prohibited from removing the fixture from the real estate. In the event a real estate mortgage foreclosure sale produces a surplus, the chattel mortgagee should share in that surplus in the same extent as junior real estate lienors.

Where the fixture mortgagee has priority, he or she may remove the fixture from the real estate, but must "reimburse any encumbrancer or owner who is not the debtor for damage caused by the removal." Under Revised Article 9 of the UCC, where a real estate mortgage that is junior to the fixture mortgagee is foreclosed, the fixture lender has the additional right—the fixture mortgagee can forego removal and instead have a senior claim on the real estate foreclosure proceeds.

E. MECHANICS' LIENS AND RELATED CONCEPTS

1. Parties Protected

Virtually every segment of the construction industry—contractors, subcontractors, materials suppliers, and in some states, design professionals—is granted liens for labor, services or materials furnished or contracted to be furnished for improvements to real estate.

2. Types of Statutory Schemes

a. Pennsylvania Type

A subcontractor or supplier is afforded a direct lien right, even though the general contractor has been paid in full. The lien is measured by the value of the subcontractor's or supplier's contribution to the project.

b. New York System

The maximum aggregate amount of liens that may be collected out of the property is the contract price under the main contract between the general contractor and the owner, less payments properly made to the general contractor.

3. Procedure

There are several key dates and time periods that are crucial to lien enforcement. These are the date of completion of the lien claimant's work; the time period during which a lien claim must be filed and recorded; and the time period during which a lien foreclosure proceeding must be commenced.

4. Lien Priority

Assuming the appropriate procedure is followed, the date of claimant's lien will generally relate back for priority purposes to some earlier date. Different dates utilized include: (a) the date of commencement of the work of construction; (b) the date the particular lienor provides materials or service; (c) date of filing the claim; and (d) the date of the general contract. The date of commencement of work on the project is probably the most commonly-used date.

5. Consent of the Owner

Statutes usually provide that property is lienable only if the improvements were made with the owner's consent. Hence, work contracted by a tenant may not give rise to a lien on the landlord's interest unless the landlord consented to it.

6. Waiver of Mechanics' Liens

a. In the General Contract

In states that follow the Pennsylvania approach, "no-lien" language in the general contract bars subsequent lien filings by subcontractors and suppliers as well as by the general contractor. New York-type states usually refuse to enforce such waivers.

b. Waivers During or After Construction

Lien waivers are effective as to work already completed. As to future work, they are enforceable in some states, but in others are construed narrowly or held to be invalid as against public policy.

7. Constitutionality of Mechanics' Liens Statutes

Sniadach-Fuentes attacks against mechanics' liens statutes will fail so long as a lienor is required to file the lien within a relatively short time after the work's completion and so long as the lien is not permitted to subsist for a period of more than a few months without a hearing being required.

F. FUTURE ADVANCES MORTGAGES

The most prevalent examples of future advances mortgages include construction mortgages, "open-end" mortgages, "home equity" mortgages, and mortgages securing fluctuating lines of credit in a commercial context.

1. **Reasons for Use**

   The future advances mortgage is advantageous to borrowers because they need not pay interest on funds until they are actually advanced. In construction loans, future advance provisions allows lenders to monitor the progress of construction in order to make sure that the loan proceeds are being used for their intended purpose.

2. **Mortgage Formats**

   Some future advances mortgages disclose both their nature and the terms and conditions of the future advances. Two other formats are in common use: (1) the mortgage may simply specify a certain amount, as if it had already been advanced, even though some of the funds are intended to be advanced at a later time. (2) The form may state the amount of the initial advance and state that it secures future advances, even though the time and amount of such advances are not spelled out.

3. **Optional vs. Obligatory Advances**

   A discretionary advance is referred to as "optional." If the mortgage or collateral agreements impose a contractual obligation on the lender to make future advances, such advances are "obligatory."

4. **Optional vs. Obligatory Advances: Priority Rules**

   If a future advance is obligatory, it takes its priority from the date of the original mortgage and thus is senior to the liens that arise between that date and the time of the advance. If the advance is optional, it will be junior to any intervening third party lien of which the future advances mortgagee has notice.

5. **What is an Optional Advance?**

   Construction loan advances are often alleged to be optional (and hence to lose priority to intervening mortgages or mechanics' liens) To forestall this allegation, a construction lender should be guided by three principles. First, it must not reserve too much discretion, but must have a genuine contractual obligation to lend. Second, the lender must use the controls and assert the conditions which are contained in the loan agreement. Third, the lender should make no further advances after the occurrence of any event which is defined by the documents as a mortgagor default.

6. What Constitutes Notice?

Under the majority rule, an optional advance loses priority to an intervening lien only when the future advances mortgagee has actual knowledge of such a lien. Under a minority view, the advancing mortgagee will be on constructive notice of any recording by an intervening lienor.

7. Special Types of Optional Advances

All advances made by a lender to protect security (e.g., to pay delinquent taxes or to remedy waste) relate back to the date of the advancing lender's mortgage and take priority over all intervening liens, even if the advances are optional.

8. Waiver by Future Advances Mortgagee

Certain actions by the future advances mortgagee can so mislead intervening lienors as to cause subordination of otherwise senior obligatory future advances to such intervening liens.

9. Statutory Modification

Several states permit future advances to take the same priority as the original mortgage irrespective of their optional character. Some confer priority as against all intervening liens, while others confer it only over mechanics' lienors.

10. The "Cut–Off Notice" Concept

In about a dozen states, statutes provide that all future advances take the original mortgage's priority, but allow the mortgagor to issue a "cut-off notice" to the mortgagee, stating that no more future advance will be drawn down. This notice is binding on the mortgagee. Its effect is to free up any equity value the mortgagor has in the property, so that it can be used to secure subordinate mortgage loans. The Restatement (Third) of Property (Mortgages) adopts the cut-off notice concept.

11. Optional Advances Under "Home Equity Loans"

If the lender under a "home equity" loan is obligated to advance funds whenever mandated by the borrower, such advances will have priority over intervening liens. If the lender has too much discretion to refuse advances, they may be deemed optional and therefore subordinate to intervening liens. A few states have adopted statutes to protect home equity lenders against this risk.

12. Dragnet Clauses

A dragnet clause is a mortgage provision that purports to make the mortgaged real estate serve as security for other, unspecified, debts that the mortgagor may already owe or may incur in the future to the mortgagee. Such clauses are generally upheld and are effective against intervening lienors to the same extent as optional future advances in other contexts. However, because they are normally not bargained for, courts tend to construe them narrowly against the mortgagee.

G. THE STOP NOTICE REMEDY

This type of legislation gives unpaid subcontractors and suppliers the right to make and enforce claims against the construction lender, and in some instances, the owner, for a portion of the undisbursed construction loan proceeds.

1. Scope of the Remedy

The remedy is available even though the owner-developer has defaulted and is no longer entitled to further construction loan advances. However, it is ineffective if no loan proceeds remain in the hands of the construction lender.

2. Criticism of the Remedy

Some have argued that the stop notice remedy is likely to be used by unscrupulous claimants to blackmail the owner and construction lender into payment of inflated claims.

3. Constitutionality

Stop notice legislation has been upheld against *Sniadach-Fuentes* procedural due process attacks.

H. THE EQUITABLE LIEN CLAIM

When neither the mechanics' lien nor the stop notice statute provides subcontractors or suppliers with an adequate remedy, they will often attempt to claim an equitable lien on either the undisbursed loan funds or on the land itself.

1. Exclusivity of Statutory Remedies

One argument against the imposition of an equitable lien is that the mechanics' lien and stop notice statutes were intended to be exclusive remedies for claimants who have supplied labor or materials.

2. Equitable Liens on Undisbursed Construction Loan Proceeds—Judicial Theories

Both unjust enrichment and third party beneficiary theories have been utilized successfully by unpaid subcontractors and suppliers to impose an equitable lien on the undisbursed loan proceeds. The former theory has been applied where undisbursed loan proceeds exist and the construction lender has purchased the land and improvements at a foreclosure sale of the construction mortgage. Under the latter theory, the subcontractor or supplier is given an equitable lien on the undisbursed proceeds because she or he is deemed to be the beneficiary of the construction loan agreement between the lender and the developer. Finally, an equitable estoppel argument may sometimes be used to benefit a lien claimant who has detrimentally relied on representations by the construction lender that the lien claimant would be paid.

3. Equitable Liens on the Property

Even though no undisbursed loan funds exist, the unpaid subcontractor or supplier can sometimes assert an equitable lien against the improved real estate itself. So long as the debt from the owner to the lien claimant is proved and the land which was improved is identifiable, an equitable lien will be imposed, at least if no bona fide purchaser has acquired title to the property.

I. SUBORDINATION AGREEMENTS

A subordination is a voluntary act by the holder of a mortgage or lien by which the holder accepts a lower priority and grants the holder of some other interest a higher priority.

1. Subordination Agreements as a Two Stage Process

When a vendor is selling land to a developer and is accepting a purchase-money mortgage for part of the price, the vendor will agree to subordinate his or her purchase-money mortgage to a potential construction loan. At this stage, the subordination agreement is executory. After the construction loan is arranged, the seller will then usually execute a second subordination document describing the construction loan more specifically.

2. Actions to Enforce Executory Subordination Agreements

Most courts refuse to enforce subordination agreements that are too vague and indefinite or that fail to define and minimize the risk that the subordination will impair or destroy the seller's security. An executory subordination agreement should (according to the Restatement) at least spell out the following features of the loan gaining priority: the new lender or type of lender; an upper limit on the initial amount of the debt; and an upper limit on the interest rate. If the proceeds of the future mortgage loan will be used for improvements to the real estate, and the subordinating mortgagee is relying on those improvements as security (as will ordinarily be the case), the subordination should include a statement requiring use of the future loan proceeds for that purpose, and a reasonable description of the improvements.

3. Actions to Reverse Priorities After Construction Loan Default

When an action has been brought after a construction loan default, the court is normally dealing with a second subordination agreement that refers specifically to the terms of the construction loan. Consequently, the problem of indefiniteness often is obviated. Even where indefiniteness is still a problem, some courts find that the seller is estopped from raising that issue where there has been detrimental lender reliance.

4. Conditional Subordination

Where the subordination of seller's purchase money mortgage to a construction loan is expressly conditional upon application of the loan proceeds to construction costs, courts will protect the lender's priority only to the extent that disbursements are utilized for construction purposes. A few courts will even imply such a condition where the parties did not express it.

■ XI. GOVERNMENT INVOLVEMENT IN THE MORTGAGE MARKET

A. GOVERNMENT AGENCY INVOLVEMENT IN MORTGAGE FINANCE

1. Regulators of Mortgage Lenders

a. Savings and Loan Associations

The Office of Thrift Supervision (OTS) regulates federally-chartered thrift institutions (savings and loan associations and savings banks). State-chartered thrifts are governed by state agencies, typically called "Savings and Loan Commissions". Most thrifts, both state and federal, have their deposits insured by the Savings Association Insurance Fund (SAIF), which is administered by the Federal Deposit Insurance Corporation (FDIC), although some savings banks have deposit insurance through the Bank Insurance Fund (BIF).

b. Banks

Like thrifts, banks may be either federally-chartered ("national banks") or state-chartered. National banks are chartered by the Office of the Comptroller of the Currency (OCC), a division of the U.S. Treasury Department. All national banks and most state banks are insured by the BIF, administered by the FDIC. Many of the larger state banks, as well as all national banks, are also members of the Federal Reserve System, managed by the Federal Reserve Board (FRB), which provides a supply of credit to them. Mortgage lending by state-chartered banks is governed by state agencies, often called "Banking Commissions."

c. Credit Unions

Credit unions may be either federally-chartered or state-chartered, but federal credit unions are far more important in terms of total assets. They are regulated by the National Credit Union Administration (NCUA).

2. Providers of Mortgage Funds

a. Loans to Lenders

A system of twelve regional Federal Home Loan Banks makes short term loans to thrifts in the form of "advances." Such advances have been an important source of funds to thrifts during times of tight credit. The FRB operates a much larger "credit window" for national banks and FRB-member state banks.

b. **Secondary Market Purchasers**

There are two main federal or quasi-federal agencies that buy loans on the secondary market: (1) Fannie Mae (formerly the Federal National Mortgage Association) and (2) Freddie Mac (formerly the Federal Home Loan Mortgage Corporation). Both are privately owned but federally-chartered entities that purchase mortgages on the secondary market from a wide variety of sources.

In addition, numerous states have housing finance agencies to support the housing market by borrowing money through the sale of tax-free notes and bonds and by diverting that money to housing. In some cases the agencies provide funds by means of purchasing mortgages on the secondary market

c. **Issuers of Mortgage Securities**

The Government National Mortgage Association (GNMA), a component of the U.S. Department of Housing and Urban Development (HUD) operates a program under which it guarantees repayment on securities issued by private lenders and collateralized by pools of FHA-insured and VA-guaranteed mortgage loans. This mortgage-backed securities program has been popular, and following its example, numerous lenders now issue securities *without* a GNMA guarantee or any other form of government backing. The Tax Reform Act of 1986 defined a new type of entity, termed a REMIC (Real Estate Mortgage Investment Conduit), which enjoys favored tax treatment for this sort of activity.

d. **Real Estate Investment Trusts (REITs)**

A REIT is similar to a mutual fund, except that it invests in either equity ownership in, or mortgages on, real estate. Profits made by the REIT are passed through and taxed to its investors.

3. **Agencies Which Spread Mortgage Risk**

a. **The Federal Housing Administration (FHA)**

The FHA is a federally-operated insurance company that insures a wide variety of mortgages on residential housing. The FHA collects an insurance premium that is paid by the mortgagor; currently the premium is 1.5% at the time of loan closing, plus an additional 0.5% per year, paid in monthly installments with the mortgage payment.

b. Veteran's Administration (VA)

The VA operates a home loan guarantee program for eligible veterans. A fee, varying in amount from 1.25% to 2%, is charged at closing for the guarantee, but the fees are insufficient to make the program actuarially sound, and losses are paid primarily out of appropriated funds.

c. Private Mortgage Insurers (PMI's)

PMI's are privately-owned corporations which insure mortgages in much the same manner as FHA and VA.

B. ACTS OF CONGRESS PREEMPTING STATE MORTGAGE LAW

1. Due–On–Sale Clauses

Section 341 of the Depository Institutions Act of 1982 expressly preempts state law which limits the enforceability of due-on-sale clauses in mortgages, and expressly makes such clauses enforceable, with certain limited exceptions for intrafamily transfers and other transfers that are not arms-length sales.

2. Alternative Mortgage Instruments

The Alternative Mortgage Transaction Parity Act of 1982 authorizes all types of state-chartered financial institutions to make mortgage loans of the same types approved by federal agencies for the analogous federally-chartered institutions.

3. State Usury Laws

Congress preempted state usury laws for first mortgage residential loans by Section 501 of the Depository Institutions Deregulation and Monetary Control Act of 1980. Under the preemption, there is no interest rate ceiling.

All states had the option to avoid the federal preemption by enacting legislation prior to April 1, 1983 stating that they did not want the preemption to apply to loans made in that state. About a dozen states so opted.

4. Mortgage Foreclosure Procedures

Since 1981, a federal statute has authorized a form of non-judicial power of sale foreclosure for multifamily apartment project mortgages held by the Department of Housing and Urban Development (HUD). In 1994 a similar act for single-family home mortgages was enacted.

C. PREEMPTION OF STATE LAW BY FEDERAL AGENCY REGULATIONS

When mortgage loans are made by institutions which are chartered or regulated by federal agencies, those institutions may be free to disregard state law, because (1) there are specific contrary federal regulations, or (2) there is a general federal preemption as a result of pervasive federal control.

1. Redlining and Mortgage Disclosure

Federal law includes the Home Mortgage Disclosure Act (HMDA), the Equal Credit Opportunity Act (ECOA), and Community Reinvestment Act (CRA). The OTS has adopted detailed regulations governing record keeping, reporting, and examination for all federally insured savings associations.

2. Cradle–To–Grave Preemption

Numerous cases state that the OTS regulations "occupy the field" of federal savings and loan associations and regulate them "from cradle to grave." These cases, however, deal with internal corporate operations, relations with members, etc., and should not be taken to refer to all aspects of mortgage contracts.

3. Express Federal Regulation Preemption

A regulation of OTS states that the agency "hereby occupies the entire field of lending regulation for federal savings associations." However, the regulation seems to be less than absolute; it also states that state rules of contract and commercial law, real property law, homestead, tort law, and criminal law are not preempted if they affect the lending operations of federal S & Ls only incidentally, and if they are consistent with the standards of safety and soundness.

D. LOANS HELD BY FEDERAL INSTRUMENTALITIES

When a federal agency or instrumentality holds a mortgage loan which is in default, the agency's range of remedies is not necessarily limited by state law restrictions. The applicable law is clearly federal. However, the content of federal law may be determined by adoption of an existing state law rule.

1. The *Kimbell* Test

In *United States v. Kimbell Foods, Inc.*, the United States Supreme Court adopted the following test to be applied in determining whether the federal courts should adopt state law as the rule of decision:

a. Is the nature of the federal program such that uniform federal law is required?

b. Would adoption of state law frustrate specific objectives of the federal program?

c. Would a uniform federal rule disrupt local commercial relationships predicated on state law?

2. Post–*Kimbell* Cases

Some post-*Kimbell* decisions involving mortgage remedies have adopted the *Kimbell* analysis and have applied state law as the rule of decision on the ground that no important federal interest would be frustrated by doing so. Others have discerned a sufficient federal interest and applied a federal common law rule. It is difficult to see a clear pattern in the cases.

3. Ability of Secondary Market Agencies to Preempt State Law

It is unclear whether the federally-sponsored secondary market agencies, Fannie Mae and Freddie Mac, have the regulatory power to preempt state mortgage law.

■ XII. ALTERNATIVE MORTGAGE LOAN INSTRUMENTS

A. MORTGAGE FORMS AND "AFFORDABILITY"

1. Graduated Payment Mortgage (GPM)

This type of loan carries monthly payments which increase annually by some specified percentage during the early years of the loan, and then remain constant thereafter. The increases are agreed upon when the loan is made and do not depend on future interest rates or market conditions. GPM loans may be FHA-insured, VA-guaranteed, or conventional.

2. Mortgage Buy–Downs and Pledged Accounts

Under a "buy-down" a mortgage lender is given (often by a seller of real estate) a substantial front-end payment to induce it to reduce the mortgage interest rate that it would otherwise require.

3. The Growing–Equity Mortgage (GEM)

The GEM is a mortgage loan that is fully amortized over a significantly shorter term than the traditional twenty-five or thirty year mortgage. Payments typically are initially sufficient amortize the loan over thirty years, but rise by an agreed percentage each year, with the additional funds being credited to principal.

A variant is the bi-weekly mortgage, under which the borrower makes a payment every two weeks equal to one-half of the regular monthly payment that would amortize the loan over 30 years. This results, in effect, in one extra month's payment each year, and reduces the loan term by a surprisingly degree.

4. The Shared–Equity Mortgage (SEM)

Under this mortgage format, a purchaser-occupant and another person (often a relative) become co-owners and co-mortgagors of real estate. Usually the non-occupant pays all or a substantial part of the down payment and is entitled to share in any appreciation when the real estate is sold. The latter person may also make a specific fraction of the monthly mortgage payments.

5.   The Reverse Annuity Mortgage (RAM)

This mortgage form, intended mainly for elderly retired borrowers, involves the disbursement of the loan proceeds by the lender by periodic installments over a long term period. Interest is accrued rather than paid currently. Thus, the balance on the loan rises steadily over its life.

B.   MORTGAGE FORMS AND THE "PORTFOLIO LAG" PROBLEM

1.   The Adjustable Rate Mortgage (ARM)

An ARM permits the lender to adjust the interest rate on the mortgage from time to time in accordance with fluctuations in some external index of market interest rates.

2.   The Shared Appreciation Mortgage (SAM)

This form of mortgage gives the lender the right to recover, as "contingent interest," some agreed percentage of the property's appreciation in value, as measured when it is sold or is appraised at some fixed date in the future. In return, the lender is willing to charge a lower fixed interest rate than the market would dictate on a standard mortgage.

3.   The Price–Level Adjusted Mortgage (PLAM)

Under this mortgage format, the loan balance is adjusted annually to reflect changes in price levels during the previous year—i.e., by the amount of inflation which actually occurred. The interest rate on that balance, however, remains the same for the life of the loan. Because the principal amount is indexed to inflation, a sustained period of high inflation can cause the balance (and thus the monthly payments) to rise far above the original amount borrowed. PLAMs are not widely used in the United States.

■ XIII. COMMON INTEREST OWNERSHIP; CONDOMINIUMS, COOPERATIVES AND PLANNED COMMUNITIES

A. CONDOMINIUMS—BASIC CONCEPTS

Each condominium purchaser acquires a fee simple ownership in the unit together with an undivided tenancy in common interest with other unit owners in the common areas.

1. Creating the Condominium

a. The Declaration

The condominium is created by a recording of a declaration. The declaration will contain, among other things, a legal description of the underlying land, a description of the building or buildings that will comprise the project, a legal description for each unit and a description of the common areas.

b. The By–Laws

If the declaration is the constitution of the condominium, the by-laws are the legislation that governs its day to day operation.

2. The Common Areas

The common areas normally consist of all of the condominium project except for the interior of each unit.

a. Ownership and Management

While a board of directors of the owners' association will manage the common areas, common area ownership is held by the unit owners as tenants in common.

b. Restrictions on Partition or Sale

Statutes prohibit partition of the common areas, as well as the separation of unit ownership from common area ownership.

3. The Owners' Association

While this association can be unincorporated, it often is organized as a not-for-profit corporation. The unit owners elect a board to manage the condominium. The board, in turn, often hires a management company to carry out actual day to day management.

4. Financing the Condominium

a. New Construction

A developer will first arrange for a construction loan to build the condominium and, in addition, obtain a commitment by a long term lender to provide financing for each of the individual units. As each condominium unit is sold, the construction lender releases its lien from that unit so that the long term lender will be assured of getting a first purchase money mortgage on the purchaser-mortgagor's unit.

b. Resale of Condominium Units

Condominium unit resales are handled in essentially the same fashion as detached houses in a subdivision. Thus a purchaser may (1) pay off the seller completely in cash; (2) assume an existing first mortgage loan already on the unit; (3) obtain third party purchase money financing; (4) obtain purchase money financing from the seller, or (5) utilize a combination of the above methods.

5. The Unit as an Independent Mortgage Entity

When a unit owner defaults on her mortgage, the foreclosure sale purchaser will obtain title to the foreclosed unit and to the percentage interest in the common areas attributable to that unit. These two property rights are inseparable.

6. The Unit for Real Estate Tax Purposes

The failure of one unit owner to pay real estate taxes will result in only the foreclosure of the tax lien on that unit and will not affect title to other units in the condominium.

7. Delinquency in Payment of Assessments

The delinquent owner becomes personally liable for any arrearages, and the owners' association has a lien on the defaulting owner's unit and accompanying interest in the common areas.

8. **Mechanics' Liens**

When labor or materials are supplied for one unit, any mechanics' lien that may arise attaches only to that unit and its accompanying percentage interest in the common areas. If labor or materials are furnished to the common areas, any mechanics lien will attach to each of the units and its accompanying percentage interest in the common areas. An individual unit owner may release such a lien with respect to her unit by payment of a percentage of the lien amount that is the same as that person's percentage ownership of the common areas.

9. **Liability for Common Area Torts**

a. **Association Liability**

The association, like a landlord, is increasingly required to exercise due care for the safety of the residents in those areas under its control.

b. **Director's Liability**

Generally, a director will be liable for injury if her action, including any claimed reliance on expert advice, was clearly unreasonable under the circumstances known to her at that time.

c. **Unit Owner Liability**

While, in theory, unit owners are jointly and severally liable for tort damage claims arising out of use of the common areas, several states have ameliorated this liability. In some states, for example, unit owner liability is limited to a percentage of total damages equal to his undivided ownership percentage in the common areas.

10. **The Condominium Governing Body as Legislator**

The governing body of the condominium owners' association operates much like a city council for the condominium. In assessing the validity of a regulation or by-law enacted by the governing board or the association, one must focus on several issues:

a. Were Applicable Procedural Requirements Followed?

b. Do the Governing Documents Provide Substantive Authority for the Regulation?

    c.   Does the Regulation Satisfy a "Reasonableness" Test?

    d.   Does the Regulation Violate the U.S. or State Constitutions?

B. HOUSING COOPERATIVES

The members of a housing cooperative are shareholders in a non-profit corporation, and the corporation owns the fee simple title to an apartment building or group of buildings. Each shareholder is also a lessee as to a particular apartment, and the corporation is the landlord.

1. Financing the Cooperative

Cooperatives are financed with construction mortgages, but there normally are no individual loans to those persons who ultimately purchase the units. Rather, the construction mortgage on the project is either converted to a long term loan or another long term lender pays off or "takes out" the construction loan and takes a new permanent first mortgage on the cooperative property. Each unit purchaser thus takes subject to this blanket mortgage on the project.

2. The Unit Purchaser's Payment Obligations

Each month the unit owner will make a payment to the cooperative corporation consisting of her unit's proportional share of the debt service on the blanket mortgage, real estate taxes, insurance and common area maintenance.

3. Default by the Unit Purchaser

If a cooperative member defaults on his monthly payment (rent) he may be dispossessed and the cooperative may foreclose its lien on the member's shares.

4. Disadvantages of Cooperative Ownership

If either the blanket mortgage goes into default and is foreclosed or the cooperative building is sold for failure to pay real estate taxes, the individual unit owner's interest will be completely wiped out. In addition, institutional financing for resale of a cooperative is often difficult to obtain.

5. **Resale of Cooperative Units**

After a cooperative unit has been occupied for some time, the unit's share of the blanket mortgage may be paid down so much that it is difficult for a new buyer of the unit to pay the difference between the unit's share of the blanket mortgage and the unit's market price. Hence some additional (junior) financing is often needed. However, financing on the security of the unit buyer's share of stock and leasehold interest may be problematic. In states in which cooperatives are popular, state-chartered financial institutions have been authorized to make such loans on the security of individual units. In addition, all of the major federal housing agencies authorize or approve such loans.

C. THE PLANNED COMMUNITY

The Planned Community (PC) typically is a subdivision in which an individual owns a fee simple absolute in a specific parcel of real estate and a membership or shareholder's interest in a corporation or association that, in turn, owns and manages the common areas.

1. **Cooperatives and Condominiums Distinguished**

Both cooperatives and condominiums entail the ownership of one's unit. In neither form of development does the individual own outright the land on which the unit sits. In the PC however, each owner typically owns in fee simple absolute the ground beneath his or her unit.

2. **Ownership of the Common Properties**

The common areas and recreational facilities in a PC usually are owned by a not-for-profit corporation or association, the shareholders or members of which are the unit owners.

3. **Government of the Common Areas**

The homeowners' association is responsible for managing the common areas. This task usually is delegated to a smaller committee of owners or board of directors who, in turn, may hire a management company to carry out the actual day-to-day management chores.

4.   Levying Assessments

The homeowners' association and, in some instances, the board of directors have authority to levy assessments to raise funds for management, repairs and improvements to the common properties. An unpaid assessment constitutes a lien on the unit of the delinquent owner.

D.   CONDOMINIUMS—SECOND GENERATION LEGISLATION

Many states have adopted "second generation" condominium legislation to deal with numerous problems that arose under the FHA Model Act and similar earlier statutes. The most significant example of second generation legislation is the Uniform Condominium Act, which was originally promulgated in 1977 (1977 UCA) and, in a slightly revised version, in 1980 (1980 UCA).

1.   Condominiums on Leaseholds

Most second generation statutes, including both versions of the UCA, authorize leasehold condominiums.

2.   The "Flexible" Condominium

a.   Problems Under First Generation Statutes

First generation legislation made it extremely difficult to amend a declaration once it was recorded.

b.   Second Generation Approach

Such legislation often specifically permits the developer or his successor to provide in the declaration that the condominium may be contracted or expanded within a time certain (usually seven years) after the filing of the declaration.

3.   Allocation of Common Area Interests, Votes and Common Expense Liability

While first generation legislation usually required a single common basis, (usually tied to the initial "value" assigned to a unit) to govern the unit owner's percentage ownership interest in the common areas, voting, and assessments for common area expenses, second generation legislation, in general, is more flexible in this regard.

4. Lien for Unpaid Assessments

While under most first generation legislation, a first mortgage will take priority over the lien for unpaid assessments, both versions of the UCA reverse that priority and give the association's lien priority to the extent of unpaid assessments due during the six months immediately preceding the lien enforcement proceeding.

E. CONFLICTS BETWEEN CONDOMINIUM DEVELOPER AND PURCHASER

1. Quality of Construction

Condominium, cooperative and PUD purchasers generally are afforded the same sort of protection against defects in design and construction that is given to purchasers of detached dwellings. Both versions of the UCA, however, contain implied warranty provisions that are markedly pro-purchaser.

2. Rescission Based on Material Change or Failure to Meet Completion Date

Courts have held that a purchaser has a right to rescind a condominium earnest money contract based on material changes in the condominium project or because the unit was not completed according to contract specifications within a reasonable time after the agreed closing date. Both versions of the UCA afford the purchaser fifteen days after the receipt of certain disclosure documents to rescind for any reason.

3. Developer Liability for Assessments On Unsold Units

Generally, courts, in interpreting first generation legislation, have been unwilling to permit developers to avoid or limit their payment of assessments with respect to unsold units. 1977 UCA § 3–114 provides that "common expenses shall be assessed against all the units in accordance with the common expense liability allocated to each unit."

4. **Developer Self–Dealing While in Control of Owners' Association**

   a. **Judicial Approach**

   While earlier decisions were unsympathetic to purchaser attacks on developer self-dealing, recent results suggest an increasing willingness to allow owners' associations either to rescind "sweetheart" contracts or to recover from the developer, for the benefit of the association, unreasonable profits gained from such agreements.

   b. **Legislative Regulation**

   Both versions of the UCA deal with developer self-dealing in two ways. First, they impose on all executive board members appointed by the developer a fiduciary liability for all of their acts or omissions as board members. Second, they confer the power on the association to avoid management contracts, recreational leases and certain other contracts entered into prior to the time the unit purchasers take control of the association. Moreover, Congress has conferred broad authority to terminate self-dealing and unconscionable contracts entered into prior to the assumption of control by the unit owners. See the Condominium and Cooperative Abuse Relief Act of 1980.

5. **Control of the Owners' Association**

   While most first generation legislation is silent on the control issue, institutional lenders and secondary market purchasers generally insist that the condominium documents provide for purchaser control of the owners' association after 75% of the units have been sold. The 1980 UCA currently uses the 75% rule, but also imposes certain time restrictions on developer control.

6. **Disclosure as Purchaser Protection**

   An increasing number of states, either as part of second generation legislation or by statute, impose substantial disclosure requirements on condominium developers.

7. **Other UCA Purchaser Protections**

   a. The developer's promotional material must specify "what need not be built."

b. Structural and mechanical components of buildings must be "substantially completed" prior to the recording of the declaration.

c. Before a unit can be conveyed, a certificate of substantial completion of that unit must be recorded.

d. Casualty insurance with a minimum coverage of 80% of the cash value of the insured property must be carried, and if there is a failure to do so, notice must be provided to unit owners.

e. Class actions for violation of the act, the declaration or by-laws, including punitive damages and reasonable attorneys' fees, are specifically authorized.

8. **Priority as Between the Construction Lender and the Unit Purchasers**

    a. **The Deposit as an Equitable Lien**

        In most jurisdictions the condominium purchaser, as a contract vendee, has an equitable lien on the realty to secure the return of the earnest money in the event the vendor-developer defaults.

    b. **Construction Mortgage vs. Equitable Lien**

        The equitable lien will be junior to the construction mortgage if it arises after the mortgage has been recorded, or, if the construction mortgage is subsequent in time to the execution of the purchase agreement and the mortgagee has no notice of the purchaser's contract.

    c. **Subordination of Purchaser's Equitable Lien**

        There is a strong argument that language contained in pre-construction purchase agreements that purports to subordinate the purchaser's interest to the construction mortgage may be deemed too vague or unfair to enforce.

    d. **Purchase Agreement Subsequent to Construction Mortgage: Arguments for Purchaser Priority**

        First, if the construction loan default is caused in part by the construction lender's failure to supervise the disbursement of loan funds and the general progress of the project, the purchaser might argue that he or she is a third party beneficiary of the construction loan agreement. Second, the purchaser may be able to rely on cases that permit subcontractors and suppliers to assert an equitable lien on any undisbursed construction loan proceeds when a mechanics' lien claim is unavailable to them.

e. Statutory Escrow Requirements

Many second generation statutes require the developer to hold earnest money deposits in escrow until construction is completed and the units have been conveyed to their purchasers.

9. Third Generation Approach to Common Interest Ownership

In 1982, the National Conference of Commissioners on Uniform State Laws promulgated the Uniform Common Interest Ownership Act (UCOIA) which consolidates the Uniform Condominium Act (UPA), the Uniform Planned Community Act (UPCA) and the Model Real Estate Cooperative Act (MRECA). UCOIA created the term "common interest community" to describe collectively the condominium, cooperative and PUD governed by the other three acts. The latter acts, together with UCOIA, were designed to afford states maximum flexibility in dealing with common interest ownership.

F. RESTRICTIONS ON UNIT OWNER TRANSFER

1. Cooperatives

In many cooperatives, control over membership takes the form of an express prohibition on the alienation of a member's corporate shares without the consent of the corporate landlord. Since courts generally uphold tenant covenants not to assign or sublease without the landlord's consent, the tendency has been to uphold such covenants in the cooperative context.

2. Condominiums

The control over condominium transfer is typically exercised through a right of first refusal conferred upon the owners' association or its board of directors.

a. Right of First Refusal as an Unreasonable Restraint on Alienation

Such a right will be deemed reasonable and thus not violate the rule against unreasonable restraints on alienation so long as the association does not utilize it to exclude prospective purchasers because of race, creed, or national origin.

b. **The Right of First Refusal as a Violation of the Rule Against Perpetuities**

Some states, either generally or with particular reference to condominiums, have adopted statutes exempting rights of first refusal from the rule against perpetuities. Moreover, most commentators agree that the rule should not be applicable to such rights in the condominium context.

c. **Prohibition on Leasing as an Unreasonable Restraint on Alienation**

There is growing support for the view that a prohibition on the owner's ability to lease his or her unit is not an unreasonable restraint on alienation.

G. CONVERSION OF RENTAL HOUSING TO CONDOMINIUMS AND COOPERATIVES

1. Statutory and Ordinance Regulation of the Conversion Process

Numerous legislatures and city councils have responded to protests about the conversion process by enacting a wide variety of regulatory measures. Some municipalities have gone so far as to impose moratoria on condominium conversion. Most regulation, however, is much more modest in its scope. For example, both versions of the UCA deal with conversion in two ways. First, the converter is required to provide substantial information in the public offering statement about the general physical condition of the building and the converter's estimate of its useful life. Second, 120 days written notice of intent to convert must be afforded existing tenants and, for a 60–day period from the date of that notice, the tenants have a pre-emptive right to purchase their units at the public price.

2. Legal Attacks on Condominium Conversion Regulation

Such regulation has been subjected to a wide variety of constitutional and related attacks, although usually without much success. Conversion moratoria have been upheld against constitutional taking and equal protection attacks. Some decisions have sustained attacks on local ordinances regulating conversions, on the ground that they conflict with or are preempted by state legislation.

H. THE TIME SHARING CONCEPT

1. The Nature of the Ownership

a. Interval Estate

Under this form of ownership, the purchaser receives two distinct interests. First, she acquires an estate for years for a time period in each year during which she is entitled to occupancy. This estate will vest annually for a fixed number of years, usually equal to the reasonable life of the building. Second, she obtains a vested remainder in the unit as a tenant in common with other interval owners.

b. The Time Span Estate

This concept involves the conveyance to each purchaser of a percentage undivided tenancy in common interest in fee simple, coupled with a right to occupy the unit during specified times. This concept is also known as "time sharing ownership."

c. The Fee Simple Estate

Under this method, the purchaser receives a fee simple absolute estate which is described as conferring the right to possession during a specified period of each year

d. Other Ownership Approaches

Numerous other and varied methods of interval ownership have developed over the last decade. Many involve ownership of an interest in a corporation and points that can be used for occupancy at a wide variety of vacation properties.

e. The License or Contract Right Approach

Under this form of "ownership" the purchaser does not receive an interest in real estate, but merely a license or contract right to use a specific unit during a certain week or weeks for a predetermined number of years.

2. Some Problem Areas

a. Limitations on the Right to Partition

When the time span estate is utilized, restrictions on the right to partition are included in the declaration. Usually the right is suspended for a period that approximates the reasonable life of the building. Such a suspension will probably not be deemed to be an unreasonable restraint on alienation.

b. **Bankruptcy of the Developer**

Under the first three timeshare ownership methods described above, ownership is not jeopardized by developer bankruptcy. As to the fourth category of ownership, Congress in 1984 amended § 365 of the Code to give the purchaser essentially the same protection in developer bankruptcy as is afforded an installment land contract vendee when a vendor goes into bankruptcy.

c. **Liability for Common Area Injury**

If one of the first three methods of time share ownership listed above is utilized, the owners will have joint and several liability for damage claims arising out of the common areas.

d. **Liability of Co-Owners for Injuries to Third Parties Occurring in Unit**

To the extent that the time share involves the ownership of separate real property interests, the negligence of the owner of one time period in a particular unit probably cannot be imputed to owners of other time periods in that unit. However, if the time span method is employed, it entails undivided tenancy in common ownership in the unit itself, and there is some danger that the negligence of the owner of one time period can be imputed to other time period owners.

3. **Legislative Regulation of Time Sharing**

Almost half of the states have statutes that specifically recognize time sharing ownership. The Model Real Estate Time–Share Act (MRETSA), issued by the National Conference of Commissioners on Uniform State Laws in 1980, parallels both versions of the UCA and extends many of the latter's consumer protection provisions to time share purchasers. A second model act, the Model Timeshare Act, jointly drafted by the American Land Development Association and the National Association of Real Estate License Law Officials, is less complex and detailed than MRETSA and affords developers greater flexibility.

4. Management, the Owners' Association and the Time–Share Owner

For a variety of reasons, time-share owners usually exercise significantly less control over the management of the project than do their counterparts in traditional condominium developments.

Perspective

■ THE SUBJECT IN GENERAL

This Black Letter covers two major topics. The first two Parts of the Black Letter deal with the first topic: the buying and selling of real estate, typically called "conveyancing." In many law schools this material is covered in the first-year Property course, but other schools blend it into an advanced course called "Property II," "Modern Real Estate Transactions," "Real Estate Finance," or the like. That is the reason we have included it here.

The second topic has traditionally been called "mortgages." It is covered in this outline beginning with Part III. Today, it has been expanded to include deeds of trust, installment contracts, and other real estate security devices in addition to mortgages. The course you take may include only this material, and may exclude conveyancing. If so, you can simply disregard Parts I and II of the Black Letter.

For many years real estate finance law was considered a stable, even humdrum, topic. Since the mid–1960s, however, it has become a remarkably fast-moving field with which even practitioners who are involved full-time have difficulty keeping up. The principal reasons for this change are three:

- First, the growth of consumerism, with its concern that individuals (who are usually mortgagors rather than mortgagees) understand transactions and are treated fairly.

- Second, a volatile national economy characterized by widely fluctuating interest rates, which has caused providers of mortgage capital to seek new legal relationships that will protect themselves from the risks and uncertainties of the market.

- Third, the development of an extensive secondary market for mortgage debt, involving the sale of individual mortgages by originating lenders to other investors and the creation and marketing of securities backed by mortgage pools—a process called "securitization."

All of these conditions seem likely to be permanent fixtures in the law of real estate finance and development. We have tried to treat them in the most up-to-date manner possible in this Black Letter. For example, we have included numerous references to the new Restatement (Third) of Property (Mortgages) which was published in mid–1997. This Restatement represents the first time the American Law Institute produced a Restatement on real estate security and is indicative of the growing importance this body of law is to the national and international economy. We have also included many references to the Uniform Nonjudicial Foreclosure Act (UNFA), adopted by the Commissioners on Uniform State Laws in 2002. While UNFA has not yet been adopted by any state legislature, it provides an excellent perspective for studying the foreclosure process.

But basic concepts must be mastered first. It will do you little good to attempt to understand the growth of the federally-sponsored secondary mortgage market until you first grasp the elemental concepts of assignments of the mortgagee's interest. You cannot understand the plethora of new types of mortgage repayment formats until you have first mastered the notion of the traditional level-payment fully-amortizing loan. Modern "arrearages" legislation makes no sense without a knowledge of the common-law equity of redemption. There are countless examples of this general idea—that new developments grow out of ancient principles which must be understood first.

■ PREPARING FOR EXAMINATIONS

We have organized this Black Letter to help you in this natural progression from old (but still highly relevant) to new ideas. Indeed, we would suggest that there is one particular topic in the course which, if you understand it well, can be a key to virtually everything else you will study, and particularly to good examination performance. That topic is the "omitted junior lienor," covered in Part IX of the Black Letter. To grasp it requires a synthesis of numerous fundamental notions of mortgage law: the equity of redemption, mortgage priority, the functioning of the foreclosure process, the principle of notice, the role of deficiencies and surplus, and so on. If you go into a final examination in this field with a clear understanding of the "omitted junior lienor" problem, you are not likely to have trouble with any of the basic concepts of the course. Hence, we commend this topic to you for particularly careful study.

Of course, the same principles of good examination writing which work well in other courses will work well in this one too. However, we can also offer some specific observations which we think will help you perform well on real estate finance examinations.

1. *Check all applicable sources of law.* Remember that real estate finance law can be both court-made and statutory, and that the statutory law can be both state and federal. Federal statutes have assumed increasing importance in recent years. As you answer examination questions, use a mental check list of three parts: court-made law, state statutes (including the Uniform Commercial Code), and federal statutes (including federal constitutional principles). Don't forget to consider the application of all three sources of law to the problem. This technique can be particularly important in such topics as due-on-sale clauses, redemption, validity of power-of-sale foreclosure, and the rights of assignees of the mortgagee's interest.

2. *Don't cut off issues.* Don't let your resolution of debatable preliminary issues preclude your discussion of later issues. This is probably the most common error students make on essay examinations. An illustration may be helpful. Suppose the question involves an installment contract sale of land; the purchaser has made a number of late payments which have been accepted without objection, but now the vendor has declared a forfeiture. There is a good argument that the acceptance of late payments constitutes a waiver of strict performance, so that the vendor cannot now forfeit the contract without first giving the purchaser notice and an adequate time to begin making timely payments. If this argument prevailed in court, the court would never reach the question of whether forfeiture is a proper remedy, since in effect the court would conclude there is presently no breach.

However, on an examination you should first give your conclusion on the waiver issue, and then go on to deal with the forfeiture issue no matter how you resolved the waiver point. For example, you might conclude that there had been a waiver, and then say, "However, if the court decides that there is no waiver, it will be necessary for the court to consider the enforceability of the forfeiture clause of the contract. Here is the way the court would analyze that clause . . . " The point is not to deal with the first issue so conclusively that you never discuss the second issue at all.

3. *Don't confuse the two types of redemption.* The term "redemption" is a constant source of confusion on examinations. The reason is that it has two quite distinct meanings in the law of mortgages. The first is pre-foreclosure equitable redemption, sometimes called the "equity of tardy redemption," a common law right which some states have modified by statute but which all states recognize. The second is post-foreclosure statutory redemption, which is recognized in only about half of the states and exists only to the extent allowed by statute. These two types of redemption frequently differ from one another in several important ways: who can exercise them, what amount must be paid to redeem, who must be paid, and what time limits are imposed on redemption. On an examination, it is extremely important to distinguish the two types of redemption. With which type is the question concerned? Are both types possibly relevant? Be very careful not to mix up the two, or to discuss one when only the other is pertinent.

■ ADDITIONAL READING MATERIAL

We don't believe that most students will need extensive outside readings beyond their own casebooks and this Black Letter. However, you may run into particular topics which you have trouble grasping without additional help. We think (with a pardonable lack of modesty) that the best source for the real estate finance material is Nelson & Whitman, Real Estate Finance Law (West Group, 4th ed.2001). It is the only modern one-volume hornbook in the field, and it develops most topics in considerably greater depth than this Black Letter or your casebook, while still keeping them at a level students can follow readily. A two-volume Practitioner's Series version of the hornbook is also available, but you probably won't need to consult it. In addition to the material in the single-volume book, it covers subrogation and marshaling in more detail, contains a chapter on financing of common-interest communities, and includes numerous forms.

In the conveyancing field, the best single volume source at this writing is Stoebuck & Whitman, Property (West Group, 3d ed.2000), chapters 10 and 11. There are several useful multivolume treatises that cover conveyancing. Powell on Property is kept up to date and is good in many areas, as is the relatively new Thomas edition of Thompson on Property.

I

Contracts for the Sale of Land

■ ANALYSIS

Most real estate transfers are preceded by contracts of sale. A contract is not legally required, but is highly convenient. Some period of time, typically 30 days to 90 days, transpires between the contract's execution and the "closing" or transfer of title. During this time, the purchaser will usually arrange for the necessary financing from a lending institution, may need to sell other real estate, and may investigate such matters as title, zoning, the physical condition of improvements on the land, and other such important matters. The seller may also need to make similar arrangements.

Contracts of this type are often termed "earnest money contracts," since the purchaser usually makes a payment (anywhere from a few hundred dollars to as much as 10% of the price or more) at the time the contract is signed. These funds may be held directly by the seller, or may be held by a real estate broker or a lawyer in a trust account until the closing occurs. The deposit is not legally essential to the validity of the contract, but it acts as an incentive for the buyer to perform, since the buyer who fails to complete the contract may be faced with litigation to recover his earnest money.

A.   The Statute of Frauds

The English Statute of Frauds was enacted in 1677. Every American state has adopted a version of the Statute, and most track the English act's language very closely. See Stoebuck & Whitman, Property § 10.1 (3d ed.2000).

1.   Requirement of a Writing

The Statute requires that the contract or "some memorandum or note thereof" be in writing. Hence, a written contract is only one way to meet the Statute's requirement. Any writing which contains the necessary elements will do, whether it was intended to memorialize the contract or not. For example, a check, a letter, a set of escrow instructions, or a deed may suffice.

Example: Sellers entered into an oral contract with Byers to sell land to him. Later, Sellers wrote a letter to his friend Jones, which said in part, "I have agreed to sell my farm, Blackacre, to Byers for $20,000. He is going to pay me cash." Sellers later refused to perform the contract; Byer sued to enforce it. (*Result:* Byer will prevail if he can produce evidence in court of the content of this letter.) See *Hines v. Tripp*, 139 S.E.2d 545 (N.C.1965).

There is no requirement that the writing itself be introduced as evidence. If it has been destroyed prior to trial, its existence can be established by other evidence. See *Reed v. Hess*, 716 P.2d 555 (Kan.1986).

2. Admission of Contract's Existence

The cases are divided, but some hold that if the defendant admits there was a contract in pleadings, depositions, or in open court, the Statute of Frauds is deemed satisfied without a writing. Other cases reject this view on the ground that it would encourage perjury. See *Restatement (Second) Contracts* § 129, Comment d (1981), which appears to approve enforcement of the contract unless the defendant affirmatively denies its existence.

3. Multiple Pieces of Paper

The writing may be shown by more than one piece of paper, so long as all of the essential elements are present when the papers are considered together. It is necessary to prove that the papers refer to the same transaction, and a few courts require internal references in the signed documents to the unsigned ones. See *In re Estate of Looney*, 975 S.W.2d 508 (Mo.Ct.App.1998).

4. Writing Need Not be a Contract

The writing, to satisfy the Statute of Frauds, need not be the contract itself. It can be a letter, a check, a set of notes, a memorandum, a pleading, or any other document, so long as it contains the necessary elements. See, e.g., *Roberts v. Karimi*, 79 F.Supp.2d 174 (E.D.N.Y. 1999) (affidavit filed in a different lawsuit satisfied Statute of Frauds).

5. Consequences of a Lack of Writing

If there is no sufficient writing, neither party can enforce the contract against the other, either at law for damages or in equity for specific performance. However, the contract is merely unenforceable, and not void (by the majority view) and it may have important legal consequences despite the absence of the writing. These consequences include the following:

a. If both parties fully perform, the resulting legal relationships are identical to those which would have existed if there had been a writing. Thus, neither can rescind after performing by claiming that the contract is a nullity.

b. Partial performance by a party may make the contract enforceable in equity. This process is discussed below.

c. Rescission and restitution (for example, for fraud), and perhaps even damages for fraud can be obtained despite the lack of the writing. See *GMH Associates, Inc. v. Prudential Realty Group*, 752 A.2d 889 (Pa.Super.Ct.2000).

d. Tortious interference with the contract by a third party is actionable notwithstanding the lack of a writing.

6. Elements Which the Writing Must Contain

The cases do not require that every matter agreed to by the parties orally must be included in the writing. In general, the following elements are necessary:

a.   The *names of the parties* or some other identification of them.

b.   An *identification of the land*. A few cases require a detailed legal description, but most courts will accept a more general description if it can be made unambiguous by resort to extrinsic evidence.

> *Example:*   Davis agreed to sell land to Brown, but the writing described the land only by Davis' statement, "I agree to sell Brown my farm." If the evidence shows that Davis owns only one farm and that it was the subject of the party's negotiations, most courts will enforce the contract. See *Seabaugh v. Sailer*, 679 S.W.2d 924 (Mo.App.1984).

c.   Some words indicating an *intent to sell* the land.

d.   *The price* need not be mentioned if the parties did not agree on one; the court will assume that a reasonable price is intended. If a price was, in fact, agreed to, the cases are divided as to whether the writing must include it; most recent cases require that it be set out. See *Busching v. Griffin*, 465 So.2d 1037 (Miss.1985).

e.   If the seller is financing the sale by entering into an installment contract or a purchase money mortgage, the cases are divided as to whether the detailed *terms of this financing* must be included in the writing. Some cases are very strict and others extremely lenient on this point. See *McDonald v. Cosman*, 6 P.3d 956 (Mont. 2000), enforcing the contract although the writing did not state the amount of the monthly payments on the contract debt.

f.   The date of closing need not be included even if the parties agreed to a date. If no date was agreed to, the courts will assume that a reasonable time is allowed. Other matters such as title quality, risk of loss, insurance, repairs, payment of taxes, date of possession, and the like are usually considered so minor that they do not need to appear in the writing. See the excellent discussion in *Zurcher v. Herveat*, 605 N.W.2d 329 (Mich.Ct.App. 1999).

7.   The Signature

Most American statutes require the writing to be signed by "the party to be charged or his agent." Thus, the contract must be signed by the person who is resisting its enforcement in the law suit. A contract may not necessarily be mutually enforceable, since it is quite possible that only one of the parties has signed it.

a.   A few statutes require "the vendor" to sign rather than "the party to be charged." However, courts in these jurisdictions are unlikely to enforce contracts against the purchaser if only the vendor has signed unless there is evidence that the purchaser saw and assented to the writing. See *Schwinn v. Griffith*, 303 N.W.2d 258 (Minn.1981).

b.   The courts are very liberal with respect to the nature of the "signature." It may be anywhere on the document and may be in any form, such as ink, pencil, rubber stamp, or typewriting. A few statutes require the document to be "subscribed"—a term which some courts construe to mean signed at the end of the writing.

B.   Rescission and Modification

Even if an appropriate writing has been created at the time a contract is formed, the parties may attempt to modify or rescind it without employing a writing for that purpose. Are such actions effective?

1.   Oral Rescissions

Courts nearly always enforce oral rescissions on the ground that the parties' action has not created a contract for the sale of land, and hence, does not fall within the statute. The result of the rescission is to eliminate the existence of the contract rather than to create one. *Niernberg v. Feld*, 283 P.2d 640 (Colo.1955).

2.   Oral Modifications

A modification results in a new contract whose terms are partly those of the old contract and partly of the agreement which modifies it. If this new contract would fall within the statute of frauds (i.e., it is a contract for the sale of land) courts conclude that *the new contract cannot be enforced.* See *Johnston v. Curtis*, 16 S.W.3d 283 (Ark.Ct.App.2000). Thus, the original contract (assuming it was supported by an adequate writing) is still in effect.

3.   Enforcing Oral Modifications by Estoppel

Most oral modifications reduce one party's performance or make it less onerous. If that party detrimentally relies upon the modification, the other may be estopped from enforcing the original contract terms. See *Imperator Realty Co. v. Tull*, 127 N.E. 263 (N.Y.1920). If the parties fix a specific date for performance (even if they agree that this time is "of the essence"), an oral statement by one that the other may have additional time will often be given effect. The party who waived strict performance may change his or her mind and revoke the waiver if this is done early enough that the revocation does not cause hardship. However, if the waiving party attempts to revoke the waiver immediately before the original date of performance arrives, the waiver will be binding despite its oral character.

Example: Carr contracted to sell his house to Baker, with closing to occur on August 1. The contract stated that time was of the essence. On July 1, Baker asked for a 45–day extension and Carr orally agreed to it. Relying on the extension, Baker delayed completion of his financing arrangements. On July 28, Carr telephoned Baker, informed him that the oral extension of time was unenforceable, and insisted on closing on August 1. When Baker failed to perform on August 1, Carr sued for damages for breach of contract. (*Result:* A court will very probably conclude that Carr is estopped to deny the validity of the extension, and will enforce it. On the other hand, if Carr had attempted to revoke the time extension on July 10, he would probably be permitted to do so.) See *Delves v. Kingdom Voice Publications, Inc.*, 464 So.2d 1327 (Fla.App.1985).

C. The Part Performance Doctrine

The statute of frauds often leaves parties unable to enforce a contract which they clearly made and relied upon. This result seems unjust, and the courts have developed the part-performance doctrine to overcome it. *Part performance is a judicially-created exception to the Statute, and permits the courts to enforce a contract in equity even though there is no sufficient writing to satisfy the Statute of Frauds.* See Stoebuck & Whitman, Property § 10.2 (3d ed.2000); *Collins v. Morris*, 716 A.2d 384 (Md.Ct.App.1998). Note that part performance is merely a substitute for a *writing*. It is still necessary to prove offer, acceptance, consideration, and the other elements of a contract, but these matters may be proved by oral testimony. See *Creyts Complex, Inc. v. Marriott Corp.*, 98 F.3d 321 (7th Cir.1996).

1. Acts of Part Performance

The term "part performance" is a misnomer, for the acts in question are not necessarily performances required by the contract itself. Three types of acts (all by the purchaser) are generally recognized by the courts.

a. Payment of all or a substantial part of the purchase price.

b. Taking possession of the property.

c. Making substantial improvements on the land.

In recent years several courts have disregarded these standard categories, and using the "estoppel" approach described below, have enforced oral contracts on the basis of *other acts* of reliance, such as a purchaser's sale of other real estate or a seller's eviction of his tenants to make the property vacant in preparation for the instant sale. See Restatement (Second) Contracts, § 129 (1981); *Jacobson v. Gulbransen*, 623 N.W.2d 84 (S.D.2001), adopting this broader approach and terming it "promissory estoppel;" *Kolkman v. Roth*, 656 N.W.2d 148 (Iowa 2003) (same). But other courts have refused to expand the part performance doctrine beyond the standard three acts mentioned above; see *Berg v. Ting*, 886 P.2d 564 (Wash. 1995).

2. Which Acts are Required?

Most courts require a combination of at least two of the acts listed above, and a few courts require all three. A few decisions recognize possession or improvements alone as sufficient, but none of them will accept payment alone. Four states (Kentucky, Mississippi, North Carolina, and Tennessee) do not recognize the part performance doctrine at all.

3. Rationales for Part Performance

a. The Evidentiary Rationale

Some courts regard the statute of frauds' function as evidentiary in nature. These courts regard part performance as a substitute for the evidence which a writing would provide, and thus see the acts as justifying enforcement of the contract. Cases taking this approach usually say that the acts of part performance must be "unequivocally referable" to the contract—that is, that they cannot be explained on any ground other than the existence of a contract. See *In re Deppe*, 215 B.R. 743 (Bankr.D Minn. 1997). There are very few if any cases in which there is no other conceivable explanation for a party's payment, possession, or improvements to real estate. Hence, the "unequivocal referability" test is usually not applied very literally. The real question is whether the acts point to the presence of a contract with reasonable clarity.

b. Estoppel

Courts which use this approach to part performance focus on the unfairness to the party who claims that a contract exists but who cannot enforce it because of a lack of a writing. They sometimes say that the plaintiff must show that he or she would suffer "irreparable injury" if the contract were not enforced. This statement is probably too strong to be taken literally, but it does indicate the importance of the plaintiff's showing hardship as a part of the proof under the part performance doctrine. See *Gegg v. Kiefer*, 655 S.W.2d 834 (Mo.App.1983) ("a grossly unjust and deep-seated wrong" must be shown).

c.   **Mixing the Two Theories**

Some courts include both statements about "unequivocal referability" and "irreparable injury" in their formulations of part performance Thus, they seem to invoke both an evidentiary and an estoppel theory of part performance, rather than clearly electing one approach or the other. As a California court recently paraphrased the Restatement of Contracts, "Two distinct elements underlie application of the part performance exception: 'first, the extent to which the evidentiary function of the statutory formalities [of the statute of frauds] is fulfilled by the conduct of the parties; second, the reliance of the promisee, providing a compelling substantive basis for relief in addition to the expectations created by the promise.' "*Sutton v. Warner*, 15 Cal.Rptr.2d 632 (Cal.App.1993).

d.   **Which Party Can Use Part Performance?**

Obviously, the three traditional acts of part performance (payment, possession, and improvements) are acts which only a purchaser can perform. Does this mean that only a purchaser can use the doctrine to overcome the lack of a writing? A court which uses an estoppel theory of part performance would probably so conclude, since the acts show only injury to the purchaser. On the other hand, courts using an evidentiary approach sometimes permit even the vendor to use the purchaser's acts as evidence of the existence of a contract.

Example: Simes entered into an oral contract to sell his farm to Phillips. Prior to the closing, Phillips moved onto the farm and constructed a barn at a cost of $10,000. Simes refused to close and ordered Phillips off the land. Phillips sued to enforce the contract. (*Result:* A court which follows the estoppel theory would probably let Phillips enforce the contract if it were convinced of the "irreparable" nature of his injury. A court following the evidentiary theory would focus instead on whether Phillips' acts could be explained in some other way, such as by the notion that he was Simes' tenant. Since agricultural tenants seldom spend so much on valuable improvements on the land, the court might well conclude that Phillips' acts were "unequivocally referable" to a contract of sale.)

Whether Simes could enforce the contract if Phillips were the defaulting party raises a different issue. A court which followed the evidentiary theory would probably permit Simes to do so, reasoning that Phillips' acts were evidence on which either party could rely. A court adopting the estoppel approach would not permit Simes to enforce the contract, since the acts of part performance do not indicate any injury to Simes. See *Pearson v. Gardner*, 168 N.W. 485 (Mich.1918).

Note that if a court is willing to adopt a broad estoppel approach, and to consider acts other than the traditional three (the purchaser's payment, possession, and improvements), it is easy to imagine cases in which the *vendor* has done acts of detrimental reliance and hence can enforce the contract without a writing. The vendor may, for example, have contracted to purchase other real estate in reliance on the belief that the present real estate is under a contract of sale. See *Rutt v. Roche*, 87 A.2d 805 (Conn.1952) (vendor evicted his tenant and applied for a new mortgage loan in reliance on the contract of sale; court found part performance and enforced the contract for vendor).

e.   Enforcement in Equity Only

The part performance doctrine only makes available equitable relief to the plaintiff, usually in the form of an action for a specific performance. Several recent cases have continued to follow the traditional rule that the doctrine is unavailable in an action at law. See, e.g., *Haugland v. Parsons*, 863 S.W.2d 609 (Mo.App.1992). Restatement (Second) of Contracts § 129 agrees. There seems to be no good policy rationale for this distinction. A small minority view allows the plaintiff to obtain damages under part performance; see *Miller v. McCamish*, 479 P.2d 919 (Wash.1971).

f.   Standard of Proof

Even when all of the elements of part performance described above are met, courts frequently insist that the proof of the contract's terms be extraordinarily "clear and convincing" or the like. See, e.g., *Peterson v. Petersen*, 355 N.W.2d 26 (Iowa 1984).

D.   Remedies for Breach of a Real Estate Contract

When one party breaches a real estate sales contract, the other may have a variety of legal and equitable remedies. The principal legal remedy is an action for damages. Equitable remedies include specific performance, restitution, and a possible lien on the land. In addition to these formal remedies it is very common, when a breach is committed by the purchaser, for the seller to retain the purchaser's earnest money deposit as liquidated damages.

1. Damages

The general measure of "loss of bargain" damages is the difference between the contract price and the market value of the land on the date of the breach. See Stoebuck & Whitman, Property § 10.3 (3d ed.2000). The general formula applies to both the buyers and sellers. Hence, the buyer can get damages only if the property's value has risen above the contract price, while the seller can recover damages only if the value has fallen below the contract price.

Example 1: Adams agreed to sell land to Barnes for $100,000. Subsequently, the land's value rose to $120,000. If Adams refuses to complete the sale, Barnes is entitled to damages of $20,000, but if it is Barnes who breaches the contract, Adams is entitled to no recovery of loss-of-bargain damages.

Example 2: Adams agreed to sell land to Barnes for $100,000. Later, the value of the land declined to $80,000. If Barnes refuses to complete the contract, Adams can recover $20,000 in damages, but if it is Adams who breaches the contract, Barnes can recover no loss-of-bargain damages.

a. Events Occurring After the Breach

In general, changes in value which occur after the date of breach are irrelevant. Thus, in the first example above, if the value of the land increases to $130,000 by the date of trial, Barnes' damages are still limited to $20,000. However, if the seller resells the land to a third party shortly after the breach, or enters into a contract to resell the land, the selling price may be treated by a court as strong evidence of value as of the date of breach.

b. Good Faith Failure of Title

About half of the American courts refuse to grant a purchaser loss-of-bargain damages if the seller's breach is a result of a title failure which was not a product of the seller's bad faith. The courts that follow this rule give the purchaser only restitution—that is, return of the earnest money paid, plus any out-of-pocket expenses such as title, attorney, brokerage, and other similar costs. *Kramer v. Mobley*, 216 S.W.2d 930 (Ky.1949). The other half of the American courts give the purchaser full loss-of-bargain damages even if the seller acted in good faith. See Donovan v. Bachstadt, 453 A.2d 160 (N.J.1982).

1) **Bad Faith**

If the seller's title failure is a result of his or her own actions, or if the seller knew of the title defect when entering into the contract, all American courts will award the purchaser full loss-of-bargain damages.

2) **Origin and Development of the Rule Limiting Damages**

The rule originated with *Flureau v. Thornhill,* decided in England in 1776. It has been widely criticized, mainly on the ground that a breach by the seller is equally harmful to the buyer whether it is a result of good faith or bad faith. There is a trend toward eliminating the limitation and giving full loss-of-bargain damages. *Beard v. S/E Joint Venture,* 581 A.2d 1275 (Md.1990); West's Ann.Cal.Civ.Code § 3306, as amended in 1983.

c. **Special Damage Recovery**

In addition to loss-of-bargain damages, a non-breaching party may recover additional damages of several types if the necessary facts can be shown. All such damages are subject to the foreseeability requirement of *Hadley v. Baxendale,* 9 Exch. 341 (1854).

1) **Expenditures in Reliance on the Contract**

The non-breaching party may have expended funds because he expected the contract to be completed. Some such expenditures are directly related to performance of the contract, such as (in the case of a purchaser) title examination, survey, engineering, and other similar costs. Foreseeability is seldom a problem with these costs. Other expenditures may be less directly related to the contract, but nevertheless foreseeable: the expenses of moving, the costs of buying or selling other property, or the renovation of the property in question. See *Ruble v. Reich,* 611 N.W.2d 844 (Neb. 2000). If the damages are considered too speculative by the court, they will be denied; see *Johnston v. Curtis,* 16 S.W.3d 283 (Ark. App. 2000).

2) **Lost Profits**

If the non-breaching purchaser had already arranged a resale of the property at a profit, the purchaser might well be able to recover the loss of that profit as an additional element of damages. If the purchaser planned to use the land for the operation of a business, the loss of profits from that business might be an additional element of damages. However, in all lost profits cases foreseeability is usually a difficult element of proof. The courts are typically conservative in awarding damages in these cases. See *Guard v. P & R Enterprises, Inc.*, 631 P.2d 1068 (Alaska 1981).

3) Increased Interest Expense

If the purchaser is required, as a result of the seller's breach, to buy other property at a later time, the delay may result in higher interest costs on a purchase-money mortgage. This element of damages is particularly obvious if the breaching seller agreed to finance the sale at an attractive interest rate. Several recent cases have awarded damages for higher interest which the purchaser was forced to pay. The usual approach is to measure the difference between the payment stream which would have been due under the original financing and that under the new financing which the purchaser was forced to accept, and to discount this difference to a present value. See *Hutton v. Gliksberg*, 180 Cal.Rptr. 141 (Cal.App.1982). But see *Wall v. Pate*, 715 P.2d 449 (N.M.1986), holding such damages non-foreseeable.

4) Damages for Partial Breach

In some cases, the seller's breach will be serious enough to justify the purchaser's refusal to perform the contract, but the purchaser may nevertheless desire to proceed. For example, there may be a title defect which is acceptable to the purchaser despite the fact that the contract did not require the purchaser to take subject to it. Similarly, the land which the seller can convey may be smaller in area than that covered by the contract, but may nonetheless be sufficient for the purchaser's purposes. In such cases, the purchaser may wish to proceed with the contract, but to have an abatement of the purchase price to account for the deficiency. This abatement is equivalent to recovery of damages for the defect, and is generally allowed by the courts.

a) Measure of Damages or Abatement

If the defect or deficiency is not a result of the seller's bad faith, there is a split of authority as to the proper method of measuring the abatement. The issue is analogous to that of

Flureau v. Thornhill, discussed above. Some cases measure the abatement by computing a pro-rata share of the original contract price, while others employ the land's market value at the date of breach.

> *Example:* Jones contracted to sell 10 acres of land to Smith at a price of $5,000 per acre. A survey prior to closing disclosed that Jones only owned nine acres of land. On the closing date, the land's value had risen to $6,000 and Smith desired to complete the purchase with an abatement of the price. (*Result:* Some courts would hold that Smith is entitled to reduce the price by $5,000, the value of one acre as fixed by the contract. Other courts would permit him to reduce the price by $6,000, the market value of one acre at the date of breach.) See *Hardin v. Hill,* 423 P.2d 309 (Mont.1967).

b) Sales in Gross

Where the contract provides for the sale of a certain number of acres of land, but does not assign a price on a per-acre basis, the courts are more reluctant to permit any abatement for a deficiency in acreage. This is especially true if the contract calls for a number of acres, "more or less." See *Perfect v. McAndrew,* 798 N.E.2d 470 (Ind.App.2003). Nevertheless, an abatement is often ordered if the deficiency is very large or if the seller has affirmatively misrepresented the size of the area to be conveyed. See *Branton v. Jones,* 281 S.E.2d 799 (Va.1981); *Snow's Auto Supply Inc. v. Dormaier,* 696 P.2d 924 (Idaho App.1985).

2. Liquidated Damages and Retention of Deposit

In the great majority of land contracts, the purchaser makes an earnest money deposit of funds with the seller or the seller's real estate broker. If the purchaser subsequently breaches, the seller commonly attempts to retain these funds as liquidated damages, while the buyer may bring an action for restitution of them. The courts reach a wide range of conclusions on these facts, and the matter is highly controversial. See Stoebuck & Whitman, Property § 10.4 (3d ed.2000).

a. **Liquidated Damages or Forfeiture?**

The courts usually resolve the retention-of-deposit question by purporting to decide whether the retention would be a valid liquidation of damages or an invalid penalty or forfeiture. Most courts purport to focus on two questions:

1. Were the actual damages difficult or impossible to measure?

2. Was the amount of the liquidated sum a reasonable estimate of the probable actual damages? See *Kelly v. Marx*, 705 N.E.2d 1114 (Mass.1999).

The majority of cases focus on the reasonableness of the amount. In theory, reasonableness is determined as of the date the contract is formed, but many cases also examine reasonableness in relation to the seller's actual damages as of the date of breach. See *Shanghai Investment Company, Inc. v. Alteka Co.*, 993 P.2d 516 (Haw.2000). Cf. *Watson v. Ingram*, 881 P.2d 247 (Wash.1994), requiring reasonableness only at the date of the contract. See also. *Mason v. Fakhimi*, 865 P.2d 333 (Nev.1993) (deposit must be reasonable at *both* date of contract and date of breach). Some courts have adopted rules of thumb, such as validating any retention of a deposit which does not exceed 10% of the sales price; see *Vines v. Orchard Hills, Inc.*, 435 A.2d 1022 (Conn.1980); West's Ann.Calif.Civ.Code § 1675 (presumption that 3% of purchase price or less is reasonable). Other courts are much more liberal to vendors; see Vitolo v. O'Connor, 636 N.Y.S.2d 163 (N.Y. App.Div.1996) (forfeiture of 23 percent down payment upheld); U.S. v. Ponnapula, 246 F.3d 576 (6th Cir.2001) (forfeiture of 15% down payment upheld under Tennessee law).

b. **Preclusion of Other Remedies**

In many states there is authority that retention of a deposit is permissible whether any clause in the contract refers to such a right or not. It can be argued that inserting a clause can have a negative effect on the seller's position since it may preclude assertion of other remedies for the seller.

1) Preclusion of Damages

It seems intuitively obvious that a clause providing for liquidated damages must be in lieu of actual damages; otherwise the vendor gets to "have his cake and eat it too!" The majority of cases take this view; see *Catholic Charities of Archdiocese of Chicago v. Thorpe*, 741 N.E.2d 651 (Ill.App.2000). However, it is fairly common for a court to permit recovery of actual damages if the clause is drafted so that the seller's retention of the deposit is clearly optional. *Alexsey v. Kelly*, 614 N.Y.S.2d 734 (App.Div.1994). See *Community Devel. Service, Inc. v. Replacement Parts Mfg., Inc.*, 679 S.W.2d 721 (Tex.App.1984), in which the court found the liquidated damage clause unenforceable, thus allowing the vendor to recover much greater actual damages.

2) Preclusion of Specific Performance

There is no inherent conflict between a liquidated damages clause and a seller's right to specific performance. In general, the courts will give the seller the choice as between these remedies unless the clause makes it very clear that retention of the deposit was regarded by the parties as the seller's only remedy. *Conner v. Auburn Partners, L.L.C.*, 852 So.2d 755 (Ala.Civ.App. 2002); *Dewey v. Wentland*, 38 P.3d 402 (Wyo.2002).

c. Election of Remedies

The courts view the retention of deposits with disfavor and often impose procedural restrictions. For example, they commonly require the seller to elect to retain or return the deposit within a short time after the breach has occurred; if the deposit is not returned, they may well conclude that the seller is barred from seeking other remedies. *Dowding v. Land Funding Ltd.*, 555 P.2d 957 (Utah 1976).

3. Specific Performance

Either the vendor or purchaser may generally obtain an order of specific performance which compels the other party to complete the contract. The court may effectuate the order by a judicial conveyance of the property or by an order holding the defendant in contempt until he or she performs the contract. See Stoebuck & Whitman, Property § 10.5 (3d ed.2000).

a. Rationale—Property Unique

The remedy of specific performance is generally justified on the ground that real property is unique, and thus that the remedy at law (damages) is always inadequate. When a purchaser seeks specific performance, this argument is sensible, since the purchaser will receive the land itself if the action is successful. It makes less sense to argue the uniqueness of the land from the viewpoint of a seller-plaintiff, since the seller is receiving only money and not the land. However, if the contract is not performed the seller will be forced to market the land in some other fashion, a burden which may be accentuated by the land's unique characteristics.

Real estate is not very liquid, and may be quite difficult to resell, particularly if market conditions have deteriorated. This is perhaps the best explanation for the courts' willingness to give sellers specific performance.

It is very widely held that the remedy is mutual and that either party may specifically enforce the contract against the other. However, a few cases have cast doubt on the notion that a seller should always be able to obtain specific performance.

Example: Builder constructed a 3,600–unit luxury condominium project and placed the units on the market. Byers signed a contract to purchase one of the units, but subsequently her job was transferred to a new location and she refused to complete the purchase. Builder sought specific performance. (*Result:* The court may hold that since the units are so similar and numerous, they are not unique and only damages should be allowed.) See *Centex Homes Corp. v. Boag,* 320 A.2d 194 (N.J.Ch.1974). One case refused to apply similar reasoning to deny specific performance to a condominium *buyer. Giannini v. First Nat'l Bank of Des Plaines,* 483 N.E.2d 924 (Ill.App.1985).

b. Circumstances Under Which Specific Performance Is Unavailable

There are some situations in which specific performance is impractical or unrealistic and will not be ordered by a court.

1) Lack of Ability to Perform

If a seller has no title to the property or has already sold it to a third party who is outside the court's power in the case, the seller obviously can neither obtain nor be subjected to a decree of specific performance. Langemeier v. Urwiler Oil & Fertilizer, Inc., 660 N.W.2d 487 (Neb.2003). Similarly, a buyer cannot obtain or be subjected to specific performance if the buyer does not have the money, or ability to borrow the money, to complete the purchase. *Gaggero v. Yura,* 134 Cal. Rptr. 2d 313 (Cal.App.2003).

2) Contrary Contract Language

The contract itself may exclude specific performance as a remedy. It is also possible that the wording of a liquidated damages clause, as noted above, may be construed to exclude specific performance.

3) Property Being Purchased for Resale

If the purchaser's only purpose in buying the property is to resell it to a third party, some courts refuse specific performance on the ground that the purchaser's loss is only pecuniary and can be easily measured and fully compensated by money damages. *Watkins v. Paul*, 511 P.2d 781 (Idaho 1973). Other courts grant specific performance in order to forestall additional litigation by the subvendee.

c. Fairness and Vagueness

The courts frequently impose a higher standard of contract specificity when asked to specifically enforce a contract than when asked to award damages. In addition, it is widely held that a contract ought not to be specifically enforced if such enforcement would be unjust or unfair. The injustice need not rise to the level of fraud or deception, but may simply be overreaching or harsh dealing. Some cases refuse specific enforcement merely because the purchase price is unfair. This is particularly likely if there is a great disparity in the sophistication or bargaining power of the parties. Ironically, a concern for fairness may result in making specific performance difficult or nearly impossible to obtain.

Example: Jones contracted to sell his house to Smith for $75,000. Later, Jones announced to Smith that he would refuse to go through with the sale. If the house's value has fallen below $75,000, specific performance is not generally an attractive remedy to Smith; unless the house has unique characteristics which are desirable to him, he would probably prefer to buy elsewhere in light of the decline in value. On the other hand, if the house has risen in value, a court might well conclude that specific performance would be unjust from Jones' point of view and refuse to award it to Smith. Thus, if the court takes the "injustice" doctrine very seriously, specific performance may be legally available only in cases in which it is financially unattractive. See Maggs, Remedies for Breach of Contract Under Article Two of the U.L.T.A., 11 Ga.L.Rev. 275 (1977). But several recent cases have given the purchaser specific performance despite sharp rises in value.

d. Damages in Addition to Specific Performance

Even if a decree of specific performance is entered by the court, a long time will usually have passed since the originally agreed closing date. This delay may well have cost one or both of the parties significant amounts of money for which they may be entitled to additional compensation. For example, the purchaser may have been deprived of the occupancy of the property, and may have paid rent at another location during the interim. On the other hand, the purchaser may have saved the interest expense, taxes, maintenance, and other costs which would have been incurred if the purchaser had been in possession of the property under the contract. These "savings" offset the rentals which the purchaser has paid at the other location, but may still leave a net loss; if so, the purchaser is entitled to recover that amount as damages. *Matrix Properties Corp. v. TAG Investments*, 644 N.W.2d 601 (N.D.2002).

The delay may also have required the purchaser to obtain a mortgage loan at a higher rate of interest because of a generally rising interest rate market. If so, he or she can probably recover the present value of the difference in payment streams. See *Housing Authority v. Monterey Senior Citizen Park*, 210 Cal.Rptr. 497 (Cal.App.1985). Similar damages can be recovered by the vendor if the purchaser delays in performing; see *Dato v. Mascarello*, 557 N.E.2d 181 (Ill.App.1989) (vendor can recover additional mortgage loan interest, additional property taxes, etc.).

Example: Paul contracted to sell Mary a commercial store building. Mary refused to close on the agreed date, and Paul, who had already arranged to move his business, was required to leave the space vacant for one year pending a decree of specific performance. During that year, he paid taxes, mortgage interest, and insurance on the vacant building, totaling $20,000. Paul can show that he made good faith efforts to rent the building during the year of vacancy, but was unable to do so. (*Result:* Paul can recover the $20,000 in damages from Mary in addition to getting a decree of specific performance against her.) See *Talerico v. Olivarri*, 796 N.E.2d 1083 (Ill.App.2003).

4. Vendor's Lien

Courts of equity recognize an implied lien, similar to a mortgage, in favor of the vendor for the unpaid portion of the purchase price on land. See Stoebuck & Whitman, Property § 10.6 (3d ed.2000).

a. Before Closing

Prior to transfer of title, the lien is on the purchaser's equitable interest, and is of little practical consequence since the vendor still has legal title and prefers, in most cases, an action for damages or specific performance.

b. After Closing

After title has been transferred, a grantor's lien is imposed on the legal title in the purchaser's hands, and is of much greater importance. Even here, however, the lien is not asserted very often, since if the grantor has not received the full price at the time of closing, he or she will usually have obtained some more specific security device, such as a mortgage or deed of trust, to secure payment of the remaining portion of the price. *Krajcir v. Egidi*, 712 N.E.2d 917 (Ill.App.1999).

c. Enforcement

Enforcement of the vendor's lien is usually by either judicial foreclosure by sale or strict foreclosure. Foreclosure by sale requires a court hearing and a court-supervised sale of the property, much like foreclosure of a mortgage. *Sewer v. Martin*, 511 F.2d 1134 (3d Cir.1975). In strict foreclosure, the court will order the purchaser to pay the remaining price within some specified time period, and if he or she fails to do so, will simply award the property back to the seller. The result is much like forfeiture of an earnest money deposit, except that it occurs after legal title has passed. Strict foreclosure is objectionable if it results in a forfeiture of an amount greatly in excess of the actual damages suffered by the vendor. See *Riffey v. Schulke*, 227 N.W.2d 4 (Neb.1975).

d. Rights of Bona Fide Purchasers

If the purchaser in whose hands the property is subject to the lien transfers it to another person, the question arises whether the transferee is also bound by the lien. Since the lien is equitable in nature, it will generally be unenforceable as against a good faith purchaser for value. Since most land sale contracts are unrecorded, transferees are probably good faith purchasers in the great majority of cases. Even knowledge of the existence of the prior contract may not deprive the transferee of BFP status unless he or she had reason to know that the price was still partly unpaid. See *Manz v. Johnson*, 531 S.W.2d 934 (Tex.Civ.App.1976).

5. Restitution

The term restitution indicates that a party to a contract has received back from the other party something which he or she paid in or contributed at some prior stage in the contract's life. While a party may make restitution voluntarily, a court may also order it. This occurs most commonly in connection with rescission of the contract. See Stoebuck & Whitman, Property § 10.7 (3d ed.2000).

a. **Relationship to Rescission**

Two forms of rescission exist. One is a voluntary agreement between the parties under which they agree to "unwind" the contract, with each returning to the other whatever has been paid or contributed and with no further obligation on either to perform. In its other meaning, rescission is an order of a court, given as a remedy for breach of contract, which places the parties back in the position which they held before the contract was entered into. *Thus if one party commits a material breach, the other is generally entitled to demand a rescission, and simultaneously to seek restitution of the amount he or she has paid.*

Example: Frank agreed to sell 10 acres of land to Bill for $50,000. Prior to the closing, the land's value declined to $40,000. Bill discovered that Frank owned only 9 acres, a breach of contract which Bill (and the court) considered material. (*Result:* Bill may obtain an order from the court rescinding the contract and ordering any earnest money he has paid be returned to him. In effect, he has seized upon Frank's breach as a ground for rescission and restitution, and thus, as a technique for getting out of an unattractive bargain.)

b. **Restitution Is a Mutual Remedy**

One who seeks and obtains restitution must also be willing to give restitution to the other party. Thus, when a party who is innocent gets restitution, the other party, even though guilty of a breach of contract, will also have returned whatever payment or contribution he has made to the contract. This restitutionary recovery may offset the damages for which the breaching party is liable.

Example: Abel signs a contract to sell land to Baker for $100,000. Baker pays $30,000 toward the price but then refuses to make any additional payments. Abel resells the land to a third party for $95,000, leaving Baker liable for $5,000 in loss-of-bargain damages. Even though Baker is in breach, he is entitled to restitution of the payments he made, since the contract cannot be performed. However, he remains liable for the $5,000 in damages, and hence can recover only $25,000 by way of restitution. *Vines v. Orchard Hills, Inc.*, 435 A.2d 1022 (Conn.1980).

6. **Vendee's Lien**

When a purchaser demands restitution under the principles discussed above, the courts recognize an equitable lien on the real estate in his or her favor as an aid to restitutionary recovery. See Stoebuck & Whitman, Property § 10.8 (3d ed.2000). No specific language in the contract is needed to create the lien. It must, however, be foreclosed by judicial action. It is inferior in priority to any other liens or interests created prior to the contract of sale, and to any subsequent liens if it is made expressly subordinate to them. Like the vendor's lien discussed earlier, it cannot be asserted against a bona fide purchaser who has bought the property from the vendor.

Example: Vern contracts to sell land to Paul, but subsequently breaches the contract. Paul brings an action to recover his earnest money, and petitions the court to declare an equitable vendee's lien on the land to assist his recovery. Vern has placed two recorded mortgages on the land, the first before entering into the contract with Paul, and the second after the contract. (*Result*: The first mortgage clearly has priority over Paul's lien. The second is junior to Paul's lien if the second mortgagee had notice of Paul's contract rights. Such notice might result from the recordation of the contract of sale, or might be actual notice. See *Stahl v. Roulhac*, 438 A.2d 1366 (Md.App.1982)).

In the example above, even the second mortgage would have priority over Paul's lien if the contract of sale contained a clause expressly subordinating Paul's rights to those of subsequent mortgagees. Such clauses are commonly inserted in sale contracts on subdivision houses or condominium units to be built in the future, for example. See *Arundel Fed. Sav. & Loan Ass'n v. Lawrence*, 499 A.2d 1298 (Md.App.1985).

E. Time of Performance

It is not essential that the parties fix a date of performance in their contract, and if they do not, the court will infer that a reasonable time was intended. In most cases the contract fixes a time, which may or may not be "of the essence." See Stoebuck & Whitman, Property § 10.9 (3d ed.2000).

1. Time of the Essence

The parties may make time "of the essence" by so stating in the contract or by other language which indicates that the time of performance is important to them. In the absence of such language, the court will assume that time is not of the essence unless there are other circumstances, such as a rapidly fluctuating market or specific plans of one party which depend on the time of performance and which are known to the other party, which indicate that the time of performance is of great significance. *Kossler v. Palm Springs Developments, Ltd.,* 161 Cal.Rptr. 423 (Cal.App.1980).

2. Duties and Remedies if Time is Not of the Essence

If time is not of the essence, a party who tenders performance late may still enforce the contract, so long as he or she is not unreasonably late. In other words, late (but reasonable) performance is not a sufficiently "total" breach to discharge the innocent party from the duty to perform, and permit him or her to rescind or abandon the contract. Delays of 30 to 90 days or more are commonly considered reasonable, and sometimes much longer periods are accepted by the courts. *Krotz v. Sattler,* 586 N.W.2d 336 (Iowa 1998) (10–year delay not unreasonable, where neither party attempted to perform contract in the interim). However, the party who is late is liable for damages caused by the delay as such. Such damages might include lost rents or profits, additional interest payments, higher taxes, or the like. *Richardson v. Van Dolah,* 429 F.2d 912 (9th Cir.1970).

3. Duties and Remedies if Time is of the Essence

If the contract or the surrounding circumstances make time of the essence, a late tender of performance by one party fully excuses the other from performing. Thus one who is late has no right to enforce the contract judicially at all. The lateness of the tender is a total breach, and also gives rise to liability for loss-of-bargain damages. This follows even if the tender is only late by a matter of hours. *Doctorman v. Schroeder,* 114 A. 810 (N.J.1921).

4. Notice Making Time of the Essence

Even if time was not originally made essential in the contract, either party can make it such by a notice to the other within a reasonable time prior to the agreed closing date. This may seem like a power to modify the contract unilaterally, but it is very widely recognized. EC, L.L.C. v. Eaglecrest Mnfg, Home Park, 713 N.Y.S.2d 391 (N.Y. App. Div. 2000) (notice given 10 days before closing date was sufficient). However, if the notice is given an unreasonably short time prior to the date of performance, it will be ineffective and time will not be considered essential. *3M Holding Corp. v. Wagner,* 560 N.Y.S.2d 865 (App.Div.1990) (notice mailed 4 days prior to closing date was ineffective).

5. Waivers of Strictly Timely Performance

Even if time is of the essence, courts often find waivers of strict performance from oral or written statements or from the parties' actions. The statute of frauds does not bar oral waivers. If one party accepts the other's late performance without objection, or orally states that it will be acceptable, a waiver will often be found. *Leiter v. Eltinge,* 54 Cal.Rptr. 703 (Cal.App.1966).

F. Conditions in Realty Sales Contracts

Contracts of sale frequently include conditions to a party's duty of performance. A condition is some event or fact which must occur or exist in order for a party to be under a duty of performance. The condition may be entirely outside the control of the parties, or it may depend on some action by one of the parties. In the latter case, courts frequently infer a duty on the party who must take action to use good faith efforts to make the condition occur. See *Bryant v. City of Atlantic City,* 707 A.2d 1072 (N.J. Super.1998)

Suppose, for example, that Ames agreed to sell his farm to Baker, and the contract included the following conditions: "Ames is obligated to sell only if (1) the county adopts a zoning ordinance by July 1, and (2) Ames is able to purchase another suitable farm in Randolph County." The first condition is outside the parties' control. The second is, to some extent, within Ames' control and most courts would probably infer a duty on Ames' part to use good faith efforts to locate and purchase a suitable farm in Randolph County. Thus, clause (2) will be viewed as containing both a condition and a covenant or promise which Ames has a duty to perform. See Stoebuck & Whitman, Property § 10.11 (3d ed.2000).

1. Precedent and Concurrent Conditions

A condition precedent is one which must occur before a party has a duty of performance. A concurrent condition, on the other hand, is one which is expected to occur simultaneously with the party's performance.

Example: Smith executed a contract to sell his house to Taylor. Since Taylor did not have cash, he inserted a clause in the contract providing "Taylor's obligation to purchase is conditioned upon his obtaining a mortgage loan for $58,000 or more, with an interest rate not to exceed 10%, and with an amortization period of 25 years or more." This language will be read as a condition precedent, and if the necessary financing is not obtained despite the buyer's good faith efforts to obtain it, the buyer will be excused from performing the contract. See *Barber v. Jacobs,* 753 A.2d 430 (Conn.App.2000). As mentioned above, the courts will almost invariably read the condition as imposing a duty of good faith on the part of the purchaser to attempt to obtain the loan. *Ouellette v. Filippone,* 745 A.2d 161 (R.I.2000).

2. Waiver of Conditions

If a condition has been inserted in a contract for the sole benefit of one party, that party may waive it and proceed to enforce the contract. Financing conditions, such as the one in the example above, are usually viewed as benefitting only the buyer. Thus, in that example, the buyer could enforce the contract even if he was unable to obtain the financing as described. But if a condition is intended to benefit the non-waiving party or both parties, no unilateral waiver is allowed.

Example: Sherman contracted to sell vacant urban land to Brown. The contract included a clause making the closing conditional upon the rezoning of the land for shopping center purposes. In most cases, the condition would be construed to benefit only the buyer, who would be hopeful of building the shopping center. However, if the seller owned adjacent land and also hoped to be benefitted by the construction of the shopping center, the condition might be deemed of mutual benefit, so that neither party alone could waive it. See *LaGrave v. Jones*, 336 So.2d 1330 (Ala.1976).

3. Concurrent Conditions and Tender

The "closing" of the real estate contract usually involves the delivery of the deed by the seller and the payment of the purchase money by the buyer. *These performances are usually regarded as concurrent conditions, so that neither party is obligated to perform unless and until the other party has tendered his or her own performance.* Thus, neither is in breach until he or she has been "put in breach" by the other party's tender of performance. *Century 21 All Western Real Estate v. Webb*, 645 P.2d 52 (Utah 1982).

A tender may be accomplished by physically holding out the necessary document, such as a deed or check. Most modern cases will also accept a truthful communication, made to the other party, that one is ready, willing, and able to perform. See Stoebuck & Whitman, Property § 10.10 (3d ed.2000).

Example: Stuart contracted to sell his house to Burton, with closing to occur on March 1. Time was not made of the essence. Neither party made a tender on March 1, but on March 10, Stuart wrote to Burton and told him that since he had failed to close, Stuart was "canceling the contract." Burton then sued for specific performance. (*Result:* Such a "cancellation" is ineffective since Stuart did not tender a deed to Burton. Until Stuart makes a tender, he cannot excuse himself from his own duty to perform the contract, and he has no claim for damages or any other remedy against Burton.) *Pelletier v. Dwyer*, 334 A.2d 867 (Me.1975).

4. Circumstances Excusing Tender

In some cases a tender is unnecessary, and a party who does not tender has full remedies available. These circumstances include the following:

a. The opposing party has clearly repudiated the contract.

b. Other circumstances make it obvious that the opposing party is unwilling to perform.

c. The opposing party's evasive conduct has made a tender impossible or very difficult.

d. The opposing party's performance has become impossible.

Example: Stuart contracted to sell his house to Burton, with closing to occur on March 1. On February 28, Burton discovered that Stuart had already sold the house the previous week to Jones. Burton can hold Stuart liable for breach without the necessity for making a tender of the purchase money to Stuart, since it is obvious that Stuart cannot perform the contract. *Kessler v. Tortoise Development, Inc.*, 1 P.3d 292 (Idaho 2000).

Even if a tender is excused by these factors, courts often will give the innocent party a remedy for breach only if she or he was *in fact* ready, willing, and able to perform. *Jewell v. Rowe*, 500 N.Y.S.2d 787 (App.Div.1986).

G. Quality of Title

The parties to a real estate sale contract may agree that the title will be of any particular quality they desire. Titles may be highly questionable, free of any doubt whatever, or somewhere in between. *Unless the parties agree to the contrary, however, the law will infer in every realty sales contract a covenant that the vendor's title will be "marketable."* (The term "merchantable" has the same meaning.) *Laba v. Carey*, 327 N.Y.S.2d 613, 277 N.E.2d 641 (N.Y.1971).

1. Marketable Title

A marketable title is one which is free of all reasonable risk of attack. It need not be absolutely perfect, but any defects in it must be sufficiently minor that a reasonable purchaser or lending institution would not object to them. See Annot., 18 A.L.R. 4th 1311 (1982); Stoebuck & Whitman, Property § 10.12 (3d ed.2000).

2. Types of Title Defects

Almost any defect which may prevent the vendor from transferring a fee simple absolute title can impair marketability. Typical illustrations include the following.

a. Flaws in the Chain of Ownership

A title may be unmarketable because some conveyance in the chain of title was *forged, undelivered, obtained by fraud or duress, or executed by a minor*. Some cases, probably a minority, would hold that a deed in the chain which is *unrecorded* renders title unmarketable, even though it can be shown to have existed in fact. A title derived from *adverse possession* may well be considered unmarketable unless the facts which support the adverse possession are very clear or have been established by a quiet title action or other judicial proceeding.

b. Encumbrances

A wide variety of *encumbrances* may make title unmarketable. They include outstanding leases, restrictive covenants, mortgages, easements, party wall agreements, options, contracts of sale, and various types of liens. Some cases hold the title marketable despite the encumbrance if the purchaser knew of it when the contract was formed, if it is readily visible from an inspection of the land, or if it is beneficial to the land. *Ford v. White*, 172 P.2d 822 (Or.1946). Moreover, the encumbrance won't make title unmarketable if it will be removed or paid off at the time of closing (with the funds the purchaser is paying the seller). *Jensen v. Bledsoe*, 593 P.2d 988 (Idaho 1979).

c. Actions Depriving the Vendor of Title

The vendor may be unable to convey marketable title because *he or she has lost the title* to some other person, such as an adverse possessor or to the government in an action in eminent domain.

d. Reasonable Threat of Litigation

If litigation challenging the land's title is threatened and has a plausible likelihood of success, the title is unmarketable. *Stewart Title Guar. Co. v. Greenlands Realty*, 58 F. Supp.2d 360 (D. N.J. 1999). However, if the litigation's merits are not reasonably debatable or have no rational justification, the title is marketable.

e. Other Matters Making Title Unmarketable

Some types of legal problems with property might be thought not to relate to title as such, but nevertheless have been treated by the courts as rendering title unmarketable, and therefore as grounds for the purchaser's objection. They include *encroachments* by improvements on the subject property on a neighboring parcel or vice versa, and existing *violations of zoning ordinances. Existing violations of other local codes,* such as building, housing, and subdivision codes, are sometimes held to constitute an encumbrance on title. See *Radovanov v. Land Title Co. of America,* 545 N.E.2d 351 (Ill.App.1989) (housing code violation); 71 Cornell L.Rev. 1 (1985). Similarly, there is case authority that an *existing violation of restrictive covenants* in a subdivision will make title unmarketable; *Coons v. Carstensen,* 446 N.E.2d 114 (Mass.App.1983). Case law is mixed and meager on these issues of code and covenant violation.

3. Timing of Marketable Title

The title need not be marketable until the date fixed for transfer of legal title. The traditional view was that even a complete absence of title was no ground for objection until the closing date. However, some recent cases have given the purchaser a right of rescission prior to closing if it appeared very unlikely that the vendor could cure the title defects. If the buyer discovers defects which make the title objectionable, he or she must notify the seller of them specifically and allow a reasonable time for cure. If the notice is given only a short time before closing, its effect will be to extend the closing date to allow the vendor a reasonable time to cure the problems. However, no time need be allowed if the defects are incurable. *Cohen v. Kranz,* 238 N.Y.S.2d 928, 189 N.E.2d 473 (N.Y.1963).

4. Merger

The right of the purchaser to object to defects which make title unmarketable lasts only until a deed is delivered and accepted. When this occurs, the contract's covenants of title are said to be "merged into the deed" and can no longer be the basis of legal action. This merger occurs only with respect to *title* covenants and not those relating to such matters as the physical condition of the property, improvements, and the like. *Richardson v. Hardin,* 5 P.3d 793 (Wyo. 2000). Merger is inapplicable to cases of fraud or mistake. See *Knudson v. Weeks,* 394 F.Supp. 963 (W.D.Okl.1975).

5. Relation of Title Covenants to the Deed

The fact that a contract contains covenants of title does not dictate the type of deed which must be used. A deed is not a title, but simply a mechanism for conveying a title, and a marketable title will pass just as well by a quitclaim deed as by a deed that contains extensive covenants or warranties of title. Thus, a contract which calls for a quitclaim deed does not negate the implied covenant that title will be marketable. See *Wallach v. Riverside Bank*, 100 N.E. 50 (N.Y.1912). Likewise, a contract clause stating that title will be marketable does not suggest that a warranty deed must be given by the seller. In general, the contract will state what type of deed is to be used, and if no statement is made the courts will usually look to local practice and custom.

H. Equitable Conversion

The doctrine of equitable conversion helps the courts answer two important sets of questions about real estate contracts. The first set of questions deals with *characterization* of the interests of the parties between the time they enter into the contract and the date legal title is transferred. It helps to determine whether a particular party's interest should be considered real estate or personal property in various types of disputes. The second set of questions deals with *risk*. When some event, such as a fire, occurs which harms the value of the property, equitable conversion helps to determine which of the parties must bear the loss. See Stoebuck & Whitman, Property § 10.13 (3d ed.2000).

1. Origin of the Doctrine

The concept of equitable conversion developed from the willingness of the courts to enforce a real estate sale contract in equity, by specific performance, at the behest of either party. Having taken this stance, the English courts began saying that equity should consider as having been done that which would be ordered done. Thus, they began treating the contract, during its executory period, as if it had already been performed for some purposes. The great majority of American courts continue to take this approach, sometimes following it with no apparent consideration of the underlying policies in the case.

2. Characterization Upon the Death of a Party

The most common characterization question arises when one of the contracting parties dies during the executory period. *Equitable conversion treats the vendor's interest as personal property and the purchaser's interest as real estate, even though no closing has yet occurred.*

a. Death of the Vendor

If the vendor dies, the "bare" legal title descends to his or her heirs or devisees, but they hold it subject to a duty *to convey to the purchaser at closing. However, the proceeds of the sale go to the vendor's personal representative, and after the debts of the estate are paid, they will be turned over to the legatees or next of kin—the recipients of the vendor's personal property.* If the vendor was intestate, the heirs and next of kin are usually the same persons, but if there is a will which gives the realty and personality to different persons, the legatees will be delighted and the devisees will be disappointed by the application of equitable conversion. *Clapp v. Tower*, 93 N.W. 862 (N.D.1903). Courts will sometimes refuse to follow this approach if it seems to conflict with the testator's intent.

1. If the will is made after the contract is formed, and it specifically identifies and devises the land, some cases have rejected equitable conversion and given the proceeds of the sale to the devisees. *Father Flanagan's Boys' Home v. Graybill*, 132 N.W.2d 304 (Neb.1964).

2. Where the will is made before the contract is formed, a few states have reversed equitable conversion by statute in cases of the vendor's death, and give the devisees the right to the purchase money.

b.   Death of the Purchaser

If the purchaser dies during the executory period, his or her interest descends as real estate to the heirs or devisees, and they receive the legal title when the closing occurs. *However, the doctrine of "exoneration" requires the purchase price to be paid by the purchaser's personal representative out of the personal property assets of the estate, thus reducing the amount passing to the legatees or next of kin.* Some states have eliminated or weakened the doctrine of exoneration by statute, but in others it still operates.

3.   Claims of Judgment Creditors

In most states, a statute provides that a judgment becomes a lien on the defendant's real property in the county where the judgment is docketed. If the judgment is docketed during the executory period of a contract of sale, equitable conversion may effect the lien's validity.

a.   Judgments Against the Vendor

If a judgment is docketed against the vendor, it may be argued that under equitable conversion his or her interest is no longer real property, and thus that the lien does not attach. The cases often turn on the specific language of the lien statute, and *a slight majority reject the equitable conversion doctrine, permitting the lien to attach.* See *Marks v. City of*

Tucumcari, 595 P.2d 1199 (N.M.1979). Denying the enforceability of the lien against the vendor, see *Stephens v. Jenkins*, 439 S.E.2d 849 (S.C.1994).

b. Judgments Against the Purchaser

If a judgment is obtained against the purchaser, it is the judgment creditor who will argue for equitable conversion, since the doctrine would characterize the purchaser's interest as real estate and subject it to the judgment lien. *The majority of cases follow equitable conversion in this context.* See *Fulton v. Duro*, 687 P.2d 1367 (Idaho App.1984), affirmed 700 P.2d 14 (1985). Thus, it is entirely possible that both the vendor's and purchaser's interests can be subjected to judgment liens. Some courts reach the same result by construction of the judgment lien statute.

4. Other Characterization Questions

Equitable conversion has occasionally been used to resolve many other characterization questions, such as determining the meaning of the word "owner" or a similar term under various contracts, the construction of state inheritance or estate tax statutes which operate on real property, and even the determination of whether a sale by co-owners works a severance of a joint tenancy.

5. Risk of Loss

Equitable conversion regards the purchaser as the owner of the real estate during the contract's executory period. *As a result, it requires the purchaser to complete the contract and to pay the full price even if some unforeseen event causes a loss in value to the property before the closing.*

Example: Sterling agreed to sell a valuable peach orchard to Barnes. Prior to the closing, an unexpected freeze destroyed many of the trees, greatly reducing the property's value. After Barnes refused to perform, Sterling brought an action for specific performance. (*Result:* Barnes must pay the full agreed price, even though the value he is receiving is far less than that for which he bargained.) See *Bleckley v. Langston*, 143 S.E.2d 671 (Ga.App.1965).

This result is subject to reversal by appropriate contract language. Thus, in the example above, if the contract had stated, "in the event the trees on the premises are not in substantially as good condition at closing as on the date of this contract, purchaser may rescind the contract," Barnes would not have been compelled to perform.

a. Criticisms of Equitable Conversion

As a tool for allocation of risk, equitable conversion has been severely criticized. The results it produces are usually contrary to the parties' expectations, since the parties generally assume that the risk is on the vendor until closing. In addition, the vendor is far more likely than the purchaser to carry insurance against the loss. Finally, the vendor is usually in possession and is therefore in a better position to take precautions that might prevent the loss. See *Skelly Oil Co. v. Ashmore,* 365 S.W.2d 582 (Mo.1963).

b. Minority View

A substantial minority of states have modified or rejected equitable conversion in the context of risk of loss. About twelve states have adopted the Uniform Vendor and Purchaser Risk Act, which denies the vendor the right to enforce the contract if a material loss occurs while he or she has the risk. Under the act, the risk does not shift until either possession or legal title is transferred to the purchaser. A few states have reached a similar position through judicial decisions.

c. Non-physical Losses

Losses in value may be due to factors other than physical damage. The property's value might fall because of a rezoning, a change in local codes, or an eminent domain action. Equitable conversion is commonly used to allocate the risk in these cases as well. See *Arko Enterprises, Inc. v. Wood,* 185 So.2d 734 (Fla.App.1966). The Uniform Vendor and Purchaser Risk Act, mentioned above, applies to physical damage and eminent domain, but does not apply to other sorts of changes in legal status which might reduce the property's value.

6. Impact of Casualty Insurance

If one of the parties carries casualty insurance, the question arises whether its presence varies the results discussed above. Sometimes the same party will have both insurance and the risk of loss, and in that happy situation no problem exists; the insurance will indemnify the insured party for his or her loss. Unfortunately, it often happens that the party with the risk is not the party with insurance.

a. Risk on Purchaser, Vendor Insured

The most common situation is that in which the vendor has an insurance policy (which has usually been carried for some time) while the purchaser, under equitable conversion, has the risk of loss. *Most modern courts are unwilling to permit the seller the windfall of recovering the full price of the land and also collecting from the insurer.* They generally permit the vendor to enforce the contract only on condition that the price is abated to the extent of the insurance recovery. *Hillard v. Franklin*, 41 S.W.3d 106 (Tenn.App.2000).

b. Purchaser Insured, Risk on Vendor

Here the positions of the parties are reversed, with the purchaser carrying insurance and the law imposing the risk of loss on the vendor. Can the purchaser collect the insurance proceeds and at the same time avoid the contract of purchase or complete the contract at an abated price? Many cases allow the insurer to avoid paying the claim on the ground that, if the purchaser takes the position described here, there is no loss, and therefore nothing for the insurer to indemnify. See *Sanford v. Breidenbach*, 173 N.E.2d 702 (Ohio App.1960). Moreover, if the insurance company pays the claim, the vendor may argue that the insurance was intended for his or her benefit as well, even though the vendor was not named as an insured in the policy. This argument has prevailed in several cases, particularly if the contract stipulated that the purchaser would carry insurance. *Nevada Refining Co. v. Newton*, 497 P.2d 887 (Nev.1972).

7. Time of Conversion

Equitable conversion clearly does not occur until there is a fully formed contract of sale. An unexercised option, for example, is not enough. Neither is an oral contract which is unenforceable under the Statute of Frauds, or a contract unenforceable for other reasons, such as insufficient specificity. If the seller's title is defective, there is no conversion until the defects are cured, at least for purposes of the seller's shifting away the risk of loss.

a. Actual Enforcement

Equitable conversion does not depend on actual enforcement of the contract. If the contract is enforceable at the critical time (the loss, the death of a party, etc.), it does not matter that the contract is later rescinded or abandoned. *Frietze v. Frietze*, 437 P.2d 137 (N.M.1968).

b. Unfulfilled Conditions

There is considerable dicta in the cases that no conversion occurs until all conditions in the contract have been fulfilled. However, a large number of cases disregard this rule in practice and find a conversion despite the presence of unfulfilled conditions. This is particularly true where the condition in question is also a covenant, or one which the party has a good faith duty to fulfill. In practical result, equitable conversion is usually delayed only by conditions which are dependent on the actions of some third party.

REVIEW QUESTIONS

1. T or F   S agreed to sell land to B by oral contract. B gave S a $1000 earnest money check, which S endorsed. B wrote the following words on the check: "Payment toward $20,000 purchase price on cash sale of Whiteacre by S to B." Later, B refused to complete the purchase. S can enforce the contract.

2. T or F   If a contract for the sale of land is modified or rescinded by oral agreement, the original contract remains in effect.

3.   S and B entered into an oral contract under which B agreed to buy S's house. B paid $500 earnest money, moved into the house, and spent $1,000 fixing it up. Then B changed his mind, moved out, and refused to complete the sale. Can S enforce the contract?

4. T or F   V and P signed a written contract of sale under which P agreed to buy V's farm. The contract contained a clause stating "P hereby deposits $1,000 with V as liquidated damages, which V may retain in the event of P's breach of this contract." Later P refused to complete the contract. V can obtain a decree of specific performance.

5.   V agreed in writing to sell his commercial warehouse building to P. The contract provided "Closing will occur on July 1." On that date, V tendered a deed to P, but P asked for an additional week's extension to allow him time to complete his arrangements for financing the purchase. What are V's rights?

6. T or F   V agreed in writing to sell his house for all cash to P, "subject to P's obtaining a loan of $50,000 at 12% interest or less." P made no attempt to arrange any loan, but on the closing date he offered to pay cash from other sources of funds and complete the purchase. V is obligated to go through with the sale.

7. T or F   Sellers contracted to sell his house to Barnes. Nothing was said in the contract about the title. Barnes searched the title and discovered a restrictive covenant, enforceable by the neighboring owners, against operation of any commercial enterprise in the house. Since

Barnes had planned to open a law office in the house, he refused to complete the purchase. Sellers can enforce the contract against him.

*

II

Conveyances and Titles

■ ANALYSIS

J. **The Real Estate Settlement Procedures Act (RESPA)**
1. Disclosure and Informational Requirements
2. Escrow Accounts for Taxes, Insurance, and Other Items
3. Kickbacks and Unearned Fees
4. Yield Spread Premiums

A.   The Deed

The most common method of transferring land in the American legal system is the deed. However, in early English history, conveyances were usually made by "feoffment with livery of seisin." The person transferring the land met with the transferee on or within sight of the land itself, and handed over a twig or clod while reciting to witnesses that the transfer was being made. No writing was essential, although it was often the practice to prepare a written "charter of feoffment" which, while not a conveyance itself, served as a memorial or record of the transaction.

1.   Early Antecedents of the Deed

From early times in English history, writings were used to transfer certain types of interests in land. The modern deed is a descendant of these early writings, and wording drawn from ancient deed forms continues to be used in many states. The more important ones are described below.

a.   The Grant

Even in very early times, non-possessory interests and non-freehold interests, such as leaseholds, easements, and future interests were transferred by grant—that is, a written instrument under seal.

b.   The Lease and Release

The common law conveyancers developed at an early date a method of transferring a possessory fee simple without the need for traveling to the land itself. The conveyor would first grant a lease to the conveyee with a duration of, say, one year. Immediately thereafter, the conveyor would transfer the reversion to the conveyee by means of a second grant, termed a release. Both grants were in writing, and the two interests merged in the grantee, giving a fee simple absolute.

c.   The Bargain and Sale Deed

The Statute of Uses, enacted in 1536, converted many equitable interests in land into legal interests. One type of interest on which it operated was the equitable title which a purchaser has during the executory period in a land sale contract, as discussed in Chapter I. The common lawyers developed a deed that took the form of a contract of sale, but with no further payment to be made; the courts treated the document as placing legal (and not merely equitable) title in the purchaser under the Statute of Uses. This form became known as the "bargain and sale deed," since the conveyor recited that he or she had "bargained and sold" the land to the conveyee. No entry on the land was necessary.

d. The Covenant to Stand Seized

If a person who owned land made a promise to hold it for the use of (in other words, to "stand seized to the use of") another person to whom he or she was related by blood or marriage, the courts applied the Statute of Uses to treat the equitable title in the hands of the conveyee as a legal title.

2. The Modern Deed

Some of the early types of deeds described above were required to be in writing, while others were not. The English Statute of Frauds, enacted in 1677, required all deeds to be written, and every American state has adopted this rule. Even though American deeds often use the terminology of the old English deed forms, the technical terms used in England no longer have much significance in this country, and the courts will give effect to the parties' intent if the basic elements of a deed are present. For example, it is no longer necessary either to pay or to recite the payment of consideration, as was required under some of the earlier deed forms. See *Chase Fed. Sav. & Loan Ass'n v. Schreiber*, 479 So.2d 90 (Fla.1985).

3. Elements of a Deed

Deeds must contain much the same information as contracts of sale: identification of the parties, description of the land, some words indicating a present intent to convey, and the grantor's signature. The courts are quite liberal with regard to the placement of these elements in the writing. A few states still require that the grantor's signature be under seal, and a few require attestation by one or more witnesses. Nearly all require an acknowledgment by a notary public or other officer for recording purposes, even though it is not essential to make the deed valid between the parties themselves. See generally Stoebuck & Whitman, Property § 11.1 (3d ed.2000).

a. Grantee's Name in Blank

A deed with no grantee's name is obviously void. However, many courts uphold such deeds once the person to whom the deed is delivered has inserted his or her name; they imply that the grantee has authority to do so from the grantor. Some cases even uphold the authority to fill in the grantee's name after the grantor has died. See *Womack v. Stegner*, 293 S.W.2d 124 (Tex.Civ.App.1956).

b. Omission of Essential Information

A deed that omits essential information may be made valid if a person with authority from the grantor fills in the information. However, the authority must be granted in writing. *McCormick v. Brevig*, 980 P.2d 603 (Mont.1999).

c. Non-existent Grantee

If the grantee does not exist, the deed is void. Examples include a deceased grantee, the heirs of a living person, or a corporation which has not yet been formed or has been dissolved. *Moffat v. United States*, 112 U.S. 24, 31–32 (1884). However, courts frequently reform deeds of this type in order to carry out the grantor's intent. See *Haney's Chapel United Methodist Church v. United Methodist Church*, 716 So. 2d 1156 (Ala. 1998).

4. Construction of Deeds

When language in a deed is ambiguous, confusing, or conflicting, the courts resolve it by attempting to determine the parties' intent. Some common construction problems are discussed below.

a. Extrinsic Evidence

Should courts consider evidence which does not appear on the face of the document, but which is available from other sources, such as the parties' statements, the nature of the land, and the circumstances surrounding the transaction? Many old cases state that extrinsic evidence can be considered only if the ambiguity is "latent," or discernible only from outside facts, rather than "patent," or evident from the face of the deed itself. *Most modern courts have abandoned this rather peculiar distinction and will now take extrinsic evidence whether the ambiguity is latent or patent. Markstein v. Countryside I, L.L.C.*, 77 P.3d 389 (Wyo.2003).

b. Easement or Possessory Interest

Language which describes and conveys a highway or railroad is often unclear as to whether only an easement or a possessory interest is intended. For example, "a right-of-way for highway purposes" is usually construed as granting an easement, while "a strip of land for a highway right-of-way" is more likely to be considered as conveying possessory title. However, there is a good deal of inconsistency in the cases in this area. A good discussion of the arguments is found in *Brown v. State*, 924 P.2d 908 (Wash.1996).

c. Reservations and Exceptions

A *reservation* is language which creates in the grantor a new interest in the land which did not exist independently before the deed was delivered. For example, the grantor might convey a fee simple but reserve an estate for his or her own lifetime. An *exception,* on the other hand, is the retention by the grantor of some interest which did exist previously, such as a certain physical part of the land. The terms are often used incorrectly, but modern courts nearly always overlook the improper usage and give effect to the parties' intent. *Many older cases hold that it is impermissible to make a reservation or an exception to a third person rather than to a grantor, although a number of more recent cases have permitted this.* See *Michael J. Uhes, Ph.D., P.C. v. Blake,* 892 P.2d 439 (Colo.App.1995).

Example: Rogers deeded his farm to Edwards and inserted in the deed the following words: "Reserving the north 50 feet to Thomas." Thereafter, Thomas sued Edwards to quiet his title to the north 50 feet of the farm. (*Result:* Most modern courts would give effect to the reservation and hold for Thomas, even though the language is technically erroneous, since it should have been an exception rather than a reservation, and even though Thomas is a third party rather than the grantor.) *Simpson v. Kistler Invest. Co.,* 713 P.2d 751 (Wyo.1986).

5. Defects in Deeds

A deed may be defective either because it contains an inadvertent error which is contrary to the parties' intention, or because some essential formality in its execution, delivery, or the capacity of the parties is missing.

a. Reformation

If the deed does not accurately reflect the intention of one of the parties, equity will reform it if the other party was also under a mistake or was guilty of fraud, other inequitable conduct, or even silence in the face of knowledge of the error. See *Andres v. Claassen,* 714 P.2d 963 (Kan.1986). However, reformation may be precluded if the land has passed to a BFP who has relied on the deed. See *Jones v. Carrier,* 473 A.2d 867 (Me.1984).

b. The Void–Voidable Distinction

If the deed is defective in its formalities, the defect may make the deed either void or voidable. The result of the distinction is simple: *If the grantee has reconveyed the land to a BFP, a void deed will be set aside even as against the BFP, while a merely voidable deed will not. Either type of defect will be enough to set aside the deed in the hands of the grantee himself. The courts classify some types of defects as making deeds void, and others as making them merely voidable.*

c. Defects Rendering Deeds Void

Defects which are nearly always held to make the deed void include forgery, lack of delivery, and fraud in the execution or "factum." (This is fraud of such a nature that the grantor does not realize that the document he or she is signing is a deed.) See *Nixon v. Nixon*, 132 S.E.2d 590 (N.C.1963). In addition, a deed by a minor can be avoided even against a BFP if the minor disaffirms it within a reasonable time after reaching majority.

d. Defects Rendering Deeds Voidable

Defects which make a deed only voidable, and thus which cannot be asserted against a BFP, include fraud in the inducement, insanity, lack of capacity, duress, undue influence, mistake, and breach of fiduciary duty. See *Blaise v. Ratliff*, 672 S.W.2d 683 (Mo.App.1984).

Example: Easley, who was a jewelry dealer, decided to defraud Ryan of his land. Easley promised Ryan, in return for a deed of the land, that he would deliver to Ryan a certain valuable diamond that Ryan had admired. In fact, Easley had no title to the diamond, but only held it on consignment from its true owner. Ryan gave Easley the deed to the land, and Easley immediately transferred the land to Barnes, who was a BFP. When Ryan realized that he would not get the diamond, he sued Barnes for cancellation of the deed and return of the land. (*Result:* The court will hold for Barnes, the BFP. Ryan was induced by fraud to sign the deed, but there was no fraud in the execution; he knew that the document was, in fact, a deed of his land. The deed is therefore only voidable, and the BFP will prevail.)

6. Land Description

A land description defines boundaries on the earth's surface which represent the horizontal limits of the parcel. In the vertical direction, ownership is presumed to extend from the earth's center to the "sky," unless it is specifically limited to a certain height. There are a number of methods of describing land boundaries. See Stoebuck & Whitman, Property § 11.2 (3d ed.2000).

a. Metes and Bounds

A metes and bounds description is one which individually describes every line which is part of the parcel's boundaries. The lines may be described by references to natural or artificial monuments, such as "the large pine tree" or "the southeastern concrete bridge abutment." They may be identified by the boundaries of adjoining land, such as "then 150 feet along the southern boundary of the land of Rufus Smith." Most commonly today, metes and bounds descriptions are made up by successive calls of courses and distances. A course is a statement of direction. Thus, a particular boundary line might be described as "north 20 degrees east 178.45 feet." (The direction in this call is 20 degrees east of due north.) In all metes and bounds descriptions, a point of beginning, from which the first of the boundary lines commences and to which the final call will run, must be identified.

b. The Government Survey System

This system was devised by Thomas Jefferson and adopted by Congress in 1785. Most U.S. land outside the original 13 colonies has been surveyed under this system. The system is based on Principal Meridians which run north-south and Base Lines which run east-west. Additional meridians and base lines spaced out along these axes divide the land into squares about six miles on a side. These squares are called townships. Each township is divided into 36 "sections" which are about one mile square. Each section contains about 640 acres. This system is an extremely convenient way of describing agricultural land, particularly in non-mountainous areas. A typical description might read "the Southwest quarter of Section 12, Township 2 North, Range 6 East, 6th Principal Meridian."

c. The Plat

A plat is a map which meets certain standards of format and accuracy, is legally approved by some local government agency, and is filed as a permanent record in the local recording office. A plat may show only a single lot or a large number of lots. If there are multiple lots, they are usually lettered or numbered. The legal descriptions of all the lot boundaries are also shown on the plat. Thus, to describe a lot, it is only necessary to refer to the number, such as "lot 6, block A, Northfield Subdivision as shown in plat book 23, page 91, official records of Adams County." Nearly all modern housing subdivisions are described by plat.

d. Monuments

Land descriptions commonly use references to monuments which have a certain width. Examples include streets, railroad tracks, and rivers or streams. In many cases, these monuments are also easements, with the grantor of the deed owning the "underlying" estate. *In such cases, a deed which refers to the monument as a boundary will usually be held to convey to its center line or "thread" rather than merely to its edge. Carney v. Heinson, 985 P.2d 1137 (Idaho 1999).*

e. Accretion and Reliction

If a river or stream is the boundary of land, the stream may shift its location gradually over time. *If this occurs gradually by accretion (a build-up of soil on the bank) or reliction (a recession of water from the bank), the additional dry land becomes the property of the abutting owner. Application of Banning, 832 P.2d 724 (Haw.1992). Similarly, gradual erosion causes the abutting owner to lose title to the affected area. On the other hand, if the change in the stream's location is radical and rapid, the process is known as avulsion, and the boundaries of the abutting owners are not affected. Bonelli Cattle Co. v. Arizona, 414 U.S. 313 (1973); Matson v. State, 531 P.2d 836 (Wash.App.1975).*

f. Priorities in Interpretation

It often happens that land descriptions contain errors or inconsistencies. While the courts look to the parties' intent in resolving them, they have also developed a list of priorities, so that a description term which is higher on the list will normally take precedence over a conflicting one which is lower. See Comment, 7 U. Puget Sound L.Rev. 355 (1983). *The usual priorities are as follows:*

1) Natural monuments

2) Artificial monuments and marked and surveyed lines

3) Adjacent tracts or boundaries

4) Courses or directions

5) Distances

6) Area or quantity

Example: A call of a boundary line in a deed reads "then south 30 degrees east 145 feet to the old white oak tree." In fact, the tree is south 40 degrees east and the distance is 150 feet. (*Result:* The boundary line will be held to run to the tree, a natural monument, even though that is contradictory to the course and distance as stated in the deed.) *Providence Properties, Inc. v. United Virginia Bank,* 251 S.E.2d 474 (Va.1979).

B. Delivery, Acceptance, and Escrow of Deeds

A deed is effective only when it is delivered. Once delivery has occurred, however, what happens to the deed has no legal significance. It can be destroyed or thrown away with impunity, particularly if it has been recorded so that a copy can be produced for evidentiary purposes in the event of a dispute. A deed operates to transfer title only from its original grantor to its grantee. If the grantee wishes to retransfer the land to another party, or even back to the original grantor, a new deed must be used; the grantee cannot simply hand over the deed that he or she received. See generally Stoebuck & Whitman, Property § 11.3 (3d ed.2000).

1. Delivery and Intent

Delivery does not necessarily require the manual handing over of the deed to the grantee. *The critical question is whether the grantor does some act with intent to make the deed* presently *operative.* James v. Mabie, 819 So.2d 795 (Fla.App.2002). Any act which sufficiently indicates this intent will constitute a delivery, and a few cases have found deliveries from oral statements by the grantor with no overt action at all. *Gonzales v. Gonzales,* 73 Cal.Rptr. 83 (Cal.App.1968).

Example: Farmer, who was old and feeble, wrote out a deed of his farm to Nephew and placed it in his bedroom closet. He then called Nephew to his bedside and said, "I've deeded the farm to you, and the deed is there in my closet. Go ahead and take it with you." Nephew immediately took the deed and recorded it. Upon Farmer's death, his heirs sued Nephew to quiet their title to the farm, claiming that the deed was never delivered. (*Result:* Most courts would find a valid delivery, since Farmer's intent was clearly to make a present transfer.)

If the grantor has the deed recorded, nearly all courts will apply a strong (some would say, conclusive) presumption that delivery has occurred. *Mattox v. Mattox,* 777 So.2d 1041 (Fla.App.2001).

2. Deeds as Will Substitutes

A will speaks at the testator's death. In most states, wills require much stricter adherence to formalities, such as the number of witnesses and the manner of attestation, than do deeds. Often a grantor will attempt to use a deed as the equivalent of a will, attempting to reserve the right to revoke it until death. *Courts frequently hold such a deed invalid because it is undelivered, since the grantor lacks intent to make a present transfer.*

Example: Assume the same facts as the previous example, except that Farmer said to Nephew, "I've deeded the farm to you. The deed is in my closet, and when I am gone, you should take it and record it." (*Result:* Most courts would probably find no effective delivery, since the grantor's intent seems to have been that the deed would take effect only when the grantor died. See *Wiggill v. Cheney,* 597 P.2d 1351 (Utah 1979)). However, some courts would probably find that an immediate transfer occurred, subject to a retained life estate in the grantor. If the deed had been placed where Nephew had more direct access to it, such as a safety deposit box jointly held by Farmer and Nephew, the courts would be somewhat more likely to uphold the delivery.) See *Lenhart v. Desmond,* 705 P.2d 338 (Wyo.1985).

3. Conditional Deliveries

The traditional view, and still the majority, is that a grantor may not impose an oral *condition on the delivery of a deed. Most cases hold that the deed is valid and disregard the condition.* A growing minority enforce the condition and allow title to pass only if it has been fulfilled.

Example: Farmer handed Niece a deed of his farm and said, "I am about to have exploratory surgery. If the doctors find that I have cancer, the farm is yours." (*Result:* The majority view gives Niece title whether Farmer has cancer or not, while the minority view gives her title only if Farmer does have cancer. *Chillemi v. Chillemi,* 78 A.2d 750 (Md.1951)).

4. Deeds Conveying Future Interests

The rule against conditional delivery should not be confused with cases in which the deed conveys a future interest. A future interest can readily be made conditional upon the happening of a future event, and if such conditions are spelled out in writing in the deed itself, they are valid and enforceable.

Example: Farmer handed a deed to Niece. The deed stated "Farmer hereby conveys farm to Niece, with Niece to have possession only if Farmer is diagnosed as having cancer within the next 30 days." (*Result:* The deed is a valid conveyance of a springing executory future interest.) *Tennant v. John Tennant Memorial Home,* 140 P. 242 (Cal.1914).

5. Acceptance

Delivery is not complete unless the grantor accepts the deed. *However, acceptance is presumed if the conveyance would be beneficial to the grantee, even if the grantee does not know about the deed or its delivery. If the grantee does not want to receive the land, he or she can refuse to accept it, and no title will pass.*

6. Escrows

An escrow is an instrument, such as a deed, which is deposited with a custodian with instructions that it should be delivered to the grantee on the occurrence of some future condition. See Stoebuck & Whitman, Property § 11.4 (3d ed.2000). Speaking more loosely, the escrow is the entire arrangement under which such a deed is deposited and then delivered. In many areas of the nation, escrows are routinely used to carry out sales transactions. An escrow may also be created with the grantor's own death as the condition of its fulfillment, thus allowing the deed to serve as a will substitute.

a. Relation Back

When the conditions of an escrow are fulfilled and the deed is delivered to the grantee by the escrow agent, the delivery "relates back" to the time the deed was handed to the custodian. Under this theory, which is widely accepted, the deed can be delivered to the grantee even if the grantor has died or become incapacitated after placing the deed in escrow. This is a very useful result, but it follows only if there is an enforceable contract of sale between the grantor and grantee. Moreover, the grantor must not have reserved any power to recall the deed from the custodian. *Malcolm v. Tate*, 267 P. 527 (Or.1928).

Example: Venton contracted to sell his land to Parsons. He placed a deed to Parsons in the hands of the Acme Escrow Company, with the condition that it be delivered when Parsons tendered the remaining purchase price. However, neither the contract nor the escrow instruction were in writing. Venton died before the deed was delivered, and his heirs sued to quiet their title to the land. (*Result:* unless there are acts of part performance by Parsons, the contract of sale is unenforceable under the Statute of Frauds. Without an enforceable contract, no "relation back" of the escrow will occur. Hence Venton's death makes the delivery ineffective, and Venton's heirs will prevail. See *Jozefowicz v. Leickem*, 182 N.W. 729 (Wis.1921). The escrow instructions themselves are not required by the Statute of Frauds to be in writing, but if they had been written, they might have supplied the necessary memorandum to satisfy the statute of frauds.)

b. Unauthorized Delivery by Escrow Agent

If the grantee persuades the escrow agent to deliver the deed to him even though some conditions are unsatisfied, the delivery is ineffective and no title passes to the grantee. Even if the grantee has resold the land to a BFP, the majority of cases hold that the grantor will still prevail. See *Watts v. Archer*, 107 N.W.2d 549 (Iowa 1961). This result has been severely criticized on the ground that the BFP has no means of protecting himself or herself, while the grantor is at least partly at fault since he or she could have selected a more reliable escrow agent. There is case law indicating that the grantor may be estopped to contest the delivery if he or she fails to assert title within a reasonable time after learning of the BFP's claim.

c. Death Escrows

Where the escrow is made conditional upon the grantor's death, special rules apply. The delivery out of escrow will be valid despite the grantor's intervening death even though there is no underlying contract. Moreover, the courts often say that the delivery of the deed to the escrow agent passes immediate title to a future interest to the grantee. Under this view, the grantor retains only a life estate. This concept makes it unnecessary to say that the ultimate delivery of the deed to the grantee "relates back", since the delivery by the grantor to the escrow agent is the only legally important delivery.

> *Example:*   Farmer made a deed of his land to Nephew and deposited it with his friend, Earl, with instructions that it be delivered to Nephew upon Farmer's death. He reserved no power to get the deed back from Earl. Later, Farmer changed his mind and demanded a return of the deed, which Earl gave to him. Upon Farmer's death, his heirs claimed the land as against Nephew. (*Result:* Nephew would probably prevail. It does not matter that the conveyance was gratuitous, with no underlying contract. Most courts would treat the delivery of the deed to Earl as passing title to Nephew by way of a future interest, subject only to Farmer's retained life estate. Farmer would have no power to call back the transaction.) *Vasquez v. Vasquez*, 973 S.W.2d 330 (Tex.App.1998).

An escrow with a more elaborate condition, such as "upon my death if the grantee survives me" or "upon my death if the grantee cares for me for the rest of my life" is usually not considered a death escrow, and will not relate back unless there is an enforceable underlying contract. *Raim v. Stancel*, 339 N.W.2d 621 (Iowa App.1983).

d. Duties of Escrow Agents

An escrow agent is the agent of both parties until the closing of the escrow. Thereafter, the escrow holder is the grantor's agent with respect to the purchase money and the grantee's agent with respect to the deed. *The escrow holder has a duty of reasonable care and skill, and is a fiduciary in the narrow sense that he or she must carry out the escrow instructions with complete fidelity and accuracy.* An escrow agent that breaches these duties is liable in damages. *Butko v. Stewart Title Co.*, 991 P.2d 697 (Wash.App. 2000). Consequential damages may be included, and punitive damages are recoverable if the default was reckless or willful. *Miller v. Craig*, 558 P.2d 984 (Ariz.App.1976). See 17 Pac.L.J. 309 (1985).

Some courts have also held that an escrow agent has a duty to disclose to one party the fraud of another party of which the escrow agent gains actual knowledge. *Mark Properties, Inc. v. National Title Co.*, 14 P.3d 507 (Nev.2000). However, the agent has no duty to investigate or discover fraud or misdealing by one party against another. *Triple A Management Co., Inc. v. Frisone*, 81 Cal.Rptr.2d 669 (Cal.App. 1999).

Escrow agents generally do not have a duty to protect the parties from other risks or losses outside the scope of the escrow instructions. See, e.g., *Schultz v. Rhode Island Hospital Trust Nat'l Bank*, 94 F.3d 721 (1st Cir.1996) (escrow holder had no duty to verify that purchasers' down payments, deposited in escrow, were cash rather than promissory notes).

7. Estoppel by Deed

Suppose a grantor executes and delivers a deed at a time when the grantor has no title, or has a lesser title than the deed purports to convey. Assume that the grantor later obtains from a valid source all or part of the title described in the deed. *The cases uniformly hold that the grantor is then estopped to deny that the title thus obtained belongs to the grantee.* Moreover, most modern cases treat the title as passing to the grantee automatically, so that no action in court is necessary to obtain it. *McNeal v. Bonnel*, 412 S.W.2d 167 (Mo.1967).

a. Type of Deed

The estoppel doctrine operates only if the deed given by the grantor contains some representation about the quality of the title being conveyed. Warranty deeds virtually always meet this test, while most quit-claims do not unless they contain explicit representations as to the quality of the title conveyed. *Zayka v. Giambro*, 594 N.E.2d 894 (Mass.App.1992).

b. Preclusion of Other Remedies

If the grantee does not want the title and would prefer to pursue an action for damages for breach of a covenant of title in the deed, the modern cases uniformly permit the grantee to exercise this choice.

c. Rights of BFPs

Suppose that after receiving the title, the grantor makes a second deed to a bona fide purchaser. Who will prevail as between the two grantees? If the first deed is recorded (as it usually is) it is possible that the second grantee will find it in the course of a title search; if this occurs he or she will not be a BFP. However, in a jurisdiction which indexes its public records by the name of the party, the first deed is quite difficult for the second grantee to find, since a search must be made in the grantor index for years earlier than the year in which the grantor obtained title. This is a sufficiently burdensome duty that the majority of courts considering the question have regarded the first deed as unrecorded, so that the subsequent grantee may treat it as void under the recording acts. *Schuman v. Roger Baker & Assoc.*, 319 S.E.2d 308 (N.C.App.1984). This reasoning would not apply in a tract-index jurisdiction.

C. Practical Location of Boundaries

If the owners of adjacent parcels of land are uncertain about the exact location of their common boundary, they may enter into an informal relationship which fixes it on the ground. The courts tend to uphold these determinations, and have developed four distinct doctrines, discussed below, for doing so. In effect, they permit a transfer of a portion of the land from one owner to another. See Stoebuck & Whitman, Property § 11.8 (3d ed.2000). However, the courts do not technically consider a transfer to have taken place. Instead, they regard the boundaries as having simply been redefined by the parties' actions. Thus, no writing is necessary to satisfy the Statute of Frauds. Note that these doctrines are different from adverse possession, and none of them require the sort of hostility or lack of permissiveness which is necessary for adverse possession.

1. Boundary by Agreement

The parties may fix their boundary by an explicit (though oral) agreement if they are uncertain or unaware of the correct location, or if a dispute as to the true location exists between them. After reaching agreement, the parties must take and relinquish possession to the agreed line. Some cases insist that this possession must continue for a "long time," and a few courts require the parties to mark the new boundary on the ground. See *Miller v. Stovall*, 717 P.2d 798 (Wyo.1986).

2. Boundary by Acquiescence

Even without an explicit agreement, adjacent owners may make a line their boundary by long recognition and acceptance of it. Generally speaking, silence by one party in the face of the other's action (such as erecting a fence) is sufficient acquiescence. The time of acquiescence must be lengthy, and the majority of decisions adopt the period of the adverse possession statute. Under this theory, it is essential that the line be marked on the ground (as by a fence or other barrier). *Seddon v. Edmondson*, 411 So.2d 995 (Fla.App.1982).

3. Boundary by Estoppel

If one owner erroneously represents to the other that the boundary between them is located in a certain place, and if the second owner reasonably relies upon those representations and takes costly detrimental action, the party who represented the line's location is estopped to deny its accuracy, and the boundary is shifted accordingly. The majority of cases find an estoppel only if the person who makes the representation knows that the statements are inaccurate, but a substantial minority will estop him or her irrespective of state of mind. *Burkey v. Baker*, 492 P.2d 563 (Wash.App.1971).

4. Boundary by a Common Grantor

If a grantor marks a line on the ground and sells parcels on both sides by reference to it, the purchasers must regard the line as binding, even though it is, in fact, erroneously located with respect to the deed description. This doctrine operates only if the parcels of land are described by lot numbers, rather than by metes and bounds descriptions. *Phillippe v. Horns*, 196 N.W.2d 382 (Neb.1972).

5. Binding on Successors

A boundary fixed by any of the methods described above is binding on the successor owners of the affected parcels. *Jedlicka v. Clemmer*, 677 A2d 1232 (Pa. Super. 1996). Hence, if the owner whose parcel has been reduced in size by the boundary change sells the land by means of a warranty deed that describes the land using the original boundaries, the owner will be in breach of the deed warranty. *Egli v. Troy*, 602 N.W2d 329 (Iowa 1999).

D. Dedication

A dedication is a mode of conveyance of land from a private owner to the public generally or to a specific public body, such as a city or state government. It requires an offer to dedicate by the owner, which may be by words or by acts indicating an intent to transfer the property to the public. It also requires an acceptance by the public, which may be accomplished either by public use or by an official resolution of the governing body. See Stoebuck & Whitman, Property § 11.6 (3d ed.2000).

1. Acts of Dedication

An offer to dedicate may be found from a variety of actions, such as an oral statement by the owner or the filing of a map or plat on which certain areas are marked and dedicated to the public. An owner who permits the public to use the land for a long period of time will often be found to have made an offer of implied dedication. It is difficult to distinguish this sort of dedication from the creation of a prescriptive easement in favor of the public. *Gion v. City of Santa Cruz*, 84 Cal.Rptr. 162, 465 P.2d 50 (Cal.1970). Cf. *Application of Banning*, 832 P.2d 724 (Haw. 1992), finding the implied dedication doctrine to be inconsistent with state statutes encouraging owners to allow public recreational use of their land. Some courts find an implied dedication only where there is specific evidence of the owner's intent to dedicate.

2. Type of Interest Dedicated

The dedicating party can specify whether the interest he is transferring is, for example, an easement or a possessory estate. In the absence of an explicit statement, the courts will determine the parties' probable intent. For example, road and street dedications are usually deemed easements, while park and school sites are more likely to be considered possessory estates. The dedicator can also impose a use restriction, either by way of covenants running with the land or by the granting of a defeasible estate. *Wheeler v. Monroe*, 523 P.2d 540 (N.M.1974).

3. Acceptance

A variety of acts can constitute an acceptance of an offered dedication. *Stafford v. Klosterman*, 998 P.2d 1118 (Idaho 2000). Acceptance can be found from the local government's taking over of maintenance or construction of improvements on the land, from approval of a plat which shows areas marked for public use, or from long and substantial public use of the land. The most common form of acceptance is a resolution of the local governing body. *Christiansen v. Gerrish Township*, 608 N.W.2d 83 (Mich. App. 2000). If there is no acceptance before the dedication is revoked, the dedication is ineffective; *General Auto Service Station v. Maniatis*, 765 N.E.2d 1176 (Ill.App.2002).

E. Covenants of Title

In general, deeds are not presumed to contain covenants concerning the quality of the title they convey; the covenants, if any, must be expressed. A "quitclaim" deed is one which contains no covenants of title, while a "warranty" deed is one which explicitly contains one or more such covenants. In a number of states, statutes imply certain covenants of title from the use of specific words in a deed, such as "grants" or "conveys and warrants." See Stoebuck & Whitman, Property § 11.13 (3d ed.2000). In some areas it is customary to use "special warranty deeds" that contain some, but not all, of the six covenants discussed below, or that warrant the title only against the acts of the grantor and not acts of previous owners. See *State Bank v. Brekke*, 602 N.W.2d 681 (N.D.1999); *Egli v. Troy*, 602 N.W.2d 329 (Iowa 1999).

1. Distinctions Between Contract Covenants and Deed Covenants

A covenant of title in a deed is similar to the implied covenant of marketability of title found in contracts of sale. However, there are several differences. First, the deed covenants take effect only when the deed is delivered, and at that point the contract's title covenants are "merged into the deed," and can no longer provide a basis for suit. Second, the deed covenants can be violated only by an actual defect of title, not a mere risk or doubt about the title's quality. See *Lewis v. Jetz Service Co.*, 9 P.3d 1268 (Kan.App.2000). Third, the only remedy for violation of a deed covenant is damages, while contract covenants may also give rise to rescission or to specific performance with partial abatement of the price.

2. Present Covenants

Three of the traditional title covenants are termed "present" because they are violated, if at all, only at the moment the deed containing them is delivered. No eviction of the grantee is necessary to establish a breach of these covenants. The statute of limitations begins to run on such violations at the moment of delivery of the deed, whether the grantee realizes the title is defective or not. *These covenants are generally held not to "run with the land" so as to benefit a remote grantee.* The present covenants are as follows:

a. Covenant of Seisin

This covenant is a promise, in substance, that the grantor owns the estate in the land which he or she is purporting to convey.

b. Right to Convey

In most cases this covenant is identical to the covenant of seisin. However, one might lack seisin but still have a right to convey under a power of appointment or as an attorney in fact.

c. Covenant Against Encumbrances

An encumbrance is a mortgage, lien, easement, lease, or other outstanding interest which impairs the grantor's title to the property. Sometimes courts find that an encumbrance does not violate this covenant if it is openly visible or was known to the grantee. See *McKnight v. Cagle*, 331 S.E.2d 707 (N.C.App.1985).

On the other hand, some cases recognize existing violations of zoning, housing, or other local codes as breaches of the covenant against encumbrances, particularly if enforcement proceedings by the local government have begun. *Brunke v. Pharo*, 89 N.W.2d 221 (Wis.1958); *Bianchi v. Lorenz*, 701 A.2d 1037 (Vt.1997). This isn't strictly logical; such code violations don't literally affect title at all.

3. Future Covenants

These covenants are considered violated only when the grantee is "evicted" or disturbed in his possession by the person claiming the outstanding interest. The statute of limitations begins to run only at that time. Moreover, these covenants are usually held to "run with the land" and benefit a later grantee who is evicted. See Bridges v. Heimburger, 360 So.2d 929 (Miss.1978). The future covenants are as follows:

a. Warranty and Quiet Enjoyment

Technically these are two separate covenants, but they are essentially identical in content. They promise that the title will be as described in the deed, and will not be subject to any encumbrances. *Northeast Petroleum Corp. of New Hampshire v. Vermont*, 466 A.2d 1164 (Vt.1983). They also promise that the grantor will defend the grantee if he or she is evicted.

b. Further Assurances

This is a promise by the grantor to execute any document that might be needed in the future to perfect the title which the original deed purported to transfer. It is the only one of the title covenants which is sometimes enforced by specific performance rather than damages.

4. What is an Eviction?

The future covenants are breached only by an eviction. See *Brown v. Lober*, 389 N.E.2d 1188 (Ill.1979). An eviction may be a physical interference with the grantee's possession, or it may be only a reasonable response to a serious threat from the third party claimant. For example, if the grantee surrenders possession voluntarily to the holder of paramount title, or buys that title from its holder, an eviction has occurred. *Garcia v. Herrera*, 959 P.2d 533 (N.M.App.1998). Note, however, that there is no eviction unless the person claiming paramount title actually has it; if the claim is later determined in court to be meritless, the grantee has not been evicted even if he or she moved off the land or paid off the third party. *Jarrett v. Scofield*, 92 A.2d 370 (Md.1952).

5. Damages

The party who makes a title covenant cannot be held liable in damages for more than the amount received when he or she sold the land. This is true even though the land may later rise sharply in value, so that the damage recovery available to the grantee may be entirely inadequate to compensate for the actual loss. A few New England states have adopted a minority rule allowing recovery of the land's value as of the date of eviction. If the breach affects only a physical fraction of the land, the grantee's recovery is limited to damages equal to that pro-rata proportion of the sale price received by the grantor. *Hillsboro Cove, Inc. v. Archibald*, 322 So.2d 585 (Fla.App.1975).

6. Additional Elements of Damage

The grantee is generally allowed to recover interest on the award of damages he receives. Some cases compute the interest for the full period since the land was acquired, while others allow interest only for any period of time the grantee was actually deprived of possession as a result of the title defect. If the grantee has expended money in attorneys' fees and court costs in litigating the title with a third party, these expenses can also be recovered in an action on the covenant of title. Some cases allow this recovery only if the grantee notified the grantor of the litigation and requested the grantor to represent the grantee in it. Ironically, no recovery of costs and attorneys' fees is allowed if the third party who claimed a paramount interest was found, in fact, not to have one. *Outcalt v. Wardlaw*, 750 N.E.2d 859 (Ind.App.2001).

F. The Recording System

All American states operate recording systems which assist the public in determining who has title to any given parcel of land. See Stoebuck & Whitman, Property §§ 11.9–11.11 (3d ed.2000). These systems do not involve the government in making any affirmative representations about the title. Instead, they act much as libraries of documents which have been executed and entered into the system by their parties. Anyone is welcome to examine the records and to draw his or her own conclusions about the title. See *Woodward v. Bowers*, 630 F.Supp. 1205 (M.D.Pa.1986). About ten states also operate a parallel system, usually termed the "Torrens" or title registration system, which *does* make affirmative statements about the title. This system is not widely used except in a few localities, and is discussed in a subsequent section.

1. Limitations of the Recording System

The recording system sometimes yields erroneous results to title searchers. There are several reasons for such errors. First, there is no assurance that recorded documents are, in fact, valid and enforceable. For example, they may be forged or undelivered. Recording them does not cure such defects. Second, there are a number of events and claims which are outside the coverage of the recording system, and which thus may affect the title to land even though nothing is recorded concerning them. Examples include acquisition of adverse possession titles and prescriptive easements. Third, a complete search may require the tracing of title instruments back as much as two hundred years, a difficult task. Searchers commonly limit their searches to a shorter period, and assume the risk that there may be an earlier title defect. Fourth, there is the possibility that the searcher may make a clerical error or a mistake of judgment, and thus reach an incorrect conclusion.

2. Basic Operation

No one is required to record any document, and unrecorded conveyances are valid as between the parties. However, the system provides a strong incentive to record by threatening a grantee with loss of priority as against later grantees from the same grantor if the first conveyance is unrecorded. *In other words, recording acts protect subsequent purchasers from prior unrecorded interests.* To illustrate, assume Owner deeds land to A. Subsequently, Owner makes a second deed of the same land to B. If A fails to record, and if B is otherwise qualified under the local recording act as described below, B will own the land and A will have nothing (except a possible claim against Owner on the basis of unjust enrichment or on a covenant of title in A's deed.) In reaching this result, the recording acts reverse the common law, under which A would own the land under the principle of "first in time is first in right"—in other words, that A got it first, and Owner had nothing left to transfer to B.

What must B do in order to have the benefit of the recording act? First, B must show that A failed to record. If A immediately recorded A's conveyance, B can never prevail over A under the recording acts. But A's failure to record is not enough, by itself, for B to win. B must also meet the standard set by the act in question. What is that standard? The statutes take three distinct approaches:

a. "Notice" Type Statutes

About half the states have so-called "notice" statutes, which typically require B, in order to prevail against A, to take without notice of A's claim and to pay value . . . in other words, to be a bona fide purchaser–a "BFP."

b. "Race" Type Statutes

Three states (Delaware, North Carolina, and Louisiana) require that B, in order to prevail against A, must record B's deed before A records. They are termed "race" statutes because one can visualize a fictitious race between A and B to the recording office.

c. "Notice–Race" Type Statutes

Nearly half the states have this sort of statute, which combines the features of both of those described above. In order to prevail against A, B must take without notice, pay value, *and* record before A records.

Example: Owens owned land in fee simple. He gave a mortgage on his land to Abel, but Abel did not record it. Subsequently, Owens gave another mortgage on the same land to Baker, who also failed to record. Baker had no knowledge of Abel's mortgage, and Baker made a contemporaneous loan to Owens, thereby giving value for the mortgage. Later Abel recorded his mortgage, and finally Baker recorded his. When Owens defaulted on both mortgages, Abel and Baker sought a judicial declaration as to which mortgage had priority. *Result:* in a "notice" type jurisdiction, Baker's mortgage will have priority. His claim is tested as of the time he took the mortgage, and at that point he gave value and lacked notice of Abel's rights. The fact that Abel later recorded is irrelevant under a notice statute. However, in a race or notice-race statute, Abel's mortgage will have priority. This is because under such a statute, Baker can prevail only if he records first. In this example, Abel recorded before Baker, so Baker cannot have the benefit of the recording act in those types of states. See *Prochaska v. Midwest Title Guar. Co.,* 932 P.2d 172 (Wash.App.1997), in which the prior conveyance was held to have priority under a race-notice statute even though it was recorded only *nine minutes* before the subsequent conveyance.

Note carefully that the foregoing example is interesting only because A failed to record. If A had immediately recorded his own mortgage when he obtained it, no recording act would ever operate to deprive him of priority. Note also that A's knowledge or notice of B's claim is irrelevant. For example, A may know about B's mortgage at the time A records, but that does not matter. It is also irrelevant whether A pays value or not. The only party whose BFP status is of interest is B, the *subsequent* taker.

3. Interests and Conveyances Outside the Recording Acts

If a particular interest or conveyance is not covered by the recording acts, it cannot be divested by failure to record it. This means that a searcher may examine the records carefully and yet find no indication that certain types of adverse claims exist. State law varies, but interests which are commonly considered outside the acts include short-term leases (less than 1–3 years' duration), unfiled mechanics' liens (which, if eventually filed within the allowable time, relate back to the date the work was commenced), and the dower or curtesy claims of undisclosed spouses.

In addition, records of some types of conveyances are usually maintained in offices other than the usual recording office, and need not be recorded there. These include wills and intestacy transfers, takings by eminent domain, transfers to trustees in bankruptcy, and local property tax and assessment liens. Finally, as noted above, some interests are created by processes which do not involve a document, and hence which cannot be recorded. These include adverse possession, easements by prescription, implication, and necessity, some types of dedications, and adjustments of boundaries by practical location.

4. Payment of Value

All recording acts (except those in the three pure "race" states) protect subsequent transferees only if they pay value. Most of the cases require the payment of an amount which is substantial in relation to the property's value, but is not necessarily equal to the full market value. Obviously, donees who receive gifts of land do not qualify. The payment must be actual, and not merely a promise to pay in the future. However, if the grantee gives a negotiable promissory note and it is, in fact, negotiated to a holder in due course, value is considered to have been paid.

a. Judgment Creditors

In most states, a judgment is a lien on the defendant's land in the county in which the judgment is obtained. *The majority of cases hold that the judgment creditor has not paid value, and thus will not be protected as against a prior unrecorded conveyance by the judgment debtor (the defendant).* A minority of jurisdictions protect judgment creditors by statute. See *Osin v. Johnson*, 243 F.2d 653 (D.C.Cir.1957).

b. Security for Preexisting Debt

The value given must be contemporaneous with the receipt of the interest in the land. Antecedent value does not count under the recording acts. Suppose a creditor takes a mortgage or other interest in land to secure what was previously an unsecured debt. The great majority of cases hold the lender in this situation to have given no value unless it also makes some further concession, such as granting an extension of time to pay the debt or promising to forbear bringing suit, at the time the mortgage is received. *Gabel v. Drewrys Ltd., U.S.A., Inc.*, 68 So.2d 372 (Fla.1953).

c. **Conveyance in Satisfaction of Preexisting Debt**

A transfer of land in full payment of a preexisting debt is regarded as being given for value. Suppose a creditor has made an unsecured loan, and the debtor subsequently transfers land to the creditor in satisfaction of that debt. The cases are divided, but the better view, adopted by most recent cases, is that value has been paid, since the creditor's claim against the debtor has been released or discharged.

Example: Bank loaned Abel $10,000, taking Abel's unsecured promissory note. Abel owned valuable land which he then deeded to Cary; Cary failed to record the deed. When Abel's note fell due, the Bank demanded payment. Abel instead offered the Bank a mortgage on his land, which the Bank assumed he still owned, as security for the debt. The Bank took the mortgage and Abel then disappeared. The Bank sued to foreclose the mortgage, but Cary argued that he owned the land free of the mortgage, since his deed was delivered prior to its execution. (*Result:* In most jurisdictions, Cary would prevail despite the fact that he failed to record. The recording acts would not protect the Bank because it gave no contemporaneous value when it took the mortgage from Abel. However, if Abel had given the Bank a deed in satisfaction of the debt rather than a mortgage securing it, most modern cases would hold that the Bank would prevail, and it would have title to the land free of Cary's mortgage.) *Fox v. Templeton*, 329 S.E.2d 6 (Va.1985).

5. **Taking Without Notice**

To be a bona fide purchaser, one must take without notice of the prior unrecorded conveyance. There are three main potential sources of notice: actual knowledge, constructive notice of facts which would be learned from a visit to the property, and constructive notice of information found in the public records. If a purchaser gains notice from any of these sources of facts which suggest a title defect, he or she is placed on "inquiry notice" of any additional facts which a reasonable investigation of the original information would produce. This is true whether any actual investigation is made or not.

a. Actual Notice

A purchaser may gain knowledge of title defects from statements of the seller or third parties such as neighbors, from an actual visit to the property or an actual examination of the public records, or from prior business dealings with the land or its former owners. *Caruso v. Parkos*, 637 N.W.2d 351 (Neb.2002).

b. Rights of Parties in Possession

Every purchaser is held to notice of facts which would have been discovered by inspecting the property and making an inquiry of anyone in possession. *Gordon v. Madison*, 9 S.W.3d 476 (Tex.App.2000). However, no inquiry is necessary if the seller personally is in possession, or if possession is otherwise consistent with the record title. About half the cases also excuse any inquiry of a possessor who is a former owner, at least if it has been a relatively short time since he or she transferred the land. *First Savings & Loan Assoc. v. Avila*, 538 S.W.2d 846 (Tex.Civ.App.1976).

1) If there are several parties in possession and one of them is the record owner, most cases impose no duty on the purchaser to make inquiry of the other possessors. *Kane v. Huntley Financial*, 194 Cal.Rptr. 880 (Cal.App.1983).

2) If the party in possession is a tenant, the purchaser will be held to notice of any rights of extension, renewal, options to purchase, or other similar rights of the tenant even if they were negotiated after the original lease was signed and do not appear in it. Thus, an inquiry of the tenant is necessary to learn whether such rights exist. *Vitale v. Pinto*, 500 N.Y.S.2d 283 (App.Div.1986).

c. Notice From the Public Records

The records themselves give constructive notice of facts which are mentioned in instruments in the chain of title to the land. Thus, a purchaser has notice of documents which are not themselves recorded, but which are described or referred to in recorded instruments. This can be very burdensome if the reference is vague or indefinite, and a few states impose no duty of inquiry in such cases. In a few other states, statutes limit the duty of inquiry to cases in which the prior conveyance referred to is itself recorded.

Example: Carey purchased land from Baker. Before completing the purchase, Carey searched the title and read the deed by which Baker had bought the land from Abel. That deed contained the following statement: "Subject to a utility easement for lines and poles in favor of Municipal Utility Company." However, the instrument which created the easement itself was unrecorded. The utility company subsequently attempted to erect power lines and poles, and Carey brought an action to enjoin them. (*Result:* Carey is subject to the utility easement. Even though the easement was unrecorded, Carey could have learned its details by a relatively simple inquiry directed to the utility company. Hence, he will be held to constructive notice of the details of the easement.) *Himes v. Schiro,* 711 P.2d 1281 (Colo.App.1985).

Some courts hold that, if a document is recorded but was defectively acknowledged (notarized), it will give no constructive notice. *In re Crim,* 81 S.W.3d 764 (Tenn.2002).

d. Other Sources of Constructive Notice

It is widely held that various types of official records beyond those in the recorder's office give constructive notice. These include property tax and special assessment records maintained by cities, counties, and special districts, as well as various types of liens and claims of local government agencies. Court records are also commonly held to give constructive notice. This is particularly true of pleadings reflecting any judicial action which may affect land titles. On the other hand, documents and maps in various administrative offices of local or state government usually are not held to give constructive notice; see *First American Title Ins. Co. v. J.B. Ranch, Inc.,* 966 P.2d 834 (Utah 1998) (map in county clerk's office imparted no notice).

Under the doctrine of *lis pendens,* a purchaser who buys land whose title is in litigation will be bound by the court's decree as fully as the original parties. Thus purchasers are held to notice of information about the litigation that could be found in the relevant court docket. In many states, statutes provide that notices of *lis pendens* can be recorded in the real estate records, but these recording provisions do not necessarily override the common law *lis pendens* doctrine, so it is usually still necessary to check the court docket as well. *Chrysler Corp. v. Fedders Corp.,* 670 F.2d 1316 (3d Cir.1982).

e. Quitclaim Deed

A good deal of older authority holds that one who takes by quitclaim deed cannot be a bona fide purchaser. The clear majority of modern cases reject this rule. *Palamarg Realty Co. v. Rehac*, 404 A.2d 21 (N.J.1979).

f. Unrecorded Documents in the Chain of Title

A purchaser is generally held to notice of the contents of documents in his or her own chain of title even if they are not recorded. A few cases go farther, holding (quite illogically) that one cannot be a bona fide purchaser if any of the essential links in his chain of title are unrecorded. They may take this position even though the defect in title is entirely unrelated to the unrecorded link in the chain. See *Messersmith v. Smith*, 60 N.W.2d 276 (N.D.1953).

g. The Shelter Principle

Once a bona fide purchaser has perfected title through the operation of the recording acts, he or she can pass that perfected status along to future grantees even if they do not qualify as BFP's.

Example: Abel gave a mortgage on his land to Zimmer, but Zimmer failed to record. Later, Abel conveyed by deed to Baker, who was a BFP for value, having no knowledge of Zimmer's mortgage. Baker immediately recorded. Subsequently, Baker contracted to sell the land to Carson, but before Carson bought it, Zimmer visited Carson and informed Carson of the mortgage. Carson proceeded with the purchase and then brought a judicial action to have the mortgage declared unenforceable. (*Result:* Carson will prevail, and the land is no longer subject to the mortgage. While Carson himself was not a BFP (since he had notice), he is entitled to the same protection as his grantor, Baker, under the "shelter" principle described above.) *Corey v. United Savings Bank*, 628 P.2d 739 (Or.App.1981).

h. Purchases in Installments

If a purchaser is paying for the land in installments, he or she may get notice of a prior unrecorded conveyance after making some payments but before making the remainder. (If the prior conveyance is recorded after payments by the purchaser have begun to be made, that recording will *not* result in constructive notice to the purchaser; only actual notice will do. See *Henson v. Wagner*, 642 S.W.2d 357 (Mo.App.1982)). The cases attempt to protect the purchase "pro tanto", giving protection to the extent of the payments already made while in good faith. Several methods have been developed to do this.

1)   Most cases award the land to the prior grantee, but give the installment purchaser a lien on the land to aid in recovery of his or her payments with interest.

2)   A few cases give the installment purchaser a fractional interest as a tenant in common with the prior grantee, with the fraction based on the proportion of the purchase price already paid.

3)   A few cases permit the installment purchaser to complete the purchase by paying the remaining installments to the prior grantee.

> *Example:*   Jones deeded his land to Smith, but Smith failed to record and did not take possession. Later, Jones entered into an installment contract to sell the same land to Clark for payments of $1,000 per year for 20 years. Clark took possession and made payments for 10 years. At that point, Smith visited Clark and informed him of Smith's ownership of the land. Clark refused to vacate the land, and Smith sued for possession. (*Result:* The most common judicial resolution of the problem would award the land to Smith, but give a lien on the land to Clark to permit him to recover the payments that he had made on the first 10 years of the contract, with interest.) *Westpark, Inc. v. Seaton Land Co.,* 171 A.2d 736 (Md.1961).

6.   Indexes to the Record

The typical recording office may contain thousands of volumes which hold millions of individual recorded documents. Thus, some sort of index is essential to permit searchers to locate and read the documents that affect the land in which they are interested. Two types of indexes are used:

a.   Name Indexes

In all states, indexes are maintained by the names of the parties to the document. Two sets of index books are maintained, one of them alphabetically by the last names of grantors and the other alphabetically by last names of grantees.

b.   Tract Indexes

In about half a dozen states, and on a county option basis in a few other states, tract indexes are also maintained. A page or set of pages in the index book is devoted to listing all documents which affect a particular tract of land, such as a quarter-quarter section or a block in a subdivision.

c.   Content of the Index

The index books do not contain full copies of the documents. Rather, they give the names of the parties, the date of the instrument and the date of its recording, and the book and page number in the "deed books" where the full document itself can be found. In some states, the index entry will also include a "brief legal description" of the land affected by the document. Increasingly, counties are maintaining their indexes on computer data bases rather than in hard-copy books.

7.   Search Methods

In a tract index system, the search is relatively simple. The searcher simply runs his or her eye down the appropriate column on the relevant page in the index books, makes note of all documents which affect the land being searched, and then reads those documents. In a name index system, the search is much more complex. It consists of three steps:

a.   The Grantee Index

The searcher begins with the putative present owner and finds his or her name in the grantee index. The index entry gives the name of the grantor who conveyed the land to the present owner, and *that* person's name is then sought in the grantee index. This process is continued from name to name in the grantee index until a chain of title is constructed back to the sovereign, or as far back as the searcher believes it is prudent to go.

b.   The Grantor Index

Next, each of the persons identified in the chain of title in the previous step must now be checked in the grantor index to determine if they made any conveyances which are adverse to the chain of title.

c.   Review of Full Copies of Documents

Finally, the searcher looks up the actual copy of each document thus identified and checks it for execution, completeness, etc.

d.   Other Sources

Whether a name or tract index system is used, the searcher must also check various sources outside the recorder's office such as the bankruptcy court, local trial court dockets, tax and assessment lien records, and perhaps various local government offices.

8. Improper Indexing

If a document is brought to the recorder's office and is copied into the deed books, but is improperly indexed or not indexed at all, it is very unlikely that a searcher will be able to find it. Perhaps the recorder is liable for negligence in such a case, but who should stand the loss as between the party who recorded the instrument and a later bona fide purchaser? The cases are split, with the traditional majority view treating the document as recorded despite the mis-indexing, and thus penalizing the subsequent BFP. See *Haner v. Bruce*, 499 A.2d 792 (Vt.1985). This rule has been strongly criticized, and most of the recent cases reject it; see, e.g., *Waicker v. Banegura*, 745 A.2d 419 (Md.App.2000); *Coco v. Ranalletta*, 733 N.Y.S.2d 849 (Sup.Ct. 2001). See also *First Citizens Nat'l Bank v. Sherwood*, 817 A.2d 501 (Pa.Super.2003) (misindexed document gives constructive notice if a reasonable search would have located it).

9. Chain of Title Problems

Certain types of adverse conveyances are difficult or impossible to find in a name index recording system, even though they are in fact copied into the deed books and are accurately indexed. There are four general types of such problems, the first three of which arise only in name (grantor-grantee) index systems and not in tract index systems:

a. The Wild Deed

Assume that a searcher has identified a chain of title from the sovereign to A, then to B, then to C. However, the searcher does not know that B also made an adverse deed to X, which X failed to record. X then deeded to Y, and Y recorded. In a name index system, it is impossible for the searcher to discover the X–Y deed, since the searcher does not know the name of either X or Y, and cannot look either of them up in the index books. The cases uniformly treat the X–Y deed as if it were unrecorded. See *Palmer v. Forrest, Mackey and Assoc.*, 304 S.E.2d 704 (Ga.1983); 4 American Law of Property § 17.17 (1952).

b. The Late–Recorded Deed

Assume the same chain of title as above. B makes an adverse conveyance, unknown to the searcher, to X. X fails to record. B then conveys to C in the known chain of title, but C does not pay value and is therefore not a BFP. Sometime later, X finally records the old deed from B. For a searcher to find this deed, the searcher must examine the grantor index under B's name not only during the period when B owned the land, but for a period from that time forward to the present date. This is a great deal of additional effort, and a large minority of the cases treat the B–X deed as unrecorded, thus making the extra search effort unnecessary. *Morse v. Curtis*, 2 N.E. 929 (Mass.1885).

c. The Early–Recorded Deed

Assume the same title chain as above. Before B acquires title to the land from A, B gives a warranty deed of the same land to X. X records it immediately. Later, B obtains the title from A. The doctrine of estoppel by deed would ordinarily pass title to X instantaneously. But if this is so, it means that a title searcher must look under B's name in the grantor index not only during the time when B owned the land, but for a lengthy prior period as well, to see if B made an adverse conveyance *before acquiring title* which would operate under estoppel by deed. A slight majority of the cases consider the B–X deed to be unrecorded, thus making the extra search effort unnecessary. *Sabo v. Horvath*, 559 P.2d 1038 (Alaska 1976).

d. The Deed Which Conveys One Parcel and Encumbers Another

Assume A owns parcels 1 and 2. A sells parcel 1 to X, and in the deed imposes an encumbrance, such as a lease, a mortgage, or a restrictive covenant, on parcel 2. Later, A sells parcel 2 to B. Is B bound by the encumbrance? Unless the "brief description" column in the index for the A–X deed mentions that it affects parcel 2 as well as parcel 1, the searcher can be sure of discovering the deed's impact on parcel 2 only by reading every deed A has made of any land in the county. The cases are divided on this point, with some holding that the A–X deed should be deemed unrecorded insofar as it affects parcel 2. See *Krueger v. Oberto*, 724 N.E.2d 21 (Ill.App.1999) (A–X deed deemed unrecorded). This last chain of title problem, unlike the three previous problems, can arise in a tract index system as well as a name index system. *Guillette v. Daly Dry Wall, Inc.*, 325 N.E.2d 572 (Mass.1975).

G. Marketable Title Acts

Under the recording system, even very old instruments may represent title defects. For example, a deed in the chain of title 100 years ago may have conveyed a fee simple defeasible rather than a fee simple absolute. Thus, it is risky for a searcher not to examine title all the way back to a sovereign's conveyance. However, such a search can be extremely laborious. Marketable title acts attempt to limit the necessary period of search. About 18 states have such acts.

1. The Root of Title

A root of title is usually defined by the acts as a deed in the chain of title recorded earlier than some fixed number of years before the search being made. Forty years is the most common period. If a search were being made in 2005, for example, a deed recorded in 1970 would not be the root of title, but a deed in 1950 would be. In principle, no search of the records prior to 1950 would be necessary.

2. Effect of the Acts

The acts provide in substance that no interest created prior to the root of title will affect the title. Exceptions are generally made if the old interest is referred to in a post-root instrument, if the instrument creating it is re-recorded during the post-root period, or if the person claiming the interest has been in possession for the full post-root period.

3. Interests Not Cut Off

A number of types of interests are exempt from the extinguishing effect of the usual marketable title act. These exemptions vary from state to state, but often include claims of the United States Government, rights of state and local governments, visible easements, utility and railroad easements, and mineral rights. See *H & F Land, Inc. v. Panama City–Bay County Airport Dist.*, 736 So.2d 1167 (Fla.1999) (act extinguished an easement of necessity that arose before the root of title, was not visible, and had not been asserted in any recorded document after the root of title). Because of the exceptions, the searcher who does not go back beyond the root of title is taking a significant risk. The exceptions tend to militate against the effectiveness of the acts.

4. Acts Cutting Off Certain Future Interests

Several states have adopted specialized statutes that cut off old future interests, such as possibilities of reverter and rights of entry, that are created in association with defeasible fee estates. These statutes are more limited in scope than marketable title acts. They typically extinguish future interests arising earlier than some fixed period (e.g., 30 years ago) unless the holder of the interest re-records it within a fixed time (e.g., 5 years) after adoption of the statute. See *Severns v. Union Pacific Railroad Co.*, 125 Cal.Rptr.2d 100 (Cal.App.2002).

H. Torrens Title Registration

In ten states there is an alternative to the conventional recording system. It is termed the "Torrens" or title registration system, and involves the issuance of a certificate of title by the local government, similar to the certificates used for motor vehicles. *The certificate is theoretically conclusive and represents the government's affirmative statement as to who holds the title to the land.* The certificate not only shows the names of the parties holding the fee title, but also shows "memorials" which identify all liens or encumbrances against the title. Claims to the land not shown on the certificate are extinguished. See *Petition of McGinnis,* 536 N.W.2d 33 (Minn.App.1995) (adverse possessor's claim could not be asserted against registered land).

1. Initial Registration

Entrance into the system is voluntary, and it is not widely used except in a few locations, such as Minneapolis–St. Paul, Minnesota and some areas of Hawaii and Massachusetts. To register one's land, an owner must go through a judicial proceeding similar to a quiet title action. The cost can be substantial—as much as several thousand dollars. See *Rael v. Zachery,* 876 P.2d 1210 (Colo.1994), holding that an initial registration proceeding could not constitutionally be binding on a party claiming an interest in the land who was not served with process but could have been identified by reasonable diligence.

2. Transfers Under the System

A transfer of land, or the creation of a lien or encumbrance against it, is not binding until registered on the certificate. When the fee title is transferred, a new certificate is issued. In some jurisdictions duplicate certificates are issued to mortgagees who hold first liens on the property.

3. Indemnity Fund

To compensate persons whose interests are cut off by an error of the registrar, a fund is created through the collection of payments from all persons registering or transferring their titles. For example, if a person's mortgage were inadvertently eliminated from the certificate by the registrar's negligence, the fund would pay off that mortgage.

4. Problems With the System

The title registration system was introduced in the United States around the turn of the Twentieth Century, and at its peak was in use in about 20 states. It has always been vigorously opposed by the title insurance companies and many title lawyers, since if it were highly successful it might threaten their livelihood. Its growth has been slow as a result of the non-mandatory nature of registration and the high initial cost. See note, 11 Wm. Mitch.L.Rev. 825 (1985). Indemnity funds have often been considered inadequate. California's was wiped out in 1937 by a single claim, and the California statute was subsequently repealed. In recent years several states, including Illinois and New York, have prospectively repealed their registration systems, thus permitting the registration of no new land titles.

I. Title Insurance

A title insurance policy is the insurance company's promise to indemnify the insured party if the title to land is not in the condition stated on the face of the policy, and if the insured suffers a loss as a result. Two types of policies are issued, insuring owners and mortgagees respectively. Nearly all mortgage lenders in the United States require mortgagee's policies. Owner's policies are somewhat less common, although they are nearly universally issued when realty is sold in many Western and Southwestern states. The policy is typically issued at the time a sale of land is consummated and, in effect, represents a substitute for an attorney's title opinion based on a search of the records. The title company itself may make an examination in its own private "title plant" or may base its policy on a search done by an attorney or one of its employees in the public records.

1. Exceptions and Exclusions

The title insurance company obviously does not wish to insure against defects in title of which it is aware. Thus, the policy will contain a schedule of exceptions which lists the encumbrances or other title matters that have been discovered in its search, and which are therefore not insured against. In addition, the policies typically contain a number of standard exclusions for such matters as zoning and other police power regulations, rights of eminent domain, matters which a survey would disclose, rights of parties in posses-sion, and unfiled mechanics' liens. Despite these exclusions, the coverage of title insurance policies is generally broader than can be obtained by a lawyer's search of the records. For example, the title policy will protect against forgeries, undelivered instruments, rights of undisclosed spouses, and the like, which even a very careful attorney's search may not disclose. Moreover, if a title defect results in a loss to the insured, the title insurer is liable without the necessity of proving negligence.

2. Effective Date

A title policy insures the title as of a specific date. The title company undertakes no liability for events occurring after that date that may impair the title. The company's liability is also limited to the face amount of the policy, even though the land may later rise in value so that the policy's coverage is inadequate. The coverage of an owner's policy's does not generally run with the land so as to benefit future grantees from the insured owner. However, the protection will run to an heir or devisee of the insured owner or the successor corporation of an insured corporate owner. A lender's policy runs to the benefit of any subsequent assignee of the mortgage.

3. Protection of Insured as a Warrantor

The insured owner might resell the land and give a warranty deed. If the seller is later sued on the warranty, the title policy will usually protect him or her, and will provide indemnification for any judgment which the seller is required to pay, provided that the title defect in question existed at the time the title policy was issued.

4. Tort Liability

Several recent cases have held title insurers liable for negligently searching title on tort rather than contract theories. See *Bank of California v. First American Title Ins. Co.*, 826 P.2d 1126 (Alaska 1992); *Tess v. Lawyers Title Ins. Corp.*, 557 N.W.2d 696 (Neb.1997). However, there are also recent cases rejecting any right of the insured to recover in tort. See *Barstad v. Stewart Title Guar. Co.*, 39 P.3d 984 (Wash.2002); *Focus Inv. Associates, Inc. v. American Title Ins. Co.*, 992 F.2d 1231 (1st Cir.1993). From the viewpoint of the insured, a tort theory may have several advantages.

a. The insured may bring the action even though he or she did not file a claim within the time limits fixed by the policy (commonly 60 to 90 days after discovering the title defect).

b. The insured may claim consequential or punitive damages.

c. The insured may get damages for mental distress. See *Jarchow v. Transamerica Title Insurance Co.*, 122 Cal.Rptr. 470 (Cal.App.1975). The Jarchow case was based on negligence in issuing a preliminary title report, and was effectively overruled by the legislature, which in 1982 enacted Cal.Ins.Code § 12340.11, which provides that a preliminary report is not an abstract of title, and that the duties of abstractors do not apply to title insurers issuing such reports.

d. Liability may flow from the issuance of a preliminary title report by the insurer, even though an actual policy of title insurance was never issued.

J. The Real Estate Settlement Procedures Act (RESPA)

Congress enacted the Real Estate Settlement Procedures Act (RESPA), 12 U.S.C. § 2601 et. seq., in 1974 to curb abuses that were thought to exist in residential real estate closings. Many of these abuses related to the marketing of ancillary "settlement services" such as title insurance, real estate brokerage, credit reports, and the like. RESPA applies to all "settlements" of "federally-related" mortgage loans—essentially all transactions in which any federal agency or federally-insured or regulated financial institution is involved.

1. **Disclosure and Informational Requirements**

One of RESPA's goals is to inform home buyers of the choices that they can make in purchasing settlement services, and to encourage them to shop for the most favorable prices. The statute requires that the following information be provided, and prohibits the charging of a fee for it.

a.   A uniform settlement statement (called the "HUD–1" form) must be used for all loans and home sales covered by RESPA. There is no private right of action for failure to complete the form accurately, although doing so may give rise to a cause of action under state law. *Washington Mut. Sav. Bank v. Superior Court*, 89 Cal.Rptr.2d 560 (Cal.App.1999).

b.   Lenders must send a special informational booklet prepared by HUD (currently entitled "A Home Buyer's Guide to Settlement Costs") to each loan applicant within 3 days of receipt of the loan application.

c.   Lenders must give loan applicants, with the booklet, a "good faith estimate" of their probable settlement costs.

d.   Lenders must inform borrowers, at the time of loan application, about the probability that "servicing" of their loans (i.e., the collection of payments and handling of questions and complaints) will be transferred by the lender to some other entity. If an actual transfer of servicing of a loan occurs, the borrower must be notified in writing by both the original and new servicer.

e.   Sellers of real estate may not require that buyers purchase title insurance from any particular title company.

2. **Escrow Accounts for Taxes, Insurance, and Other Items**

Mortgage lenders often require borrowers to create escrow accounts, and to pay into them monthly a portion of the property's annual taxes, insurance premiums, and sometimes other recurring charges, such as ground rents or condominium association assessments. Under RESPA, the monthly payment into the escrow account is limited to 1/12 of the estimated annual charges for these items. In addition, when a loan is initially made and an escrow account is created, a lender may not require more than one-sixth of the annual charges to be paid in by the borrower as a "cushion" over and above the amount estimated to be needed to pay the actual charges when due.

3. Kickbacks and Unearned Fees

No one may give or receive a fee or thing of value in return for a referral of settlement service business. No one who receives a fee for providing a settlement service may split it with another person except for services actually performed by the recipient. However, the following types of payments are permitted.

a. Payments may be made to lawyers, title companies, lenders, and other providers for services actually rendered.

b. Salaries or fees may be paid to employees and other persons for services rendered or goods or facilities provided.

c. Real estate agents are permitted to split commissions.

d. "Controlled business" refers to arrangements in which someone who has the ability to refer settlement service business makes referrals to an entity in which the referrer has at least a 1% ownership interest. A typical example is a real estate agent or a lender that owns an interest in a title company and refers business to that company. Controlled business arrangements are permitted so long as all of the following limitations are met:

    1. The relationship is disclosed to the customer when the referral is made.

    2. The person making the referral provides the customer with an estimate of the range of charges usually made by the provider to whom the referral is made.

    3. The customer is not required to use that particular provider.

    4. The referrer receives nothing of value for the referral except a return on its ownership interest.

e. Settlement service providers are permitted to "mark up" the cost of various services they purchase from other parties. See, e.g., *Boulware v. Crossland Mortg. Corp.*, 291 F.3d 261 (4th Cir.2002) (lender did not violate

RESPA by charging borrower $65 for a credit report that cost the lender only $15 to obtain); *Krzalic v. Republic Title Co.*, 314 F.3d 875 (7th Cir. 2002) (title company did not violate RESPA by charging borrower $50 to record mortgage when county recorder's fee was only $36). HUD issued a policy statement in 2001 disagreeing with this interpretation.

4. Yield Spread Premiums

Mortgage brokers often assist borrowers in obtaining loans. The borrower may pay an interest rate higher than the lender's "par" or market rate, and the lender may then pay the present value of the difference (termed a "yield spread premium") to the broker. In a number of suits, borrowers have argued that such payments are illegal referral fees under RESPA. However, HUD issued policy statements in 1999 and 2001 approving the practice if the compensation of the broker was for services performed and was reasonably related to the value of the services provided. Several federal courts have deferred to HUD's interpretation and found that payment of a yield spread premium is permissible. *Bjustrom v. Trust One Mortgage Corp.*, 322 F.3d 1201 (9th Cir.2003); *Heimmermann v. First Union Mortg. Corp.*, 305 F.3d 1257 (11th Cir.2002); *Glover v. Standard Fed. Bank*, 283 F.3d 953 (8thCir.2002).

REVIEW QUESTIONS

1. T or F Granny was elderly and had poor vision. Nephew approached her and told her that he had a letter for her to sign. However, he instead gave her a deed, which she signed, transferring her land to Nephew. Nephew then recorded the deed and sold the land to a bona fide purchaser. Granny can recover the land.

2. A deed contained the following language as part of a metes and bounds description: "Thence to Thompson Road, which is the boundary of Fred Thompson's farm." In fact, Thompson's farm extended toward the subject property 100 feet beyond Thompson Road. How far will the call in the instant deed be considered to extend?

3. T or F Mother made a deed of her land to Daughter as grantee and handed it to Daughter, saying "Your father and I are considering a divorce. If we get one, the land is yours; otherwise, I will keep it." Mother did not get a divorce, but Daughter recorded the deed and took possession of the land. Mother can recover title from Daughter.

4. T or F George sold his land to Evelyn by deed containing all covenants of title. Ten years later Evelyn discovered that the land was subject to

an easement for power lines. However, no power lines were ever erected and the electric company made no objection to Evelyn's use of the portion of the land over which the easement ran. The statute of limitations for deed covenants is five years. Evelyn can recover against George on some of the covenants of title.

5.   O owns land in fee simple absolute. He deeds it to A, who is a bona fide purchaser for value but who fails to record. O then places a mortgage on the land to the B Bank, which makes a contemporaneous loan to O and immediately records the mortgage. The Bank has no notice of A's rights. Under which type(s) of recording acts does the Bank have a valid mortgage on the land?

6.   Vendor and Purchaser entered into an enforceable contract of sale for land. Vendor signed a deed of the land and placed it with Escrowee, with instructions to deliver the deed to Purchaser when Purchaser deposited the remaining purchase price. However, Purchaser bribed Escrowee to give him the deed without payment of the price. Purchaser then recorded the deed and sold the land to B, a bona fide purchaser. What are Vendor's remedies?

III

Introduction to the Law of Real Estate Finance

■ ANALYSIS

A.   Impact of English History

Today's substantive law of mortgages, as well as much of the procedure related to it, have been influenced to a substantial degree by English legal history. While the modern mortgage has its antecedents in both the Roman law and the English common law, it was English Chancery that made the most enduring contribution to contemporary mortgage law. See generally Nelson & Whitman, Real Estate Finance Law § 1.2. (4th ed.2001).

1.   The Common Law Mortgage

The English common law mortgage of the 14th and 15th century was a conveyance of a fee simple subject to a condition subsequent. For example, suppose Lender loaned $5,000 to Borrower to be repaid in one year, the loan to be secured by a "mortgage" on Blackacre. Borrower (as grantor) would convey Blackacre to Lender (as grantee) and his heirs, but on the condition that if on the due date Borrower repaid the $5,000, he would have the right to reenter and terminate Lender's estate. Note several important attributes of this transaction. First, the lender obtained legal title to Blackacre. Second, with that title went the right to collect rents and profits. These fruits of possession were important because at this stage of English legal development, the collection of any interest was considered to be usurious and thus unlawful. Note that this mortgage transaction was decidedly pro-mortgagee. If, for any reason, the borrower-mortgagor did not pay the debt in full on law day, he forfeited all interest in Blackacre.

2.   The Intervention of Equity Courts: The Equity of Redemption

Gradually this common law mortgage yielded to the moderating influences of English Chancery. Mortgagors who had failed to satisfy the mortgage debt on law day would seek redress from Chancery. At first, Chancery intervened to allow the mortgagor to "pay late" or "redeem tardily" if the latter was able to establish a good reason for his default such as fraud, accident, misrepresentation or duress. By the 17th century, however, the mortgagor routinely was able, as a matter of right, to redeem the land by payment of the mortgage debt, so long as he or she tendered the principal and interest (by now the collection of interest was legally permissible) within a reasonable time after the law day. It was no longer necessary to establish specific grounds for equitable relief. This right to "pay late" became known then and is referred to today as the mortgagor's *equity of redemption* or, sometimes, the *equity of tardy redemption*. The mortgagee did retain the right to keep possession of the mortgaged land until the debt was paid, but was required to "account" for any rents collected by crediting them to the mortgage debt.

3. The Equitable Remedy of Foreclosure

As the above material illustrates, the English law of mortgages had by now become decidedly pro-mortgagor. Even though the mortgagor had defaulted, the mortgagee faced the prospect that mortgagor could sue to redeem in equity. Because the mortgagee and potential purchasers of the mortgaged land could not forecast with assurance what a "reasonable" time for redemption might be, title to that land was clouded and often unmarketable. Consequently, Chancery developed the *mortgagee's right to foreclosure*. After a default by mortgagor at law day, the equity court at the mortgagee's request would fix a reasonable period of redemption for the mortgagor. If the latter did not pay within that period, the mortgagor's redemption right was forever barred and title to the mortgaged land vested absolutely in both law and equity in the mortgagee. This type of foreclosure was called *strict foreclosure*, because no sale of the land was involved.

B. The American Development

Mortgage law as developed by English Chancery was adopted in this country relatively intact. American courts readily recognized the mortgagor's equity of redemption and most of its implications. Stated another way, the mortgagor not only had the right to redeem tardily, but also the right to *insist upon being foreclosed.* Any attempt by the mortgagee to have the mortgagor waive that right, either in the mortgage or in agreement contemporaneous therewith, was deemed to be an invalid *clog on the mortgagor's equity of redemption.* This rule "as a corollary to the original creation of the equity of redemption, was developed to prevent evasion [of that redemption right] by ingenious and determined mortgagees who utilized a wide variety of clauses which, while recognizing the existence of the equity of redemption, in practical effect nullified or restricted its operation." Nelson & Whitman, Real Estate Finance Law § 3.1 (4th ed.2001). For example, if mortgage language or a separate agreement limited the mortgagor's right to pay to one month after the due date of the mortgage debt, it was unenforceable. This anti-clogging doctrine is alive and well in this country today; we will cover it in greater detail in the next chapter.

In many respects, however, mortgage law in this country developed its own uniquely American attributes. Some of these are described briefly here.

1. Foreclosure by Sale

Strict foreclosure is used relatively rarely in this country. Rather, foreclosure is generally by public sale. Under this method, the property is sold to the highest bidder and the proceeds of the sale are used to pay off the mortgage debt. If the land sells for more than the mortgage debt, the surplus will be paid to the mortgagor or others who derive their rights through the mortgagor. If the sale brings less than the mortgage debt, the mortgagee can obtain a judgment for the deficiency against the mortgagor. The most common type of foreclosure by sale is *judicial foreclosure,* a court-supervised proceeding in which all persons interested in the land are made parties. It is time-consuming and costly but is nevertheless the only foreclosure option in the majority of states. The other method of foreclosure is by *"power of sale"*, a non-judicial process by which, after varying degrees and types of notice to interested parties, the property is sold at a public sale either by a trustee designated in the documents, a public official, some other third party or, in some instances, by the mortgagee itself.

2. Statutory Redemption

Many states not only recognize the judicially created equity of redemption, but have enacted "statutory redemption" legislation. While lawyers and courts often confuse these two types of redemption, it is important to realize that they are distinctly different concepts. This legislation permits the mortgagor to redeem *after* the foreclosure sale for various periods of time, as short as a few months in some jurisdictions and as long as eighteen months in others. Note that while the equity of redemption allows the mortgagor to redeem until a valid foreclosure sale, statutory redemption is usually available only after that valid foreclosure has occurred.

3. The Title, Lien and Intermediate Theories of Mortgage Law

American courts recognize one of three theories of mortgage law. *The title theory* is the direct descendant of the English common law mortgage we considered earlier in this Part. Under this theory, the mortgagee has the legal title, and thus the right to possession of the mortgaged real estate, until the mortgage debt is satisfied. In the United States this right to take possession is rarely, if ever, exercised until default by the mortgagor. Under the *lien theory,* followed by a majority of states, the mortgagor retains both the legal and equitable title, and thus the right to possession, to the mortgaged land until a valid foreclosure has taken place. The mortgagee owns a security interest only. Finally, the *intermediate theory,* in effect in a few states, gives the right to possession to the mortgagor until default, and to the mortgagee thereafter.

For the vast majority of mortgage transactions the above mortgage theories will have little practical significance. After all, even title mortgagees rarely exercise their possessory rights, and it is doubtful that modern courts would allow them to do so in the absence of a default by the mortgagor. On the other hand, many lien state mortgagees are able to avoid the disadvantages of that theory by intelligent mortgage drafting. Indeed, the importance of these theories may traditionally have been overemphasized, especially by academics. Nevertheless, such theories can be significant in commercial mortgage transactions where the cash flow from rents is deemed a significant part of the mortgagee's security. Mortgagees have a special interest in ensuring that mortgagors in default do not divert the rents to purposes other than mortgage payments. Moreover, in jurisdictions where foreclosure is a slow and cumbersome process, the mortgagee's ability to obtain possession or its equivalent quickly can be crucial in preventing waste or deterioration to the mortgage security. The significance of these theories will be examined in greater detail in Chapter V.

4. The Deed of Trust as a Mortgage Variant

In many jurisdictions the deed of trust is the most commonly used mortgage instrument. Usually a trustor (analogous to the mortgagor) conveys Blackacre to a trustee (often the lender's attorney, employer, or officer) to be held as security for the payment of a debt by the trustor to the beneficiary (analogous to the mortgagee). Upon default, and at the request of the beneficiary, the trustee conducts a public foreclosure sale. It is important to remember that while the labels for the parties may seem unfamiliar, the deed of trust is essentially a mortgage with a power of sale. Traditional mortgagor protections such as the equity of redemption and the prohibition against clogging that redemption right are applicable to deeds of trust as well as mortgages. Moreover, in many states, statutes regulating deeds of trust apply to mortgages with power of sale as well.

Thus, deeds of trust are utilized primarily to facilitate ease of foreclosure rather than to avoid more basic substantive mortgage law. You should assume, unless the context clearly suggests otherwise, that the mortgage law principles examined in this volume apply to deeds of trust as well as mortgages. Unlike the deed of trust, certain other land financing devices are viewed as *mortgage substitutes* rather than *mortgage variants*. They are utilized precisely to avoid the impact of the mortgagor's equity of redemption, the anti-clogging doctrine, statutory redemption, and other pro-mortgagor substantive mortgage law concepts. Such instruments include the "absolute deed as a mortgage" and the installment land contract. These instruments will be examined in detail in Chapter IV.

C. Some Basic Mortgage Law Principles

1. The Long Term Installment Mortgage and the Acceleration Clause

Most mortgages today are amortized or repaid in equal installments over a substantial number of years. Normally the last installment payment completely pays off the principal balance. Prior to the 1930s, however, mortgages were of the "balloon" type. Usually these involved short terms of 3 to 5 years during which borrowers usually made interest payments only or some minimal reduction payments on principal. The entire principal balance came due or "ballooned" at the end of the period. While a few home loans made by financial institutions today have a "balloon" feature, it is more frequently found in commercial real estate loans and in second mortgage loans made by sellers of real estate to their purchasers.

The key to any installment mortgage, whether it is evenly amortized over a long period of time or is of the balloon variety, is the acceleration clause. This clause enables the mortgagee, in the event of mortgagor default, to declare the entire principal balance due and payable.

2. Some Basic Mortgage Priority Principles

Most laypersons sense intuitively that a "second" mortgage is not as desirable from the lender's perspective as a "first" or "senior" mortgage. They also know that junior mortgages carry a higher interest rate than first mortgages and that this is because of the higher degree of risk associated with such mortgages. *Underlying these pervasive popular perceptions is a fundamental mortgage priority rule: The purchaser at a foreclosure sale of a senior mortgage will acquire a title that is free and clear of all mortgages or other liens or interests junior or subordinate to the mortgage being foreclosed. Stated another way, if the proper procedure is used, the foreclosure of a senior lien wipes out all liens and other interests that are junior to it.*

Example: E–1 holds a $80,000 first mortgage on Blackacre. E–2 holds a $25,000 second mortgage. The E–1 mortgage is in default, the debt has been accelerated, and foreclosure is imminent. The fair market value of Blackacre free and clear of liens is $85,000. What is the maximum amount purchaser at the foreclosure sale should be willing to pay and what type of title will she obtain? (*Result:* Because a first mortgage is being foreclosed, the E–2 lien will be wiped out and thus the purchaser should be willing to pay a maximum of $85,000, because she will acquire a title to Blackacre that is free and clear of liens.)

A corollary of this priority principle is that the purchaser at the foreclosure sale of a junior lien takes title subject to any liens or other interests senior to the mortgage being foreclosed. Thus, a purchaser at the foreclosure sale of such a mortgage should be willing to pay at most an amount that equals the fair market value of the land being foreclosed free and clear of liens, less the amount of any senior liens remaining on the land.

> **Example:** Same facts as the preceding example, except that it is the E–2 mortgage that is about to be foreclosed. What is the maximum amount a purchaser at the foreclosure sale would be willing to pay and what type of title will she obtain? (*Result:* Because a second mortgage is being foreclosed, purchaser will acquire a title subject to the E–1 mortgage. Consequently, she should be willing to pay at most $5,000, the fair market value of Blackacre free and clear of liens ($85,000) less the amount of senior liens [E–1's $80,000 first mortgage]).

REVIEW QUESTIONS

1. T or F   After a default in an English common law mortgage of the 14th and 15th centuries, the lender's remedy was foreclosure by public sale.

2. T or F   Once English equity created the remedy of foreclosure it no longer permitted the mortgagee to take possession of the mortgaged land prior to default.

3. How does strict foreclosure differ from foreclosure by sale?

4. T or F   The Deed of Trust is a mortgage substitute.

5. T or F   Under the lien theory of mortgages, the mortgagee holds legal title to the mortgaged real estate, but the mortgagor holds the equitable title.

6. T or F   A balloon mortgage is usually for a shorter term than the more traditional evenly-amortized mortgage loan.

*

IV

The Use of Mortgage Substitutes

■ ANALYSIS

A. The Rule Against Clogging the Equity of Redemption

The perception of many mortgage lenders is that mortgage law is generally "pro-mortgagor." This perception has been reinforced by modern judicial interpretation of the mortgagor's "equity of redemption" and the rule prohibiting "clogs" on that equity. The former concept, as indicated earlier, affords the mortgagor the right to redeem by payment of the mortgage debt at any time prior to a valid foreclosure of the mortgage. The latter ("anti-clogging") doctrine *renders unenforceable and void any agreement by the mortgagor that is part of the original mortgage transaction and that purports to cut off or modify that right of redemption.*

Example 1: A mortgage on Blackacre states that "in the event mortgagor defaults under this mortgage, she waives any right to be foreclosed and agrees that title to the mortgaged real estate shall vest immediately in mortgagee." Mortgagor fails to pay as promised and mortgagee declares a default. Two months thereafter, mortgagor tenders the full amount of the debt then due and owing. No foreclosure has occurred. (*Result:* The mortgage language is unenforceable and the redemption is effective.)

Example 2: A mortgage on Blackacre states that "in the event mortgagor defaults under this mortgage, she agrees that her right to redeem shall terminate two months after mortgagee declares a default." Mortgagor fails to pay as promised and mortgagee declares a default. Three months thereafter, mortgagor tenders the full amount of the debt then due and owing. No foreclosure has occurred. (*Result:* The mortgage language is unenforceable and the redemption is effective.)

Example 3: Mortgagor executes and delivers a mortgage on Blackacre to mortgagee. In connection with this transaction, mortgagor also executes and delivers to mortgagee a quitclaim deed to Blackacre. The parties agree that "in the event of default under the mortgage, mortgagee shall have the right to record the quitclaim deed and, upon so doing, all of interest of mortgagor in Blackacre shall immediately terminate." Mortgagor defaults and mortgagee records the quitclaim deed. Two months later, mortgagor tenders the full amount due and owing on the mortgage debt. No foreclosure has occurred. (*Result:* The recording of the deed is ineffective and the redemption is valid). See, e.g., *Panagouleas Interiors, Inc. v. Silent Partner Group, Inc.,* 2002 WL 441409 (Ohio App.2002).

Sometimes courts use the clogging principle to deny specific performance of an *option to purchase* mortgaged real estate that is granted to the mortgagee as part of the mortgage transaction. Technically, such an option is a clog because it allows the mortgagee to obtain title to the land without being forced to go through foreclosure. However, under the approach of the Restatement such options are invalid only if their enforceability is expressly dependant upon mortgagor default. See Restatement (Third) of Property (Mortgages) § 3.1 comment d (1997).

Finally, note that the clogging doctrine is not violated by *fully executed subsequent transactions.* Thus, a subsequent *deed in lieu of foreclosure* is not an invalid clog. The rationale is that once the mortgagor decides to "give up," she or he is no longer influenced by sanguine overconfidence or the "mirage of hope." On the other hand, courts sometimes invalidate *subsequent executory agreements* as clogs. They are also invalid under the Restatement approach. See Restatement (Third) of Property (Mortgages) § 3.1 comment f (1997). This situation occurs where a mortgagor in default avoids foreclosure and obtains a further grace period by giving the mortgagee a quitclaim deed which is placed in escrow, to be recorded if the mortgagor defaults yet another time. Here, the "mirage of hope" may still be operating because the mortgagor is purporting to waive future redemption and foreclosure rights.

Example 1:   Mortgagor delivers a mortgage on Blackacre to mortgagee. Several months thereafter, mortgagor defaults and mortgagee threatens foreclosure. Mortgagor and mortgagee agree that in lieu of foreclosure, mortgagor will deliver to mortgagee a quitclaim deed to Blackacre and mortgagee will release mortgagor from the mortgage debt. Both the deed and release are executed and delivered. Several months thereafter, mortgagor tenders the full amount of the mortgage debt to mortgagee. (*Result:* Mortgagor's attempt to redeem is ineffective because mortgagor's equity of redemption was terminated by delivery of the quitclaim deed).

Example 2:   The facts are the same as in the prior example, except that after mortgagor's initial default, she delivers to mortgagee a quitclaim deed to Blackacre with the agreement that if the mortgage debt is paid off within the next six months, the deed will be returned to mortgagor. However, if mortgagor fails to pay as promised, the deed is to be recorded. Mortgagor fails to satisfy the mortgage debt within the six month period and mortgagee records the deed. Two months later, mortgagor tenders to mortgagee the full amount of the mortgage debt. (*Result:* Mortgagor's attempt to redeem is effective because mortgagor's equity of redemption was not terminated by recording of the quitclaim deed.)

In addition, legislatures often reinforce mortgagor rights by limiting the mortgagee's right to accelerate the mortgage debt and by establishing statutory periods after the foreclosure sale during which the mortgagor is permitted to "redeem." Finally, as we have noted earlier, many states require that mortgages be foreclosed by judicial action only, a relatively time-consuming and costly process.

Because of the above and certain other considerations, many lenders utilize land financing devices that they hope will avoid the application of the substantive law of mortgages. The use of such mortgage substitutes, however, often fails to accomplish this result, and in some instances creates more problems for the lender than would have been the case had a traditional mortgage format been utilized. The remainder of this Chapter focuses on such commonly used mortgage substitutes.

B. The Absolute Deed

Because of their roots in the common law mortgage, typical mortgage documents in use today utilize "deed" terminology. In other words, the mortgagor purports to "convey" the mortgaged premises to the mortgagee. However, the mortgage document will also contain language of "defeasance" that makes it clear that if the mortgagor pays the debt in a timely fashion, the "conveyance" will become ineffective.

It is not uncommon, however, for lenders to utilize as a security device an absolute deed from the borrower to the lender containing no defeasance language. This deed is often accompanied by an oral agreement by the lender-grantee to reconvey to the borrower-grantor if the debt is paid according to its terms. Sometimes this agreement to reconvey is in a collateral writing. The lender believes that in the event of a default by the grantor-borrower, foreclosure will be unnecessary because the lender has already acquired title to the real estate.

The impetus for using an absolute deed transaction rather than an ordinary mortgage usually comes from the lender rather than the grantor-borrower. Occasionally a grantor-borrower may view such a transaction as an effective mechanism for concealing his or her real estate ownership from third party creditors. In such a setting, a recorded absolute deed to Blackacre may satisfy the lender's requirement for security and simultaneously make it appear to grantor-borrower's other creditors that the grantee-lender, and not the grantor-borrower, is the owner of Blackacre. See *Beelman v. Beelman*, 460 N.E.2d 55 (Ill.App.1984) (absolute deed used as security for loan at borrower's request in order to conceal his ownership of the real estate from the Internal Revenue Service).

1. The Absolute Deed Unaccompanied by a Collateral Writing: Extrinsic Evidence

It is the overwhelming rule that parol evidence is admissible to establish that an absolute deed was intended to serve as security for a debt or obligation, even though there is no evidence of fraud, mistake, ignorance, duress or undue influence. In a few states, this principle is embodied in a statute. Sometimes the mortgage thus established is referred to as an "equitable mortgage" because the above doctrine has its origin in English chancery. However, in view of the pervasive procedural merger of law and equity in this country, parol evidence is admissible to establish security intent whether the proceeding is characterized as legal or equitable. See Nelson & Whitman, Real Estate Finance Law § 3.6 (4th ed.2001); Restatement (Third) of Property (Mortgages) § 3.2 (1997).

A few states limit or reject the majority approach. For example, one or two states require that the party seeking to establish an absolute deed as a mortgage must prove that defeasance language was omitted because of ignorance, mistake, fraud, or undue advantage. A few others prohibit proof of security intent unless the evidence of defeasance is in writing. See generally Nelson & Whitman, Real Estate Finance Law § 3.6 (4th ed.2001).

a. Burden of Proof

Although a few cases suggest that security intent must be established by a mere preponderance of the evidence, the overwhelming majority of courts demand that the evidence be clear and convincing.

The reason for the heavy burden of proof is understandable. In general, there is a public policy interest in the stability of written real estate transactions and in discouraging false swearing by a grantor who may regret having sold his or her real estate and who then seeks to avoid the consequences of the sale by attempting to redeem the property from a "mortgage." Moreover, the majority burden of proof discourages debtors who wish to conceal their ownership of real estate from creditors by putting title in the name of the mortgage. Finally, although the absolute deed intended as a mortgage is a relatively frequent occurrence, it is important to stress that the vast majority of absolute deed transactions are exactly what they purport to be—complete transfers of the grantor's interest. Accordingly, it is probably justifiable to require a heavier burden of proof than is usually called for in civil cases.

b. Parol Evidence Rule Inapplicable

The parol evidence rule normally bars extrinsic evidence that would vary the terms of a written instrument which the parties have executed with the intention that it be the complete expression or embodiment of their entire agreement. The usual explanation for holding the rule inapplicable to the absolute deed situation is that the absolute deed was not intended to embody the whole agreement of the parties. Consequently, the oral agreement simply supplements the deed concerning a matter with which the deed does not purport to deal.

c. Statute of Frauds Not a Bar

Generally the Statute of Frauds requires that the creation and transfer of interests in land be in writing. Thus, it could be argued that the statute is violated in the absolute deed setting because the grantor seeks to establish by extrinsic evidence an agreement by the grantee to reconvey to the grantor. Some courts avoid application of the statute by emphasizing that rules of law designed to prevent fraud should not be used to produce fraud and "that it would be a virtual fraud for the grantee to insist upon the deed as an absolute conveyance of the title, which had been intentionally given to him, and which he knowingly accepted, merely as security, and therefore in reality as a mortgage." *Smith v. Smith*, 45 So. 168, 169 (Ala.1907). Perhaps the best explanation for why the statute should not prevent the use of extrinsic evidence to establish an absolute deed to be a mortgage is that such a use literally does not violate the statute. Under this reasoning, the judicial determination that an absolute deed is a mortgage does not create in or transfer to the grantor an interest in land. Rather, the parol evidence merely shows that the grantor never parted with the beneficial interest in the land.

d. Factors That Establish an Absolute Deed as a Mortgage

While no single factor is necessarily controlling in determining whether an absolute deed constitutes a mortgage, the following checklist of factors is often crucial in finding an intent that the real estate is security for a debt or obligation.

1) Presence of a Debt or Obligation

The most important factor in determining whether an absolute deed is intended as security is whether there is a debt or obligation owing from the grantor to grantee that was unaffected by the conveyance. The debt may have existed prior to the conveyance or have been created contemporaneously with it.

Example: Grantor conveys Blackacre to grantee. Grantee remains in possession of a grantor's pre-conveyance promissory note. (Strong presumption of a mortgage transaction is raised.) *Thomas v. Klemm,* 43 A.2d 193 (Md.1945).

Note, however, that it is not necessary to establish the existence of a promissory note. Rather, where the totality of the facts indicate that the transaction was intended as a mortgage, a court may "impute the existence of an enforceable debt." *Johnson v. Cherry,* 726 S.W.2d 4, 7 (Tex.1987). Moreover, although there is authority to the contrary, the better view is that the debt or obligation need not be the *personal* liability of any person. Just as "formal" or "legal" mortgages may secure "non-recourse" obligations, the same should be true in the "absolute deed" context. See Restatement (Third) of Property (Mortgages) § 3.2(a) (1997).

2)   **Actual Statements of the Parties**

For example, it would be helpful if third parties could testify that grantee stated: "If grantor pays off the debt, she will get her land back."

3)   **Disparity Between the Amount Received by the Grantor and the Fair Market Value of the Land Conveyed**

Normally rational people, other than in gift transactions, do not transfer land without receiving a purchase price that at least approximates the fair market value of the land. To the extent that the value of the land is substantially greater than the amount advanced by the grantee, this is exceptionally strong evidence that the advance constituted a loan and therefore that the deed was a disguised mortgage. On the other hand, to the extent that the disparity between the amount advanced and the fair market value of the land is relatively small, this indicates that the transaction was a sale and not a mortgage.

4)   **Possession**

Retention of possession by the grantor is usually evidence that the conveyance is a mortgage unless, for example, the grantee is able to establish that the grantor retained possession as the grantee's lessee.

5)   **Payment of Real Estate Taxes**

To the extent that the grantor continues to pay the real estate taxes, this is indicative of a mortgage and not a sale. However, to the extent that the grantee can show that the grantor and grantee were in a lessor-lessee relationship, the payment of real estate taxes may be of less importance, since under "net" lease arrangements, it is not uncommon for the lessee to pay real estate taxes.

6) Improvements by Grantor

In the absence of a long-term lease, parties do not normally make substantial improvements to land unless they at least believe they own a beneficial interest in that land. Thus, such improvements by the grantor would be evidence that the conveyance was intended as security for a debt or obligation.

7) Nature of the Parties

To the extent, for example, that the grantee is in the business of making mortgage loans, this would be strong evidence of a security transaction. On the other hand, if the grantee is known as a land speculator who often buys and sells real estate, it would be much more difficult for the grantor to establish clear and convincing evidence of a security transaction.

e. Effect of Success in Establishing an Absolute Deed as a Mortgage

Once an absolute deed is established as a mortgage, it will be treated, as between the parties, as if it were a regular or "formal" mortgage. All of the substantive and procedural rules of mortgage law will be applicable. Thus the grantor will have the equitable right to redeem, and, if the state law so provides, the benefit of statutory redemption. If the grantee has been in possession, he or she will be held accountable for the application of rents and profits to the mortgage debt. Moreover, since the absolute deed obviously will not contain a power of sale (which would otherwise permit non-judicial foreclosure), the grantee will be required to foreclose the "mortgage" by judicial action.

2. The Absolute Deed With Collateral Written Instrument of Defeasance

If a collateral writing contains language of defeasance or a promise to reconvey upon payment of money acknowledged to be a debt and if the court is convinced that the two instruments were executed as part of a single transaction, the transaction will be treated as a mortgage. See Cunningham and Tischler, Disguised Real Estate Security Transactions in Substance, 26 Rutgers L.Rev. 1, 15–19 (1972); Nelson & Whitman, Real Estate Finance Law § 3.4 (4th ed.2001); Restatement (Third) of Property (Mortgages) § 3.2(c) (1997).

a. Use of Parol Evidence to Establish Single Mortgage Transaction

Parol evidence can always be introduced to establish that the two instruments really constituted one transaction. The parol evidence rule is inapplicable to bar its admission because such evidence is not utilized to contradict or vary the writings, but rather to establish that the documents were part of a single security transaction.

b. Timing of the Two Writings

The two writings need not be executed simultaneously in order for both to be treated as part of a single security transaction. The fact that the written agreement of defeasance is executed after the absolute deed does not bar mortgage treatment so long as the parties actually agreed to the defeasance at the time of executing the deed.

Since, as we observed earlier, courts allow a party to utilize extrinsic non-written evidence to establish that an absolute deed is intended as security, it should follow *a fortiori* that a written evidence of a defeasance should be admissible for such a purpose.

c. Nature of the Collateral Writing

While there is some authority to the contrary, under the prevailing view the collateral writing need not satisfy the same formalities required for executing the absolute deed.

Example: Grantor delivers a fully acknowledged absolute deed to grantee and receives $5,000 from the grantee. Six months later, in a letter to grantor, grantee acknowledges that "if you pay off the $5,000 debt with interest by next year, I will redeem the land to you." 18 months later, grantor tenders the $5,000 with interest and grantee refuses to reconvey. Grantor sues to establish the transaction as a mortgage and to redeem from it. (*Result:* Parol evidence will be admissible to establish that the deed and the letter were part of the same transaction. See a. above.)

C. The Conditional Sale

In the two types of absolute deed situations previously considered, we examined first the situation where extrinsic non-written evidence is utilized to establish that an absolute deed was intended as security. Next, we looked at the conceptually easier situation where the evidence of defeasance or an agreement to reconvey is in writing. Now we focus on absolute deed transactions where there not only is a second written document, but the document contains no language of defeasance or agreement to reconvey. Rather, the separate document professes expressly to be an instrument such as a contract or option to resell to the grantor the property described in the absolute deed. See *Sannerud v. Brantz*, 928 P.2d 477 (Wyo.1996). This type of transaction is referred to as a *conditional sale*. This type of transaction is relatively common and can take a variety of forms. The two most common are described below:

1. A sale and conveyance of the land by grantor to grantee with an option in grantor to repurchase it.

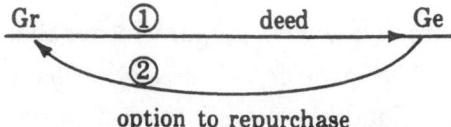

2. A sale and conveyance by grantor to grantee and a lease by grantee to grantor with an option in grantor to repurchase.

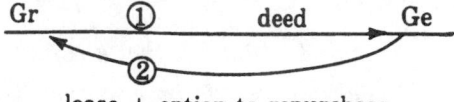

1. Reasons For Use

As in the case of the absolute deed transaction, the conditional sale is often motivated by the desire on the part of the lender-grantee to avoid the consequences of the borrower-grantee's equity of redemption and the accompanying rules of mortgage law. However, there can be other reasons for using such a transaction. One such reason can be state usury law. The lender may seek to characterize the difference between the sale price and repurchase price as simply part of the purchase price and not as interest, thus avoiding the usury statute's limitations on the amount of interest that one may charge.

Example: Lender agreed to lend $10,000 for one year to a borrower who had Blackacre to offer as security. Lender desired to collect 50% per annum interest on the $10,000 loan and borrower was willing to pay it. However, state usury law limited the rate of interest borrower could pay to 20% per annum. Thus, a single promissory note carrying a 50% interest rate secured by a mortgage on Blackacre would on its face violate state usury law. The parties may choose to characterize the loan as a sale to lender for $10,000 with a one-year option to repurchase in favor of the borrower at a repurchase price of $15,000.

Sometimes the conditional sale is motivated by income tax law considerations. Under federal income tax law, ordinary income generally is taxed at a higher rate than capital gain. Interest income is normally considered to be ordinary income. On the other hand, gain from the sale of land usually is treated as a capital gain. Thus, a lender sometimes seeks to characterize a loan transaction as a sale and option to repurchase so as to enable the difference between the "sale" price and the repurchase price to be treated as capital gain rather than ordinary income.

Example: Same facts as in above example except that 50% interest does not violate the state usury law. Lender, however, desires to have the $5,000 treated as capital gain rather than as interest income. By characterizing the loan transaction as a sale and repurchase of land, the lender may for tax purposes improperly attempt to report the $5,000 gain as profit from the sale of real estate.

2. Use of Extrinsic Evidence

Extrinsic evidence is admissible to establish that a conditional sale was intended as a security transaction. While some courts impose a burden of proof requiring clear and convincing evidence of security intent, others hold that a mere preponderance of evidence of such intent is sufficient.

Some courts require less proof of security intent in the conditional sale setting than in situations involving the use of parol evidence to show that an absolute deed was intended as security. In a sense this relaxed burden in the conditional sale situation is understandable. In the former context, after all, the grantor is attempting to convince a court that the absolute deed is not what it purports to be. In the conditional sale situation, however, the second document clearly establishes that the grantor retained *some* right to reacquire the conveyed real estate. On the other hand, it could be argued that the conditional sale situation should require at least as heavy a burden of proof as that required where the only written document is the absolute deed. In the former case, after all, the extrinsic evidence establishing that the parties intended a security transaction squarely contradicts the second written document. Its use cannot be justified on the ground that it merely fills out a part of the transaction that the parties did not cover in the absolute deed. See Nelson & Whitman, Real Estate Finance Law § 3.18 (4th ed.2001). The Restatement mandates a "clear and convincing" standard in both absolute deed and conditional sale contexts. See Restatement (Third) of Property (Mortgages) §§ 3.2(b), 3.3(b) (1997).

3. Factors Establishing a Conditional Sale as a Mortgage

The crucial question is whether the parties intended what was characterized as a conditional sale to be a real estate security transaction. Thus the factors enumerated in Section B(1)(d) of this Chapter in connection with utilizing extrinsic evidence establishing an absolute deed to be security are also important in the conditional sale setting. As in the absolute deed setting, probably the most important factor is the extent of the disparity between the amount received by the grantor and the fair market value of the land conveyed. On the other hand, certain of those factors may be of minimal importance in certain conditional sale transactions. For example, if there has been a sale and a lease-back, the retention of possession by the grantor may not be indicative of a security transaction because it is consistent with the grantor's status as a lessee. Moreover, in such a situation the significance of the grantor's payment of real estate taxes is neutralized if a lease requires such payment by the grantor-lessee.

D. Two Problems Common to Absolute Deed and Conditional Sale Transactions

1. Use of Specific Language Negating a Mortgage Transaction

Occasionally a grantee will include special language in an absolute deed or conditional sale setting that specifically negates the creation of a mortgage or debt transaction. Where other credible evidence supports a finding that the parties intended to create a mortgage transaction, a court will not be bound by specific contract or deed language negating such an intent. *Downs v. Ziegler*, 477 P.2d 261 (Ariz.App.1970). According to the Restatement, such language "is relevant to the issue of the parties' intent, but does not preclude a determination that the parties intended a mortgage transaction." Restatement (Third) of Property (Mortgages) § 3.3(c) (1997).

2. Application of the Same Burden of Proof to Grantor and Grantee

While there is authority that the burden of proof is the same for grantee as well as grantor, there are persuasive arguments that a heavier burden should apply to a grantee who seeks to establish that an absolute deed or conditional sale is a mortgage.

Most attempts to establish a mortgage will be by the grantor. However, this will not always be the case. For example, suppose that the value of the deeded land has dropped significantly and that the grantor has substantial assets to satisfy any personal liability on the mortgage debt to the grantee. The grantee may very well want to establish that what appears to be an absolute deed or a conditional sale is actually a loan and security transaction.

Since, however, the grantee-mortgagee probably controlled the language and format of the transaction, it could be argued that he or she should bear a heavier proof burden than should the grantor in establishing that the transaction was not what it purports to be. Indeed, according to the Restatement, "if the grantee was the party who insisted on insertion of the security-negating language, he probably should be estopped from attacking his own prior attempt to negate security intent." Restatement (Third) of Property (Mortgages) § 3.3, comment c (1997).

E. The Installment Land Contract

The most commonly used mortgage substitute is the installment land contract. In many areas this device is also known as a "contract for deed" or "long term land contract." Its economic function is identical to that of a purchase-money mortgage loan provided by a seller; both provide financing by the seller of the unpaid purchase price for the sale of real estate.

In the typical installment land contract, the vendee goes into possession and agrees to make monthly installment payments until the balance is paid off. During this period, the vendor retains legal title. When the contract is paid off, the vendee receives from the vendor a deed to the land. Such contracts may be amortized over periods of time varying from as little as two years to as long as 20 or 30 years. Sometimes, even though monthly payments are based on amortization periods of twenty years or longer, the balance of the contract will become due or "balloon" within, say, three to five years.

1. Distinguished from Earnest Money Contracts

The installment land contract should be distinguished from the ordinary executory contract for the sale of land. The latter is known as an "earnest money contract," a "binder" or a "marketing contract." This type of contract governs the buyer and seller of real estate during the period from the date of the bargain to the date of the closing. During this relatively short period, usually thirty to ninety days, such important matters as title examination and buyer's financing are attended to. At the closing date, the seller usually delivers a deed to the buyer and mortgages or security agreements, if any, are executed. The installment land contract, on the other hand, is a purchase money financing device. Like a mortgage, it governs the relationship of the parties throughout the life of the debt. The earnest money contract, however, in most important respects ceases to govern the parties after the closing takes place. Indeed, in some situations, the earnest money contract will specify that the parties will execute an installment land contract at the closing date. In short, it is helpful to remember that the installment land contract is a financing or security device while the earnest money contract is not.

2. The Forfeiture Remedy

Virtually every installment land contract provides that time is of the essence and that when a vendee defaults, the vendor has the option to declare the contract terminated, to retake possession of the premises and to retain all previous payments as liquidated damages. This clause normally relieves the vendor from all further obligations under the contract. Vendors rely on this remedy in the overwhelming majority of cases. It is the availability of this remedy that leads vendors to conclude that the installment land contract is a "pro-vendor" financing device. This remedy seems especially attractive to sellers of land in jurisdictions where the substantive law governing mortgages is perceived to be weighted heavily in favor of the mortgagor. Moreover, it is this remedy that has attracted the most judicial and legislative attention.

3. Other Remedies for Vendee Breach

Notwithstanding the pervasive reliance on the forfeiture remedy, a vendor may occasionally opt for certain contract remedies.

a. Specific Performance for the Price

Under this remedy vendor tenders title to the land and vendee is ordered to pay the remainder of the contract purchase price. Many courts, however, require as a condition precedent for granting specific performance for the price, that the contract contain an acceleration clause (allowing vendor to declare the entire debt due and payable upon vendee breach). Normally, a vendor would utilize this remedy where the vendee has assets to satisfy a judgment for the price and the land is now worth less than the contract price. In this relatively rare situation, the forfeiture remedy should not be utilized because the vendor would get back land that has dropped in value. Specific performance, on the other hand, would recover for the vendor the full contract price.

b. Specific Performance for the Installments Due

This remedy would give the vendor the amount of past due installments plus interest. Generally, the vendor will utilize this remedy only where the absence of any acceleration clause makes specific performance for the full price impossible.

c. Foreclosure of the Vendee's Rights

This remedy, where permitted, allows the vendor to treat the installment land contract as a mortgage and results in a judicial sale of the land. If the sale brings more than the contract price, the surplus will go to vendee. If the sale yields less than the contract amount, a deficiency judgment against the vendee can be obtained. Note that in using this remedy, the vendor is choosing to treat the installment land as a mortgage.

d. Strict Foreclosure

Some states, including a few of those that normally do not foreclose installment land contracts by judicial sale, will grant a vendor strict foreclosure of the contract. Typically, a court will fix a redemption period during which the vendee may enforce the contract by tendering the balance due. If, however, the vendee fails to redeem, the contract is canceled and title to the land is confirmed in the vendor. Some courts will award strict foreclosure only where the vendor can establish that the value of the land does not exceed the contract balance.

e. Suit for Damages

Generally, when a land contract vendee defaults, the vendor's damages are measured by the difference between the contract price and the fair market value of the land as of the date of vendee's breach. The pursuit of this remedy, however, is only possible where the vendee has abandoned the land. This is so because where the forfeiture remedy is necessary to regain the land, a subsequent action for damages will probably be barred by the election of remedies doctrine. See Section 7 of this Part. Moreover, the vendor faces the unenviable prospect of having to convince a court or jury that the land, as of the date of breach, was worth less than the contract price. Obviously, if the vendee has assets to satisfy a judgment, vendor would be better off, where possible, suing for specific performance for the price or seeking to foreclose the contract as a mortgage. If the foreclosure sale yields less than the contract price, vendor can then obtain a judgment for the deficiency.

4. Comments on the Forfeiture Remedy

Traditionally, installment land contract forfeiture provisions were routinely enforced in favor of the vendor. Today, while such clauses are occasionally enforced, (see e.g., Russell v. Richards, 702 P.2d 993 (N.M.1985)) it nevertheless can safely be said that in no jurisdiction will a default by a vendee automatically result in enforcement of the forfeiture provision.

Initially, courts enforced forfeiture clauses relatively automatically on the assumption that they were merely carrying out the intent of the parties. In other words, the installment land contract was treated as a creature of the law of contracts rather than the law of mortgages. Today, however, because of legislative intervention and changing judicial perspectives, the installment land contract is increasingly taking on the mantle of mortgage law. In a variety of ways, legislatures and courts are limiting the forfeiture remedy, especially in situations where the vendee has built up a substantial equity in the property. The trend, however, has been uneven, and the law varies greatly from jurisdiction to jurisdiction.

5. Legislative Limitation on Forfeiture

At least a dozen states have adopted statutes limiting the harshness of the forfeiture remedy. Such statutes often mandate "grace periods" during which the defaulting vendor can defeat forfeiture by payment of the late install- ments or "arrearages." Such statutes also specify that cancellation or forfei- ture of the vendee's rights may only be accomplished by following a specified non-judicial procedure. Commonly, the vendor is required to serve notice of intent to forfeit on the vendee and others having a record interest in the real estate. Notice by publication may also be required. Normally, the vendee's grace period begins to run from the date the vendor initiates the statutory procedure. If the vendee cures his or her default within the requisite time period, the forfeiture is avoided. However, failure to cure results in a forfeiture of the land and the prior payments to the vendor. See Nelson & Whitman, Real Estate Finance Law § 3.28 (4th ed.2001).

With respect to the states where such statutes exist, two observations are important: first, the harshness of common-law forfeiture has been alleviated. In some situations, the statutory grace periods are similar to the rights afforded to defaulting mortgagors under the law of mortgages. Second, the presence of such statutes tends to institutionalize or formalize the forfeiture concept. Courts in these states have largely limited their intervention to making sure that the technical requirements of the statutes have been fulfilled.

6. Judicial Limitations on Forfeiture

Absent statutory regulation, many courts in recent years have found a variety of ways to limit enforcement of forfeiture clauses. Certain of these judicial approaches have utilized contract principles, while many courts have gone a long way toward simply treating installment land contracts as mortgages. Some courts seem to apply an often-confusing amalgam of contract and mortgage law. The following catego- ries illustrate some of the major approaches used in the judicial assault on forfeiture clauses.

a. Waiver by Vendor as an Excuse for Delinquency

Frequently, a vendor will accept one or several late payments before finally losing his or her patience and attempting to enforce forfeiture. The vendor may then bring an action for a judicial declaration of forfeiture and the vendee may counterclaim for specific performance. The vendee may tender the balance of the purchase price or, in some situations, insist on the opportunity to reinstate the contract by payment of arrearages. In either case, the vendee will claim that the vendor's past pattern of acceptance of late payments constitutes a waiver of the time provisions of the contract. The cases are confusing and difficult to reconcile. In some cases, rather innocuous forbearances by the vendor have resulted in a finding of waiver, while in other cases, substantial leniency by the vendor has proven to be unavailing.

Claims of waiver present courts with a difficult dilemma. To some extent the waiver concept provides a workable basis for invalidating unreasonable attempts to invoke forfeiture. On the other hand, to the extent that courts are relatively generous in finding waiver, the more they may encourage other vendors to be ungenerous with tardy vendees, for fear that their forbearance will defeat any future attempts to enforce forfeiture.

b. Recognition of an Equity of Redemption

Some jurisdictions have held that a vendee in default should have the right, within a reasonable time, to pay the balance on the contract or, in a few instances, the arrearages, before losing the land. Some courts view this right as unconditional, while others limit it to situations where the vendee has paid a substantial amount on the contract (*Petersen v. Hartell*, 707 P.2d 232 (Cal.1985)) or where forfeiture would be unconscionable for some other reason. Some of these jurisdictions, however, may nevertheless permit forfeiture where the vendee has been guilty of gross negligence or bad faith. See Nelson & Whitman, Real Estate Finance Law § 3.29 (4th ed.2001).

Note that the above issues will frequently arise in the context of a specific performance request by the vendee. Often this claim will be interjected as a counterclaim after the vendor has sought judicial termination of the vendee's interest. Some courts, in referring to vendee's right to tardy payment, refer to it in "equity of redemption" mortgage law terminology, while others grant the relief on the general grounds of fairness. It should be emphasized, however, that if the vendee fails to come up with the requisite amount, the land will be forfeited to the vendor. Note that this is the equivalent of giving the vendor strict foreclosure.

Example 1: Vendor and vendee entered into installment land contract for the sale of farm land. Vendee had paid almost 35% of the total purchase price. Vendee then defaulted on one installment by fifteen days and vendor refused to accept late payment. Vendor sued for termination of the contract. Vendee then counterclaimed for specific performance, tendering the unpaid balance of the contract. (*Result:* specific performance granted. Enforcement of forfeiture determined to be inequitable.) *Nigh v. Hickman,* 538 S.W.2d 936 (Mo.App.1976). See also *Petersen v. Hartell,* 707 P.2d 232 (Cal.1985); *Jenkins v. Wise,* 574 P.2d 1337 (Hawaii 1978).

Example 2: Similar facts to above example except that not only had farmer vendee paid one-third of the purchase price, he also had made substantial improvements to the land. After he fell substantially in default, vendor sued to have the contract canceled. (*Result:* vendee given six months to pay entire purchase price or lose the land to vendor. However, if vendee paid arrearages within ten days, he was given eighteen months to pay the balance of the purchase price.) *Nelson v. Robinson,* 336 P.2d 415 (Kan.1959).

Example 3: Vendor and vendee executed an installment land contract for property containing a fourplex. Vendee made no payments in 1968, 1969, 1970, 1971, 1972, 1974, 1975. A minimal payment was made in 1973. Vendor during this time provided money for vendee to make improvements to the building. After vendor sought a judicial declaration of forfeiture, vendor counterclaimed for specific performance. (*Result:* forfeiture granted. Vendee's apparent bad faith and negligence were so substantial that forfeiture was considered justifiable.) *Curry v. Tucker,* 616 P.2d 8 (Alaska 1980).

c. Restitution

In some jurisdictions that do not yet recognize a vendee's equity of redemption or where a vendee is unwilling or unable to redeem, a court may grant forfeiture, but temper its harshness by requiring the vendor to return the payments made by vendee on the contract to the extent they exceed vendor's actual damages. Vendor's damages are usually measured as the sum of the fair rental value of the property during the period of vendee's occupancy, plus such incidental damages as repairs and a sales commission on resale.

Example: On May 1, 2003, vendor and vendee contracted to sell a warehouse building for $60,000. Vendee made a $20,000 down payment and agreed to pay the balance by making three annual installments of $10,000 plus interest at the rate of 12 percent on the unpaid balance on May 1 of each succeeding year until the balance is fully paid. Vendee made the first installment payment of $10,000 plus $4,800 in interest on May 1, 2004. Vendee defaulted on the second installment and vendor immediately brought an action to terminate the vendee's interest. Vendee counterclaimed for restitution. The fair rental value of the premises until the date of trial was $14,000. (*Result:* vendor gets the land back but must pay vendee $19,800. This amount is determined by subtracting $15,000 [the fair rental value of the premises until vendee vacates] from $34,800 [the down payment of $20,000 plus the first installment of $14,800].)

Note that where the vendee's down payment is relatively small and the period of amortization relatively long, it is less likely that the vendee's payments will exceed the fair rental value of the property. See generally Nelson & Whitman, Real Estate Finance Law § 3.29 (4th ed.2001).

Courts often use rental value in computing the restitution to the vendee, as illustrated in the example above, but the computation is flawed in several respects. In the example, the vendor parted with an asset having a value of $40,000 (the purchase price less the down payment) on May 1, 2003. The vendor recovered the land two years later when the forfeiture occurred. If the land was worth the same amount ($60,000) as on the date of the original contract, the vendor has accrued a $20,000 benefit by virtue of the forfeiture. However, the land's value may have changed, either positively or negatively, and changes in value should be at the purchaser's risk. However, the "rental value" measure of restitution fails to take such changes into account.

Another serious flaw in the computation in the example is its failure to recognize the time value of money. In effect, the example pretends that everything happened at once, while in fact two years have elapsed during which the vendor's $40,000 asset has been unavailable to the vendor. The computation uses rental value as a proxy for interest, but it is a poor proxy. It would be far more accurate for the courts to use actual interest at the contract rate. If that were done in the example above, the vendor would have no loss attributable to the first year of the contract (since the vendee actually paid the $4,800 interest that accrued during that year). The vendor would be entitled to $3,600 interest for the second year, and should be required to give restitution of all of the value received in the forfeiture over and above a return of principal (the $30,000 balance remaining on the contract price) plus interest of $3,600. If one assumes that the land is still worth $60,000 at the date of the forfeiture, the vendor should give restitution of $60,000 minus $33,600, or $26,400. If a judicial decree is necessary to legitimate the forfeiture, and if the vendor's title is not marketable until that decree is entered, the vendor should be entitled to further interest until that date.

The analysis in the foregoing paragraph treats the forfeited installment contract like a mortgage that has been foreclosed with a foreclosure sale price equal to the property's fair market value. Properly understood, rental value has nothing to do with it. The courts, however, have demonstrated little insight into this matter, and often perform only the simplistic analysis given in the original example above.

d. Foreclosure as a Mortgage

Several states, including Florida, Indiana, Kentucky, Nebraska, New York and Oklahoma, generally treat installment land contracts as mortgages, at least in those situations where the vendee has made more than nominal payments on the contract. The Restatement unambiguously provides that an installment land contract "creates a mortgage." Restatement (Third) of Property (Mortgages) § 3.4(b) (1997).

Note that the effect of equating the installment land contract with a mortgage is to afford the tardy vendee greater rights than do those courts that simply recognize, directly or indirectly, a vendee's equity of redemption. (See Section 6(b) of this Chapter supra.) The latter courts generally provide the vendee in default the right to redeem by paying off the contract balance (or in some instances the arrearages). Failure to redeem, however, results in vendee losing the land to the vendor. Where a court treats the contract as a mortgage, however, the vendee not only has the right to redeem, but failing such redemption, has the additional right to insist that the property be sold at a public foreclosure sale. Any sale surplus over the contract balance would go to vendee. If the property sold for less than the contract debt, vendor could obtain a deficiency judgment against the vendee.

Example: Vendor and vendee entered into an installment land contract to sell Blackacre for $14,300. Vendee made a down payment of $3,800. The balance was to be paid off at $120 per month including interest at 8½%. After the down payment, vendee defaulted on seven payments during a twenty-one month period. Vendor brought suit to enforce forfeiture. Vendee did not counterclaim for specific performance or to redeem because she could not raise the amount of the contract balance. Vendee sought to have her contract treated as a mortgage. (*Result:* public foreclosure sale must be ordered.) *Sebastian v. Floyd,* 585 S.W.2d 381 (Ky.1979).

7. Election of Remedies

To the extent that a jurisdiction recognizes forfeiture as a valid remedy, a vendor who obtains a forfeiture is usually barred from seeking to recover the mortgage equivalent of a deficiency judgment. The vendor is said to have elected the forfeiture remedy and can have nothing in addition.

Note that election of remedies can be a particular problem when the value of the land described in the installment land contract is no longer worth the contract price. To the extent that the vendee is financially sound, the vendor may be able to forego the forfeiture remedy and sue for specific performance for the price. See *Glacier Campground v. Wild Rivers, Inc.,* 597 P.2d 689 (Mont.1978). Or perhaps, if the law of the jurisdiction or the language of the contract permits, the vendor could choose to treat the installment land contract as a mortgage and foreclose it. To the extent that the foreclosure sale brings less than the contract price, the vendor could, unless barred by anti-deficiency legislation, then seek a deficiency judgment. However, if the vendor chooses to pursue the forfeiture remedy, he or she is barred from obtaining other relief. Moreover, courts reach the same result even where the contract obligation to the vendor is represented by a separate promissory note.

Example 1: Vendee and vendor executed an installment land contract for the sale of Blackacre. The total purchase price was $100,000, of which vendee paid $10,000 in cash at the date of the contract and agreed to pay the balance in nine equal annual install-ments of $10,000, together with interest at 14% per annum. After making the first annual installment payment, vendee defaulted on the second. Vendor chose to invoke forfeiture and thereafter discovered that the land was now worth $60,000. (*Result:*vendor will be unable to collect from the vendee the difference between the balance due on the contract [$80,000 plus interest] and the fair market value of the land [$60,000].)

Example 2:   Same facts as in Example 1, except that in addition to executing the installment land contract, vendee also executed a separate promissory note in favor of vendor for the amount of $100,000. After forfeiture, vendor then sought to recover the $20,000 by suing on the promissory note. (*Result:* once vendor effects forfeiture of the contract, there is an entire failure of consider-ation for the promissory note, and it becomes unenforceable by vendor or any person who is not a holder in due course.) *Nemec v. Rollo,* 562 P.2d 1087 (Ariz.App.1977).

A few courts distinguish between promissory notes given as part of the contract "down payment" and those that finance the balance of the purchase price. According to these courts, the "down payment" type note survives the termination of the contract and can be enforced, but the "contract balance" note is unenforceable. See *Novus Equities Corp. v. EM–TY Partnership,* 381 N.W.2d 426 (Minn.1986).

Note that the election of remedies doctrine, as a general contract law or remedies concept, has been subjected to substantial criticism. Hence some courts, in the installment land contract context, reject the election of remedies rule as a specific principle, but apply a similar or related rationale. For example in Iowa, the vendor who has opted for forfeiture is barred from further relief on the ground that "the contract between the parties has been terminated, thereby extinguishing any right to recover the unpaid purchase price." *Gray v. Bowers,* 332 N.W.2d 323, 325 (Iowa 1983). Sometimes an estoppel analysis is substituted for the election of remedies rule. Under this approach, "the proper inquiry should be whether the [vendee] has relied on [acts or statements by the vendor] and therefore would be unfairly prejudiced by the assertion of a different inconsistent remedy. If so the [vendor] should be bound to the remedy earlier chosen." *Keesee v. Fetzek,* 681 P.2d 600 (Idaho App.1984).

8. Mortgaging the Vendee's Interest

As the vendee pays off an installment land contract and particularly if the land increases in value, the vendee's interest becomes increasingly valuable. Thus, it is common for a vendee to borrow money by mortgaging his or her interest.

a. Mortgageability

Most states hold that a vendee's interest is mortgagable. Fincher v. Miles Homes, 549 S.W.2d 848 (Mo.1977): Nelson & Whitman, Real Estate Finance Law § 3.35 (4th ed.2001).

b. Rights of the Vendee's Mortgagee to Notice

The majority of cases hold that the vendor cannot declare and enforce a forfeiture without first providing the vendee's mortgagee who has recorded a mortgage notice of intention to invoke forfeiture and an opportunity to protect itself. A minority approach limits the duty to notify to those situations where the vendor has actual knowledge of the mortgage on the vendee's interest. See Nelson & Whitman, Real Estate Finance Law § 3.35 (4th ed.2001).

Example: Vendee paid off $40,000 of a $75,000 installment land contract. Vendee gave a mortgage to Finance Co. to secure a $25,000 loan and Finance Co. recorded the mortgage. Vendee defaulted under the land contract and vendor decided to invoke the forfeiture provision. (*Result:* in majority of states, vendor must give at least mailed notice to Finance Co.)

Note that under the majority approach, recording by the vendee's mortgagee constitutes valid constructive notice to the vendor. Thus, the vendor will be required to examine the title to the land prior to invoking forfeiture. In a minority jurisdiction, however, vendee's mortgagee must provide the vendor with actual knowledge that there is a mortgage on the vendee's interest in order to obligate the vendor to notify the mortgagee of the vendor's intent to invoke forfeiture.

Unlike both the majority and minority approaches, Oregon takes the extreme position that the vendor has no obligation to provide notice to the vendee's mortgagee even where he or she has actual knowledge of the mortgagee's existence. See *Estate of Brewer v. Iota Delta Chapter, Tau Kappa Epsilon Fraternity, Inc.,* 692 P.2d 597 (Ore.1984).

c. Criticism of the Minority Rule

One commentary identifies several arguments against the minority approach: "The better policy would be to protect the mortgagee's interest if the mortgage has been recorded. If the burden of providing actual notice to the vendor is placed on the mortgagee and the mortgagee fails to prove such notice, his rights will be lost. As one commentator pointed out: 'It would be far more equitable to place a burden of notification on the party who seeks to extinguish the rights of another completely, than to penalize for failure to give notice one who seeks only the opportunity to perform obligations under the contract.' There are other reasons why the constructive notice rule would be preferable. When a vendor seeks forfeiture he usually consults an attorney. Mortgagees, however, quite commonly receive and record mortgages without the benefit of counsel. The vendor's lawyer would have knowledge of a constructive notice rule and would search the record for potential mortgages. A mortgagee acting alone would lose his interest in the land by relying on the commonly accepted tenet that recording provides protection. Adoption of the actual notice rule would reward ignorance. A vendor who did not search the public record would be in a better position than one who checked the record and discovered the mortgage." Note, Mortgages—Mortgage of a Vendee's Interest in an Installment Land Contract—Mortgagee's Rights Upon Default, 43 Mo.L.Rev. 371, 373–374 (1978).

9. Rights of Judgment Creditors of the Vendee

In most jurisdictions, statutes provide that a judgment is a lien on all "real estate" of the judgment debtor in the county in which the judgment is obtained. Frequently, the question arises as to whether a judgment against an installment land contract vendee attaches to that vendee's interest. Is the vendee's interest treated as "real estate" for purposes of the judgment lien statutes? *Most states hold that the vendee's interest is real estate for purposes of such statutes and that a judgment creditor of a vendee thus obtains a valid lien on the vendee's contract interest.*

Example 1: Vendee paid off $40,000 of a total installment land contract price of $100,000. The land then had a fair market value free and clear of liens of $100,000. A creditor of the vendee then obtained a $15,000 judgment against the vendee in a county where the land described in the contract is located. Vendee then gave a $30,000 mortgage to Bank to obtain money to send vendee's child to college. Vendee then defaulted on the mortgage and Bank foreclosed. (*Result:* because the judgment against the vendee is a valid lien on the vendee's interest and because it was perfected prior to the Bank's mortgage, the purchaser at the foreclosure sale will buy the vendee's interest *subject to* the judgment lien.)

Example 2:   Same facts as in the above example, except that the judgment creditor obtained the judgment before the mortgage was given to the Bank. (*Result:* because the judgment creditor has a valid lien and because it is senior to the mortgage lien, a judgment sale purchaser will obtain the vendee's interest free and clear of Bank's mortgage.)

Courts reach the above results on one of two theories:

1)   Equitable Conversion

Under this theory, at the time an earnest money contract or an installment land contract is executed, the vendee's interest is considered in equity as real estate for purposes of the judgment lien statutes.

2)   Statutory Interpretation

A few courts reject the application of equitable conversion because of difficulties they believe the doctrine creates in numerous other contexts. Rather, such courts simply hold that the legislature intended that a vendee's contract interest be considered "real estate" for purposes of the language of the judgment lien statutes. See *Cascade Security Bank v. Butler,* 567 P.2d 631 (Wash.1977).

10. Mortgaging The Vendor's Interest

The vendor's interest in an installment land contract is clearly mortgagable. Suppose a creditor makes a loan, and takes as security the borrower's interest as a vendor under an installment land contract. How should the creditor "perfect" this security interest? Prior to 2000, the correct method of perfection was uncertain and the cases were in disarray. Some cases took the traditional approach that the primary asset involved was only an interest in real property. In effect, this approach treated the transaction as a simple mortgage on a fee interest in real estate. Consequently, the creditor would take and record in the real estate records a *real estate mortgage.* See e.g., *In re Shuster,* 784 F.2d 883 (8th Cir.1986). At the other extreme, some courts held that the vendor's interest under an installment land contract was essentially personal property, and could be perfected simply by filing a financing statement under UCC Article 9. See, e.g., *In re Huntzinger,* 268 B.R. 263 (Bkrtcy.D.Kan.2000).

Still other courts held that either method was sufficient (see *Security Bank v. Chiapuzio*, 304 Or. 438, 747 P.2d 335 (1987); or that both methods had to used together. See *Bullitt, Trustee for Heide v. Mading King County Enterprises, Inc.*, 915 F.2d 531 (9th Cir.1990). Finally, a few courts held that the right to the contract payments was a personal property right, perfectible under Article 9, while the right to assert the security interest in the real estate was a real property right, separately perfectible by recording in the real estate records. See *In re Freeborn*, 94 Wash.2d 336, 617 P.2d 424 (1980).

This issue was greatly clarified by Revised UCC Article 9, promulgated in 2000 and adopted by most states by 2003:

> "perfection of a security interest in a right to payment or performance also perfects a security interest in a lien on personal or real property securing the right, notwithstanding other law to the contrary."

UCC § 9–308(e). *Thus, one who takes a security interest in an installment contract vendor's interest does not have to record in the real estate records in order to perfect as to both the right to payments and the real estate security for those payments.* Perfection under Article 9 is sufficient. However, when and how does a lender to a vendor perfect under Article 9? Consider the following analysis:

> Under Revised Article 9, the proper method of perfecting a security interest in an account is the filing of a financing statement [in most states, in the Secretary of State's office] unless a so-called "isolated" transfer is involved. An isolated transfer is one "which does not by itself or in conjunction with other assignments to the same assignee transfer a significant part of the assignor's outstanding accounts or payment intangibles." UCC § 9–309(2). Thus, the proper method of perfection depends on whether the account "is a significant part of the assignor's outstanding accounts." If the definition of "isolated" is met, a security interest in an account is automatically deemed perfected when it attaches and no filing is needed. This would seem to create a distinction, for example, between an individual who sold a home on installment contract and then pledged his rights to a bank as collateral for a loan, and someone who had sold a number of real estate parcels and then pledged rights under one of those contracts to the same bank. The bank would arguably need to file in the former case but not the latter. In the first case, the contract in question is the only one the vendor has entered into, so it appears to be a significant part—perhaps 100%—of the accounts the vendor possesses. This seems an odd and unexpected distinction, at least for real estate lenders. Unfortunately, the definition is so vague and

uncertain in application that no creditor can safely rely on it. The only sensible course for a creditor to follow is to file in every case.

Whitman, Transfers by Vendors of Interests in Installment Land Contracts: The Impact of Revised Article 9 of the Uniform Commercial Code, 38 Real Prop. Prob. & Tr.J. 421, 429–30 (2003).

Example 1:   Vendor, under an installment land contract for the sale of Blackacre, had the right to collect $50,000 plus interest over the remaining five years of the contract. Lender loaned $20,000 to vendor and took a mortgage on Blackacre and recorded it in the real estate records. X, having no actual knowledge of the foregoing loan, then loaned money to vendor. X took and filed a financing statement under Article 9 of the U.C.C. (*Result:* as between lender and X, X's lien claim to the contract proceeds will have priority over that of the lender).

Example 2:   Same facts as in Example 1, except that Lender took and filed a financing statement under Article 9 of the UCC. (*Result:* as between lender and X, lender's lien claim to the contract proceeds will have priority over that of X).

Note that even though a lender files under Article 9 there may still be good reasons to record an assignment in the real estate records. While such a recording is unnecessary and irrelevant for Article 9 purposes, recording may be important and desirable for three reasons:

(1) Suppose a vendor defaults on the obligation to the lender and the lender steps into the vendor's shoes. Suppose further that the contract vendee pays off the contract. The lender will then, as vendor, need to deliver the vendee a fulfillment deed. Unless an assignment to the lender has previously been recorded, the lender's fulfillment deed will appear in the records as a "wild deed"–not connected to the preexisting chain of title. Consequently the vendee's title may be treated as unmarketable.

(2) Suppose the vendee defaults on the land contract. In the absence of a recorded assignment, a dishonest original vendor (without informing the lender) may declare a forfeiture under the land contract. The vendor might then make a competing outright sale of the real estate to another person. A court could very well hold that after the contract has been terminated by forfeiture, an "account" for UCC

purposes no longer exists and hence Article 9 ceases to apply. Consequently, the subsequent purchaser might take free and clear of the lender's security interest under the normal operation of the recording acts.

(3) Suppose, after making an assignment to a lender, the vendor colludes with the contract vendee to improperly release the vendor's interest to the vendee by recording a fulfillment deed. If the land records contains no evidence of the assignment, it will appear that the fulfillment deed is proper and that the vendee has unencumbered title to the real estate. The vendee may then turn around and convey the premises to a bona fide purchaser. Under the normal operation of the recording act, a BFP will prevail against the unrecorded claim of the lender-assignee. The recording of the assignment would prevent this result.

See Whitman, supra, at 444–45; Wertheim, *Revised Article 9 of the U.C.C. and Minnesota Contracts for Deed*, 28 Wm. Mitchell L.Rev. 1483 (2002).

11. Rights Of Judgment Creditors Of The Vendor

In seeming contradiction of the doctrine of equitable conversion, courts often treat the vendor's interest in an installment land contract as "real estate" for purposes of judgment lien statutes. One court has stated the general approach as follows: "The doctrine of equitable conversion generally does not apply. . . . The majority rule is that a judgment lien against the vendor after the making of the contract sale, but prior to making and delivery of the deed, extends to all of the vendor's interest remaining in the land and binds the land to the extent of the unpaid purchase price." *First Security Bank of Idaho v. Rogers*, 429 P.2d 386 (Idaho 1967). Accord: *Bedortha v. Sunridge Land Co.*, 822 P.2d 694 (Ore.1991); *First Mustang State Bank v. Garland Bloodworth, Inc.*, 825 P.2d 254 (Okla.1991). However, a significant and growing number of cases are characterizing the vendor's interest as personalty. See e.g., *Cannefax v. Clement*, 818 P.2d 546 (Utah 1991).

Note, however, that if the vendor's contract rights are characterized as personalty, a judgment against vendor does not constitute a lien on that interest. While a judgment becomes a lien on the judgment debtor's real estate from the moment the judgment is obtained, it creates no interest at all in the debtor's personal property until an actual execution sale of that property is held.

Example 1: Under an installment land contract, vendor still had the right to collect $50,000 over the next four years. X obtained a judgment in the county where the contract land was located against vendor for $20,000. Y then obtained a $40,000 judgment in the same county. Y held an execution sale on the judgment and she purchased at the sale for $40,000. (*Result:* Y has made a serious error. Because under the majority rule the vendor's interest is real estate, the judgments were both liens on that interest. Their relative priority is determined by the date each judgment was obtained. Thus, since Y's judgment was obtained second, Y purchased the vendor's interest *subject to* X's unpaid $20,000 lien).

Example 2:   Same facts as in Example 1, except that the parties were in a jurisdiction that treats the vendor's interest as personalty for purposes of the judgment lien statute. In such a setting, the date of entry of the judgment establishes no priority; rather, the first execution sale passes title to the personalty free and clear of any other judgment no matter when it was obtained. Thus, in our example, even though Y's judgment was obtained after X's, Y purchased at her execution sale a title free and clear of any lien claim by X.

F. The Negative Covenant as a Mortgage Substitute

Occasionally, a lender in a loan transaction with a borrower will require the borrower to execute a promise not to encumber or transfer, so long as the loan remains unpaid, certain of the borrower's real estate. The question is whether such a negative covenant constitutes an equitable mortgage on that real estate.

1.   Reasons for Use

Many lenders believe the negative covenant will, in the event of a borrower's default, give them the option of proceeding against the borrower either as a secured or as an unsecured creditor. If, for example, at the time of default, the borrower has sufficient assets to satisfy a judgment, the lender may decide simply to proceed as an unsecured creditor. By taking such an approach, the lender would in some jurisdictions avoid certain pro-mortgagor concepts such as a "one action" rule, an antideficiency statute (see X infra), and perhaps other substantive and procedural limitations on creditors who are real estate mortgagees. On the other hand, if the defaulting borrower has no other assets, the lender wants the option, notwithstanding the above limitations, to proceed as a secured real estate mortgagee. In other words, the use of the negative covenant illustrates a lender attempt "to have it both ways" or "to have one's cake and eat it too." See generally Nelson & Whitman, Real Estate Finance Law § 3.38 (4th ed.2001).

2. Judicial Treatment

In the absence of other evidence of intent to create a mortgage, a debtor's promise to a lender not to encumber or transfer an interest in debtor's real estate does not create a mortgage, lien or security interest in that real estate. At most, the promise confers an in personam *contract right in the lender against a borrower who violates the covenant.* This is the vast majority view, and is also the Restatement position. See Restatement (Third) of Property (Mortgages) § 3.5 and comment b (1997). Moreover, under the Restatement, "[o]nly if the negative covenant is accompanied by specific language of grant or conveyance or by words such as 'mortgage', 'security', 'security interest', 'lien', or language of similar import to refer to the lender's interest, will extrinsic evidence normally be admissible to establish that a mortgage on real estate was intended." Id.

Example 1: Borrower executed a promissory note to Bank–1 in the amount of $60,000. Borrower also executed an instrument entitled "Covenant Not to Encumber or Convey Real Estate." This instrument identified certain real estate and stated that so long as Borrower remained indebted to Bank–1, he would not cause any mortgage, conveyance or other lien to be placed on such real estate. A year later Borrower gave a mortgage on the above real estate to Bank–2 which had notice of the covenant. Bank–1 brought suit to foreclose on the covenant as an "equitable mortgage." Bank–2 asserted that Bank–1 did not have a valid lien on which to foreclose. (*Result:* Bank–1 has no lien. The creation of a lien requires an affirmative act and the intention to do so cannot be implied from an express negative covenant.) *Equitable Trust Co. v. Imbesi,* 412 A.2d 96 (Md.1980).

Example 2: Same facts as in Example 1, except that prior to Bank–2 taking a mortgage from Borrower, Bank–1 sued to enjoin Borrower from executing and Bank–2 from accepting a mortgage. (*Result:* an injunction is arguably available to prevent Borrower from violating his promise.) See Nelson & Whitman, Real Estate Finance Law § 3.38 (4th ed.2001).

3. Scholarly Criticism

Commentators seem to be in unanimous agreement that a negative covenant does not create a mortgage. See 4 American Law of Property, § 16.38;

Coogan, Kripke and Weiss, The Outer Fringes of Article 9: Subordination Agreements, Security Interests in Money and Deposits, Negative Pledge Clauses and Participation Agreements, 79 Harv.L.Rev. 229, 264 (1964). According to Professor Gilmore, the "debtor's covenant not to encumber property . . . should be treated, as on the whole the case law has done, as a covenant 'mere personal'—good enough to give rights against the covenantor for breach, to bring an acceleration clause into play, to constitute 'an event of default' under a loan agreement, but not good enough to give rights, whether they be called legal or equitable in the property." Gilmore, Security Interests in Personal Property, 1017 (1965).

REVIEW QUESTIONS

1. T or F   A mortgage contains a provision that states: "In the event of a default herein, mortgagor agrees to convey title to the mortgaged real estate to mortgagee." A default occurs and mortgagor refuses to convey. A court will order mortgagor to convey.

2. T or F   An absolute deed may be established as a mortgage if the mortgagor proves, by a preponderance of the evidence, that the parties intended a mortgage transaction.

3. T or F   In a sense it should be easier to establish that a conditional sale is a mortgage than to do so with respect to an absolute deed.

4. T or F   The conditional sale transaction is primarily used to avoid the application of mortgage law.

5. T or F   A written agreement that, during the life of lender's unsecured loan to borrower, the latter will not mortgage or transfer Blackacre constitutes a mortgage on Blackacre in lender's favor.

6. What is the difference between an earnest money contract and an installment land contract?

7. Explain how restitution may mitigate forfeiture as an installment land contract remedy.

8. When would a vendor consciously choose specific performance instead of forfeiture as a remedy for vendee breach?

9. T or F   Most legislative regulation of installment land contracts ultimately inures to the vendor's benefit.

10.   T or F   One who holds a mortgage on a vendee's interest in an installment land contract can, by recording the mortgage, insure that he will receive notice of any attempt by the vendor to invoke forfeiture.

11.   Assume that a prudent lender makes a loan to an installment land contract vendor and desires to have security in the vendor's interest. Why would the lender perfect its interest under Article 9 of the UCC as well as in the real estate records? How should the Article 9 security interest be perfected?

*

V

Rights and Duties Prior to Foreclosure

■ ANALYSIS

A. Theories of Title and the Right to Possession

As was noted in III supra, three "theories" of mortgage law exist in the United States—the title, lien and intermediate theories.

1. The Title Theory

Under this theory, legal "title" is in the mortgagee until the mortgage has either been satisfied or foreclosed. This theory represents the evolutionary remains of the original English common law mortgage described in III supra. You will remember that the common law mortgage actually gave possession to the mortgagee who used the fruits of possession—the rents and profits—as a substitute for the interest or return on investment that was prohibited by usury laws. Once the charging of interest was no longer prohibited, the mortgagee collected interest on the mortgage debt and the mortgagor was permitted to remain in possession of the mortgaged premises. Moreover, the development by English chancery courts of the "equity of redemption" or the right to redeem the mortgage debt after default at any time until foreclosure reflected the fact that equity regarded the mortgagor as the "owner" of the mortgaged land. What remains of this development is the notion that from the time the mortgage is executed, the mortgagee obtains legal, although not equitable, title. As a consequence, *the mortgagee has the right to collect rents and profits until the mortgage debt is paid or foreclosure has occurred.* The theory is recognized in less than ten states and most of these are in the East and South.

Note, however, that title theory mortgagors are almost always unaware that the mortgagee has legal title. This is because mortgage forms routinely grant mortgagor the right to possession until a default occurs. Indeed, taking possession of the mortgaged premises is usually the farthest thing from the mortgagee's mind. On the other hand, once default occurs, the taking of possession to protect the property and collect rents and profits becomes an important pre-foreclosure mortgagee option.

2. The Lien Theory

At least forty American states take the position that the mortgagee acquires only a "lien" on the mortgaged premises and that both legal and equitable title remain in the mortgagor until a valid foreclosure takes place. The Restatement also adopts the lien theory. See Restatement (Third) of Property (Mortgages) § 4.1(a) (1997). Under the lien theory the mortgagor retains the right to possession and to the rents and profits until foreclosure. While many lien theory states protect the mortgagor's possessory rights zealously, some enforce mortgage language that confers the right to possession on the mortgagee if the mortgagor defaults. In view of the fact that most mortgagees control the language of the mortgage document, it is fair to say that these latter states are *de facto* title theory jurisdictions. However, under the Restatement, any agreement contemporaneous with the mortgage "which grants the mortgagee, as mortgagee, the right to possession in the future" is generally unenforceable. Restatement (Third) of Property (Mortgages) § 4.1(b).

3. The Intermediate Theory

Under this approach, in effect in a handful of jurisdictions, the lien theory is applied until default and the title theory thereafter. In other words, a mortgagee has the right to possession and to collect rents and profits after the mortgagor defaults. Since even title theory mortgagees rarely, if ever, reserve the right to take possession prior to default, there is little practical difference between the intermediate theory and the title theory.

4. The Mortgagee in Possession

Even in strict lien theory states, if the mortgagee is "let" into possession by the mortgagor or takes possession after the mortgagor abandons the premises or in good faith after purchasing at an invalid foreclosure sale, the mortgagee then becomes a "mortgagee in possession" and may remain in possession until the mortgage has either been satisfied or foreclosed. Stated another way, once a mortgagee so qualifies, a court will not put the mortgagor back into possession unless the mortgage debt has been paid. Nelson & Whitman, Real Estate Finance Law § 4.24 (4th ed.2001); Restatement (Third) of Property (Mortgages) § 4.1(c) (1997).

5. Duties of the Mortgagee in Possession

The status of a mortgagee in possession is a two-edged sword. The mortgagee is entitled to the rents and profits on the one hand, but on the other he or she is held to strict duties with respect to the management of the property. *Sometimes it is said that the mortgagee has the duty of a provident owner—to manage the property in a reasonably prudent and careful manner so as to keep it in a good state of preservation and to use the rent collected for no other purpose than to credit it to the debt.* More specifically, these important rights and responsibilities may be summarized as follows:

a. Rents

A mortgagee may either rent the mortgaged property or occupy it himself. Reasonable diligence must be used to keep the property rented and for a reasonable rental amount. The rents, less reasonable expenses, must be applied to the mortgage debt.

b. Maintenance and Repairs

The mortgagee is not only liable for destructive acts, he or she must make reasonable affirmative efforts to make necessary repairs. The mortgagee will be credited for such expenditures from the rents collected. Stated in financial terms, the duty to maintain and repair, however, is limited to the greater of the rents and profits the mortgagee actually receives or such rents as a reasonably prudent mortgagee should have collected. *In other words, the mortgagee has no obligation to be out of pocket to make repairs.*

c. Improvements

Normally a mortgagee in possession will not be permitted to make improvements to the mortgaged real estate. This rule is designed to protect the mortgagor. To permit such improvements would add to the mortgage debt and thus make it more difficult for the mortgagor to redeem.

d. Compensation for Services

There is substantial authority that even though a mortgagor would have been justified in hiring a third person for services or repairs, he cannot do the job himself and obtain compensation for doing so. Other jurisdictions, either by statute or judicial decision, allow the mortgagee a reasonable compensation for his services.

e. Liability for Tort

The mortgagee in possession is liable in tort for injuries to third persons arising through negligence in the use of the property or in failure to carry out duties normally imposed on the owner or possessor of real estate.

6. The Assignment of Rents Clause

A mortgagee commonly requires a mortgage provision or a separate agreement that "assigns" to the mortgagee the rents and profits to the mortgaged real estate as additional security for the mortgage obligation. In rare instances the assignment will give the mortgagee immediate access to the rents. In that event, the rents will supplement or substitute for annual or monthly installments on the mortgage obligation. In most cases, however, the mortgagee's right to collect the rents is triggered by mortgagor default. *Virtually all states, whether "title", "lien," or "intermediate", hold that such assignments are valid and enforceable. Moreover, rents from real estate are deemed to be realty and are governed by the law of real property security. See UCC § 9–104(j), providing that the Code is inapplicable "to the creation or transfer of an interest in or lien on real estate, including a lease or rents thereunder."*

a.   What Is Meant By "Valid and Enforceable"?

Once we say that assignments are "valid and enforceable", unanimity ends. Courts approach assignments in a variety of ways and are often hopelessly confused. To aid in understanding this area, we need to digress and focus on three preliminary issues. First, we need to determine when the assignment is effective to create a valid lien on the rents between the mortgagor and mortgagee. Next, we must ascertain when it is effective ("perfected") against third parties. Finally, we must determine when the mortgagee has the right to collect (enforce or foreclose upon) the rents and profits.

Sometimes a mortgagee will employ a so-called *"absolute assignment"* under which the mortgagee purports to acquire present ownership of the rents, but the clause defers the mortgagee's right to actually collect rents until the mortgagor defaults. If this strikes you as inherently contradictory, you are entirely correct. The use of "absolute assignment" language is unfortunate and creates needless confusion. Despite the broad language of the clause, we are obviously not dealing with an outright sale or transfer of the *substantive ownership* of the rents, but rather with *mortgaging* them as additional *security* for the loan. The parties will readily concede that once the loan is paid, the right to collect the rents ends. In other words, the "absoluteness" of the assignment is largely a fiction.

Nonetheless, some states recognize this form of assignment as giving significant advantages to the mortgagee. They hold that the assignment is effective between the parties upon execution and, as against third parties, upon recording. Moreover, once default occurs, they allow the mortgagee to take possession of the rents without taking any "affirmative action." Indeed, one court has stated that the "absolute assignment does not create a security interest but instead passes title to the rents. [It] is not security but a *pro tanto* payment of the obligation." *NCNB Texas National Bank v. Sterling Projects, Inc.*, 789 S.W.2d 358 (Tex.App.1990). See *In re Jason Realty, L.P.*, 59 F.3d 423 (3d Cir.1995).

The fictitious "absolute assignment" described above was developed by lawyers for mortgagees in response to decisions like that of the Texas Supreme Court in *Taylor v. Brennan*, 621 S.W.2d 592 (Tex.1981), holding that an ordinary (non-"absolute") assignment of rents is presumed to create only an inchoate security interest or pledge that is neither effective nor perfected "until the mortgagee obtains possession of the property, or impounds the rents, or secures the appointment of a receiver, or takes some similar action." This is also sometimes referred to as the "American common law" view. Here the mortgagee presumably has nothing until the requisite affirmative action takes place. Note, however, that in some of these "inchoate lien" states, the affirmative action required is sometimes nominal, such as mailing a notice to the mortgagor or making a demand for possession.

In a slight variation on the above "inchoate lien" approach, some courts hold an ordinary security assignment of rents may be effective upon execution, but that perfection requires not only recording, but some type of affirmative action (such as taking possession or obtaining the appointment of a receiver) as well.

Most jurisdictions follow a broad "middle ground" approach. They hold that a security assignment of rents is *effective* against the mortgagor upon execution and *perfected* against third parties by recording, but *enforcement* (collection of the rents) requires some additional *affirmative action*. Sometimes this latter requirement may be onerous. For example, the appointment of a receiver or the taking of possession of the real estate by the mortgagee may be required. In other jurisdictions, the affirmative action requirement is satisfied by such nominal acts as mailing notice to the mortgagor or simply *requesting* the appointment of a receiver.

The Restatement takes a middle ground approach to security interests in rents. A mortgage (that is, a security assignment) on rents becomes effective against the mortgagor upon its execution and delivery to the mortgagee and is "perfected" against third parties when it is recorded or when the latter receive actual notice of it. The mortgagee normally may commence collection of the rents upon default simply by delivering a demand to the mortgagor and others holding mortgages on the real estate. See Restatement (Third) of Property (Mortgages) § 4.2 (1997).

In sum, it is unfortunate that some states have made it so difficult to perfect an ordinary security assignment on rents, and doubly unfortunate that lenders' lawyers felt it necessary to develop the fictitious and confusing "absolute assignment, but with possession deferred until default," as described above, in an effort to overcome these difficulties.

Example: Debtor gives Bank takes a mortgage on Blackacre, commercial real estate, together with an assignment of rents. Both the mortgage and assignment are recorded. Thereafter,

Creditor obtains a judgment against Debtor. Creditor records the judgment in the county where Blackacre is located (or takes whatever steps are required to make the judgment a lien on Blackacre). Bank and Creditor each claim a senior lien on the rents. (*Result:* If Blackacre is in a jurisdiction that follows the "inchoate lien" or "American common law" approach, Creditor's judgment lien is senior to Bank's assignment. This is because the assignment is not perfected upon recording but only after the requisite "affirmative action" takes place. If Blackacre is in a jurisdiction that follows the Restatement or "middle ground" approach, the Bank's assignment is senior to Creditor's judgment lien on the rents. See *In the Matter of Millette*, 186 F.3d 638 (5th Cir.1999).

b. Consistency With the Lien Theory

The enforcement of an assignment of rents clause to some extent conflicts with the philosophy of the lien theory of mortgages. That theory stresses that the mortgagor normally has the right to possession, and therefore the right to rents and profits, until there has been a valid foreclosure. To enforce the assignment clause, in effect, allows the mortgagor to waive in advance the major benefit of the lien theory. Of course, to the extent that a lien jurisdiction permits the mortgagor, in the mortgage or contemporaneously therewith, to give the mortgagee the right to possession on mortgagor default, it would seem to follow automatically that such a jurisdiction would enforce an assignment of rents clause.

c. Enforcement Not a Clog on the Equity of Redemption

The enforcement of an assignment of rents clause does not violate the prohibition on "clogging." Even though such an agreement is usually contained in the mortgage or in a document executed contemporaneously therewith, it is not an invalid clog because even after the assignment is enforced, the mortgagor has the right to redeem the debt at any time until a valid foreclosure has taken place.

d. Reasons for Use

The clause is used for several reasons. First, it enhances the mortgagee's security position by allowing it to reach the rents and profits without actually incurring many of the responsibilities that we saw were incident to being a mortgagee in possession. Second, as we shall see in the following material, the presence of the clause may enhance the mortgagee's ability to have a receiver appointed. Finally, an assignment of rents clause may give the mortgagee an enhanced claim to rents vis á vis the mortgagor's subsequent creditors or trustee in bankruptcy.

B. The Appointment of a Receiver

An equitable receivership entails the judicial appointment of a third person to go into possession of the mortgaged property to preserve it and to collect rents.

1. Reasons for Use

Mortgagees usually prefer the appointment of a receiver to taking possession themselves. While a title theory mortgagee has the right to take possession on default, the mortgagee in possession, as we have just seen, incurs relatively strict and undesirable accounting responsibilities and other obligations incident to being a possessor of real estate. Lien theory mortgagees view the receivership as an even more important remedy because of the doctrinal roadblocks to mortgagee possession found in lien theory jurisdictions. Finally, mortgagees, whether in a title or lien state, may prefer a receivership to enforcement of an assignment of rents provision. The latter remedy is, after all, of little value if the mortgaged property is vacant or only partially rented. A receiver can take possession, find new tenants, and attempt to reestablish a cash flow from the real estate.

2. Standard for Appointment

Generally the standard for the appointment of a receiver varies little as among title, lien or intermediate theory states. Normally, the mortgagee must show that the security is inadequate and the establishment of some "distinct equitable ground, such as danger of loss, waste, destruction or serious impairment of the property to warrant the appointment of a receiver." Grether v. Nick, 213 N.W. 304, 306 (Wis.1927). In addition, some courts require that the mortgagor be insolvent. See Mutual Benefit Life Insurance Co. v. Frantz Klodt & Son, Inc., 237 N.W.2d 350 (Minn.1975). Note that the above standard is highly manipulable. In some jurisdictions, for example, waste means affirmative physical destruction of the mortgaged real estate, while in others the failure to pay taxes could constitute waste. See American Medical Services, Inc. v. Mutual Federal Savings & Loan Association, 188 N.W.2d 529 (Wis.1971).

Under the Restatement, a mortgagee is entitled to a receivership if *(1) the mortgage is in default; (2) the security is inadequate; and (3) the mortgagor is committing waste.* Restatement (Third) of Property (Mortgages) § 4.3(a). Waste is defined broadly to include not only physical destruction and the failure to repair, but also the failure to pay taxes or to comply with a wide variety of mortgage covenants.

In theory, it would seem that a receiver should be more easily obtained in a title than in a lien jurisdiction because, after all, since the mortgagee can utilize ejectment to get possession for him or herself, it would seem to follow *a fortiori* that an independent third party receiver would be appointed rather easily. Interestingly, however, the judicial standard for appointment differs little, if at all, as between title and lien jurisdictions. Indeed, in a few title jurisdictions, the mortgagee's right of possession may actually be a roadblock to the appointment of a receiver because a court may view the mortgagee's right to obtain possession as an adequate remedy at law.

Example 1: Bank had a senior mortgage on Blackacre, an apartment building, with a balance of $200,000. Mortgagor ceased making mortgage payments on principal or interest and was insolvent. Mortgagor also diverted the rents from the mortgaged property for various other personal and business uses. The fair market value of the mortgaged real estate was $300,000. Bank requested the appointment of a receiver. (*Result:* receivership denied. Insolvency of the mortgagor and diversion of the rents above are an insufficient basis for appointment. Here the value of the real estate exceeded the mortgage debt by $100,000 and there was no proof of some "distinct equitable ground," such as waste or failure to pay taxes.) See *Dart v. Western Savings & Loan Association,* 438 P.2d 407 (Ariz.1968).

Example 2: Same facts as above, except that the value of Blackacre was $205,000 and the mortgagor failed to repair a badly deteriorated roof. (*Result:* A receiver would probably be appointed because the security was close to being impaired and waste was arguably being committed.)

3. Impact of Other Factors on Appointment

a. Receivership and Assignment of Rents Clauses

In many jurisdictions, neither the presence of a mortgage clause authorizing the appointment of receiver upon default nor an assignment of rents clause enhance the chances of appointment. As Professor Glenn said, "no such contract provision should force a court of equity to exercise its discretion in favor of a party who stands in no need of aid. . . . If the security is plainly adequate a receiver will not be appointed, despite the presence in the mortgage of a rent pledge or receivership clause or both." 2 Glenn, Mortgages, § 175.1.

On the other hand, the clauses may sometimes be considered a relevant factor, favorably influencing a court to appoint a receiver. In some jurisdictions these provisions can be crucial. For example, while in California, in the absence of such clauses a receiver will not be appointed unless "the property is probably insufficient to discharge the mortgage debt," the presence of either of such clauses establishes, upon mortgagor's default, a "rebuttable, evidentiary, showing of the [mortgagee's] entitlement to appointment of a receiver." *Barclays Bank of California v. Superior Court*, 137 Cal.Rptr. 743 (Cal.App.1977).

Under the Restatement, the clauses are extremely useful to the mortgagee. If the mortgage documents contain either an assignment of rents or a receivership clause, the only requirement for the appointment of a receiver is that the mortgage be in default. Restatement (Third) of Property (Mortgages) § 4.3(b) (1997).

b. Statutory Provisions

Some states by statute provide for the appointment of a receiver as a matter of right where the mortgage contains a receivership clause. See McKinney's N.Y. Real Prop.Law § 254(10). Others tie the appointment to the existence of a rents and profits clause. Minnesota statutes provide, for example, with respect to certain mortgage loans that "if by the terms of an assignment, a receiver is to be appointed upon the occurrence of some specified event, and a showing is made that the event has occurred, the court shall, without regard to waste, adequacy of the security, or solvency of the mortgagor appoint a receiver. . . . " Minn.Stat.Ann. § 559.17(2)(a).

4. Ex Parte Receiverships

Several jurisdictions appoint receivers by *ex parte* order. This entails the appointment of a receiver, usually pending a judicial foreclosure, without affording notice or an opportunity for a hearing to the mortgagor or other interested parties. Several courts have considered the problem of whether this practice is constitutional in light of the requirements of *Fuentes v. Shevin*, 407 U.S. 67 (1972) and its progeny. In *Fuentes*, the United States Supreme Court invalidated certain state replevin statutes on 14th Amendment procedural due process grounds because they did not provide for an opportunity to be heard before chattels were taken from the possessor, even on a temporary basis, pending a trial on the merits. In an *ex parte* receivership, the mortgagor can lose both possession of the mortgaged real estate and the ability to collect its rents with *no* prior notice or an opportunity to be heard.

Thus far, courts have upheld ex parte receiverships against a procedural due process attack by applying one of two theories: First, the practice is constitutional because the ex parte appointment is under judicial supervision and the mortgagor has a right to a hearing on the probable validity of the underlying claim immediately after the appointment. Second, even assuming the unconstitutionality of such a practice, where the mortgage provides for the appointment of a receiver, "without notice and hearing," there is a valid waiver of the mortgagor's due process rights. See *Friedman v. Gerax Realty Associates*, 420 N.Y.S.2d 247 (N.Y.Sup.Ct.1979) and *Manufacturers Life Ins. Co. v. Patterson*, 554 N.E.2d 134 (Ohio App.1988).

We will consider these procedural due process and waiver problems further in Chapter IX *infra* in connection under power of sale real estate foreclosure.

C. Waste

The doctrine of waste is designed to protect the value of the real estate security from harm due to the mortgagor's acts or failures to act. See Restatement (Third) of Property (Mortgages) § 4.6.; Leipziger, The Mortgagee's Remedies for Waste, 64 Cal.L.Rev. 1086 (1976). Waste is in the nature of a tort, and thus does not depend on the presence of mortgage language prohibiting waste. Historically, waste occurred only when the land or improvements were physically damaged. In modern American law, however, a variety of other acts or failures by the mortgagor can also constitute waste. The mortgagee's remedies for waste include damages, injunctions, and foreclosure of the mortgage. As noted in Section B supra, a showing of waste may also assist the mortgagee in obtaining appointment of a receiver. Parties other than the mortgagor who damage the real estate security can be held liable for waste, but the mortgagee's range of remedies against them is more limited.

1. What Constitutes Waste?
The following are typically regarded as acts of waste.

(1) *Physical damage to the real estate security*, including such acts as demolishing valuable improvements and removing fixtures, unless the mortgagor replaces them with items of equal or greater value. Removal of timber may be considered waste if it is not consistent with "good husbandry."

(2) *Failure of the mortgagor to make reasonably necessary repairs* on the property. See *Prudential Insurance Co. v. Spencer's Kenosha Bowl, Inc.*, 404 N.W.2d 109 (Wis.App.1987)(However, if the repairs are required by a catastrophic

natural occurrence, such as an earthquake, hurricane, or the like, the courts generally do not require the mortgagor to repair. See *Krone v. Goff*, 127 Cal.Rptr. 390 (Cal.Ct.App.1975)). Most courts would take the same view if the damage were caused by a third party without the mortgagor's fault.

(3) *Failure of the mortgagor to pay property taxes.* Such taxes are a prior lien on the real estate, and thus failure to pay puts the mortgage lien at risk in a tax foreclosure action. *Travelers Ins. Co. v. 633 Third Associates*, 14 F.3d 114 (2d Cir.1994) ("from the secured creditor's vantage point, a tax lien on the secured property may be as costly as a leaky roof"). However, a substantial minority of cases hold that failure to pay taxes is not waste; see *Chetek State Bank v. Barberg*, 489 N.W.2d 385 (Wis.App.1992).

(4) *Failure of the mortgagor to comply with mortgage covenants dealing with the physical condition of the premises.* These might include promises to construct improvements, to insure the property against casualty loss, or to demolish undesirable structures. In essence such covenants are contractual extensions of the common-law waste concept.

(5) *Failure of the mortgagor to remit rents to the mortgagee, when a valid mortgage on the rents has been enforced.* The enforcement of mortgages on the rents is discussed in Chapter V(A)(6). The mortgagor who withholds rents when the mortgagee is entitled to them is liable for "waste of rents." See *Taylor v. Brennan*, 621 S.W.2d 592 (Tex.1981).

The cases of waste listed above are illustrative, but courts may be flexible in finding waste in other instances in which the mortgagor's acts have harmed the property's value. See, e.g., *Duncan v. First American Title Co.*, 648 F.Supp. 296 (D.Nev.1986), in which the land's value was largely dependent on the existence of certain federal grazing permits. The mortgagor repeatedly violated Bureau of Land Managements regulations, causing the government to cancel the permits. The court held the mortgagor liable for waste.

However, *the courts have generally been unwilling to hold that failure of the mortgagor to keep prior liens current is waste.* Such a holding would be logical, since failure to pay a prior mortgage debt, for example, is just as apt to cause loss to a junior mortgage as is failure to pay property taxes. But the case law does not yet extend this far.

2. Remedies for Waste

Three remedies are traditionally available to the mortgagee for waste: *damages, an injunction, and foreclosure* of the mortgage. Of course, foreclosure merely for waste alone is quite rare; but if a foreclosure occurs on account of other defaults and the proceeds are insufficient to fully satisfy the mortgage obligation, it is clear that the mortgagee can also recover directly from the mortgagor the amount of the waste. Foreclosure is not available if the waste was caused by a third party rather than the mortgagor. Even when the mortgagor commits the waste, recovery is limited by the three following important principles.

a.   Loan balance

The mortgagee may never recover more than the owed balance owed on the mortgage debt, no matter how severe the waste. The reason is that full payment of the debt is the only purpose of holding the security. Moreover, *all recoveries for waste must be applied on the mortgage debt*.

b.   Amount of waste

The actual harm or damage suffered by the real estate forms a ceiling on the amount of waste recovery. In the case of physical harm, the damage may be measured either by the reduction of market value that results, or by the cost of repair. *Bell v. First Columbus Nat'l Bank*, 493 So.2d 964, 970 (Miss.1986) (mortgagee may have its choice of these measures of damage unless mortgagor can show that one of them would cause unjust enrichment).

c.   Impairment of security.

All lien-theory states, and some title-theory states, agree that the mortgagee's recovery of *damages for waste may not exceed the amount by which the security has been impaired.* Similarly, a mortgagee may not enjoin waste or foreclose on account of waste unless its security is impaired (or in the case of an injunction, impairment is threatened). Finally, an injunction may require the mortgagor to restore the property from waste only to the extent needed to prevent security impairment. However, there is widespread disagreement on how to determine whether, and to what extent, there has been impairment of security. Among the theories sometimes used are the following:

1)   Debt equivalency rule

This rule holds that there is no impairment of security unless the property's value is reduced below the balance owing on the mortgage debt. See *Payne v. Snyder*, 661 S.W.2d 134 (Tex.App.1983). Such an approach is very disadvantageous to mortgagees, since it allows them no margin of security.

2) **Reasonable margin of security rule**

Under this approach, the mortgagee may claim damages if the property's value has fallen so much that the mortgagee's margin of security is unreasonably low. See *Finley v. Chain*, 374 N.E.2d 67 (Ind.Ct.App.1978) (test: has the remaining debt been rendered "unsafe?") The difficulty is in determining what is unreasonable. The margin of security is usually stated in terms of the loan-to-value ratio, with a smaller ratio indicating a greater margin of security. Is 90% reasonable? 80%? The test is extremely imprecise.

3) **Original loan-to-value ratio rule**

Here the courts ask what was the loan-to-value ratio when the original loan was made, and then permit the collection of sufficient damages (applied toward the debt, of course) to restore the ratio to that same level. See *Duncan v. First American Title Co.*, 648 F.Supp. 296 (D.Nev.1986).

Example: Edwin makes a loan of $80,000 to Roberta, secured by a mortgage on Blackacre which has a value of $100,000. Hence, the original loan-to-value ratio is 80%. During the ensuing five years, regularly scheduled amortization payments reduce the loan balance to $70,000 while Blackacre's value increases to $120,000. Roberta then commits waste, reducing Blackacre's value by $40,000 to $80,000. Under the "original loan-to-value ratio," Edwin is entitled to a loan balance of 80% of $80,000, or $64,000. Hence, Edwin can recover $6,000 in damages for waste in order to bring the loan balance down from $70,000 to $64,000.

4) **Pre-waste loan-to-value ratio rule**

This approach takes the view that the mortgagee is entitled to a sufficient recovery to reduce the loan-to-value ratio to the same level as just prior to the waste.

Example: The facts are the same as in the previous example. The loan-to-value ratio prior to the waste was $70,000/$120,000, or 58.3%. Under this rule, Edwin is entitled to a loan balance of 58.3% of $80,000 (the post-waste value of the property), or $46,666. Hence Edwin can recover $33,334 in damages for waste in order to bring the loan balance down from $70,000 to $46,666.

This approach seems to give the mortgagee an excessive recovery, by in effect allowing the mortgagee to continue to benefit from the rise in property value that had occurred before the waste was committed.

5) Scheduled loan-to-value ratio rule

Under this approach, the mortgagee can recover enough damages to bring the loan-to-value ratio to the same level that would have existed if all payments on the loan had been made on time and if the property's value had not changed upward or downward since the time the mortgage loan was made. This approach is adopted by Restatement (Third) of Property (Mortgages) § 4.6, and is believed to be the fairest compromise between the interests of the mortgagor and mortgagee.

Example: The facts are the same as in the two previous examples. Under the "scheduled loan-to-value ratio" approach, Edwin's scheduled ratio was $70,000/$100,000, or 70%, at the time of the waste. Hence Edwin is entitled to recover in damages to give a loan balance of 70% of $80,000 (the post-waste value of the property), or $56,000. Hence Edwin can recover $14,000 in damages for waste in order to bring the loan balance down from $70,000 to $56,000.

6) No margin of security required if mortgage is foreclosed

The tests for impairment of security mentioned above all assume that the mortgage has not been foreclosed and will continue to exist. However, if a foreclosure has already occurred, or if the recovery for waste is being sought in a foreclosure proceeding, it is entirely unnecessary to give the mortgagee any "margin of security" recovery, since there will no longer be a security relationship. Hence, the mortgagee can recover only an amount that, when added to foreclosure recovery, will fully satisfy the mortgage debt. This recovery is limited, of course, to the actual damage resulting from the waste. See *Finley v. Chain*, 374 N.E.2d 67 (Ind.Ct.App.1978).

Example: The facts are the same as in the three previous examples. Edwin forecloses the mortgage, and the high bid at the foreclosure sale is $80,000. This is more than sufficient to pay Edwin's $70,000 debt in full, so Edwin can recover nothing in addition for waste. See Cornelison v. Kornbluth, 542 P.2d 981 (Cal.1975). If the high bid at the sale had been lower (say, $60,000), Edwin could recover $20,000 for Roberta's waste, thus fully discharging the debt owed to Edwin.

d. Waste liability in the absence of liability on the mortgage debt

A mortgage may contain a "non-recourse" clause exempting the mortgagor from personal liability on the mortgage debt. Whether such a clause also excludes liability for waste depends on the wording and construction of the clause. See *United States v. Haddon Haciendas Co.*, 541 F.2d 777 (9th Cir.1976) (clause prohibiting a deficiency judgment did not prohibit recovery for waste). The California courts have held that the antideficiency statute also bars recovery of damages for waste unless it was committed in "bad faith." *Cornelison v. Kornbluth*, 542 P.2d 981 (Cal.1975). However, no other courts have adopted this view.

3. Waste by Successors of the Mortgagor

Successor owners of the mortgaged real estate may be held liable for waste even if they did not assume the mortgage debt and have no personal liability on it. See *Prudential Ins. Co. v. Spencer's Kenosha Bowl, Inc.*, 404 N.W.2d 109 (Wis.App.1987). Thus waste recovery may be available to the mortgagee even if a deficiency judgment is not. However, leasehold tenants and persons taking nonpossessory interests in the real estate (easements, covenants, and the like) are exempt from waste liability unless they actually cause physical damage to the real estate.

4. Waste by Persons With No Interest in the Real Estate

When waste is committed by a third party who has no interest in the real estate, the third party may be held liable for damages or subjected to an injunction. *McCorristin v. Salmon Signs*, 582 A.2d 1271 (N.J.Super.1990). However, unless the mortgagor authorized the waste, he or she is not personally liable for it and (as noted earlier) cannot be subjected to foreclosure on its account. The following additional limitations also apply.

a. No liability absent notice of mortgage.

A third party who commits waste is liable only if he or she had notice of the existence of the mortgage on the real estate. Third parties are often hired by mortgagors to do demolition work on land, and the cases are divided as to whether they are bound by constructive notice of the mortgage from the fact that it is recorded. The better view is that they cannot reasonably be put to the burden of examining the title before commencing work. Contra, see *U.S. Financial v. Sullivan*, 112 Cal.Rptr. 18 (Cal.Ct.App.1974), holding the contractor to constructive notice. The mortgagor who hires such work done may be liable for waste irrespective of the third party contractor's notice.

b. Impairment of security test not applicable.

When a waste action is brought by the mortgagee against a third party, *there is no requirement of a showing that security has been impaired*, and the third party is liable for the full extent of the waste (limited, of course, to discharge of the mortgage debt balance).

D. Mortgagee Liability for Environmental Contamination

A mortgagee is not ordinarily responsible to third parties, private or governmental, for the physical condition of the mortgaged premises or for injuries that occur on it. Only by becoming a mortgagee in possession or by acquiring title through foreclosure or a deed in lieu of foreclosure does the mortgagee assume the normal responsibilities of ownership. However, the enactment by Congress in 1980 of the Comprehensive Environmental Response, Compensation, and Liability Act ("CERCLA") and similar state statutes significantly increased the potential for mortgagee liability. See 42 U.S.C.A. § 9601 et seq.

1. An Overview of CERCLA

CERCLA confers broad authority on the Environmental Protection Agency ("EPA") either to order responsible parties to clean up a hazardous waste site or to do it itself and charge those parties for its costs. If EPA chooses the latter option, "it may recover its response costs from any one or more of the persons enumerated in * * * the Act, including: (1) the current *'owner and operator'* of the waste site; (2) any person who owned or operated the waste site when any hazardous dumping occurred; (3) the hazardous waste generators; and (4) the hazardous waste transporters." Burkhart, Lender/Owners and CERCLA: Title and Liability, 25 Harv.J.Legis. 318, 327 (1988).

A *strict liability* standard generally applies to responsible parties under CERCLA. Consequently, there is no need to prove that a defendant was negligent, at fault, or even had knowledge of the presence or dangers of the hazardous substances. This liability is *joint and several*. Thus all responsible parties are equally liable and any one may be forced to pay the entire liability unless that defendant can prove that the damage is divisible and that there is a reasonable basis for apportioning liability.

2. The Mortgagee and CERCLA

Why should a mortgagee be concerned about CERCLA? Indeed, mortgagees appear to be exempt from liability because CERCLA excludes from the definition of "owner and operator" a "person, who, without participating in the management of a * * * facility, holds indicia of ownership primarily to protect his security interest in the * * * facility." However, this exemption has proven to be much more apparent than real for mortgagees. At least two important questions confront mortgagees. *First,* when does pre-foreclosure oversight of a mortgagor's operations represent impermissible "participation in management"? *Second,* when mortgagees acquire ownership through foreclosure or a deed in lieu, do they continue to enjoy the "security interest" exemption, or will they now be treated as "owners" of the premises? Pre–1995 judicial responses to these questions were hardly reassuring for the mortgage lending community.

a. Participation in Management

In *United States v. Fleet Factors Corp.,* 901 F.2d 1550, 1557 (11th Cir.1990), a controversial federal appellate opinion, the court stated that a "secured creditor may incur * * * liability * * * by participating in the financial management of a facility to a degree indicating a capacity to influence the corporation's treatment of hazardous wastes. It is not necessary for the secured creditor actually to involve itself in the day-to-day operations of the facility in order to be liable—although such conduct will certainly lead to the loss of the statutory exemption. Nor is it necessary for the secured creditor to participate in management decisions related to hazardous waste. Rather, a secured creditor will be liable if its involvement with the management of the facility is sufficiently broad to support the inference that it could affect hazardous waste disposal decisions if it so chose."

This language from the *Fleet Factors* decision was extremely worrisome for mortgagees. They were concerned that a mortgagee who had unexercised "capacity to influence" a mortgagor's environmental management could lose the CERCLA "security interest" exemption.

b. Acquiring Title by Foreclosure or Deed in Lieu

Once a mortgagee acquires ownership of the premises at a foreclosure sale or through a deed in lieu, does it lose the benefit of the "security interest" exemption? In *United States v. Maryland Bank & Trust Co.,* 632 F.Supp. 573 (D.Md.1986), the federal district court held that a mortgagee loses the exemption through purchase at a foreclosure sale. According to the court, the purpose of the security exemption was to protect mortgagees in those states that follow the "title" theory of mortgages under which, as we noted earlier in this Chapter, the mortgagee holds legal title from the date the mortgage is executed until the obligation is satisfied by payment or foreclosure. While there was authority contrary to the *Maryland Bank* case, mortgagees were fearful that taking title to contaminated property through foreclosure or a deed in lieu exposed them to potentially huge CERCLA liability. Faced with this potential for liability, mortgagees often simply refused to foreclose or otherwise acquire mortgaged real estate where contamination was an actual or potential problem.

3. The 1992 EPA Lender Liability Regulation

Largely in response to the foregoing concerns, the EPA in 1992 promulgated a regulation interpreting the CERCLA security interest exemption. See 40 CFR §§ 300.1100, 300.1105. This regulation appeared to allay most mortgagee misgivings about CERCLA. First, it provided broad protection for mortgagees in the pre-foreclosure stage. All pre-loan activities of the mortgagee were deemed irrelevant to liability unless the liability was predicated on some other ground than the loan (such as the mortgagee's being a prior owner, a generator or a transporter). Even *actual knowledge* by the mortgagee of contamination at the time of making the loan would not make the mortgagee liable. After the loan is closed, the mortgagee would trigger liability only by engaging in "actual participation in management" of the facility. The *Fleet Factors* dictum that unused power could be characterized as "participation in management" was rejected. Instead the regulation provided that "participation in management" meant only (1) decision-making control over the mortgagor's environmental compliance; or (2) overall control of the facility at a level comparable to that of a manager of the enterprise, encompassing day-to-day control of either environmental compliance or substantially all the operational aspects other than environmental compliance. Moreover, a large number of post-mortgage acts to protect security were insulated from liability by the regulation. After default, most *workout practices,* including exercising remedies under the mortgagor's warranties, covenants or representations, restructuring the loan, or exercising an assignment of rents, were protected.

Most important, *the regulation extended the security interest exemption to protect the mortgagee after it acquired ownership, whether by foreclosure or deed in lieu.* Acquisition of title would not make the mortgagee liable so long as it attempted to sell or divest itself of the property in a reasonably expeditious manner. The regulation created a *"safe harbor"* which *per se* protected the mortgagee if it either listed the property for sale within 12 months of acquisition or began advertising of the property within such a period. However, a mortgagee would lose the exemption if, within 6 months after foreclosure, it rejected or did not act within 90 days on a written *bona fide* offer of a fair price for the property. Moreover, if the mortgagee took the necessary steps to dispose of the property, it could *"maintain business activities"* or otherwise operate the property without CERCLA liability so long as it did not cause further contamination.

However, the foregoing attempt to protect mortgagees from CERCLA liability came to naught when in *Kelley v. EPA*, 15 F.3d 1100 (D.C.Cir.1994), the United States Court of Appeals for the District of Columbia held that the EPA exceeded its authority in promulgating the Regulation.

4. 1996 Congressional Amendments to CERCLA

Lenders finally obtained their desired protection from CERCLA liability when Congress enacted the Asset Conservation, Lender Liability, and Deposit Insurance Protection Act of 1996 (the "1996 Statute"). The 1996 Statute largely codifies the Regulation. Indeed, the 1996 Statute expressly provides that the Regulation shall be deemed to have been validly issued and effective. See 1996 Statute § 2504(b),(d). The following is a summary of the impact of the Regulation and the 1996 Statute on mortgagees:

a. Pre–Loan Activities

A mortgagee may engage in a wide variety of "due diligence" actions and other pre-loan activities, including:

- negotiating loan terms

- requiring and conducting environmental inspections

- requiring post-inspection cleanups

- requiring compliance with applicable law

- requiring representations, warranties, covenants and other promises.

Most importantly, *a mortgagee may knowingly make loans secured by contaminated real estate.*

b. Post–Closing Activities

A mortgagee may monitor the loan and mortgagor's activities closely, including the following acts:

- monitoring and inspecting the real estate

- requiring post-closing cleanup

- monitoring mortgagor's business

- reviewing mortgagor's financial statements

- requiring compliance with applicable law

- providing financial or other advice or counseling

- otherwise monitoring and enforcing the terms and conditions of the loan

On the other hand, mortgagee still *must not "participate in management."* However, this means "actually participating in the management or operational affairs of a * * * facility; and does not include merely having the capacity to influence, or the unexercised right to control * * * facility operations." Moreover, a mortgagee will be deemed to "participate in management" *only if it:*

1) exercises decision-making control over the environmental compliance related to the * * * facility, such that the [mortgagee] has undertaken responsibility for the hazardous substance handling or disposal practices related to the vessel or facility; or

2) exercises control at a level comparable to that of a manager of the * * * facility, such that the [mortgagee] has assumed or manifested responsibility—

   - for the overall management of the * * * facility encompassing day-to-day decision-making with respect to environmental compliance; or

   - over all or substantially all of the operational functions (as distinguished from financial or administrative functions) of the * * * facility other than the function of environmental compliance.

c. Post–Default Activities and Acquisition of Title

Once the loan goes into default, mortgagee may engage in a wide variety of "work-out" activities without being considered to "participate in management." These include:

- renegotiating and restructuring loan terms

- extending payment and engaging in other acts of forbearance

- providing advice, counseling or guidance in administrative or financial matters.

Most important, the 1996 Statute makes it clear that *a mortgagee may take title to the real estate by foreclosure or a deed in lieu without becoming an "owner and operator" subject to CERCLA liability. This protection applies after acquisition of title so long as the mortgagee "seeks to sell * * * the facility at the earliest practicable, commercially reasonable time, on commercially reasonable terms."* 1996 Statute § 2502(b), codified at 42 U.S.C.A. § 9601 (20)(E)(ii).

Recall that the 1992 regulation provided a much more specific *"safe harbor"* for mortgagees who took title through a deed in lieu or foreclosure. However, since the 1996 Statute ratified the Regulation, the mortgagee apparently will be able to claim the benefit of the "safe harbor" provision of the regulation as well as the more general "commercially reasonable" statutory standard.

Finally, as noted earlier in connection with the regulation, while a mortgagee is taking the necessary steps to dispose of the property, it may "maintain business activities" and otherwise operate the facility so long as it does not cause further contamination.

E.   Insurance Proceeds and Real Estate Taxes

Mortgagees nearly always require mortgagors to carry casualty insurance on the mortgaged premises for obvious reasons; in the event of a casualty loss, the insurance proceeds serve as substitute security for the real estate, which might lose enough value as a result of the casualty to become inadequate security. *General Star Indem. Co. v. Pike County Nat'l Bank*, 706 So.2d 227 (Miss.1997). Because the insurance proceeds are regarded as a replacement for the property and not a replacement of the debtor, the mortgagee will be entitled to claim the insurance proceeds even if the mortgage debt was "non-recourse" and imposed no personal liability. *San Roman v. Atlantic Mutual Insurance Co.*, 672 N.Y.S.2d 396 (N.Y.App.Div.1998). Of course, the amount of the mortgage debt always imposes a ceiling on the mortgagee's recovery, even if the insurance proceeds are larger in amount; if there are no junior liens, the mortgagor is entitled to the excess proceeds. *Bank of Richmondville v. Terra Nova Ins. Co.*, 694 N.Y.S.2d 206 (N.Y.App.Div.1999).

The "substitute security" principle will be applied only if the mortgage (or other loan documents) require the mortgagor to carry the insurance. Restatement

(Third) of Property (Mortgages) § 4.7 (1997). Hence, if the mortgagor voluntarily purchased insurance coverage that was not required by the lender, the lender will have no claim to the proceeds. *Foothill Village Homeowners Association v. Bishop*, 81 Cal.Rptr.2d 195 (Cal.App.1999). But if the mortgage requires the mortgagor to carry the insurance, and the mortgagor simply fails to include the lender's name as an insured on the policy, the lender will nonetheless be permitted to assert its claim on the insurance proceeds. *Castle Ins. Co. v. Vanover*, 993 S.W.2d 509 (Ky.App.1999).

Insurance policies on mortgaged property usually specifically insure both parties, "as their interests may appear." Two types of such policies are the "loss payable policy" (also known as the "open" policy) and the "standard mortgage policy." See generally Nelson & Whitman, Real Estate Finance Law § 4.14 (4th ed.2001).

1. The Loss Payable Policy

This type of policy, which is almost never used today, is issued to the mortgagor with language providing that the loss be payable to the mortgagor and to the mortgagee as their interests may appear. The mortgagee is a mere appointee of the mortgagor to receive payment, and its right to recover is completely dependent on the right of the mortgagor. Thus, if a mortgagor breached a condition that would bar mortgagor recovery, the mortgagee's recovery would be barred as well.

Example: Mortgagor and mortgagee are covered by a loss payable type policy on Blackacre on which mortgagee has a $50,000 mortgage. Mortgagor stores gasoline and other hazardous chemicals on the insured property in violation of a policy provision prohibiting such storage. A fire caused by such storage destroys the building, leaving a lot worth $10,000. (*Result:* mortgagee will not be able to collect from the insurance policy, since mortgagor is barred from recovery because he or she violated the above policy provision.)

2. The Standard Mortgage Policy

This type of policy not only insures the mortgagee, but also provides that the coverage "shall not be invalidated by any act or neglect of the mortgagor or owner of the within described property, nor by any change in title or ownership of the property, nor by the occupation of the premises for purposes more hazardous than are permitted by this policy." The effect of this policy is to insure the mortgagee as completely as if he or she had taken out a separate policy directly from the insurer, free from the conditions that restrict the mortgagor.

Example: Same facts as in last example except that a Standard Mortgage policy is in effect. (*Result:* the mortgagee will be covered by the policy, since the mortgagee's rights are not dependent on those of the mortgagor. Thus, the mortgagor's violation of the policy terms will not bar recovery by the mortgagee.)

3. Impairment of Security as a Limitation on the Mortgagee's Recovery

If the conditions outlined above for recovery of insurance proceeds by the mortgagee are satisfied, title theory states usually allow the mortgagee to recover the full amount of the proceeds provided, of course, that they do not exceed the amount of the mortgage debt. *However, in lien theory states, the mortgagee's recovery is limited to the amount that the casualty has impaired the security.* This is the same test applied by the courts in cases of recovery for waste.

Unfortunately, there is little consensus in the lien theory case law about how to measure impairment of security. A number of cases have held that security is impaired only if the property is now worth less than the mortgage debt. *Ginsberg v. Lennar Florida Holdings, Inc.*, 645 So.2d 490 (Fla.App.1994). This is manifestly unfair to the mortgagee, since it may have the effect of increasing the loan-to-value ratio to virtually 100%, despite the fact that the mortgagee originally bargained for a much lower (and less risky) loan-to-value ratio. Alternatively, some cases allow a sufficient recovery to restore the loan-to-value ratio to a "reasonable" level; see *Stevensen v. Goodson*, 924 P.2d 339 (Utah 1996) (no recovery if debt is "adequately secured"); others require restoration of the loan-to-value level that existed when the loan was made, or at the time of the loss; see *First Western Fin. Corp. v. Vegas Continental*, 692 P.2d 1279 (Nev.1984).

The Restatement takes the same view of impairment of security when a lender claims insurance proceeds as when a lender claims recovery for waste: that the recovery should be sufficient to return the lender's loan-to-value ratio to the level it was scheduled to have at the time the casualty occurred. Restatement (Third) of Property (Mortgages) §§ 4.6(c); 4.7(a) (1997). This is believed to be the fairest method of determining inadequacy of security. See the illustrations in the section of this Chapter dealing with waste on pp. 255–256 supra.

4. Restoration of the Premises

Today most commonly used mortgage forms specifically provide for the disposition of the insurance proceeds after a casualty loss. For example, the pervasively-used Fannie Mae–Freddie Mac mortgage and deed of trust form for 1–to–4–family homes provides that "insurance proceeds shall be applied to restoration or repair of the property damaged, if the restoration or repair is economically feasible and Lender's security is not lessened. If the restoration or repair is not economically feasible or Lender's security would be lessened, the insurance proceeds shall be applied to the sum secured by this Security Instrument with any excess paid to the Borrower."

However, suppose the mortgage requires the borrower to carry insurance, but contains no specific language governing the distribution of the proceeds. What is the is the default rule? Under the traditional and majority view, the mortgagor has no right to insist that insurance proceeds be used for restoration of the property. Thus, the mortgagee will be permitted to apply the proceeds toward either restoration or prepayment of the mortgage debt, at the mortgagee's option. See, e.g., *General G.M.C. Sales, Inc. v. Passarella*, 481 A.2d 307 (N.J.Super.1984); *English v. Fischer*, 660 S.W.2d 521 (Tex.1983); Randolph, A Mortgagee's Interest in Casualty Loss Proceeds: Evolving Rules and Risks, 32 Real Prop. Prob. & Tr.J 1 (1997). The mortgagee's right to apply the proceeds toward the debt is not conditioned on a showing that application of the proceeds to restoration would impair the mortgage security. Indeed, the mortgagee prevails even though the value of the property remaining after the casualty is greater than the mortgage debt. This view is supported by the following argument:

> There may be cases in which the mortgagee will be adequately protected by a holding that allows the mortgagor to use the fire insurance proceeds to rebuild. But there will be times when the mortgagee will be placed at risk by having his mortgage on an existing building converted to a construction mortgage for a new building. [This] creates too much potential for dispute and litigation. * * * The parties could dispute the value of the security after a fire, especially if the property is not insured at full market value. Disagreement could also arise as to the value of the repairs or the replacement structure, the amount of progress payments, and other matters. * * * [T]he mortgagee should not be forced into partnership with the mortgagor in rebuilding the structure, and the mortgage loan should not be converted into a construction loan.

General G.M.C. Sales, Inc. v. Passarella, 481 A.2d 307 (N.J.Super.1984).

a.   Criticism of the Majority Approach

There is a strong argument that if rebuilding would restore the mortgaged premises to their pre-casualty condition, the mortgagee's security would not be impaired and the proceeds should be made available for rebuilding purposes if the mortgagor so desires. In other words, the mortgagee would be getting exactly what was bargained for—a fully secured mortgage transaction. To be sure, to permit the mortgagor to opt for rebuilding may well force the mortgagee to litigate the extent and sufficiency of the repairs. On the other hand, it is the *mortgagor* who has paid the insurance premiums. Moreover, while permitting the mortgagee to utilize the insurance proceeds to pay the mortgage debt, strictly speaking, benefits the mortgagor by removing or diminishing the mortgage lien from the real estate, often the mortgagor will not be able to obtain outside financing sufficient to rebuild the premises. For a decision rejecting the majority approach and adopting the foregoing reasoning when the mortgage was silent on the point, see *Starkman v. Sigmond*, 446 A.2d 1249 (N.J.Super.1982).

b. California Approach

Only one decision, a California case, has endorsed the presumption in favor of using the insurance proceeds to rebuild *even where the mortgage specifically gave the mortgagee the option to rebuild or to have the debt prepaid.* There the Court of Appeals held that "the right of a [mortgagee] to apply insurance proceeds to the balance of a [mortgage debt] must be performed in good faith and with fair dealing and that to the extent that the security *is not impaired the [mortgagee] must permit* those proceeds to be used for the cost of remodeling." *Schoolcraft v. Ross*, 146 Cal.Rptr. 57 (Cal.App.1978).

c. The Restatement Approach

The Restatement adopts the minority approach described in *Starkman v. Sigmond*, supra, in situations where the mortgage makes no provision for the application of the insurance proceeds. Thus, "if restoration of the loss or damage * * * is reasonably feasible within the remaining term of the mortgage with the funds received by the mortgagee, together with any additional funds made available by the mortgagor, and if after restoration the real estate's value will equal or exceed its value at the time the mortgage was made, the mortgagee holds the funds received subject to a duty to apply them, at the mortgagor's request and upon reasonable conditions, toward restoration." Restatement (Third) of Property (Mortgages) § 4.7(b) (1997).

How does the Restatement deal with a mortgage provision that specifically gives the mortgagee the option to permit rebuilding or to require prepayment? According to the commentary to § 4.7, "[w]hile such a provision may be enforced, it may also be disregarded on the ground that it is an unconscionable term of the contract * * * or that enforcement would violate the mortgagee's duty of good faith and fair dealing." Restatement (Third) of Property (Mortgages) § 4.7, comment e (1997).

5.   Mortgagee Purchase at Foreclosure Sale—Effect on Insurance Proceeds

Suppose that either before or after a casualty loss, a mortgagee purchases the mortgaged real estate at a foreclosure sale by bidding in the amount of the debt (what is known as a "full credit bid"). Since normally such a bid by the mortgagee destroys the mortgage debt, does the destruction of that debt also terminate the mortgagee's interest in the insurance proceeds?

a.   Loss Payable Policy

Cases uniformly prohibit the mortgagee from recovering on the policy. Since technically only the mortgagor's interest is insured and the mortgagee is merely an appointee to collect the proceeds, when the mortgagee bids in the amount of the debt, that debt is extinguished and the mortgagee's policy interest is terminated.

b.   Standard Mortgage Policy

Here the results depend upon *when* the loss occurs. If the loss occurs *after* the foreclosure sale purchase by the mortgagee for the amount of the debt, the mortgagee is permitted to recover. However, if the purchase follows the casualty loss, courts typically deny the mortgagee recovery on the policy.

Where the loss occurs after the foreclosure purchase, statutes and the common law of insurance normally permit the mortgagee to recover on the policy. The rationale is that the policy "specifically protects the mortgagee's interest in the mortgaged real estate and creates an independent contractual claim by the mortgagee against the insurer. Consequently, a change in the mortgagee's status from lienholder to owner, as a result of foreclosure, does not defeat the mortgagee-owner's right to the insurance proceeds because the standard policy is designed to accommodate the mortgagee's change in status." Restatement (Third) of Property (Mortgages) § 4.8 comment b (1997); 4 Couch, Insurance § 65:59 (3d ed 2002); *Travers v. Universal Fire & Cas. Ins. Co.*, 34 S.W.3d 156 (Mo.App.2000).

Why is the mortgagee denied recovery from the insurance carrier when the loss precedes the foreclosure purchase? In this setting, the mortgagee either will have known or could have discovered the loss before bidding at the sale. Thus, a mortgagee could very well be tempted to bid in the amount of the debt, unfairly discouraging third party bidders, and then attempt to collect the insurance proceeds as well. Moreover, the mortgagee can always protect itself by bidding in what the property is actually worth. If a third party winds up purchasing for more than the debt, the mortgagee will have been made whole in cash from the foreclosure sale proceeds. If, on the other hand, the mortgagee or third party purchases at the sale for less than the debt, the mortgagee can obtain a deficiency judgment which, in turn, can be satisfied out of the insurance proceeds; *Intercounty Mortg. Corp. v. McCrof Realty, Inc.*, 690 N.Y.S.2d 25 (N.Y.App.Div.1999).

Another, perhaps simpler, explanation is that when the mortgagee makes a full credit bid, the mortgage debt is extinguished, just as if it had been fully paid. Hence, there is no further debt to be collected out of the insurance proceeds, and the unpaid indebtedness is always a limitation on the lender's application of the insurance proceeds. See *Norwest Mortgage, Inc. v. State Farm Fire & Cas. Co.*, 118 Cal.Rptr.2d 367 (Cal.App.2002); *Fire Ins. Exchange v. Bowers*, 994 S.W.2d 110 (Mo.App.1999); Nelson & Whitman, Real Estate Finance Law § 4.16 (4th ed.2001); Restatement (Third) of Property (Mortgages) § 4.8 comment a (1997).

Suppose, however, the mortgagee makes a full credit bid without actual knowledge of the earlier casualty loss? A few decisions have come to the aid of the mortgagee in this setting by: (1) setting aside the foreclosure sale; (2) reforming the mortgagee's bid to reflect the actual value of the property after the loss; or (3) allowing the mortgagee to recover on the policy the difference between the amount of the foreclosure bid and the value of the damaged property. See, e.g., *Fireman's Fund Mortg. Corp. v. Allstate Ins. Co.*, 838 P.2d 790 (Alaska 1992), allowing reformation of the foreclosure sale where the lender was unaware of the casualty loss. Most courts, however, refuse to rescue the mistaken mortgagee, and their approach is sound from a practical and policy perspective. The mortgagee can avoid this problem with minimal effort. "An inspection or telephone inquiry immediately prior to the foreclosure sale will obviate any possible prejudice to the mortgagee." Restatement (Third) of Property (Mortgages) § 4.8 Comment a, Reporters' Note (1997).

6. **Interest on Escrow or Reserve Accounts for Insurance and Taxes**

    Just as mortgagees have a strong interest in making sure that insurance proceeds are available to substitute for real estate security destroyed or damaged by casualty, so too they seek to ensure that real estate taxes and special assessments are always paid when due. This is important because tax and assessment liens normally have priority over all mortgage liens. Stated another way, the foreclosure of a real estate tax lien, no matter when it came into being, wipes out every other lien on the foreclosed real estate.

For this reason, mortgagees often require mortgagors to pay monthly, in addition to their installments of principal and interest on the mortgage debt, an amount equal to one-twelfth of the estimated annual real estate taxes and insurance premiums on the mortgaged real estate in an escrow or reserve account. Some mortgagees set up special savings accounts for this purpose on which a normal passbook interest rate is paid. A few, in effect, pay the mortgagor the same rate of interest on the reserve account that the mortgagor pays on the mortgage debt. Most mortgagees, however, absent a statutory or regulatory requirement to pay interest, deposit escrow payments in non-interest bearing accounts which permit the mortgagee to commingle the escrow funds with its own.

Absent a statutory or regulatory mandate, most courts have refused to require mortgagees to account for income or interest earned by the mortgagee on escrows or reserves for taxes and insurance.

a. Judicial Challenges

At least four theories have been advanced to justify compelling the mortgagee to account to the mortgagor for profits from escrow accounts, but none of them have garnered much judicial support. One argument is that the escrow account constitutes an express trust or a constructive trust. See *Kronisch v. Howard Sav. Institute*, 392 A.2d 178 (N.J.Super.1978), rejecting these theories. A second argument is that a resulting trust arises, analogous to situations in which one person gives money to another to purchase property for the first person's benefit. This approach was rejected in *Carpenter v. Suffolk Franklin Sav. Bank*, 346 N.E.2d 892 (Mass.1976). Finally, it has been argued that if the escrow account is, by the terms of the mortgage, pledged as additional security for the mortgage debt, a "pledge" has been created on which interest must be paid under Article 9 of the Uniform Commercial Code. This theory was adopted in *Madsen v. Prudential Federal Savings and Loan Ass'n*, 558 P.2d 1337 (Utah 1977), but appears to have been based on the somewhat unique language of the mortgage in that case, and has not been accepted elsewhere. Nearly all mortgages in use today expressly disclaim any duty on the part of lenders to pay interest or profits from escrow accounts to borrowers. Hence, there is no common law theory that borrowers can use successfully to recover such interest or profits.

b. **Statutory and Other Regulation of Escrow and Reserve Deposits**

About 14 states have enacted legislation regulating escrow accounts and requiring mortgagees to pay interest to the mortgagors on escrowed funds. While generalization is hazardous, it is safe to say that most of this legislation applies to residential loans only and either mandates the payment of a minimum interest rate in the two-to-three percent range or such higher rate as may be set by certain state administrative agencies. See Nelson & Whitman, Real Estate Finance Law § 4.19 (4th ed.2001).

Currently no federal law or regulation requires mortgagees to pay interest on escrow accounts. Indeed, an Office of Thrift Supervision regulation provides that "federal savings associations may extend credit as authorized under federal law * * * without regard to state laws purporting to regulate or otherwise affect their credit activities." The regulation then specifically lists "escrow accounts, impound accounts, and similar accounts" as illustrations of the types of state laws preempted. 12 C.F.R. § 560.2(b)(6) (2004). This regulation preempts any state law prohibiting federally-chartered thrift institutions from requiring escrow accounts. *Goudreau v. Standard Federal Savings and Loan Association*, 511 A.2d 386 (D.C.App.1986). In addition, it invalidates state legislation that would require such institutions to pay interest on escrow accounts. See *Wisconsin League of Financial Institutions, Ltd. v. Galecki*, 707 F.Supp. 401 (W.D.Wis.1989).

7. **Escrow Accounting Under RESPA**

Section 10 of the Real Estate Settlement Procedures Act (RESPA) imposes some important restrictions on the way lenders handle escrow accounts on home loans. See 12 U.S.C.A. § 2609. A lender is permitted to collect, on a monthly basis, no more than one-twelfth of the estimated annual amount to be paid out for the escrowed items (e.g., property taxes, insurance, and so forth). In addition, lenders are permitted to maintain in the account a "cushion" of no more than one-sixth of the estimated annual amount of those items. The cushion's purpose is to provide the lender with some protection in cases in which the taxes, insurance, or other items are larger than estimated, or in which the borrower misses some monthly payments, potentially resulting in an insufficiency in the account. By the majority view, there is no private right of action for damages for a lender's violation of the RESPA limitations; see *State of Louisiana v. Litton Mortg. Co.*, 50 F.3d 1298 (5th Cir.

1995). However, they could form the basis for a borrower's refusing to contribute an amount above the legal maximum, and would arguably support a suit for restitution of the excess funds being held in the account; see *Heller v. First Town Mortg. Corp.*, 1998 WL 614197 (S.D.N.Y.1998).

a. Aggregate vs. Individual Item Accounting

During the late 1980s a controversy arose as to whether lenders should calculate the one-sixth cushion on an aggregate or an individual item basis. This issue is significant only if the escrow account includes two or more items, such as property taxes and casualty insurance premiums. If only one item is being escrowed (e.g., property taxes), the question is irrelevant.

The reason the accounting controversy arises is that, when more than one item is being escrowed, each item is usually paid out of the account at a different time during the calendar year. For example, property taxes may be payable in November–near the end of the tax year–while insurance premiums are payable in, say, June–near the anniversary date of the original loan. Hence, if the lender calculates the cushion so that each individual item's balance is reduced, at its lowest point in the year, to one-sixth of its annual amount, the total balance in the account will *never* drop to one-sixth of the total of the annual amounts of the two items. In effect, since the items are on different annual schedules, the balance on each of them will be relatively high when the balance on other item reaches its lowest point, just after it is paid out.

Consumer advocates and a group of state attorneys general argued that lenders had a responsibility under RESPA to maintain no more cushion than would be required to make the *total* balance in the account drop, at its lowest point in the year, to one-sixth of the aggregate annual amount of all of the items combined. Lenders disagreed, arguing that the individual item method (which most lenders had historically employed) was simpler to calculate and was permitted by RESPA. The statute itself was ambiguous and could be read either way. See Note, 12 Bridgeport L. Rev. 789 (1992).

b. HUD's Resolution of the Controversy

In 1994 HUD (after much debate and confusion) finally published a regulation that resolved the controversy. See 24 C.F.R. § 2500.17, effective in 1995. *That regulation requires lenders to use the aggregate method.* The result is lower average balances in lenders' escrow accounts (a benefit to borrowers), but greater complexity in accounting. Indeed, HUD has issued a number of subsequent clarifying regulations to resolve questions raised by lenders about the proper method of implementing the aggregate method.

REVIEW QUESTIONS

1. Why would a mortgagee prefer to be in a title rather than a lien theory state?

2. When can a lien theory mortgagee validly be in possession of the mortgaged premises?

3. T or F A mortgagee in possession has a duty to account for the proceeds of the property.

4. T or F Any attempt at enforcement of an assignment of rents clause executed contemporaneously with the mortgage should be considered an invalid clog on the mortgagor's equity of redemption.

5. T or F The appointment of a receiver should be easier to obtain in a title than in a lien jurisdiction.

6. T or F Receivership and assignment of rents clauses in a mortgage do not affect the mortgagee's chances of getting a receiver appointed.

7. T or F A mortgagee who forecloses and purchases at the foreclosure sale becomes an "owner and operator" and loses its CERCLA "security interest" exemption.

8. T or F Most commonly used mortgage forms give the mortgagee the option of applying casualty insurance proceeds either to prepay the debt or to restore the damaged premises.

9. T or F Mortgagees require the monthly payment into a reserve or "escrow" account of $\frac{1}{12}$ of the estimated real estate taxes on the mortgaged real estate in order to be able to reinvest those funds at a profit.

*

VI

Transfer by the Mortgagor

A. Transferability of the Mortgagor's Interest

During periods when interest rates are rising, it is common for purchasers of real estate to wish to "take over" mortgagor-sellers' lower-than-market-interest mortgage loans. This sort of transaction has several potential advantages, the most obvious of which is that the interest rate on the old loan may be preserved in the hands of the purchaser, saving considerable money over time. In addition, the purchaser hopes to avoid some of the "closing costs"—loan fees and appraisal and credit report costs—associated with the obtaining of a new loan, as well as the delay that new loan approval often entails.

This section deals with the methods and implications of "taking over" mortgages. In general we will discover that the mortgagor has a broad common law freedom to alienate his or her interest. This relative freedom has displeased mortgagees who, in periods of rising interest rates, naturally desire to be able to "call in" existing lower-than-market-interest mortgages in order to relend the money at higher current interest rates. Moreover, mortgagees sometimes have a justifiable concern that particular purchasers may increase the risk of nonpayment of the mortgage. To allay that concern, mortgagees often utilize a device called a "due-on-sale" clause to deter transfers by mortgagor-sellers. Because such clauses have enormous economic implications for the housing and lending industry, this Chapter will examine their use in detail. See generally, Nelson & Whitman, Real Estate Finance Law §§ 5.1–5.26 (4th ed.2001).

1. In General

A mortgagor's interest or "equity" is normally freely transferable. However, the mortgagor cannot escape personal liability on the mortgage debt by transferring the real estate to a purchaser-grantee. The mortgagor normally remains personally bound to pay the debt unless expressly discharged by agreement with the mortgagee.

2. Transfer "Subject To" the Mortgage

A sale of real estate with the mortgage remaining in place may occur in either of two ways: by the grantee's *assuming* the mortgage debt, or by the grantee's merely taking *subject to the mortgage*, but without an assumption. When a transfer is made simply "subject to" an existing mortgage, the grantee does not become personally liable to either the mortgagee or the mortgagor. The implications and practical application of the above principle can be explained by a simple hypothetical. Suppose mortgagor-grantor agrees to sell Blackacre to grantee (G–1) for a total price of $50,000. At the date of closing, mortgagor-grantor conveys Blackacre to grantee. Grantee in turn pays

$15,000 in cash to mortgagor and takes "subject to" an existing $35,000 mortgage held by a mortgagee (E–1) and previously placed on Blackacre by grantor.

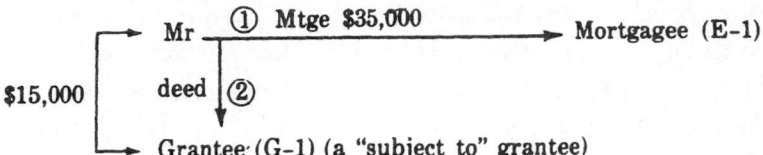

Note that there are several important consequences flowing from this transaction. First, G–1 is not personally liable on the mortgage debt. Thus if E–1 chooses to sue on the mortgage note G–1 has a valid defense. Moreover, if E–1 forecloses the mortgage and, because Blackacre has dropped in value, the purchaser at the sale pays only $30,000 for Blackacre, E–1 cannot obtain a $5,000 deficiency judgment against G–1. Second, even though G–1 is not personally liable on the mortgage debt, G–1 has the right to make the payments on that debt, and has a strong incentive to do so, since if the payments are not made, foreclosure by E–1 will destroy G–1's interest in Blackacre and G–1's $15,000 investment may well be wiped out. Finally, the mortgagor-grantor remains personally liable on the mortgage debt.

3. Assumption Transfers

A grantee-purchaser who "assumes" an existing mortgage becomes personally liable for payment of the mortgage debt.

An "assumption" is simply an express promise by G–1 to pay the mortgage debt. The promise may be made to MR, to E–1, or to both of them. Even if E–1 is not a direct party to G–1's promise to pay, E–1 is considered a third party beneficiary of that promise, and hence can enforce it.

Suppose in our prior example, G–1 "assumes" the $35,000 mortgage. If so G–1 has *two motivations* to pay off the mortgage debt. First, a foreclosure sale will wipe out G–1's $15,000 cash investment in the land. Second, E–1 will be able either (1) to obtain a personal judgment for $35,000 if E–1 opts simply to proceed on the mortgage note or (2) to obtain a deficiency judgment against G–1 if there is first a foreclosure and the sale yields less than the mortgage debt.

4. Assumption Transfers—How Created

Frequently an assumption agreement is contained in the deed to the assuming grantee. The deed will refer to an existing mortgage and recite that the grantee "assumes and agrees to pay said mortgage according to its terms."

Note, however, that such deed language is not a condition precedent to the establishment of a valid assumption. Extrinsic evidence—other writings or express oral statements—may be used to show that an assumption was intended. The admission of such evidence violates neither the Statute of Frauds nor the parol evidence rule. See Nelson & Whitman, Real Estate Finance Law §§ 5.6, 5.7 (4th ed.2001).

Example 1:   Same facts as in previous example, except that the deed to G–1 contained only "subject to" language and no assumption agreement. The mortgage went into default and E–1 sued G–1 to obtain a personal judgment on the mortgage note. E–1 now seeks to admit the earnest money contract between MR and G–1 which stated that G–1 "will assume the existing mortgage on the premises." (*Result:* extrinsic evidence in the form of other writings is admissible to show assumption intent.)

Example 2:   Same facts as in Example 1, except that the earnest money contract simply said that G–1 would take "subject to" the mortgage. E–1 seeks to introduce evidence that G–1 stated at the closing that "I understand that I am becoming liable on the mortgage debt." (*Result:* such evidence is admissible to show assumption intent.)

The absence of express assumption language in the deed or the earnest money contract is probably less of an obstacle to finding an assumption in a single family dwelling housing transaction than in the sale of apartment houses or other commercial real estate. In the single family dwelling transaction, most sellers and buyers probably believe that the buyer's "taking over" of an existing mortgage means that the buyer is becoming personally liable. In the sale of rental real estate, on the other hand, the buyer and seller are generally more sophisticated about the significance of assumption transfers, and the use of simple "subject to" language is strong evidence that the buyer took title to the land without becoming personally liable on the mortgage debt.

5. The Implied Assumption Problem

A few states hold that where, in a transaction with a conveyance "subject to" the mortgage, the full value of the land is agreed on as the purchase price and the purchaser deducts the mortgage amount from it, the purchaser becomes personally liable for the mortgage debt. These states include Maryland, New Jersey, Oklahoma, and South Carolina. Pennsylvania reaches a similar result, finding an implied obligation on the part of the grantee to indemnify the mortgagor who pays off the mortgage debt.

Most states disagree with this view, and insist on a showing of an express assumption. The promise to pay the mortgage debt is not considered to "touch and concern" the land, and thus does not "run with the land" to bind future owners automatically; see *In re Ormond Beach Assoc. Ltd. Partnership*, 204 B.R. 336 (Bankr.D.Conn.1996).

In states following the "implied assumption" approach, transfers of mortgaged land are usually viewed as assumption transactions. This is because in most cases the stated purchase price specified in the earnest money contract is what the parties believe to be the true value of land free and clear of liens. Such a contract may say, for example, "purchaser agrees to pay $10,000 in cash at closing and the balance of the purchase price of $25,000 by taking subject to a $15,000 mortgage now on the premises." In "implied assumption" jurisdictions, when the grantee does not intend to undertake personal liability, the deed should provide, after the "subject to" language, that "said mortgage is not being assumed by the grantee."

6. Rights of Grantor Against Non–Assuming Grantee

Whenever real estate is transferred subject to, or with assumption of, a mortgage, the original mortgagor is regarded as a surety. *This suretyship status does not restrict the rights of the mortgagee against either the mortgagor or the grantee. However, it gives the grantor-mortgagor certain rights against the grantee, which are designed to place the ultimate responsibility for payment on the grantee and the real estate.* These rights are much more extensive when the grantee assumes the mortgage debt than when the grantee merely takes "subject to." The most important and frequently-used of these rights is subrogation, and it is available (although with somewhat different consequences) against both assuming and "subject-to" grantees, as explained below.

In a subject-to transaction, the grantor-mortgagor's subrogation rights work as follows. When the mortgage debt becomes due or is accelerated, the mortgagor may pay it in full and become subrogated to the rights of the mortgagee. Since those rights are exclusively against the real estate, the mortgagor may then foreclose the mortgage and apply the proceeds of the foreclosure sale toward reimbursement of the mortgagor's outlay to pay the mortgage debt. See Restatement (Third) of Property (Mortgages) § 5.2. However, subrogation in this context does not give the mortgagor any personal right of action against the grantee, since the mortgagee had no such right.

Example: Mortgagor conveyed Blackacre to grantee who took "subject to" a $25,000 mortgage. Grantee defaulted and mortgagor attempted to pay the mortgage balance to the mortgagee, who refused to accept mortgagor's payment. (*Result:* mortgagor has a right to compel mortgagee to take payment. Mortgagor will then be subrogated to the rights of the mortgagee, and may foreclose the mortgage against the grantee).

The mortgagor has subrogation rights because the law confers such rights on one who makes a payment under a legal duty to pay, but where another person would be unjustly enriched by the payment in the absence of subrogation. If the mortgagor had no subrogation rights, the grantee would be unjustly enriched by the mortgagor's payment. See *Zastrow v. Knight,* 229 N.W. 925 (S.D.1930). For a minority view, however, that the mortgagor has no subrogation rights in the "subject to" context, see *Best Fertilizers of Arizona, Inc. v. Burns,* 570 P.2d 179 (Ariz.1977).

"One-action" statutes may assist the mortgagor in the above situation. Under the one-action concept, in effect in about half a dozen states, there can be only one action for the enforcement of a mortgage secured debt, that being a foreclosure proceeding in which a deficiency judgment may be obtained. Where this concept is applicable, the mortgagor may be able to compel the mortgagee to foreclose against the grantee prior to going against the mortgagor personally. The latter's personal liability would then be limited to the deficiency, if any, resulting from the foreclosure sale.

7. Rights of Grantor Against Assuming Grantee

In addition to the rights of the mortgagor described above, applicable in the non-assumption case, the mortgagor also has personal rights against an assuming grantee because of the contract of assumption between the mortgagor and the grantee. See Nelson & Whitman, Real Estate Finance Law § 5.10 (4th ed.2001); Restatement (Third) of Property (Mortgages) § 5.1. Thus, when the grantee fails to pay the mortgage debt according to its terms, the mortgagor may do all of the following:

a. Subrogation

The mortgagor may pay the mortgage debt in full, and may then be subrogated to both the mortgage and the note or other obligation. Thus, *the mortgagor may either sue the grantee directly on the note (in the absence of a one-action rule), or may foreclose the mortgage against the grantee and then recover from the grantee any deficiency that may result.* See *Thompson v. Miller,* 79 S.E.2d 643 (Va.1954).

b. Reimbursement

If the mortgagor makes any payment, total or partial, on the mortgage debt (i.e., to cure arrearages), *the mortgagor may immediately sue the grantee personally for reimbursement.* Any costs or attorneys' fees paid by the mortgagor may also be reimbursed. See *Kyner v. Clark*, 29 F.2d 545 (8th Cir.1928). This sort of action differs from subrogation in that (1) it is not secured by the mortgaged real estate, and (2) it does not require full payment of the mortgage debt first.

c. Exoneration

If the debt is due or in default, *the mortgagor may obtain a court order compelling the grantee to pay it.* This right is not dependent on the mortgagor having paid anything at all on the debt. It is premised on the view that the mortgagor is entitled to be free from the risk of having to discharge the mortgage. See *Riedle v. Peterson*, 560 N.E.2d 725 (Mass.App.Ct.1990).

8. Mortgagee's Rights Against Assuming Grantees

It is universally held that the mortgagee has a right to recover personally from an assuming grantee. Courts use either of two theories to support this conclusion.

a. The Third Party Beneficiary Theory

The substantial majority of jurisdictions permit the mortgagee to recover against the assuming grantee on a third party beneficiary theory. The mortgagee is deemed to be a beneficiary of the assumption contract between the mortgagor and the grantee.

b. The Subrogation or Derivative Theory

Although the conceptual underpinnings of this theory are obscure, the upshot is that the mortgagee has a right to stand in the shoes of the mortgagor and thus to be subrogated to the mortgagor's rights against an assuming grantee. Since the mortgagor, as we have seen, has a right to recover from an assuming grantee personally upon breach of the assumption agreement, the mortgagee has the same right. The mortgagee's right is thus a derivative one. See Nelson & Whitman, Real Estate Finance Law §§ 5.12, 5.13 (4th ed.2001).

9. Mortgagee's Rights Against Successive Grantees

Commonly, mortgaged property will have an unbroken chain of assuming grantee-owners. In such a situation each of them becomes and remains liable to the mortgagee until the mortgage debt is paid. The mortgagee may apply successfully against each successive assuming grantee whatever theory enabled the mortgagee to reach the first assuming grantee.

Example: Mortgagor conveyed to G–1 who assumed an existing $50,000 mortgage. G–1 then conveyed to G–2 who also assumed. G–2 failed to pay the mortgage according to its terms. Mortgagee either sued G–2 personally on the mortgage debt or foreclosed and sought a deficiency judgment against G–2.

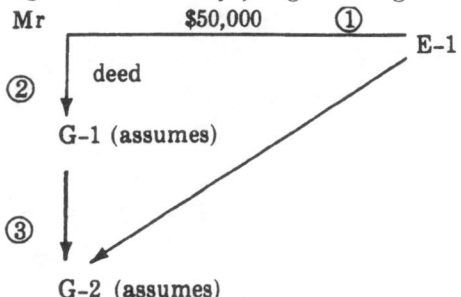

(*Result:* If the jurisdiction follows a third party beneficiary theory and E–1 is viewed as a creditor beneficiary of the assumption contract between mortgagor and G–1, E–1 will also be deemed a creditor beneficiary of the assumption contract between G–1 and G–2. To the extent that a subrogation-derivative theory is applicable, since E–1 is permitted to stand in the mortgagor's shoes to reach G–1, so too will it be permitted to reach G–2 by being able to stand in the shoes of G–1, the next succeeding grantee-debtor.)

10. Break in the Chain of Assumptions

Courts disagree as to whether a mortgagee can hold an assuming grantee liable when any earlier grantee in the chain of ownership failed to assume the mortgage debt.

a. The Third Party Beneficiary Theory

If, in the immediately preceding example, G–1 did not assume, but G–2 did, whether the mortgagee will be able to reach G–2 depends on how a jurisdiction interprets its third party beneficiary doctrine. The cases are divided. Those rejecting liability for G–2 require that the promisee (G–1) be personally liable on the obligation. Restatement (Third) of Property (Mortgages) § 5.1(c)(1), takes the view that the transferee who assumes is liable "whether or not the transferor is personally liable."

b. The Subrogation–Derivative Theory

Under this approach, the mortgagee can reach a subsequent assuming grantee because it has the right to stand in the mortgagor's and subsequent grantee-debtor's shoes. In our problem, since G–1, the preceding grantee, is *not a grantee-debtor,* there are no shoes in which the mortgagee can stand.

11. Grantee's Assertion of Mortgagor's Defenses Against the Mortgagee

The general rule is that an assuming or subject-to grantee cannot utilize any defenses the mortgagor may have against the mortgagee.

The underlying basis for this rule is that a grantee who assumes or takes subject to an existing mortgage has subtracted the amount of the mortgage from the purchase price in calculating the amount of cash paid for the transfer. If the grantee were then permitted to raise defenses to the mortgage debt, the grantee would be unjustly enriched. See Nelson & Whitman, Real Estate Finance Law § 5.17 (4th ed.2001).

Example: Mortgagor's $100,000 mortgage debt violated the state's usury law. Under the usury law, the debt was unenforceable by mortgagee against the debtor-mortgagor. Mortgagor sold the property to a grantee for $120,000. Grantee paid mortgagor $20,000 in cash and agreed to pay the balance by assuming the $100,000 mortgage. (*Result:* Grantee will not be permitted to raise usury as a defense to an action on the debt by mortgagee against grantee.)

Note that some have argued that while the above rule may prevent a windfall for a buyer-grantee, it confers one on the mortgagee instead. This is because the mortgagee is able to enforce an obligation that violates the public policy of the state simply because the person who was the initial party to the obligation has transferred it. Hence, some states are unwilling to construe their usury statutes to bar the grantee's raising of the defense. See *Michigan Wineries, Inc. v. Johnson*, 242 N.W.2d 568 (Mich.App.1976), affirmed 262 N.W.2d 651 (Mich.1978).

12. Release of the Mortgagor Upon a Transfer of the Real Estate

When a mortgagor transfers the real estate, whether with or without an assumption by the grantee, we have noted above that the mortgagor remains personally liable to the mortgagee on the mortgage debt. However, *the mortgagor may be released from that liability.*

a. Express Release by the Mortgagee

The mortgagor may be discharged by the mortgagee's giving an express release. See *Bruno v. First Fed. Sav. & Loan Ass'n*, 772 P.2d 1198 (Idaho 1989). Of course, the mortgagee has no duty to give a release, but the mortgagor may successfully negotiate for it, particularly if the grantee has strong credit, income, and other desirable characteristics.

b. Duty to Provide Release Under Federal Regulations

A regulation of the Office of Thrift Supervision (which has interpretive authority under § 341 of the Garn–St. Germain Depository Institutions

Act of 1982) provides that if the mortgage contains a due-on-sale clause, *the mortgagee is required to release the original mortgagor if the grantee and the mortgagee agree in writing that the grantee will assume the loan, and agree as to the interest rate the grantee will pay.* 12 C.F.R. § 591.5(b)(3). It is uncertain whether the mortgagee can evade this duty by imposing arbitrarily high credit standards on the grantee, or by refusing to put the agreement with the grantee in writing.

c. Discharge of Liability Under FHA–Insured Home Loans

By federal statute, a mortgagor under an FHA-insured or VA home loan may seek a release of liability when selling the home to an assuming grantee. If the FHA or VA finds that the grantee qualifies under their standards, the mortgagor will be released. See FHA Mortgage Letter 90–9 (Mar. 20, 1990); 38 C.F.R. §§ 4209, 4232, 4285.

13. Discharge of the Mortgagor After Transfer of the Real Estate: The Suretyship Defenses

As already noted, once the mortgagor transfers the real estate, the mortgagor becomes a surety, with the grantee (in the case of an assumption transfer) or the real estate (in the case of a transfer without assumption) becoming primarily liable. The law has traditionally been highly solicitous of sureties; a surety is generally discharged from his or her duties in a variety of situations in which actions of the obligee (here, the mortgagee) impair the surety's position. The mortgagor-surety is said to have a "suretyship defense" in such cases. The discharge is granted on the grounds that the actions of the mortgagee (1) have made it less likely that the grantee or the land will satisfy the debt, and (2) have made it more difficult for the mortgagor to assert recourse (that is, subrogation, reimbursement, and exoneration) against the grantee and the land if the mortgagor is required to pay the debt.

To understand this last statement you must realize that, in all of the cases discussed below, the mortgagee's action (in releasing the grantee or the real estate, or in modifying or extending the time for payment on the mortgage debt) *is binding on the mortgagor in asserting recourse against the grantee* unless the mortgagee, as explained in section 14(c) below, has "preserved" the recourse of the mortgagor by an express agreement with the grantee. For example, if the mortgagee gives the grantee an additional year to pay the debt, the mortgagor may not assert recourse against the grantee until that extra year has elapsed. Similarly, if the mortgagee releases some of the real estate from the lien of the mortgage, the mortgagor may not assert recourse (by way of subrogation) against that real estate. These results may seem surprising, but they are quite well established.

The following paragraphs summarize the situations in which a discharge of a mortgagor may occur on account of the mortgagee's actions. The Restatement (Third) of Property (Mortgages) § 5.3 (1997) takes the position that "the transferor of mortgaged real estate may be discharged from personal liability by receiving from the mortgagee an express release from the obligation secured by the mortgage, or by virtue of suretyship defenses under the the Restatement (Third) of Suretyship and Guaranty §§ 37–49 (1996)."

a. **Release of the Assuming Grantee.**

In general, *if the mortgagee releases an assuming grantee from liability for the debt, the mortgagor is also completely discharged.* See *Prigal v. Kearn*, 557 So.2d 647 (Fla.Dist.Ct.App.1990). The Restatement (Third) of Suretyship and Guaranty § 39 makes an adjustment to this view, however. It holds that if the mortgagee, in granting the release, makes clear that it intends to continue to hold the mortgagor liable, the mortgagor will not necessarily be completely discharged, but will only be discharged to the extent that the release of the grantee would otherwise cause the mortgagor a loss. This approach may indeed result in a complete discharge, since the release makes it impossible for the mortgagor to have personal recourse (e.g., by way of subrogation or reimbursement) against the grantee. However, if the grantee was insolvent or had few assets, and hence would have been unable to pay the mortgage debt anyway, the mortgagor's right of recourse will have had little or no value, and the mortgagor's discharge is limited to that amount.

Note that the discharge discussed in this subsection applies only to *assuming* grantees. In a "subject-to" transfer, the grantee has no liability to be released.

b. **Release or Impairment of Security by the Mortgagee.**

If the mortgagee releases *all* of the real estate from the mortgage, *the better view is that the mortgagor is released to the extent of the value of the land released.* Restatement (Third) of Suretyship and Guaranty § 42; *In re Roth*, 272 Fed. 516 (N.D.Ohio 1920). This principle applies whether the transfer was an assumption or was merely "subject to." In effect, this approach presumes that the mortgagor's position is prejudiced only to that extent. An alternative view, that the mortgagor is *completely* discharged, has been followed in the majority of states; see *Haberl v. Bigelow*, 855 P.2d 1368 (Colo.1993).

1) Partial release of security

If only part of the real estate is released, the Restatement (Third) of Suretyship and Guaranty § 42 holds that *the mortgagor is discharged only to the extent that the security becomes inadequate to cover the debt.* Thus, if the debt was originally oversecured, a release of only part of the land may result in little or no discharge. In this respect the Restatement distinguishes between total and partial releases of the security.

2) Other forms of impairment of security

The mortgagor may also be discharged if the mortgagee takes actions that impair the effectiveness of the real estate as collateral. Such actions include failing to record the mortgage, voluntarily subordinating it to other liens, following improper procedures in foreclosing, or authorizing the commission of waste or the demolition of improvements. In all of these cases, the Restatement's position is that the mortgagor is discharged by the amount that the mortgagee's misconduct reduces the amount of the debt that can be recovered from the real estate. However, some case law gives the mortgagor a complete discharge; see *Chrysler First Business Credit Corp. v. Kawa*, 914 P.2d 540 (Colo.App.1996) (release of mortgage completely discharged mortgagor).

c. **Modification of the Obligation by the Mortgagee**

If the mortgagee and the grantee enter into a modification of the terms of the mortgage obligation, the mortgagor is discharged. Most of the cases hold that the discharge is total (or, in the case of a subject-to transfer, is equal to the value of the real estate). See *First Fed. Sav. & Loan Ass'n v. Arena*, 406 N.E.2d 1279 (Ind.App.1980). However, the Restatement (Third) of Suretyship and Guaranty § 41 takes the view that the discharge is only to the extent that the modification would otherwise damage the mortgagor. Under this approach, many types of modifications would result in no discharge at all because they cause no damage. See, e.g., *Bank USA v. Sill*, 582 N.E.2d 310 (Ill.App.1991), holding that a reduction of the interest rate and the monthly payment, without any extension of maturity, actually benefitted the mortgagors and did not discharge them.

Example: Mortgagor has a mortgage on her house with an interest rate of 11% per annum. She sells her house to Grantee, who assumes the debt. Immediately thereafter, Mortgagee and Grantee agree to increase the interest rate to 12%. A year later Grantee defaults in payment and Mortgagee demands that Mortgagor pay the debt. The balance on the debt is

$111,000, but would have been only $110,000 if the interest rate had not been increased. (*Result*: Under the Restatement, Mortgagor is discharged from liability to the extent of the $1,000 in increased balance, but remains liable for the $110,000 sum that would have been due in the absence of the modification.)

The mortgagor is entitled to the benefit of any *advantageous* modifications, at least if the obligation is to pay money. For example, if the interest rate is decreased, the mortgagor is thereafter liable only at the lower rate. On the other hand, a disadvantageous modification is not binding against the mortgagor unless he or she consented to it. Thus, if the interest rate is decreased, the mortgagor may still discharge the obligation to the mortgagee at the original rate. In effect the mortgagor is entitled to perform either the original or modified version of the obligation, at the mortgagor's option. See Restatement (Third) of Suretyship and Guaranty § 41(c).

d.   Extension of Time to Pay by Mortgagee

An extension of time is simply a particular type of modification of the mortgage obligation. *The traditional view is that such an extension, granted by the mortgagee to an assuming grantee of the real estate, will completely discharge the original mortgagor. Moss v. McDonald,* 772 P.2d 626 (Colo.Ct.App.1988). If the grantee merely took subject to the mortgage and did not assume it, the mortgagor will be discharged to the extent of the value of the land at the time of the extension (since that is the only asset against which the mortgagor had recourse). *Branch Banking & Trust Co. v. Kenyon Inv. Corp.,* 332 S.E.2d 186 (N.C.App.1985).

The rationale for these cases seems to be that a time extension would increase the mortgagor's risk if the mortgagor were not discharged. In many cases this is true. An automatic discharge seems a Draconian result, however. In other cases, the time extension is not harmful to the mortgagor's position, and indeed may be quite beneficial. For example, the added time may allow the grantee to put his or her financial house in order and cure an existing default, or may allow the real estate to rise in value and cover more of the mortgage debt. In such cases, the mortgagor's position is improved and the risk lessened by the extension.

Restatement (Third) of Suretyship and Guaranty § 40(b) takes a more moderate approach. *Under the Restatement the mortgagor is discharged only to the extent that the time extension would otherwise cause loss to the mortgagor.*

Example: Mortgagor borrows $100,000 from mortgagee. The debt is secured by a mortgage on mortgagor's real estate (worth $100,000), and is due in one year. During Year 1 mortgagor sells the mortgaged real estate to grantee, who takes subject to, but does not assume liability on, the promissory note and mortgage. Thereafter, at grantee's request and without mortgagor's consent, mortgagee extends to grantee an additional year to pay the note. At the end of Year 2 grantee defaults in payment on the note. Mortgagee makes a claim against mortgagor for the balance owing on the note. The balance owing on the mortgage debt at the end of Year 2 remains $100,000, but the value of the real estate has declined during Year 2 from $100,000 to $90,000. (*Result*: Under the Restatement (Third) of Suretyship and Guaranty approach, mortgagor is discharged from liability for $10,000, but remains liable to mortgagee for $90,000. Under the traditional approach, mortgagor is discharged from liability by $100,000, the value of the real estate at the time the extension was granted).

When a time extension is given to the grantee, the mortgagor (to the extent not discharged as discussed above) has the choice of paying either on the original or the modified schedule. See Restatement (Third) of Suretyship and Guaranty § 40(c).

14. Methods of Avoiding the Suretyship Defenses

The suretyship defenses are potentially very harmful to the mortgagee's position, but there are certain actions the mortgagee can take to preserve its claim against the mortgagor.

a. Mortgagor's consent to mortgagee's action

A mortgagee who wishes to give the grantee a release of personal liability or of security, a modification of the obligation, or a time extension, *may avoid discharging the mortgagor's liability by securing the mortgagor's consent to the action.* If the mortgagor approves the action, the mortgagor cannot later assert a discharge on account of it. See Restatement (Third) of Suretyship and Guaranty § 48. The consent may be given:

1) In the original mortgage itself, in which case, it may be termed a "survival" clause or "waiver of defenses" clause; or

2) Before the mortgagee's granting of the release, modification, or extension; or

3) At the time of the granting of the release, modification, or extension, by the mortgagor's joining in it; see *Zellner v. Hall*, 80 S.E.2d 787 (Ga.1954); or

4) After the release, modification, or extension is given.

Example: A mortgage contains the following clause: "In the event of a release of security, extension of time, or modification of this note by any successor of the maker hereof, the payee's rights against the maker are reserved." The mortgagor sells the real estate to a grantee, and the grantee and the mortgagee enter into an agreement increasing the interest rate and extending the term of payment. (*Result:* The mortgagor is not discharged by this modification, and remains fully liable on the mortgage debt. *However, the reservation of rights provision will be construed strictly against the mortgagee and must specifically mention all of the possible types of modifications.*) See *First Fed. Sav. & Loan Ass'n v. Arena*, 406 N.E.2d 1279 (Ind.App.1980);

b. A "Preservation of Recourse" Clause in the Release or Extension Agreement

The mortgagee may effect a "preservation" of the mortgagor's recourse. See Restatement (Third) of Suretyship and Guaranty § 38. This is accomplished by providing in express terms, in the release or extension, that the mortgagee retains the right to seek performance of the obligation from the mortgagor, and that the mortgagor will continue to have the corresponding rights of recourse against the grantee as though the modification or extension had not occurred. In effect, the "preservation" clause tells the grantee, "I'm releasing you (or extending your time for payment), but the original mortgagor is not." It thus provides a clear warning to the grantee.

This sort of "preservation" clause may or may not be acceptable to the grantee. It obviously makes the release or extension less attractive to the grantee, since the risk remains that the mortgagor will assert recourse against the grantee on the obligation's original terms. In some cases, however, the transferee may well be willing to accept that risk in return for the mortgagee's release or extension.

Use of a "preservation of recourse" clause does *not* necessarily prevent the mortgagor's discharge under the suretyship defenses discussed above. However, it does have the potential to reduce the extent of the mortgagor's discharge. The reason is that, as discussed above, a discharge under the suretyship defenses is ordinarily measured by the loss the transferor would otherwise suffer from the release or extension. When a preservation of recourse is employed, both the transferor's duties (to the mortgagee) and rights of recourse (against the transferee) are unchanged by the release or extension. Hence, it is less probable that any loss will result to the transferor, and thus less probable that a discharge will occur. Nevertheless, if a loss would result to the mortgagor on account of the release or extension (for example, because during the time extension the grantee's financial position deteriorates, and the grantee is no longer able to reimburse the mortgagor who is forced to pay the debt), the mortgagor is still discharged to that extent.

B. Restrictions on Transfer: The Due–On Clauses

Beginning largely in the 1960s, mortgagees began to use two relatively new types of restraints on the mortgagor's ability to transfer or mortgage the property: the *due-on-sale* and *due-on-encumbrance* clauses. *These clauses give the mortgagee the option of declaring the entire debt due and payable if the mortgagor respectively either transfers or encumbers the mortgaged real estate without the consent of the mortgagee.*

Some mortgage forms include both the due-on-sale and due-on-encumbrance concepts in the same clause. However, due-on-encumbrance language is much less commonly utilized than due-on-sale language. For example, the mortgage form specified for use by lenders who sell mortgages to the Federal National Mortgage Association (FNMA) and the Federal Home Loan Mortgage Corporation (FHLMC) contains only a due-on-sale clause. That clause states: "If all or any part of the property or an interest in it is sold or transferred * * * without lender's prior written consent lender may, at its option, require immediate payment in full of all sums secured by this Security Instrument". The clause goes on to incorporate federal law, which provides that

> a lender may not exercise its option pursuant to a due-on-sale clause [on a 1–to–4–family dwelling] upon the creation of a lien or other encumbrance subordinate to the lender's security instrument which does not relate to a transfer of rights of occupancy in the property.

12 U.S.C.A. § 1701j–3(d)(1). Thus, the net effect is that the clause in the FNMA/FHLMC form is "due-on-sale" but not "due-on-encumbrance."

Mortgagees utilize due-on clauses for two purposes: First, to protect against a new grantee who may endanger the mortgage security or who is a greater credit risk than the mortgagor; and secondly and more importantly, to enable the mortgagee to insist on a payoff of lower-than-current-market-interest rate loans. Due-on-encumbrance provisions, while occasionally used for interest rate reasons, are largely intended to protect the mortgagee against an increased risk of default. That risk arises because junior mortgage financing both increases the mortgagor's total debt burden and reduces the mortgagor's economic "stake" in the mortgaged real estate. This is a particular concern to mortgagees in the commercial real estate market.

Due-on clauses engendered a torrent of litigation during the 1970's and early 1980's. However, in 1982 Congress resolved most of this controversy by enacting Section 341 of the Garn–St. Germain Depository Institutions Act of 1982 (the "Garn Act"). This legislation provides very broadly that due-on clauses are enforceable according to their terms, notwithstanding contrary state law. Nevertheless, some understanding of the pre-Garn Act judicial and legislative controversy concerning due-on clauses is necessary for a complete understanding of the Garn Act itself. Consequently, we first explore briefly some of this pre-Garn Act background.

1.   Judicial Approaches to Due–On–Sale Clauses

Prior to the enactment of the Garn Act, due-on-sale clauses were often attacked by borrowers as unreasonable restraints on alienation. However, courts had difficulty fitting these clauses into standard "restraint on alienation" doctrine. Obviously, the clauses do not directly prohibit a sale or transfer; they merely allow the mortgage lender to insist on a payoff of the loan if a transfer occurs. Hence, they were usually classified as "indirect" restraints, and thus as valid if reasonable.

Two primary approaches developed in the judicial decisions. Under one approach, due-on-sale clauses were regarded as reasonable on their face, and hence enforceable unless there was specific evidence of overreaching or inequitable conduct by the mortgage lender in accelerating the loan. See, e.g., *Martin v. Peoples Mut. Sav. & Loan Ass'n*, 319 N.W.2d 220 (Iowa 1982). This approach implicitly recognized that the lender's objective of "calling" the loan in order to lend the funds at a higher, current-market interest rate was valid and reasonable.

The alternative approach viewed this objective as invalid and unreasonable. Under it, the courts held that the lender could not enforce the clause unless the transfer would increase its risk of nonpayment or its risk that the security would be inadequate. (Commonly, this meant a showing that the proposed purchaser of the real estate had a weak credit rating or insufficient income to make the loan payments, using the lender's usual standards.) The lender had the burden of making this showing. About a dozen states adopted this approach, most during the 1970s and early 1980s. See, e.g., *Wellenkamp v. Bank of America*, 148 Cal.Rptr. 379, 582 P.2d 970 (Cal.1978).

Thus by the time of the Garn Act's enactment in 1982, the case law was severely divided, with the majority of decisions permitting lenders to enforce the clauses automatically (in the absence of specific overreaching), but a large minority permitting enforcement only if the lender could prove the transfer would increase the lender's risk.

2. State Statutory Regulation of Due–On–Sale Clauses

Several states enacted statutes in the late 1970's and early 1980's that limited the enforcement of due-on-sale clauses. While this legislation varied, many of the statutes prohibited either acceleration of the mortgage debt or an increase of the mortgage interest rate with respect to mortgages on residential property unless the mortgagee could establish that the mortgage security would be impaired. Other legislation disallowed enforcement of the clauses in cases in intrafamily and other non-arms'-length sale cases, or imposed limits on the amount of the fee or interest rate increase that a lender might impose in return for allowing a transfer.

3. Federal Regulation of Due–On–Sale Clauses

In 1976 the Federal Home Loan Bank Board (FHLBB) issued a regulation which created an express right in federally-chartered savings and loan associations to employ due-on-sale clauses to increase the interest rate on outstanding mortgages. 12 C.F.R. § 545.8–3(g). Contrary to state law in many states (e.g., California), the lender was not required to show an increased risk to its security in order to exercise its rights under the clause. Conflicting state law was preempted.

The FHLBB regulation was considered by the U.S. Supreme Court in *Fidelity Federal Sav. & Loan Ass'n v. de la Cuesta*, 458 U.S. 141 (1982). The Court held that: (1) The FHLBB intended to preempt state law; (2) the regulation in fact conflicted with state law (in California), despite the fact that it merely authorized, and did not require, S & L's to employ due-on-sale clauses; (3) the FHLBB was acting within its statutory authority under § 5(a) of the Home Owners Loan Act, which authorized the FHLBB to prescribe rules providing for the "operation and regulation" of S & L's; and (4) the regulation's merits might be debatable, but it was a reasonable and, therefore, a valid exercise of FHLBB authority.

4.   Policy Arguments

During the late 1970s and early 1980s, controversy over the enforceability of due-on-sale clauses became increasingly heated. Interest rates had moved upward to unprecedented levels. Most institutional lenders (banks and savings associations) held portfolios of mortgage loans that were yielding average returns much lower than current rates on new loans. Indeed, many savings associations were paying higher interest rates to their savings depositors than they were earning from their mortgage loan portfolios. As a result, their net worth was steadily deteriorating. Lenders strongly desired to use due-on-sale clauses to clear the older, lower-yielding loans from their portfolios when the owners of the underlying real estate parcels entered into sales. But in a dozen or so states, like California, that had adopted the "increased risk" approach to determining enforceability, it was usually impossible for lenders to make the showing of increased risk that was necessary to accelerate the loan.

The problem was, in a sense, exacerbated by the FHLBB regulation mentioned above. With respect to federally-chartered savings associations, that regulation preempted state law. The result was that, in states like California, federally-chartered savings associations could call their loans in when the underlying real estate was sold, while state-chartered associations generally could not. This sort of discrimination seemed intolerable to the state-chartered institutions.

Congress came under strenuous pressure from the lending industry to eliminate this disparity of treatment and to promulgate a nationwide policy that would apply to all lenders in all states. The Garn Act was the result of this pressure.

5.   The Garn–St. Germain Act

The Act was effective October 15, 1982 and broadly preempts state laws that restrict the enforcement of due-on clauses. It thereby makes such clauses generally enforceable. Congress delegated to the Federal Home Loan Bank Board (now the Office of Thrift Supervision) the authority to issue regulations interpreting the Act, and in April, 1983, the Board issued a final regulation entitled "Preemption of State Due-on-Sale Laws" ("Regulation"). The following material analyzes the more important provisions of the Act and the regulation, their scope, and the complex problems of interpretation they have engendered. See Nelson & Whitman, Real Estate Finance Law § 5.24 (4th ed. 2001).

a. Lenders Covered

The Act covers any "person or government agency making a real property loan." According to the Regulation, the foregoing definition includes, without limitation, individuals, Federal associations, state-chartered savings and loan associations, national banks, state-chartered banks and state-chartered mutual savings banks, Federal credit unions, state-chartered credit unions, mortgage banks, insurance companies and finance companies which make real property loans, manufactured-home retailers who extend credit, agencies of the Federal government, [and] any lender approved by the Secretary of Housing and Urban Development for participation in any mortgage insurance program under the National Housing Act.

b. Loans Covered

The Act covers every "loan, mortgage, advance, or credit sale secured by a lien on real property, the stock allocated to a dwelling unit in a cooperative housing corporation, or a residential manufactured home, whether real or personal property." Although the Act makes no reference to mortgages on leasehold interests, the Regulation provides that a loan is secured by a lien on real property if it is made on the "security of any instrument * * * which makes * * * a leasehold or subleasehold * * * specific security for payment of the obligation secured by the instrument."

c. Types of Transfer Restrictions Covered

The Act preempts state law only with respect to due-on-sale clauses that "authoriz[e] a lender, at its option, to declare due and payable sums secured by the lender's security instrument if all or any part of the property, or an interest therein, securing the real property loan is sold or transferred without the lender's prior written consent." Thus a clause that does not authorize the lender to accelerate the debt, but merely allows the lender to collect a fee or to increase the interest rate on the loan does not literally fall within the Act's definition.

d. Time of Transfer

The Act applies to all mortgage *loans*, whether consummated before or after October 15, 1982, the effective date of the Act. However, a *transfer* is covered only if it is made after the Act's effective date.

e. Transfers in Which Due-on-Sale Enforcement is Prohibited

The Act expressly enumerates several types of transfers that may not be used as the basis for due-on-sale acceleration. These include:

(1) the creation of a lien or other encumbrance subordinate to the lender's security instrument which does not relate to a transfer of rights of occupancy in the property;

(2) the creation of a purchase money security interest for household appliances;

(3) a transfer by devise, descent, or operation of law on the death of a joint tenant or tenant by the entirety;

(4) the granting of a leasehold interest of three years or less not containing an option to purchase;

(5) a transfer to a relative resulting from the death of a borrower;

(6) a transfer where the spouse or children of the borrower become an owner of the property;

(7) a transfer resulting from a decree of a dissolution of marriage, legal separation agreement, or from an incidental property settlement agreement, by which the spouse of the borrower becomes an owner of the property;

(8) a transfer into an inter vivos trust in which the borrower is and remains a beneficiary and which does not relate to a transfer of rights of occupancy in the property; or

(9) any other transfer or disposition described in regulations prescribed by the Federal Home Loan Bank Board.

Note that many of the foregoing transfers involve intra-family, involuntary, or a variety of "non-sale" or "non-substantive" transactions. When a transfer of one of these types is involved, the Act is preemptive: acceleration under a due-on-sale clause is prohibited even if permitted by state law. *However, the above transfers are insulated from acceleration only if the mortgaged real estate contains "less than five dwelling units."* This means that a *due-on-encumbrance* clause in a mortgage on a 1–to–4–family home is unenforceable under paragraph (1) of the exceptions above.

The Regulation modifies the Act's exceptions to due-on-sale enforcement in another important respect. It adds to the "further encumbrance" exception by making it clear that a transfer by installment land contract does not constitute "[t]he creation of a lien or other encumbrance subordinate to the lender's security instrument." Thus any attempt to circumvent a due-on-sale clause by using an installment land contract, rather than a regular deed, as the transfer mechanism, will be unsuccessful. This result is consistent with the great majority of pre-Garn Act state decisions.

Suppose the due-on-sale clause is contained in a mortgage on a farmhouse together with significant acreage, and one of the above types of transfers occurs. The Regulation is silent as to enforceability of the clause. Since most farms contain less than five dwelling units, the 1983 amendment would appear literally to apply, thus restraining enforcement of the clause. But this conclusion is by no means certain.

f. Estoppel

In certain relatively rare situations, a mortgagee may be held estopped to assert, or may be held to have waived its rights under an otherwise enforceable due-on-sale clause. Suppose a mortgagor requests permission to transfer and receives no reply from the mortgagee. Nonetheless, the proposed transfer is consummated. *If the mortgagee delays acceleration of the mortgage debt for a significant period of time, a court may be convinced that any subsequent attempt to enforce the clause as to that transfer is barred by waiver or estoppel principles.* The probability of this result will be increased if the transferee has made significant improvements to the mortgaged real estate or has entered into substantial commercial relationships with respect to that real estate, prior to a belated attempt by the mortgagee to accelerate the mortgage debt. The Garn Act itself does not seem to bar a borrower's use of the estoppel concept as a defense to due-on enforcement.

g. Release of the Original Mortgagor Under the Act

When a mortgagee waives its right to accelerate under a due-on-sale clause (typically after a higher interest rate or "assumption fee" is agreed upon) and the transferee assumes (rather than merely takes "subject to") the existing mortgage, *the Regulation appears to require that the mortgagee release the original mortgagor from personal liability* on the mortgage debt. See 12 C.F.R. § 591.5(b)(4). However, the Regulation is not entirely clear on this point, and one court has held that the lender is not automatically obligated to give such a release in these circumstances; see *Bank USA v. Sill*, 582 N.E.2d 310 (Ill.App.1991).

h.   Does the Due–On Clause Bind Successor Owners?

The usual due-on clause refers only to transfers by "the mortgagor." Suppose the original mortgagor makes a sale of the property with the mortgagee's consent. Is the second owner (and other successors in the future) bound by the clause as well? The answer is yes, at least where (as is nearly always the case) the mortgage itself contains a "boiler-plate" clause stating that its covenants are binding on the "heirs, successors, and assigns" of the original parties. See *Howell v. Murray Mortg. Co.,*, 890 S.W.2d 78 (Tex.App.1994); *Esplendido Apartments v. Metropolitan Condominium Assoc.*, 778 P.2d 1221 (Ariz.1989).

6.   Concealment of the Transfer

It is not unusual for the parties to a real estate transaction to attempt to avoid an acceleration of the mortgage debt by concealing the transfer from the mortgagee. Moreover, to decrease the risk of discovery of the transfer by the mortgagee, the parties usually arrange to have the purchaser make the monthly mortgage payment to the seller-mortgagor or to a third party who, in turn, makes the payment to the mortgagee under the name of the mortgagor. Despite the parties' precautions, mortgagees often learn of these transactions through a variety of means. For example, a mortgagee may monitor the public records for new real estate recordings affecting its mortgages. Similarly, ownership transfers may become apparent when, in its escrow capacity, the mortgagee receives real estate tax statements that evidence a new owner or when, after a new casualty insurance policy has been issued, a new mortgagee's policy is also issued. Some mortgagees keep abreast of transfers through a program of regular inspection of the properties on which they have mortgages.

a.   Effect of Failure to Record Transfer

Some purchasers attempt to enhance the concealment by not recording the transfer. If the grantee goes into possession, that possession constitutes constructive notice of the grantee's interest in most jurisdictions and should protect against mortgages and other liens that are subsequently created by or arise against the mortgagor-grantor. However, there are a few states where possession alone does not confer constructive notice. Even where it does, if subsequent liens arise through the mortgagor, the grantee is faced with the practical difficulty of proving he or she was in possession on the crucial dates those liens arose.

b. Duty to Notify the Mortgagee of Transfer

Do attempts at concealment violate an implied duty to notify the mortgagee on the part of the mortgagor and his transferee? If so, will the mortgagee be able to recover damages based on the difference between the interest rate specified in the mortgage and the market rate at the time of the transfer? The limited case law suggests that the transferee has no such duty to notify the lender; the lender's sole remedy is to accelerate the loan when it discovers the transfer. See *In re Ormond Beach Assoc. Ltd. Partnership*, 204 B.R. 336 (Bankr.D.Conn.1996) (non-assuming grantee does not become personally liable on the debt because it concealed a transfer of the property); *Esplendido Apartments v. Metropolitan Condominium Assoc.*, 778 P.2d 1221 (Ariz.1989) (grantee is not liable for damages because the transfer to it was concealed). However, some mortgagees now include, in addition to a due-on clause, specific mortgage language requiring the original mortgagor to notify the mortgagee in the event of a transfer. Where such language is used, it will probably justify an action for damages against the mortgagor, because the mortgagee surely has a valid interest in discovering the identity of a prospective transferee.

c. Ethical Problems

Is a lawyer acting unethically if he or she counsels a client to conceal a transfer, or arranges the details of the transaction? It is necessary to distinguish two issues: (a) Is the lawyer under an ethical obligation to inform, or not to inform, the lender that a transfer has occurred? (b) Is the lawyer under an ethical obligation to avoid advising or assisting in the concealed transfer? The comments below are based on the Model Code of Professional Responsibility (1969) (MCPR), the Model Rules of Professional Conduct (1983) (MRPC), and the Restatement (Third) of the Law Governing Lawyers (2000) ("Restatement").

1) Duty to Inform or Not to Inform the Lender

A lawyer has a duty not knowingly to reveal a confidence of his or her client. See MCPR, D.R. 4–101(B) and (C); MRPC 1.6. Exceptions are made for disclosures necessary to prevent the client from committing a crime that would result in death or bodily harm, or that are based on "fraudulent" conduct by the client; see MCPR, D.R. 7–102(B). The relevant opinions consistently treat "fraudulent" as referring only to criminal conduct or something very close to it. Hence, there is probably a duty on the lawyer's part not to disclose a real estate transfer to a mortgage lender against the client's wishes.

2) **Duty to Avoid Advising or Assisting in the Transfer**

The concealment of a transfer is at most a breach of contract (and perhaps not even that if the mortgage does not specifically require the borrower to report the transfer). However, the relevant rules require the lawyer to withdraw from representation only when the client's conduct is "illegal" or "fraudulent." MCPR, D.R. 7–102(A)(7); MRPC 1.2(d); Restatement § 44(2)(a). There is no prohibition on advising a client to breach a contract. Again, the term "fraudulent" is generally taken to include only criminal or quasi-criminal activity. This approach is adopted in the due-on-sale situation by Oregon Ethics Opinion 464, exonerating a lawyer who assisted a client in a concealed real estate sale. The "terminology" section of MRPC's Preamble provides:

> "Fraud" or "fraudulent" denotes conduct having a purpose to deceive and not merely negligent misrepresentation or failure to apprize another of relevant information.

It is difficult to conceive of a court's finding nondisclosure of a real estate transfer to be fraudulent in this sense.

A lawyer may nonetheless feel uncomfortable in assisting a client in a concealed transfer. If the client insists on proceeding contrary to the lawyer's advice, the lawyer is plainly entitled to withdraw from representation; see Restatement § 44(3)(f) (lawyer who considers the client's action "repugnant or imprudent" may withdraw).

7. Restrictions on Transfer in Installment Land Contracts

Installment land contract vendors have traditionally included contract clauses prohibiting assignment by the vendee without the vendor's consent. Violation of such a clause constituted a default, and therefore was ostensibly a ground for forfeiture. These clauses differ from the due-on-sale clause, where enforcement results not in forfeiture of the real estate to the mortgagee, but rather acceleration and foreclosure by public sale. In restraint-on-alienation terminology, prohibition of assignment thus represents a forfeiture type of direct restraint.

a. General Judicial Approach

While early authority sustained prohibitions against vendee transfer, contemporary courts have been more unsympathetic toward enforcement of such restraints. This shift in attitude has been evidenced in two ways. First, courts often construe the no-transfer language narrowly against the vendor. See *Conner v. First Nat'l Bank*, 439 N.E.2d 122 (Ill.App.1982) (transfer by trustee holding the vendee's interest to a successor trustee held not to constitute a "conveyance or assignment" for purposes of a no-transfer provision).

Second, even where the transfer is within the scope of prohibition, *courts increasingly enforce no-transfer clauses only where the vendor establishes that enforcement is reasonable under the circumstances of the individual case*. This probably means that the vendor will have to demonstrate that the transfer will result in security impairment. Moreover, forfeiture of the vendee's interest may seem an excessive penalty for violation of a no-transfer clause. Thus, courts may avoid a forfeiture by permitting the vendee to redeem by payment of the balance of the contract price to the vendor or, failing that, by foreclosing the contract at a public sale.

b. **Garn Act Coverage of Installment Land Contracts**

While the Garn Act itself does not specifically mention installment land contracts, its preemption does apply to any "loan, mortgage, advance, or credit sale secured by a lien on real property." Does an installment land contract vendor retain a "lien on real property", as well as legal title? The Regulation answers affirmatively, and is probably correct. While a few courts have had conceptual difficulty with the notion that one can have legal title to land and a lien on it simultaneously, there is substantial authority that the installment land contract vendor retains a "vendor's lien" for the unpaid purchase price.

However, many no-transfer clauses in installment contract simply do not meet the definition of a "due-on-sale" clause that appears in the Garn Act. The reason is that they baldly prohibit transfers, rather than authorizing the lender, "at its option to declare due and payable sums secured by the * * * "contract if the property is transferred without the lender's consent. Presumably the Garn Act has no effect at all on an outright prohibition on transfer.

Even if the Garn Act applies, the federal preemption does not necessarily mean that a contract vendor can have forfeiture. As noted earlier, where prohibitions against vendee transfer are upheld, it is likely that only non-forfeiture remedies (such as vendee redemption or vendor foreclosure) will be upheld. The federal preemption does not change this. Literally, the Act only validates the clause which makes the debt "due"—i.e., that accelerates the debt. The remedies available to the vendor after acceleration occurs are a matter of state law, and it would be very surprising for a state court to decree forfeiture, with its attendant harshness, merely because the purchaser had made an unconsented transfer of her interest. A more plausible course would be for the court to permit foreclosure of the contract as a mortgage. It could hardly be argued that such an approach would conflict with the federal preemption.

REVIEW QUESTIONS

1. T or F   A conveys to B "subject to" a $50,000 mortgage in favor of E. At a subsequent foreclosure sale of E's mortgage P purchases for $40,000. E sues B to collect a $10,000 deficiency judgment. E will succeed.

2. T or F   Extrinsic evidence is admissible to establish that a "subject to" transfer was intended to impose personal liability for the mortgage debt on the grantee.

3. T or F   Under the Restatement of Contracts, Second, a mortgagee cannot recover a personal judgment against an assuming grantee who took title from a grantee who was not personally liable on the mortgage debt.

4. Mortgagor conveyed Blackacre to G, who assumed an existing $50,000 mortgage in favor of E. G later had difficulty in making the monthly payments and, after much negotiation, G and E agreed that G would make no further payments for a year, at which time G was to resume payments at a slightly higher interest rate. Mortgagor then filed suit for a declaratory judgment that she was no longer liable on the mortgage debt. How should the court rule?

5. T or F   Due-on-sale clauses are restraints on alienation.

6. What is the installment land contract equivalent of a due-on-sale clause?

7. T or F   The consequences of enforcing an installment land contract prohibition on transfer are much more harsh than enforcing a due-on-sale clause in a mortgage.

8. Harold owned a 10 unit apartment building with a mortgage on it containing the FNMA/FHLMC type due-on-sale clause described earlier in this Chapter. On August 1, 2003, Harold and Wendy were divorced. Pursuant to the

terms of the property settlement agreement, Harold immediately thereafter conveyed the apartment building to Wendy, who was by then his ex-spouse. The mortgagee now wishes to enforce the due-on-sale clause because current market interest rates far exceed the fixed interest rate in the mortgage. Will the mortgagee be able to do so?

9. On March 10, 2003, Seller agrees to sell her house to Buyer who wishes to assume an existing 8% mortgage loan executed in 1996. The mortgage contains a due-on-sale clause like the one described in the preceding question. In order to avoid immediate enforcement of the due-on-sale clause, Buyer and Seller agree that Seller, as lessor, will grant a 35 month lease to Buyer, as lessee. The lease gives Buyer the option to purchase the house at an agreed upon price at any time during the lease period. Assuming the option is not exercised until the end of the lease term, will such a transaction protect the parties from mortgagee enforcement of the due-on-sale clause during the lease term?

*

VII

Transfer by the Mortgagee

■ ANALYSIS

D.   Participations
1.   Rights of the Participants After Default
2.   Lead Lender Misconduct
3.   Lead Lender Bankruptcy

It is a common practice for mortgagees to sell some or all of their mortgage loans to other investors shortly after their origination. The sale of a loan is loosely referred to as an "assignment" of the mortgage. Such sales are most often made by "mortgage bankers," whose business consists of originating loans for immediate sale to other institutional lenders. Other originating lenders, such as savings and loan associations and commercial banks, may retain in their own portfolios some of the mortgage loans they originate, while selling others.

The market in which these sales occur is commonly referred to as the secondary mortgage market. Numerous entities, both private and governmental, actively participate in purchasing mortgage loans in the secondary market. Some of the agencies and their significant economic impact on the housing industry are described in XI, *infra.* Two of the largest, Fannie Mae and Freddie Mac, are federally-chartered corporations. This Chapter focuses on the legal rights and obligations that ensue from secondary market transactions.

In recent years it has become increasingly common for a pool or package of mortgage loans to be "securitized." Securitization is a process by which the mortgage loans are assigned to and held by a custodian or trustee. Debt securities are then issued in the capital markets and sold to investors, with the payments to the investors being derived from payments made on the underlying mortgages. These securities may take one of several forms:

• The pool of mortgage loans may be divided into fractional shares, and the securities sold to investors may represent ownership interests in the mortgage notes in the pool. Such securities are often known as "**participation certificates**" or "PCs." See *Bankers Trust (Delaware) v. 236 Beltway Investment*, 865 F.Supp. 1186 (E.D.Va.1994).

• The pool of mortgage loans may be pledged as collateral for a set of debt securities that are sold to investors with the understanding that each investor will be entitled to receive a fractional share of the payments of principal and interest made by the mortgagors on the underlying mortgage loans. These are usually termed "**pass-through**" securities, since the mortgage payments are passed through directly to the securities investors. These securities differ from the PCs mentioned above because here the mortgage loans serve as collateral for the securities, while in the PC arrangement the securities are actual shares of ownership in the mortgage loans. The Government National Mortgage Association (GNMA) guarantees payment on pass-through securities of this type, collateralized by FHA and VA residential mortgage loans. See *U.S. v. Logan*, 250 F.3d 350 (6th Cir.2001).

• The pool of mortgage loans may be pledged as collateral for a set of securities that do *not* individually represent fractional shares of the payments of principal and interest (although in the aggregate, the payouts on the securities must, of course, mirror the payments being made on the mortgage loans). The securities may be issued in as many as ten to twenty different classes or "tranches," each of which has different characteristics in terms of interest rate, timing of payment of principal and/or interest, and priority of payment vis á vis the other securities issued out of the same pool. Each "tranche" may appeal to somewhat different investors. The mortgages employed to make up a pool of this type are usually large loans on commercial property, and the securities are often termed "**commercial mortgage-backed securities**" or simply "CMBS." See *Recupito v. Prudential Securities, Inc.*, 112 F.Supp.2d 449 (D.Md.2000).

No matter which form of mortgage securitization is involved, all securitizations require that the mortgages be assigned to a trustee or custodian to be held for the benefit and protection of the securities investors. Hence, the problems discussed in this chapter, involving the transfer of notes and the assignment of mortgages, are equally applicable to securitizations as to the traditional sale of mortgages on the secondary mortgage market.

A. Nature of the Mortgagee's Interest

1. The Twofold Nature of the Mortgagee's Interest

A real estate mortgagee owns two interests: the personal obligation owed by the mortgagor, usually evidenced by a promissory note, and the interest in the real estate that is the security for that obligation.

2. Primary Importance of the Obligation

When the mortgagee's interest is transferred, the primary object of the transfer is the personal obligation, usually represented by a promissory note. The mortgage security in land being transferred is an important but subsidiary aspect of the transaction. Thus, the security follows the obligation unless the parties express a contrary intent (which is rare indeed). Whoever is the transferee of the note automatically obtains the benefit of the mortgage on the land. See Restatement (Third) of Property (Mortgages) § 5.4(a).

3. Governing Law

Generally, a transfer of the mortgagee's interest is governed by the law of contracts and real property. Where the obligation secured, however, is a promissory note, Article 3 of the Uniform Commercial Code governs its transfer. (All references to the Article 3 of the UCC here are to the 1990 Revision.)

B. Rights and Obligations of the Assignee Vis à Vis the Mortgagor

1. Qualifying as a Holder in Due Course (HDC)

Holder in Due Course status confers significant benefits on an assignee of a note and mortgage, and is highly sought after. *Holder in due course status can be achieved only by satisfying two requirements: (1) the promissory note itself must be negotiable and (2) the process by which the note is transferred must be a proper negotiation.* See Nelson & Whitman, Real Estate Finance Law § 5.29 (4th ed.2001).

a. Negotiability

Negotiability requirements are governed by UCC § 3–104(a) and are fairly complex. The basic requirements for negotiability include the following.

- *The note must contain the maker's **unconditional promise***

- *to pay a **fixed amount** of money (with or without interest)*

- *on **demand** or at a **definite time***

- *It must be payable to "**order**" or "**bearer**".*

- *It may not state any **other undertaking** or instruction to do any act in addition to the payment of money (with certain exceptions mentioned below).*

Because of the prohibition on including "other undertakings," it is risky to include in the note a clause generally incorporating the terms of the mortgage by reference; see *Resolution Trust Corp. v. 1601 Partners, Ltd.,* 796 F.Supp. 238 (N.D.Tex.1992). Such an incorporation clause may result in reading into the note conditions or additional promises contained in the mortgage that will destroy the note's negotiability.

However, certain specific references to the mortgage in the note are permitted, and will not impair its negotiability; see UCC § 3–104(a)(3):

- The note may include "an undertaking or power to give, maintain, or protect collateral." For example, it may state that it is secured by a mortgage on real estate, and may include or incorporate mortgage provisions dealing with protection of the real estate, such as payment of taxes and insurance premiums and avoidance of waste.

- The note may incorporate by reference specific provisions of the mortgage dealing with prepayment and acceleration rights, since these provisions simply define the amount of money to be paid. For example, a statement in the note referring to a due-on-sale clause in the mortgage is permissible.

- The note may include authority for the holder of the note to confess judgment and to dispose of the collateral, and it may include a waiver by the maker of any law intended to protect him or her.

Example 1:   R executed a promise to build a driveway across Blackacre for E's benefit. The promise was secured by a mortgage on Blackacre. (*Result:* the promise is not a negotiable note because it does not "contain a promise to pay a fixed amount of money").

Example 2:   A $25,000 promissory note payable to Safety Savings and Loan Association is secured by a first mortgage on Blackacre. In addition to the usual terms, the note also contains a covenant by the maker (mortgagor) to purchase certain additional real estate from the mortgagee. (*Result:* The note is non-negotiable. With the exceptions noted above, the note may not contain a promise "to do any act in addition to the payment of money." UCC § 3–104(1)(b).)

Example 3:   First Bank extends a line of credit, up to $1 million, to Bob Borrower. Bob's note promises to repay "$1 million, or so much thereof as Bob has borrowed from time to time." (*Result:* The note is non-negotiable because the promise is not to pay a "fixed amount of money." *Yin v. Society Nat'l Bank*, 665 N.E.2d 58 (Ind.App.1996)).

Example 4:   Lender requires Borrower to sign a note which imposes a covenant that "mortgagor shall use this real estate only as his personal residence." (*Result:* The note is non-negotiable because it contains an additional undertaking besides the promise to pay, and the undertaking does not relate to giving, maintaining, or protecting the collateral. See *Insurance Agency Managers v. Gonzales*, 578 S.W.2d 803 (Tex.Civ.App.1979)).

Consider the following types of notes that are sometimes used in real estate transactions:

- Under the pre–1990 version of Article 3, a note on which the interest rate was to be adjusted in the future in accordance with some external rate index (an "ARM" or adjustable rate mortgage) was usually held to be non-negotiable because it did not provide for payment of a "sum certain"; see *Northern Trust Co. v. E.T. Clancy Export Corp.*, 612 F.Supp. 712 (N.D.Ill.1985); *Taylor v. Roeder*, 360 S.E.2d 191 (Va.1987). The 1990 version of the UCC reversed this view, and ARM notes can now be negotiable. "The amount or rate of interest may be stated or described in the instrument in any manner and may require reference to information not contained in the instrument." UCC § 3–112(b). See *Resolution Trust Corp. v. Maplewood Investments*, 31 F.3d 1276 (4th Cir.1994).

- Under the pre–1990 version of Article 3, a non-recourse note (one that imposed no personal liability on the debtor, and permitted collection only out of the real estate) was considered nonnegotiable because it was not an "unconditional" promise to pay; see. However the revised version of Article 3 reversed this rule, providing that a note is not considered conditional "because payment is limited to resort to a particular fund or source." UCC § 3–106((b)(ii).

b. Negotiation

To constitute a proper negotiation, a promissory note must be transferred by **indorsement** (if the note is payable to an identified person, as is almost always the case with notes secured by real estate) and **delivery of possession** of the original note. UCC § 3–201.

The delivery must be of the original note; a photocopy will not do. One indorses a promissory note in much the same fashion as a check. An indorsement normally will consist of language similar to the following on the back of the note:

"Pay to the order of Fannie Mae."

[Signature of payee/transferor"]

If there is not enough space to write the endorsement on the note, it can be written on a separate piece of paper (called an "allonge") which is affixed to the note and made a part of it. UCC 3–204(a). But if the allonge is not firmly affixed, a court may well disregard it; see Adams v. Madison Realty & Devel., Inc., 853 F.2d 163 (3d Cir.1988).

c. Taking in Due Course

For the transferee to hold "in due course" under UCC § 3–302, the note must not be obviously **forged, altered, irregular or incomplete**. The assignee must take it **for value**, in **good faith**, and without **notice** that

- it is overdue or has been dishonored

- it (or another note in the same series) is in default in payment

- it contains an unauthorized signature or has been altered

- someone else has a claim to it

- the maker or someone else has a defense or a claim in recoupment to it.

Normally the good faith and notice requirements are treated by the courts as much the same thing: one who has notice of a defect cannot take in good faith. The notice requirement is satisfied if the assignee has either actual knowledge or "reason to know". In other words, a person cannot be "willfully ignorant of information of which an ordinary person would have become aware." On the other hand, constructive notice from filings in the public records will not deprive a holder of HDC status; UCC § 3–302(b).

Example 1: Payee sold a promissory note and mortgage to an assignee. The note was properly indorsed, but it contained evidence of erasure and modification of the note language stating the due date. In fact, the note was overdue. (*Result:* The assignee will be held to have knowledge of the note's contents, including the discrepancies described above. Thus the assignee cannot be a HDC.) See Nelson & Whitman, Real Estate Finance Law § 5.29 (4th ed.2001).

Example 2: Payee was an aluminum siding contractor who obtained a note and mortgage from Homeowner as payment for siding installation. Payee indorsed and sold the note and mortgage to Finance Company. Homeowner later refused to pay the note, claiming that Payee had defrauded Homeowner by lying about the quality of the siding. (*Result:* if Finance Company had a long course of dealing with Payee and knew of Payee's general practice of defrauding his customers, the court may hold that Finance Company lacked good faith and is not a HDC, even though Finance Company had no specific knowledge of the fraud in this transaction. *United States Finance Co. v. Jones*, 229 So.2d 495 (Ala.1969)).

2. The Rights of an Assignee Who is a HDC

a. Personal Defenses

*The great advantage of being a HDC is that the holder takes free of certain of the defenses against collection or foreclosure that the maker (mortgagor) of the note could have utilized against the original holder-mortgagee. These defenses are called "personal" defenses and include: "**failure or lack of consideration, breach of warranty, unconscionability** and **garden variety fraud** (fraud in the inducement)."* White and Summers, Uniform Commercial Code § 14–10 (4th ed.1995).

Example: Maker-mortgagor hired mortgagee to construct a "shell" house on Blackacre. To finance the construction, maker-mortgagor executed and delivered to mortgagee a promissory note for $9,700 secured by a mortgage on Blackacre. Mortgagee assigned the note and mortgage to assignee, a HDC. After making installment payments for four years, maker-mortgagor defaulted and assignee filed an action to foreclose. Maker-mortgagor defended by attempting to prove that the actual value of the "shell house" was greatly less than the purchase price. (*Result:* assignee prevails. Maker-mortgagor's defense is inadequacy of consideration, which may not be raised against an HDC. Such a defense will be ineffective both in a suit on the note and in a mortgage foreclosure action.) See *Colburn v. Mid–State Homes, Inc.*, 266 So.2d 865 (Ala.1972).

b. "Real" Defenses

A HDC takes subject to certain defenses known as "real defenses." These are described in UCC § 3–305(a)(1):

- *infancy*, to the extent that it is a defense to a simple contract

- *duress, lack of legal capacity, or illegality* of the transaction which nullifies the maker's obligation

- *fraud* that induced the party to sign the instrument with neither knowledge nor reasonable opportunity to obtain knowledge of its character or its essential terms (usually called "fraud in the execution")

- *discharge in insolvency* proceedings.

> *Example:*   Waterproofing, Inc. persuaded Frank, an elderly man with no close relatives, that the basement in Frank's home needed waterproofing to protect against serious structural problems. Frank was only partially sighted and showed some evidence of senility. Frank paid $2,000 in cash of the $7,000 waterproofing charge and, as maker-mortgagor, executed and delivered to Waterproofing, Inc. as mortgagee a $5,000 promissory note secured by a mortgage on his house. Frank did not know that he had mortgaged his house; rather Waterproofing, Inc. told him that he had signed an unsecured promissory note. Waterproofing, Inc. then sold the note and mortgage to Third Federal Savings and Loan, a HDC. Shortly thereafter the sole shareholder of Waterproofing, Inc. skipped town and Frank obtained no waterproofing service at all. Frank refused to make any payments on the promissory note, and Third Federal initiated a foreclosure action on the mortgage on Frank's house. Frank then hired a lawyer who argued that Frank had "real" defenses. (*Result:* Foreclosure action against Frank will probably be dismissed. Even though Third Federal is an HDC, Frank's physical and mental infirmities, Waterproofing, Inc.'s affirmative misrepresentations as to the character of the instruments, and Frank's inability to discover their true character are probably sufficient to give Frank a "real" defense, such as fraud in the execution or incapacity.)

3. Non–HDC Status

As we have just seen, an assignee of the mortgagee's interest can fail to be treated as an HDC for one of three reasons. First, the note itself may be non-negotiable. Second, the process by which the assignee obtained the note may not have been a negotiation. Third, even if the note is negotiable and was negotiated, it may have been obviously irregular or the assignee may not have taken it for value, in good faith and without notice. However, even a non-HDC is not necessarily subject to all defenses; as explained below, he or she may still be free of defenses based on "latent equities".

a. The Patent–Latent Equity Distinction

If the defense to enforcement of the note and mortgage can be asserted by the maker-mortgagor, it is referred to as a "patent" equity. If the defense is capable of being raised by a third party, it is commonly is called a "latent" equity.

Example 1: Under the law of the jurisdiction, a transfer by one spouse without the consent of and signature of the other is presumed fraudulent as to the non-joining spouse. Maker-mortgagor executed and delivered to mortgagee a non-negotiable note secured by a mortgage on Blackacre. Mortgagee assigned the note and mortgage to A. Because maker-mortgagor's spouse did not join in the mortgage, the defense to be asserted against A resides in a third party (maker-mortgagor's spouse) and will be referred to as a latent equity.

Example 2: T held title to Blackacre subject to a trust agreement for the benefit of B. However, the trust agreement was not recorded and from the recorded documents it appeared that T held title in his personal capacity. T executed a mortgage to Blackacre to ME in violation of the terms of the trust, which stated that B's consent was required for any mortgage. The defense that B may raise to foreclosure of the mortgage resides in a third party and is a latent equity. (See Scott, Trusts § 284 (Fratcher ed. 1989)).

b. Raising Patent Equity Against Transferee

Patent equities may be raised against an assignee of the mortgagee to the same extent that they could have been raised against the original mortgagee. UCC § 3–305(a)(2) provides that holders who are not HDCs are subject to any defense "that would be available if the person entitled to enforce the instrument were enforcing a right to payment under a simple contract."

c. Estoppel Certificates

An assignee of a note and mortgagee who believes that HDC status may be lacking often quite wisely insists on obtaining an estoppel certificate from the maker-mortgagor before taking the assignment. In this document, the maker-mortgagor states that the note is valid and that it is not subject to defenses by the maker-mortgagor. Such a certificate is actually more powerful and valuable to an assignee than the HDC doctrine because *it protects the assignee against the maker-mortgagor's assertion of both real and personal defenses.* However, estoppel certificates only protect the assignee against patent equities. The maker-mortgagor's certificate cannot, of course, create an estoppel as to third party claims (latent equities).

d. Raising Latent Equities Against the Maker–Mortgagor

As mentioned above, UCC § 3–305(a)(2) allows the assertion of "simple contract" defenses against non-HDCs. In effect, the UCC adopts state case law in this situation. The prevailing view under these cases is that the assignee who pays value for the note and has no notice of latent equities takes free of them. The "simple contract" defenses are not available because they are being asserted by third parties, not by the assignor. Hence the assignee of the note has no way to discover them by demanding an estoppel certificate before purchasing the note.

4. Limitations on the Holder in Due Course Doctrine

The holder in due course doctrine, as we have seen, provides the assignee of a negotiable note and mortgage with a large measure of insulation from maker-mortgagor defenses. The doctrine has been subject to special criticism when it shields assignees from defenses that relate to the quality of consumer products purchased "on time". In the real estate setting the "consumer" is usually someone who gives a note secured by a mortgage on his or her home to a home improvement contractor. In the past four decades courts, legislatures and regulatory bodies have imposed substantial limitations on the HDC doctrine in a wide variety of consumer lending contexts.

a. The Close–Connectedness Concept

Some courts hold that holder in due course status may be denied to an assignee of a negotiable note who is too closely connected to the original payee. Based on closeness alone, notice may be imputed or good faith denied even though there is no direct evidence to establish the knowledge otherwise required to deny HDC status. The standards for finding a "close connection" are somewhat elastic. One well-known opinion expressed them as follows:

> When it appears from the totality of the arrangements between [seller] and financer that the financer has had a substantial voice in setting standards for the underlying transaction, or has approved the standards established by the [seller], and has agreed to take all or a predetermined or substantial quantity of the negotiable paper which is backed by such standards, the financer should be considered a participant in the original transaction and therefore not entitled to holder in due course status.

Unico v. Owen, 232 A.2d 405 (N.J.1967).

b. Legislation and Other Regulation

1) The UCCC

While many state legislatures have modified the HDC protection in a variety of consumer lending contexts, the most significant state legislation limiting or modifying the HDC doctrine is contained in the Uniform Consumer Credit Code (UCCC) which, in either its 1968 or 1974 version, has been enacted in at least 12 states. This legislation is extremely complex and subject to variation in many of the adopting states. In general, it abolishes HDC status for many assignees of vendor home improvement mortgages (usually junior liens) and a limited class of first mortgages as well. Where the original note and mortgage run to a third party lender (a "consumer loan") and the debtor is able to establish a close connection between the provider of goods and services and the third party lender, both the lender and subsequent assignees are "subject to all claims . . . arising from that sale" although only to the extent of the amount owing to the lender when he receives notice of the claim. For more detailed coverage of the UCCC see Nelson & Whitman, Real Estate Finance Law § 5.30 (4th ed.2001).

2) The Federal Trade Commission Holder in Due Course Rule

Under a "trade regulation rule" adopted by the Federal Trade Commission in 1975 entitled "Preservation of Consumer's Claims and Defenses," it is an unfair trade practice for certain sellers of goods and services to finance a sale without including in the debt instrument specific ten-point-type bold-face language that makes the holder subject to the maker's claims and defenses. See 16 CFR § 433.1–.2. Loans originated by third party lenders to finance sales of consumer goods and services are also covered by the above requirement if a very broad close-connection test is satisfied. (Close connection exists if the seller of goods or services refers consumers to the lender or is affiliated with that lender by common control, contract or business arrangement). See 16 CFR § 433.1(d).

The FTC rule applies only to natural persons who purchase goods or services for personal, family or household use in amounts of $25,000 or less. Real estate mortgages are affected by the rule only if they secure payment for such goods or services. Thus, for example, a

$15,000 note and mortgage given to a home improvement contractor as a result of the latter having built an addition to the maker-mortgagor's house is covered by the FTC rule. On the other hand, the rule is inapplicable to real estate mortgages arising from sales of *interests in real estate*, whether the mortgagee is the vendor or a third party. Consequently, the typical purchase money real estate mortgage, whatever its lien priority status, is unaffected by the rule.

3) The Uniform Land Security Interest Act (ULSIA)

The ULTA was adopted by the Commissioners on Uniform State Laws in 1975 and amended extensively in 1977, but was not enacted in any state. In 1985 the Commissioners split off the portion of the ULTA that dealt with real estate security (mortgage) transactions and relabeled it the Uniform Land Security Interest Act (ULSIA). ULSIA has had no more success in the state legislatures than ULTA did, but it may nonetheless be influential in the drafting of more piece-meal state legislation.

Unlike both the FTC rule and the UCCC, the ULSIA does not attempt to deal with the situation of a third-party lender who provides financing for a consumer sale and who is closely related to the seller. In such cases the lender is apparently considered to be unaffected by the consumer's claims of fraud, failure of consideration, and the like growing out of the sale transaction, and does not need the HDC doctrine to buttress this position.

However, the ULSIA does take a very aggressive position in precluding use of the HDC doctrine by assignees of *junior* (e.g., second, but not first) *mortgages given by "protected parties"* (owner-occupants who give mortgages on their homes). Neither the HDC doctrine nor any "waiver of defenses" clause in the note or contract will prevent the maker of such mortgages from asserting the full range of common-law defenses. ULSIA § 206. See generally Nelson & Whitman, Real Estate Finance Law § 5.30 (4th ed.2001).

5. Payment to Assignor as a Defense

After the original mortgagee assigns the note and mortgage, to whom should the maker-mortgagor make payments? Obviously, if the assignee notifies the mortgagor of the assignment, payments made to the original mortgagee after such notice cannot be raised by the mortgagor as a defense to an action by assignee to collect the debt or to foreclose the mortgage. The following material, however, focuses on the situation where no notice of the assignment is given and the mortgagor innocently continues to make mortgage payments to the original mortgagee. All references below are to the 1990 version of UCC Article 3. See generally Nelson & Whitman, Real Estate Finance Law § 5.33 (4th ed.2001).

a. Negotiable Notes

UCC § 3–602 provides that a negotiable note is paid, and the payor is discharged, ". . . to the extent that payment is made . . . to a person entitled to enforce the instrument." Section 3–301 informs us that the phrase "person entitled to enforce" includes a holder to whom the note has been negotiated. However, that phrase also includes any person to whom the note is delivered for the purpose of giving the right of enforcement, even if that person is not a holder; see § 3–203(a),-(b). For example, a transfer by delivery of the note without an indorsement will not constitute the transferee a holder, but the transferee is still entitled to enforce the note.

Why is payment to the *actual* possessor of the note necessary to discharge it? The rationale for this result is provided by U.C.C. § 3–203 comment 1:

> [A negotiable] instrument is a reified right to payment. The right is represented by the instrument itself. The right to payment is transferred by delivery of possession of the instrument "by a person other than its issuer for the purpose of giving to the person receiving delivery the right to enforce the instrument."

The UCC sections cited above are widely understood to vest the power to discharge the obligation *exclusively* in the person "entitled to enforce" the note, even though the Code does not expressly so state. Hence, *if the original payee has delivered possession of the negotiable note to another for the purpose of transferring the right of enforcement, payment to the original payee is not recognized as discharging the obligation.* The payment does not "count" against the assignee. This is true whether or not the assignee is a holder or is "in due course" and is true even if the payor has received no notice that the note has been transferred.

Example: Maker-mortgagor made 40 monthly installment payments of $450 each to mortgagee on a mortgage whose balance was $45,000 after the 40th payment was made. After the latter payment, mortgagee assigned the note and mortgage to an assignee, who did not notify mortgagor of the transfer. Mortgagor thereafter made ten more monthly installment payments to mortgagee. Assignee then declared the mortgage in default, accelerated the debt and commenced foreclosure. Mortgagor defended on the ground that acceleration and foreclosure were improper because no default existed. (*Result:* foreclosure is permissible. Payment to the mortgagee is not a valid payment of the mortgage debt. Thus, not only is there a valid basis for acceleration and foreclosure, but the ten monthly payments made to the mortgagee after the assignment cannot be credited to the amount of principal and interest due and owing on the debt.) *Groover v. Peters,* 202 S.E.2d 413 (Ga.1973).

This result has been widely criticized in the context of notes secured by mortgages. It is obviously unrealistic for a mortgagor to demand to see the note itself before making each installment payment to the original mortgagee. Yet in principle the UCC would require precisely that sort of vigilance by mortgagors. See Whitman, Reforming the Law: The Payment Rule as a Paradigm, 1998 B.Y.U. L. Rev. 1169 (1998).

Fortunately, in practice mortgagors are rarely harmed by this rule. This is because today most institutional purchasers of mortgages on the secondary market designate the original mortgagee as agent to service (collect payments on) the loan. Payment to the mortgagee under such circumstances constitutes valid payment to the assignee. If the secondary market assignee wishes to assign the servicing to some other agent, or to assume direct servicing of the loan, it will routinely notify the mortgagor of that fact. Hence, the real risks to mortgagors from the "reified right to payment" theory usually arise in the context of non-professional mortgagees and assignees. Still, the rule is troublesome enough.

b. Nonnegotiable Notes

Where the note is nonnegotiable, the UCC provisions mentioned above are inapplicable. There is, however, some case authority for the same result, at least in the context of a final payoff of the note. See *Assets Realization Co. v. Clark,* 98 N.E. 457 (N.Y.1912); *Johnstone v. Mills,* 22 B.R. 753 (Bankr.W.D.Wash.1982). However, *the better rule is that the assignee of a nonnegotiable note takes subject to all payments made to the assignor before the mortgagor received notice of the assignment.* Restatement (Third) of Property (Mortgages) § 5.5 agrees that such payments are binding on the assignee.

Example: Same facts as in previous example except that the note is nonnegotiable. (*Result:* Foreclosure is impermissible. Payment to the mortgagee after the assignment constituted valid payment of the mortgage debt because no notice of the assignment was given to mortgagor. Thus no grounds for acceleration and foreclosure exist.) *In re Kennedy Mortgage Co.*, 17 B.R. 957 (Bankr.N.J.1982) (dictum); contra, but finding the payment effective on an estoppel theory, *Rodgers v. Seattle–First Nat'l Bank*, 697 P.2d 1009 (Wash.App.1985).

c.   Suggested Alternative Rule

Some have argued that the law with respect to negotiable notes should be changed to make payment to the original mortgagee binding until notice of the assignment is provided to the mortgagor. This is the rule under UCC § 9–318(3) with respect to payments on accounts secured by personal property. Moreover, such an approach would be more consistent with the modern reality of computerized records and the operation of the secondary market. Mortgage notes are often stored in a central vault a substantial distance from where mortgage payments are customarily handled and are thus rarely physically available to a mortgagor who wants to insure that payment is being made to the proper party. At this writing (early 2004) a change in Article 3 along these lines has been proposed, but has not yet been finally adopted.

6.   Other Payment and Recording Act Problems

a.   Effect of Recording the Mortgage Assignment

A few cases and statutes provide that the recording of the assignment constitutes constructive notice of it to the mortgagor. This is a minority view and represents a completely unrealistic approach; few, if any mortgagors routinely search the public records prior to making their mortgage payments, and the burden of doing so would be immense. As a practical matter, statutes and cases taking this approach remove the protection that maker-mortgagors of nonnegotiable notes would otherwise expect and have.

Suppose, however, the mortgagor sells the real estate to a grantee after the mortgage assignment has been recorded. Here, it makes excellent sense to hold that the recordation is constructive notice to the grantee. The reason is that the grantee is expected to search the public records anyway, in order to determine whether the mortgagor's title is satisfactory. Hence, holding the grantee to notice of the recorded assignment imposes no additional burden at all. The majority of the cases do impute such notice to grantees.

Example: Rogers borrows money from Eaton and gives Eaton a nonnegotiable note secured by a mortgage. Eaton assigns the note and mortgage to Able, who records the assignment but does not notify Rogers that he now holds the note and mortgage. *Result:* If Rogers now pays Eaton the balance due on the loan, the better view considers the mortgage to be satisfied. The recordation of the assignment has no effect on Rogers. However, if Rogers sells the real estate to Grant, and Grant purports to pay off the loan to Eaton, the payment will not be effective as against Able. Since Able had reason to search the records (when he bought the land), he is deemed to have notice of the assignment to Able.) See *In re Kennedy Mortgage Co.,* 17 B.R. 957, 965 n. 5 (Bankr.D.N.J.1982)).

Note that if the note is negotiable the above rule is superfluous because, as we saw earlier, under present Article 3 a payment to anyone other than the possessor of a negotiable note is ineffective. This is true whether the assignment is recorded or not. On the other hand, we also saw if the note is nonnegotiable, payment by the mortgagor to the original mortgagee constitutes valid payment if it was made prior to the time notice of the assignment was given to the mortgagor. In most jurisdictions, recording of the assignment is held to give no notice to the mortgagor. However, where a grantee takes the mortgagor's interest after the recording of the assignment, the recording does constitute constructive notice of the assignment to the grantee. Consequently, recording saves assignees of nonnegotiable notes the trouble of giving actual notice to those who may subsequently buy the land.

b. Wrongful Satisfaction of the Mortgage by the Original Mortgagee

Where a note and mortgage are assigned, but the assignee fails to record the assignment before the original mortgagee (1) records a release of the mortgage and (2) the mortgagor conveys to a grantee who is a bona fide purchaser for full value, the grantee will take the land free and clear of the mortgage even if the assignee never receives payment of the mortgage debt.

Example: Rogers borrows money from Eaton and gives Eaton a note secured by a recorded mortgage. Eaton indorses the note and assigns the mortgage to Able, who does not record the assignment. Then Rogers and Eaton collude; Eaton (who has no legal authority to do so) releases the mortgage on the public record, and Rogers sells the land, purportedly free and clear of the mortgage, to Grant, a good faith purchaser for value. Rogers and Eaton split their ill-gotten gains and disappear. (*Result:* Grant prevails over Able; the land is free of the mortgage. *Brenner v. Neu*, 170 N.E.2d 897 (Ill.App.1960)).

This result follows even if the note is negotiable and the assignee is a HDC. This situation presents a conflict between the UCC and the law of negotiability on the one hand and the real estate recording system on the other. The result reflects ultimate victory for the innocent land buyer who relies on the public records. See Nelson & Whitman, Real Estate Finance Law § 5.34 (4th ed.2001). If the note in question is nonnegotiable, it is all the more clear that the BFP grantee of the land will prevail, since there is then no competing UCC policy to weigh against the recording act argument made by the grantee.

c. **Wrongful Satisfaction by a Trustee Under a Deed of Trust**

A trustee under a deed of trust has two alternative functions. One is to reconvey the land to the mortgagor if the mortgage debt is paid. The other is to foreclose if there is a default in payment of that debt. When the original beneficiary (mortgagee) assigns the note, the trustee normally is not replaced. Consequently, potential subsequent grantees are entitled to assume that the trustee is acting in accordance with the noteholder's instructions when reconveying the land to the mortgagor.

Example: Blackacre (which was worth $50,000 free and clear of liens) was owned by R, subject to a deed of trust that was security for R's $25,000 indebtedness to E. E then sold the note that represented that indebtedness to A, who promptly recorded the assignment. R and T, the trustee under the deed of trust, then carried out the following scheme without A's knowledge. T recorded a release of the deed of trust. R then conveyed Blackacre to G, who paid $50,000 in cash to R (who in turn paid part of it to T as compensation for T's disloyal service to E). A, after discovering what had happened, sought a judicial declaration that her note was still secured by a deed of trust on Blackacre. (*Result:* G owns

Blackacre free and clear of the deed of trust. G is entitled to rely on the release by T, notwithstanding G's notice of the assignment.)

C.   Assignment of the Note and Mortgage for Security Purposes

Mortgagees often obtain loans by pledging their notes and mortgages as security. In essence, what results might be termed a mortgage on a note and mortgage. Sometimes an individual mortgagee may borrow money by pledging a single note and mortgage as security. More commonly, a mortgage banker will obtain short-term commercial bank financing by delivering a package of notes and mortgages to the bank as collateral. When the mortgage banker finds permanent purchasers for those notes and mortgages on the secondary market it will often pay off the short-term loan and take them back from the bank. This practice is called *"mortgage warehousing"*. Often the package of loans is delivered to the lender with no formal assignment or endorsements. Sometimes, no physical delivery at all takes place and the mortgage banker simply designates itself as custodian for the lender. As we shall see, this is a particularly risky procedure.

1.   The Application of UCC Article 9 to Transfers of Mortgage Notes as Security.

As we have already seen, a transfer of a promissory note will automatically assign the mortgage that secures the note; no separate assignment is necessary (although it may well be desirable for the reasons discussed above). This is equally true of a transfer as security as it is of an outright transfer by sale of the note.

However, when a mortgage note is assigned as security, we must also be concerned with "perfection" of the assignee's security interest. *Perfection of security interests in promissory notes ("instruments") is governed by UCC Article 9.* As the drafters of Revised Article 9 expressed it,

> The security interest in the promissory note is covered by this Article even though the note is secured by a real-property mortgage. Also [the creditor's] security interest in the note gives [the creditor] an attached security interest in the mortgage lien that secures the note. * * * One cannot obtain a security interest in a lien, such as a mortgage on real property, that is not also coupled with an equally effective security interest in the secured obligation."

UCC 9–109, Official Comment 7. Perfection under Article 9 is critically important in two distinct contexts:

- Assume that the original mortgagee, having transferred the note as security to an assignee, experiences financial distress and gives *another* security interest in the note to another creditor. (This might be termed "double-pledging" the note, a phenomenon that is shockingly common.) Which assignee would be entitled to the payments made on the note? The answer is the second if it perfected, unless the assignment to the first was already perfected. See UCC § 9–322(a)(1) ("Conflicting perfected security interests * * * rank according to priority in time of filing or perfection); UCC § 9–322 (a)(2) ("A perfected security interest * * * has priority over a conflicting unperfected security interest").

- Assume that the original mortgagee, having transferred the note as security to an assignee, becomes insolvent and files bankruptcy. A trustee in bankruptcy has the "strong-arm" power, under § 544(a) of the Bankruptcy Code, to act as a perfected judgment lien creditor of the bankrupt as of the date of bankruptcy. Acting under this power, the trustee might claim the note as against the first assignee. If the court found that the assignee was unperfected and thus that the bankruptcy trustee prevailed, the payments on the note would go to the bankruptcy estate and benefit the mortgagee's general creditors, and the assignee would be limited to a pro-rata share of those payments.

While these examples refer only to perfection of the security interest in the note, Revised Article 9 makes it clear that *perfecting as to the note will automatically perfect as to the mortgage or other collateral for the note*. Under § 9–308(g), "Perfection of a security interest in a right to payment or performance also perfects a security interest in a lien on personal or real property securing the right, notwithstanding other law to the contrary." Perfection as to the note automatically takes care of the mortgage as well. *It is not necessary to record a mortgage assignment in order to perfect as to the real estate collateral.*

2. How is Perfection Accomplished?

UCC Article 9 characterizes a promissory note (whether it is negotiable or not) as an "instrument," and it provides two distinct methods of perfecting security interests in instruments:

- Perfection can be accomplished by the assignee's *taking possession* of the original note. (This was the only method recognized by the previous version of Article 9.) As we shall see, this is the safest method. UCC § 9–313(a). Incidentally (but very importantly), taking possession really does require the physical moving of the note. The courts are very disinclined to accept anything less than a manual transfer of possession to the secured party-assignee. For example, it is most unwise for the assignee to leave the note in the hands of the mortgagee-assignor as the assignee's "trustee," "nominee," "agent," or the like. See *In re Executive Growth Investments, Inc.*, 40 B.R. 417 (Bkrtcy.C.D.Cal.1984).

- Perfection can also be accomplished by *filing a financing statement* (a so-called UCC–1 form), typically with the Secretary of State's office. UCC § 9–312(a).

Both methods are acceptable. However, a later perfection by possession supersedes an earlier perfection by filing unless the later taker has actual knowledge of the earlier one. See UCC § 9–330.

3. Which Method of Perfection Should be Used?

Revised Article 9 introduced the concept of perfection by filing because financings secured by mortgage notes and other consumer notes are often for short periods of time and involve large numbers of notes. Transferring physical possession of the notes to the creditor and back again can be burdensome, and notes can become lost or mislaid. Filing is obviously much easier, since a single filing can list a large number of notes, cam be accomplished electronically in most states, and costs only a small fee.

However, perfection by filing is a sort of "second-rate" perfection since, as noted above, it can be "trumped" by the debtor's later giving actual possession of the notes to a different creditor who does not know about the first assignment. The drafters believed that filing would a sufficient perfection to protect the assignee against a subsequent trustee in bankruptcy of the assignor–the second of the two perfection scenarios described above. However, it quite clearly *will not protect the assignor in the "double-pledging" case*–the first of the perfection scenarios described above–if the second assignee gets possession of the note and does not know about the first assignment.

Hence, a wise creditor will not perfect merely by filing unless the creditor completely trusts the debtor not to "double-assign" the note. If the creditor has any qualms at all about the business ethics of the debtor, the creditor had better go to the extra trouble of taking possession of those notes. By the same token, for any creditor who does get possession, the fact that there has been a prior filing is simply irrelevant; the filing imparts no constructive notice to such a person, and there is no need for a creditor who is taking possession of the note to do a UCC search.

4. How Does a Security Assignee Realize on the Security?

Assume that a creditor has taken and perfected a security interest in a note and mortgage as collateral for a debt owed by the mortgagee. Now assume that the mortgagee defaults on that debt. How does the creditor realize (or in mortgage parlance, foreclose) on the note and mortgage? Article 9 offers three basic methods:

- The creditor can place the mortgage loan on the secondary mortgage market and sell it to another investor. This is known as *"disposal"* of the collateral; UCC § 9–610(a). Such a sale must be a "commercially reasonable" disposition; see U.C.C. § 9–610(b). Appropriate notice must be given to the pledgor and others entitled to such notice, as outlined in U.C.C. §§ 9–611 to 9–614. Note carefully that this is *not* a foreclosure of the underlying mortgage, and it is not necessary to conduct an auction-type sale, as is typically used for mortgage foreclosures.

- The creditor can, in effect, step into the original mortgagee's shoes and notify the mortgagor to make all further payments to or for the benefit of the creditor. The creditor may then enforce the obligations of the mortgagor by means that would have been available to the mortgagee, including a foreclosure of the mortgage or a suit on the note. This is known as *"collection"* of the underlying obligation; U.C.C. § 9–607(a).

- The creditor can accept (and assume ownership) of the underlying note and mortgage in full or partial satisfaction of the mortgagee's debt. This is known as *"acceptance;"* see UCC § 9–620. As a practical matter, it differs little from "collection," discussed above.

Whichever method of realization on the security is used by the creditor, it is very convenient for the creditor to be able to memorialize its actions in the public real estate records. For example, if the creditor uses the "collection" remedy and subsequently finds it necessary to foreclose the underlying mortgage, in many states it will be necessary for the creditor to be able to establish a chain of ownership of the mortgage by recorded documents. To accomplish this, *UCC § 9–619 allows the creditor to record a "transfer statement"* reciting that the mortgagee defaulted to the creditor, that the creditor exercised its post-default remedies with respect to the underlying note and mortgage, and that a transferee (which may be the creditor, or in the case of a "disposal," a third party) has acquired the rights of the mortgagee in the note and mortgage. Thus, the transfer statement can fill the gap in the chain of title to the mortgage.

D. Participations

Sometimes a mortgage lender, rather than selling and assigning a note and mortgage to single secondary market investor, will sell fractional interests in one or more mortgage loans to multiple investors. This is often referred to as the sale of "participation" interests. The originating or "lead" lender may sell fractional interests in a single large mortgage loan, or may assemble a large portfolio of loans and then to sell fractional interests in the portfolio. In either situation, the fractional interests will be evidenced by participation certificates (PCs). The certificates, in turn, will refer to and be governed by a detailed participation agreement. See Nelson & Whitman, Real Estate Finance Law § 5.35 (4th ed.2001); *In re Autostyle Plastics, Inc.*, 1999 WL 1005647 (W.D.Mich.1999).

Participants sometimes argue (usually after the underlying loans have gone into default) that the lead lender has misled them as to the quality of the underlying loans or the qualifications of the borrowers. See, e.g., *Southern Pacific Thrift & Loan Ass'n v. Savings Ass'n Mortg. Co.*, 82 Cal. Rptr. 2d 874 (Cal.App.1999). In general, the lead lender does not owe a fiduciary duty to the participants. Its liability for misrepresentations is governed by the general law of fraud and the terms of the participation agreement.

1. Rights of the Participants After Default

Where one or more loans go into default almost all courts today, in the absence of a contrary agreement, grant a pro-rata priority among the participants.

Example: E–1 held a mortgage loan with a $400,000 principal balance. E–1 sold a 25% participation interest in the loan to E–2 and a 50% participation interest to E–3. The mortgagor defaulted in payment on the loan, the mortgaged real estate was foreclosed and the foreclosure purchaser paid $300,000. The mortgagor was judgment-proof and thus a deficiency judgment was uncollectible. (*Result:* as among the three participants, unless the participation agreement contains contrary language, each participant's share of the foreclosure proceeds will be determined by multiplying the foreclosure proceeds by that party's participation percentage. Thus, E–1's share would be 25% of $300,000 or $75,000, E–2's share would be the same, and E–3's share would be 50% of $300,000 or $150,000. Each winds up losing 25% of its initial investment.)

A few early decisions took the position that the participants should not share the proceeds on a pro-rata basis, but that each would be assigned a priority based on the order that such participant received its participation interest. Under this approach in the above example, E–1 received its participation interest first, E–2 second, and E–3 last, so the $300,000 would be divided as follows: E–1, having initially invested $100,000 would receive the full amount. E–2, having the same initial investment would receive that full amount. E–3, on the other hand, being third in priority, would receive the remaining $100,000 and thus wind up losing $100,000 or half of its initial investment.

As between the lead lender and the participants, under the better and majority view, absent a guarantee of payment, the participants have no special priority vis-à-vis the lead lender. See *Domeyer v. O'Connell,* 4 N.E.2d 830 (Ill.1936). This rule is consistent with the result reached in the foregoing example. There are a few contrary cases, which follow a variety of approaches. Some hold that the lead lender is a trustee who should not be permitted to recover from the mortgage security at the other participants' expense. Others take the position that delivery of the participation interests to each of the participants creates an implied agreement by the lead lender to subordinate its interest to those of the participants. These priority rules are seldom of practical importance today because the participation agreement itself almost always delineates the priorities of the parties in detail, and it is quite common for some participants to be given a higher priority than others or than the lead lender.

2. Lead Lender Misconduct

Because the original loan instruments remain in the lead lender's hands, there are many opportunities for specific misconduct on its part. For example, the lead lender could reassign or "double-assign" some or all of the notes and mortgages. In theory, it could purport to sell an unlimited number of additional participation interests. It could pledge some or all of the loans to secure new or existing debts. Historically few precautions were taken against such potential misconduct because most institutional lenders had confidence in the integrity of their fellow lenders. In recent decades, well-publicized financial misdealings by major banking institutions have made loan participants reevaluate this lax attitude.

To avoid some of the above problems the participants can insist that the notes be marked so as to provide notice to non-participant third parties that they are subject to participants' rights. While this expedient will be effective in preventing most lead lender misconduct, it will create practical complications. For example, where the portfolio contains numerous loans, it would require that every time one is paid off, consent to cancellation of the note would be required of each participant. Hence, this approach is more workable where the participation is in a single large loan.

An alternative method of preventing misdealing by the lead lender is to insist that the original mortgage documents be placed in the hands of an independent trustee or custodian, such as a bank or trust company which has no other involvement in the transaction. A detailed set of instructions is necessary to delineate the conditions under which the trustee is to release possession of the mortgage documents. This approach is more practical when the participation is in a portfolio consisting of a large number of small loans.

3. Lead Lender Bankruptcy

When a lead lender goes into bankruptcy, its general creditors or trustee in bankruptcy may claim that the participation arrangement was not sufficient to transfer ownership of the notes to the participants and therefore, they remain a part of the bankrupt lead lender's estate. Two arguments are sometimes advanced to support this position.

a. Loan of Money by Participants to Lead Lender

According to this argument, the participation really amounts to a loan of money by the participants to the lead lender with the notes and mortgages constituting security for the loan. See *In re Coronet Capital Co.*, 142 B.R. 78 (Bankr.S.D.N.Y.1992). In order to be insulated from the "strong-arm" powers of the trustee in bankruptcy, it is essential that these security interests in the underlying mortgage loans be perfected under UCC Article 9. However, such perfection can be accomplished only by the filing of a UCC financing statement or by transfer of physical possession of the mortgage notes to the participants or their representative (*In re Churchill Mortg. Inv. Corp.*, 233 B.R. 61 (Bankr.S.D.N.Y.1999). Often these steps are not taken, leaving the participants vulnerable to attack by the lead lender's trustee in bankruptcy.

To help avoid this argument, the participation agreement should make it absolutely clear that a sale, not a collateral security arrangement, is intended. It is also helpful if possession of the underlying mortgage documents has been transferred to an independent custodian who represents the participants, as discussed above. With proper precautions, the participation will survive an attack in bankruptcy. See *In re Okura & Co. (America), Inc.*, 249 B.R. 596 (Bankr.S.D.N.Y.2000).

b. Assignment of Mortgage Loan Proceeds

Under this argument, the participants do not receive property interests in the notes themselves but rather only assignments of the loan proceeds.

Only the lead lender, as assignor, so this theory goes, has the right to enforce the mortgage notes and thus the participants have no ownership interests.

This seems at best to put form over substance. The lead lender's capacity to enforce the underlying notes and mortgages is readily explained on the ground that the lead lender is the agent of the participants for that purpose. An equally plausible position is that the lead lender is a trustee for the participants and that therefore the former's legal title is being held for the participants as the beneficial owners of the notes. Either argument ought to be sufficient to withstand attack from the lead lender's general creditors or claims of its trustee in bankruptcy.

c. Buttressing the Participant's Position by Drafting

To enhance the participants' positions, the participation agreement should include the following provisions:

1) a statement that a transfer of ownership is intended;

2) a disavowal of the idea that a loan to the lead lender was intended;

3) the lead lender should specifically be designated as either an agent or trustee for the participants and its powers should be spelled out by using agency or trust language; and

4) the interest yield to the participants and the term of the participation should be tied to the yield and terms on the mortgage or mortgages in the portfolio rather than computed on some independent basis. See Nelson & Whitman, Real Estate Finance Law § 5.35 (4th ed.2001); *Came Realty LLC v. DeMaio*, 746 N.Y.S.2d 555 (Sup.Ct.2002).

REVIEW QUESTIONS

1. T or F   The secondary mortgage market refers to lenders who deal in second or junior mortgages.

2. T or F   A promissory note secured by a real estate mortgage is non-negotiable if it includes any reference to the mortgage.

3. T or F   A, a dishonest lawyer, persuaded M, his client, who had a fourth grade education and virtually no legal or commercial sophistication,

to execute a $10,000 promissory note payable to the order of A and a mortgage on Blackacre to secure it. A told M that the documents gave A a power of attorney to deal with personal injury litigation that A had commenced on M's behalf. A then sold the note and mortgage to H, a holder in due course. M has a valid defense to any action by H to collect the note or to foreclose the mortgage.

4. Why would a transferee of a promissory note and mortgage utilize an estoppel certificate?

5. T or F "Close connection" is a judicial doctrine aimed at expanding holder in due course protection to greater number of holders of promissory notes.

6. T or F A negotiable promissory note secured by a mortgage was assigned by the original mortgagee to a transferee who was a holder in due course. Maker-mortgagor, who was not notified of the transfer, continued to make monthly payments to the original mortgagee. Payments made to the original mortgagee must be credited on the mortgage debt.

7. Suppose the promissory note referred to in last question was non-negotiable. Would your answer be different? Explain.

8. T or F Mortgagee, under a promissory note secured by a mortgage on Blackacre, assigned the note and mortgage to Assignee, who promptly recorded the assignment. Mortgagor then conveyed Blackacre to G, a grantee, who continued to make mortgage payments to the original mortgagee. Assignee will not be required to credit against the mortgage debt any payments made by G to the original mortgagee after the assignment was recorded.

9. T or F A negotiable promissory note secured by a mortgage was assigned to a holder in due course who did not immediately record the assignment. The original mortgagee then satisfied the mortgage of record and the mortgagor sold and conveyed to a grantee who paid full value for Blackacre, had no knowledge of the assignment and who immediately recorded his deed. The holder in due course then recorded the assignment. The grantee owns Blackacre subject to the mortgage.

10. T or F A valid pledge of a promissory note and mortgage to secure a loan to the holder is governed by Article 9 of the UCC.

11. T or F Four lenders, E–1, E–2, E–3 and E–4, in chronological order, each took a 25% participation interest in a mortgage on Blackacre. The mortgage then went into default and at the time of default had a $1,000,000 balance. The mortgage was then foreclosed and the sale yielded $500,000. Mortgagor was judgment-proof so no deficiency judgment was sought against him. The participation agreement was silent on the priority of the parties' claims to foreclosure proceeds. Thus, E–1 and E–2 should each receive $250,000 and E–3 and E–4 should take nothing.

*

VIII

Discharge of the Debt and Mortgage: By Payment or Otherwise

■ **ANALYSIS**

A. Prepayment of the Mortgage Debt

Most laypersons tend to assume that a mortgage debt is prepayable. This belief probably stems from a cultural attitude that tells us that if prompt payment of debts is desirable, early payment must be even more commendable. However, this instinct is a substantial misperception of the law.

1. At Common Law

There is no right to prepay a mortgage debt before it is due, unless the terms of the obligation expressly authorize prepayment. See *Russo Enterprises, Inc. v. Citibank*, 699 N.Y.S.2d 437 (App.Div.1999); *Brannon v. McGowan*, 683 So.2d 994 (Ala.1996); Nelson & Whitman, Real Estate Finance Law § 6.1 (4th ed.20011994). This rule is derived from *Brown v. Cole*, 14 L.J. (N.S.) Ch. 167 (1845), where the court stated that if mortgagors "were allowed to pay off their mortgage money at any time after the execution of the mortgage, it might be attended with extrinsic inconvenience to mortgagees, who generally advance their money as an investment." Today, there may also be undesirable income tax consequences for prepayment. For example, for the seller of real estate who takes back a mortgage or installment land contract, prepayment in the year of sale can destroy entirely the advantages of installment reporting under § 453 of the Internal Revenue Code.

a. Recent Authority Rejecting the Common Law Rule

While the foregoing rule is plainly still the majority view, *a few recent cases have permitted prepayment where the documents were silent on the point.* See, e.g., *Mahoney v. Furches*, 468 A.2d 458 (Pa.1983). Two other states, Florida and North Carolina, have taken the same view by statute. Restatement (Third) of Property (Mortgages) § 6.1 adopts this trend, stating that, "In the absence of an agreement restricting or prohibiting payment of the mortgage obligation prior to maturity, the mortgagor has a right to make such payment in whole or in part." This trend is reasonable and desirable. Most borrowers probably assume that they have the right to prepay, and it is hardly burdensome for lenders to include a specific clause prohibiting prepayment if they do not wish to receive their money early.

b. "Lock-in" clauses

A "lock-in" clause is a provision that specifically prohibits prepayment prior to a certain date. *The courts uniformly enforce such clauses.* See, e.g., *George v. Fowler*, 978 P.2d 565 (Wash.App.1999). Restatement (Third) of

Property (Mortgages) § 6.2 agrees, stating that "an agreement that prohibits payment of the mortgage obligation prior to maturity is enforceable."

2. Prepayment Fees

Many mortgagees permit prepayment, but exact a charge or "prepayment fee" for the privilege of doing so. Such fees are relatively rare in home mortgage loans, but are widely used in loans on commercial property. A variety of formulas are used to calculate the fee. Examples include:

- Six months' interest on the amount by which prepayments in a 12 month period exceed 20% of the original principal amount.

- A fixed percentage (e.g., 2%) of the amount being prepaid. (This percentage may decline over time as the loan grows closer to maturity.)

- The difference between the interest the lender would have earned on the mortgage loan for the remaining term and the interest it would earn on the same sum if invested in U.S. government securities of an equivalent term. (This sort of clause is sometimes referred to as a "yield maintenance" fee.)

3. Reasons for Using Prepayment Fees

There are two major reasons why institutional lenders utilize prepayment fees. The traditional justification for such provisions is that the mortgagee's fixed costs of making a loan are not recaptured entirely at the inception of the loan, but are amortized over the life of the loan. Thus the collection of a fee, in theory, compensates for those costs. Second, the prepayment fee is used as a rough economic complement to the due-on-sale clause. While the due-on-sale clause allows a mortgagee to "call back" funds lent at lower than market interest rates, prepayment penalties tend to "lock in" loans that were made at higher than current market interest rates. In other words, the fee discourages the borrower from "shopping around" for refinancing at lower interest rates, and helps the lender maintain its yield on the loan when market rates have dropped.

Prepayment fees are very widely upheld by the courts. Indeed, outside of the bankruptcy context, there are very few cases refusing to enforce a prepayment fee. See Whitman, Mortgage Prepayment Clauses: An Economic and Legal Analysis, 40 UCLA L.Rev. 851 (1993).

4. Judicial Attacks on Prepayment Fees

a. The Usury Argument

Prepayment fees are not regarded as usurious because they represent a charge for returning money and not interest for the right to use money. See Boyd v. Life Insurance Co. of the Southwest, 546 S.W.2d 132 (Tex.Civ.App.1977).

b. Restraint on Alienation

Prepayment penalties are not considered an unreasonable restraint on alienation. See Carey v. Lincoln Loan Co., 998 P.2d 724 (Or.App.2000). Even a complete prohibition of prepayment for 11 years has not been deemed an unreasonable restraint on alienation. See *Hartford Life Insurance Co. v. Randall*, 583 P.2d 1126 (Or.1978). However, if a prohibition on prepayment is combined with a prohibition on sale of the property subject to the mortgage, the combination plainly *is* a restraint on alienation, since the owner cannot sell the property either free of the loan or subject to it. *Terry v. Born*, 604 P.2d 504 (Wash.App.1979).

c. Liquidated Damages vs. Penalty Analysis

A few courts have analyzed prepayment fees as a form of liquidation of damages. However, outside of the bankruptcy context the fee is nearly always found to be a reasonable estimate of the actual damages, and not to be an invalid penalty. See, e.g., *TMG Life Ins. Co. v. Ashner*, 898 P.2d 1145 (Kan.App.1995).

In *Lazzareschi Investment Co. v. San Francisco Federal Savings & Loan Ass'n*, 99 Cal.Rptr. 417 (Cal.App.1971) fee equal to 6 months' interest was upheld as reasonable, in part because it complied with a regulation of the Federal Home Loan Bank Board (FHLBB) governing prepayment penalties in residential transactions. Because the court actually was dealing with a non-residential transaction, it left the impression that the mortgagee could have charged an even higher penalty had it so chosen.

Example: A clause in a purchase money mortgage required a fee of 50% of any amount prepaid. The mortgagee-seller included the provision to avoid the negative federal income tax consequences that could have resulted if more than 30% of the total purchase price had been paid during the year of sale. (*Result:* the above penalty is valid because it was deemed to be "reasonably related to the [mortgagee's] anticipated risk of incurring increased tax liability upon the occurrence of the prepayment.") *Williams v. Fassler*, 167 Cal.Rptr. 545 (Cal.App.1980).

The *Lazzareschi* court held that the 6 months' penalty was reasonable because it was commonly utilized and, in a different context, actually authorized by a federal regulatory agency. It is probably safe to say that a fee equal to 6 months' interest is generally valid. On the other hand, one cannot say that a 50% penalty is valid beyond the confines of the *Williams* case unless the same federal income tax considerations make it reasonable. In other words, when the penalty is that large, it can be valid only when it is deemed to be reasonable under the facts and circumstances of the individual case.

The "reasonableness" test is often mentioned by the courts, but has little practical meaning, since virtually all prepayment fees have been held reasonable. One rare exception is *Automotive Finance Corp. v. Ridge Chrysler Plymouth L.L.C.*, 219 F.Supp. 2d 945 (N.D. Ill., Sept. 13, 2002), in which the court found unreasonable, and refused to enforce, a 15% fee in a loan to an auto dealership; the loan was not secured by a mortgage. The Restatement (Third) of Property (Mortgages) § 6.2 discards the reasonableness test, and simply provides that *"an agreement requiring the mortgagor to pay a fee or charge as a condition of such [pre-]payment is enforceable."* This seems perfectly sensible; after all, if prepayment can be entirely prohibited, as it can, what can be wrong with conditioning prepayment on the payment of any fee imaginable?

5. Acceleration by Mortgagee After Mortgagor Default

Most prepayments result from the mortgagor's desire to refinance at a lower rate, but they can also arise from a variety of circumstances that are, in a sense, beyond the mortgagor's control. The most obvious of these situations is the mortgagor's default in the payment of the loan and subsequent acceleration by the mortgagee. Once a mortgagor defaults and the mortgagee accelerates and initiates foreclosure, should the mortgage debt (for purposes of the mortgagor's right to redeem or for purposes of calculating the amount of a possible sale surplus or deficiency) include the amount of the prepayment charge?

Most of the cases prohibit the collection of the charge where the default and acceleration is caused by an honest inability to pay. At least three theories have been used to justify denial of the fee: (1) Once an acceleration has occurred, the principal sum is due and the payment is no longer "pre." (2) By accelerating, the lender has waived its claim to the prepayment fee. (3) The prepayment fee clause is intended to govern only "voluntary" prepayments, not a payment required by the lender. In the words of one court, the "lender loses its right to a prepayment charge when it elects to accelerate the debt. This is so because acceleration, by definition, advances the maturity date of the debt so that payment thereafter is not prepayment but instead payment after maturity." *Matter of LHD Realty Corp.*, 726 F.2d 327, 330–331 (7th Cir.1984). See also, *George H. Nutman, Inc. v. Aetna Business Credit, Inc.*, 453 N.Y.S.2d 586 (N.Y.1982).

a. Intentional Default to Avoid Fee

Where a mortgagor intentionally defaults and triggers acceleration and foreclosure in order to avoid the payment of a prepayment charge, the court will probably enforce the fee. In this setting, the mortgagor's plan would be to exercise his or her equitable right to redeem prior to foreclosure by paying an accelerated mortgage debt that would not include the prepayment fee. Although there is scant case authority on point, in this context the prepayment charge should be collectible. Unlike the situation where the mortgagor defaults in the payment of the loan without the prepayment clause in mind, here the mortgagor *chooses default as the means of prepayment.* As one court has noted, "should such intentional defaults become a problem, . . . we believe courts could deal with the difficulty by denying the acceleration exception in appropriate cases." *Matter of LHD Realty Corp.*, 726 F.2d 327, 331 (7th Cir.1984).

b. Mortgage Clause Specifically Requiring Payment of Fee Upon Default and Acceleration

Several recent cases hold that, even where the mortgagor's default is not part of an intentional plan to avoid payment of the fee, the mortgagee may still collect the fee if the mortgage documents specifically provided for it in the context of default and acceleration. *Biancalana v. Fleming*, 53 Cal.Rptr.2d 47 (Cal.App.1996); *General Mortg. Assoc. v. Campolo Realty & Mortg. Corp.*, 678 So.2d 431 (Fla.App.1996). See Stark, New Developments in Enforcing Prepayment Charges After an Acceleration of a Mortgage Loan, 26 Real Prop. Prob. & Tr. J. 213 (1991).

6. Other Involuntary Prepayments

Courts often refuse to permit the collection of prepayment penalties if the payment is "involuntary," as, for example, where it is the result of casualty loss and the collection of insurance proceeds or of the exercise of the condemnation power. See *Chestnut Corp. v. Bankers Bond & Mortg. Co.*, 149 A.2d 48 (Pa.1959) (insurance proceeds); *Clinton Capital Corp. v. Straeb*, 589 A.2d 1363 (N.J.Super.Ch.1990) (eminent domain award); Nelson &

Whitman, Real Estate Finance Law § 6.3 (4th ed.2001). However, if the documents clearly state that the fee is due in this context, there is authority that it will be enforced. *Melin v. TCF Financial Corp.*, 1995 WL 265064 (Minn.App.1995); *Village of Rosemont v. Maywood–Proviso State Bank*, 501 N.E.2d 859, 862 (Ill.App.1986).

Under Restatement (Third) of Property (Mortgages) § 6.3, the enforceability of the fee in this context depends on the lender's position with respect to use of the insurance or condemnation proceeds. If it would be feasible to use the proceeds for restoration of the property, but the lender nonetheless insists that they be paid toward the loan balance instead, the lender may not also collect the prepayment fee.

7. Prepayment Charges Incident to Due–On–Sale Enforcement

Mortgagees sometimes attempt to collect prepayment penalties incident to due-on-sale clause enforcement. State law consistently has been unsympathetic to this type of "double dipping." A few state statutes prohibit the enforcement of a prepayment penalty where it is triggered by the mortgagee's enforcement of a due-on-sale clause. Several courts have reached the same result without the benefit of a statute. See *Tan v. California Fed. Sav. & Loan Ass'n*, 189 Cal.Rptr. 775 (Cal.App.1983). These cases often assert that once a mortgagor has exercised the due-on-sale clause and accelerated the mortgage debt, payment by the mortgagor is then legally due and by definition cannot be a "prepayment." Alternatively, they reason that the prepayment is "involuntary" and hence not covered by the prepayment fee clause. See Nelson and Whitman, Real Estate Finance Law § 6.5 (4th ed.2001).

Nonetheless, if the mortgage clearly provides that the fee will be payable in the event of an acceleration resulting from an unconsented transfer of the property under the due-on-sale clause, it is very likely that the courts will enforce the fee. *Eyde Bros. Development Co. v. Equitable Life Assur. Soc'y*, 888 F. 2d 127 (6th Cir.1989). By analogy to the position of the Restatement on prepayment fees resulting from eminent domain or casualty insurance payments, it would be reasonable, in the due-on-sale context, to ask whether the lender is accelerating because of the undesirable credit characteristics of the new owner of the property, or simply because rates have risen and the acceleration will allow the lender to reap higher profits. The fee would be enforced in the first situation, but not in the second. However, there is no case authority supporting this view.

A regulation of the Office of Thrift Supervision (12 C.F.R. § 591.5(b)), prohibits prepayment penalty collection in a variety of due-on-sale enforcement contexts. The regulation, as paraphrased in the Board's preamble, prohibits:

> prepayment penalties with respect to loans on the security of borrower-occupied homes if a lender
>
> (1) exercises a due-on-sale clause by written notice,
>
> (2) commences a foreclosure proceeding to enforce a due-on-sale clause or to seek payment in full as a result of invoking such a clause, or
>
> (3) fails to approve within 30 days the completed credit application of a qualified transferee to assume the loan in accordance with its terms, and thereafter, within 120 days of the lender's receipt of such application, the borrower transfers the home to that transferee and prepays the loan in full.

8. Prepayment Fees in Bankruptcy

When the borrower is in bankruptcy, the collection of a prepayment fee will be decided by the bankruptcy court. As a practical matter, the issue is usually not enforceability *per se* of the fee, but rather whether it is enforceable as a *secured claim*. A claim that is valid but unsecured is likely to be virtually uncollectible. On the other hand, a claim that is secured may be collectible in full if debt is oversecured—that is, the real estate security is significantly more valuable than the principal balance owing on the mortgage debt.

Under Bankruptcy Code § 506(b), *prepayment fees (and a variety of other miscellaneous charges) are treated as secured claims only if they are reasonable.* The bankruptcy courts have been extremely aggressive in finding prepayment fees to be unreasonable if they appear to exceed the actual damages suffered by the lender as a result of the prepayment. See Gould, Conflicting Approaches to Recovery of Pre-payment Premiums under § 506(b), 18 Am. Bankr. Inst. J. 22 (1999). Often these decisions purport to employ the "liquidated damage/penalty" analysis discussed above, but they are *much* more likely to find that the fee is a penalty than are state courts. See, e.g., *In re Wiston XXIV Ltd. Partnership*, 170 B.R. 453 (D.Kan.1994); *In re A.J. Lane & Co.*, 113 B.R. 821, 823 (Bankr.D.Mass.1990).

9. Yield Maintenance Clauses

Most of the prepayment fee clauses presented to bankruptcy courts in recent years have been so-called "yield maintenance clauses," which purport to give the lender the economic equivalent of loss that the lender sustains if prepayment is made when interest rates have fallen. Such clauses are usually structured to give the lender the present value of the difference between the interest rate on the loan and the rate on U.S. Treasury obligations of the same maturity as the remaining loan term. In effect, this assumes that the lender will reinvest the prepaid funds in Treasury debt–a bit farfetched, since what the lender will in fact do in most cases is to make another mortgage loan with the prepaid funds. However, there is no generally-available index of interest rates on commercial mortgage loans, and the Treasury rate may be seen by the courts as an acceptable substitute. Bankruptcy courts have varied in their treatment of these yield maintenance clauses.

a. Use of Treasury Rate as an Index

Most recent bankruptcy cases have sustained the use of a Treasury rate as an index in calculating the prepayment fee. See, e.g., *In re Hidden Lake Ltd. Partnership*, 247 B.R. 722 (Bankr.S.D.Ohio 2000) ("use of the Treasury obligation as a reference point for the calculation, although generally overcompensating [the lender], is not an unreasonable estimate"); *In re Vanderveer Estates Holdings, Inc.*, 283 B.R. 122 (Bkrtcy.E.D.N.Y.2002).

b. Other Faults in Yield Maintenance Clauses

Bankruptcy courts have routinely struck down yield maintenance clauses that failed to discount the difference between the loan rate and the reinvestment index rate to present value. *In re Schwegmann*, 264 B.R. 823 (Bankr.E.D. La.2001); In re *A.J.Lane & Co.*, 113 B.R. 821 (Bankr.D.Mass.1990). They have also been unwilling to enforce clauses with large "floor" fees that were to be added to the present value calculation; see *In re Kroh Bros. Development Co.*, 88 B.R. 997 (Bankr.W.D.Mo.1988).

10. Statutory and Regulatory Limitations

a. State Legislation

Many states have legislation governing prepayment fees, but they vary a great deal. The one common element in nearly all such legislation is that it is limited to residential real estate. Sometimes prepayment penalties are prohibited altogether. More common, however, are statutes that limit penalties to 1–3% of the principal balance, depending on the number of years the loan has been outstanding.

b. Office of Thrift Supervision (Federal Savings Associations)

At one time a federal regulation limited the amount of prepayment fees that could be charged by federally-chartered savings and loan associations. This regulation was subsequently repealed. Currently, the regulations of the OTS provide that "subject to the terms of the loan contract, a Federal savings association may impose a fee for any prepayment of a loan." 12 C.F.R. § 560.34. It is clear that this regulation preempts any contrary state law, so that Federally-chartered savings association may impose prepayment fees even when state-chartered institutions are prohibited by state statute from doing so; see 12 C.F.R. § 560.2(b)(5).

c. Comptroller of the Currency (National Banks)

The Comptroller of the Currency has not adopted a regulation that would generally preempt state law with respect to prepayment fees charged by national banks. However, in Interpretive Letter No.744 (Aug.21, 1996), the OCC's chief counsel took the view that prepayment penalties are "interest" within the meaning of 12 U.S.C. § 85. Under that statute, national banks are permitted to charge the same amounts as "interest" to customers in other states as would be legal under state law in the state where the bank is located. In effect, the home state's law is "exported" to the state of the customer's residence, even if the latter state would not allow the charging of the item. As a practical matter, this reasoning would allow a national bank located in a state that did not limit prepayment fees to charge the same fees nationwide. This principle (but not its application to prepayment fees) was sustained in *Smiley v. Citibank (South Dakota) N.A.*, 116 S.Ct. 1730 (1996). Whether the OCC's characterization of prepayment fees as "interest" is correct is debatable, however.

d. Federal National Mortgage Association (FNMA) and Federal Home Loan Mortgage Corporation (FHLMC)

The current Fannie Mae–Freddie Mac single-family note form permits prepayment without penalty. However, the Fannie Mae multi-family form provides for a "yield maintenance" type of fee in the event of prepayment.

B. Late Payment Charges and Default Interest

Mortgages commonly require the payment of "late payment charges" or "late fees" on the failure of the mortgagor to tender timely payment of a mortgage loan installment. While practice varies, such charges are often calculated as a percentage of the late installment and, less frequently, as a percentage of the principal balance. Sometimes the penalty is a fixed dollar amount, but usually it is the lesser or greater of a percentage and a fixed dollar amount.

As an alternative to, or in addition to, a simple fee for late payment, the loan documents may provide for a "default interest rate"—i.e., that the interest rate on the loan will be higher during any period that the payments are delinquent.

1. **Judicial Approaches to Late Payment Charges and Default Interest**

   There have been two judicial approaches to enforcement of late payment charges and default interest rates. Some courts have employed a "liquidated damages/invalid penalty" analysis similar to that discussed in the prepayment fee context. Others have treated the charges as agreements for the payment of interest and have adopted a usury analysis.

   a. **Liquidated Damages vs. Penalty Analysis**

   Under this approach, *a late payment charge or default interest rate will be struck down as an invalid penalty if it is not a reasonable effort to estimate the mortgagee's actual damages* resulting from late payment. *Hitz v. First Interstate Bank*, 44 Cal.Rptr.2d 890 (Cal.App.1995) (late fee held unenforceable); *Feller v. Architects Display Bldgs., Inc.*, 148 A.2d 634 (N.J.App.Div.1959) (interest increase from 17% to 33% upon default held unenforceable). Late fees calculated as a percentage of the unpaid principal balance of the loan are more likely to be invalidated as an unlawful penalty than charges based on a percentage of the late payment. However, the majority of the cases sustain and enforce both late fees up to 5% or 6% of the late payment, and default interest "kick-ups" of 5% to 6%; see *MetLife Capital Financial Corp. v. Washington Ave. Associates L.P.*, 732 A.2d 493 (N.J.1999), upholding a 5% late fee without requiring proof by the lender of actual damages, on the theory that the fee was a reasonable advance estimate of likely damages; *Mattvidi Assoc. L.P. v. NationsBank of Virginia*, 639 A.2d 228 (Md.Spec.App.1994) for a comprehensive listing of the cases. Occasionally a court will sustain a much greater rate; see, e.g., *In re Dixon*, 228 B.R. 166 (W.D.Va.1998), upholding a default interest increase from 18% to 36%.

   Example: A mortgage provided that in the event of late payment by mortgagor, the mortgagee became entitled to a late payment fee of 2% of the principal balance of the mortgage. The mortgagor challenged the fee judicially on the ground that it was an invalid penalty. (*Result:* charge measured against the unpaid principal balance is punitive and an invalid penalty.) *Garrett v. Coast & Southern Federal Savings & Loan Ass'n*, 108 Cal.Rptr. 845, 511 P.2d 1197 (Cal.1973).

   Example: A mortgage provided that in the event the mortgagor's payments were delinquent, the interest rate on the loan would increase from 9% to 24% per annum. The mortgagor challenged the increased interest judicially on the ground that it was an invalid penalty. (*Result:* case remanded to determine whether the increased interest was punitive and invalid.) *Stuchin v. Kasirer*, 568 A.2d 907 (N.J.App.Div.1990).

Note that if a court finds a late fee invalid as a penalty, the *borrower remains liable for the actual damages* resulting from his or her delinquency. *Hitz v. First Interstate Bank, supra.*

If a mortgage provides for a balloon payment of principal, applying the late fee provision to that final payment can produce a very large fee. Hence, unless the language of the loan documents is very clearly to the contrary, courts are likely to construe them as applying only to monthly payments, and not as imposing the late fee on a late final payment; see *Art Country Squire, L.L.C. v. Inland Mortg. Corp.*, 745 N.E.2d 885 (Ind.App.2001). On the other hand, default interest, if otherwise reasonable, is readily applied to balloon payments; *Fourth Fed. Sav. Bank v. Nationwide Assoc.*, 701 N.Y.S.2d 814 (S.Ct.1999).

b. Late Fees as Usury

Under this approach, late payment charges are tantamount to interest payments and are usurious if they cause the overall interest to exceed the legal maximum. See *Ford v. Staats*, 1998 WL 1184108 (Mass.Super.1998). Some courts refuse to characterize late payments as the payment of interest for usury law purposes because the mortgagor has it in his or her power to avoid the penalty by timely payment of the installment. Other courts may be reluctant to treat late fees as usurious because of the often harsh penalties imposed on usurious transactions, such as the total loss of interest (and sometimes principal). Where the charge is expressed as a default interest rate, it is much easier for a court to conclude that it is within the scope of the usury statute.

c. Late Fees and Default Interest in Bankruptcy

When the borrower is in bankruptcy, the question often arises whether a late fee or default interest is recognized as a secured claim, assuming the security real estate is sufficient to cover it. If the claim is deemed unsecured, it will usually be largely or wholly uncollectible. Bankruptcy Code § 506(b) governs this question, and requires that the fee or additional interest be "reasonable." The bankruptcy courts have been quite vigorous in holding large late fees or interest increases to be unreasonable and thus unsecured, even if they might have been sustained under state law liquidated damage or usury principles. See *In re Timberline Property Development, Inc.*, 136 B.R. 382 (Bankr.D.N.J.1992) (late fee of 5% of delinquent installment held unreasonable); *In re Hollstrom*, 133 B.R. 535 (Bankr.D.Colo.1991) (default interest of 36% held unreasonable). In addition, a bankruptcy reorganization plan under Chapter 11 may treat the defaulted mortgage debt as reinstated, thus completely eliminating the running of default interest; see *In re Sylmar Plaza, L.P.*, 314 F.3d 1070 (9th Cir.2002), sustaining such a plan despite the mortgage lender's argument that it was promulgated in bad faith.

2. Legislative and Regulatory Limitations

a. State Statutes

A growing number of states regulate late fees by statute. Almost all of these statutes have in common a requirement that late charges be calculated as a percentage of the late installment rather than of the principal balance of the loan. Some limit the penalty to the *lesser* of a nominal amount such as $5 or $10 and a percentage of the late payment. Grace periods before any penalty may be exacted are also common features of this legislation. However, most states' statutes do not regulate default interest provisions, except in the sense that the total interest may become usurious. See generally Nelson & Whitman, Real Estate Finance Law § 6.8 (4th ed.2001).

b. Uniform Consumer Credit Code

Section 2.203 of the 1968 Uniform Consumer Credit Code (UCCC) and § 2.502 of the 1974 UCCC generally limit late charges to the lesser of $5 or 5% of the late installment with respect to real estate installment loans for personal, family, household or agricultural purposes whose interest rates exceed 12% per annum. There is a 10 day grace period. At least 11 states have enacted the Code in one of its versions.

c. Federal Regulation

1) FHA and VA Loans

As to home mortgages insured by the Federal Housing Administration (FHA), late payment penalties are limited to 4% of each installment due that is more than fifteen days late. 24 C.F.R. § 203.25. The maximum late charge for mortgages guaranteed by the Veterans Administration (VA) is also 4% of any installment that is delinquent more than fifteen days. 38 C.F.R. § 36.4212(d). The same VA regulation also prohibits the charging of a higher interest rate upon default.

2) Loans by Federally–Regulated Lenders

With respect to all loans made to consumers, federally-regulated lenders may not charge a late fee when the only delinquency is the borrower's failure to pay a previously-assessed late fee. See 12 C.F.R. § 227.15 (banks belonging to the Federal Reserve System); 12 C.F.R. § 535.4 (federal savings associations); 12 C.F.R. § 706.4 (federal credit unions).

3) Federal Savings Associations

Office of Thrift Supervision (OTS) regulations authorize federally-chartered savings and loan associations to include late charge provisions in their home loan documents, and they impose no substantive limitations on the amount of the charges. See 12 C.F.R. § 560.33. Since these regulations are preemptive of state law, a federal association may charge late fees without regard to state statutes limiting the amounts of such fees. See *Collins v. Union Federal Sav. & Loan Ass'n*, 662 P.2d 610 (Nev.1983).

The OTS regulations, however, impose certain procedural limitations on late charges. An association may not impose a charge more than one time for the same late installment. Each payment received must be applied to the longest outstanding installment due. The association may not deduct late charges from regular installment payments, but must collect them separately. Finally, no charge may be assessed unless a payment is more than 15 days late.

4) Federal Secondary Market Agencies

Fannie Mae requires collection, on non-federally insured or guaranteed home mortgages, of a late charge of 4% of the late installment (or such lesser amount if there is a state law limitation) after a 15 day grace period. Freddie Mac permits, but does not require, the collection of a maximum 5% late charge after a 15 day grace period.

C. Payment and Redemption

Common sense suggests that when the obligation secured by a mortgage is fully performed, the mortgagee has a duty to discharge or release the mortgage, and to do so in a fashion that can be memorialized in the public records, so that the title to the real estate will no longer appear to be encumbered by the mortgage. This is indeed the law, but matters are a bit more complex. The precise effect of paying off the obligation depends on who pays and why.

1. Payment by One Who is Primarily Responsible for the Obligation

When one who has primary responsibility for the mortgage debt pays it in full, the mortgage is automatically extinguished. See *United States v. Hoffman*, 826 P.2d 340 (Ariz.App.1992). This result is termed a "redemption" of the real estate from the mortgage. A partial payment ordinarily will not suffice, unless the mortgagee accepts it as the equivalent of payment in full. See Restatement (Third) of Property (Mortgages) § 6.4(a) (1997).

a. Who Is Primarily Responsible?

Obviously the original mortgagor is primarily responsible for payment if he or she still owns the mortgaged real estate. This is so even if the debt is "non-recourse," so that the mortgagor has no personal liability on it. In addition, a grantee who presently owns the real estate is considered primarily responsible, whether he or she assumed the mortgage debt or merely took subject to it. Likewise, a cotenant or the holder of limited interest, such as a life estate, is considered primarily responsible except to the extent that someone else has a duty to reimburse him or her for part of the payment made.

b. When Can Payment Be Made?

A redemption of the mortgage can be made only when payment is due, or prior to that time if the mortgagee is willing to accept it or applicable prepayment principles permit it. This includes the case in which the debt has matured naturally, as well as any situation in which the mortgagee has accelerated the debt under an appropriate clause in the mortgage or the debt instrument. Acceleration may occur because of a default in payment or a failure to perform some other mortgage covenant. It may also occur under a due-on-sale, due-on-encumbrance, or similar clause.

c. Payment Must Be in Full

A partial payment will not extinguish the mortgage, unless the mortgagee voluntarily accepts it in lieu of payment in full. The payment must include the full principal balance of the debt, all accrued interest, and any other legally-demanded charges, such as prepayment fees, trustees' fees, and costs and attorneys' fees if the mortgagee has expended them in collection efforts. See Annot., 46 A.L.R.3d 1362 (1972).

d. Payment not Good until Received

The payment is not considered to have been made when it is mailed or transmitted, but only when it is actually received by the mortgagee. *Nguyen v. Calhoun*, 129 Cal.Rptr.2d 436 (2003); *Ciuffetelli v. Apple Bank For Savings*, 208 F.3d 202 (Table) (2d Cir.2000) (unpublished).

1) Exception for Partial Release Clauses

Some mortgages, particularly on raw land that is expected to be subdivided, contain clauses requiring the mortgagee to release individual lots or parcels from the mortgage upon payment of specified portions of the full mortgage debt. Such clauses are effective, and govern over the requirement that payment must ordinarily be in full. See Annot., 41 A.L.R.3d 7 (1972).

e. The Payor's Right to a Written Discharge

Even though in theory the discharge of the mortgage is instant and automatic, *the mortgagee has a duty to give the payor a written document in recordable form, showing that the mortgage has been extinguished.* See *Bartold v. Glendale Federal Bank*, 97 Cal.Rptr.2d 226 (Ct.App.2000) (beneficiary of deed of trust has a duty to instruct trustee to reconvey immediately upon receipt of full payment). If the mortgagee refuses, the payor may apply to a court for an order compelling issuance of such a paper. A mortgagee who refuses in bad faith to provide a discharge may be held liable for damages. In most states there are also statutory penalties against mortgagees who fail to provide a discharge within some fixed time, such as 15 or 30 days after a written demand for a discharge from the mortgagor. See, e.g., *Nay v. First Finan. Bank*, 79 P.3d 1124 (Okla.Civ.App.2003).

f. Agreement Not to Extinguish the Mortgage

Sometimes the payor and the mortgagee do not want to extinguish the mortgage, even though a payment in full is made. This is often the case with "line of credit" or "home equity" mortgages, in which the borrower and lender expect that the balance on the loan will be drawn down, repaid, and drawn down again numerous times. It would be inconvenient if a new mortgage had to be executed and recorded for each of these cycles. Hence, if the parties agree that the mortgage will remain in effect, no discharge will occur. See *Raintree Realty & Constr., Inc. v. Kasey*, 447 S.E.2d 823 (N.C.Ct.App.1994) (based on statute).

2. Payment by One Who is Not Primarily Responsible for the Obligation

When someone who holds an interest in the real estate subordinate to the mortgage, but who is not primarily responsible for the obligation, pays it in full, the mortgage is not extinguished. Instead, the mortgage and the obligation are deemed assigned to the payor by operation of law under the principle of subrogation. See Nelson & Whitman, Real Estate Finance Law, § 10.4 (4th ed.2001). This allows the payor to use the mortgage to assist in gaining reimbursement from the person who *is* primarily responsible. Such a payment accomplishes a redemption of the payor's interest from the mortgage; hence, the term "redemption" does not always mean the extinction of the mortgage. As with payments by those who are primarily responsible, payment in the present context must be in full; there is no redemption or subrogation on the basis of partial payment (unless the mortgagee voluntarily accepts it as payment in full, of course).

a. What Payors Are Not Primarily Responsible?

A variety of persons might wish to pay a mortgage debt to protect their interests, even though they are not primarily responsible for payment. They include guarantors, holders of junior mortgages and other junior liens, and tenants under junior leases. See *Matter of Forester*, 529 F.2d 310 (9th Cir.1976). Similarly, a tenant in common or a life tenant is not primarily responsible to the extent that someone else (e.g., another tenant in common or the holder of a future interest) has a duty to reimburse the payor for part of the payment; hence, to that extent, the mortgage is considered assigned to the payor rather than extinguished.

Example: A and B are equal tenants in common of mortgaged property, and each has a duty to the other to pay one-half of the mortgage debt. The debt is due and B refuses to pay anything, so A pays the entire debt. As to one-half of the debt, the mortgage is extinguished. As to the other one-half, the mortgage is regarded as assigned to A by subrogation, and as affecting only B's one-half interest in the property. A may foreclose the mortgage against B's half interest if necessary to obtain reimbursement for one-half of the payment A made. See *Snider v. Basinger*, 132 Cal.Rptr. 637 (Cal.Ct.App.1976).

Example: Mr is in default on a mortgage loan, and the mortgage is threatening foreclosure. G has guaranteed payment of the loan. To forestall foreclosure, G pays the mortgage debt is full. G is subrogated to the mortgagee's rights on the note and mortgage, and is entitled to an assignment of them. *Harley J. Robinson Trust v. Ardmore Acres, Inc.*, 6 F.Supp.2d 640 (E.D.Mich.1998).

b. When Can Payment Be Made?

A redemption of the mortgage by one who is not primarily responsible for payment can be made only when payment is due. This may occur as a result of maturity of the debt or an acceleration by the mortgagee under an appropriate clause. *However, prepayment is not permitted, even if the mortgagee is willing to accept it.* Those who are not primarily responsible for payment have no right to interfere with the debt relationship by voluntarily prepaying the loan.

c. The Payor's Right to a Written Assignment

Even though in theory the assignment of the mortgage to the payor under the principle of subrogation is instant and automatic, *the mortgagee has a duty to give the payor a written document in recordable form, showing that the mortgage has been assigned.* See *United States v. Boston & Berlin Transportation Co.*, 237 F.Supp. 1004, 1008 (D.N.H.1964). If the mortgagee refuses to give such a document upon reasonable request, the payor may apply to a court for an order compelling it, and may also recover damages if the refusal was in bad faith. *2301 Jerome Avenue Realty Corp. v. Di Paolo*, 737 N.Y.S.2d 816 (Misc.2002).

3. Subrogation in Favor of a Refinancing Lender

Often a mortgagor will obtain a new mortgage loan in order to refinance an existing loan. This is especially common when interest rates have been falling, so that the rate on the existing loan is above current market rates. The new lender will ordinarily obtain a title examination or title report in order to verify that the existing mortgage is the first and only lien on the property. Hence, the new lender expects that, when the existing mortgage is discharged by the new funds being lent, the existing mortgage will disappear and the new lender's mortgage will have first priority on the property.

Sometimes, however, this plan goes awry. There is in fact a second mortgage or other junior lien on the property, a fact not mentioned to the refinancing lender by the borrower, and (because of an error, usually by the title insurance company) not reported to the refinancing lender in the title report. After the refinancing is completed and the old first mortgage has been discharged, the second mortgage holder takes the position that it now has a first lien, and that the refinancing mortgage is subordinate to it.

In order to combat this argument, the refinancing lender will argue that it has a right of equitable subrogation to the position and priority of the mortgage that was paid off with the funds the refinancing lender advanced. If this argument is successful, the refinancing lender's problem is solved, for it will step into the shoes of the old first lien and will have the priority it expected to receive. In effect, it will benefit from an assignment of the old first mortgage by operation of law to it, with the priority of that mortgage intact. This seems a fair result, since it imposes no hardship on the junior mortgagee, who simply remains in the same junior position it had previously. On the other hand, if subrogation is denied, the junior mortgagee receives an unwarranted and unexpected promotion in priority–a windfall.

In American law there are three distinct views of the refinancing lender's subrogation claim, outlined below.

a. Subrogation Granted Only if Refinancing Lender Has No Constructive Notice of Intervening Lien

Under this view, followed in a minority of jurisdictions, the refinancing lender will be held to have had notice of the junior lien if it is recorded, as is virtually always the case. Courts following this view consider that the equitable remedy of subrogation should not be exercised in favor of a party who could have known or discovered its predicament. *The practical effect of this view is to deny subrogation to the refinancing lender in essentially all cases.* See *Harms v. Burt*, 40 P.3d 329 (Kan.App.2002); *Metmor Financial, Inc. v. Landoll Corp.*, 976 S.W.2d 454 (Mo. App.1998). This reluctance to grant subrogation is difficult to understand in light of the fact that subrogation harms no one, while refusal to grant it gives the intervening lienor an unwarranted promotion in priority.

b. Subrogation Granted unless the Refinancing Lender Has Actual Knowledge of Intervening Lien

Under this view, the refinancing lender is entitled to subrogation unless it actually discovered the junior lien, whether through a title examination or by means of other sources of information. This is likely the majority view; see *Metrobank for Sav. v. National Community Bank*, 620 A.2d 433 (N.J.Super.1993). The mere fact that the junior lien is recorded will not suffice to deny subrogation under this approach; *Citibank Fed. Sav. Bank v. New Plan Realty Trust*, 748 A.2d 24 (Md.App.2000).

c. Subrogation Granted if the Refinancing Lender had a Reasonable Expectation of Gaining Priority

This is the view most favorable to refinancing lenders. It holds that, even if the refinancing lender had actual knowledge of the junior lien, it should still be entitled to subrogation if it reasonably expected to obtain the priority of the mortgage that it paid off. See *Houston v. Bank of America FSB*, 78 P.3d 71 (Nev.2003); *Suntrust Bank v. Riverside Nat. Bank*, 792 So.2d 1222 (Fla.App.2001); *East Boston Sav. Bank v. Ogan*, 701 N.E.2d 331 (Mass.1998); *Aames Capital Corp. v. Interstate Bank*, 734 N.E.2d 493 (Ill.App.2000). This is a minority view, but appears to be gaining ground, and is adopted by Restatement (Third) of Property (Mortgages) § 7.6, cmt. e (1997).

d. The Relevance of Title Insurance

In most cases, the refinancing lender will have obtained a title insurance policy insuring its new mortgage as a first lien. Hence, if the court refuses to apply the doctrine of subrogation, the loss will ultimately be borne by the title insurer rather than the refinancing lender. Several recent cases have taken the view that, since it was the title company's fault that it failed to discover and report the intervening lien, subrogation should be refused so that the title company will not be able to avoid the consequences of its negligence. See, e.g., *Centreville Car Care, Inc. v. North American Mortg. Co.*, 559 S.E.2d 870 (Va. 2002); *Kim v. Lee*, 31 P.3d 665 (Wash.2001), as amended by 43 P.3d 1222 (Wash.2001). This seems a bizarre form of reasoning. If a legal rule is adopted that gives purchasing insurance the effect of increasing risk, the rule will run precisely counter to the economic efficiency that insurance is designed to achieve. The presence or absence of title insurance should be irrelevant to the decision to grant subrogation.

e. Harm to the Holder of the Intervening Interest

Subrogation should be applied only if it will do no harm to the holder of the intervening junior interest. This is not always the case. For example, if the interest rate on refinancing loan is *higher* than on the preexisting loan that it replaces, the intervening lienholder can quite plausibly argue that granting subrogation will harm it, and hence should be denied. See *Indymac Mortg. Holdings, Inc. v. Kauffman*, 2001 WL 1683779 (Tenn.App.2001, not reported in S.W.2d), taking this view. While this is often taken by the courts as a sign that subrogation should be denied, the better view, we believe, is that it should only be denied *pro tanto*, to the extent of the prejudice to the intervening lienor.

f. Use of an Assignment

As we have seen above, the application of the equitable principle of subrogation to assist a refinancing lender in assuming the priority of the mortgage that was paid off is an uncertain and problematic undertaking.

However, there is a simple way the refinancing lender can avoid these problems, and that is to obtain an actual, written assignment of the old lender's mortgage. The old lender has an obligation to give an assignment, rather than a discharge, if one is requested. See Restatement (Third) of Property (Mortgages) § 7.6, cmt. a (1997); *Payne v. Foster*, 135 N.Y.S.2d 819 (App. Div.1954). Refinancings are routinely handled this way in New York state in order to avoid the payment of a new mortgage recording tax; perhaps lenders throughout the nation should adopt it.

If, after taking an assignment, the refinancing lender wishes to join with the borrower in modifying the terms of the loan, that may certainly be done. However, the lender is subject to the risk of a partial loss of priority to the extent that the new loan terms are materially prejudicial to or increase the risk of loss to the intervening lienor. See Restatement (Third) of Property (Mortgages) § 7.3(b) (1997).

4. Tender as the Equivalent of Payment

Sometimes a mortgagee will improperly refuse to accept a payment in full, even though the debt is due or has been accelerated. *In such a case, the tender of the payment—that is, a present offer to pay immediately in full, coupled with present ability to do so—has the same effect, discussed above, as payment itself would have.* Specifically, tender will stop the running of interest on the debt and will entitle the payor to a document showing that the mortgage has been extinguished or assigned, as the case may be. The tender must be the equivalent of cash; a mere tender of another promissory note is not effective; *Federal Nat'l Mortg. Ass'n v. McAuliffe*, 641 N.Y.S.2d 115 (App.Div.1996). It must be for the full debt, including any valid fees, accrued interest, and attorneys' fees. *Metropolitan Credit Union v. Matthes*, 706 N.E.2d 296 (Mass.App.1999). It must be a present offer to pay, not merely an offer to pay in the future; *Hansen v. Little Bear Inn Co.*, 9 P.3d 960 (Wyo.2000).

a. Tender Must Be Unconditional

To be effective, the tender must not be conditioned on some further agreement or performance by the mortgagee. For example, if the mortgagor tenders payment on the condition that the mortgagee also release another mortgage on other real estate, the tender is ineffective. See *Cardella v. Giancola*, 747 N.Y.S.2d 31 (App.Div.2002). However, the payor may properly tender on the condition that the mortgagee give a release of the debt and mortgage, since these acts are the duties of the mortgagee in any event.

b. Tender Must Be Kept Good

To be effective, the tender must be kept good. This means that the payor must continue to be ready, willing, and able to make the payment in full. This might be accomplished by putting the funds in an escrow or trust account or paying them into court, but these acts are not required if the payor continues to have immediate access to the funds and willingness to pay them. See *Brinton v. Haight*, 870 P.2d 677 (Idaho App.1994).

D. Mortgages Securing Non–Monetary Obligations

A mortgage is enforceable only if the obligation it secures is readily reducible to a money equivalent at the time of its enforcement. See Restatement (Third) of Property (Mortgages) § 1.4 (1997).

Example: Seller of a grocery business agreed not to compete with the buyer for 3 years within a radius of 20 miles. To secure this promise, seller, as mortgagor, gave buyer, as mortgagee, a mortgage on Blackacre, seller's vacation home. Within a month or two, seller opened a grocery business a few blocks away from the store she sold to buyer. Buyer brought an action to foreclose the mortgage on Blackacre. Seller-mortgagor moves to dismiss the action. (*Result:* motion to dismiss should probably be granted because damages resulting from the violation of the covenant not to compete are at best speculative. The covenant is not readily reducible to a money equivalent and therefore there is no valid mortgage).

There are good reasons for the above rule. First, suppose the mortgagor defaults and foreclosure occurs. Unless the mortgage debt can be reduced to a money equivalent, it will be impossible to determine the amount of a deficiency judgment or to allocate surplus among junior lienholders or to the mortgagor. Second, it will be difficult, if not impossible, to obtain second mortgage financing on land burdened by a "non-monetary" senior mortgage. This is because bidders at a junior lien foreclosure sale should bid, at most, the fair market value of the land less the amount of any senior lien. If the latter amount cannot be determined because it is not capable of being reduced to a money amount, intelligent bidding at the second mortgage foreclosure sale becomes impossible. Finally, if the mortgage does not secure an obligation with a monetary equivalence, it will be impossible for junior interest-holders to redeem, since they cannot determine what amount to tender. See generally, Nelson & Whitman, Real Estate Finance Law § 2.2 (4th ed.2001).

The law does not require that the obligation be stated directly in monetary terms, provided that its monetary value can be determined. In this category are promises to construct buildings (see *Pawtucket Institution for Savings v. Gagnon*, 475 A.2d 1028 (R.I.1984)) or to install utilities or other improvements on real estate (see *Jeffrey Towers, Inc. v. Straus*, 297 N.Y.S.2d 450 (N.Y.App.Div.1969)).

Mortgages to secure promises of support present especially difficult problems. The grantor—typically an elderly person—conveys title to real estate to a younger relative in return for the latter's promise to care for the grantor during his or her life. The grantee's promise is secured by a mortgage on the conveyed real estate in favor of the grantor-mortgagee. Courts tend to construe these mortgages liberally in favor of the mortgagee. See, e.g., *Thompson v. Glidden*, 445 A.2d 676 (Me.1982). Thus, there is authority that mortgages securing promises of financial or physical support are enforceable. Id; Restatement (Third) of Property (Mortgages) § 1.4 illus. 2 & 3 (1997). However, some courts go so far as to read into the transaction an "implicit promise of peace, harmony and emotional well-being" in addition to the specific promise of physical support. Id. "Where such promises of emotional support are present, it is highly questionable whether the mortgage should be regarded as a mortgage at all, since it is difficult to see how the obligation can be reduced to a sum of money." Nelson & Whitman, Real Estate Finance Law § 2.2 (4th ed.2001). See Restatement (Third) of Property (Mortgages) § 1.4 illus. 4.

E.   Merger, Deed in Lieu of Foreclosure and Related Problems

1.   An Introduction to Merger

The basic merger concept is deceptively simple. The theory is that when a mortgagee's interest and fee title coincide and meet in the same person, the lesser estate, the mortgage, merges into the fee title. As a consequence, the mortgage and, in some instances, the debt may be destroyed.

Note that the above doctrine, like the equitable conversion concept, is applied unevenly and is often honored in the breach. Courts often avoid its application where unjust results would occur. Focus carefully on two fact patterns that are utilized below to illustrate these aspects of the merger concept.

2.   Mortgagee Foreclosure Purchase Where Mortgagee Owns Both Junior and Senior Mortgages: Merger and Destruction of Debt

a.   Mortgagee Purchase at Junior Sale

Suppose, as is not uncommon, a holder of both junior and senior mortgages, a Bank, forecloses the junior and purchases at the foreclosure sale. This situation can be illustrated by the following diagram:

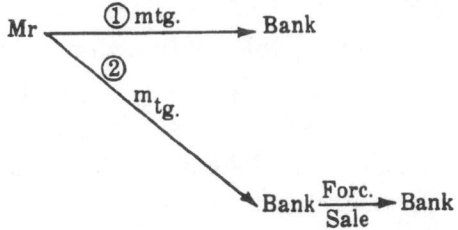

Here, unless there is *clear* evidence of a contrary intent, courts hold that the foreclosure purchase by Bank destroys Bank's right to sue Mr personally on the first mortgage debt. See *Mid Kansas Federal Savings and Loan Ass'n. v. Dynamic Development Corp.*, 804 P.2d 1310 (Ariz.1991). The underlying logic for this result is that when Bank purchased at the foreclosure sale of the second mortgage, it presumably followed the basic rule for bidding at junior lien sales; that is, it bid, at most, the fair market value of the land less the amount of the senior lien. Thus, Bank should not be able to collect on the first mortgage debt because it has already subtracted that amount in arriving at its bid at the foreclosure sale of the junior lien.

1) Criticism of the Above Result

The above analysis is logical and fair if one assumes that the land was worth at least an amount equal to the sum of the two mortgage debts. Thus, if the first mortgage debt is $20,000, the second mortgage debt is $10,000 and the fair market value of the land free and clear of liens is $30,000, and the Bank purchases for $10,000 (fair market value less $20,000) it makes sense to destroy the senior debt. In such a case, the mortgagee would be unjustly enriched if it were permitted to become the owner of land worth at least an amount equal to the sum of the two mortgage debts and also allowed to collect on the senior debt. But where the land is not worth at least the sum of the two debts, to apply the merger doctrine to destroy completely the senior debt shortchanges the Bank. For example, suppose the fair market value of the land free and clear of liens is $10,000 and the two mortgages are in the same amounts described above. If the Bank purchases for $10,000 at the foreclosure of the second mortgage, it obtains land that is worth $10,000. To allow it to recover the other $20,000 personally against Mr would not result in unjust enrichment. See Nelson & Whitman, Real Estate Finance Law § 6.16 (4th ed.2001).

Note the Restatement simply rejects the merger doctrine as it applies to the law of mortgages. See Restatement (Third) of Property

(Mortgages) § 8.5 (1997). Accordingly, in the foregoing problem unjust enrichment principles, rather than merger, would be applied to reach the same result. Thus, where the foreclosed real estate is at least the sum of the two mortgage obligations, the concept of unjust enrichment would deny the Bank the right to recover on the senior obligation. On the other hand, where the fair market value of the real estate is less than the sum of the two obligations, "the mortgagor would be unjustly enriched if the mortgagee is prevented from recovering on the senior obligation." Id., comment c(2).

2) **Avoidance of the Merger Result**

In any event, if both junior and senior mortgages are both in default, the mortgagee can avoid the merger problem by bringing one judicial foreclosure action of both mortgages simultaneously. The court could order *one* sale for the sum of both debts. If the sale brought less than that sum, the court could enter a deficiency judgment for the difference. A similar approach will not work with power of sale foreclosure because power of sale legislation ordinarily does not provide for the foreclosure of more than one mortgage at a time.

b. Mortgagee Purchase at Senior Sale

Suppose, instead of foreclosing the junior mortgage, the mortgagee forecloses the senior mortgage. This situation is illustrated by the following diagram:

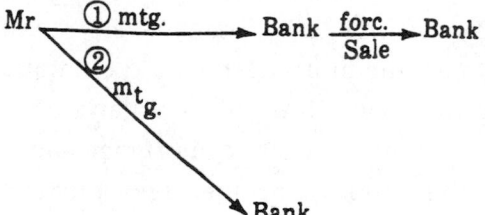

The general rule in the above situation is that the purchase of the mortgaged property by Bank at the foreclosure sale of the senior mortgage does not destroy the Bank's ability later to collect on the second mortgage debt. Remember that a purchaser at a senior foreclosure sale should pay, at most, the fair market value of the land free and clear of liens. Thus, to indulge in a presumption that the Bank subtracted the amount of the junior lien from its bid is illogical.

3. The Merger Doctrine and Mortgage Extinguishment: The Deed in Lieu of Foreclosure

It is a common practice for a mortgagee to take a conveyance of the mortgaged real estate from the mortgagor in satisfaction of the mortgage debt and as a substitute for foreclosure. This practice is often attractive for both parties. It allows the mortgagee to avoid the expense and delay associated with foreclosure, and especially with judicial foreclosure. Moreover, the potential for obtaining a deficiency judgment may be of no value to a mortgagee if the mortgagor is of questionable solvency. The mortgagor, on the other hand, may wish to avoid a personal judgment, which, even though currently uncollectible, could later come back to haunt her in the event her financial fortunes improve. Unfortunately, the deed in lieu raises the risk of so many pitfalls for mortgagees that its disadvantages may well outweigh its positive attributes.

a. The Merger Problem

The deed in lieu of foreclosure, unlike an actual foreclosure, does not cut off junior liens. Hence, if the mortgagor placed additional liens on the real estate after granting the mortgage in question, the senior mortgagee will *at least* have to foreclose later to wipe out those junior liens. More important, a junior lienor may well argue that since, as a result of the deed in lieu, both the fee title and the mortgage have merged in the mortgagee, the *mortgage* has been destroyed. The net effect, is arguably to promote the junior lienor to first lien status.

Normally, however, courts reject this merger argument and hold that the first mortgage will be preserved or reinstated as against any junior lienholders. *Miller v. Martineau*, 983 P.2d 1107 (Utah App. 1999). Courts here commonly apply the presumption that the mortgagee, the person in whom the mortgage and fee interests were merged, intended a result most favorable to itself. In this case, that means keeping the mortgage alive so that it can be foreclosed later against junior liens, if any. However, if circumstances indicate that merger is intended or would be just, a court may order it; see *United States Leather, Inc. v. Mitchell Mfg. Group, Inc.*, 276 F.3d 782 (6th Cir. 2002).

In any jurisdiction that adopts the Restatement position and rejects the merger doctrine completely, that doctrine cannot prejudice the mortgagee who takes a deed in lieu. Such a mortgagee will be permitted to keep its mortgage alive and to foreclose against any junior lienor in order to avoid the unjust enrichment of the latter interest. "The junior lienholder suffers no unjustifiable injury in these settings, but is in the same position as if there had been a judicial foreclosure to which the junior lienor was not made a party: the junior lien is not terminated, but neither is it elevated. To reach a contrary result would confer on the junior lienor an unbargained-for windfall." Restatement (Third) of Property (Mortgages) § 8.5 comment b (1997). Note, however, that the deed in lieu mortgagee who either *assumes* an existing junior lien or takes with *actual knowledge* of its existence will be deemed to have waived the right to foreclose against it. Id.

b.   Protecting the Mortgagee in the Deed in Lieu Transaction

Note that even if the merger concept is deemed to be irrelevant in the deed in lieu situation, mortgagees must be exceedingly careful in any event. This is because, as we mentioned earlier, *a deed in lieu of foreclosure does not operate like foreclosure.* It does not cut off junior liens. While it will not be promoted in priority, it continues as an encumbrance on the mortgagee's title. The only way to insure that the mortgagee does not become embroiled in such problems is to conduct a thorough title search *before* taking a deed in lieu to determine whether intervening liens exist. If such liens do not exist, it is normally safe to take a deed in lieu. If intervening interests are discovered, the only prudent alternative is to foreclose.

4.   Other Difficulties With the Deed in Lieu

Even assuming that no intervening liens exist and that the merger doctrine is thus inapplicable, the deed in lieu can raise two less important problems. First, it can be argued that the deed in lieu is really a mortgage disguised as a deed. This is a concept we examined earlier in Chapter III supra. The second argument that could be advanced is the notion that equity can set aside transactions that are unfair and unconscionable.

a.   The Absolute Deed as Mortgage Problem

As we noted earlier, grantor-mortgagors are occasionally successful in establishing by clear and convincing evidence that an absolute deed in favor of a grantee-mortgagee was actually intended as a mortgage. In the deed in lieu situation, mortgagors-grantors occasionally succeed in persuading courts to view the deed as a mortgage. This is exactly what happened in the leading decision by the United States Supreme Court in *Peugh v. Davis*, 96 U.S. 332 (1877). In nearly all cases reaching this result, the court perceives the deed in lieu transaction as unjust and overreaching, and as failing to compensate the mortgagor fairly for the loss of his or her ownership of the real estate.

b.   The Unfairness and Unconscionability Problem

As one commentator has noted, "there is an underlying idea that the mortgagor and mortgagee are not of equal bargaining strength. It is therefore entirely possible, especially if the consideration paid is dispro-portionately less than the value of the equity or if none is paid where the equity has value, that the whole transaction will be construed as unfair or unconscionable. The court will either permit the mortgagor to redeem at this point or restore the original mortgagor-mortgagee relationship." Note, Mortgages—Improvements—Absolute Deed in Lieu of Foreclo-sure, 31 Mo.L.Rev. 312, 315 (1966).

REVIEW QUESTIONS

1. T or F   There is normally a right to prepay a mortgage debt.

2. T or F   Prepayment charges constitute interest for usury law purposes.

3. T or F   A prepayment charge of more than 6 months' interest is an invalid penalty.

4. T or F   A late payment charge is more likely to be upheld if it is calculated a percentage of the late installment rather than of the principal amount of the debt.

5.   Aged aunt pays niece $20,000 and the latter promises to give her aunt love and affection so long as the aunt lives. The latter promise is secured by a mort-gage on niece's house. If niece fails to carry out her promise, is the mortgage a valid lien on niece's house?

6.   How does the deed in lieu of foreclosure create merger problems?

*

IX

Foreclosure

■ ANALYSIS

K. **Servicemembers Civil Relief Act**
1. Statutes of Limitation
2. Section 202 Stay
3. Installment Land Contracts
4. Mortgages and Deeds of Trust
5. Section 207 Limitation on Mortgage Interest Rates
6. Section 107 Waiver of Rights by Serviceperson–Mortgagor

L. **Bankruptcy**
1. Classification Of Bankruptcy Proceedings
2. The Automatic Stay
3. Straight Bankruptcy
4. The Trustee's Avoidance Powers
5. The Chapter 11 Reorganization
6. Chapter 13 "Wage Earner" Plan
7. Family Farmer Bankruptcy Act of 1986 (Chapter 12)
8. Setting Aside Pre–Bankruptcy Foreclosures
9. Right to Rents During Pendency of a Bankruptcy Proceeding
10. Installment Land Contracts in Bankruptcy

A. Determining the Foreclosure Amount: Problems of Acceleration

Virtually all mortgages today include acceleration clauses which give the mortgagee, in the event of mortgagor's default, the right to declare the entire debt due and payable. Moreover, acceleration is permitted not only for failure to make timely installment payments on the mortgage debt, but also for defaults in compliance with other covenants in the mortgage itself, such as failure to pay taxes or maintain insurance coverage or for the commission of waste. Another common cause for acceleration is the triggering of a due-on-sale clause by a transfer of the mortgaged real estate. Once acceleration has taken place as a result of a nondebt default, foreclosure normally cannot be prevented, for example, by payment of back taxes or by reinstatement of insurance coverage, but only by tendering the full amount of the accelerated debt.

1. Notice as a Condition Precedent

Absent a mortgage provision to the contrary, the traditional view is that notice to the mortgagor is not required for a valid acceleration. Rather, what is required is that the mortgagee perform some affirmative, overt act evidencing its intention to take advantage of the acceleration clause. Cure of the default prior to the occurrence of that affirmative act destroys the right to accelerate for that particular default.

What constitutes sufficient affirmative action will vary to some extent depending on the type of foreclosure being utilized and the facts of a particular case. For example, if judicial foreclosure is used, generally the mere commencement of the action constitutes the requisite affirmative action. Whether the mere commencement of a power-of-sale foreclosure would similarly suffice is more doubtful.

There is a growing view is written notice to the mortgagor is a condition precedent to a valid acceleration. See *In re Crystal Properties, Ltd.*, 268 F.3d 743 (9th Cir.2001). The Restatement provides that "acceleration becomes effective on the date specified in a written notice by the mortgagee to the mortgagor delivered after default." Restatement (Third) of Property (Mortgages) § 8.1(a) (1997).

Whether the mortgage foreclosure is by judicial action or power of sale, the prudent mortgagee will mail to the mortgagor a notice of intent to accelerate unless default is cured, and then, assuming the mortgagor does not correct the default, a second notice informing the mortgagor that acceleration has taken place. There is, however, no general legal requirement that a notice of default be given before acceleration, and many commercial mortgages contain no provision for such a notice of default.

2. Judicial Limits on Acceleration

a. Waiver
A mere failure to accelerate on the first default does not operate as a waiver of the option to foreclose because of later defaults. However, acceleration may be defeated where there has been a consistent prior pattern of acceptance of late payments by the mortgagee. See Dorn v. Robinson, 762 P.2d 566 (Ariz.App.1988). Some courts view such mortgagee forbearance as desirable creditor behavior and thus do not want to discourage such activity by readily finding waiver.

b. Hardship as a Ground for Defeating Acceleration
Generally, a mortgagor will not be relieved from the enforcement of an acceleration clause for a default occurring because of his or her negligence, inadvertence, mistake or accident unless the mortgagee is guilty of fraud, bad faith, or other conduct that would render enforcement of the acceleration clause unconscionable. This is also the Restatement view. See Restatement (Third) of Property (Mortgages) § 8.1(d) (1997).

Example: On July 1, 1996, a quarterly installment of principal and interest is due under a promissory note secured by a mortgage on Blackacre. The note provides for a three-week grace period for each installment. Prior to leaving on a business trip to Europe on June 18, 1996, mortgagor directs his bookkeeper to prepare a check for the July 1 payment. Because of an arithmetical error, the bookkeeper computes the interest as $4,219, which is $401 less than the correct amount. Mortgagor signs the check and departs for Europe. Thereafter, the bookkeeper discovers the mistake. Bookkeeper then informs mortgagee of the mistake and forwards the incorrect check to the mortgagee with a promise that the balance would be forthcoming upon mortgagor's return from his trip on July 5. When mortgagor returns, the bookkeeper forgets to inform him about the error. One day after the expiration of the grace period, mortgagee accelerates the full mortgage obligation. When mortgagor receives notice of the acceleration, he tenders the full amount of the installment, but mortgagee refuses the tender. Mortgagee proceeds with judicial foreclosure and mortgagor defends on the ground that the acceleration was unconscionable. (*Result:* the acceleration is effective). *Graf v. Hope Building Corp.,* 171 N.E. 884 (N.Y.1930).

However, a significant minority of decisions hold that a mortgagor will be protected from defaults that are a result of accident or a mistake while acting in good faith, or in unusual circumstances beyond mortgagor's control.

Example: Mortgagor serviceman stationed in the Philippines made prompt monthly mortgage payments for a 3 year period. Then two lapses of a month and a half and 3 months occurred. Mortgagee accepted late payments for those periods and collected late charges as well. A payment was made on September 10, 1973, but it did not include the installment due on September 1. Mortgagee accelerated and sued to foreclose. (*Result:* Mortgage reinstated. The court stated: "Though the personal hardship arising from the [mortgagor's] daughter's need of stateside hospitalization [does not] excuse payment, the distance between mortgagor and mortgagee's agent because of military obligations of the mortgagor is not to be ignored. . . . The total evidence indicates a good faith effort . . . to meet the mortgagee's conditions of bringing the account current.") *Federal Home Loan Mortgage Corp. v. Taylor,* 318 So.2d 203 (Fla.App.1975).

3. Statutory and Regulatory Limitations

a. State Statutes

A growing number of states have enacted "arrearages" legislation permitting the mortgagor to defeat acceleration by tendering the amount that would have been due in the absence of default and acceleration. Some of these statutes also provide that acceleration caused by defaults such as failure to pay taxes or insurance premiums can be defeated by performing the obligation that caused the acceleration.

Note that such legislation can be subject to abuse by mortgagors who default repeatedly, with the knowledge that they can defeat foreclosure merely by payment of arrearages. To combat this inclination, some statutes require the mortgagor to pay attorney's fees and other mortgagee expenses. Others limit the number of reinstatements within a fixed time period. See Nelson & Whitman, Real Estate Finance Law § 7.7 (4th ed.2001).

b. **Federal Agency Guidelines**

Both the Federal Housing Administration (FHA) and the Department of Veterans Affairs (VA) have issued guidelines governing loans insured or guaranteed by those agencies. Such guidelines extend the time which must elapse between default and foreclosure and require the mortgagee to permit reinstatement by payment of arrearages. See Nelson & Whitman, Real Estate Finance Law § 7.7 (4th ed.2001).

c. **Fannie Mae–Freddie Mac Standard Form Provisions**

The Fannie Mae–Freddie Mac residential mortgage form contains substantial limitations on the acceleration process. Not only does it require detailed mailed notice and a 30 day grace period as a condition precedent to acceleration, it also affords the mortgagee the right to defeat acceleration until 5 days prior to foreclosure by the payment of arrearages and mortgagee's reasonable attorney's fees.

Note that the above provisions may be omitted from the Fannie Mae–Freddie Mac mortgage form only when state law is more protective of the mortgagor with respect to pre-acceleration requirements and the ability to defeat acceleration once it has occurred. Because most institutional lenders wish to retain the option of selling their mortgages to these two secondary market entities, they will be likely to use the Fannie Mae–Freddie Mac form. Thus vast numbers of mortgagors in states that have not enacted legislation regulating acceleration, or whose legislation is less restrictive than the requirements of the Fannie Mae–Freddie Mac form, will nevertheless have substantial protection against abuse of the acceleration process.

4. **The Absence of an Acceleration Clause**

The failure to provide an acceleration clause in the usual installment payment mortgage can have extremely undesirable consequences for a mortgagee. In the event of mortgagee default such a mortgagee has two options. First, the mortgagee can wait, in some instances for many years, for all of the installments to come due, and then foreclose for the entire unpaid amount. The other alternative is to foreclose based on mortgagor's default on one or more installments. Since the latter alternative is more likely to be utilized, we need to focus on how one forecloses for default in the payment of installments.

a.   Property Capable of Physical Division

In relatively rare circumstances where the mortgaged real estate is capable of physical division, a court could order a foreclosure sale of only so much property as will be needed to satisfy the unpaid installments. The mortgage will continue unimpaired on the unsold portion of the land as security for the balance of the mortgage debt as it comes due.

Example: A $50,000 mortgage that did not contain an acceleration clause was to be paid in 5 equal annual installments of $10,000 plus accrued interest. The mortgagor defaults on the first payment. The mortgagee foreclosed. (*Result:* If the property is, for example, farmland capable of being physically divided, the court will divide it and sell approximately ⅕ of it at a foreclosure sale. The mortgage will remain on the unsold ⅘ of the land to secure the payment of the remaining $40,000.)

b.   Property Incapable of Physical Division

In this situation, courts have taken at least two approaches:

1)   **Sale Free and Clear**

A court could order all of the property sold free and clear of the mortgage lien, even though the entire debt is not due and owing. If, as is likely, a surplus results, the court could, in effect, supply the missing acceleration clause for the mortgagee and utilize the surplus to prepay the entire debt.

2)   **Sale Subject to the Mortgage**

More likely the court would order all of the property sold to satisfy the unpaid installment, but subject to the remaining balance of the mortgage debt.

Example: Same facts as in 4(a) above except that the court determined the land could not be physically divided. The court ordered all of the land sold for default in the $10,000 installment, but subject to the remaining $40,000 debt. (*Result:* a purchaser at the foreclosure sale will buy *all* of the land, but subject to a $40,000 mortgage. The purchaser thus should pay at most the fair market value of the land less $40,000, the amount of the lien remaining on the land. Surplus, if any, could either be given to the mortgagor or used to reduce the $40,000 remaining debt. If the sale brings less than $10,000, however, she could add the deficiency amount to the $40,000 mortgage that remains on the land).

5. Marshaling

Questions of marshaling arise when the same debt is secured by a mortgage on two or more parcels of land. In the absence of marshaling, the decision as to the order in which the parcels will be foreclosed is normally made by the mortgagee. However, in some situations the mortgagee might elect an order of foreclosure which is unnecessarily damaging to other parties. *The court conducting the foreclosure has equitable discretion, under the marshaling concept, to require a specific order of sale of the parcels to avoid or minimize these harsh consequences.* See Nelson & Whitman, Real Estate Finance Law § 10.9 (4th ed.2001). More specifically, under the Restatement, upon application to the court by a subordinate interest, the mortgagee must first foreclose against "parcels on which no subordinate interests exist" and, if doing so does not satisfy the mortgage obligation, then foreclose upon parcels on which subordinate interests exist. As to the latter parcels, the mortgagee must foreclose on "those with subordinate interests created more recently" before "those with subordinate interests at a more remote time." Restatement (Third) of Property (Mortgages) § 8.6(a). These statements capsulize the two most common forms of marshaling; they are described in greater detail below.

a. The "Two Funds" Rule

This rule holds that, where a mortgage creditor has the right to foreclose on two parcels of property, while another creditor has junior mortgage rights in only one of the parcels, the senior creditor should be compelled to foreclose first against the parcel which is otherwise unencumbered. This approach minimizes the risk of the junior mortgagee's being unnecessarily wiped out. See *In re Beeman*, 224 B.R. 420 (Bankr.W.D.Mo.1998).

Example: Ozzie owned two parcels of land, P–1 and P–2. He borrowed $50,000 from Mary, giving her a mortgage on both parcels. Later he borrowed an additional $10,000 from Margaret, giving her a mortgage only on P–1. Upon his default to Mary and her action to foreclose, the court will require that parcel P–2 be foreclosed first, and P–1 sold only if the sale of P–2 does not produce sufficient funds to satisfy Mary's debt. *Indiana Lawrence Bank v. PSB Credit Services, Inc.*, 706 N.E.2d 570 (Ind.App.1999).

b. The "Inverse Order of Alienation" Rule

This rule may be thought of as an extension of the two funds rule. Where a mortgagee has a lien on several parcels, some of which have been sold by the mortgagor after the imposition of the mortgage, and others of which are retained by the mortgagor, the mortgagee may be required by the marshaling concept to foreclose first on the land retained by the mortgagor, and then (if necessary to satisfy the debt) to foreclose on the other parcels in the inverse order of their transfer by the mortgagor. This requirement is imposed only where the grantee(s) did not assume the duty to pay the debt.

> *Example:* Ozzie owned parcels P–1, P–2, and P–3. He borrowed $50,000 from Mary, giving her a mortgage on all three parcels to secure the debt. He then sold P–2 to Gary, and later sold P–3 to Gertie, both subject to the mortgage. They did not assume the debt, but expected Ozzie to pay it. Ozzie kept P–1. Upon his default, Mary brought a foreclosure action. Under marshaling concepts, the court would require that Mary first foreclose on P–1. If this sale did not bring sufficient funds to satisfy the debt, Mary would next be required to foreclose on P–3. (That is, the last parcel alienated would be the first alienated parcel to be foreclosed upon.) If a deficiency still remained, Mary would be permitted to foreclose on P–2. *Pongetti v. Bankers Trust Sav. & Loan Ass'n*, 368 So.2d 819 (Miss.1979).

If Gary and Gertie had assumed specific portions of the debt at the time they purchased their parcels, the marshaling rule above would not be applied; indeed, it is likely that Mary would be compelled to foreclose on P–2 and P–3 *before* foreclosing on P–1. See Nelson & Whitman, Real Estate Finance Law § 10.11 (4th ed.2001).

c. No Prejudice to Senior Mortgagee

Neither the "inverse order" rule nor the "two funds" rule will be applied where doing so would prejudice the rights of the senior mortgagee. For example, if the parcel which would otherwise be held in abeyance for future foreclosure is declining rapidly in value, the court may order it sold immediately. Moreover, marshaling concepts are never employed as an ultimate bar to the foreclosure of all of the parcels of land subject to the mortgage. They merely control the order in which the parcels will be sold.

B. Methods of Foreclosure

1. Major Methods

a. Judicial Foreclosure

Judicial foreclosure by sale is the predominant method of foreclosure in the United States. It may be expressly authorized by statute or may be incident to a court's inherent equitable powers. It is the exclusive method in slightly less than half of the states and an authorized method everywhere. While judicial foreclosure produces the firmest and most marketable title, it is complicated, costly, and time-consuming. Because it is a judicial proceeding, it entails the normal incidents of litigation: service of process on all persons who are necessary parties, formal pleadings, a judicial trial, a court-supervised foreclosure sale, a possible deficiency proceeding, and in some instances, an appeal.

b. Power of Sale Foreclosure

This method is now permitted in more than half of the states. After varying types of notice the mortgaged real estate is sold at a public sale. The sale is conducted either by a public official, such as a sheriff, by some other private party, or, in some rare situations by the mortgagee itself. In order to utilize this method of foreclosure, the mortgage must contain a power of sale. The most common power of sale mortgage instrument is the deed of trust. Under this instrument, the mortgagor-trustor conveys the property to a trustee who holds it in trust for the mortgagee-beneficiary. In the event of foreclosure, the trustee executes the power of sale by holding a public sale of the mortgaged property. While the title that results from a power of sale foreclosure is somewhat less secure than a judicial foreclosure title, it is significantly less costly, complicated and time-consuming than its judicial counterpart.

2. Minor Methods

a. Judicial Strict Foreclosure

This is a judicial proceeding but there is no sale, public or otherwise, of the mortgaged real estate. Rather the court orders the mortgagor to pay the mortgage debt within a judicially determined reasonable period of time. If the debt is not paid within this time period, title to the property vests in the mortgagee. In the event the property is not worth the amount of the mortgage debt, the mortgagee can obtain a deficiency judgment. On the other hand, there is no possibility of the mortgagor obtaining the equivalent of surplus if the property is worth more than the mortgage debt. This apparent mortgagee advantage has been held not to violate mortgagor's equal protection rights under the 14th Amendment. See *Dieffenbach v. Attorney General of Vermont*, 604 F.2d 187 (2d Cir.1979). Strict foreclosure is still used in Vermont and Connecticut, and in certain other jurisdictions in very limited circumstances.

b. Entry Without Process

Under this method, a mortgagee after default may take possession of the mortgaged property without legal intervention. Then, after the expiration of a time period that varies from one to three years, the mortgagor's equity of redemption is barred. The mortgagee's entry must be peaceable. This method is used in a few New England states.

c. Action at Law for a Writ of Entry

This method is similar to the latter method, except that the mortgagee's entry can come only after a judicial determination of default and the amount owing, and a judgment for possession. Note that in both *Entry without Process* and the *Action at Law for a Writ of Entry* the result is strict foreclosure.

d. Scire Facias

This is a type of legal, as opposed to equitable, judicial foreclosure and, for the most part, is used only in Delaware. It is similar to the remedy at law available to an execution creditor. After a default, a mortgagee obtains from the court a writ of scire facias, which is an order to the mortgagor to show cause why the mortgaged property should not be sold to satisfy the mortgage debt. If the mortgagee prevails at trial the mortgagee obtains a judgment for the amount owing and a writ of *levari facias* will issue directing that an execution sale be held to satisfy the judgment.

C. Judicial Foreclosure

1. Use in Power of Sale States

As we noted earlier, judicial foreclosure is the usual method of foreclosure in slightly less than half of the states, but it is available and used occasionally in every jurisdiction. Since we noted that it is both more time-consuming and costly than power of sale foreclosure, why would a mortgagee in a power of sale state ever utilize judicial foreclosure? The answer is at least fourfold. First, through inadvertence or otherwise, the mortgage form used may not have contained a power of sale. In such a situation judicial foreclosure is a necessity. Second, judicial intervention may be necessary to correct other defects in the mortgage. For example, if there is an error in the legal description of the mortgaged land, judicial aid may be needed to reform it. While in theory one could go to court to obtain the correction and then foreclose the corrected mortgage nonjudicially by power of sale, this obviously will entail greater effort than to allow the court to perform both functions. Third, if the mortgage is in the form of an absolute deed, since it obviously contains no power of sale, judicial foreclosure is needed. Finally, when there are other liens on the mortgaged real estate and priority is uncertain, judicial foreclosure is needed to determine the priority of these liens. This will enable potential foreclosure purchasers to determine the state of the title they will be bidding on and thus to calculate their maximum bids. If power of sale foreclosure were used, the uncertain lien priority could discourage bidding and create title difficulties for the successful bidder.

2. The Necessary–Proper Party Distinction

There is a substantial body of case law as to who is a "necessary" party or a "proper" party for purposes of judicial foreclosure. An important thing to remember is that what you have learned about those terms in a civil procedure course may have minimal relevance in the mortgage foreclosure context because, in this latter setting, they seem to have taken on their own special meaning.

a. The Purpose of Foreclosure

Sometimes it is said that foreclosure should, if successful, terminate the rights of all parties whose interests in the land are "subject to" or "subordinate" to the mortgage being foreclosed. This is correct, but why is it so? *The answer is found in a more basic and descriptive purpose of foreclosure, which is to give the purchaser at the foreclosure sale the same title to the land that the mortgagor had when the mortgage being foreclosed was executed.*

Keep this statement in mind when you focus on the following diagram.

In this case E–1's mortgage was perfected prior to E–2's mortgage. However, the judgment lien against MR became effective after E–2's mortgage was perfected. Lastly, MR granted an easement for roadway purposes to X. Note that when E–2 took her mortgage the only other interest in the land besides that of MR was E–1's mortgage. Suppose then E–2's mortgage goes into default and foreclosure. The purpose of the foreclosure sale is to give whoever buys the same title MR possessed when E–2 took her mortgage.

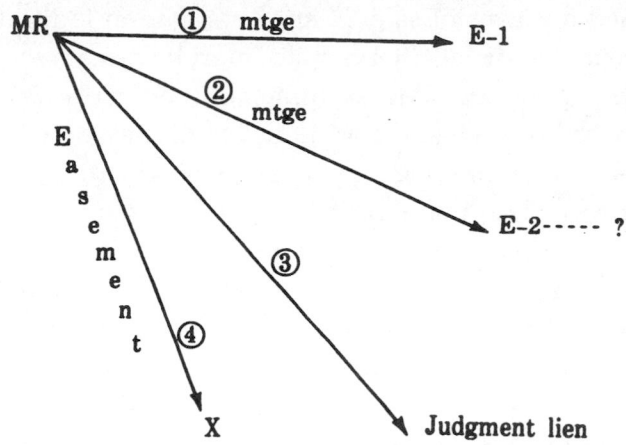

b. Necessary Parties

Keep the purpose of foreclosure and the above diagram in mind in considering who is a necessary party. *Essentially, a party is "necessary" if failure to join him or her in the action will not accomplish the purposes of foreclosure described above.* Remember also that an unjoined party cannot have his or her interest terminated. In the above diagram, suppose E–2 forecloses her mortgage judicially. Judgment lienor is a necessary party in the sense that the failure to join him will mean his judgment is still valid and thus the foreclosure will not accomplish its purpose, which is to wipe out junior interests and to give P the same title MR had when the mortgage to E–2 was executed. X, the easement holder, would be a necessary party for the same reason. E–1, on the other hand, is not a necessary party because failure to join E–1 will not defeat the basic purpose of E–2's foreclosure. While it is true, of course, that failure to join E–1 means that E–1's mortgage will not be affected, P will nevertheless acquire exactly the same title MR had when E–2 took her mortgage—fee simple title subject to a mortgage in favor of E–1.

As a rule of thumb, all persons junior to the mortgage being foreclosed are "necessary" parties. These include the owner of the equity of redemption (that is, the title to the land), junior lienors, junior lessees and easement holders, and junior mechanics' lienholders. If the original mortgagor no longer owns the equity of redemption, he or she nevertheless is usually made a party because it may be necessary to do so in order to obtain a deficiency judgment.

c. Proper Parties

It is occasionally useful to join as parties certain unconsenting persons even though they do not qualify as necessary parties, in the sense that their interests will be cut off by the foreclosure. Such persons can be considered "proper" parties.

The most obvious proper party is a lienholder who is senior to the mortgaged being foreclosed. Such a lienholder is not a necessary party because he is not subordinate to the mortgage being foreclosed, nor will failure to join him result in the foreclosure sale purchaser acquiring a different title than the mortgagor had at the time the foreclosed mortgage was executed. Still, there are situations when it is highly desirable that the senior lienholder be brought into the proceeding without his consent. When then will a court treat such a senior lienor as a "proper party"?

3. The Senior Lienholder as a Party

The general rule is that a senior lienholder cannot be made a party without his or her consent. However, he or she may be made a party without consent where the foreclosing mortgagee is seeking to ascertain the amount and terms of the senior lien or where the actual priority status of the "senior" lien is unclear. If the senior lien is due and payable some courts hold that the property may be sold free and clear of liens in what amounts to a joint foreclosure. The proceeds of the sale will be used to pay off all liens in order of their priority.

Note that the above two exceptions are both aimed at encouraging potential purchasers to bid at the junior lien foreclosure sale. After all, if a potential purchaser is unable to ascertain the balance and terms of the senior mortgage or, indeed, whether that mortgage is even senior, bidding may very well be discouraged. If a court orders a joint foreclosure, it deprives the senior lienholder of one of the advantages of being senior—the right to decide when or whether to foreclose. However, in some instances a sale free and clear of liens is likely to encourage higher bidding at the foreclosure sale. Moreover, since the senior lienholder is paid first out of the sale proceeds he or she arguably does not have a legitimate grievance.

4. The Lessee as a Party

If a lease is senior to the mortgage being foreclosed, the lease is unaffected by the foreclosure. The foreclosure purchaser obtains the mortgagor-lessor's interest and becomes the lessee's landlord. If the lease is junior, joinder of the lessee in the foreclosure proceedings terminates the lease and lessee's obligations under it.

Where a junior lease is pro-landlord or the lessee a desirable tenant, a foreclosing mortgagee will sometimes intentionally not join a junior lessee as a foreclosure party. Under the majority rule the lessee, even though an intentionally omitted necessary party, is unaffected by the foreclosure and is still bound by the lease. This gives a senior foreclosure mortgagee the option of selling the premises subject to the lease or free and clear of it depending on how the mortgagee assesses the desirability of the lease from a landlord's perspective. This approach arguably confers on the mortgagee a bonus for violating the normal foreclosure maxim that encourages joinder of all necessary parties. To discourage such mortgagee manipulation, some states give the unjoined junior lessee the option of staying out of the foreclosure procedure, and thus continuing to be bound by the lease, or of intervening and becoming a party to the proceeding in order to get the lease terminated. See Nelson & Whitman, Real Estate Finance Law § 7.12 (4th ed.2001).

Lessees in a strong bargaining position often are able initially to insist that a prior mortgagee subordinate the mortgage to the lease. This is a common practice in with major "anchor" tenants in shopping centers, for example. The long term mortgagee in such a situation has an interest in solid stable tenants who will provide a steady cash flow for servicing the mortgage. Thus the mortgagee will often be willing to subordinate the mortgage to such otherwise junior lessees. In those jurisdictions where an omitted junior lessee has the option of intervening in the foreclosure for the purposes of terminating the lease, the mortgagee may actually prefer to be subordinate to important lessees so that if the mortgagee purchases at a foreclosure sale, those lessees will be required to continue to comply with their leases.

An alternative approach, more widely used, involves an agreement between the mortgagee and the lessee. If their bargaining power is fairly evenly balanced, the agreement will consist of three elements: (1) a subordination of the lease to the mortgage; (2) a "nondisturbance" promise by the mortgagee, assuring the lessee that even if a foreclosure occurs, the lessee will not be disturbed and its lease will not be terminated, so long as the lease itself is not in default; and (3) an agreement by the lessee to "attorn" to any purchaser of the property at a foreclosure sale, recognizing the purchaser as a legitimate substitute for the original lessor and paying rent to the purchaser accordingly. When these three elements are combined, the overall agreement is usually known as a "Subordination, Nondisturbance, and Attornment Agreement," abbreviated "SNDA."

5. The Omitted Party Problem

Under certain circumstances a necessary party is deemed to be bound by a foreclosure proceeding even though she was never formally made a party to it. These circumstances include the following:

- In the few states with pure "race" type recording acts, where the necessary party acquires her interest prior to foreclosure, but she does not record her interest by the time the foreclosure proceeding commences. In these jurisdictions, the unrecorded party is bound even though the mortgagee may have had actual knowledge of that party prior to or during the pendency of the foreclosure proceeding.

- In the majority of states with "notice" or "notice-race" type recording acts, where the necessary party acquires her interest prior to foreclosure, but she does not record her interest prior to the foreclosure sale and the foreclosure sale purchaser buys without notice of the unrecorded interest.

- Where the *lis pendens* doctrine operates to bind a necessary party who acquires his interest in the mortgaged real estate *after* the commencement of the foreclosure proceeding. In almost all states, however, this binding effect occurs only if the mortgagee files a formal *notice of lis pendens* prior to the time the necessary party acquires his interest.

Generally, however, omitted necessary parties are governed by the following rules.

a. The Omitted Owner

If the owner of the equity of redemption or any part of it is omitted from a judicial foreclosure proceeding, the proceeding as to that person is void and that person's right to redeem is unaffected. *Patel v. Khan*, 970 P.2d 836 (Wyo. 1998). Thus, such a person has the right to redeem the land by paying the mortgage debt to the foreclosure sale purchaser.

An owner of the equity of redemption has the right, until there has been a valid foreclosure of it, to redeem *the land* by payment of the mortgage debt to the mortgagee. Where a judicial foreclosure omits that person, that right continues unaffected by the foreclosure. Nevertheless, while the purchaser at the foreclosure sale does not acquire the omitted owner's interest, he or she does acquire the mortgagee's interest. Thus, if the omitted owner chooses to redeem *the land* he or she will do so by tendering the full amount of the mortgage debt to the foreclosure sale purchaser.

b. The Omitted Junior Lienor and the Foreclosure Sale Purchaser

1) The Junior Lienor's Remedies

The junior lienor who was omitted from a judicial foreclosure has two remedies. First he or she can foreclose the junior mortgage subject to the first (which is regarded as still alive for this purpose). Second, the junior lienor may "redeem" by paying the foreclosure purchaser the amount of the mortgage debt.

2) The Foreclosure Sale Purchaser's Remedies

The purchaser at the foreclosure from which the junior lienor was omitted has three possible alternative remedies. First, the purchaser, as an assignee of the rights of the senior mortgagee, can reforeclose the senior mortgage. Second, the purchaser standing in the shoes of the foreclosed mortgagor, may "redeem" by paying the junior lienor the amount of that lien. Finally, in certain limited circumstances the sale purchaser, standing in the shoes of the senior mortgagee, may obtain strict foreclosure against the junior lienor.

3) Junior Lienor vs. Foreclosure Sale Purchaser

If both the omitted junior lienor and the sale purchaser choose to redeem, the latter will prevail. Since, in the absence of foreclosure, the mortgagor could always have forced the junior lienor to accept payment of the junior debt, the sale purchaser, as a successor to the rights of the mortgagor, can pay off the junior lien and terminate completely the latter's interest in the foreclosed real estate.

4) Explanation of the Three Principles

As the foregoing rules indicate, when the omitted party is a junior lienor rather than an owner, the situation becomes extremely complicated. *Moreover, the extent to which you have a thorough understanding of these rules in large measure determines the extent to which you understand the law of mortgages.* Thus you will need to proceed through the following materials carefully and slowly. For further explanation, see Nelson & Whitman, Real Estate Finance Law § 7.15 (4th ed.2001).

5) The Omitted Junior Lienor's Options

Remember that the above rule states that the omitted junior has two rights. He has a right to foreclose his lien because it was not wiped out by the defective foreclosure. *Lenexa State Bank v. Dixon*, 559 P.2d 776 (Kan. 1977). If this occurs, the purchaser at the junior foreclosure sale will buy the land subject to a first mortgage in favor of the purchaser at the senior foreclosure sale. The status of the purchaser at the first sale is changed from owner to mortgagee. Note that the first mortgage is "revived" for this purpose and that the revived mortgage amount is the *balance owing on it prior to the first foreclosure sale*. This latter sum may be more or less than the amount the purchaser at the first sale paid for the property. If it is more, the original purchaser gets a windfall if the buyer at the second sale ultimately pays off the senior lien. On the other hand, if the purchaser at the first sale paid more than the amount of the senior lien, not only will he be deprived of title to the property, he will receive a lien that is worth less than his original investment.

We also said that the omitted junior lienor has the right to redeem. *Kuehl v. Eckhart*, 608 N.W.2d 475 (Iowa 2000). This is because the junior lienor, like the owner of the equity of redemption, has certain equitable redemption rights. The junior lienor's right is to pay off a senior lien in default and be subrogated to the senior lienor's rights. This right derives, in part, from the notion that a person should be able to pay off another to protect one's interest. *But note* that this right to redeem is not the same nor as desirable as the owner's redemption right. The latter's equitable redemption right is to pay off a mortgage in default and redeem *the land*. The junior lienor's right in redeeming is *to purchase the senior mortgage*. Because this option will normally require the junior lienor to invest a significant amount of money simply to acquire another lien, this option probably is not often exercised.

6) The Options of the Foreclosure Sale Purchaser

Now focus on the foreclosure sale purchaser's remedies. First, we said that he or she could reforeclose the first mortgage. The purchaser has this right as an assignee of the first mortgagee's rights. This time, of course, the foreclosure presumably will be handled correctly and the junior lienor made a party. The junior will be able to bid at the new senior sale. The sale proceeds will be used to pay off both liens in order of their priority and any surplus beyond that amount will go to the reforeclosing party. Of course, having purchased once before, the prior purchaser may choose to do so again; this time, since he is an assignee of the first mortgage, he will be able to bid up to the amount of the first mortgage debt without being "out of pocket."

The foreclosure sale purchaser's second, and most important, remedy is to redeem by paying the omitted junior the amount of his lien. *Pease Co. v. Huntington Nat'l Bank*, 495 N.E.2d 45 (Ohio

App.1985). The purchaser has the right to do this because in addition to being an assignee of the first mortgagee's rights he is also a successor to the mortgagor's interest as well. After all, while the foreclosure sale may have been ineffective as to the junior lienor, it was valid as to the mortgagor, and thus, the mortgagor's rights had to go to someone. Since the mortgagor prior to foreclosure had the right to redeem "the land" by paying off any lien on the land in default, so then may the sale purchaser, as a successor to mortgagor's rights, do the same.

Suppose, however, that the junior lienor and the foreclosure purchaser both choose to exercise the right to redeem. Who wins? How do we break the circle of redemptions? As the above rule suggests, the sale purchaser will always win. This is because, as we have seen earlier, the purchaser is standing in the foreclosed mortgagor's shoes. Surely the junior lienor never had the right to redeem the land from the mortgagor. His sole right *vis à vis* the mortgagor was to have his debt satisfied. Thus, he surely has no right to redeem from a foreclosure purchaser, who, as the mortgagor's successor, has paid the junior debt.

If the junior lien is for a relatively minor amount and the value of the land is worth more than the sum of the two liens, the sale purchaser will in all probability take the junior lienor out of the picture by deciding to redeem.

The third remedy possibly available to the foreclosure sale purchaser is *strict foreclosure*. If ordered, it amounts to a judicial decree that the junior lien will be canceled unless the junior pays off the senior mortgage debt within a court-determined period. In effect, the court orders the junior to "put up or shut up". Note that this remedy takes from the junior the right to foreclose the junior lien, a right he clearly would have been able to exercise had no foreclosure of the senior taken place. Thus, we confront the irony that even a defective foreclosure, under some circumstances, may destroy a significant junior lienor right.

This injustice to the junior lienholder is more apparent than real. First, strict foreclosure is simply unavailable in many states. Second, in those states that do sometimes grant it, the sale purchaser must often overcome substantial roadblocks. The remedy is clearly unavailable if the junior lienor was intentionally omitted from the proceeding. Moreover, some courts require not only that the sale purchaser have bought without knowledge of the junior's existence, but also that the junior lienor knew of the foreclosure proceeding and did not alert the purchaser of his existence. While other courts may be somewhat more flexible, they require at a minimum that the omission be the result of inadvertence or good faith mistake. One factor that can be persuasive in favor of strict foreclosure is that the court is convinced that the land is worth no more than the senior lien, so that the junior lienholder's position really has no security value anyway.

Under the Restatement, there is a presumption against the use of strict foreclosure in this setting and, accordingly, the remedy is available only where the sale purchaser "can establish that the omission was the result of inadvertence or mistake and that the fair market value of the mortgaged real estate does not exceed the amount of encumbrances senior to the junior lien." Restatement (Third) of Property (Mortgages) § 7.1, comment b (1997).

c. Omitted Parties: Statutory Redemption vs. Equitable Redemption

Up to this point we have focused on the omitted junior lienor's equitable right to redeem. However, such parties in some states also have statutory redemption rights. While we cover statutory redemption in substantial detail later in this work, some understanding of how it works is necessary at this point to assess completely the rights of omitted parties.

1) Nature of Statutory Redemption

In about half the states, statutory redemption legislation permits the mortgagor, subsequent grantees, and sometimes junior lienors to redeem after the foreclosure sale for periods of time as short as a few months or as long as 18 months. Such legislation was enacted in part to give mortgagors an extra time period in which to find alternative financing to save their property. Another purpose was to put pressure on the mortgagee at the foreclosure sale to bid at least up to the amount of the mortgage debt. To enforce this latter purpose, the redemption amount *almost always is the foreclosure sale price and not the mortgage debt.* While such legislation has been subjected to substantial criticism that in practice it deters third party bidding, we will consider those matters in Chapter X, *infra.*

2) The Omitted Owner and Statutory Redemption

The omitted owner does not have the option of choosing between equitable redemption and statutory redemption. This is because the equitable right accrues at mortgage maturity and ends when there is a valid foreclosure. Statutory redemption, however, begins only when a valid foreclosure has taken place. Since there has been no valid foreclosure of the omitted owner, statutory redemption is simply inapplicable. There are times when an omitted owner would be delighted to have the choice. This would especially be true when the omitted owner was a non-assuming grantee of the original mortgagor.

Example: Mortgagee foreclosed judicially on a $20,000 mortgage on Blackacre. G–1, a non-assuming grantee, was omitted from the proceeding. Mortgagee purchased at the sale for $12,000 and obtained a deficiency judgment against the original mortgagor for $8,000. The latter party is now insolvent. G–1 seeks to redeem, pursuant to statutory redemption, by tendering $12,000 to mortgagee-purchaser. (*Result:* The only redemption available to G–1 is equitable. Statutory redemption would be applicable only if G–1 had been *validly* foreclosed. Thus, G–1 must pay $20,000, the mortgage debt, rather than $12,000, the foreclosure sale price, in order to redeem the land.) See *Portland Mortg. Co. v. Creditors Protective Ass'n,* 262 P.2d 918 (Or.1953)

3)   The Omitted Junior Lienor and Statutory Redemption

Under the prevailing view, an omitted junior lienor, like an omitted owner, may exercise only the equitable right to redeem.

For the omitted junior lienor, the choice of equitable redemption or statutory redemption can be more significant than for an omitted owner. Unlike an omitted owner who redeems the land, when an omitted junior lienor redeems equitably, he or she is merely redeeming a senior mortgage. On the other hand, if the omitted junior is permitted to proceed statutorily, in most jurisdictions, he or she would get *title* to the land. Moreover, while a mortgagor who redeems statutorily for a foreclosure sale price significantly less than the mortgage debt may still be personally liable for a deficiency judgment, the junior lienor, who has no personal liability, would be more than pleased to get the land for a bargain basement amount. It has been argued that since junior lienors normally have statutory redemption rights, "unless it were to be held that the statutes applied only to those subsequent lienors whose liens were cut off by foreclosure, it would seem that the omitted lienor also possesses that right." (Note, 88 U.Pa.L.Rev. 994, 1003 (1940).) But the prevailing view is that of Professor Glenn: "[statutory redemption] comes into effect at and with foreclosure . . . but the statute envisages those only whom foreclosure has barred. It follows that one who has never been foreclosed cannot resort to statutory redemption. [His] remedy . . . is redemption in equity after the ancient mode." Glenn, Mortgages, § 238 (1943).

Note, however, that if an omitted junior lienor acquires her lien *after* the commencement of the foreclosure proceeding and the filing by the foreclosing mortgagee of a *notice of lis pendens*, she will be bound by the foreclosure. As a validly foreclosed lienor, she will thus qualify for statutory redemption. See *Land Associates v. Becker*, 656 P.2d 927 (Or.1982).

D. Power of Sale Foreclosure

As noted at Section (B)(1) above, power of sale foreclosure is the predominant foreclosure method in slightly more that half the states. After varying degrees of notice, the property is sold at public sale, normally by a public official or a third party trustee or, less frequently, by the mortgagee. Notice requirements vary from states that require mailed notice to everyone junior to the mortgage to those that require only notice by publication. However, most require, in addition to publication, at least mailed notice to the mortgagor and the owner of the equity of redemption.

1. Effect of Power of Sale Foreclosure

If the mortgagee complies with the statutory notice requirements referred to above, power of sale foreclosure normally accomplishes the identical purposes achieved by judicial foreclosure, but with a considerable saving in the cost and time burdens associated with the latter. In other words, properly executed, power of sale foreclosure will terminate all interests junior to the mortgage being foreclosed and put the foreclosure purchaser into the shoes of the mortgagor as of the time the foreclosed mortgage was executed.

2. Stability of Power of Sale Titles

In spite of its substantial advantages in terms of cost and time, power of sale foreclosure produces titles that are somewhat less stable than those produced by judicial foreclosure. There are at least three reasons for this. First, supervision by a judge or clerk of court at the various stages of the judicial foreclosure process probably reduces significantly the number of errors that can arise in an unsupervised setting. Second, because judicial foreclosure is an adversary proceeding, the presence of other parties in the proceeding increases substantially the likelihood that potential procedural and substantive defects will be called to the court's attention. Finally, because of the very nature of a civil action, the concept of judicial finality provides the ultimate insulation against subsequent attack on judicial foreclosure decree. After all, the trial court foreclosure decree will, if there is no appeal, become final within a short period of time, or if an appeal takes place, within a short period thereafter. Perhaps the only defect in a judicial foreclosure that will be cured only by the finality concept or the passage of time is the omitted necessary party problem. This is because such persons can always attack the foreclosure collaterally after the periods for direct review have expired. Power of sale foreclosure, on the other hand, encompasses none of the procedural checks and relatively few of the finality concepts associated with judicial foreclosure. True, the passage of time helps to solidify an otherwise defective power of sale title. However, this is accomplished over a relatively long time period and largely by means of such debatable concepts as statutes of limitation, laches and related notions.

3. Classification of Power of Sale Foreclosure Defects

Power of sale foreclosure defects are classified in three ways. The most serious defects render a foreclosure void. The purchaser at the foreclosure sale and subsequent grantees acquire nothing. This is true even if the sale purchaser is a bona fide purchaser. Such a foreclosure may be void, for example, if it is based upon a forged mortgage, or more commonly, if the mortgage debt was not in default. At the other extreme are foreclosure defects that are so inconsequential as to have no impact on the validity of the sale. These may include minor typographical errors or minor discrepancies in the notice of sale. Finally, between the two foregoing extremes are defects that render the sale voidable. In this context, "voidable" means that a court will set the sale aside because of the defect unless the land has passed into the hands of a bona fide purchaser. Most power of sale defects fit into the "voidable sale" or "inconsequential" category.

4. Who is a Bona Fide Purchaser?

A foreclosure sale purchaser will be treated as a BFP and thus take free of voidable defects if value has been paid and if the purchaser (a) has no actual knowledge of the defects; (b) is not placed on reasonable notice of the defects from recorded instruments; and (c) the defects are not such that a person attending the sale exercising reasonable care would have discovered them.

A subsequent grantee who did not attend the foreclosure sale will be treated as a BFP, free of voidable defects, if value has been paid and (a) she had no actual knowledge of the defects and (b) was not placed on reasonable notice from recorded instruments.

A mortgagee that purchases at its own foreclosure sale will not be treated as a BFP.

5. Specific Defects

The following material deals with some of the more commonly raised grounds for setting aside a power of sale foreclosure. Note that very often one alleged defect alone will not be enough to affect the validity of a foreclosure, but the cumulative impact of that defect operating in conjunction with others strengthens the chances of a successful attack. For a more detailed consideration of these defects, see Nelson & Whitman, Real Estate Finance Law § 7.21 (4th ed.2001).

a. Inadequacy of Foreclosure Sale Price

Inadequacy of the price alone normally will not invalidate a sale, absent fraud, unfair dealing, or other irregularity in the sale process. Courts articulate two main standards for invalidating a sale based on price inadequacy. Many courts require that, in the absence of some other defect or irregularity, the price be "grossly inadequate." Other courts require a disparity between the sale price and fair market value so gross as to "shock the conscience of the court."

In applying these two standards, courts have invalidated sales for one-seventh and one-sixtieth of fair market value, but have upheld sales for one-half, one-third, one-fourth, one-fifth, or even one-twentieth of fair market value. See Nelson & Whitman, Real Estate Finance Law § 7.21 (4th ed.2001).

The Restatement adopts the "grossly inadequate" standard. Under this standard, "a court is warranted in invalidating a sale where the price is less than 20 percent of fair market value and, absent other foreclosure defects, is usually not warranted in invalidating a sale that yields in excess of that amount. * * * [I]n extreme cases a price may be so low (typically well under 20 percent of fair market value) that it would be an abuse of discretion for the [trial] court to refuse to invalidate it." Restatement (Third) of Property (Mortgages) § 8.3 comment b (1997). See *Krohn v. Sweetheart Properties, Ltd.*, 203 Ariz. 205, 52 P.3d 774 (2002).

Note that courts do set aside sales where prices exceed the grossly inadequate standard but other defects in the sale process existed.

Sometimes these "other defects" may be relatively minor. See *In re Edry*, 201 B.R. 604 (Bkrtcy.D.Mass. 1996) where the court set aside a sale of real estate for slightly more than 50% of fair market value, but the mortgagee failed to use pictorial advertizing which, even though it was not required by statute, was customarily used by foreclosing mortgagees in the area.

b. Time of Sale

Defects involving the time of sale can arise in two situations. First, a sale is sometimes held on a different day or hour than specified in the notice of sale. Second, the actual sale may be held at a time consistent under the notice of sale, but at an unusual day or hour for such sales in that community. For example, a Montana court invalidated a sale which was held on a day when the ashfall from a Mt. St. Helens volcanic eruption had brought normal commercial transactions to a standstill. The inherent danger in both instances is that potential third party bidders will not attend the sale and that therefore the sales price will be lower than it should be. The same could be said for holding a sale on September 11, 2001, the day of the World Trade Center tragedy. While generalizations are hazardous, the greater the disparity between the actual time of sale and the time it should have taken place, the greater the likelihood that the sale will be set aside.

c. Place of Sale

Statutes normally require that the foreclosure sale take place in the county in which the land is located. Failure to do so renders the sale void. Absent a statutory requirement, if the mortgage specifies a place of sale, and that mortgage provision is violated, the sale is probably rendered voidable. Finally, the sale is also voidable if the actual place of sale varies significantly from the place specified in the advertised notice of sale.

d. Sale by Parcel or Bulk

Often the person exercising the power of sale has the alternative of selling it in parcels rather than in bulk. This option will arise where the mortgaged property is a subdivision or agricultural acreage. The method of sale chosen should be the one most beneficial to the mortgagor. *Normally, this creates a presumption in favor of selling in parcels because "a sale in parcels or lots opens the field to a greater number of bidders, is conducive to a better price, tends to prohibit odious speculation upon the distress of the debtor, and enables him to redeem some of the property without being compelled to redeem it all." J.H. Morris, Inc. v. Indian Hills, Inc.,* 212 So.2d 831, 843 (Ala.1968). Similar principles are embodied in some states' statutes (see, e.g., Minn.Stat.Ann. § 580.08), and a few states give the mortgagor or junior lienholders the right to designate the method of sale. Normally, sales that violate these principles are held to be voidable.

e. Chilled Bidding

Where a mortgagee or a trustee under a deed of trust engages in irregular conduct that suppresses bidding, this "chilled bidding" sometimes results in the sale being set aside. Such conduct falls into two general categories. First, there can be collusion between the mortgagee or trustee and potential bidders to hold down the bidding. Such "intentional chilled bidding" is often held to render the sale void. The second type can include a myriad of situations where a mortgagee or trustee inadvertently acts or fails to act in such a manner as to suppress bidding. For example, the published notice of foreclosure could simply refer to a senior lien that no longer exists; or a trustee could make incorrect statements at a sale concerning the physical condition of the mortgaged premises. Where such activity in fact suppresses bidding it can render the sale voidable.

f. Mortgagee Purchase Under Mortgage With Power of Sale

Where a mortgage contains a power of sale in the mortgagee, the mortgagee traditionally could not purchase at that sale. Such a sale was normally rendered voidable. In states that utilize a mortgage with a power of sale, the above problem is obviated by legislation that directs a public official, usually the sheriff to conduct the foreclosure sale. In other states using this device, courts permit mortgagees to purchase at their own sale, but apply a closer degree of scrutiny than would be the case in a deed of trust setting, where the power of sale is exercised by a third party. See *Williams v. Resolution GGF OY*, 630 N.E.2d 581 (Mass.1994), stating that "when a party who is intrusted with a power to sell attempts to become the purchaser, he will be held to the strictest good faith and the utmost diligence * * * "

6. Nature of the Trustee's Duties Under a Deed of Trust

In a trustee's sale under a deed of trust, the fact that the mortgagee purchases is rarely a practical problem. Judicial opinions often wax eloquent about the fiduciary obligations the trustee under a deed of trust owes to both the grantor (mortgagor) and the beneficiary (mortgagee). Nevertheless, because the trustee represents parties whose interests are often antithetical, courts do not purport to apply normal trust law standards to such persons. For example, as the California Supreme Court noted:

The similarities between a trustee of an express trust and a trustee under a deed of trust end with the name. "Just as a panda is not a true bear, a trustee of a deed of trust is not a true trustee." * * * The trustee under a deed of trust does not have a true trustee's interest in, and control over, the trust property. Nor is it bound by the fiduciary duties that characterize a true trustee.

Monterey S.P. Partnership v. W.L. Bangham, Inc., 777 P.2d 623, 628 (Cal.1989). If anything, the trustee under the deed of trust is more like a common agent of the parties to the instrument.

Given this *sui generis* nature of the trustee's function, it is important to focus on certain specific questions concerning the trustee's role.

a. Mortgagee (Beneficiary) Purchase at Trustee's Sale

So long as a trustee is not employed by or otherwise closely associated with the mortgagee, it is permissible in every jurisdiction for the mortgagee to purchase at the sale.

b. Trustee Purchase at Sale

A trustee, without at least the express consent of the mortgagor or his successor, may not purchase the premises for his or her own account. Such a sale is voidable. A few states' statutes reverse this position, and authorize the trustee to purchase at the sale.

c. Trustee an Employee or Part Owner of Mortgagee

Courts take a variety of approaches to this type of apparent conflict of interest. Some courts hold that where the connection between the trustee and mortgagee is substantial, purchase by the mortgagee is really an indirect purchase by the trustee and thus voidable. See *Whitlow v. Mountain Trust Bank,* 207 S.E.2d 837 (Va.1974). An alternative judicial approach holds that where, for example, the trustee is an important officer of the mortgagee, the deed of trust in effect becomes a mortgage and thus the law of mortgages, rather than of trust deeds applies. Such a sale to the mortgagee is voidable because the mortgagee is treated as if he had purchased at his own sale. See *Mills v. Mutual Building & Loan Ass'n,* 6 S.E.2d 549 (N.C.1940). Many other courts, however, hold that mere close connection between the trustee and the mortgagee does not in itself render a mortgagee purchase voidable. See *Perry v. Virginia Mortg. and Inv. Co., Inc.,* 412 A.2d 1194 (D.C.App.1980). Rather, such circumstances merely place the burden on trustees to prove "faithfulness to their trust" absent specific evidence of fraud, self-dealing or over-reaching by the trustee. This burden, however, is satisfied if the trustee shows compliance with the affirmative duties under the deed of trust and the statute to advertise and sell the property and to pay all proper expenses and indebtedness. In a number of states this approach has been codified by statute.

Note, however, that even where legislation or case law permits "close connection" between the trustee and the mortgagee, the trustee who is also the attorney for the mortgagee may pose special problems. At least one court has suggested that such a dual role may violate the attorney's obligations under the state's Code of Professional Responsibility. See *Cox v. Helenius*, 693 P.2d 683 (Wash.1985).

d. Trustee Duty to Ascertain Whether Foreclosure is Justified

"Absent unusual circumstances known to the trustee, he may, upon receiving a request for foreclosure from the [mortgagee], proceed upon that advice without making any affirmative investigation and without giving any special notice to the [mortgagor]." Spires v. Edgar, 513 S.W.2d 372, 378 (Mo.1974).

e. Trustee Duty to Disclose Title Defects to Sale Purchasers

Many courts take a *caveat emptor* approach, holding that the trustee "owes no duty except to refrain actively from doing anything to hamper [purchasers] in their search for information or to prevent the discovery of defects by inspection. He is under no duty to make representations or to answer questions; but if questions are asked and he undertakes to answer, then such answers must be full and accurate—nothing must then be concealed." *Feldman v. Rucker*, 109 S.E.2d 379, 386 (Va.1959). In other jurisdictions, trustees with knowledge of title defects must disclose them to potential purchasers if they are not readily observable upon reasonable inspection by a purchaser. See *McPherson v. Purdue*, 585 P.2d 830 (Wash.App.1978).

f. The "Commercially Reasonable" Standard

A few courts have borrowed the "commercial reasonableness standard from Article 9–504 of the Uniform Commercial Code and applied it power of sale real estate foreclosure. The leading case is *Wansley v. First National Bank of Vicksburg*, 566 So.2d 1218 (Miss.1990), where the court ruled:

> Subject to our otherwise governing statutes, we declare that, if the secured creditor is authorized to foreclose by power of sale, after the

debtor's default and upon compliance with the deed of trust or other instrument, the secured creditor may sell any or all of the real estate that is subject to the security interest in its then condition or after any reasonable rehabilitation or preparation for sale. *Every aspect of the sale, including the method, advertising, time, place and terms, must be commercially reasonable.* This is an objective standard."

Note that because the mortgagee in this case was seeking a deficiency judgment, it is not clear whether the foregoing "commercially reasonable" standard also applies to suits to set aside a sale. Certain observations, however, are appropriate. Note that the standard is "subject to our otherwise governing statutes." Thus, if a statute mandates a certain practice or procedure, it will govern no matter how "reasonable" the trustee's actions in disposing of the real estate. For example, if the foreclosure statute mandates a "public" sale, it is extremely unlikely that a court would uphold a private disposition of the real estate, no matter how "reasonable" and common such a practice is in the chattel security context.

What then is the value of the "commercially reasonable" approach? Does it serve any purpose? It clearly does in those situations where the applicable statute is silent as to a particular issue. In *Wansley* the trustee was a part-owner and lawyer for the mortgagee. Here, in the absence of a statute requiring otherwise, the court was able to conclude that, notwithstanding this conflict of interest, it was not "commercially unreasonable" for this lawyer to serve as trustee and to conduct the sale.

g. The Impact of Presumption Statutes

Several states have statutes that provide that recitals of statutory compliance contained in a trustee's deed create prima facie evidence of compliance with statutory requirements "relating to the exercise of the power of sale and sale of the property described therein, including recitals concerning any mailing, personal delivery and publication of the notice of default, any mailing and publication and posting of notice of sale, and the conduct of the sale." Utah Code Ann. § 57–1–28. As to bona fide purchasers, some of these statutes also state that the recitals create conclusive evidence of compliance. Id.

These statutes are important for at least two reasons. First, they create a general rebuttable presumption that the statutory requirements have been satisfied and that the sale is valid. Thus, they enhance the stability of foreclosure titles. More important, they suggest that any defect in the foreclosure proceeding which is contradicted by a recital in the trustee's deed renders the sale only *voidable* and not void. As we noted earlier in this Chapter, if a defect renders a sale void, the sale passes no title even to a bona fide purchaser and thus the defect can be raised against such a purchaser. If, however, the defect merely renders the sale voidable, it cannot be set aside against a BFP.

Does this mean that a sale to a BFP may not be set aside even though the deed of trust obligation was not in default or the loan documents were forged? Probably not. A more acceptable reading of these statutes is that they cover defects that arise in connection with the *mechanics* of exercising the power of sale and not those that relate to whether there was a *substantive* basis to foreclose in the first place. Any other result would seem not only inherently unfair but arguably unconstitutional as well.

h. Failure to Provide Notice to Junior Interests—Should a Judicial Foreclosure Analogy Apply?

Suppose a power of sale foreclosure statute requires mailed notice to junior lienors, and the foreclosing mortgagee or trustee fails to comply with the requirement. Logically, the rights of a foreclosure purchaser in such a setting should rise no higher than those of purchaser at a judicial foreclosure sale where a necessary party is omitted. If such were the case, a junior interest holder who is given no notice should be unaffected by the sale and the parties should be governed by the analysis of Section (C)(5) of this Chapter. However, in many states the situation is complicated by presumption statutes of the type we just considered. There are decisions in these states holding that such legislation insulates a bona fide purchaser from the claims of a junior lienor who was not properly notified, a result that clearly is inconsistent with the rights of omitted junior lienors in the judicial foreclosure setting. See *Glidden v. Municipal Authority of Tacoma*, 758 P.2d 487 (Wash.1988). As a reaction to the latter decision, Washington enacted legislation mandating that where the trustee fails to give the required notice to a junior interest, the latter "shall be treated as if such person was a holder of the same lien or interest and was omitted as a party defendant in a judicial foreclosure proceeding." West's Rev.Code Wash.Ann. § 61.24.040(7).

7. Remedies for Defective Power of Sale Foreclosure

There are three main remedies against defective power of sale foreclosure: an injunction against sale; a suit to set aside the sale; and an action for damages for wrongful foreclosure.

The selection of the appropriate remedy will depend upon several variables, including when the defect was discovered, the nature of the defect and, in the case of a completed foreclosure sale, whether the sale purchaser or subsequent grantee is a BFP. Note also that these remedies are available not only to the mortgagor or subsequent grantees, but to former junior lienholders as well. See generally, Nelson & Whitman, Real Estate Finance Law § 7.22 (4th ed.2001).

a. Injunction Against Sale

When the sale has not yet been consummated, the most common remedy for the mortgagor or other injured party is the injunction suit.

1) Substantive Grounds

Because most of the typical defects we concentrated on in the previous material will not yet have occurred, injunction suits most often will be based on defenses to the obligation or related matters. Examples would include such defenses as the absence of a default, the invalidity of acceleration, or the fact that some of the land described by the proposed sale is not covered by the mortgage being foreclosed.

2) Procedural Considerations

Very often the injunction suit is accompanied by a request for temporary injunctive relief. Normally the plaintiff must post an injunction bond to protect the mortgagee in the event it is established that the temporary relief was wrongfully issued. In determining whether to grant temporary relief, a court must balance the hardships that would be imposed on plaintiff from failure to issue such relief against those that mortgagee would suffer in the event it is granted. While technically the temporary injunction stage is not "on the merits," as a practical matter probable ultimate success on the merits is an important consideration in a court's decision whether to grant temporary relief.

3) Tender as a Requirement for Injunctive Relief

Some courts require, based on the maxim that "one who seeks equity must do equity", that the mortgagor tender the balance owing on the mortgage debt as a condition precedent to injunctive relief. This requirement makes little sense at a litigation stage in which the issue being litigated may well be whether the debt in fact is due. Moreover, if temporary relief is being sought, there will usually be an injunction bond to protect the mortgagee from frivolous claims. Most important, the requirement of tender is inconsistent with the right, inherent in the mortgagor's equity of redemption, to insist upon a valid foreclosure.

While some courts apply the same tender requirement to junior lienors, it makes even less sense in the junior lien setting than when the mortgagor is bringing suit. Because both have an interest in a possible sale surplus, the junior lienor, like the mortgagor, has the right to redeem the senior lien; but only the mortgagor has the *obligation* to do so.

b. The Suit to Set Aside the Sale

This remedy encompasses not only the substantive grounds discussed above that would justify an injunction suit, but can also be a vehicle for raising defects that were inherent in the foreclosure process itself. For example, most of the defects considered in Section D(5) of this Chapter would normally be raised in a suit to set aside the sale. The remedy is available to the holders of junior interests injured by the sale as well as mortgagors.

1) Tender as a Condition Precedent

More courts require tender in the suit to set aside than in the injunction situation. However, for the same reasons considered above in connection with the injunction remedy, the tender requirement is an unfair burden on those who have a right to insist on a valid foreclosure process.

2) Unavailability Against a BFP

If the defect is one which renders a sale only voidable and if the defendant acquired title as a BFP, the suit to set aside the sale is unavailable. If the defect rendered the sale void, the remedy is available irrespective of the BFP status of the defendant.

Example 1: At a power of sale foreclosure, the trustee at the sale mistakenly, but innocently, mentioned that mechanics' liens against the premises were senior to the mortgage being foreclosed. As a result, third parties at the sale decided not to bid. Mortgagee purchased and later sold to a grantee who was a BFP. Mortgagor filed a suit to set aside the sale. (*Result:* Remedy is unavailable because the subsequent grantee was a BFP and the defect [unintentional chilled bidding] was one that at most rendered the sale voidable.)

Example 2: Same facts as above except that the trustee and mortgagee conspired to chill the bidding by having the trustee intentionally assert the existence of the fictitious mechanics' liens. (*Result:* Suit to set aside is available notwithstanding the fact that the grantee was a BFP. Since intentional chilled bidding generally renders a sale void, the BFP status of the grantee is irrelevant.)

c. Damages for Wrongful Foreclosure

If the sale has been completed and the mortgagor or junior lienor cannot bring a suit to set aside the sale because of the above considerations, the only remaining remedy is an action for damages for wrongful foreclosure against the foreclosing mortgagor or trustee.

1) Measure of Damages—Mortgagor

Most courts measure the mortgagor's damages as the difference between the fair market value of the mortgaged real estate and the aggregate amount of liens as of the date of the defective foreclosure sale. Some courts simply refer to this measure of damages as the mortgagor's equity.

Example: At the date of the defective sale the fair market value of Blackacre was $70,000. The total amount of liens against it, including the mortgage that was defectively foreclosed, equaled $62,000. The land is now in the hands of a BFP. Mortgagor sued for damages. (*Result:* Damages will be $8,000 [$70,000 less $62,000 the aggregate amount of liens on the property as of the date of foreclosure].)

Some have argued that the mortgagor should have the option of measuring the damages at either the date of the defective foreclosure sale or the date of the suit for damages. This approach would deny the wrongdoer the fruits of his or her wrongdoing if the land went up in value after the foreclosure. On the other hand, when the land goes down in value, it arguably is fair to utilize the date of foreclosure because, but for the foreclosure proceeding clouding mortgagor's title, he arguably would have been able to sell the property before it decreased in value. See Nelson & Whitman, Real Estate Finance Law § 7.22 (4th ed.2001).

2)   Suit for Damages by Junior Lienor

Where the junior lienor is bringing suit for damages for wrongful foreclosure, the measure of damages is the difference between the fair market value of mortgaged real estate and the amount of any senior liens thereon as of the date of the wrongful foreclosure. In no event may the junior lienholder recover more than the amount of his or her lien.

Example: As of the date of a defective foreclosure sale of a first mortgage on Blackacre, the fair market value of Blackacre was $100,000. The amount of the first mortgage was $65,000. There was also a $25,000 second mortgage on Blackacre. Second mortgagee sued for damages for wrongful foreclosure. (*Result:* Second mortgagee will recover $25,000. [Although $100,000 less $65,000 equals $35,000, in no event may junior lienor recover more than the amount of the junior lien].)

3)   Damages as an Alternative to the Suit to Set Aside

Suppose that a defect renders the foreclosure sale void or, alternatively, that it is only voidable, but the purchaser is not a BFP. Should the mortgagor's only remedy be a suit to set aside the sale or should he or she have the option to say to the purchaser, "Keep the land; I want damages."? *The majority of courts allow the mortgagor to sue for damages even though a suit to set aside would be available. A minority of jurisdictions hold that "to recover damages at law it is necessary to show that the land went to an innocent holder so that the plaintiff's interest in it was lost." Bowen v. Bankers' Life Co.,* 239 N.W. 774 (Minn.1931).

E. Power of Sale Foreclosure—Constitutionality

As we noted earlier, power of sale foreclosure legislation provides varying degrees of notice to interested parties. Some statutes, for example, provide for mailed notice to persons who would be necessary parties in a judicial foreclosure proceeding. At the other extreme are a few states which require only notice by publication. Most, however, require mailed notice to the mortgagor and owner of the equity of redemption (if a different party), but do not require such notice to junior lienholders. Moreover, almost no power of sale legislation provides for a hearing, judicial or otherwise, prior to foreclosure.

Two general questions are thus presented. First, does a power of sale foreclosure involve the requisite state or federal action to invoke the protection of the due process clause? Second, if sufficient state or federal action is present, does the particular power of sale procedure violate the notice and hearing requirements of procedural due process under the Fourteenth and Fifth Amendments?

1.　Constitutional Notice Requirements

Assuming that power of sale legislation constitutes state or federal action for Fourteenth and Fifth Amendment purposes, such legislation violates the notice requirements of those Amendments if it requires less than mailed notice to those parties who in a judicial foreclosure would be characterized as necessary parties.

Mullane v. Central Hanover Bank and Trust Co., 339 U.S. 306 (1950) held that notice by publication to beneficiaries of a common trust fund failed to meet procedural due process standards. Rather, the means used must be "reasonably calculated to reach interested parties." Moreover, the Court also stated that "where the names and addresses of those affected by a proceeding are at hand, the reasons disappear for resort to means less likely than the mails to apprize them of its pendency." In *Mennonite Board of Missions v. Adams*, 462 U.S. 791 (1983), the Court relied on *Mullane* in holding that notice by publication and posting to a mortgagee of real estate being sold for nonpayment of taxes violated the notice requirements of the due process clause of the Fourteenth Amendment. According to the Court, "when the mortgagee is identified in a mortgage that is publicly recorded, constructive notice by publication must be supplemented by notice mailed to the mortgagee's last known available address, or by personal service. But unless the mortgagee is not reasonably identifiable, constructive notice alone does not satisfy the mandate of *Mullane*." Several courts have applied *Mullane* to invalidate notice by publication to the mortgagor in the power of sale foreclosure context. See, e.g., *Ricker v. United States*, 417 F.Supp. 133 (D.Me.1976). *Contra: Federal Deposit Insurance Corporation v. Morrison*, 747 F.2d 610 (11th Cir.1984).

While almost all of the litigation concerning the constitutionality of power of sale notice requirements has focused on the mortgagor, it seems clear that other junior interests, as well, are equally entitled to the minimum notice guaranteed by the Fourteenth Amendment.

Statutes that fail to provide for notice by mail or personal service to junior lienors are probably defective. The message of *Mennonite* seems unmistakable. If notice by publication or posting is insufficient for mortgagees whose liens face destruction by the foreclosure of a real estate tax lien, so too it must be for those whose liens are jeopardized by senior mortgage foreclosure. Moreover, it probably does not matter whether the junior lienor is a home seller who takes back a purchase money second mortgage or a sophisticated institutional second mortgage lender. According to *Mennonite*, "personal service or mailed notice is required even though sophisticated creditors have means at their disposal to discover whether property taxes have not been paid and whether tax sale proceedings are therefore likely to be initiated. . . . [A] party's ability to take steps to safeguard its interests does not relieve the state of its constitutional obligation." Nor will requiring such notice to a junior lienor impose an unfair burden on the foreclosing mortgagee. As one recent case explains, a "simple title scan from the time that the property was acquired by the current owner to the initiation of the foreclosure proceedings would have provided notice of [junior mortgagee's] interest in the property. * * * Certainly, this process is not oppressive to the foreclosing party in terms of the amount of time, money or effort expended." *Island Financial, Inc. v. Ballman*, 607 A.2d 76, 80 (Md.App.1992).

A few states require mailed notice or personal service both for the mortgagor and owner of the equity of redemption, but mailed notice to other interest holders only if they previously have recorded a specific request to receive it. The foregoing considerations probably doom these statutes as well. See *Island Financial, Inc. v. Ballman*, 607 A.2d 76 (Md.App.1992). Under such legislation, an interested party could be wiped out without being provided a notice "reasonably calculated to provide actual notice." As emphasized in the prior paragraph, while *Mennonite* "fashioned its rule from the view of the least sophisticated creditor[s]", it clearly refused to weaken 14th Amendment protections for their more sophisticated and powerful counterparts. Note, 49 Mo.L.Rev. 385, 392 (1984). In the last analysis, "request for notice" provisions probably satisfy the constitutional notice requirement only where the junior interest is not "reasonably ascertainable" from a search of the records. This may be the case, if at all, only in extremely complicated title search situations such as those involving multiple recorded mineral interests and their assignments. See *Davis Oil Co. v. Mills*, 873 F.2d 774 (5th Cir.1989).

Mortgagees sometimes attempt to "cure" notice deficiencies in power of sale legislation by providing mailed notice to all persons junior to the mortgage being foreclosed, even though the applicable statute does not require it. It can be argued that when such notice is in fact provided, the complaining party suffers no injury and therefore lacks the constitutional requirement of standing. On the other hand, in *Wuchter v. Pizzutti*, 276 U.S. 13 (1928), the Supreme Court held that a nonresident motorist service of process statute that required only service on the secretary of state violated the Fourteenth Amendment due process clause even though the secretary of state in that case actually mailed notice to the nonresident defendant. See Comment, The Constitutionality of Maine's Real Estate Foreclosure Statutes, 32 Maine L.Rev. 147, 171 (1980); Nelson & Whitman, Real Estate Finance Law § 7.25 (4th ed.2001).

2. Constitutional Hearing Requirements

Assuming the requisite state or federal action is present, power of sale legislation violates the hearing requirement of the Fourteenth and Fifth Amendments to the extent that there is no requirement of a hearing at which interested parties can challenge the legal right to foreclose and the propriety of the decision to do so.

Fuentes v. Shevin, 407 U.S. 67 (1972), invalidated a state replevin statute because it did not provide for an opportunity for a probable cause hearing before chattels were taken temporarily from the possessor, pending a trial on their merits. *Mitchell v. W.T. Grant Co.*, 416 U.S. 600 (1974) modified *Fuentes* by upholding a similar Louisiana procedure where the judge, not a clerk, issued the seizure order and there was a right to an "immediate" probable cause hearing thereafter. However, power of sale statutes usually make no provision for hearing at any time, before or after the final deprivation of title to mortgagor's real estate. Most courts considering the issue have utilized *Fuentes* and *Mitchell* to invalidate power of sale legislation on hearing grounds. See *Ricker*, supra; *Garner v. Tri–State Development Co.*, 382 F.Supp. 377 (E.D.Mich.1974). *Contra: Guidarelli v. Lazaretti*, 233 N.W.2d 890 (Minn.1975).

The hearing required by procedural due process must be automatically triggered by the power of sale legislation itself. Thus, the ability to bring an injunction suit to enjoin a pending foreclosure, based either on the common law or on general statutory authorization existing independent of power of sale legislation, does not satisfy the hearing requirement. See generally, Nelson & Whitman, Real Estate Finance Law § 7.25 (4th ed.2001). On the other hand, there is authority that when the United States is the foreclosing mortgagee, federal agency regulations, rules or practice that provide for an administrative hearing may be sufficient to satisfy procedural due process requirements even though the state power of sale statute that was utilized was deficient with respect to constitutional hearing requirements. *United*

States v. Ford, 551 F.Supp. 1101 (N.D.Miss.1982). The agency hearing officer, however, must be sufficiently "neutral". It is doubtful, for example, that this standard is satisfied where the hearing officer is an agency executive who is put in the position of evaluating a foreclosure decision made by a fellow administrator which has already been approved by a higher official who is a supervisor of both persons. See *Johnson v. United States Department of Agriculture*, 734 F.2d 774 (11th Cir.1984).

A more difficult case is presented if the power of sale legislation specifically provides for the mortgagor's right to sue to enjoin the pending foreclosure. See, e.g., Rev.Code Wash. § 61.24.130. While one must concede that the hearing is literally provided for in the power of sale legislation, it is triggered only by the mortgagor affirmatively filing suit. Consequently, the procedure is still constitutionally suspect. To bring a separate suit inevitably requires the services of a lawyer or at least a reasonably sophisticated lay mortgagor. On the other hand, if a hearing is automatically required by the power of sale legislation, most mortgagors should be able to answer a summons and appear to state their case without the aid of legal counsel.

3. Enforceability of Waiver Provisions

Even assuming that power of sale foreclosure is constitutionally deficient in one or both of the areas considered above, such objections, in theory at least, are capable of being waived either in the mortgage itself or in a separate agreement. In all probability, however, such attempts at waiver will be either constitutionally unsound or, for practical purposes, unworkable.

In *Fuentes*, supra, the Supreme Court recognized that waiver was possible, but it refused to find an actual waiver in that case. The contract there provided that in the event of default, "Seller at its option may take back the merchandise." This and similar language in other contracts were deemed ineffectual for several reasons: the language did not specifically refer to a waiver of constitutional rights; there was a lack of awareness by the parties of the significance of the waiver; and there was no bargaining over the terms of the waiver by parties who were equal in bargaining position. See also *Ricker*, supra.

If waiver could be achieved simply by spelling out what rights were being waived and making sure that the mortgagor understood what the waiver encompassed, that result could be accomplished by appropriate drafting. However, to the extent that some type of equality of bargaining position is required, a valid waiver will be difficult, if not impossible, to achieve. Very few, if any, mortgage transactions could satisfy such a requirement. Moreover, a title examiner evaluating a five-year-old power of sale foreclosure would be hard pressed to ascertain from the recorded mortgage whether such equality existed.

Finally, even if it were possible and practical to enforce a waiver against a mortgagor, it would be even more difficult against a junior lienholder or other holders of subordinate interests in the real estate. It could be argued that such parties are on notice from recorded prior documents and that they therefore implicitly consent to the terms of a waiver contained in a prior recorded mortgage. However, it is doubtful that constitutional rights can be waived so indirectly. Moreover, even if such a waiver were effective against subsequent grantees and junior mortgagees, on the theory that the takers of consensual liens normally examine the record beforehand, it could hardly be applicable to such parties as junior judgment creditors or mechanics lien claimants who normally do not make such an examination. See Nelson & Whitman, Real Estate Finance Law § 7.26 (4th ed.2001).

4. The State Action—Federal Action Problem

It is clear that most power of sale legislation is inconsistent with the notice and hearing components of Fourteenth and Fifth Amendments. But such legislation can be unconstitutional only if for purposes of the Fourteenth Amendment, "significant state involvement" exists or in the case of the Fifth Amendment, sufficient "federal action" is established. In early cases invalidating power of sale foreclosure on constitutional grounds, the government was the mortgagee (*Ricker*, supra) or the court either assumed sufficient governmental action or treated the latter issue in a cursory fashion. But the opponents of power of sale legislation appear to have won numerous early due process battles only to have largely lost the overall "governmental action" war.

a. Power of Sale and "State Action"

State action litigation has focused on five theories: "direct" state action; the "encouragement" theory; the governmental function theory; the judicial enforcement theory; and the "pervasiveness" theory. Although the United States Supreme Court has not decided the state action question in the power of sale context, its decisions in related areas and the opinions of other courts directly dealing with power of sale foreclosures makes it increasingly unlikely that state action can be found on any of the five theories.

1) Direct State Action Theory

State action under this theory exists when state officials act directly to enforce rights arising from a state statute. In *Fuentes*, supra, state action was found, albeit without analysis, because the replevin statute provided for the writ to be issued by a clerk of court and seizure of the chattel was to be carried out by the sheriff. Recent decisions have rejected this argument in the power of sale context on the ground that the intervention of public officials is limited largely to ministerial functions. See *FNMA v. Howlett*, 521 S.W.2d 428 (Mo.En Banc 1975). Indeed, in most power of sale jurisdictions a foreclosure normally will be consummated without the knowledge, much less the participation, of any public official other than perhaps the recorder of deeds. In a few states the sheriff (e.g., Minnesota) or some other type of public official (e.g., the public trustee in Colorado) actually conducts the foreclosure sale. In view of this it is important to emphasize the Supreme Court's statement in *Lugar v. Edmondson Oil Co., Inc.*, 457 U.S. 922 (1982) in characterizing the state action in the *Fuentes-Mitchell* line of cases: ". . . in each case the Court entertained and adjudicated the defendant debtor's claim that the procedure under which the private creditor secured the disputed property violated federal constitutional standards of due process. Necessary to that conclusion is the holding that private use of the challenged state procedures *with the help* of state officials constitutes state action for purposes of the Fourteenth Amendment." Thus, it would seem that in the few states where a public official conducts the foreclosure sale, there is a strong argument that private mortgagees are acting "with the help" of state officials; there is therefore a persuasive case for finding state action with respect to those statutes.

2) The "Encouragement" Theory

Those who assert this theory argue that state action is present when state statutes "encourage" objectionable, but otherwise private, activity. The theory is based on *Reitman v. Mulkey*, 387 U.S. 369 (1967), which involved the adoption by California voters of a state constitutional amendment that protected a person's right to refuse to sell or rent his property to anyone for any reason. The United States Supreme Court, 5–4, adopted a California Supreme Court finding that the sole purpose of the amendment was to invalidate state antidiscrimination statutes and held that it made the state an impermissible "partner" in racial discrimination.

Courts have rejected the argument that state power of sale legislation "encourages" this type of foreclosure and therefore makes the state a partner in it. Such courts stress that power of sale foreclosure existed prior to legislative authorization and that, in any event, the "encouragement" theory is relevant only in racial discrimination settings. See *Howlett*, supra.

3) Governmental Function Theory

This approach would find state action when a private person performs a function that is inherently governmental in nature. Thus, the "company town" in *Marsh v. Alabama*, 326 U.S. 501 (1946) was held to the same First Amendment standards as a municipal corporation because running a town was deemed to be a governmental function. Lower federal court decisions have rejected the application of this theory to foreclosure on the ground that foreclosure of mortgages has never been the exclusive prerogative of the state. Moreover, the United States Supreme Court in *Flagg Brothers Inc. v. Brooks*, 436 U.S. 149 (1978) used similar reasoning in rejecting the governmental function argument as applied to a Uniform Commercial Code provision that provided for the private sale of goods to enforce a warehouseman's lien.

4) The Judicial Enforcement Theory

Under this theory, the origin of which is *Shelley v. Kraemer*, 334 U.S. 1 (1948), state action occurs when state courts enforce the rights of private parties. In the *Shelley* case, the Supreme Court held that specific judicial enforcement of a racially restrictive covenant constituted state action in violation of the Fourteenth Amendment equal protection clause. Even though most power of sale foreclosures do not involve direct judicial intervention, courts can become involved in ejecting a holdover mortgagor or in subsequent quiet title actions. In either situation judicial recognition of the power of sale foreclosure would be involved. However, the Supreme Court has been especially hesitant to expand the *Shelley* concept beyond the racial covenant setting. State court decisions have refused to expand the *Shelley* concept, emphasizing the limited role of courts in power of sale foreclosure. See *Howlett*, supra.

5) The Pervasiveness Theory

This theory emphasizes that state action can be found where statutory regulation pervasively governs otherwise "private" activity. The Supreme Court rejected this argument in the context of a constitutional challenge to public utility service termination practices. The Court stated that "the fact that the regulation is extensive and detailed . . . does not by itself convert its action into that of the State for purposes of the Fourteenth Amendment. [T]he inquiry must be whether there is a sufficiently close nexus between the state and the challenged action of the regulated entity so that the action of the latter may be fairly treated as that of the state itself." *Jackson v. Metropolitan Edison Co.*, 419 U.S. 345 (1974). State courts in confronting this argument in the power of sale context have thus far been unable or unwilling to find the required nexus. See *Barrera v. Security Building & Investment Corp.*, 519 F.2d 1166 (5th Cir.1975).

Note that the foregoing analysis leads to at least three observations: First, most power of sale legislation fails to comply with the notice and hearing requirements of the Fourteenth Amendment. Second, nongovernmental mortgagees may continue to use such legislation because courts have been almost entirely unwilling to find the requisite state action necessary to invoke application of the Fourteenth Amendment. Third, where the state statutes provide for a government official such as a sheriff or public trustee to conduct the foreclosure sale, there is a strong argument that state action exists.

b. Power of Sale and "Federal Action"

1) The Government as Foreclosing Mortgagee

Where a direct instrumentality of the state or federal government is the foreclosing mortgagee, courts cannot avoid the notice and hearing defects inherent in power of sale foreclosure. In such cases it is not the power of sale legislation, but rather the foreclosing mortgagee itself that supplies the requisite governmental action. In the case of a direct instrumentality of a state as foreclosing mortgagee, Fourteenth Amendment state action is supplied. Where a direct federal instrumentality is involved, the requisite federal action exists for purposes of the Fifth Amendment. In the *Ricker* case, supra, for example, the Farmers Home Administration (FmHA) foreclosed a mortgage under a Maine nonjudicial foreclosure statute. Because the government was the mortgagee, the court went directly to the Fifth Amendment due process issues and invalidated the foreclosure. Had the mortgagee been a private entity, a preliminary issue would have been whether sufficient Fourteenth Amendment state action existed. Based on the existing case law, it is very likely that governmental action would not have been found and that the foreclosure would have survived unscathed. *Thus, stated simply, power of sale foreclosure may continue to be used by private mortgagees but not by many of their governmental counterparts.* Hence, we need to consider which governmentally-related mortgagees are subject to the requirements of due process.

a) Direct Governmental Instrumentalities

The Farmers Home Administration (FmHA), the Department of Veterans Affairs (VA) and the Federal Housing Administration (FHA) will probably each be considered direct instrumentalities of the United States. See *Ricker*, supra; *Rau v. Cavenaugh*, 500 F.Supp. 204 (D.S.D.1980). A similar conclusion is likely with respect to direct state government agencies, such as state housing finance agencies.

b) The Government National Mortgage Association (GNMA)

GNMA is a corporation wholly-owned by the United States government that purchases federally-insured or guaranteed mortgages on the secondary market. Strangely, the Court of Appeals for the Eighth Circuit in *Warren v. Government National Mortgage Ass'n*, 611 F.2d 1229 (8th Cir.1980) held that GNMA as a foreclosing mortgagee under Missouri power of sale legislation should not be considered the federal government for purposes of the Fifth Amendment. While the reasoning is unclear, the court may have been saying simply that GNMA, because of its unique role as a corporation dealing on the secondary mortgage market, acts for the most part like a private corporation and therefore should not be treated as a direct federal instrumentality. On the other hand, the opinion can easily be read more broadly for the proposition that even a direct instrumentality of the United States can foreclose without "federal government action" being triggered so long as the federal agency simply follows state power of sale statutes and "neither mandate[s] nor approve[s] the method of foreclosure to be followed in the event of default." Finally, perhaps the court was suggesting that even the United States can act in a proprietary or commercial, as opposed to governmental, fashion and that foreclosure of mortgages can be classified as proprietary or commercial activity. If either of the latter interpretations is accurate and either were to be accepted by other circuits, then even FmHA, the VA and the FHA could be treated, in their role as foreclosing mortgagees, as nongovernmental and insulated from the requirements of Fifth Amendment due process. Under such an approach the *Ricker* case, supra, for example, should never have reached the constitutional issues.

Warren may be dubious authority in light of *Lebron v. National Railroad Passenger Corporation,* 513 U.S. 374 (1995). That case involved the question whether the National Railroad Passenger Corporation ("Amtrak") could impose content-based restrictions on the leasing of billboard space for political purposes in the Pennsylvania Station in New York City. The United States Supreme Court reversed, 8–1, a Second Circuit holding that Amtrak was not a government entity for First Amendment purposes. According to the Supreme Court, "where, as here, the Government creates a corporation by special law, for the furtherance of governmental objectives, and retains for itself permanent authority to appoint a majority of the directors of that corporation, the corporation is part of the Government for purposes of the First Amendment." Id. at 974. Note that while Amtrak's preferred stock was wholly owned by the United States, railroads and other private entities owned common shares. GNMA, on the other hand, is wholly owned by the United States.

c)   Other Quasi–Federal Entities

Fannie Mae and Freddie Mac are both federal-chartered corporations that purchase large quantities of mortgage loans on the secondary market. Both are completely privately owned, but the President of the United States appoints some of their directors, and they are subject to heavy federal regulation.

Fannie Mae and Freddie Mac are probably not be considered to be acting as the federal government when they are foreclosing mortgages under state power of sale legislation. As one commentator has observed, "both [Fannie Mae] and [Freddie Mac] will satisfy the first prong of the [*Lebron*] test, because they were both formed by the government to further governmental objectives. The second prong, however, is not met by either [Fannie

Mae] or [Freddie Mac]. [Fannie Mae] is entirely owned by the private sector and has only a minority of directors appointed by the government. [Freddie Mac] is also owned by the private sector and also has only a minority of directors appointed by the government." Blegen, *The Constitutionality of Power of Sale Foreclosures by Federal Government Entities,* 62 Mo.L.Rev. 425, 444–446 (1997).

2) Federal Action Premised on Federal Subsidy and Regulation

Many federal programs involve subsidy to the mortgagor or substantial other regulation of the initial loan transaction. The VA program, for example, normally involves private lenders, but the federal government pays most of the cost of the mortgage guaranty and substantially regulates the details of the mortgage transaction. The 1960s and 1970s witnessed several programs under which the FHA paid part of the mortgagor's monthly mortgage payment directly to private mortgagees. Such transactions were subject to substantial federal regulatory scrutiny.

Where the foreclosing entity is non-federal, the cases indicate that the presence of substantial federal subsidy and regulation will not trigger a finding of federal action. To the extent, however, that the foreclosing entity is federal or quasi-federal and such subsidy and regulation exist, the chances of finding federal action are enhanced.

F. The Uniform Nonjudicial Foreclosure Act

While power of sale foreclosure has existed for at least 100 years, remarkably little national uniformity has been achieved. In 1974 the National Conference of Commissioners on Uniform State Laws adopted the Uniform Land Transactions Act (ULTA). ULTA covered numerous aspects of real property law, and a major portion was devoted to land security. In 1985, the Conference split these mortgage-related provisions off into a separate act, the Uniform Land Security Interest Act (ULSIA). Despite aggressive advocacy by the Conference, no state adopted either ULTA or ULSIA.

During the late 1990's, the Conference decided to try again to achieve uniformity in the real estate foreclosure context. The result was the Uniform Nonjudicial Foreclosure Act (Act) which was promulgated by the Conference in 2002. The Act is the product of years of drafting and reflects the thinking of many of the nation's prominent land finance scholars and practitioners. For a full exploration of the

Act, see Nelson and Whitman, *Reforming Foreclosure: The Uniform Nonjudicial Foreclosure Act,* ___ Duke L.J. ___ (2004). The following is a brief description of the important provisions of the Act.

1. Methods of Foreclosure

The Act provides for three methods of foreclosure and permits the secured creditor to elect the method to be used. The first is foreclosure by auction sale, the method currently pervasively use d in this country, conducted by a representative of the foreclosing creditor. The second method is foreclosure by negotiated sale. Such a sale will be consummated in much the same way as other real property sales. The real estate will probably be listed with a real estate broker and advertised extensively. Under this second method, the mortgagee notifies the debtor and junior lien holders of the"foreclosure amount" that it is willing to offer for the property, and they can simply disapprove the sale if they are dissatisfied with that amount. If one or more of them rejects this amount, the foreclosing creditor has three choices: (1) to discontinue the negotiated sale and resort to a different method of foreclosure; (2) to exclude the objecting party from the effect of the foreclosure, so that the objector will be unaffected by the foreclosure; or (3) to pay off the objecting party, if that person holds a lien. The third foreclosure method authorized by the Act is foreclosure by appraisal. This method does not liquidate the property, but rather leaves it in the hands of the mortgagee who will have the burden of liquidating it after the foreclosure is completed. This foreclosure method is in reality a form of "strict foreclosure," but with more substantial protections for those being foreclosed. The mortgagee chooses the appraiser, but the appraiser must meet reasonable professional standards of qualification and may not be mortgagee's employee. As with foreclosure by negotiated sale, the secured creditor notifies the debtor and junior lien holders of the "foreclosure amount" that it is willing to offer for the property. Any debtor or junior lienor who is dissatisfied with the amount can simply disapprove it and, as with a foreclosure by negotiated sale, the foreclosing creditor must either exclude the objector from the foreclosure, pay off the objector, or discontinue the foreclosure by appraisal and employ a different method of foreclosure.

2. Notice Provisions

The Act uses a "two-notice" system. Debtors, but not other junior interests, are given a notice of default and a 30–day period of cure before a notice of foreclosure may be issued to them. After the cure period has expired foreclosing creditor is permitted accelerate the debt and give a notice of foreclosure. Then an original notice of foreclosure must be given to all parties whose interests will be extinguished by the foreclosure. The foreclosure cannot occur earlier than an additional 90 days after the notice of foreclosure is given. Thus, a minimum of 120 days will ordinarily elapse between the debtor's default and the date of foreclosure. During the 90–day period, any affected persons have the right to redeem the real estate from the mortgage, but they must usually pay the accelerated balance due to do so. In addition to these two notices, all affected parties will receive further warning that the foreclosure is about to occur. In the case of foreclosure by auction, a copy of the advertisement of the sale must be given to them; it may be included with the notice of foreclosure or sent separately. If foreclosure is by negotiated sale, the affected parties must be given a notice informing them of the proposed sale. In the case of foreclosure by appraisal, they will receive a copy of the appraisal report, informing them of the date that the foreclosure will take effect.

3. Due Process Concerns

The Act provides for notice to all those whose interests in the foreclosed real estate are put at risk by foreclosure. It also affords an opportunity for any other person who wishes to receive notice of the foreclosure to file a request for such notice in the public records. Thus, assuming state or federal action is present, the notice provisions of the Act satisfy due process requirements.

What about the due process requirement for a hearing? The Act provides residential debtors the right to an informal meeting with a responsible representative of the secured creditor to present reasons why the foreclosure should not go forward. This meeting, which will be held only if it is affirmatively requested, is intended to guard debtors against the fundamental unfairness of a mistakenly-conducted foreclosure. The creditor's representative must have available at the meeting the evidence of the debtor's default. This right to a meeting may satisfy the due process hearing requirement if a government agency is foreclosing under the Act. The Act does not obligate creditors to hold a meeting with nonresidential debtors or with subordinate lienholders. Thus, there may still be constitutional hearing issues as to these latter parties.

4. Redemption

As we have emphasized earlier, mortgaged real estate may be redeemed in either of two ways: by equitable redemption before foreclosure and by statutory redemption for some fixed period of time after foreclosure. All states recognize equitable redemption, but only about half of the states have statutes permitting redemption after foreclosure. The Act recognizes the fundamental right to equitable redemption until the date of foreclosure, but does not permit post-foreclosure redemption.

5. Deficiency Liability

In general, no matter which of the three foreclosure methods is used, the Act permits recovery of a deficiency by the foreclosing creditor if there is personal liability on the obligation. However, residential mortgagors who act in good faith are exempt from deficiency liability. In addition, deficiency liability is limited by the "fair market value" concept: a debtor may present proof of the property's fair market value, and may have the amount of the deficiency limited as though the foreclosure amount was at least 90 percent of fair market value. This limitation is available to all debtors if the foreclosure was by auction, but is available only to residential debtors in the case of a foreclosure by negotiated sale or by appraisal.

6. Protections for Residential Debtors

The Act recognizes two classes of debtors: residential debtors and everyone else. Residential debtors are assumed to need additional legal protections from foreclosing creditors that are not essential to other persons. "Residential debtor" includes both a person who owns a home on which a mortgage exists, and anyone who is personally liable on an obligation that is secured by a home. "Home" is used here as a shorthand for "residential real property," which must be owner-occupied and contain no more than four dwelling units. Thus, "residential debtor" encompasses not only the usual consumer borrowers on home mortgage loans, but also relatives who guarantee their loans and purchasers who buy homes subject to, or with an assumption of, existing mortgages. The most important protections for residential debtors have already been considered above.

G. Disposition of Foreclosure Surplus

1. Common Law Rule

When the foreclosure sale price exceeds the amount needed to satisfy the mortgage being foreclosed and the costs of sale, the disposition of this surplus is governed by one underlying principle: that the surplus represents what is left of the foreclosed real estate. From this principle flow two corollaries: (1) the liens and other interests terminated by the foreclosure attach to the surplus in the order of priority they enjoyed prior to the foreclosure and (2) the foreclosed mortgagor's claim to the surplus is junior to the claims of all holders of valid interests that were terminated by the foreclosure.

Example: The following liens existed on Blackacre in order of their priority: a first mortgage in favor of E–1 for $50,000, a second mortgage in favor of E–2 for $20,000, a judgment lien in favor of J for $5,000. E–1's mortgage was foreclosed and P paid $80,000 at the sale. (*Result:* After the costs of sale are satisfied, $50,000 will be used to pay off E–1. The balance of the proceeds will be used first to pay E–2 in full, then to pay J in full, and the balance of $5,000 will be paid to the foreclosed mortgagor.)

2. Effect of Statutes

Statutes in many jurisdictions codify the common law approach described above. On the other hand, some statutes on their face award the surplus to the "mortgagor, his heirs, successors and assigns" and make no mention of junior lienholders. Such statutes, however, are almost always construed in favor of junior lienors by interpreting the word "assigns" broadly to include the junior lienholder as an assignee on the theory he acquired his lien "through or under the mortgagor." *Brown v. Crookston Agricultural Ass'n,* 26 N.W. 907 (Minn.1886).

3. Mortgage Form Language

To the extent that mortgage forms purport to award surplus to the "mortgagor, heirs and assigns," and are silent as to junior lienors, courts will, by analogy to judicial interpretation of such statutory language, in all likelihood give priority to junior lienors over the mortgagor. Given the strong common law rule favoring the junior lienors over the mortgagor with respect to surplus, unless the mortgage language specifically and unambiguously subordinates the junior lienors' claims to surplus to that of the mortgagor, courts will probably interpret mortgage language in a manner that is consistent with the common law.

Suppose, however, that language in the senior mortgage makes it crystal clear that the mortgagor's claim to surplus supercedes those of junior lienors. Under the Restatement, even such specific language will be ineffective. "This result is supported by logic and sound policy. To be sure, such language on its face purports to reserve for the mortgagor the right to any senior foreclosure surplus and to deny access to it by foreclosed junior mortgagees and other junior interests. However, having reserved the right to that senior surplus, mortgagor clearly remains free to assign that right thereafter. Thus, any subsequent creation by the mortgagor of a junior mortgage * * * surely carries with it an assignment by mortgagor to those junior parties of the right to any senior surplus. Only specific language in the *junior* mortgage reserving for mortgagor the right to senior surplus will accomplish mortgagor's intended purpose." Restatement (Third) of Property (Mortgages) § 7.4, Comment c, Reporters' Note (1997).

4. Claims of Those Senior to Foreclosed Mortgage

An important corollary of the common law rules governing the disposition of surplus is that *only one whose interest in the foreclosed real estate was terminated may share in the surplus.* This means that senior lienors have no right to utilize the surplus created by a junior foreclosure sale to prepay all or part of the first mortgage debt. See *Armand's Engineering Inc. v. Town and Country Club, Inc.,* 324 A.2d 334 (R.I.1974); Nelson & Whitman, Real Estate Finance Law § 7.32 (4th ed.2001).

5. Junior Liens Not Yet in Default

The majority of courts allow junior interests whose liens are not yet in default to share immediately in a senior foreclosure surplus. Such junior lienors are in effect prepaid. This is also the position of the Restatement. See Restatement (Third) of Property (Mortgages) § 7.4, Comment b (1997). *There is some authority, however, that would order the surplus held in trust by the court until the junior debt becomes due and payable.*

Note that it is extremely rare for a junior lien not to be in default if senior lien is in foreclosure. Moreover, even if the payments on a junior mortgage are being kept current, most junior mortgages will contain a "cross default" provision that permits acceleration of the junior debt in the event there is a default under a senior mortgage.

6. Remedies When Priority of Junior Claimants is Unclear

Where a mortgage has been foreclosed judicially and a surplus results, any ambiguities or dispute as to the priority of junior liens can be resolved by the same court that ordered foreclosure. On the other hand, where such problems arise after a power of sale foreclosure a judicial determination of lien priority is not immediately available. The foreclosing mortgagee or trustee will not want to risk potential liability by paying the surplus to the wrong junior claimant. In some states, statutes authorize the payment of surplus into court. Absent such a procedure the prudent stakeholder should seek judicial guidance by filing an interpleader action. See Nelson & Whitman, Real Estate Finance Law § 7.32 (4th ed.2001).

H. Reacquisition of Title by Holder of the Equity of Redemption and Related Issues

It is an axiom of mortgage law that the valid foreclosure of a mortgage not only terminates the owner's equity of redemption, but also all other junior interests in the real estate as well. But where the foreclosure purchaser is the mortgagor or other holder of the equity of redemption, many courts depart from this rule.

1. Foreclosure Purchase by Mortgagor or other Equity Holder

Under the prevailing view, a mortgagor or other holder of the equity of redemption who purchases the mortgaged real estate at a foreclosure sale acquires title subject to any lien or other interest that was junior to the foreclosed mortgage. Restatement (Third) of Property (Mortgages) § 4.9(a) (1997).

Example: Mortgagor borrows money from E–1 and gives E–1 a note secured by a mortgage on Blackacre. The mortgage is promptly recorded. Mortgagor then borrows money from E–2 and gives E–2 a promissory note secured by a mortgage on Blackacre. The E–2 mortgage is promptly recorded. The E–1 obligation goes into default and is accelerated. At a foreclosure on the E–1 mortgage, mortgagor purchases at the sale.(*Result:* E–2 still has a valid lien on Blackacre.)

There are several reasons for the foregoing result. First, when the mortgagor purchases the property at the foreclosure sale, he or she in effect is *paying the senior lien*. If this payment had taken place prior to the foreclosure, the junior mortgage would have moved into the first position. See *Old Republic Insurance Co. v. Currie,* 284 N.J.Super. 571, 665 A.2d 1153 (1995). More important, according to the Restatement,

> where a mortgagor is personally obligated on a junior lien, or where the mortgagor simply contains the usual warranties of title, it would be undesirable and inequitable to allow the mortgagor to profit by violating those obligations. Even where the mortgage obligation is completely "non-recourse," the mortgagor agrees to the satisfaction of that obligation out of the mortgaged real estate. Thus, actions by the mortgagor that undermine the ability of the mortgagee to realize on the benefits of that agreement should be discouraged.

Restatement (Third) of Property (Mortgages) § 4.9, comment b (1997). There is contrary authority. See *Mooney v. Provident Savings Bank,* 308 N.J.Super. 195, 705 A.2d 816 (1997).

Example: Mortgagor borrows money from E–1 and gives E–1 a promissory note secured by a mortgage on Blackacre. The mortgage is promptly recorded. Mortgagor then borrows money from E–2 and gives E–2 a promissory note secured by a mortgage on Blackacre. The E–2 mortgage is promptly recorded. Mortgagor then sells and conveys Blackacre to G–1 who either simply takes subject to the E–1 mortgage or assumes it. The E–1 mortgage then goes into default, is validly accelerated and a foreclosure sale occurs. G–1 purchases at the sale. (*Result:* E–2 still has a valid lien on Blackacre.)

As the foregoing example illustrates, the foregoing rule burdens not only the original mortgagor, also all of his or her grantees, whether they assume or simply take subject to the mortgage. In any transfer transaction the purchase price paid by the grantee is almost always reduced by the value of any senior liens which are to remain on the real estate. "To permit the transferee under such circumstances to acquire title through a senior lien foreclosure and, in so doing, to destroy junior liens, would enable the transferee to acquire the real estate for less than originally contemplated. Such unjust enrichment of the transferee should be discouraged." Restatement (Third) of Property (Mortgages) § 4.9, comment b (1997).

The same rule applies even where a mortgagor or grantee purchases the real estate from the foreclosure purchaser. In that case, junior liens are revived except in any situation where the foreclosure purchaser was a bona fide purchaser.

2. Foreclosure Purchase by Holder of Junior Interest: Impact on Other Junior Interests

A holder of a junior interest who purchases real estate at the foreclosure sale of any senior lien on that real estate acquires title free and clear of the interest of the holder of the equity of redemption and of any interest that was junior to the foreclosed lien. Restatement (Third) of Property (Mortgages) § 4.9(b) (1997).

Example :   Mortgagor borrows money from E–1 and gives E–1 a promissory note secured by a mortgage on Blackacre. The mortgage is promptly recorded. Mortgagor then borrows money from E–2 and gives E–2 a promissory note secured by a mortgage on Blackacre. The E–2 mortgage is promptly recorded. Mortgagor then borrows money from E–3 and gives E–3 a promissory note secured by a mortgage on Blackacre. The latter mortgage is promptly recorded. The E–1 mortgage then goes into default, is validly accelerated and foreclosed. The purchaser at the foreclosure sale is E–3. (*Result:* E–3 takes title to Blackacre free and clear of the interests of both Mortgagor and E–2.)

Why should we draw a distinction between a foreclosure purchase by the holder of the equity of redemption and a purchase by other junior interests?

"As against the mortgagor or other holder of the equity of redemption, a mortgagee has no duty to pay senior liens * * *. On the other hand, the holder of the equity of redemption does have * * * an obligation (often personal) to pay other liens on the real estate." Restatement (Third) of Property (Mortgages) § 4.9, comment c (1997).

I. Statutory Redemption

Once a valid foreclosure has occurred, the equity of redemption or equitable right to redeem from the mortgage ends. In about half the states, a statutory right to redeem begins. There is great variety in this state legislation. While in some jurisdictions it is available in both power of sale and judicial foreclosure, in others it is unavailable after power of sale foreclosure. The redemption period varies from a few months to 18 months. Some states limit the redemption right to the foreclosed mortgagor or owner, while others also authorize redemption by junior lienors. In most states, the mortgagor has the right to possession during the statutory period, while in a few others that right is conditioned upon the posting of a bond. In a few jurisdictions the sale purchaser has the possessory right during the redemption period. In almost all of the states the redemption amount is the foreclosure sale price plus interest, costs, and other incidental items. Redemption, for purposes of most statutes, means redeeming *the title* or *the land*.

1. Purpose of Statutory Redemption

There are at least four legislative goals underlying statutory redemption: (1) to allow the mortgagor an additional time period to obtain refinancing; (2) to permit a financially hard-pressed mortgagor additional use of the real estate; (3) to encourage those who bid at the foreclosure sale to offer a fair price (since the lower the foreclosure sale price the greater the chances that there will be redemption from the purchaser) and (4) where junior lienors are allowed to redeem, to allow them to protect their security that would be otherwise lost. Goals (3) and (4) are related, since where junior lienors have redemption rights a potential sale purchaser may tend to bid higher because he or she knows that the property can be taken away by subsequent redemption by one or more junior lienors as well as the mortgagor.

2. Criticisms of Statutory Redemption

Several criticisms of statutory redemption have been advanced. First, some have argued that the additional period to redeem may be viewed by the mortgagor as simply an additional grace period and thus discourage prompt payment of the mortgage debt. Second, because potential foreclosure purchasers know that the title can be taken away from them at any time during the redemption period, bidding may in reality be discouraged. This will especially be the case where the party redeeming from the purchaser is required to pay only a relatively low statutory rate of interest on the sale price. Third, in situations where a mortgagor has little likelihood of redeeming, but the statute allows the mortgagor to remain in possession during the redemption period, the mortgagor may be encouraged to "milk" the property and to avoid necessary maintenance. See Comment, The Statutory Right to Redeem in California, 52 Calif.L.Rev. 846 (1964).

3. The Operation of Typical Statutes

A thorough understanding of what statutory redemption is intended to accomplish is possible only by focusing specifically on how two typical state statutes work.

a. Strict Priority Approach

This approach is illustrated by Minn.Stat.Ann. §§ 580.23, 580.24. After the foreclosure sale, the mortgagor or his successor generally has a 6 month period (in certain situations 12 months) to redeem by payment of the foreclosure sale price plus a statutory rate of interest to the sale purchaser. The mortgagor's right to redeem is preemptive—in other words, if the mortgagor redeems there can be no further redemption. If, however, the mortgagor fails to redeem within the specified period, then junior lienholders each have a 5 day period, in order of their pre-foreclosure priority, to redeem by paying the sale purchaser the foreclosure price (including interest), plus the amount of the lien of any lienor who has redeemed in a previous 5 day period.

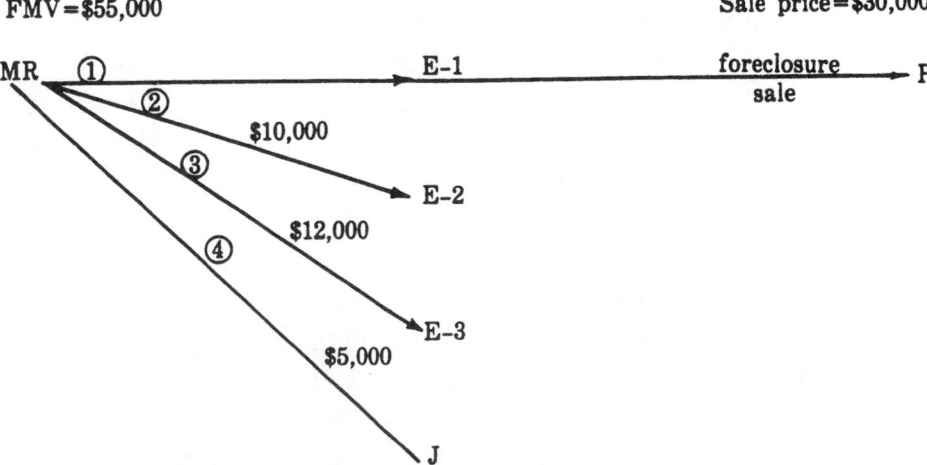

Suppose that a senior mortgage was foreclosed and the purchaser at the sale paid $30,000 for the mortgaged real estate that now has a fair market value of $55,000. At the time of the sale, E–2 had a second mortgage with a balance of $10,000. E–3 had a third mortgage with a balance of $12,000 and J had a $5,000 judgment lien on the property junior to all of the other liens.

Under the Minnesota scheme, MR has the right for 6 months to redeem from P by paying $30,000 plus interest. If MR redeems, redemption ends. If MR fails to act during that period, then E–2 has a 5 day period to redeem by paying the same amount to P as MR would have paid. If E–2 redeems, then E–3 has 5 days to redeem from E–2 by paying E–2 an amount equal to the sales price plus the amount of E–2's lien including interest or approximately $40,000. ($30,000 + $10,000). Finally, J can then redeem by paying E–3 approximately $52,000 ($30,000 + $10,000 + $12,000). Thus, for J redemption is a risky redemption. If the land is worth $55,000 and he or she must pay $52,000 for it, $3,000 of the $5,000 judgment can be satisfied out of the value of the land. On the other hand, J may correctly conclude that putting up $52,000 to recoup part of a $5,000 loss may not be worth it. Note that if any junior lienor allows the 5 day period to run without redemption, the next junior lienor in redeeming need not add the amount of that prior lien in calculating the redemption amount. Thus if E–2 fails to redeem, E–3 can redeem by paying P $30,000 plus interest. J then could redeem by paying E–3 $42,000 etc.

b. The Scramble Method

Under the "scramble method" there is no exclusive redemption period for the mortgagor. During the redemption period, redemption may be made from the purchaser by both mortgagors and junior lienholders, although if redemption is ever made by the mortgagor, redemption ends. As between junior lienholders, each may redeem at any time irrespective of their priority. However, priority is relevant in determining how much a redeeming lienor must pay. Now focus again on the fact situation utilized in explaining the "strict priority approach". If E–3 redeems first, the price paid to P will be the $30,000 purchase price plus interest. If then E–2 redeems from E–3, because of E–2's prior seniority, he or she will pay E–3 only the foreclosure purchase price plus interest and not the amount of E–3's lien. E–3, then, since his or her judgment is still unsatisfied, can redeem from E–2 by paying E–2 what E–2 paid plus interest and the amount of E–2's lien, in other words approximately $40,000 ($30,000 + $10,000). E–2 will then be barred from further redemption because he or she will have been fully paid. If MR now redeems, he will have to pay whatever E–3 paid plus interest and that will end all further redemption. J will then have no further rights.

4. Redemption by Mortgagor: Revival of Liens

When a mortgagor redeems statutorily many courts, using a variety of rationales, hold that all liens existing prior to the foreclosure sale are revived, including, to the extent of any deficiency, the lien under which the real estate was sold. Some courts reach the same result as to junior liens, but not as to a deficiency lien. Other courts hold that while junior liens are revived if redemption is by the original debtor-mortgagor, they are not revived if it is by a subsequent grantee.

An argument for revival, at least as against the mortgagor, is that we do not want to encourage him to destroy by default, foreclosure and redemption, the liens that he had created. See, e.g., *Farmers Production Credit Ass'n v. McFarland*, 374 N.W.2d 654 (Iowa 1985). On the other hand, it has been argued that under the ideal redemption statute, no pre-sale liens would be revived after a redemption by the mortgagor or a successor. Such is the approach taken by the California statutory redemption scheme. See West's Ann.Cal.Code Civ.Pro. § 729.080(e). Such a system would be designed to put pressure on the foreclosing mortgagee to bid at least the amount of the debt and on the junior lienors to bid above that amount, out of fear that a low sale price could result in a mortgagor redeeming, and removing from the grasp of such lienors, land possibly worth enough to satisfy one or more of such claims. See Cal. Legislative Committee Comment § 729.080(e) (1982); Nelson & Whitman, Real Estate Finance Law § 8.6 (4th ed.2001).

It should be noted, of course, that even where there is no revival of junior liens, the former lienholders normally can, in the case of redemption by a debtor-mortgagor, reduce their personal claims against him to a judgment and thus regain their liens on the formerly mortgaged property. However, even if a former junior lienor is permitted to reestablish her lien in this fashion, it may prove to be a Pyrrhic victory. In the meantime other liens may have intervened or, worse yet, the mortgagor may have filed bankruptcy, in which case the newly acquired judgment liens may well be avoided by the bankruptcy trustee. California flatly prohibits this approach. Under its statute, "once a lien is extinguished a lien may not be created on the same property to enforce the same claim or judgment." Cal. Legislative Committee Comment § 729.080(e) (1982).

5. Redemption by Junior Lienor: Revival of Liens

Under most statutes, redemption by a junior lienor gives the latter the same title the foreclosure sale purchaser would have obtained had there been no redemption. In other words, unlike in the mortgagor redemption situation, there is no revival of junior liens.

Since under this approach, junior liens are not revived, other junior lienors are arguably encouraged to use the redemption system as a mechanism for satisfying their liens. Since redemption probabilities increase, this approach may also put increased pressure on bidders at the sale to bid up the price to avoid subsequent loss of the land through redemption. Nelson & Whitman, Real Estate Finance Law § 8.7 (4th ed.2001).

J. Anti–Deficiency Legislation

Absent legislation, a mortgagee has two options for collecting the mortgage debt. First, the mortgagee may simply sue on the note, obtain a judgment, and then attempt to collect it from any of the mortgagor's property. To the extent the judgment is not satisfied in this fashion, the lender may foreclose on the real estate for the balance. Alternatively, the mortgagee may first foreclose on the real estate and, if the sale yields less than the mortgage debt, a deficiency judgment may then be obtained. Usually the amount of the deficiency is determined by subtracting the foreclosure sale price from the mortgage debt. If the foreclosure is judicial, the deficiency judgment is obtained from the same court that ordered foreclosure. In a power of sale situation, the mortgagee must bring an action at law for the deficiency judgment.

In many states deficiency judgments are closely regulated by statute. Much of this legislation is the product of the great depression of the 1930's when depressed land values resulted in foreclosure sales that often yielded prices far below the amount of the mortgage debt on the land.

1. The One Action Rule

California and a few other states follow a "one action rule." While it is not technically anti-deficiency legislation, it affects how a deficiency can be obtained. Under this rule, the mortgagee must first bring a foreclosure action and then seek a deficiency judgment in that action. The rule might aptly be called a "security first" rule. If the mortgagee first sues on the note, the mortgagor may have that action dismissed. On the other hand, if the mortgagor fails to raise the one action defense in a suit on the note, and the mortgagee obtains a personal judgment on the note, the mortgagee will be barred from using foreclosure to collect any part of the judgment that remains uncollected.

Example 1:   A promissory note with a current balance of $50,000 was secured by a mortgage on Blackacre in a state with a one action rule. After default, mortgagee brought an action on the note.

Mortgagor moved to dismiss (*Result:* motion should be granted. The one action rule prohibits any action but foreclosure).

Example 2:   Same facts as above, but the mortgagor failed to raise the one action rule as a defense in the action on the note. A judgment was entered against the mortgagor. Mortgagee was able to collect only $15,000 from other assets of the mortgagor. Mortgagee brought a foreclosure action on Blackacre to collect the remaining $35,000. Mortgagor filed a motion to dismiss (*Result:* motion granted. While the judgment on the note is valid because mortgagor failed to raise the one action rule, a foreclosure on Blackacre is barred.)

Note that the purpose of the rule is to protect the mortgagor from a multiplicity of actions and to compel a mortgagee to exhaust the mortgaged real estate before attempting to collect the mortgage debt from unencumbered assets. Some states apply the same rule in the power of sale context. In this setting it is more commonly referred to as the "security first" principle. See Nelson & Whitman, Real Estate Finance Law § 8.2 (4th ed.2001).

2.   Fair Value Legislation

The most significant and enduring anti-deficiency legislation of the great depression is the "fair value" legislation in effect in a significant number of states. Instead of defining the deficiency as the difference between the foreclosure sale price and the mortgage debt, it is calculated as the difference between the mortgage debt and the "fair value" of the foreclosed real estate. Sometimes, instead of "fair value" such legislation will use such terms as "true market value", "appraised value" or "actual value".

Sometimes the "fair value" is determined by a jury, sometimes by the court, and in some instances by appraisers. The legislation was largely designed to prevent unjust enrichment of the mortgagee by prohibiting him or her from purchasing the property for significantly less than the mortgage debt, obtaining a deficiency judgment for the difference between the debt and sale price and then reselling the real estate at its fair market value. A few states have adopted the "fair value" limitation by judicial decision. The Restatement adopts the "fair value" approach; see Restatement (Third) of Property (Mortgages) § 8.4 (1997). So does the Uniform Nonjudicial Foreclosure Act § 608(c), authorizing the court, in determining the amount of a deficiency, to substitute 90% of fair market value for the foreclosure amount if the former is larger.

Even though the "fair value" limitation is largely aimed at prohibiting unjust enrichment of the mortgagee, the majority of states apply it even to third party foreclosure purchasers. This is because limiting the application of the fair value determination to mortgagee purchasers may discourage mortgagees who contemplate obtaining a deficiency judgment from taking part in the foreclosure bidding and thus may remove a significant impetus to higher bidding by third parties. Moreover, irrespective of who purchases at the foreclosure sale, it is arguably good policy to protect the mortgagor from the double burden imposed by the loss of his or her real estate and an unfairly measured deficiency judgment.

Example: In a "fair value" jurisdiction, mortgagee foreclosed on a $60,000 mortgage on Blackacre and purchased at the sale for $35,000. Mortgagee then sought a deficiency judgment in a jurisdiction that utilizes a jury to determine the fair value of the foreclosed real estate. The jury determined that the fair value was $55,000. (*Result:* the court will enter a deficiency judgment for $5,000, the difference between the mortgage debt and the "fair value" of the real estate).

3. Prohibition of Deficiency Judgments in Power of Sale Foreclosure

Several states, including California, prohibit deficiency judgments after power of sale foreclosure.

The states that have such a prohibition tend also to have power of sale legislation that is relatively pro-mortgagee in other respects. For example, in California, when a deed of trust with power of sale is utilized, no statutory redemption is permitted. Other states may have believed that the "no deficiency" rule was a fair trade-off for the enactment of a power of sale system that was relatively quick and summary in nature.

On the other hand, a prohibition on power of sale deficiency judgments does not necessarily mean that the mortgagor is shielded from personal liability on the mortgage debt. If a mortgagee simply decides to forego foreclosure and no "one action" or "security first" principle is applicable, the mortgagee may still sue on the debt and attempt to collect it from the mortgagor's general assets.

4. Prohibition of Deficiency Judgments in Foreclosure of Purchase Money Mortgages

a. General Nature of the Prohibition

Several states prohibit deficiency judgments in a variety of situations involving purchase money mortgages. In some states the prohibition bars only deficiency judgments in favor of vendor-mortgagees, while in others the bar applies to third party lenders as well as vendors.

Such legislation is designed "to discourage land sales that are unsound because the land is overvalued and, in the event of a depression in land values, to prevent the aggravation of the downturn that would result if defaulting purchasers lost the land and were further burdened under personal liability". *Bargioni v. Hill*, 28 Cal.Rptr. 321, 378 P.2d 593 (Cal.1963). The overvaluation argument seems questionable. The theory is that seller-mortgagees will be encouraged to set lower selling prices because they will be forewarned that in the event of a mortgagor default they will be forced to look primarily to the land, and not to the mortgagor's other assets, to satisfy their debt. In any period of high interest rates and significantly reduced institutional mortgage lending, purchase-money lenders are often sellers of single family dwellings. It seems doubtful that significant numbers of such sellers are even aware of the deficiency limitations, much less take them into account in setting the sale price for their homes. And to the extent that deficiency limitations are a factor in sales price decisions, they may well tend to discourage seller financing during a period when, but for such financing, substantial numbers of such transactions simply could not take place.

b. As a Bar to Mortgagor Liability

Some states interpret limitations on purchase-money mortgage deficiency judgments to prohibit any mortgagor personal liability on the mortgage debt, both before and after foreclosure. See, e.g., Mid Kansas Federal Savings and Loan Ass'n v. Dynamic Development Corp., 804 P.2d 1310 (Ariz.1991); Ross Realty Co. v. First Citizens Bank & Trust Co., 250 S.E.2d 271 (N.C.1979).

Example: V conveyed Blackacre to MR who paid $5,000 in cash at the time of the conveyance and gave to V a promissory note for $45,000, secured by a mortgage on Blackacre, to cover the balance of the $50,000 sales price. MR paid the note down to a $40,000 balance and then defaulted. V then filed an action seeking a personal judgment against MR for $40,000, the balance due on the note. MR filed a motion to dismiss. (*Result:* Motion to dismiss granted. V's only remedy in a jurisdiction that interprets purchase-money mortgage deficiency legislation to bar all personal liability of the mortgagor is to foreclose the mortgage. V can neither first sue MR personally on the note nor seek a deficiency judgment after a foreclosure of the mortgage).

Some states have even used such legislation to prohibit mortgagor liability on a promissory note where a purchase money mortgage securing it had previously been released by the mortgagee. See *Barnaby v. Boardman*, 330 S.E.2d 600 (N.C.1985).

5. Deficiency Judgments and Installment Land Contracts

a. The Election of Remedies Problem

Even in the absence of anti-deficiency legislation, the election of remedies doctrine bars an installment land contract vendor from first invoking forfeiture and then seeking to recover the difference between the contract price and what the land is worth. See IV, Section E, supra.

b. Vendor Proceeding as a Foreclosing Mortgagee

Suppose that a vendor has the option of treating the installment land contract as a mortgage and elects to do so. The foreclosure sale of the real estate brings a price that is less than the contract price. In the absence of anti-deficiency legislation, the vendor can then seek a deficiency judgment for the difference between the contract price and the foreclosure sale price. The extent to which anti-deficiency legislation will bar a deficiency judgment against a vendee will depend on whether such legislation, either by specific language or by judicial interpretation, encompasses installment land contracts.

In some states anti-deficiency legislation specifically covers foreclosure by a contract vendor. In North Dakota, for example, fair value legislation is specifically applicable to contract vendors. In other words, any deficiency judgment after the foreclosure of an installment land contract will be measured by the difference between the foreclosure sales price and the fair value of the land and not by foreclosure sale price-contract price difference. See N.D.Cent.Code § 32–19–06. In California, the statutory prohibition on purchase-money mortgage deficiency judgments also prohibits such judgments in "any sale of real property for failure of the purchaser to complete his contract of sale. . . . " West's Ann.Cal.Civ.Code § 580(b). Where such specific statutory language is absent, however, courts have tended to be reluctant to extend purchase money mortgage deficiency prohibitions to installment land contracts. See *Glacier Campground v. Wild Rivers, Inc.*, 597 P.2d 689 (Mont.1978).

K. Servicemembers Civil Relief Act

Since World War I, federal law has conferred a variety of protections against creditors and other third parties on members of the military and their families. Until 2003, these protections were codified and popularly referred to as the The Soldiers' and Sailors' Civil Relief Act of 1940. As a result of the Iraq War, in 2003 Congress renamed the prior legislation the "Servicemembers Civil Relief Act" ("the Act") and at the same time included significant amendments that in some cases either modify or expand the protections of the prior Act. The Act provides certain protections to servicepersons with respect *to installment land contracts and mortgages on real estate executed prior to entrance on active duty.* While it does not extinguish any rights and obligations of mortgagors or mortgagees, certain proceedings may be stayed or extended and remedies altered in order to prevent undue hardships or pressure caused by military service. While numerous provisions affect normal debtor-creditor relationships, we will emphasize only some of the more important sections that significantly alter mortgage law relationships. Citations are to 50 U.S.C.A. App. §§ 501–596.

1. Statutes of Limitation

Section 526 in a broad manner tolls all statutes of limitation that otherwise would run against a service person. This section specifically has been held applicable to statutory redemption periods after real estate foreclosure. For example, a mortgagor's period of statutory redemption under state law normally is extended by a period equal to the mortgagor's period of service.

Example: MR executed a mortgage on Blackacre on June 1, 1999. On June 15, 1999, MR enlisted in the U.S. Army. In October 1999, MR went into default and the mortgage was foreclosed judicially on March 1, 2000. Under local law, there was a one year statutory redemption period. On June 15, 2002, MR was discharged from military service. A week later she tendered the statutory redemption amount to the foreclosure sale purchaser. The latter refused the tender and MR filed suit to enforce her statutory rights. (*Result:* the foreclosure sale purchaser must accept MR's tender. The statutory period is extended for 3 years (MR's period of service) from March 1, 2001, the date the statutory redemption period normally would have expired. MR thus would have the right to redeem at any time until March 1, 2004). See *Illinois National Bank v. Gwinn*, 61 N.E.2d 249 (Ill.1945).

While several lower appellate decisions had held in a tax sale redemption that the predecessor of section 526 did not protect "career" servicepersons who could not show that military service prejudiced their ability to redeem, the United States Supreme Court, in a case involving a career U.S. Army officer, unanimously rejected such an interpretation. In *Conroy v. Aniskoff*, 507 U.S. 511 (1993), the Court concluded that "Congress included a prejudice requirement whenever it considered it appropriate to do so, and * * * its omission of any such requirement was deliberate."

2. Section 525 Stay

Under this section, during military service or within 90 days thereafter, a service person-debtor is authorized to petition a court to stay any civil action or proceeding Such a stay which must be for a period of not less than 90 days is conditioned upon the service person proving that military service had a material effect on his or her ability to ability to appear. Additional stays are also authorized under this section. If an additional stay is refused the court must appoint counsel to represent the servicemember in the action or proceeding.

Example: E–1 commences either a judicial or power of sale foreclosure of a mortgage or deed of trust against Mortgagor, a protected servicemember. sends a letter explaining why military service has a material effect on her inability to appear and this letter is supported by a similar letter from her commanding officer. (*Result:* A court is authorized to stay the foreclosure for not less than 90 days and to authorize additional stays. If an additional stay is denied, counsel for the servicemember must be appointed. This section is available irrespective of whether the mortgage or deed of trust was executed prior to or during the servicemember's current service.)

3. Installment Land Contracts

Section 532 makes it a criminal offense for the vendor to exercise any right or option such as termination of the contract, repossession of the land, or rescission, except by a court order, with respect to most contracts executed prior to vendee's entry into the military. If such a judicial action is filed, and the court believes that military service has materially effected the vendee's ability to pay, the court has broad powers to order a stay "the proceedings for a period of time * * * as justice and equity require." If a court decides to authorize forfeiture or termination of the contract, it may condition such relief on payment of all or part of the vendee's prior payments on the contract. The court "may make other disposition as is equitable to preserve the interests of the parties."

4. Mortgages and Deeds of Trust

Section 533 provides that after default in a mortgage executed prior to the mortgagor's entrance into military service, the mortgagee cannot sell, foreclose or seize the mortgaged real estate during the period of service plus 90 days thereafter without a court order. Moreover, the court may grant stays and other relief to the mortgagor similar to that authorized in the installment land contract setting. Note that, as a practical matter, this means that power of sale foreclosure against a serviceperson is prohibited. Failure to comply with the statute is not only a criminal act, but it also probably renders a foreclosure without the required court approval absolutely void.

5. Section 527 Limitation on Mortgage Interest Rates

A mortgage obligation bearing an interest rate in excess of 6 percent that was incurred by a servicemember (or with a spouse jointly) prior to military service shall not bear interest in excess of 6 percent unless the mortgagee establishes that the ability of the servicemember to pay interest in excess of that amount is not materially affected by reason of his or her military service. Thus, for example, if a mortgagor-servicemember had executed a 8 percent mortgage and then was called to active duty during the Iraq War, upon written notice to the mortgagee, the interest rate must be reduced to 6 percent unless the mortgagee establishes that the ability to pay the higher amount is not materially affected by the military service.

6. Section 517 Waiver of Rights by Serviceperson–Mortgagor

A serviceperson-mortgagor may waive the protections of the Act if the waiver is "made pursuant to a written agreement of the parties that is executed during or after the servicemember's period of military service. The written agreement shall specify the legal instrument to which the waiver applies * * *." Such a waiver may cover the rights conferred by the Act on both mortgagors under mortgages and deeds of trust and contract vendees under installment land contracts. Note, however, that a waiver is ineffective if it is contained in a pre-service mortgage or is executed at any time prior to entry into the service. On the other hand, if the waiver concerning the pre-service mortgage is entered into after entry into military service or thereafter, it is enforceable. Suppose, however, a servicemember executes a mortgage while on active duty. Section 517 seems to provide that a waiver incident to the execution of the mortgage is effective. Lenders who deal with servicepersons who seek mortgage loans may well be encouraged routinely to obtain such waivers. Thus Section 517 seems in this context to be inconsistent with the traditional state protections afforded mortgagors through the prohibition against clogging the equity of redemption and similar concepts.

L. Bankruptcy

1. Classification Of Bankruptcy Proceedings

There are four types of bankruptcy proceedings: Chapter 7 ("straight bankruptcy"), Chapter 11, Chapter 13, and Chapter 12. Straight bankruptcy entails the liquidation of the debtor's non-exempt assets to satisfy his or her creditors according to the priority and amount of their claims. Such a proceeding ultimately discharges the debtor of most pre-bankruptcy debts. It is the most common type of bankruptcy proceeding. Chapter 11 proceedings, on the other hand, provide for the reorganization of corporate and other business debtors. Rehabilitation, not liquidation, is the goal of such proceedings. Reorganization plans can result in extension and reduction of debts and broad judicial control over both secured and unsecured creditors. Chapter 13 is to some extent a Chapter 11 equivalent for individuals. Such proceedings are aimed at the rehabilitation of the debtor by extension and reduction of both unsecured and certain secured claims. Such a proceeding may be used by any individual who owes less than $250,000 in unsecured debt and $750,000 in secured debt (the latter amounts will be adjusted for inflation in 1998 and every three years thereafter). Finally, Chapter 12, enacted in 1986, in large measure extends Chapter 13 protections to the "family farmer." While the structure and substance of the two proceedings are very similar, a farmer can qualify for Chapter 12 relief so long as his or her aggregate indebtedness is less than $1,500,000. Thus Chapter 12 is more readily available to farmers than its Chapter 13 counterpart.

2. The Automatic Stay

Under Section 362(a)(1) of the Bankruptcy Reform Act of 1978 (the Code), all foreclosure proceedings, whether judicial or power of sale, are automatically stayed by the filing of any of the four types of bankruptcy proceedings. The stay is applicable whether or not the foreclosure was initiated prior to the bankruptcy petition. Moreover, in Chapter 13 proceedings the stay is also applicable to foreclosure and other proceedings against third persons who have guaranteed the bankrupt's consumer debt or put up property to secure it.

The impact of the stay on the real estate mortgagee can be substantial. From the date of the bankruptcy filing all proceedings against the debtor come within the jurisdiction of the bankruptcy court. For example, a mortgagee can be in the middle of a complex judicial foreclosure in state court, and the filing of a bankruptcy proceeding will bring that action to an absolute halt. Indeed, when and if that state court foreclosure action is ever consummated is largely within the discretion of the bankruptcy court and the trustee.

3. Straight Bankruptcy

As we noted above, the filing of a petition in straight bankruptcy, as in all bankruptcy proceedings, results in an automatic stay of any pending or planned foreclosure proceeding. However, the trustee in such a proceeding normally has a legitimate interest in mortgaged real estate only if the mortgagor-debtor has "equity" in that real estate—the amount by which its fair market value exceeds the mortgage debt. If such equity does not exist, the trustee normally will release the real estate to the mortgagee, who then can proceed to foreclose. If equity is found to exist, the real estate will be sold by the bankruptcy court, either (1) subject to the existing mortgage, or (2) free and clear of the existing mortgage. If the latter course is chosen, the mortgagee's lien will be transferred to the sale proceeds.

Note that because liquidation of the mortgagor-debtor is the purpose of straight bankruptcy, such a proceeding usually harbors relatively few unpleasant surprises for the real estate mortgagee. Most such proceedings are consummated relatively rapidly, and normally the mortgage security and lien priority will be preserved. It is true that in some instances, a trustee may delay temporarily the disposition of income-producing real estate in an attempt to accumulate some of those rents for the benefit of unsecured creditors. This problem we will examine a bit later. By and large, however, assuming the mortgagee's lien is valid, the most significant impact of a straight bankruptcy on the mortgagee will be the potential loss of part or all of its deficiency judgment, and that will usually pose no problem to the prudent mortgagee who made sure initially that the debt was well-secured.

Example 1: E had a valid first mortgage on Blackacre with a $50,000 balance. On February 1 MR, the mortgagor, went into default and E began foreclosure proceedings. On February 15, MR filed a petition for straight bankruptcy. (*Result:* the foreclosure proceedings are automatically stayed. If the trustee determines that Blackacre is worth $50,000 or less, normally the stay will be lifted and E will be free to foreclose. As to any possible deficiency judgment, however, E will be treated as a general unsecured creditor.)

Example 2:   Same facts as above except that the trustee determined that Blackacre is worth $65,000 free and clear of liens. (*Result:* the trustee may either (1) sell Blackacre subject to the $50,000 mortgage, [in which case E's lien will remain attached to Blackacre in the hands of a new grantee] or (2) sell it free and clear of the $50,000 lien. If, for example, the land sold for $60,000, E would have a peremptory right to $50,000 and $10,000 would be available for the general unsecured creditors.)

Suppose, as in Example 1, that the trustee abandons the mortgaged real estate because the mortgagor lacks equity in it. Normally the mortgagee is then free to foreclose under state law. However, then we must determine the amount of the mortgage debt for foreclosure purposes. Is it the unpaid balance on the mortgage or is it only the appraised value of the real estate as determined in the Chapter 7 proceeding? All personal liability of the mortgagor, of course, will be discharged at the conclusion of the bankruptcy proceeding. Does this mean that during or after bankruptcy the mortgagor may redeem the mortgage simply by paying the mortgagee the appraised value of the real estate as established in the bankruptcy proceeding? Or what if the mortgagee opts to foreclose and, because the land has appreciated in value since the bankruptcy proceeding was completed, the sale yields more than that appraised value. Is the mortgagor entitled to this excess as surplus or should the mortgagee be able to capture the post-bankruptcy appreciation?

In *Dewsnup v. Timm,* 502 U.S. 410 (1992), the United States Supreme Court answered most of the foregoing questions in the mortgagee's favor. Dewsnup, a Chapter 7 debtor, owed $120,000 on a debt secured by a mortgage on farm land that, as of the date of the bankruptcy proceeding, was worth $39,000 and thus had been abandoned by the trustee. Dewsnup sought to reduce the mortgagee's lien to $39,000, the fair market value of the land, and to redeem the land for the reduced amount. He relied on section 506(d) of the Code, under which a lien is void "to the extent that [it] secures a claim against the debtor that is not an allowed secured claim." Thus, under Dewsnup's analysis, the mortgagee would lose and Dewsnup, the mortgagor, would gain the benefit of any increase in the value of the land prior to the time it chooses to foreclose. The Supreme Court, 6–2 rejected Dewnup's attempt to "strip down" the mortgagee's lien to the value of the land. Because mortgagee's claim was secured by a lien and was otherwise fully allowed under section 502 of the Code, it was impermissible to classify it as "not an allowed secured claim" for purposes of section 506(d). The Court chose to de-emphasize section 506(a), which provides that "an allowed claim of a creditor secured by a lien on property to which the estate has an interest * * * is a secured claim to the extent of the value of such creditor's interest in the estate's interest in such property."

As a result of *Dewsnup*, debtor-mortgagors and trustees in Chapter 7 will not be permitted to bifurcate a mortgage debt into secured and unsecured claims so as to deprive the mortgagee of any post-valuation increase in the value of the real estate. Stated another way, even though the unsecured portion of the mortgage debt technically is discharged, the mortgagee still will be able to collect it out of any subsequent appreciation in value of the real estate.

4. The Trustee's Avoidance Powers

Because the trustee represents the interests of the bankrupt's unsecured creditors, her primary goal is to enlarge the asset pool available to satisfy their claims. Since each mortgage invalidated usually serves that purpose, she will be especially watchful for opportunities to attack vulnerable security interests. The Code affords her an impressive arsenal of weapons in this regard.

a. Section 558

Section 558 gives the trustee "the benefit of any defense available to the debtor" against the mortgagee, even if the debtor waives it after the commencement of bankruptcy. Thus, for example, to the extent that a debtor would be able to invalidate a mortgage based on fraud, usury, incapacity or other grounds, so too will the trustee.

b. Section 544(a)(3)

This Section affords the trustee, irrespective of knowledge on her part, the status of a bona fide purchaser of real property from the debtor who has perfected under state law. Such status can be utilized whether such a purchaser actually exists or not. Consequently, the trustee will always be able to defeat any mortgage of the debtor that is unrecorded as of the commencement of bankruptcy. Because she is deemed to have perfected under state law, the type of state recording act (e.g., whether race-notice, notice, or pure race) and its requirements become irrelevant.

c. Section 551

Under this provision, a trustee who uses her powers under the Code to avoid a senior lien becomes subrogated to the rights of the senior lienor up to the amount of the senior debt. Suppose, for example, that after a mortgage on Blackacre is executed, but never recorded, a second mortgage is recorded by another lender who has actual knowledge of the unrecorded mortgage. The debtor-mortgagor then files a bankruptcy petition. While section 544(a)(3) enables the trustee to avoid the unrecorded mortgage, it does not itself prevent the second mortgage from being promoted in priority. Section 551 then becomes important. Under the latter provision, a trustee who avoids a senior lien becomes subrogated to the rights of the senior lienor up to the amount of the senior debt. Suppose, for example, the unrecorded mortgage has a balance of $10,000 and the recorded second mortgage a balance of $20,000. If the real estate is sold by the bankruptcy court for $25,000, the trustee, as subrogee, has a right to $10,000 and the second mortgagee will receive $15,000.

d. Section 548 (Fraudulent Transfers)

Under section 548 of the Code, transfers made by the debtor within one year of bankruptcy may be set aside by the trustee if they were made with the intent to hinder, delay, or defraud any creditor to which the debtor was or became indebted. For example, suppose a debtor, in order to conceal his substantial equity in Blackacre, grants mortgagee a mortgage on it for no consideration within a year of filing a bankruptcy petition. The trustee will be able to set aside the mortgage.

Moreover, the trustee may also set aside certain "constructively fraudulent" transfers. Under section 548(a) of the Code, the trustee "may avoid any transfer of an interest of the debtor * * * that was made * * * within one year before the date of the filing of the petition, if the debtor voluntarily or involuntarily * * * received less than reasonably equivalent value in exchange for such transfer * * * and was insolvent on the date such transfer was made * * * or became insolvent as a result of such transfer." A *deed in lieu of foreclosure* given to a mortgagee by an insolvent debtor within one year of bankruptcy may be set aside if the debtor received "less than reasonably equivalent value" for the transfer. Normally courts have equated "reasonably equivalent value" with 70% of fair market value. Thus, suppose that an insolvent mortgagor conveys Blackacre to mortgagee in exchange for being released from a $70,000 debt. Within a year of the transfer, mortgagor files a bankruptcy petition. If the property had a fair market value of more than $100,000 on the date of the transfer, the trustee will be able to set aside the deed in lieu.

The trustee may exercise yet another fraudulent conveyance weapon. To the extent that *state fraudulent conveyance law* confers on unsecured creditors broader powers to avoid debtor mortgages than are afforded by section 548, section 544(a) of the Code empowers the trustee to take advantage of that state law.

e. Section 547 (Voidable Preference)

Many mortgages given to secure antecedent debt within ninety days of the mortgagor's bankruptcy will be voidable by the trustee as a preference under section 547 of the Code. A significant policy embodied in the bankruptcy law is that similarly situated creditors be treated equally. However, once a debtor becomes financially unstable, creditors commonly violate that policy by seeking to gain advantage vis-à-vis their creditor brethren. Often this entails acquiring real estate mortgages from the debtor to secure pre-existing debts. To the extent that such mortgages are granted by an insolvent mortgagor within ninety days of bankruptcy, and they would enable the creditor to realize more on its claim than it otherwise would in a straight bankruptcy liquidation, they constitute voidable preferences. Moreover, there is a presumption of debtor insolvency during this ninety day period. If the creditor is an "insider," the preference period is one year rather than ninety days.

Example: Mr owed E $25,000 on a promissory note dated five years earlier which was secured by a first mortgage on Blackacre. After a series of financial reverses, Mr became insolvent. Blackacre was now worth only $10,000. Because E felt insecure, he persuaded Mr to give him a mortgage on Whiteacre as additional security for the $25,000 debt. Whiteacre was worth $10,000 and E had the only mortgage on it. Twenty days after the Whiteacre mortgage, Mr filed a bankruptcy petition. Because the Trustee determined that there were virtually no unencumbered assets to satisfy unsecured creditors, he moved to set aside the Whiteacre mortgage as a voidable preference. (*Result*: The mortgage will be set aside. It was given within 90 days of bankruptcy while Mr was insolvent. Moreover, if E had not obtained the Whiteacre mortgage, E would have received in the bankruptcy proceeding only $10,000 by virtue of the Blackacre mortgage and a minuscule amount from the assets available to unsecured creditors. The Whiteacre mortgage would have allowed E to receive at least $20,000 of his $25,000 debt. Consequently, it would have allowed E to have received more than he otherwise would have realized in a Chapter 7 liquidation.)

Note that under certain circumstances, courts have held *foreclosure sales* to be voidable preferences. See Section 8(b) infra.

5. The Chapter 11 Reorganization

Because the purpose of a Chapter 11 proceeding is the rehabilitation rather than the liquidation of the debtor, the debtor typically continues to operate the estate as a "debtor-in-possession." See 11 U.S.C.A. § 1107. Parties in interest (usually creditors) may obtain the appointment of a trustee only for cause, "including fraud, dishonesty, incompetence, or gross mismanagement" on the part of the debtor or where appointment is otherwise in such parties' "best interests." See 11 U.S.C.A. § 1104(a) and (b). The appointment of a trustee is considered "an extraordinary remedy" and there is thus a strong presumption in favor of the debtor remaining in possession, at least through the plan formulation period. Moreover, the debtor-in-possession is entitled to exercise all the avoidance powers of a Chapter 7 trustee.

a. Relief From Stay

The filing of a Chapter 11 petition, like the filing of other bankruptcy proceedings, stays any pending and future state foreclosure proceedings. Consequently, mortgagees, become particularly interested in obtaining stay relief. Under section 362 of the Code, the bankruptcy court may "terminat[e], annul, modify or condition such stay (1) for cause, including the lack of adequate protection of an interest in property of such [mortgagee]; or (2) with respect to a stay of an act against property, if—(A) the [mortgagor] does not have an equity in such property; and (B) such property is not necessary to an effective reorganization."

1) Ground Number One

The first ground for relief has provided some difficulty for the bankruptcy courts. Some courts, for example, suggest that "adequate protection" exists if there is an "equity cushion" in the mortgaged real estate. Others stress that the foregoing language is designed to protect against post-filing decline in the value of the real estate. In a few instances, mortgagor failure to pay real estate taxes or to keep the mortgaged premises insured have been deemed to cause a lack of adequate protection. When such adequate protection is lacking, section 361 sets out three permissible ways to provide it.

"First, the trustee may be required to make periodic cash payments to the [mortgagee] in an amount sufficient to compensate for the decrease in value of the [mortgagee's] interest resulting from the stay. Second, the [mortgagee] may be provided with an alternative or additional lien equal in value to the decrease in the value of the [mortgagee's] interest resulting from the stay. Finally, any other relief may be granted that will give the [mortgagee] realization of the 'indubitable equivalent' of its interest in property."

Kennedy, Automatic Stays Under the New Bankruptcy Law, 12 U.Mich.J.L. Reform 343–344 (1979).

Until 1988, undersecured mortgagees sometimes successfully argued that the foregoing "adequate protection" and "indubitable equivalence" concepts required bankruptcy courts to order the payment to them of "lost opportunity costs" that were caused by the automatic stay. Thus, some courts required the periodic payment of cash equal to the interest that the creditor could otherwise earn on an amount of money equal to the value of the security. However, the United States Supreme Court, in *United Savings Association of Texas v. Timbers of Inwood Forest Associates, Ltd.*, 484 U.S. 365 (1988), held unanimously that the "adequate protection" and "indubitable equivalence" language of sections 362 and 361 of the Code do not require periodic post-petition interest payments of lost opportunity costs to undersecured creditors.

2) Ground Number Two

Under this approach two requirements must be satisfied. First, the mortgagor must lack equity in the mortgaged real estate and second, that real estate must not be necessary to an "effective reorganization." The meaning of the term "equity" has proven especially troublesome for the bankruptcy courts. Under the predominant approach, "equity" refers to "the difference between the value of the property and all encumbrances against it." A sizeable minority of decisions, however, take the position that the term "means the difference between the value of the property and the lien which is the subject of the [request for stay relief], along with any liens senior thereto." Under this view, it "makes no difference how many junior encumbrances are outstanding against the subject property so long as the [mortgagor] has a substantial and meaningful equity cushion over and above the senior encumbrances." Matter of Spring Garden Foliage, Inc., 15 B.R. 140, 143 (Bankr.M.D.Fla.1981).

Example: Blackacre had a fair market value of $100,000 free and clear of liens. Blackacre was encumbered by a $50,000 first mortgage in favor of E–1, a $30,000 second mortgage in favor of E–2 and a $40,000 third mortgage in favor of E–3. Mr then filed a Chapter 11 petition and, shortly thereafter, E–1 filed a motion to terminate the stay against foreclosure of its mortgage. Mr, as debtor-in-possession, asserted that equity still existed in Blackacre and that therefore the first requirement for stay relief was not satisfied. (*Result*: If the bankruptcy court follows the predominant approach, "the difference between the value of the property [$100,000] and all encumbrances against it" [$50,000 + $30,000 + $40,000] equals zero. Consequently, Mr "lacks equity" and the first requirement is satisfied. On the other hand, if the court uses the minority approach, it would subtract $50,000 (the amount of the lien held by E–1, the person seeking stay relief—there are no liens senior to it) from $100,000 (the fair market value of Blackacre free and clear of liens). Under this calculation, $50,000 of equity would still remain, the first requirement would not be satisfied and the motion to terminate the stay would be denied.)

If the court finds that equity exists, it must then determine whether the mortgaged real estate is "necessary to an effective reorganization." As one court has stressed, it is "not enough for a debtor to argue that the automatic stay should continue because it needs the secured property in order to propose a reorganization. The word is 'effective'." The mere fact that the real estate is essential to the survival of the mortgagor's business is insufficient. Rather, the mortgagor is required to demonstrate that there is "a reasonable likelihood of a successful reorganization within a reasonable period of time."

b. Which Stay Relief Is Preferred?

On the surface it would seem that a mortgagee should invariably prefer the "adequate protection" route to stay relief over the "no equity—necessary to an effective reorganization" approach. For example, suppose the mortgagee can establish that an "equity cushion" no longer exists in the mortgaged real estate. If such a showing is enough to show inadequate protection, why should the mortgagee run the risk that mortgagor will be able to establish that the real estate is necessary to an effective reorganization? Perhaps the answer lies in the fact that if the court finds both a lack of equity and that the property is unnecessary to an effective reorganization, it will invariably dissolve the stay because, by definition, there is no reason for the court to retain control over it. On the other hand, a finding of inadequate protection alone may simply result in a decree ordering additional protection for the mortgagee or some modification, rather than dissolution, of the stay.

c. Stay Relief Where Debtor Is a "Single Asset Real Estate" Mortgagor

The Bankruptcy Reform Act of 1994 ("1994 Act") makes it much more difficult for a "single asset real estate" debtor to use Chapter 11 for delay or reorganization purposes. "Single asset real estate" means for this purpose "real property constituting a single property or project, other than residential real property with fewer than 4 residential units, which generates substantially all of the gross income of a debtor and on which no substantial business is being conducted by a debtor other than the business of operating the real property * * * having aggregate * * * liquidated secured debts in an amount no more than $4,000,000." 11 U.S.C.A § 101(51B).

Congress accomplished this by creating a third ground for stay relief under section 362 that is applicable only to such single asset real estate debtors. Under this provision, the bankruptcy court "shall grant relief" such as by "terminating, annulling, modifying or conditioning [the] stay * * * unless not later than the date that is 90 days after the [filing of a voluntary bankruptcy petition] (or such later date as the court may determine for cause by order entered within that 90 day period)"

> (A) the debtor has filed a plan of reorganization that has a reasonable possibility of being confirmed within a reasonable time; or

> (B) the debtor has commenced monthly payments to each creditor whose claim is secured by such real estate (other than a claim secured by a judgment lien), which payments are in an amount equal to interest at a current fair market rate on the value of the creditor's interest in the real estate.

11 U.S.C.A. § 362(d)(3).

The upshot is that the single asset real estate debtor must either promptly produce a reorganization plan that has a reasonable possibility of being confirmed within a reasonable time or begin making interest payments to the mortgagee based on the value of the mortgagee's security. Such a prospect will presumably discourage Chapter 11 filings by such debtors and perhaps result in earlier foreclosure of their real estate under state law. Pending legislation would remove the $4,000,000 cap referred to above. If enacted, it would make all single asset real estate more friendly to mortgagees.

6. Chapter 13 "Wage Earner" Plan

The Chapter 13 plan pays a role for individuals analogous to Chapter 11 for business or commercial entities. The automatic stay of foreclosure applies. The rehabilitation plan must be completed within 3 years or, with bankruptcy court approval, within 5 years of its adoption. Chapter 13 may be utilized by an individual who has regular income and owes secured debt not exceeding $750,000 and unsecured debt not exceeding $250,000. Such plans may entail, for unsecured creditors, accepting not only a deferral of payment of those claims, but a substantial reduction in their amount. Real estate mortgagees (other than those holding mortgages on the debtor's principal place of residence) can be made part of the plan against their consent, and may have their claims modified so long as the following protection is provided: "(1) the plan must provide that [the mortgagee] retain his lien and the value [as of the effective date of the plan] of property to be distributed under the plan must not be less than the allowed amount of the secured claim, or (2) the plan must provide for surrender of the property securing the claim to the [mortgagee]." King, 2 Collier Bankruptcy Manual ¶ 1325.02 (1979). A real estate mortgagee who holds a claim secured only by a lien on the debtor's principal residence normally may not have its claim modified without its consent.

a. Nature of the Problem

Often the only or most significant real estate mortgage in a Chapter 13 proceeding is the mortgage on the debtor's home. While section 1322(b)(2) provides that the plan may, under certain circumstances, "modify the rights of holders of secured claims," it prohibits such modification as to any holder of a "claim secured only by a security interest in real property that is the debtor's principal residence." This latter exception "was in response to perceptions, or to suggestions advanced in the legislative hearings . . . that home-mortgagor lenders, performing a valuable social service through their loans, needed special protection against modification." Grubbs v. Houston First American Savings, 730 F.2d 236, 246 (5th Cir.1984).

Yet section 1322(b) also contains important cross-current provisions. Section 1322(b)(3) provides for the "curing or waiving of any default." Moreover, section 1322(b)(5) specifies that "notwithstanding [section 1322(b)(2)]" the plan may "provide for the curing of any default within a reasonable time and maintenance of payments while the case is pending on any . . . secured claim on which the last payment is due after the date on which the final payment under the plan is due."

b. In re Taddeo, 685 F.2d 24 (2d Cir.1982)

In *Taddeo*, the leading decision, the debtors were permitted, pursuant to their Chapter 13 plan, to defeat a pre-petition mortgage acceleration by payment of arrearages and to reinstate the mortgage's original amortization schedule. Not only did the court hold that the "concept of 'cure' in section 1322(b)(5) contains the power to de-accelerate," but also that "the ban on 'modification' in section 1322(b)(2) does not limit the [debtors'] exercise of their curative powers under either section 1322(b)(3) or (b)(5)." Consequently, the debtors were permitted to cure their default under (b)(3) and thereafter maintain their payments pursuant to (b)(5). In buttressing its conclusion, the Second Circuit rejected the argument that (b)(3) was inapplicable to home mortgages, and also emphasized that "the power to cure must comprehend the power to 'de-accelerate.' This follows from the concept of 'curing a default.' A default is an event in the debtor-creditor relationship which triggers certain consequences—here, acceleration. Curing a default commonly means taking care of the triggering event and returning to pre-default conditions. The consequences are thus nullified. This is the concept of 'cure' used throughout the Bankruptcy Code."

The *Taddeo* approach has been universally adopted. *Thus, even though the home mortgage may not be "modified," the Chapter 13 debtor will be permitted to "de-accelerate" a pre-petition acceleration. As a result, he or she will be able to pay off the arrearages over the period of the plan so long as current mortgage installments are also being paid.*

c. May Non-default Balloons Be De-accelerated Under *Taddeo*?

Suppose that the total principal balance of a home mortgage debt becomes due, not as a result of acceleration based on mortgagor's failure to make timely installment payments, but rather because the terms of the loan call for a final "balloon" payment which mortgagor has failed to pay. Prior to the Bankruptcy Reform Act of 1994 ("1994 Act"), it was unlikely that such a mortgagor would be able to use *Taddeo* and its progeny to de-accelerate the balloon in order to pay it off on installment basis under the plan. Indeed, as one federal appellate decision concluded, to permit de-acceleration under such circumstances would constitute an impermissible "modification" under section 1322(b)(2). According to this court, "when a debt has been accelerated, 'cure' results in the reinstatement of the original payment terms of the debt. But when, as here, a debt has already matured, 'cure' * * * cannot aid the debtor, since reinstatement of the original terms of the debt will merely make the debt immediately due and payable." *In re Seidel*, 752 F.2d 1382 (9th Cir.1985). However, the 1994 Act provides that "in a case in which the last payment on the original payment schedule * * * is due before the date on which the final payment under the plan is due, the plan may provide for payment of the claim as modified * * *." Several courts hold that this statutory language overrules *Seidel* and permits acceleration of non-default balloons. See, e.g., *In re Ibarra*, 235 B.R. 204 (Bkrtcy.D. Puerto Rico 1999); *In re Wilcox*, 209 B.R. 181 (Bkrtcy.E.D.N.Y. 1996)

d. Post–Foreclosure Sale Application of Taddeo

To what extent should *Taddeo* de-acceleration be permitted after the foreclosure sale? While there pre–1994 authority that *Taddeo* could not be used to de-accelerate after a foreclosure sale *In re Glenn*, 760 F.2d 1428 (6th Cir.1985), under the then prevailing view the availability of *Taddeo* depended on whether the foreclosure took place in a statutory redemption state. In the latter type of jurisdiction, *Taddeo* had been successfully asserted. See Nelson & Whitman, Real Estate Finance Law § 8.15 (4th ed.2001). In non-statutory redemption states *Taddeo* was generally unavailing. See id. This result was justified by the argument that if the foreclosure state has statutory redemption, the sale purchaser was on notice that it was acquiring a defeasible title. On the other hand, in a non-statutory redemption state, the purchaser had a right to expect that it would be acquiring a non-defeasible title.

In the Bankruptcy Reform Act of 1994 ("1994 Act"), Congress seems to have codified *Glenn* by making the foreclosure sale the cut-off point for asserting the right to de-accelerate. Under the 1994 Act, "a default with respect to * * * a lien on the debtor's principal residence may be cured * * * until such residence is sold at a foreclosure sale that is conducted in accordance with applicable nonbankruptcy law." 11 U.S.C.A. § 1322(c)(1).

However, the following statement in the legislative history of the foregoing language casts some doubt on whether the foreclosure sale is the cut-off date in statutory redemption states: "However, if the State provides the debtor more extensive 'cure' rights (through, for example, some later redemption period), the debtor would continue to enjoy such rights in bankruptcy." Thus, for example, where state law permits redemption until the sheriff's deed is delivered to the foreclosure sale purchaser, courts are split as to whether *Taddeo* de-acceleration is proper during the post-sale, pre-delivery period. Compare *In re Ross*, 191 B.R. 615 (Bankr.D.N.J.1996) (permitting post-sale, pre-delivery de-acceleration) with *In re Little*, 201 B.R. 98 (Bankr.D.N.J.1996) and *In re Ziyambe*, 200 B.R. 790 (Bankr.D.N.J.1996) (holding that the sale itself is the cut-off). Moreover, where states have long post-sale statutory redemption periods, the foregoing legislative history raises the possibility that Chapter 13 de-acceleration will be permitted during those periods.

e. Junior Liens on the Mortgagor's Principal Residence

Although *Taddeo* permits de-acceleration of junior mortgages on the debtor's residence, such liens nevertheless enjoy the same protection from *modification* as their senior brethren. See, e.g., *In re Rubottom*, 134 B.R. 641 (9th Cir.BAP 1991); *In re Bradshaw*, 56 B.R. 742 (S.D.Ohio 1985) (proposed plan that sought to reduce interest rate on second mortgage on debtor's principal residence from 14% to 8% violated statutory prohibition against modification).

f. Bifurcation of the Undersecured Home Mortgage Prohibited

Suppose that a $100,000 obligation is secured by a mortgage on a home that is now worth only $65,000. May the $35,000 unsecured portion of that claim be modified or is the entire $100,000 claim protected against modification? Stated another way, will the debtor be permitted simply to make minimal plan payments on the unsecured portion and then be discharged of liability on it at the end of the plan? In so arguing, mortgagors relied on section 506(a) of the Code, which provides that an "allowed secured claim of a creditor secured by a lien on the property in which the estate has an interest * * * is a secured claim to the extent of the value of such creditor's interest in the estate's interest in such property * * * and is an unsecured claim to the extent of the value of such creditor's interest * * * is less than the amount of such allowed claim." Mortgagors also relied on section 506(d) which states that "to the extent a lien secures a claim against the debtor that is not an allowed secured claim, such lien is void * * *." Mortgagees, on the other hand, in defending against bifurcation, stressed the language of section 1322(b)(2), which permits modification of secured claims, but not "a claim secured only by a security interest in real property that is the debtor's principal residence."

The United States Supreme Court resolved the bifurcation issue in the mortgagee's favor. In *Nobelman v. American Savings Bank,* 508 U.S. 324 (1993), a unanimous Supreme Court determined that section 1322(b)(2)'s prohibition on modification trumped mortgagors' reliance on section 506. According to the Court, "to give effect to § 506(a)'s valuation and bifurcation of secured claims through a Chapter 13 plan in the manner [mortgagors] propose would require a modification of the rights of the holder of the security interest. Section 1322(b)(2) prohibits such a modification where * * * the lender's claim is secured only by a lien on the debtor's principal residence."

However, in the relatively uncommon situation where the "last payment on the original payment schedule * * * is due before the final payment under the plan is due," there is a split of authority as to whether the 1994 Act permits modification and bifurcation of a home mortgage. 11 U.S.C.A. § 1322 (c)(2). See *In re Paschen,* 296 F.3d 1203 (11th Cir.2002); *In re Mattson,* 210 B.R. 157 (Bkrtcy. D. Minn. 1997)(undersecured junior home mortgage may be modified under 1994 Act language). Contra: *In re Witt,* 113 F.3d 508 (4th Cir. 1997)

g. Modification Permitted Where Claim is Secured by More Than Principal Residence

Section 1322(b)(2) prohibits modification of a claim that is secured *"only by a security interest in real property that is the debtor's principal residence."* However, if the claim is also secured by other real estate or chattels, modification, and thus bifurcation, is permitted. Thus, for example, modification will probably be permitted where the mortgage includes not only the principal residence, but farm land as well.

The foregoing "only" language has proven to be a dangerous trap for many home mortgagees. The normal inclination of lenders is to take as much security as they can find. Indeed, it is normally considered prudent to do so. However, if bifurcation is to be avoided, mortgagees must resist the temptation to take additional mortgages on other real estate or security interests in the debtor's motor vehicles or other chattels. Moreover, the "only" language masks more subtle dangers for the mortgagee. Most mortgage forms contain "boilerplate" language that not only mortgages the real estate, but also "all the improvements now or hereafter erected on the property, and all easements, appurtenances, and fixtures now or hereafter a part of the property." Many forms also contain provisions mortgaging "the rents, issues and profits" of the real estate. Finally, many forms make the tax and insurance escrow accounts "additional security" for the mortgage obligation.

While a number of courts have taken the position that security interests in rents or escrow accounts do not constitute "additional security," and are probably correct in doing so, others have reached contrary results. This issue continues to plague lenders. Indeed, it threatens to make *Nobelman* a pyhrric victory. In the meantime, lenders should avoid such boilerplate in their mortgage forms.

h. Interest on Home Mortgage Arrearages

In *Rake v. Wade*, 508 U.S. 464 (1993), the United States Supreme Court upheld the mortgagee's claim that section 1325 of the Code required that debtors who are curing their defaults under a Chapter 13 plan pay interest on home mortgage arrearages. Congress responded in the 1994 Act by enacting language providing that "if it is proposed in a plan to cure a default, the amount necessary to cure the default, shall be determined in accordance with the underlying agreement and applicable nonbankruptcy law." Thus, a home mortgagee in Chapter 13 will be entitled to interest on arrearages only if such interest is required in the mortgage instruments or under state law.

i. Relief From a Chapter 13 Stay

As noted earlier, section 362(d) of the Act authorizes relief from the stay "(1) for cause, including the lack of adequate protection of an interest in property of [the mortgagor]; or (2) . . . if (A) the [mortgagor] does not have an equity in such property; and (B) such property is not necessary to an effective reorganization." However, there has been substantial disagreement about whether (d)(2), as well as (d)(1), is applicable in Chapter 13 proceedings. There is significant case law holding that it is and that a mortgagee is entitled to a stay relief under either subsection. Indeed, section 103 of the Act expressly states that Chapter 3, which includes section 362, is applicable to Chapter 13. On the other hand, there is substantial case authority to the contrary and a supporting textual argument as well. See Nelson & Whitman, Real Estate Finance Law § 8.15 (4th ed.2001).

7. Family Farmer Bankruptcy Act of 1986 (Chapter 12)

For farmers who were unable to cope with the economic hardship of the severe agricultural recession of the 1980's, Chapters 11 and 13 produced little meaningful relief. In the case of Chapter 11, substantial creditor control over the contents of the reorganization plan has made it extremely difficult to obtain approval of a plan that provides any significant chance of a successful farmer-debtor rehabilitation. On the other hand, while Chapter 13 would otherwise be an advantageous reorganization vehicle for family farmers, a debtor then qualified for its protection only if he or she had a maximum of $100,000 in unsecured and $350,000 in secured indebtedness. Since the indebtedness of most troubled family farmers far exceeded the foregoing limits, few of them could take advantage of Chapter 13.

In response to the above situation, in October, 1986 Congress enacted a new Chapter 12 of the Bankruptcy Code entitled "Adjustment of Debts of a Family Farmer with Regular Annual Income". *In large measure, Chapter 12 extends Chapter 13 protections to the family farmer, and the substance and structure of the two chapters are very similar.* In general, Chapter 12 affords important powers to the farmer-debtor, including the ability:

- to reduce secured indebtedness to the *current* value of the underlying security

- to repay the reduced amount over an extended period of time

- to satisfy unsecured claims—including those that became unsecured by the foregoing "write-down" of the security—by paying to the plan only his or her "disposable income" (income which is not reasonably necessary for family support and business operations)

When the plan is completed successfully, the farmer will be discharged of his or her unsecured indebtedness.

a. Who Qualifies for Chapter 12 Relief?

In general, an individual farmer may utilize Chapter 12 if more than 50% of his or her income is derived from farming and the aggregate indebtedness of the farming operation does not exceed $1,500,000. If the farming operation is incorporated, Chapter 12 is available so long as one family owns at least 50% of its shares. Moreover, more than 80% of the corporation's assets must be related to the farming operation and its total indebtedness may not exceed $1,500,000.

b. Who Controls the Farming Operation?

While section 1202 clearly contemplates the appointment of a trustee in every Chapter 12 case, the farmer will remain in possession of the real estate and continue to operate the farm as a "debtor-in-possession." Presumably the trustee's role, as in Chapter 13, will be passive. A debtor in possession may be removed only for "fraud, dishonesty, incompetence, or gross mismanagement." 11 U.S.C.A. § 1204. As in the Chapter 11 context, removal of the debtor-in-possession will be rare.

c. Avoidance Powers

As in the case of Chapter 13, Chapter 12 does not specifically confer avoidance powers on the debtor in possession. Nevertheless, as in the Chapter 13 context, courts will probably infer the existence of such powers. See Nelson & Whitman, Real Estate Finance Law § 8.15 (4th ed.2001).

d. Stay Relief

As in the case of Chapter 11, stay relief is governed by section 362 of the Code, which provides that the bankruptcy court may "terminat[e], annul, modify or condition such stay (1) for cause, including the lack of adequate protection of an interest in property of such [mortgagee]; or (2) with respect to a stay of an act against property, if—(A) the [mortgagor] does not have an equity in such property; and (B) such property is not necessary to an effective reorganization." However, under Chapter 12, it is substantially easier than under Chapter 11 for the debtor-mortgagor to provide "adequate protection" and thus keep the stay in effect. The three Chapter 11 methods for providing adequate protection described earlier were replaced by section 1205(b), which provides that adequate protection may be supplied by:

1) requiring the trustee to make a cash payment or periodic cash payments to such entity, to the extent that the stay under section 362 of this title, use, sale, or lease under section 363 of this title, or any grant of a lien under section 364 of this title results in a decrease in the value of property securing a claim or of an entity's ownership interest in property;

2) providing to such entity an additional or replacement lien to the extent that such stay, use, sale, lease, or grant results in a decrease in the value of property securing a claim or of an entity's ownership interest in property;

3) paying to such entity for the use of farmland the reasonable rent customary in the community where the property is located, based upon the rental value, net income, and earning capacity of the property; or

4) granting such other relief . . . as will adequately protect the value of property securing a claim or of such entity's ownership interest in property.

Section 1205(b)(3) provides specifically "for the use of farmland, the reasonable rent customary in the community where the property is located. . . . " It arguably is inconsistent to provide for reasonable rental payments based on the value of the land and yet also prohibit lost opportunity costs. Perhaps, in the case of real estate security, if "adequate protection" protects simply against a decrease in the value of the security, reasonable rental will be required only where the real estate is dropping in value.

e. Contents of the Plan

The requirements for a Chapter 12 plan are substantially similar to those for a Chapter 13 reorganization. The plan will be three years, but may be extended to five years with the permission of the bankruptcy court. See 11 U.S.C.A. § 1222(c).

The plan may *modify* the rights of both *secured* and *unsecured* creditors. Such modifications may include extensions and restructuring of payments. Interest on secured debt may be reduced. Principal may be reduced but not below the value of the security. Moreover, no special protection against modification is afforded to holders of mortgages on the debtor's principal residence, as is the case in Chapter 13. Finally, the plan may "provide for the curing or waiving of any default." Consequently, pre-foreclosure mortgage accelerations may be de-accelerated and the original payment schedule reinstated.

The foregoing process is more readily understood in the context of a specific case. In *Travelers Insurance Company v. Bullington*, 878 F.2d 354 (11th Cir.1989), the mortgagors' indebtedness was approximately $646,000 and the value of the land securing that obligation was $475,000. The indebtedness ballooned after five years and carried an interest rate that was fixed the first year at 12.5%. Thereafter the interest rate floated at one point above an index of AAA-rated corporate bonds. The mortgagor's Chapter 12 plan *bifurcated* mortgagee's claim into two parts: a secured claim for $475,000, the value of the real estate, and an unsecured claim for the remainder of $170,000. The plan converted the five year obligation into a thirty-year fixed rate mortgage of $475,000 carrying a 10.75% interest rate. The $170,000 unsecured claim was to be discharged at the end of the four year plan after having disposable income, if any, applied proportionately to it and other unsecured debt.

The bankruptcy court confirmed the plan and the Eleventh Circuit affirmed notwithstanding mortgagee's objections to the extension of the secured claim to thirty years and the mandated fixed interest rate. The court held that section 1222(b)(9) authorized the extension of the mortgage. Moreover, it concluded, "simply because a creditor subjectively would not extend a mortgage on the same terms does not mean that objectively the mortgage does not have a given value. Given that [mortgagee] has pointed to no record evidence to show that the 10.75% interest rate does not give the mortgage a present value of $475,000, while [mortgagors'] chart does tend to support the interest rate, the bankruptcy court's finding * * * is supported by sufficient evidence."

Perhaps most important, Chapter 12 abolishes the *absolute priority rule*, a common law rule that is traditionally applied in Chapter 11 reorganizations. This rule is technically not a priority rule, but rather requires that a debtor may not receive anything upon completion of the plan unless the plan provides for full payment of unsecured creditors or they consent to the plan. Consequently, under Chapter 11 the farmer-debtor may not keep the land after the completion of the plan unless the unsecured creditors accept the plan. As a result, undersecured mortgagees can use the threat of withholding their consent unless the debtor-farmer agrees to higher plan payments on the unsecured part of their claims. Under Chapter 12 the mortgagee loses this valuable negotiating tool. Under Chapter 12 the farmer-debtor can "cram down" a plan that gives holders of unsecured claims only what they would have received in a Chapter 7 liquidation. Thus, to the extent that the real estate mortgagee is undersecured, that part of the debt can be reduced to its liquidation value.

Under Chapter 11, a mortgagee has the option to give up the unsecured part of its claim and instead keep its mortgage for the full amount of the claim. Thus, if during the plan the real estate goes up in value, the mortgagee will get the benefit of that appreciation. See 11 U.S.C.A. § 1111(b)(2). But under Chapter 12, the mortgagee loses this option.

Thus, an appraisal at the time of plan confirmation will establish the amount of the secured claim. If the land goes up in value, the farmer-debtor will get the benefit of that appreciation at the completion of the plan. The mortgagee will wind up with a mortgage on the land in an amount that will not exceed the foregoing appraised value, the unsecured part of its claim will be discharged, and the debtor-farmer will own equity as well as bare title in the real estate.

8. Setting Aside Pre–Bankruptcy Foreclosures

We have already explored in the preceding section how the *Taddeo* concept may be used in certain Chapter 13 contexts to de-accelerate previously foreclosed mortgage debts. Moreover, until recently many courts utilized the fraudulent conveyance provisions of the Bankruptcy Code to set aside pre-bankruptcy foreclosures and installment land contract forfeitures. To a more limited extent, foreclosures have been subjected to successful attack as voidable preferences. These latter developments are explored in detail in this section.

a. The Foreclosure Sale as a Fraudulent Conveyance

Until recently, bankruptcy trustees frequently challenged pre-bankruptcy foreclosure sales as constructively fraudulent transfers under § 548 of the Code. Under this section, a trustee or a debtor in possession may avoid a transfer by a debtor if it can be established that (1) the debtor had an interest in property; (2) the transfer took place within a year of a bankruptcy filing; (3) the debtor was insolvent at the time of the transfer or the transfer caused insolvency; and (4) the debtor received "less than a reasonably equivalent value" for the transfer. 11 U.S.C.A. § 548(a)(2)(A).

In *Durrett v. Washington National Ins. Co.*, 621 F.2d 201 (5th Cir.1980), a controversial decision by the United States Court of Appeals for the Fifth Circuit, the court used the predecessor to § 548(a) to find, for the first time, that a foreclosure proceeding that otherwise complied with state law could be set aside if the sale price did not represent "reasonably equivalent value." In dictum the court suggested that a foreclosure price of less than 70% of fair market value failed to meet the "fair equivalency" test. Several other federal courts adopted *Durrett*. See, e.g., *In re Hulm*, 738 F.2d 323 (8th Cir.1984); *First Federal Savings & Loan Ass'n of Warner Robbins v. Standard Building Associates, Ltd.*, 87 B.R. 221 (N.D.Ga.1988). Other courts, while rejecting a "bright line" 70 percent test, endorsed *Durrett* as a general principle, but adopted the view that "in defining reasonably equivalent value, the court should neither grant a conclusive presumption in favor of a purchaser at a regularly conducted, noncollusive foreclosure sale, nor limit its inquiry to a simple comparison of the sale price to the fair market value. Reasonable equivalence should depend on all the facts of the case." *Matter of Bundles,* 856 F.2d 815, 824 (7th Cir.1988).

In *BFP v. Resolution Trust Corp.,* 511 U.S. 531, 544 (1994), the United States Supreme Court, in a 5–4 decision, rejected *Durrett* and its progeny:

> [W]e decline to read the phrase "reasonably equivalent value" * * * to mean, in its application to foreclosure sales, either "fair market value" or "fair foreclosure price" (whether calculated as a percentage of fair market value or otherwise). We deem, as the law has always deemed, that a fair and proper price, or a "reasonably equivalent value," for foreclosed property, is the price in fact received at the foreclosure sale, so long as all the requirements of the State's foreclosure law have been complied with.

Consequently, section 548 of the Bankruptcy Code now provides no grounds for invalidating noncollusive state foreclosure sales based on inadequacy of the price, so long as all other requirements of state foreclosure law have been satisfied.

b. The Installment Land Contract Forfeiture as a Fraudulent Conveyance

Does *BFP* preclude a determination that a forfeiture under an installment land contract may be a fraudulent transfer under § 548 of the Code? Suppose, for example, a vendee's installment contract interest is forfeited within a year of vendee's bankruptcy and it can be established that the real estate was worth significantly more than the remaining contract obligation. Note that here, unlike in the foreclosure sale context, there is no opportunity for a public valuation of the real estate and thus no basis for a determination that "reasonably equivalent value" was obtained. As one court explained, in holding that *BFP* does not insulate an installment land contract forfeiture from a section 548 attack,

> Debtor's real estate is worth at least $40,000. The balance remaining on the contract plus unpaid taxes total approximately $15,830. The forfeiture had the effect of canceling this debt and transferring the property to [the vendor]. Taking into account all the surrounding circumstances, the Court concludes that cancellation of debt of $15,830 in exchange for the transfer of property worth $40,000 does

not constitute reasonably equivalent value under § 548(a)(2). *Unlike the sale price received at a foreclosure sale, forgiveness of debt by a contract forfeiture is not dispositive on the issue of reasonably equivalent value.*

In re Grady, 202 B.R. 120 (Bankr.N.D.Iowa 1996) (emphasis added). On the other hand, there are decisions applying *BFP* in the installment land contract setting and refusing to set aside contract forfeitures in the section 548 context. See, e.g., *In re Vermillion,* 176 B.R. 563, 570 (Bankr.D.Or.1994), where the court concluded that "absent a debt so small as to shock the conscience, the cancellation of the remaining debt on an Oregon land sale contract through a forfeiture proceeding regularly conducted pursuant to state law is 'reasonably equivalent value' for the debtor's interest in the property within the meaning of § 548(a)(2)(A)."

c. The Foreclosure Sale as a Preference

Several courts have held that a pre-bankruptcy foreclosure sale that brings less than fair market value may also be attacked as a preference. Because of the demise of *Durrett,* the preference approach is perhaps the only viable concept left for attacking state foreclosure sales in bankruptcy based on inadequate price. Consequently, it is important to understand the theory and how it differs from *Durrett.*

1) The Preference Elements

Under section 547(b) of the Bankruptcy Code, the trustee may avoid a transaction if it was (1) a transfer of an interest of the debtor in property, (2) to or for the benefit of a creditor, (3) for or on account of an antecedent debt, (4) made while the debtor was insolvent, (5) made within 90 days before the commencement of bankruptcy (or between 90 days and one year in the case of insiders), and (6) which enables the creditor to realize more than it would have received in a Chapter 7 liquidation. At least one federal district court and three bankruptcy courts have held that a foreclosure sale can be a preference. See *In re Park North Partners, Ltd.,* 80 B.R. 551 (D.Ga.1987); *In re Winters,* 119 B.R. 283 (Bankr.Fla.1990); *In re Wheeler,* 34 B.R. 818 (Bankr.N.D.Ala.1983); *Matter of Fountain,* 32 B.R. 965 (Bankr.W.D.Mo.1983).

2) Application of the Elements

The *first element* is identical with one of the elements in section 548(a) and is satisfied by the same analysis applicable in that context. The *second, third and fifth elements* are likewise easily satisfied. If the mortgagee purchases at the foreclosure sale the transfer will be *to* a creditor; if a third party purchases, it will be *for the benefit of* a creditor. Since the foreclosure sale is a separate transfer it will always be for an antecedent debt.

The *fourth element* requires, like section 548(a), that the debtor be insolvent on the date of the sale, but the trustee's proof will be easier than in the *Durrett* context. Under section 547(f), the debtor is presumed to have been insolvent during the 90 days preceding bankruptcy and the trustee will have to prove insolvency only in cases where the presumption is rebutted or the transfer was to an insider and occurred before the 90–day period commenced.

The *sixth element* is also present where the sale brings less than fair market value, but only if the mortgagee is the purchaser. If the transfer had not occurred, the mortgagee would have been treated as a creditor with a secured claim in a Chapter 7 proceeding and would have ultimately received the full value of the debt. By virtue of purchasing at the foreclosure sale, however, the mortgagee also obtains the debtor's equity, an asset that would have gone to unsecured creditors in a Chapter 7 proceeding. Thus, the mortgagee obtains more by way of foreclosure than it would have obtained in bankruptcy. This element will not be satisfied if a third party purchases at the foreclosure sale since the mortgagee will only be allowed to retain the amount of the debt.

3) Comparison to the Fraudulent Conveyance Approach
    In some respects, the preference approach is preferable from a mortgagee's viewpoint to the *Durrett* doctrine. The pre-bankruptcy avoidance period is shortened to 90 days, although if bankruptcy is initiated during that period there may still be several years of uncertainty. In addition, since the theory only applies where the mortgagee is the purchaser, the problem of inequitable treatment of third parties is resolved. Thus, third party bidding is less likely to be discouraged than in the *Durrett* setting. On the other hand, since the focus of the preference approach is on whether the mortgagee received more than it would have received in a Chapter 7 liquidation, unlike *Durrett* it may be used to recapture property where more than 70 percent of fair market value has been paid at the foreclosure sale.

4) *In re Ehring*, 900 F.2d 184 (9th Cir.1990)
    The United States Court of Appeals for the Ninth Circuit rejected the application of section 547 in the foreclosure sale context in *In re*

Ehring. In that case a mortgagee foreclosed on a second mortgage and purchased at the sale for $200,000, the amount of the mortgage obligation. The purchase was subject to an $80,000 first mortgage. Two months later, mortgagee-purchaser entered into a contract to sell the property to a third party for $390,000. Shortly thereafter, mortgagor filed a Chapter 11 petition and sought the return of $110,000 as a voidable preference. The bankruptcy court entered summary judgment for the mortgagee-purchaser and the BAP affirmed. The Court of Appeals affirmed the two lower courts. While seeming to concede that the six elements of section 547 were literally satisfied by the foregoing facts, it refused to find the sale preferential. The court stated:

> Because the creditor appears to have received value greater than the debt that was secured, it could be argued that the creditor received "more" from the foreclosure than it would have under Chapter 7 liquidation.
>
> This analysis, however, fails to consider the reality of the transaction. If the creditor received "more" it is only because the creditor elected to purchase the property at the foreclosure sale rather than simply accepting the receipts of a sale to a third party. Had the third party out-bid the creditor, there could be no preference because the price paid would not have been transferred for an antecedent debt. Since section 547 does not reach a third-party purchaser, it is difficult to see why the existence of a preference should turn on the status of the purchaser as a creditor. * * *

Id. at 188. Accord: *First Federal Savings & Loan Ass'n of Warner Robbins v. Standard Building Associates, Ltd.*, 87 B.R. 221 (N.D.Ga.1988).

Is it fair to treat a mortgagee purchaser differently than other bidders? Arguably, yes. It is only when the mortgagee purchases, as the court acknowledges, that a windfall can occur. When a third party purchases, any excess over the mortgage debt will be used for the benefit of other creditors. Moreover, it is the mortgagee who controls if and when the foreclosure takes place. Also, the mortgagee has the advantage over other potential bidders of being able to make a full credit bid without being out of pocket. Under such circumstances, it arguably is fair to place a greater burden on the mortgagee-purchaser to avoid receiving property worth more than the mortgage obligation. In the final analysis, why should the mortgagee receive more than what is owing to it when that excess could be used to satisfy other creditors of the mortgagor? See Nelson & Whitman, Real Estate Finance Law 766–767 (4th ed.2001).

9. Right to Rents During Pendency of a Bankruptcy Proceeding

Where mortgaged real estate of a bankruptcy debtor throws off a significant rental cash flow, an important question exists between the trustee, who represents mortgagor's unsecured creditors, and the mortgagee as to who is entitled to those rents during the bankruptcy period. This issue is especially crucial for the mortgagee when the mortgage debt is not fully secured.

a. Pre–1979 Law

Prior to 1979, the federal courts of appeal were divided as to what law governed entitlement to rents during this post-petition period. A majority of the circuits took the position that the mortgagee's rights should be governed by the state law which would have applied in the absence of bankruptcy. See Nelson & Whitman, Real Estate Finance Law § 8.17 (4th ed.2001). Thus, the mortgagee was required to take those steps, either by leave of or through the bankruptcy court, as would have been necessary to activate its rights under state law. If, for example, a mortgagee was relying on a rents and profits clause, but state law required the appointment of a receiver for its activation, the majority of federal decisions required that the bankruptcy court apply the same standard. A minority of federal circuits, however, utilized a federal rule of equity that afforded the mortgagee a security interest in the rents even if state law failed to recognize such an interest. Id.

b. Butner v. United States, 440 U.S. 48 (1979)

In *Butner,* the Supreme Court endorsed the majority view and held that state law governed in determining whether the mortgagee had a valid security interest in rents collected during bankruptcy. According to the Supreme Court, the bankruptcy court "should take whatever steps are necessary to ensure that the mortgagee is afforded . . . the same protection he would have under state law if no bankruptcy had ensued."

Although *Butner* was decided under an earlier bankruptcy statute, courts have uniformly followed it in applying the current Code.

c. Post–Petition Rents: Mortgagee vs. Trustee or Debtor-in-Possession Prior to Enactment of Bankruptcy Reform Act of 1994

Before we tackle the thorny problems of how rents are treated in bankruptcy, you should now go back to Chapter V(A)(6) and review carefully how state law treats assignments of rents.

Before you do, however, note that rent assignments given to *federal agency mortgagees* whose mortgagors are in bankruptcy are governed by *federal* and not state law. This federal case law holds that a federal mortgagee perfects an assignment of rents simply by recording it. The right to collect (enforcement or foreclosure) is triggered automatically when mortgagor defaults.

Finally, note that the following explanation is based on section 552(b) of the Bankruptcy Code prior to its amendment by the Bankruptcy Reform Act of 1994 ("1994 Act").

Situation 1. Treatment of mortgagee who has taken all the necessary steps pre-petition both (1) to perfect and (2) to enforce the assignment. Generally, the trustee or debtor-in-possession may use, sell or lease estate property, including rents arising from property of the estate. 11 U.S.C.A. § 541(a)(6). However, if the rents qualify as *"cash collateral"* under section 363(a), the power of the trustee or debtor-in-possession are substantially restricted. Under this latter section, "cash collateral" includes "rents, or profits of property * * * subject to a security interest as provided in section 552(b) of this title, whether existing before or after the commencement of a case under this title."

Now focus carefully on section 552. Under section 552(a), property, such as rents, acquired after the bankruptcy petition is filed is not subject to a lien arising from *a pre-petition* security interest. However, this latter prohibition on liens on after-acquired property is itself subject to an important exception in section 552(b), which provided (prior to the 1994 Act):

> Except as provided in sections 363, 506(c), 522, 544, 545, 547, and 548 of this title, if the debtor and [the mortgagee] entered into a security agreement before the commencement of the case and if the security interest created by such security extends to property of the debtor acquired before the commencement of the case and to * * * rents of such property * * *, then such security interest extends to such rents * * * acquired by the estate after the commencement of the case to the extent provided in such security agreement and by applicable nonbankruptcy law * * *.

As a result, post-petition rents arising from an assignment that has been perfected and enforced pre-petition, qualify as "cash collateral" and are entitled to the "adequate protection" benefit provided for in section

363(e). Thus, the bankruptcy court "shall prohibit or condition such use * * * as is necessary to provide adequate protection of such interest."

Note that this does not mean the mortgagee automatically gets the rents. If, for example, the mortgagee is oversecured (i.e., the real estate is worth more than the mortgage obligation), it may be unable to gain *any* access to the rents. On the other hand, if the mortgagee is undersecured, it will usually be able to convince the court that all or a part of the rents are necessary to protect its security interest.

One final note: a few courts avoid all of the foregoing issues and simply give the mortgagee who has perfected and enforced its assignment under state law pre-petition *automatic access to the rents.* Under this approach, "when a mortgagee completes all steps necessary to enforce its rights under an assignment of rent clause pre-petition, all interests of the [mortgagor] in the rents are extinguished and the rents do not become property of the estate or cash collateral." *In re Northwest Commons, Inc.,* 136 B.R. 215 (Bankr.Mo.1991). Accord: *In re Robin Assoc.,* 275 B.R. 218 (Bkrtcy.W.D.Pa.2001). Where this view prevails, the mortgagee is clearly in the driver's seat. Rents are the debtor's lifeblood. Either it gets a reorganization that it finds attractive or it will be able to scuttle it entirely and force foreclosure of its mortgage under state law. For criticism of this approach, see Nelson & Whitman, Real Estate Finance Law 773–774 (4th ed.2001).

Situation 2. Treatment of mortgagee who has perfected its assignment of rents pre-petition, but has not enforced it prior to bankruptcy. Here courts generally permit the enforcement step, in effect, to be taken in bankruptcy. The authority for post-petition has been explained as follows:

> Section 363(c)(2) provides, in effect, for the automatic sequestration of rents that are subject to a perfected security interest. Under § 361(3), the bankruptcy court may provide adequate protection by "granting such other relief * * * as will result in the realization by such entity of the indubitable equivalent of such entity's interest" while § 105(a) grants the bankruptcy court the power to "issue any order * * * necessary or appropriate to carry out the provisions of [the Code]." We hold that under these authorities, the bankruptcy court's powers are sufficiently broad to allow it to enforce a mortgagee's security interest in rents when and to the extent a state court would do so.

In re Park at Dash Point L.P., 121 B.R. 850, 859 (Bankr.Wash.1990).

Situation 3. Treatment of mortgagee who has not even recorded the assignment pre-petition. Here the mortgagee runs afoul of the avoiding power of the trustee or debtor-in-possession who is given the status of a bona fide purchaser under section 544(a)(3) of the Code. Consequently, she will be able to defeat any mortgage given by the debtor that is unrecorded as of the date of the petition. This is true even if she had actual knowledge of the mortgage and no bona fide purchaser actually existed. As a result, the trustee will be able to avoid (invalidate) any assignment that is not recorded as of the date of the bankruptcy petition.

Situation 4. Treatment of mortgagee whose assignment was recorded, but not perfected, pre-petition, because state law requires further affirmative action for perfection.

Here the starting point is section 546(b) of the Code, which provides that "[i]f such [local] law requires seizure of such property or commencement of an action to accomplish such perfection, and such property has not been seized or such action has not been commenced before the date of filing of the petition, such interest in such property shall be perfected by notice within the time fixed by such law for such seizure."

Mortgagees often claim that the foregoing statute permits them to perfect post-petition by seeking possession or a receivership in bankruptcy court or by giving the notice referred to in the statute. Once perfected, they argue, the rents accruing thereafter become "cash collateral" subject to "adequate protection" for their benefit. There is substantial case law supporting their argument.

On the other hand, a significant number of courts reject this argument. Their position is that section 546(b) applies only when *state law* contains a "relation back" provision. As one court explains, section 546(b) was intended "to affirm the validity of statutes such as 9–301(c) of the U.C.C. which permits a purchase money security interest to be perfected within ten days after the debtor receives possession of the collateral. * * * If the particular statute has no retroactive effect, § 546(b) does not apply." *In re Multi–Group III Ltd. Partnership*, 99 B.R. 5, 9 (Bankr.D.Ariz.1989). Since state assignment of rents statutes and case law usually do not have this "relation back" attribute, these courts conclude that section 546(b) may not be used by mortgagees to perfect in bankruptcy.

d. Impact of Bankruptcy Reform Act of 1994 on Post–Petition Rents

Now go back and reread section 552(b) as it existed prior to October, 1994. See *Situation 1,* above. The 1994 Act amended section 552(b) in two important aspects. First, the language "and notwithstanding section 546(b) of this title" were inserted after the words "of this title." Second, the words "and by applicable non-bankruptcy law" were deleted.

Congressman Brooks stated, in describing the above amendments:

> Under current section 552 * * *, real estate lenders are deemed to have a security interest in postpetition rents only to the extent their security interest has been "perfected" under applicable state law procedures * * *. In a number of states, however, it is not feasible for real estate lenders to perfect their security interest prior to a bankruptcy filing; and as a result, courts have denied lenders having interests in post-petition rents the protection offered under sections 552 and 363 of the Bankruptcy Code. [Section 552(b)(2) of the 1994 Act] provides that lenders may have valid security interests in postpetition rents for bankruptcy purposes notwithstanding their failure to have fully perfected their security interest under applicable state law.

140 Cong.Rec.H10768 (daily ed.Oct.4, 1994). Some commentators and cases "have concluded that [section 552(b)(2) of the 1994 Act] establishes a federal law standard—that an assignment of rents creates an enforceable security interest in postpetition rents—thereby rendering state rent assignment laws irrelevant." Freyermuth, The Circus Continues—Security Interests in Rents, Congress, the Bankruptcy Courts, and the "Rents are Subsumed in the Land" Hypothesis, 6 J.Bankr.Law & Prac. 115, 119 (1997). However, others are doubtful that Congress intended such a sweeping change. See id.

What can we say with some certainty was accomplished by the 1994 Act? *At the very least, the mortgagee in Situation 4, above, who has recorded the assignment pre-petition, will be able to complete perfection post-petition in the bankruptcy court by using section 546(b).* The new "notwithstanding section 546(b)" language indicates that Congress wished to expand post-petition perfection under section 546 beyond situations where state law contained a "relation back" feature. Thus, a mortgagee who has recorded an assignment pre-petition, but who has not "fully perfected" (to use Congressman Brook's language) under state law will be able to do so in bankruptcy court.

Moreover, our *Situation 2* mortgagee (one who has perfected, but not enforced an assignment pre-petition) will be in an even stronger position to "enforce" post-petition. After all, since the 1994 Act makes some post-petition perfection permissible, surely this should strengthen the position of the mortgagee who has already "fully" perfected under state law.

On the other hand, it is extremely unlikely that our *Situation 3* mortgagee (one who has not even recorded pre-petition) will be able to perfect under section 546(b). This is because section 552(b)(2) remains expressly subject to section 544. The latter "strong arm" provision, as we noted above in our consideration of Situation 3, gives a trustee or debtor-in-possession the power to set aside any mortgage that is unrecorded pre-petition.

10. Installment Land Contracts in Bankruptcy

Frequently, a bankruptcy debtor will be either a vendor or vendee under an installment land contract. In this connection, section 365(a) of the Bankruptcy Code provides that the trustee (or debtor-in-possession) may "assume or reject" any "executory contract" of the debtor. The following material focuses on the extent to which the foregoing provision may be used to upset the rights and obligations of the parties to installment land contracts.

a.   Vendor Bankruptcy

When the vendee is in possession (as is almost always the case), the trustee's right to reject an installment land contract is subject to the vendee's right under section 365(i) of the Code to obtain legal title by completing the payments under the contract. If the vendee is not in possession, the trustee will be able to reject the contract and leave the vendee with a claim for damages for breach of the contract. Vendee will not be able to complete the contract and obtain title to the real estate.

Example: Vendor and vendee executed an installment land contract eight years ago that provided for a purchase price of $100,000 payable in equal annual installments of $5,000 over a 20 year period. Vendee took possession immediately and paid 8 of the annual installments. Vendor then filed a bankruptcy petition. The trustee then filed a motion under § 365 to reject the installment land contract as an executory contract. (*Result*: Because the vendee is in possession, section 365(i) affords the vendee the right to continue to make the payments under the contract and ultimately to receive legal title to the land.)

b. Vendee Bankruptcy

Suppose, in the foregoing example, that the vendor had never filed a bankruptcy petition and, instead, that the vendee defaulted on the ninth payment. Suppose further that vendee filed a bankruptcy petition prior to vendor taking any action to seek forfeiture or other remedies under state law. If the installment land contract is deemed an "executory contract" for purposes of § 365(a) of the Code, then § 365(b) provides that if the debtor has defaulted under the contract, the trustee, at the time of assumption, must cure the default, compensate the other party for any loss resulting from the default, and provide adequate assurance of future performance of the contractual obligations. If the requirements of § 365(b) cannot be satisfied, it will have the effect of forcing rejection of the contract and the vendee will lose the land. See *Shaw v. Dawson*, 48 B.R. 857 (D.N.M.1985). Thus, if the land is worth more than the balance owing on the contract, the vendor will gain that benefit.

On the other hand, if the installment land contract is characterized as a mortgage or security interest, vendor may not invoke § 365(b) and the vendor will be afforded the status of a mortgagee in the bankruptcy proceeding. See *In re Booth*, 19 B.R. 53 (Bankr.D.Utah 1982). Consequently, the vendor will be entitled only to the contract balance and not to the land. If the land is sold by a bankruptcy sale, to the extent that the sale yields more than the contract balance, the surplus will be available for the benefit of the vendee's unsecured creditors.

Courts have experienced substantial difficulty in determining whether an installment land contract should be deemed an executory contract in the vendee bankruptcy context. While there is a slight trend in the case law in favor of the "executory" categorization, prediction is hazardous. Compare *In re Terrell*, 892 F.2d 469 (6th Cir.1989) (Michigan law) (adopting the "executory contract" characterization) with *Heartline Farms, Inc. v. Daly*, 934 F.2d 985 (8th Cir.1991) (Nebraska law) (adopting the "mortgage or security device" approach). Some courts, such as *Shaw*, suggest that such a contract should be characterized as a mortgage or security device only to the extent that state law treats it as such in other contexts. Under this view, a bankruptcy court in Florida, Kentucky, Indiana, Nebraska, New York or Oklahoma, where installment land contracts generally must be foreclosed as mortgages, would reach a different result than in New Mexico, where state courts continue to resist such a characterization and continue to enforce forfeitures.

REVIEW QUESTIONS

1. What is an acceleration clause?

2. Mortgagor defaults on the fifth and sixth installments under a mortgage payable in equal monthly installments over a 120 month period. The mortgage contains no acceleration clause. What are mortgagee's foreclosure options?

3. T or F   A second mortgage is being foreclosed by judicial action. The first mortgage is a necessary party in the foreclosure action.

4. When may the senior lienholder in Question 3 be made a party to a judicial foreclosure without his or her consent?

5. T or F   Mortgagee brought a judicial foreclosure action and intentionally omitted Lessee, the holder of a lease that is junior to the mortgage being foreclosed and that is economically "pro-lessor." Mortgagee purchased at the foreclosure sale. Lessee is still bound by the lease.

6. Why is the holder of the equity of redemption who is omitted from a judicial foreclosure action in a stronger position than an omitted junior lienor?

7. Assuming that statutory redemption exists in a particular state and that it affords redemption rights to junior lienholders, would an omitted junior mortgage prefer to redeem under the statute or equitably? Does he have the option? Explain.

8. T or F   Judicial foreclosure vests a stronger title in the foreclosure sale purchaser than does its power of sale counterpart.

9. Why is it important to know whether a particular power of sale foreclosure defect renders the sale void or simply voidable?

10. T or F   Chilled bidding renders a power of sale foreclosure voidable?

11. T or F   A voidable power of sale foreclosure has occurred and the sale purchaser is not a BFP. The mortgagor has the option of suing in equity to set aside the sale or of allowing the purchaser to retain the land and suing for damages for wrongful foreclosure.

12. T or F   The mortgagor's traditional right to sue to enjoin a pending power of sale foreclosure satisfies any requirement for a hearing that may

be imposed by procedural due process under the 14th or 5th Amendments.

13. T or F   Whenever the Veterans Administration forecloses a mortgage it should use judicial foreclosure.

14. T or F   In most instances, a foreclosed junior lienholder has a superior claim to a foreclosure sale surplus to that of the mortgagor.

15. To what extent does statutory redemption discourage foreclosure bidding by third parties?

16. T or F   The "one action" rule prohibits any attempt to enforce mortgagor's personal liability on the mortgage debt.

17. T or F   On May 1, 2003, mortgagor executed a mortgage on Blackacre containing a power of sale. On May 15, 2003, mortgagor enlisted in the Navy and went on active duty a few days later. During August 2003, the mortgage went into default, the mortgagee foreclosed pursuant to state power of sale legislation and P purchased at the sale. P has marketable title to Blackacre.

18. In what manner will the holder of a mortgage on real estate that is in default be affected by the mortgagor's filing of a straight bankruptcy petition?

19. Bank held a mortgage on Blackacre, mortgagor's principal place of residence. After the mortgagor defaulted on several installments, Bank accelerated the mortgage debt and foreclosed the mortgage. Mortgagee purchased at the sale for the amount of the mortgage debt. Two weeks thereafter, mortgagor filed a Chapter 13 bankruptcy petition. Will mortgagor be able to use section 1322(b) of the Bankruptcy Code to set aside the foreclosure sale?

*

X

Some Priority Problems

■ ANALYSIS

A.   Purchase Money Mortgages

It is a common practice for a seller of land to convey title to the buyer, receiving part of the purchase price in cash and taking back, as part of the same transaction, a mortgage on the land to secure a promissory note for the balance of the purchase price. This is referred to as a "vendor purchase money mortgage." Alternatively, the seller may receive part of the purchase price in cash from the buyer and the balance in cash from a third party lender, who takes from buyer a promissory note and mortgage on buyer's new land. This mortgage is known as "third party purchase money mortgage." Both of these types of purchase money mortgages deserve special attention because of the preferred priority accorded them over certain other claimants of the buyer's newly acquired land.

1.   The Purchase Money Mortgage Priority Rule

A purchase money mortgage, whether of the vendor or third party type, executed at the same time as the deed of purchase, or as part of one transaction, is senior to any other claim or lien attaching to the land that arises against or is created by the buyer-mortgagor prior to the latter's acquisition of title. See Restatement (Third) of Property (Mortgages) § 7.2 (1997).

Example 1:   On January 10, J docketed a judgment for $10,000 against R. on January 15, V, the owner of Blackacre and R entered into an earnest money contract for the sale of Blackacre to R. The contract provided that for a purchase price of $50,000, R agreed to pay $5,000 in cash at the closing date and V agreed to take back a note and mortgage for the balance. On February 1, at the time V conveyed Blackacre to R, R paid $5,000 in cash and, three days later, delivered to V a promissory note for $45,000 secured by a mortgage on Blackacre. V had actual knowledge of J's judgment. On September 1, J held an execution sale on the judgment lien and P purchased at the sale. P then brought a quiet title suit to establish that V's mortgage was no longer a lien on Blackacre. (*Result:* P owns Blackacre subject to the mortgage in favor of V. Although the judgment under which P purchased was a valid lien on Blackacre, it was junior to V's mortgage because of the purchase money mortgage doctrine. Even though the mortgage to V was executed and delivered three days after the deed, it was part of one continuous transaction.) See *Fleet Mortgage Corp. v. Stevenson* 575 A.2d 63 (N.J.Super.1990).

Example 2:   Same facts as in Example 1, except that the $45,000 in cash came from E, a third party lender, who took back a mortgage on Blackacre. (*Result:* P owns Blackacre subject to the mortgage in favor of E. Most jurisdictions give the benefit of the purchase money mortgage priority rule to third party lenders as well as vendors.)

The traditional justification for the priority rule is that title "shoots" into the buyer and the mortgage is given back to the mortgagee so quickly that the judgment does not have time to attach before the mortgage lien. This theory, of course, breaks down when, as in the above examples, there is a considerable time period between the conveyance to the buyer and the delivery of the mortgage to the purchase money mortgagee.

While there are a variety of technical arguments in favor of the rule; see Nelson & Whitman, Real Estate Finance Law § 9.1 (4th ed.2001). However, the best justification is simply one of fairness. "Certainly the vendor should prevail over claimants of dower, curtesy, community property or homestead rights, for any of these would be acquiring a pure windfall for which they paid nothing and would be getting it out of the unpaid-for property of the vendor. As against judgment lien creditors she should win because they have not extended their credit in reliance on the right to be repaid out of any specific property, much less out of property previously owned by another and coming to the debtor unpaid for, with the seller of it relying upon that very property she has parted with for her payment. Furthermore, their judgments are obtained before their debtor receives the property to which it attaches on acquisition so they could not have relied upon it in getting their judgment lien. . . .Much the same reasoning applies to the [third-party] purchase money mortgagee to give it priority over all but the vendor. He relied upon getting security upon this very property and his money went into the payment of it. Without his advance of money, the mortgagor would never have received the property." Nelson & Whitman, Real Estate Finance Law 786 (4th ed.2001).

Suppose that the proceeds of a purchase money mortgage are used not only for acquisition of title to Blackacre, but also to *construct a building or other improvements on it.* The cases are about evenly divided as to whether to extend purchase money priority status to the proceeds used for construction on Blackacre. Compare *Resolution Trust Corp. v. Bopp,* 850 P.2d 939 (Kan.App.1993), with *Carteret Sav. Bank v. Citibank Mortgage Corp.,* 632 So.2d 599 (Fla.1994).

Example 3:   J obtains a judgment lien against R. Bank then agrees to lend

$125,000 to R to be used to acquire title to Blackacre, a vacant lot, from V and to construct building on it. Incident to V's conveyance of Blackacre to R, R executes and delivers to Bank a promissory note for $125,000 secured by a mortgage on Blackacre. $35,000 of the loan proceeds is paid to V incident to V's conveyance to R, and the remaining $90,000 is used to construct a building a Blackacre. (*Result:* Under one group of cases, Bank's mortgage is senior to J's judgment lien to the extent of the entire $125,000 advanced by Bank. Other cases take the position that Bank's mortgage is senior to J's judgment lien to the extent of $35,000, the funds used to acquire title to Blackacre, and junior to it to the extent of $90,000, the amount used to construct the building on Blackacre.)

The Restatement position gives priority to the Bank in the foregoing example to the extent of the entire $125,000. In addition, under the Restatement approach, even where the loan proceeds are used entirely for improvements on Blackacre, the mortgage will be afforded purchase money priority status so long as it was given "as part of the same transaction in which title to [Blackacre] is acquired." Restatement (Third) of Property (Mortgages) § 7.2, comment c (1997). To qualify under the "same transaction" requirement, "the mortgagor must commence negotiations with the construction lender prior to mortgagor's acquisition of title, and the actual loan must be made incident to mortgagor's acquisition of title or within a reasonable time thereafter." Id.

2. Recording Act Problems

A purchase money mortgage will normally prevail against prior liens and interests arising through the buyer, whether the purchase money mortgage is recorded or not. However, the operation of the recording acts can, in some circumstances, give priority to liens or interests acquired subsequent to the purchase money mortgage.

Under most recording acts, an unrecorded mortgage will lose priority as against a *subsequent* mortgagee who takes without notice and, in some states, records first. Even a purchase money mortgage, if unrecorded, can lose as against such a *subsequent* taker. But if the unrecorded mortgage is a purchase money mortgage, it will still prevail as against *prior* liens or interests arising through the buyer.

Example: J obtained a valid judgment against R. V conveyed Blackacre to R who paid part of the purchase price in cash to V. E, an institutional lender, provided the balance of the purchase price and took back a note and mortgage to secure it. E had actual knowledge of J's judgment. Prior to the recording of E's mortgage, R borrowed money from L, who recorded her mortgage without knowledge of E's mortgage. E then recorded. (*Result:* Because of the recording acts, L will be senior to E. L prevails against a prior unrecorded conveyance because she recorded first without actual knowledge of E. On the other hand, E is senior to J because E is a purchase money mortgagee. To protect oneself against a prior interest arising through the buyer, the purchase money mortgagee *never* need record).

3. The Vendor's Purchase Money Mortgage Preference

When there is a priority dispute between a vendor purchase money mortgage and a third party purchase money mortgage, and that dispute cannot be resolved by the recording act or agreement between the parties, preference is generally given to the vendor.

Why should the vendor be given preference when both mortgagees supply the means by which the buyer obtains Blackacre? After all, a third party lender often has a greater economic stake in Blackacre than the vendor. The vendor prevails because "the property she is relying on for payment was previously hers up to the time of sale and mortgage back; . . . she would never have parted with it except upon the belief . . . that if her buyer defaulted she would recapture the property or get paid out of it. . . .Lenders of purchase money parted only with money in which they retained no interest whatsoever, and placed their reliance for repayment of their debts on getting a security interest in other property . . . never previously owned by them." Nelson & Whitman, Real Estate Finance Law 787 (4th ed.2001). Quite simply, preference is given to those who part with real estate previously owned over those who risk not getting a bargained-for interest in property that had never belonged to them.

a. If Each Mortgagee Has Notice of the Other

Note the problem that can arise when both a vendor and third party purchase mortgage are going to be utilized in the same transaction. Normally, both will be aware of each other because of the earnest money contract, which the third party lender routinely examines prior to making a mortgage loan. Such a third party cannot gain priority simply by recording first because, in all probability, it took its mortgage with actual notice of the vendor's mortgage. Moreover, if the vendor records first, her knowledge of the third party mortgage will prevent a victory based on the recording act. Thus, the recording act does not resolve the priority dispute. Nevertheless, the above presumption will enable the vendor to prevail.

b. If Neither Mortgage Has Notice of the Other

Suppose, however, each mortgagee lacks notice of the other's mortgage. Here again, the recording acts will not vary the result because they grant priority "only to a *subsequent* purchaser without notice and here neither mortgagee can meaningfully be said to be subsequent to the other, since both mortgages arise in the same transaction." Restatement (Third) of Property (Mortgages) § 7.2, comment d (1997).

c. If One Mortgagee Has Notice and the Other Does Not

Where, however, only *one* of the parties has notice of the other, the recording acts rather than the vendor preference will govern. "Even though delivery of the mortgages is essentially simultaneous, the party lacking notice must in fairness be treated as a subsequent taker and thus eligible for the protection of the recording acts. Thus, in a jurisdiction having a notice type recording act, the lender who takes its mortgage without notice of the other's mortgage prevails." Id.

d. Priority Is Subject to the Parties' Agreement

The priority given to the vendor's purchase money mortgage over that of a third party lender is only a presumption, and is subject to any contrary agreement the parties may enter into. Thus, it is entirely possible for the vendor to subordinate his or her priority expressly. For example, the vendor's mortgage might contain a statement that "The priority of this mortgage is subordinate to a mortgage of even date herewith to First National Bank in the amount of $100,000." In most cases, the third-party institutional lender intends and expects to get priority, and hence is well-advised to insist that such subordination language be included in the vendor's mortgage or in a separate subordination agreement signed by the vendor.

e. Order of Recording as Reflecting the Parties' Agreement

As noted above, often the technical operation of the recording acts does not resolve priorities as between a vendor and a third party lender, both of whom have taken purchase-money mortgages. However, this is a subtle point that the two mortgagees may not understand. Hence, they may believe that establishing a particular order of recording of their mortgages will be an effective way of fixing the priority that they have in fact agreed upon. The courts should and generally will recognize the priority that is indicated by the order of recording of the two mortgages, if there is evidence that the mortgagees instructed the escrow agent, attorney, or title company who handled the closing to record the mortgages in the specified order *for the purpose of establishing priority*. In such a case, it is not the recording act *per se*, but rather the agreement of the parties as reflected in their conduct, that is determinative.

B.   After–Acquired Property Clauses

1.   General Validity

A mortgage that contains an after-acquired property clause purports not only to mortgage specified real estate, but also any other parcel of real estate that mortgagor subsequently acquires. *As between the mortgagor and mortgagee such clauses generally create an equitable lien on the subsequently acquired real estate. Some jurisdictions limit the coverage of the clause to subsequently acquired real estate that is functionally related to the real estate described originally.*

Example: R gave to E a mortgage on Blackacre containing an after-acquired property clause. Later R acquired title to Whiteacre. (*Result:* E has a valid lien on Whiteacre).

Note that the most commonly-advanced theory supporting the validity of an after-acquired property clause is the "specific performance" theory. Under this theory, the clause is treated as a promise to mortgage subsequently acquired real estate which will be specifically enforced when that property later is acquired. A suit to enforce the clause is, in effect, a suit for specific performance of a contract. See Nelson & Whitman, Real Estate Finance Law 793 4th ed.2001).

2.   Preexisting and Purchase Money Liens

The equitable lien that attaches to mortgagor's subsequently acquired real estate as a result of an after-acquired property clause is generally junior to preexisting liens thereon and to purchase money mortgages created in the process of its acquisition.

Example: R gave to E a mortgage on Blackacre containing an after-acquired property clause. R then acquired Whiteacre by paying part in cash and part by giving a purchase money mortgage to V, the seller. There is a preexisting mortgage on Whiteacre in favor of X. (*Result:* E has a mortgage on Whiteacre, but it is junior to both X's mortgage and V's purchase money mortgage.)

Note that V's purchase money mortgage is senior to E's lien because of the purchase money doctrine and this is so even though V has actual knowledge of the after-acquired property clause. See Section A(1) of this Chapter. However, some courts apparently confer the benefit of purchase money priority only on vendor and not on third party purchase money mortgages. See *Hickson Lumber Co. v. Gay Lumber Co.*, 63 S.E. 1045 (N.C.1909).

3. Relationship to Accession

An after-acquired property clause in a mortgage on Blackacre is utilized to ensure that the mortgagee also acquires a lien on any tracts subsequently acquired by the mortgagor. *To the extent that the mortgagor makes improvements on Blackacre, they are subjected to the mortgage on Blackacre because of the doctrine of accession or the law of fixtures.*

Example: R gave E a mortgage on Blackacre, vacant land, that contained no after-acquired property clause. R then built a house thereon. (*Result:* the house automatically "feeds" the mortgage either because of the common law of accession or the law of fixtures. The absence of the after-acquired property clause is irrelevant.) *Caveat:* Even though the house in the foregoing example becomes subject to E's mortgage, that does not mean that E's lien on the house is superior to unpaid contractors or chattel mortgagees of appliances installed in the house. Such priorities are considered in Sections D and E of this Part.

4. Recording Act Problems

Even though an after-acquired property clause may be effective to create a lien on real estate subsequently acquired by the mortgagor, recording act problems make it difficult for the beneficiary of the clause to obtain priority over other parties that acquire interests in that real estate from or through the mortgagor.

Example: R gave E a mortgage on Blackacre containing an after-acquired property clause. E recorded the mortgage. R then acquired Whiteacre. Two months later R borrowed money from Z who took and recorded a mortgage on Whiteacre. (*Result:* absent actual knowledge by Z of E's lien on Whiteacre, E's lien will be junior to Z's mortgage).

Note that if Whiteacre is in a different county than Blackacre, unless a court is willing, as the *Hickson* court was, to say that the recording of the mortgage on Blackacre "is effective notice against the world," it will not constitute constructive notice to Z because land records in this country relate only to land within the county. Even if Blackacre and Whiteacre are in the same county, it is extremely doubtful that the recording of the Blackacre mortgage would put Z on constructive notice of E's lien on Whiteacre. This is because normally a person is not on constructive notice of a recorded interest that could not have been discovered by a reasonably diligent search, or, as it is sometimes said, that is not in the chain of title of land that is being searched. As Professor Glenn once emphasized in this connection, "the mortgage [containing the AAPC] is of record all right, but the difficulty is that it will not show up in the chain of title that relates to the new property [Whiteacre]." 3 Glenn, Mortgages 1658 (1943). It would be difficult to envision that a search beyond the chain of title to Whiteacre is part of a reasonable title search. See generally Nelson & Whitman, Real Estate Finance Law § 9.3 (3d ed. 1994).

The Restatement resolves the foregoing problem by treating a recorded mortgage containing an after-acquired property provision as *unrecorded as against those who later take interests in the after-acquired real estate.* Restatement (Third) of Property (Mortgages) § 7.5, comment d (1997). Thus, under the Restatement approach, in the last example, Z's mortgage has priority over E's mortgage even where Blackacre and Whiteacre are in the same county. However, E can protect himself by "recording a notice which specifically describes the parcel of after-acquired real estate [Whiteacre], refers to the mortgage [containing the after-acquired property provision] and is in a form that provides record notice under local law. When such a notice is recorded, the after-acquired property provision becomes part of the chain of title of the after-acquired parcel [Whiteacre], and interests in [Whiteacre] that arise thereafter will be junior to the lien of the after-acquired property provision." Id.

C. Replacement, Refinancing and Modification of Senior Mortgages: Effect on Junior Lienors

As we discovered when we studied the deed in lieu of foreclosure and related merger concepts in VIII, supra, senior mortgagees occasionally inadvertently take actions with respect to their liens that give rise to claims by existing and subsequent junior lien holders that their liens have been promoted.

1. Replacement or Refinancing by Original Mortgagee

A senior mortgagee who releases its mortgage of record, and, as part of the same transaction, takes and records a new mortgage, retains the predecessor's priority as against an intervening lienor except to the extent that: (1) any change in the terms of the mortgage or the obligation it secures is materially prejudicial to the intervening lienor or (2) the senior mortgagee intends to subordinate its mortgage to the intervening lien. See Restatement (Third) of Property (Mortgages) § 7.3 (1997).

Normally, a replacement mortgage that extends the time of payment of its predecessor does not materially prejudice an intervening lienor. On the other hand, unless the original mortgage validly secures future advances (see Section F of this Chapter), where the replacement is for an increased principal amount, to that extent there will be material prejudice to an intervening lienor. Moreover, there will also be material prejudice to the intervenor to the extent that the replacement mortgage obligation carries a higher interest rate than any fixed rate predecessor.

Example 1:   On March 1, R gave E–1 a mortgage on Blackacre as security for a $50,000 loan by E–1 to R. E–1's mortgage was payable on demand. On April 1, R gave E–2 a mortgage on Blackacre to secure a $10,000 loan. On July 1, after negotiations between E–1 and R about refinancing the E–1 debt, E–1 agreed to replace the original demand note and mortgage with a note and mortgage for the same principal amount and interest rate, but payable in equal installments over the next five years. As a result, E–1 satisfied the original E–1 mortgage of record and recorded the replacement. E–2 claimed now to have a first mortgage on Blackacre. (*Result:* E–1's replacement mortgage is senior to E–2's mortgage.)

Example 2:   Same facts as in Example 1, except that the replacement mortgage delivered to E–1 secures a $60,000 obligation. (*Result:* The increase in principal amount is materially prejudicial to E–2. Thus, E–1's replacement mortgage retains it seniority over E–2's mortgage, but not with respect to the $10,000 increase in principal amount and interest accruing thereon.)

Example 3:   Same facts as in Example 1, except that the replacement mortgage obligation carries an 10% interest rate, rather than the 8% rate on its predecessor. (*Result:* the increase in interest rate is materially prejudicial to E–2. Thus, E–1's replacement mortgage retains its seniority over E–2's mortgage, but not to the extent that the increase in interest rate enlarges the obligation it secures.)

Note that a replacement mortgage can lose its priority entirely to an intervening lienor through the operation of the recording acts. For example, suppose an intervening lienor acquires its lien after the release of record of the senior mortgagee and prior to the recording of the replacement mortgage. If the intervening lienor qualifies under the typical recording act (usually by being a BFP and, in some states, by recording first as well), it will acquire senior status vis á vis the replacement mortgagee. See Restatement (Third) of Property (Mortgages) § 7.3(a)(2).

> *Example 4:*   Same facts as in Example 1, except that E–2 takes and records its mortgage after the release of record of E–1's mortgage, but before E–1 takes and records its replacement mortgage. E–2 has no knowledge of the later mortgage to E–1. (*Result:* E–2's mortgage is senior to E–1's replacement mortgage.)

Occasionally, a senior mortgagee may actually intend to subordinate the replacement mortgage to an intervening lien. "However, such an intent * * * will not be inferred in the absence of a clear statement or other proof to that effect. This will be the case even where the senior mortgagee has actual knowledge of an intervening lien at the time the replacement is recorded." Restatement (Third) of Property (Mortgages) § 7.3, comment b (1997).

2.   Replacement or Refinancing by New Mortgagee

Under the doctrine of equitable subrogation, where a senior mortgagee releases its mortgage of record, and, as part of the same transaction, a new mortgagee takes and records a new mortgage, the new mortgagee retains the predecessor's priority as against an intervening lienor except to the extent that: (1) any change in the terms of the new mortgage or the obligation it secures is materially prejudicial to the intervening lienor or (2) the new mortgagee intends to subordinate its mortgage to the intervening lien. Restatement (Third) of Property: (Mortgages) § 7.6, comment d (1997).

The equitable subrogation doctrine provides that:

> One who fully performs an obligation of another, secured by a mortgage, becomes by subrogation the owner of the obligation and the mortgage to the extent necessary to prevent unjust enrichment. Even though the performance would otherwise discharge the obligation and the mortgage, they are preserved and the mortgage retains its priority in the hands of the subrogee.

Restatement (Third) of Property (Mortgages) § 7.6(a) (1997). Note that in the prior situation we were dealing with a situation where the replacement or refinancing loan was made by the original lender. Subrogation was inappropriate in that situation since one cannot be subrogated to one's own mortgage. However, the principles we applied there were essentially similar to those for subrogation. Here we deal here with a situation where the refinancing loan is made by a *new* lender and thus the subrogation doctrine is applicable.

Not all courts take such a broad view of subrogation. A few courts, bar the application of subrogation where a mortgagee could have discovered the existence of the junior lien. This approach thus requires that the refinancing lender carry out a thorough title search prior to advancing its funds. In essence, the refinancing lender is on constructive notice of the junior lien. Other courts, however, deny subrogation to the refinancing lender only if it has actual knowledge the junior interest. See the extended discussion of these points in Chapter 8, Section C(3), supra.

What sorts of changes in the terms of the senior loan will constitute material prejudice to junior lienholders? Where the refinancing or replacement loan is for an increased principal amount such prejudice exists. So too, it exists where the new loan carries an increased interest rate. On the other hand, a extended amortization period for the new loan is normally not deemed materially prejudicial.

Where such material prejudice does exist, there will be a loss of priority to the junior lien *only to the extent of the prejudice.* The following examples are based on the Restatement approach:

Example 1: On March 1, R gave Bank A a mortgage on Blackacre as security for a $50,000 loan by Bank A to R. Bank A's mortgage was payable in equal monthly installments over 5 years at 7% per annum. On April 1, R gave Finance Co. a mortgage on Blackacre to secure a $10,000 loan. On October 1, after negotiations between Bank B and R about refinancing the Bank A debt, Bank B agreed to replace the original Bank A note and mortgage for the same principal amount and interest rate, but payable in equal monthly installments over 10 years. As a result, Bank A satisfied the original Bank A mortgage of record. Bank B recorded the replacement. Finance Co. claims to have a first mortgage on Blackacre. (*Result:* Bank B's mortgage is senior to Finance Co.'s mortgage because of equitable subrogation.)

Example 2: Same facts as in Example 1, except that the replacement mortgage delivered to Bank B secures a $60,000 obligation.

(*Result:* The increase in principal amount is materially prejudicial to Finance Co. Thus Bank B's replacement mortgage is senior to Finance Co.'s mortgage because of equitable subrogation, but not with respect to the $10,000 increase in principal amount and interest accruing thereon.)

Example 3: Same facts as in Example 1, except that the replacement mortgage obligation carries a 9% interest rate, rather than the 7% rate on its predecessor. (*Result:* the increase in interest rate is materially prejudicial to Finance Co. Thus, Bank B's replacement mortgage is senior to Finance Co.'s mortgage because of equitable subrogation, but not to the extent that increase in interest rate enlarges the obligation it secures.)

Note that in a relatively rare fact situation the replacement or refinancing mortgage can lose its priority entirely to an intervening lienor through the operation of the recording acts. For example, suppose an intervening lienor acquires its lien after the release of record of the senior mortgage and prior to the recording of the refinancing mortgage. If the intervening lienor qualifies under the typical recording act (usually by being a BFP and, in some states, by recording first as well), it will acquire senior status vis a vis the refinancing mortgage.

Example 4: Same facts as in Example 1, except that Finance Co. takes and records it mortgage after the release of Bank A's mortgage, but before Bank B takes and records its refinancing mortgage. Finance Co. has no knowledge of the mortgage to Bank B. (*Result:* Finance Co.'s is senior to Bank B's refinancing mortgage.)

3. Modification of Senior Mortgage: Impact on Junior Lienors

Suppose that the parties simply agree to modify an existing mortgage instead of releasing it of record and recording a replacement or refinancing mortgage. Here the same general principles govern priority questions as in the replacement or refinancing by the original mortgagee context.

Where the parties modify a senior mortgage or the obligation it secures, the mortgage as modified retains its priority as against a pre-modification junior lienor except to the extent that the modification materially prejudices that lienor. See Restatement (Third) of Property (Mortgages) § 7.3(b) (1997).

Lenders frequently agree to a variety of modifications in the terms of the mortgage and the obligation it secures. Perhaps most commonly the mortgagee will consent to an extension of the mortgage maturity date or a "stretching out" of the installment payments. Normally, this type of modification is not considered prejudicial to the intervening lienor. Indeed, it may well reduce the risk of foreclosure of the senior mortgage and thus prove quite beneficial to the junior lienor.

On the other hand, where we are dealing with neither a future advances mortgage or an adjustable rate obligation, a modification that either increases the principal amount or the interest rate on the senior mortgage obligation is generally materially prejudicial to the junior lienor. If the latter is ever forced to redeem the senior mortgage in order to protect its interest, the amount required to do so will be more than could have been contemplated at the time the junior lien was created. Thus, the junior lienor will gain priority, but only to the extent of the modification.

Example 1: On July 1, 1995 R gave E–1 a $100,000 note and mortgage, the entire principal balance being due and payable on July 1, 1997. The E–1 mortgage was recorded. On January 15, 1997, R gave E–2 a $25,000 note and mortgage, which mortgage was promptly recorded. On June 25, 1997, E–1 and R enter into a modification agreement in which E–1 extends the due date of the E–1 mortgage to July 1, 1998. The latter agreement was promptly recorded. E–2 now claims that the E–1 mortgage has been subordinated to his mortgage. (*Result:* The E–1 mortgage retains its senior status.)

Example 2: Same facts as in Example 1 except that at the time the due date was extended, E–1 also loaned an additional $10,000 to R. As a result, E–1 and R executed a modification agreement making E–1's original mortgage security for the additional $10,000. The modification agreement was promptly recorded. E–2 now claims that the E–1 mortgage has been subordinated to his mortgage. (*Result:* E–1's mortgage is senior to E–2's mortgage except to the extent of $10,000 and interest accruing thereon.)

Example 3: The same facts as above except that the one year extension of the E–1 debt was accompanied by an increase in the interest rate from 10% to 12%. (*Result:* E–1's mortgage is senior to E–2's mortgage except to the extent that the increase in the interest rate enlarges the obligation secured by E–1's mortgage) *Shane v. Winter Hill Federal Savings and Loan Association,* 492 N.E.2d 92 (Mass.1986).

Suppose a senior mortgage contains the following provision: "This mortgage shall also secure all extensions, amendments, modifications, or alterations of the secured obligation, including amendments, modifications, or alterations that increase the amount of the mortgage obligation or its interest rate." While there is little case law concerning the effect of such mortgage language, under the Restatement, "[i]f the mortgagor and mortgagee reserve the right in a mortgage to modify the mortgage or the obligation it secures, the mortgage as modified retains priority even if the modification is materially prejudicial to the holders of junior interests * * *." Restatement (Third) of Property (Mortgages) § 7.3(c) (1997).

Note that the presence of such "reservation of rights" language may jeopardize the mortgagor's ability to obtain further financing. Other lenders may well be unwilling to advance credit to mortgagor when the amount of the senior mortgage is uncertain because of its potential for modification. As a result, the mortgagor could thereafter be "at the mercy" of the senior mortgagee with respect to future secured borrowing unless he or she has other real estate to offer as security. The Restatement deals with this problem by permitting the mortgagor to issue a "cut-off notice" to the mortgagee that operates to terminate the mortgage modification provision. Upon receipt of this notice, the senior mortgagee then must deliver to the mortgagor a certificate in recordable form stating that the mortgagor's notice has been received. See Restatement (Third) of Property (Mortgages) § 7.3(d). The rationale for this "cut-off notice" is that once it is recorded, other lenders will no longer be deterred from extending credit to the mortgagor.

D. Fixtures

Suppose that immediately after a conveyance to a house purchaser, the seller demands the right to remove the furnace that he or she installed a few months earlier. Even if the purchase agreement made no mention of the furnace, most persons would conclude intuitively that the furnace is part of the real estate. Indeed, a court surely would hold that the furnace is a fixture, "a former chattel which, while retaining its distinct separate physical identity, is so connected with the realty that a disinterested observer would consider it a part thereof." 5 American Law of Property 3–4 (1952). Simply to reach the conclusion that the furnace is a "fixture" signifies that the furnace belongs with the real estate and that the purchaser may keep it.

Not all disputes arising over chattels affixed to real estate are so easily resolved. For example, suppose the dispute as to the furnace is not between purchaser and seller of the real estate, but rather is a conflict between a seller or third party lender who takes a purchase money chattel security interest in the furnace and a mortgagee who holds the mortgage on the real estate on which the furnace has been installed. While it is true that the furnace, as a fixture, is subject to the lien of the real estate mortgage, that does not itself preclude the chattel security claimant from also having a valid lien on the furnace, and one that may even be senior in priority to the real estate mortgagee. Unlike the house purchase transaction, where the determination that the furnace is a fixture resolves the conflict, that determination is but the first step in the resolution of any dispute between the chattel security holder and the real estate mortgagee. In order to resolve this latter problem we need to take a close look at Section 9–313 of the Uniform Commercial Code and related provisions.

1. Section 9–313 of the Uniform Commercial Code

Until recently, fixtures were dealt with in one of two versions of Section 9–313 of the Uniform Commercial Code: (1) the original 1962 version of 9–313 (1962 Code); or (2) the 1972 amended version of § 9–313 and related provisions (1972 Code). The 1972 Code has been adopted in virtually all jurisdictions and is generally more favorable to the real estate mortgagee than its 1962 counterpart. In 1998 a revised Article 9 of the UCC was promulgated and has been adopted in numerous states. While the revised Article 9 makes substantial changes in many areas of chattel security law and there has been considerable renumbering of sections, the substantive treatment of security interests in fixtures is largely the same as under the 1972 Code.

2. What is a Fixture?

The UCC is much less helpful in explaining what a fixture is than in defining what it is not. It delineates three categories of goods: "(1) those which retain their chattel characteristics entirely and are not part of the real estate; (2) ordinary building materials which have become an integral part of the real estate and cannot retain their chattel characteristics for purposes of finance; and (3) an intermediate class which becomes real estate for certain purposes, but as to which chattel financing may be preserved." 1972 Code Comment 3.

Note that if the goods fall into the first category above, they cannot become part of the real estate security. Office furniture, for example, and other unattached equipment fall into this category. On the other hand, building materials such as bricks, lumber, etc., once incorporated into a building, cannot be the subject of a chattel security; such goods then are part of real estate security only. Fixtures represent the "intermediate class" referred to above and are most important for our purposes. The goods in this category are "schizophrenic" in the sense that they can be covered simultaneously by a real estate mortgage and a chattel security device. What goods fall into this category is a matter the UCC leaves to local law. In other words, one must look largely to state case law and real estate statutes to determine what is and what is not a fixture. While states follow numerous approaches in this area, the *American Law of Property* definition spelled out in the introduction is as helpful as any; you should go back and reread it carefully.

3. The Problem of Where to File

The filing requirements for the creditor who desires to perfect a chattel security interest in a fixture depend upon the parties against whom the creditor seeks protection. If protection is sought against real estate mortgagees, there must be a *"fixture filing"* in the office where a mortgage on the real estate would be recorded, and it must be such that it can be located by a real estate title search. If the property turns out to be a fixture, filing in the real estate records automatically protects the creditor against personal claimants as well. If the only protection sought is against personal claimants, a filing in the standard UCC financing statement records will suffice. Note that if a security interest is filed only in the personal records and later the property turns out to be a fixture, the filing is still valid to protect against personal claimants.

4. Priority Rules Under the UCC

We now focus on how specific priority disputes between a real estate mortgagee and a chattel mortgagee of a fixture are resolved.

a. Prior Real Estate Mortgage

The chattel mortgagee will prevail as to a fixture if (1) it is a purchase money mortgage and (2) a fixture filing is made either before it was affixed to the real estate or within 10 days after it became a fixture.

Note that a purchase money chattel mortgagee is preferred here because the installation of the fixture often improves the value of the real estate. Moreover, since the prior real estate mortgagee took its mortgage without relying on the fixture, to afford that mortgage priority would confer on it an unbargained-for windfall. On the other hand, where the chattel mortgagee is not a purchase money lender, the real estate mortgagee will prevail. Here the chattel mortgagee is not enhancing the value of the real estate. Moreover, the real estate mortgagee may well have relied on the fixtures when its mortgage was taken.

b. Subsequent Real Estate Mortgage

The chattel mortgagee will have priority if, prior to the recording of the real estate mortgage, the goods (1) became fixtures and (2) the mortgage was perfected by a fixture filing.

Note that no distinction is drawn here between purchase money and other chattel mortgagees. The general rule here is simply that the first party to fixture file or record the real estate mortgage prevails. See *Corning Bank v. Bank of Rector*, 576 S.W.2d 949 (Ark.1979).

5. Construction Mortgages

Construction mortgagees pay out the proceeds of their loans in installments as the building progresses. In an attempt to ensure that these advances relate back to the date of the initial advance, such mortgages include "future advances" clauses. The problem for our purposes is the extent to which such advances take priority over chattel security interests in fixtures installed during construction.

"As to any goods that become fixtures during the course of construction, the construction mortgagee enjoys priority to the extent of all advances made under the mortgage to finance the construction, including the cost of acquiring the land." Adams, Security Interests in Fixtures Under Mississippi Uniform Commercial Code, 47 Miss.L.J. 831, 908 (1976).

Note that this construction mortgage priority prevails even though it is competing against a purchase money chattel security interest and even though the advances are "optional" as opposed to obligatory. See Nelson & Whitman, Real Estate Finance Law § 9.7 (4th ed.2001) "The reason for giving priority to the construction mortgagee is to prevent the double-financing of fixtures where funds to purchase the goods are obtained from the mortgagee and the fixtures are then purchased on credit from a supplier." Bailey, Secured Transactions, 289 (1976).

6. Remedies to Enforce Priority

In those situations where the real estate mortgagee has priority over a fixture mortgagee, the latter is absolutely prohibited from removing the fixture from the real estate. If a real estate mortgage foreclosure sale yields a surplus, the chattel mortgagee should share in that surplus to the same extent as junior real estate lienors.

In those situations *where the fixture mortgagee has priority* he or she may remove the fixture from the real estate, but must " 'reimburse any encumbrancer or owner who is not the debtor' for damage caused by the removal (gouges on the wall paper, changed doors, holes in the wall), but need not reimburse other parties for the diminution in value of real property caused by the absence of the goods removed." White and Summers, Uniform Commercial Code 860 (5th ed.2000). Where a state adopts Revised Article 9 and a real estate mortgage that is junior to the fixture lender is foreclosed, the fixture lender has an additional right–the fixture lender can forego removal and instead have a senior claim on the real estate foreclosure proceeds. This means the fixture lender is authorized to "claim the lesser of its debt or the value of the fixture out of the proceeds of a [foreclosure] sale of the [real estate]. Id. at 861.

E. Mechanics' Liens and Related Concepts

Mechanics' and materialmen's liens give unpaid contractors, workers, and materials suppliers liens on the real estate which they have improved. They are solely the creature of statute and exist in every state. Their provisions vary greatly from state to state; hence, case authority is usually limited to a particular jurisdiction and generalization is hazardous. See Nelson & Whitman, Real Estate Finance Law § 12.4 (4th ed.2001).

1. Parties Protected

While initially only general contractors were protected under mechanics' lien legislation, now virtually every segment of the construction industry is granted liens of varying extent for labor, services, or materials furnished or contracted to be furnished for improvements to real estate. General contractors, subcontractors, suppliers, laborers, architects, engineers, surveyors, and drafters are all covered today under most statutes.

2. Types of Statutory Schemes

There are two major classes of mechanics' lien statutes utilized in this country, the "Pennsylvania" type and the "New York" type.

a. Pennsylvania Type

This type of statute confers on the subcontractor or supplier a direct lien right of his or her own, even though the general contractor has been paid. It is measured by the value of his or her contribution to the project. Under this approach, the owner in theory could wind up paying almost twice the contract price. For example, if the owner pays the contract price to the general contractor, who in turn pays none of the subcontractors, laborers, and suppliers, the total claims of the latter could very well come close to equaling the main contract price.

b. **New York System**

Under this system the maximum aggregate amount of liens that may be collected out of the property is the contract price in the main contract between the general contractor and the owner, less payments properly made to the general contractor. See *Lincoln Lumber Co. v. Lancaster*, 618 N.W.2d 676 (Neb.2000), applying the New York system to "protected party contracting owners." The rights of the subcontractors and suppliers are thus derived from and dependent upon the main contract.

3. Procedure

Under typical statutes there are several key dates and time periods. These are the *date of completion* of the lien claimant's work, the time period during which *a lien claim must be filed and recorded*, and the time period during which a lien *foreclosure proceeding must be commenced.* Thus, suppose a plumbing contractor does work on X's house and the date of last work is April 15. If that contractor is unpaid, he or she typically must file or record a lien claim within a time period of 60 to 180 days after the date of completion of the work. If the claim is not filed, the lien is lost. If it is filed, then the claimant will usually have a period of six months to a year to begin foreclosure proceedings. If the latter time period passes without the foreclosure commencement, the lien is lost.

4. Lien Priority

Assuming the appropriate procedure is followed, the date of claimant's lien will generally relate back for priority purposes to some earlier date. Different dates are utilized:

a. **Date of Commencement of the Building**

More than half the states allow the liens of unpaid claimants to relate back to the date of commencement of the building. Thus the lien of the person who installs the sod after the building is complete can relate back to the date of first excavation for the building or in some instances, even earlier. This is sometimes referred to as "piggybacking" and it confers on mechanics' lienors an advantage over intervening lien claimants. All lien claimants are usually treated as having equal priority among themselves under this system. See *1st Choice Bank v. Fisher Mechanical Contractors, Inc.*, 15 P.3d 1100 (Colo.App.2000); *LePore v. Parker–Woodward Corp.*, 818 F.Supp. 1029 (E.D.Mich.1993).

b. **Date the Particular Lienor Provides Materials or Service**

Under this approach in situations involving new construction each unpaid lien claimant may have a different priority date, at least in jurisdictions that do not place mechanics' lien claimants on a parity as among themselves. Moreover, the task of determining numerous commencement dates, instead of just the date of building commencement, makes proof problems and the foreclosure proceeding more complex. See *Ultrawall, Inc. v. Washington Mut. Bank*, 25 P.3d 855 (Idaho 2001), employing this approach.

c. Date of Filing the Claim

This approach obviously rewards those who are quick to file a claim. This may encourage lien claim filings in marginal situations and needlessly cloud the owner's title. See *In re MBA Poultry, L.L.C.*, 251 B.R. 78 (Bankr.D.Neb.2000), construing the Nebraska statute in this fashion; *Ohio Farmers Ins. Co. v. Commercial Ctr. Contrs. Corp.*, 676 N.E.2d 928 (Ohio App.1996).

d. Date of the General Contract

Where this date is used, all mechanics' lien claimants will have their liens relate back to a date that is almost always earlier than the date of commencement of the building.

5. Consent of the Owner

Statutes usually provide that property is lienable only if the improvements were made with the owner's consent. The term "owner" is variously defined. In many instances, a lessee or life tenant may not be treated as an owner, but an installment land contract vendee, for example, may very well be so classified. Thus, work hired by a lessee will usually not permit the filing of a lien on the lessor's interest unless the lessor has authorized or consented to the contract. *F & D Electrical Contractors, Inc. v. Powder Coaters, Inc.*, 537 S.E.2d 285 (S.C. App.2000). While execution by the owner of the construction contract will normally constitute consent, so too in some instances will the owner's acquiescence in or mere knowledge of the construction. See *DCB Construction Co. v. Central City Devel. Co.*, 965 P.2d 115 (Colo. 1998).

6. Waiver of Mechanics' Liens

a. In the General Contract

In most of the states that follow the Pennsylvania approach to lien liability, "no-lien" language in the general contract bars subsequent lien filings by subcontractors and suppliers as well as by the general contractor. States having the New York type of statute usually refuse to enforce such waivers.

b. Waivers During or After Construction

Lien waivers executed by contractors and suppliers after construction begins are widely utilized by construction lenders, title insurers, and purchasers of newly constructed buildings to minimize the risk of lien filings by unpaid mechanics and suppliers. Waivers covering work already performed or materials already supplied are universally upheld by the courts. Waivers that purport to cover work to be performed in the future are enforceable in some states. But in other states, such as California and Indiana, they are either construed narrowly or held to be invalid as against public policy. See *Landvatter Ready Mix, Inc. v. Buckey*, 963 S.W.2d 298 (Mo.App.1997).

7. Constitutionality of Mechanics' Lien Statutes

Early cases upheld mechanics' lien legislation against a variety of constitutional attacks, including substantive and procedural due process, equal protection and impairment of contractual obligation. More recent constitutional litigation, in the 1970s and 1980s, involved a procedural due process attack based on the *Sniadach-Fuentes* line of cases considered earlier in connection with power of sale foreclosure. See Chapter IX supra. The meaning of these cases is debatable, but they at least stand for the proposition that prejudgment creditor remedies which deprive a debtor of a significant property interest without notice and the opportunity for a probable cause hearing are unconstitutional unless accompanied by substantial safeguards to protect the debtor's interest.

Mechanics' lien cases have focused on the *ex parte* nature of a mechanics' lien filing; usually no provision is made for a prior hearing or even the posting of a bond by the claimant or any assurance that the claim is made in good faith or based on probable cause. Such attacks, nevertheless, have usually failed either (1) because courts have been unwilling to find a significant deprivation of the owner's property rights or (2) because, even where such a deprivation is found, courts have determined that the statutory scheme provides adequate protection of the owner's interests. The "no significant deprivation" argument was cast into doubt by *Connecticut v. Doehr*, 501 U.S. 1 (1991). Nevertheless, it is probable that statutory safeguards of the owner's interest will be upheld so long as a lienor is required to file the lien within a relatively short time after the work's completion and so long as the lien is not permitted to subsist for a period of more than six months without a hearing being required. See the extended discussion of *Doehr* in Nelson & Whitman, Real Estate Finance Law § 12.6 (4th ed.2001).

F. Future Advances Mortgages

It is common for parties to enter into a present mortgage transaction in which part of the loan proceeds will not be disbursed to the borrower until some future date.

The most prevalent example is the construction mortgage, under which the loan funds are advanced, usually monthly, as the building progresses. Another form is the "line of credit" or "home equity" loan, which contemplates that the borrower may draw down funds, repay them, and draw them down again from time to time. A third example is the "open-end" mortgage, usually a home loan, in which the lender retains the option of advancing additional funds up to the original mortgage balance for such purposes as home remodeling, repair and similar reasons.

1. Reasons For Use

The most obvious advantage to a future advances loan is that the borrower need not pay interest on the funds until they are actually needed. Moreover, in the construction context, such a format allows the construction lender to monitor the loan payments to insure that the proceeds are actually being used for their intended purpose, and that the value of construction in place does not exceed the sum disbursed to date. In all future advances loans, both parties avoid the expense and inconvenience that would be required if new documents needed to be drafted and recorded for each new loan advance.

2. Mortgage Formats

Some future advances mortgages not only disclose their nature, but also carefully spell out the terms and conditions of the future advances. Often, however, they do not. Rather, two other formats are in common use: (1) the mortgage may simply specify a certain amount, as if it had already been advanced, even though some of the funds are intended to be advanced at a later time. In other words, this type of form appears on its face to be a regular non-future advances mortgage. (2) The form may state the amount of the initial advance and state that it secures future advances as well, although the time and amount of such advances are not spelled out. One version of this latter type is the "dragnet" mortgage, a concept we will look at carefully later in this section.

Both formats have been subject to attack. The first is arguably misleading, since it makes it appear that the mortgaged real estate is subject to greater indebtedness than it really is. However, this should not prejudice subsequent creditors because, if anything, it will tend to make them more conservative in their credit decisions as to the mortgagor. Existing lien creditors may, however, refrain from proceeding against the mortgagor's equity because of the mistaken impression that the mortgage debt against it is larger than it really is. Courts nevertheless uphold this type of mortgage against all creditors.

The second format survives a vagueness attack because courts normally are willing to admit extensive evidence, such as a separate written loan agreement or parol evidence to establish the actual intent of the parties. Thus, both of these forms of future advances mortgages are effective. However, if neither form appears in the mortgage documents, future advances will not be secured; *Cottingham v. Citizens Bank*, 859 So.2d 414 (Ala.2003).

3. Optional vs. Obligatory Advances

If a future advance must be made only at the lender's discretion, it is referred to as "optional". However, if the mortgage or collateral agreements impose a contractual duty on the lender to make future advances, such advances are "obligatory".

4. Optional vs. Obligatory Advances: Priority Rules

While the characterization of the advances in such a manner does not affect the enforcement of the mortgage as between the mortgagor and mortgagee, it is often critically important where intervening third party lienors are involved. Under the rule traditionally followed in the United States, if the future advance is obligatory, it relates back to and takes its priority from the date of the original mortgage, and consequently is senior to liens that arise between that date and the time of the advance. If the advance is optional, it will be junior to any intervening third party lien as to which the future advances mortgagee has notice at the time the advance is made. See *Shaw Acquisition Co. v. Bank of Elk River*, 639 N.W.2d 873 (Minn.2002); *La Cholla Group, Inc. v. Timm*, 844 P.2d 657 (Ariz.App.1992).

The most significant argument advanced for the "optional—obligatory" distinction is that "if optional advances had an absolute preference, the mortgagor, although having no right to demand the contemplated additional loan funds, would be unable to obtain financing elsewhere, for no one else would lend on a security which could be cut down by subsequent action by the first mortgagee. And, for like reason, the mortgagor would be unable to sell the property. [If the advances are obligatory], he does have a legal right to performance by the mortgagee and as great or probably a far greater actual probability of getting it from his mortgagee than he would from another lender even though [the latter] were given power to end the priority of the first." Nelson & Whitman, Real Estate Finance Law 887 (4th ed.2001).

This argument carries little weight when applied to construction mortgages, the situation where the "optional—obligatory" issue most frequently arises. Contractors and suppliers who supply credit in the form of labor and materials are usually well aware of a prior construction mortgage and have little expectation that the mortgagee lender would subordinate its mortgage to their potential mechanics' liens. They rely instead on the mortgagor's honesty and business judgment, and probably expect that the construction lender will exercise control over the loan disbursements and construction. If the deal turns sour, they then may argue that the construction loan advances were optional. But if they succeed, it is at best a windfall. It seems extremely unlikely that they were more likely to have supplied labor and materials because of the chance that if they were not paid, their lawyer might be able to convince a court that the construction lender's advances were optional rather than obligatory.

5. What is an Optional Advance?

Construction lenders frequently attempt to reserve in the loan agreement a significant amount of discretion to condition subsequent advances on satisfactory progress of the construction project. However, the construction lender needs to be guided by at least three principles to avoid having those advances characterized as optional.

a. Lender Discretion Must Not be Excessive

The lender must not reserve too much discretion, but must have a genuine contractual obligation to lend. If the lender makes the obligation conditional, the conditions must be objectively defined and not subject to the lender's control or whim.

Example: A construction loan agreement made the lender's advances conditional upon a current appraisal, retention of an architect and progress on the project, all of which had to be "satisfactory" to the lender. Advances were to be made "at such times and in such amounts as lender shall determine." No advance was due unless, in the lender's judgment, all work covered by the advance was carried out in a good and workmanlike manner. (*Result:* the advances are optional. The builder had no definite obligation to advance any funds. By reserving too much discretion, the lender rendered the advances optional.) *National Bank of Washington v. Equity Investors*, 506 P.2d 20 (Wash.1973).

b. Lender Must Assert the Rights it Has Reserved

The lender must use the controls and assert the conditions which it has reserved for itself in the loan agreement. Even if those procedural controls and conditions are far more restrictive than most prudent lenders require, so that the failure to assert them could in no wise be regarded as negligence, the lender may still be charged with making optional advances if it does not make the mortgagor hew to the line. *J.I. Kislak Mortgage Corp. v. William Matthews Builder, Inc.*, 287 A.2d 686 (Del.Super.1972), affirmed 303 A.2d 648 (Del.1973).

c. The Lender Must Not Waive Defaults

The lender must make no further advances after the occurrence of any event which is defined by the documents as a default of the mortgagor; if the lender has the right to cease making advances, it had better exercise it. See Nelson & Whitman, Real Estate Finance Law § 12.7 (4th ed.2001). But see *Home Lumber Co. v. Kopfmann Homes, Inc.*, 535 N.W.2d 302 (Minn.1995), finding that such a waiver did not make the lender's advances optional.

6. What Constitutes Notice?

Under the majority rule, an optional advance loses priority to an intervening lien only when the advances mortgagee has actual knowledge of such a lien. In the case of mechanics' liens, this means knowledge not only that work or supplies have been furnished, but also that they are unpaid and their bills overdue. A minority view holds that the advancing mortgagee is charged with constructive notice from the public records, so that all advances made after the intervening lien is recorded will be junior to that lien. See Nelson & Whitman, Real Estate Finance Law § 12.7 (4th ed.2001).

Note that in jurisdictions following the minority approach, a future advances lender must conduct a title search prior to each advance to make sure that intervening liens have not been recorded, unless the lender is absolutely certain that the advance will not be considered optional. On the other hand, in a majority jurisdiction no such search is necessary. When intervening parties become lienors, they routinely mail a notice advising future advances lenders of their existence. Several states have statutes that adopt the majority view and require the intervening lienor to send a written notice in order to attack the senior lender's priority.

7. Special Types of Optional Advances

Optional advances made by a lender to protect security, such as the payment of real estate taxes, insurance premiums, or prior liens are treated as if they were obligatory. In other words, they relate back to the date of the advancing lender's mortgage and take priority over all intervening liens. *Virginia Corp. v. Galanis*, 613 A.2d 274 (Conn.1992).

8. Waiver by Future Advances Mortgagee

Certain actions by the future advances mortgagee with respect to intervening lienors can result in the subordination of otherwise senior obligatory future advances to such intervening liens. For example, suppose a subcontractor, in the midst of construction, inquires of the construction lender as to the financial soundness of the project and is informed that sufficient funds exist to take care of all subcontractors and suppliers. In fact, however, the undisbursed funds are almost depleted. To the extent that the subcontractor relied on the misleading statement, the mechanics' liens ultimately filed may take priority over the advances made by the construction lender after the misleading statements even though the advances are obligatory. In re 5000 Skelly Corp., 142 B.R. 442 (Bankr.Okl.1992). See Nelson & Whitman, Real Estate Finance Law § 12.7 (4th ed.2001). In Missouri, the court have essentially held that, merely by virtue of making a construction loan with knowledge that improvements will be placed on the property, the construction lender has waived its priority against mechanics' liens; Dave Kolb Grading, Inc. v. Lieberman Corp., 837 S.W.2d 924 (Mo.App.1992).

9. Statutory Modification

Several states by statute permit future advances to take the same priority as the original mortgage irrespective of their optional character. See, e.g., *Perry v. Carolina Builders Corp.*, 493 S.E.2d 814 (N.C.App.1997). Usually such statutes also require a definite statement in the mortgage of the maximum amount that will be advanced under it, and withdraw priority for advances which exceed that amount. Some confer priority as against all intervening liens, while others confer it only over mechanics' lienors. See Nelson & Whitman, Real Estate Finance Law § 12.7 (4th ed.2001).

Note that the Uniform Land Transaction Act (ULTA) and the Uniform Simplification of Land Transfers Act (USLTA) adopted by the National Conference of Commissions on Uniform State Laws also substantially modify the common law treatment of future advances. Under ULTA § 3–301, for example, priority is given to any construction loan advance if it is made "pursuant to a commitment" given when the lender had no knowledge of the competing lien. An advance qualifies as "pursuant to commitment" even though it is optional. Under USLTA § 5–209, the construction advance will have priority over mechanics' liens if it is made pursuant to a commitment made "in payment of the price of the agreed improvements." See generally Nelson & Whitman, Real Estate Finance Law § 12.7 (4th ed.2001).

10. The "Cut–Off Notice" Concept

About a dozen states have adopted statutes that not only give all future advances the priority of the original mortgage, as mentioned above, but also give the mortgagor a right to issue a notice to the mortgagee terminating all further future advances. (The effect of the notice may be to make all future advances subordinate to intervening liens, or to make them unsecured, depending on the statute and the wording of the notice.)

The point of the "cut-off notice" is to free up the borrower's equity in the real estate so that it can be used as security for additional (junior) financing from other sources. In the absence of a cut-off of the senior lender's ability to make additional future advances, no junior lender will consider making a loan to the borrower, no matter how much equity value remains in the real estate, since that value might be eaten up by advances in the future by the senior lender. Thus the "cut-off notice" concept assures the senior lender of full priority for all advances made until the borrower issues a notice, but at the same time allows the borrower to get additional financing elsewhere if the senior lender is unwilling to make further advances on acceptable terms.

The Restatement (Third) of Property (Mortgages) § 2.3 (1997) adopts the cut-off notice concept. Hence, if the Restatement is followed, courts may recognize such notices (and the concomitant idea that all advances made before a notice is issued have full priority), even in states that have adopted no statute on the subject. However, only one decision has thus far indicated acceptance of the concept without statutory support, and that only in dictum. See *Shutze v. Credithrift of America, Inc.*, 607 So.2d 55 (Miss.1992).

a. Types of Loans Not Subject to Cut–Off Notices

Some types of future advance loans cannot fairly be subjected to cut-off notices because of the potential for hardship to the lender. The Restatement identifies two categories of such loans, and some of the statutes contain similar exceptions.

1) Loans in which a termination of further advances would unreasonably jeopardize the mortgagee's security for advances already made, such as a construction loan in which termination of advances would leave the project only partially completed.

2) Loans in which the further advances will benefit persons other than the mortgagor, and the mortgagee has a contractual duty to provide such benefit. One illustration is a mortgage securing

reimbursement to the lender of the lender's payout under a guaranty, a letter of credit, or some similar obligation the lender has to a third party. Here a cut-off notice would leave the lender still liable to the third party, but without any security for its reimbursement claim—obviously an unfair result.

b. Future Advances to Protect Security Are Unaffected by a Cut–Off Notice

As noted above, mortgage lenders are privileged to make expenditures necessary to protect their security, and to add the amounts to the mortgage balance, even in the absence of a specific clause authorizing them to do so. These amounts are, in a sense, future advances; they always take the priority of the original mortgage. Payments of insurance premiums, property taxes, and repairs necessitated by waste are common illustrations. Under the Restatement and most of the statutes, these advances are not affected by a cut-off notice.

11. Optional Advances Under "Home Equity Loans"

Some home equity loans are for fixed amounts and are disbursed in a single payment; thus they raise no future advance problems. Others, however, are of the "line of credit" variety, under which the borrower may execute and record a mortgage on her home, and may then borrow and repay in various amounts and at different times over many years, with the mortgage purporting to secure all disbursements up to some specified maximum. If the lender is obligated to advance funds whenever mandated by the borrower, the priority of the advances is probably beyond question. See *Kent v. Huntington Natl. Bank*, 764 N.E.2d 480 (Ohio App.2001). However, if the lender has too much discretion to refuse to make advances, all advances might be deemed optional, and thus subordinate to any intervening liens. Several states have enacted statutes to protect lenders against this possibility. While these statutes were clearly enacted with homeowners in mind, they may also apply in commercial line of credit contexts as well.

12. Dragnet Clauses

A dragnet clause is a mortgage provision that purports to make the mortgaged real estate security for other, unspecified debts that the mortgagor may already owe or may incur in the future to the mortgagee.

Note that because the lender is not obligated to make future advances, the clause creates a species of optional future advances mortgage. However, unlike other future advances mortgages such as construction loans, the lender and borrower who execute a "dragnet" mortgage usually have no specific future advances in mind. The lender normally simply includes such language in the preprinted part of a non-future advance standard mortgage form with the hope that it might come in handy later.

Such clauses are generally upheld and are effective against intervening lienors to the same extent as optional future advances in other contexts. However, because they usually are not explicitly negotiated and borrowers are frequently unaware of their presence, courts tend to construe them narrowly against the mortgagee. While courts purport to do this based on the intention of the parties, more probably they are motivated by their own concepts of fairness and mortgagee overreaching. Judicial suspicion of dragnet clauses has been especially apparent in certain specific fact situations. While these patterns do not necessarily represent a majority approach, they do illustrate situations where courts have narrowed the application of dragnet clauses. See Nelson & Whitman, Real Estate Finance Law § 12.8 (4th ed.2001); Cisar, The Enforceability of Dragnet Clauses, 18 Am.Bankr.Inst.J. 18 (Feb.1999). These situations as follows:

a. **Preexisting Debts Not Secured**

   The mortgage will only secure advances or debts incurred in the future. If the mortgagor already owes debts to the mortgagee at the time the mortgage is executed, it should be easy to identify those existing debts specifically. Hence, if they are not so identified it is assumed that the parties did not intend to secure them. Restatement (Third) of Property (Mortgages) § 2.4(b) agrees with this position. See *In re Wollin*, 249 B.R. 555 (Bankr.D.Or.2000). Contra, see *In re Smink*, 276 B.R. 156 (Bkrtcy.N.D.Miss.2001).

b. **Clause Limited to Debts of the Same Type or Character**

   Only debts of the same type or character as the original debt are secured by the mortgage. Restatement (Third) of Property (Mortgages) § 2.4(c) agrees with this position, unless the mortgage describes the additional type of loan with reasonable specificity or the test of paragraph (c) below is met. See *In re Polley*, 219 B.R. 205 (Bankr.W.D.Ky.1998); *Ralfs v. Mowry*, 586 N.W.2d 369 (Iowa 1998).

c. **The Future Loan Must Refer to the Dragnet Mortgage**

   As an extension of the foregoing concept it is sometimes held that the dragnet clause will cover future debts only if the documents evidencing those debts specifically refer back to the dragnet mortgage. See *Pearll v. Williams*, 704 P.2d 1348 (Ariz.Ct.App.1985).

d. Clause Will Not Apply to Debts That Are Secured by Other Collateral

If the future debt is separately secured, whether by another mortgage or by a personal property security agreement, it may be assumed that the parties did not intend that it also be secured by the dragnet mortgage. *Gardner v. Guldi*, 724 So.2d 186 (Fla.App.1999).

e. Clause Will Not Apply to Debts Originated by Other Lenders and Later Acquired by the Dragnet Mortgagee

The clause may be considered inapplicable to debts which were originally owed by the mortgagor to third parties, and which were assigned to or purchased by the mortgagee. *Pongetti v. Bankers Trust*, 368 So.2d 819 (Miss.1979).

f. Clause Will Not Apply to Debts on Which All of the Mortgagors Are Not Liable

If there are several joint mortgagors, only future debts on which *all* of the mortgagors are obligated (or at least of which all were aware) will be covered by the dragnet clause. See *Maries County Bank v. Williams*, 989 S.W.2d 269 (Mo.App.1999). A large number of cases reject this limitation on dragnet clauses; the cases are about evenly divided. See, e.g., *Schmidt v. Waukesha State Bank*, 555 N.W.2d 655 (Wis.App.1996), holding property which the husband had transferred to his wife to be security for a business loan obtained by the husband without the wife's knowledge or involvement.

g. Clause Is Inoperative After the Original Debt Is Paid in Full

Once the original debt has been fully discharged, the mortgage is extinguished and the dragnet clause cannot secure future loans. See *McGlaun v. Southwest Georgia Prod. Credit Ass'n*, 352 S.E.2d 558 (Ga.1987).

h. If Real Estate Is Transferred, The Clause Terminates

If the real estate is transferred by the mortgagor to a third party, any debts which the original mortgagor incurs after the mortgagee gains knowledge of the transfer are not secured by the mortgage. Restatement (Third) of Property (Mortgages) § 2.4(d) takes this position. See *Green v. Southtrust Bank*, 519 So.2d 1289 (Ala.1987).

i. Loans to a Transferee of the Mortgaged Real Estate Are Not Within the Scope of the Clause

If the real estate is transferred by the mortgagor to a grantee, advances subsequently made by the mortgagee to the *grantee* are not secured by the mortgage, even if the grantee expressly assumed the mortgage. See *Walker v. Whitmore*, 262 S.W. 678 (Ark.1924). Likewise, additional debts incurred by the *grantor* to the mortgagee after the real estate is transferred may be held not secured by the mortgage. See *Vaughn v. Crown Plumbing & Sewer Service, Inc.*, 523 S.W.2d 72 (Tex.Civ.App.1975).

Example: In 1973 R gave E a $6,000 mortgage to enable R to purchase Blackacre, a new home. The mortgage contained a dragnet clause that provided that the mortgage secured "the payment of any and all claims or demands now due or to become due now or hereafter which [E] may have or hold against [R]." In 1974, R borrowed $9,000 from E for a cattle-raising venture. In return R gave E a promissory note for $9,000 and a chattel security interest in the cattle. The cattle loan documents made no mention of the earlier dragnet clause. R defaulted on the cattle loan, E foreclosed on the collateral, and a $4,000 deficiency resulted. E then commenced a foreclosure proceeding on the Blackacre mortgage, claiming that the $4,000 deficiency was secured by that mortgage by virtue of the dragnet clause. (*Result:* the dragnet clause is unenforceable. In view of the fact that Fact Situations (b), (c), and (d) above are applicable, clause should be interpreted narrowly against E. There is thus an insufficient basis for concluding that the parties intended the cattle loan to be secured by the Blackacre mortgage). See *First Security Bank of Utah v. Shiew*, 609 P.2d 952 (Utah 1980).

G. The Stop Notice Remedy

In many jurisdictions the mechanics' lien is of little practical value to unpaid subcontractors and suppliers. Even though in at least half the states, all mechanics' liens will relate back to date of the commencement of work, construction lenders routinely record their mortgages prior to that date and, in addition, take pains to avoid making optional advances. Thus, most mechanics' liens are usually subordinate to the construction mortgage and will be wiped out in the event that mortgage is foreclosed. *Stop notice legislation in effect in at least ten states provides an alternate remedy to the unpaid subcontractors and suppliers. This legislation gives these parties the right to enforce a claim against the construction lender and, in some instances, the owner, for a portion of the undisbursed construction loan proceeds.* See, e.g., *Mechanical Wholesale Corp. v. Fuji Bank, Ltd.*, 50 Cal.Rptr.2d 466 (Cal.Dist.Ct.App.1996) for a thorough description of the California stop notice procedure.

1. Scope of the Remedy

The stop notice remedy is available even though the owner-developer has defaulted and is no longer entitled to further construction loan advances. On the other hand, it is ineffective if no loan proceeds still remain in the hands of the construction lender. The legislation imposes strict procedural and time requirements on the claimants. In addition, the claimant will be required to post a bond to protect the construction lender against damages that arise from the assertion of a wrongful claim. Unlike most mechanics' liens, the stop notice claim will survive foreclosure of the construction mortgage. If insufficient loan proceeds remain in the construction lender's hands to satisfy all stop notice claims, the claimants will share those proceeds pro-rata. See *Tabet Lumber Co. v. Romero*, 872 P.2d 847 (N.M.1994) (funds placed in an escrow account after completion of construction to remedy "punch-list" items were not undisbursed construction funds, and were not subject to a stop notice).

2. Criticism of the Remedy

Some have argued that the stop notice remedy is too likely to be used by unscrupulous claimants to blackmail the owner and construction lender into payment of inflated claims. When a significant claim arises, the construction lender will often be forced to withhold a substantial amount of the loan proceeds; consequently, completion of construction may be delayed. Moreover, when one subcontractor files, ensuing doubt about the owner's financial condition may cause other subcontractors and suppliers likewise to file. In such a situation, even more loan proceeds will be withheld and the project could grind to a halt. Some commentators have suggested procedural reforms to facilitate the hearing on the stop notice, and thus to speed up the release of withheld funds.

3. Constitutionality

As in the case of mechanics' lien legislation, stop notice statutes have been subjected to 14th Amendment procedural due process attacks utilizing the *Sniadach-Fuentes* line of cases discussed previously in this Chapter at (E)(7) supra. Such legislation, like prejudgment garnishment, freezes the owner's funds without the opportunity for a hearing. However, stop notice legislation has been upheld against procedural due process attacks. The California Supreme Court held that even though such legislation involves state action and the filing of such a claim results in more than a *de minimus* taking of property, it does not violate procedural due process because the limited deprivation it imposes on the owner is outweighed by the interest of the claimant in a relatively rapid and efficient remedy. See *Connolly Development, Inc. v. Superior Court*, 132 Cal.Rptr. 477, 553 P.2d 637 (Cal.1976).

H. The Equitable Lien Claim

Cases often arise in which neither the mechanics' lien nor the stop notice statute will provide the subcontractor or supplier with an adequate remedy. This can occur with respect to mechanics' liens because in most cases, as noted above, the foreclosure of the construction mortgage will wipe out the mechanics' lien. Moreover, the majority of states do not have stop notice statutes, and in those that do, often a subcontractor or supplier will fail to satisfy one or more of their procedural requirements. In such situations, subcontractors and suppliers may attempt to claim an equitable lien on either the undisbursed loan funds or on the land itself.

1. Exclusivity of Statutory Remedies

One argument against the imposition of an equitable lien is that the mechanics' lien and stop notice statutes were intended to be exclusive remedies for claimants who have supplied labor or materials. In some instances, the legislature has specifically said as much. See West's Ann.Cal.Civ.Code § 3254, enacted in 1967 (stop notice is the exclusive remedy as to undisbursed construction loan proceeds). On the other hand, where such specific evidence is unavailable, an intent by a legislature to preclude the imposition of equitable liens will not be readily inferred. See *Town Concrete Pipe of Washington, Inc. v. Redford,* 717 P.2d 1384 (Wash.App.1986); *Architectonics, Inc. v. Salem–American Ventures, Inc.,* 350 So.2d 581 (Fla.Ct.App.1977) (failure to file timely mechanics lien does not preclude an equitable lien claim).

2. Equitable Liens on Undisbursed Construction Loan Proceeds— Judicial Theories

While the case law is confusing and imprecise, at least two major theories have been utilized successfully by unpaid subcontractors and suppliers to impose an equitable lien on the undisbursed loan proceeds.

a. Unjust Enrichment

This theory is applicable where undisbursed loan proceeds exist and the construction lender has purchased the land and improvements at a foreclosure sale of the construction mortgage. Here courts sometimes focus on whether the construction lender has made a false statement to the lien claimant which has misled the claimant into continuing to furnish labor or materials. If, however, the question is whether the construction lender has been unjustly enriched, then the statements made should be irrelevant. Indeed, the essence of the claim should be that by purchasing the land and improvements at the foreclosure sale, the construction lender has received the benefit of the lien claimant's contribution without having to pay for it (as is shown by the fact that the undisbursed proceeds exist). See Nelson & Whitman, Real Estate Finance Law § 12.6 (4th ed.2001).

b. Third Party Beneficiary Theory

Under this approach, the subcontractor or supplier is given an equitable lien on the undisbursed proceeds because she or he is viewed as the beneficiary of the construction loan agreement between the lender and the developer. In this setting, courts often require some type of representation by the construction lender during the course of construction that the claimant will be "made whole" or "taken care of". This type of statement apparently is used by the court to satisfy a supposed third party beneficiary doctrinal requirement that *both* parties must intend to benefit the beneficiary. It seems clear, however, that this is a misperception of the law; what generally is required is only that the obligee (the owner) have the requisite intent to benefit the third party (subcontractor or supplier). Such a requirement seems easily met in construction loan situations because it seems clear that the owner, by entering into an arrangement that entails paying for improvements with borrowed funds, intends to benefit the contractor, subcontractor, and suppliers. See Nelson & Whitman, Real Estate Finance Law § 12.6 (4th ed.2001).

The problem with the third party beneficiary theory, however, is that the lien claim may be barred by the owner-borrower's default under the construction loan agreement. Where, for example, the owner has failed to make interest payments on the loan, or has defaulted in some other respect, the construction lender will argue that it no longer has an obligation to disburse additional funds under the loan agreement. The lender may further argue that since the third party beneficiary's rights are derivative of the owner-borrower, no further disbursement need be made to the lien claimant. This defense is difficult to overcome. Some courts avoid it by holding that if the lien claimant performs prior to the owner's default, the claimant's rights are "vested". Others simply choose to ignore this problem or find that by encouraging the claimant to continue work, the lender "waived" the defense.

Suppose an undisbursed loan fund still exists, but the above two theories are inapplicable. This could occur, for example, where the construction lender purchased the real estate at the foreclosure sale, but because so much of the loan proceeds was diverted from the project, it is difficult to find that the value of what was purchased, when added to the undisbursed proceeds, results in unjust enrichment of the construction lender. Or the third party beneficiary theory may fail because owner-borrower's default may be viewed as a valid defense for the lender. Perhaps there are situations where an *equitable estoppel theory* could be utilized to allow the lien claimant to prevail. Suppose, for example, the lien claimant continued work based on representations by the construction lender, however innocent, that "you'll be taken care of" or "there is plenty of money for all the subs." When the lien claimant relies to her detriment in such situations, perhaps a court should "estop" the construction lender from avoiding the consequences of those representations by imposing an equitable lien on the undisbursed funds.

The fairness of such a result could be buttressed by the argument that it would encourage construction lenders both to control disbursements and to supervise more carefully in future transactions. Nevertheless, the equitable estoppel approach can be difficult to sustain because some courts will require that the lender's statements amount to "fraud, misrepresentation, or other affirmative misrepresentation". See *Rinker Materials Corp. v. Palmer First National Bank & Trust Co. of Sarasota*, 361 So.2d 156 (Fla.1978). Cf. *Emerald Designs, Inc. v. Citibank F.S.B.*, 626 So.2d 1084 (Fla.App.1993) (proof of fraud is unnecessary where lien claimant is attempting to reach undisbursed construction loan funds and not to gain priority over a recorded mortgage).

3. Equitable Liens on the Property

Even though there are no undisbursed loan funds on which to impose a lien, the unpaid subcontractor or supplier may assert an equitable lien against the improved real estate itself. So long as the debt from the owner to the lien claimant is proved and the land which was improved is identifiable, an equitable lien may be imposed, at least if no bona fide purchaser has acquired title to the property. See *Hunnicutt Const. Inc. v. Stewart Title and Trust of Tucson Trust No. 3496*, 928 P.2d 725 (Ariz.App.1996) (BFP took free of unrecorded equitable lien). However, once again, some courts will require proof of fraud or misrepresentation, this time by the owner; see *Wal-Mart Stores, Inc. v. Ewell Industries, Inc.*, 694 So.2d 756 (Fla.App.1997).

Of course, if the construction mortgage was recorded prior to the time visible improvements were made on the mortgaged land, obligatory advances made by a construction lender will usually relate back to that date and have priority over intervening mechanics' liens. An equitable lien claim arguably should be given no higher priority than would have been afforded a mechanics' lien, had it been filed. However, we noted earlier that there are occasions when misleading statements by the construction lender that induce the prospective mechanics' lien claimant to continue work on the project can result in conferring mechanics' lien priority on that claimant as to those otherwise obligatory advances made by the construction lender after the misleading statements. Thus, in a case where similar representations are involved, but the claim is for an equitable lien, perhaps the equitable lien should at least be senior to construction loan advances made after those representations.

I. Subordination Agreements

It is a common practice for otherwise senior mortgagees to subordinate their liens to other mortgages on or interests in the mortgaged real estate. Subordinations are used in a variety of contexts. We have already noted their use in adjusting the relationships between mortgage lender and lessees in the context of commercial income-producing property. See Chapter V supra; Mears, Who's on First? Negotiating Debt and Lien Subordination Agreements in Real Estate Transactions, 13 Prob. & Prop. 19 (Feb.1999). They are also frequently used in the process of subdividing and developing raw land. In this context, normally a developer-purchaser persuades the seller of the land to finance a large portion of the purchase price by taking back a purchase money mortgage. The developer then arranges a construction loan from an interim lender to finance the construction of residential or commercial improvements. Because most construction lenders will insist on first lien status, it will be necessary to have the seller agree to subordinate his or her purchase money mortgage to that of the construction lender. Thus, an enforceable subordination agreement becomes a key element in the subdivision process. Because subordinations are so important to this process, we will examine them mainly in that context. See generally, Nelson & Whitman, Real Estate Finance Law § 12.9 (4th ed.2001).

1. Subordination Agreements as a Two–Stage Process

Initially in the subdivision process the seller and the subdivider will enter into an earnest money contract or other form of purchase agreement. As part of that agreement, the seller may agree to subordinate the purchase money mortgage to a construction loan which has not yet been arranged. By necessity, the subordination agreement at this stage is not as complete and detailed as it will be when the construction loan is secured and the conditions of the loan made more specific. At this stage, the *subordination agreement is executory.*

Once the construction loan is arranged, the seller will then usually execute a second subordination document whose terms are much more detailed and complete. Litigation concerning the executory subordination agreement is most likely to arise after a seller refuses to go through with the whole purchase agreement or simply balks with respect to the subordination agreement. At that stage, the subdivider will normally sue for specific performance of the entire contract. Litigation concerning the second subordination agreement is likely to arise only if the construction loan goes into default and there is a lien priority dispute between the seller and the construction lender.

In some cases, a single subordination clause which is part of the purchase agreement, and which purports to operate automatically as soon as the construction mortgage is recorded, is employed. Here there is no second agreement to fill in the ambiguities of the first.

2. Actions to Enforce Executory Subordination Agreements

Most courts refuse to enforce subordination agreements that are too vague and indefinite. Specificity is needed in order to define and minimize the risk that the future lien to gain priority by virtue of the subordination agreement will impair or destroy the seller's purchase-money security. See, e.g., Restatement (Third) of Property (Mortgages) § 7.7, requiring that a subordination to a mortgage to be created in the future must describe that mortgage "with reasonable specificity."

In addition, California courts have denied specific enforcement to subordination agreements because of a general statute that prohibits specific performance against a defendant if the contract is not "as to him, just and reasonable." However, this is not the majority view; the Restatement, for example, would approve enforcement of even very onerous subordinations if they were described with sufficient specificity.

Example: A purchase agreement between Seller and developer-purchaser contained the following subordination language: "Twenty acres of said land are subordinated to the purchasers for immediate improvement, and such other tracts shall be subordinated to use as the occasion may arise." (*Result:* language of the clause is too vague and indefinite to be enforced). See *Grooms v. Williams,* 175 A.2d 575 (Md.1961). Other courts, however, have enforced similar clauses. See Annot. 26 A.L.R.2d 858 (1969).

To the extent that the subordination language does not specify a maximum construction loan amount or maximum interest rate, the agreement may be considered too vague and uncertain to be enforced, since if those two factors turn out to be too high, the seller's security will be impaired. Similarly, to the extent that there is no limitation on the use of the construction loan proceeds, the subordination agreement is more uncertain, and is objectionable because of the possibility that the proceeds could be used for purposes other than improvement of seller's land, thus weakening or endangering the seller's security. In addition, to the extent that the terms of the subordination agreement are too indefinite to afford adequate protection to the seller's mortgage or deed of trust, they probably violate the California "just and reasonable" requirement. See *Handy v. Gordon,* 55 Cal.Rptr. 769, 422 P.2d 329 (Cal.1967); *Roskamp Manley Associates, Inc. v. Davin Development and Investment Corp.,* 229 Cal.Rptr. 186 (Cal.App.1986).

How much specificity is required? The Restatement, at § 7.7 Comment b, requires that the subordination to a future mortgage loan must, at a minimum, identify:

- the new lender or type of lender;

- an upper limit on the initial amount of the debt; and

- an upper limit on the interest rate.

In addition, if the proceeds of the future mortgage loan will be used for improvements to the real estate, and the subordinating mortgagee is relying on those improvements as security (as will ordinarily be the case), the Restatement requires that the subordination include a statement requiring use of the future loan proceeds for that purpose, and a reasonable description of the improvements.

3. Actions to Reverse Priorities After Construction Loan Default

When an action has been brought after a construction loan default, the court is normally dealing with a second subordination agreement that refers specifically to the terms of the construction loan. Hence the problem of indefiniteness is generally obviated. Even where indefiniteness is still a problem, some courts find that the seller is estopped from raising that issue where there has been detrimental lender reliance.

It is difficult to generalize concerning post-default litigation. While the probability that the court will uphold the subordination agreement is enhanced, the cases are hardly uniform. For example, in one case, the first subordination agreement specified that the loan proceeds be used for certain specified purposes. The second agreement contained no such limitation. The court held that "a subordination agreement should be construed, unless it expressly provides otherwise, as permitting the loan proceeds to be used only for purposes which improve the seller's security position. The court granted the seller senior lien statutes as to that part of the construction loan used for unauthorized purposes." *Miller v. Citizens Sav. and Loan*, 56 Cal.Rptr. 844 (Cal.App.1967).

4. Conditional Subordination

Where the subordination of the seller's purchase money mortgage is expressly conditional on application of the construction loan proceeds to construction costs, courts will recognize the lender's priority only to the extent the disbursements are utilized for construction purposes.

> *Example:* Under language in seller's $100,000 purchase money mortgage, the seller agreed to subordinate his interest to "a construction loan for the purpose of constructing on each lot a dwelling house with the usual appurtenances." Out of the total construction loan proceeds of $500,000, $200,000 was used by the developer in other non-related business projects and for a vacation to Europe. The construction loan went into default and lender foreclosed. Seller argued that the disbursement of loan proceeds was in violation of the subordination conditions. (*Result:* Seller's purchase money mortgage will be junior only to the $300,000 that was utilized in construction on the mortgaged real estate.) See generally Nelson & Whitman, Real Estate Finance Law 918–921 (4th ed.2001).

A few courts have applied this approach where the condition was only *implicit*. See *Middlebrook-Anderson Co. v. Southwest Savings & Loan Ass'n*, 96 Cal.Rptr. 338 (Cal.App.1971). But most courts have rejected the implied condition approach, and will look only to conditions that are expressed in the subordination itself. Hence, they refuse to find any duty on the part of the mortgagee to care for the interests of the subordinating party. See *Capul v. Fleet Bank of Maine*, 697 A.2d 66 (Me.1997); *Frick v. North Bank*, 542 N.W.2d 331 (Mich.App.1995); Nelson & Whitman, Real Estate Finance Law § 12.9 (4th ed.2001).

REVIEW QUESTIONS

1. What is a third party purchase money mortgage?

2. T or F   A prior unrecorded purchase money mortgage on Blackacre has priority as against subsequent mortgages thereon arising through the mortgagor-buyer.

3. How does the accession principle differ from an after-acquired property clause?

4. T or F   There are two mortgages on Blackacre, a first held by E–1 and a second held by E–2. E–1 and mortgagor agree to extend the due date and increase the interest rate on the E–1 mortgage. E–2's mortgage is now senior to the E–1 mortgage.

5. T or F   Acme Steel Co. supplied over 100 steel beams that were used in constructing an apartment building on Blackacre. Prior to their use in construction, the building owner gave a chattel security interest in the steel beams, which Acme promptly recorded in the appropriate office. Acme has a valid security interest in the steel beams.

6. T or F   A purchase money chattel mortgage on a fixture installed on Blackacre has priority over a prior real estate mortgage on Blackacre even though the chattel mortgage was never perfected.

7. How does the "Pennsylvania" mechanics' lien system differ from the "New York" system?

8. T or F   Language in the main contract between an owner and a general contractor that purports to waive any potential mechanics' lien claim is valid and enforceable.

9. T or F   E–1 took and recorded a mortgage on Blackacre containing a future advances clause. Initially E–1 advanced $50,000 to mortgagor out of the $75,000 authorized by the mortgage. E–2 then took and recorded a mortgage on the same land. Later, E–1 advanced the remaining $25,000 to the mortgagor. E–2's mortgage has priority over the $25,000 advance made by E–1.

10. How does a dragnet clause differ from more traditional future advances language?

11. In what manner may "stop notice" legislation be abused?

12. What judicial theories have been utilized by unpaid subcontractors and suppliers to impose an equitable lien on undisbursed construction loan proceeds?

13. T or F   Litigation over executory subordination agreements is most likely to arise after a construction mortgage goes into default and there is a lien priority dispute between the construction mortgagee and the seller-purchase money mortgagee.

14. T or F   Once a construction loan default has occurred, the seller-purchase money mortgagee will be able to get his lien promoted over that of the construction mortgage by arguing that the subordination agreement was impermissibly vague.

*

XI

Government Involvement in the Mortgage Market

■ ANALYSIS

INTRODUCTION

In recent years there has been a vast expansion of governmental involvement in the traditionally private field of mortgage law. This Chapter discusses four main areas of such involvement:

- The roles of government agencies in mortgage finance.

- The preemption of state mortgage law by federal statutes.

- The preemption of state mortgage law by federal agency regulations.

- Preemption resulting from the fact that a federal government agency is foreclosing a mortgage.

A. Government Agency Involvement in Mortgage Finance

Government agencies perform three main roles in mortgage finance. These are:

- *As regulators of privately-owned mortgage lenders.*

- *As providers of funds to the mortgage market, mainly through secondary market purchases and guaranties of mortgage securitizations.*

- *As spreaders of risk through insurance and guaranty programs.*

The Federal Government has been much more active than state governments in most of these areas, although states have some important programs as well. The discussion below will concentrate on federal agencies, but will mention state agencies where appropriate.

1. Regulators of Mortgage Lenders

The main regulatory agencies are specialized, in the sense that each of them is responsible for regulation of a particular type of financial institution. The discussion below is therefore organized by type of lender. Before we examine each of the lender types, it may be helpful to examine how much mortgage debt is held by each. Of the roughly $8.2 trillion in mortgage debt outstanding at the beginning of 2003, the following types of lenders held the percentages indicated.

Thrift institutions	9%
Commercial banks	24%

Life insurance companies	3%
Federally-related agencies	43%
Individuals and private pools	21%

Note that these are percentages of mortgage debt *held*, not mortgage debt *originated*. "Holding" refers to the long-term owner of the mortgage, not the lender that made the loan initially. For example, mortgage bankers are not on the list; they originate a large number of mortgage loans each year, but sell virtually all of them on the secondary market, primarily to federally-related agencies, and therefore hold essentially no mortgages at all.

a. Thrift Institutions

There are two general categories of thrift institutions: savings and loan associations (S & Ls), which traditionally tended to concentrate very heavily on mortgage lending, and savings banks. S & Ls could (and still can) be chartered either by federal or state government. Mutual savings banks (MSBs) historically were state-chartered in about 17 states and were permitted to engage in somewhat broader investments than the home-mortgage-oriented S & Ls.

The S & L industry came under extreme financial stress during the latter half of the 1980s, and many institutions failed. Hence, the current number of operating S & Ls today is far smaller than in, say, 1980. In 1989 Congress adopted the Financial Institutions Reform, Recovery, and Enforcement Act (FIRREA). The Act substantially revised the structure of the federal agencies that supervise S & Ls, narrowed the S & Ls' lending and investment powers, and created a new (but temporary) agency, the Resolution Trust Corporation (RTC) to manage, consolidate, and if necessary liquidate, failing S & Ls. From 1991 onward, S & Ls were required to meet a "Qualified Thrift Lender" test that, while complex, essentially requires all S & Ls to devote at least 70% of their loan portfolios to housing-related investments. FIRREA also increased the capital reserve requirements S & Ls must meet. For a judicial perspective on these events, see *Anderson v. U.S.*, 344 F.3d 1343 (Fed.Cir.2003).

FIRREA closed down the Federal Savings and Loan Insurance Corporation (FSLIC), which had historically provided deposit insurance for S & Ls and some MSBs. In its place, Congress authorized the Federal Deposit Insurance Corporation (FDIC),which had traditionally written deposit insurance only for commercial banks, to create two distinct insurance funds—the Bank Insurance Fund (BIF) for commercial banks, and the

Savings Association Insurance Fund (SAIF) for thrift institutions. As of the beginning of 2003, the BIF had assets of $4.6 trillion, and the SAIF assets of $1.9 trillion.

Since FIRREA, the Office of Thrift Supervision (OTS) has been authorized to charter federal savings banks (FSBs) as well as S & Ls; they may operate under either mutual or stock ownership, and may have their deposits insured under either the SAIF, like S & Ls, or the BIF, like commercial banks, although most of them have elected the SAIF. There has been a major trend toward the conversion of state-chartered MSBs and S & Ls to FSBs and to stock ownership, a movement motivated largely by the potential for greater capitalization that issuance of stock can provide.

So far as mortgage lending powers are concerned, federally-chartered thrifts are regulated by the Office of Thrift Supervision (OTS) while state-chartered S & Ls (including those with federal SAIF deposit insurance) are governed by state agencies, typically called "Savings and Loan Commissions" or the like. In theory, state-chartered thrifts in a particular state may have broader or narrower lending powers than federally-chartered thrifts located in the same state. However, FIRREA prohibits state-chartered thrifts that have SAIF insurance from making certain types of investments (such as direct real estate ownership and junk bonds) that are prohibited for federally-chartered thrifts. On the other hand, the lending powers of state-chartered thrifts with respect to "alternative" mortgage loans are at least equal to those of federal S & Ls under the Alternative Mortgage Transaction Parity Act of 1982, discussed in Section B(2), infra.

By mid–2003, there were fewer than 1,500 thrift institutions–less than half if the number twenty years earlier. The OTC was responsible for supervising about two-thirds of them, with the remainder supervised by the banking regulators. However, thrifts remained fairly concentrated in real estate lending: about 48% of their assets were mortgage loans on 1–to–4–family homes, and another 7% on multifamily, construction, and land development loans. Because of the decline in the overall size of the thrift industry, by 2003 thrifts held only about 9% of all mortgage loans, far less than the more than 30% they had held in the early 1980s. This lost market share had been largely absorbed by commercial banks and by Fannie Mae and Freddie Mac.

b. Commercial Banks

Banks have broader lending powers than thrifts and do not concentrate as heavily on mortgage lending. Many, however, do make large numbers of mortgage loans. Like thrifts, banks may be either federally-chartered ("national banks") or state chartered. National banks are chartered by the Office of the Comptroller of the Currency (OCC), a division of the U.S. Treasury Department. All national banks and most state banks have deposit insurance with the Bank Insurance Fund (BIF) managed by the FDIC. A significant number of the larger state banks, as well as all national banks, are also members of the Federal Reserve System, managed by the Federal Reserve Board (FRB), which provides a supply of credit to them. The three federal agencies mentioned (OCC, FDIC, and FRB) operate quite independently of one another, and the latter two have considerable influence on state-chartered banks.

With respect to mortgage lending powers, national banks are governed by Section 24 of the Federal Reserve Act, which gives the OCC full authority to regulate them. See 12 C.F.R. § 7.2000 et seq. Their powers are extremely broad. Mortgage lending by state-chartered banks is governed in each state by some state agency, often called a "Banking Commission." The regulations of the FDIC and FRB do not generally deal with mortgage lending by state banks.

Despite the fact that they do not tend to concentrate on mortgage lending, commercial banks held nearly a quarter of all mortgage debt at the beginning of 2003.

c. Credit Unions

A credit union is usually sponsored by a group of people organized for some other purpose, such as employees of a particular company or members of a labor organization. Credit unions have traditionally concentrated on consumer lending and made few mortgage loans, but in recent decades many have expanded their mortgage activity, particularly with respect to home improvement loans and second mortgages. At the beginning of 2003 there were more than 10,000 credit unions in the United States, although many were small and made few or no mortgage loans. Credit unions may be either federally-chartered or state-chartered, but federal credit unions are far more important in terms of total assets. They are regulated by the National Credit Union Administration (NCUA), both with regard to mortgage lending and in other respects. Overall, credit unions hold less than 2% of all U.S. mortgages.

2. Providers of Mortgage Funds

In the last four decades there has been a strong effort on the part of government to assure a stable and relatively low-cost flow of investment funds into the residential mortgage market. These funds have typically been raised by the sale of various types of bonds, notes, and debentures in the general capital markets (e.g., the New York Exchange), and have then been funneled into housing either by way of loans to mortgage lending institutions or by secondary market purchases from such institutions.

a. Loans to Lenders

A system of 12 regional Federal Home Loan Banks (FHLBs) cover the nation. Their main role is to borrow funds in the capital markets and to relend them to S & Ls in the form of "advances." Most advances are fairly short in maturity (a few months to a few years) and are secured by the pledging of loans from the borrowing S & Ls' mortgage portfolios. Advances have been an important source of funds to S & Ls during times of tight credit. The FHLBs are supervised nationally by the Federal Housing Finance Board (FHFB), which was created in 1989 by FIRREA.

The Federal Reserve Board (FRB) operates a much larger "credit window" for national banks and state banks that are members of the Federal Reserve System. However, relatively little of the money borrowed by banks from this source finds its way into mortgage lending.

There is little state agency activity of a type analogous to the federal activity described above. In a few states, state housing finance agencies (SHFAs) operate programs to make loans to lenders which in turn agree to use the funds for specific types of mortgage lending, usually on housing for low-income and middle-income people. Most SHFAs, however, use other techniques described below.

b. Government-sponsored Secondary Market Purchasers

Two main federal or quasi-federal agencies buy loans on the secondary market.

1) Fannie Mae

Fannie Mae, originally known as the Federal National Mortgage Association (FNMA) was created in the 1930's to buy home mortgages from local lenders, thus giving them cash liquidity. In 1968 it was converted from a government agency to a quasi-private corporation, with its stock privately held and traded. Five of its 18–

member board are Presidential appointees, with the remainder elected by its shareholders. It purchases a variety of mortgage types, including single-family and apartment loans, second mortgages, etc.

Traditionally the funds used by Fannie Mae to buy mortgages were raised by the sale of debentures and other forms of debt in the open market. However, during the past two decades Fannie Mae has, for the most part, employed a different financing technique: it acquires individual multifamily mortgages or pools of single-family mortgages from local lenders, packages them, and sells "mortgage-backed securities" (MBS) based on the mortgages themselves. One type of MBS is the "participation certificate," in which Fannie Mae sells to investors virtually all of its ownership rights in the mortgage pool. Payment on the underlying loans represented in these certificates is guaranteed by Fannie Mae. Thus the certificates are highly liquid and readily traded in the capital markets. Often, the certificates are purchased by the very lenders who provided the pools of mortgages; the certificates represent a much more liquid and easily-sold asset than the mortgages themselves.

Another type of MBS is the collateralized mortgage obligation (CMO). This security is not a participation or ownership share in the underlying mortgages, but rather is an issuance of Fannie Mae itself, secured or "collateralized" by the mortgage pool. In a CMO, a variety of different securities may be generated from the same pool of mortgages. The securities may have different maturities, payment schedules, and risks, representing different parts of the pool's interest and principal payments. The different securities may appeal to different market investors, thus making the overall package more broadly attractive.

2) Freddie Mac

Freddie Mac, originally known as The Federal Home Loan Mortgage Corporation (FHLMC) was chartered in 1970 by Congress. Its stock was held by the 12 Federal Home Loan Banks. However, in 1989 FIRREA revised the ownership structure of Freddie Mac so that it is now virtually identical to Fannie Mae.

Like Fannie Mae, Freddie Mac is a secondary market purchaser of mortgages from local lending institutions. It originally concentrated on serving the thrift industry, but now purchases loans from all sorts of lenders. Freddie Mac raises most of its funds by selling mortgage-backed securities.

While both Freddie Mac and Fannie Mae are privately-owned by shareholders, they are subject to the overall supervision and regulation of the Office of Federal Housing Enterprise Oversight (OFHEO), an office within HUD created by Congress in 1992. OFHEO sets public policy goals for Freddie Mac and Fannie Mae and imposes restrictions on their mortgage-purchasing activity to attempt to achieve these goals.

The vastness and importance of Fannie Mae and Freddie Mac can hardly be overstated. Together with a few other minor federally-related agencies, they either hold in portfolio or guarantee (in the form of mortgage-backed securities) about 43% of all of the outstanding mortgage debt in the United States.

c. Other Government Support for the Mortgage Market

1) Government National Mortgage Association (GNMA)

GNMA is a government agency—a part of the Department of Housing and Urban Development (HUD). Its principal activity is to guarantee payment on bond-like mortgage-backed securities (MBS), sold to investors by private lenders and collateralized by pools of FHA and VA home mortgages (and small numbers of mortgages guaranteed or issued by other government agencies, such as the Farmers Home Administration). The federal guarantee makes these securities more attractive to investors and hence reduces the cost of borrowing the funds. GNMA collects fees for its guarantees of these securities, and has experienced very low losses; it is self-supporting and requires no government subsidy.

The GNMA program has been quite popular; from the time of its inception in 1970 until 2002, over $2 trillion in mortgages were securitized with GNMA guarantees. GNMA guaranteed nearly $180 billion in MBS in 2002. However, because the GNMA guarantee is available only on pools of FHA and VA mortgages (and small numbers of mortgages originated under a few other federal programs), and not on conventional mortgages, and because relatively few borrowers currently want to obtain FHA or VA loans, by 2003 GNMA-guaranteed MBS accounted for only about 5% of all residential mortgages originated in the U.S. There has been discussion in Congress of authorizing GNMA to guarantee conventional mortgage loans, but no such proposal has been adopted.

2) State Housing Finance Agencies

A large majority of the states have created housing finance agencies (SHFAs) which attempt to support the housing market by borrowing money through sales of notes and bonds in the capital markets, and then by diverting that money to housing. The notes and bonds are tax-free, and therefore carry attractively low interest rates by comparison with rates on taxable instruments. A variety of techniques have been used to funnel the money into housing, including loans to lenders, secondary market purchases, and in some cases direct loans to borrowers or developers. Both single-family and multifamily housing is supported by most agencies, but the occupants must meet criteria dealing with family income, price of the housing unit, and the like.

d. Private Issuers of Mortgage Securities

The success of the mortgage-backed security programs of GNMA, Fannie Mae and Freddie Mac have stimulated many private lenders to issue securities backed by mortgage portfolios without the further security of a guarantee from GNMA or any other government agency. While the early private MBS were collateralized by home loans, during the past decade there have been many issues backed by mortgages on apartment, commercial, hotel, and other types of income-producing properties. Both traditional financial institutions and most of the principal Wall Street investment banking houses have become "conduits," issuing large packages of mortgage-backed securities, some exceeding $1 billion in size.

A variety of types of privately-issued securities have been backed by mortgages. Some, like those guaranteed by GNMA and described above, are "pass-throughs" in which the security holder receives a pro-rata share of all payments of both principal and interest made by borrowers on the underlying mortgages.

Under a more complex technique, known as the Collateralized Mortgage Obligation (CMO), the issuing lender sets up several different bands or "tranches" of maturities in the securities (e.g., 1–3 years, 4–6 years, and 7–10 years), all collateralized by the same portfolio of mortgages. The mortgage payments in the early years are used to retire the first band of securities, and so on. Some tranches may carry no payments of principal prior to their maturity; some typically have a higher priority in the cash flow from the underlying mortgage pool than others. As noted above,

Fannie Mae and Freddie Mac, as well as many types of private lenders, have issued CMO's. When they are collateralized by commercial mortgages, they are known as Commercial Mortgage–Backed Securities (CMBS). Because the different tranches appeal to different types of investors, they may be more readily marketable, and at a lower aggregate cost of funds, than single-class pass-through securities.

As mortgage-backed securities grew more popular and complex during the first half of the 1980's, issuers encountered a variety of technical tax problems. These problems were associated with the taxation of trusts (since mortgage securities are normally issued through a trust arrangement), the concept of original issue discount, and the requirement that the issuer have significant equity. In the Tax Reform Act of 1986 Congress recognized a tax-favored type of entity called the REMIC, or Real Estate Mortgage Investment Conduit. In essence, an issuer that elects to be treated as a REMIC is freed of this welter of tax problems. The REMIC provisions provided a new stimulus to private issuers of mortgage-backed securities.

e. Real Estate Investment Trusts (REITs)

A REIT is analogous to a mutual fund, except that it invests in real estate rather than in the stock market. REITs sell their own shares to investors, and in turn use the funds to acquire either equity (ownership) positions or mortgage loans on real estate, primarily of the commercial, income-producing type.

REITs were popular during the 1970s, but many of them failed during the latter part of that decade, and for a number of years few new REITs were formed. The concept gained renewed market interest in the mid–1990s, and many large and successful REITs have been created since that time.

3. Agencies That Spread Mortgage Risk

Anyone who makes mortgage loans or invests in mortgages must be concerned with the possibility of loss. *Losses arise because (1) the borrower defaults, requiring foreclosure, and (2) the property is not sufficiently valuable to cover the foreclosure expenses and outstanding indebtedness. Defaults and foreclosures also produce costs in the form of administrative time and effort expended.* In theory, borrowers who have personal liability on their mortgage loans might be sued on the debt, or for a deficiency after foreclosure, but as a practical matter it is rare for the lender to recover much by such suits.

Several federal agencies and a number of private mortgage insurance companies (PMIs) exist for the purpose of spreading mortgage risk, and thereby making mortgages more attractive investments. The proportion of all home mortgages that are insured or guaranteed by federal agencies and PMIs has varied from about 20 percent to 40 percent in recent years, with most of the total accounted for by the PMIs.

a. The Federal Housing Administration (FHA)

FHA was organized during the depression to encourage investment in residential mortgages. It is a federally-operated insurance company, a component of HUD, which promises mortgagees that they will not sustain losses in the event of mortgage default or foreclosure. FHA collects insurance premiums, creates reserves, and pays losses from those reserves. FHA operates a variety of programs, covering single-family, multifamily, condominium, cooperative, home improvements, and land development loans. When a default occurs and is not cured, the lender may, under most of the programs, either assign the loan to FHA and receive 99% of its outstanding balance, or may proceed to foreclose and acquire title to the property, and then transfer it to FHA for 100% payment.

FHA imposes limits on loan-to-value ratios under its programs; for owner-occupied single-family homes, the loan may not exceed 98.75% of the home's value if it is $50,000 or less, or 97.75% if the home is valued at more than $50,000. However, the borrower is also permitted to add the one-time front-end insurance premium (1.5% of the loan) into the loan amount, so that it is possible for the total loan to exceed 100% of the house's value.

In addition to the one-time mortgage insurance premium (MIP) of 1.5% of the loan amount, payable at closing, FHA also charges an annual MIP of 0.5% of the loan amount (not counting any portion of the loan that is used to finance the one-time MIP). This 0.5% is divided into twelve monthly installments and paid by the borrower along with his or her monthly principal and interest payments. The annual MIP must be paid for eleven years if the original loan-to-value ratio was below 90%, and for 30 years if the original loan-to-value ratio was 90% or above (as most FHA loans are). If the loan-to-value ratio was above 90%, the annual MIP is increased to 0.55%.

b. Veteran's Administration (VA)

The VA operates a home loan guarantee program for eligible veterans. Unlike FHA, which pays the lender virtually the entire amount of its loss when a foreclosure occurs, VA pays only a "guaranteed amount," leaving the lender with the risk of absorbing some loss. In effect, the mortgagee is assured of getting up to the "guaranteed amount" in addition to its recovery from the foreclosure process, toward the loan balance. If the property's value has declined so much that the foreclosure price plus the guaranteed amount do not equal the loan balance (including expenses of foreclosure), the lender will stand the difference as a loss. Such declines are uncommon, and hence losses to lenders on VA loans are fairly rare.

The "guaranteed amount" is computed on the basis of a statutory sliding scale adopted by Congress. For loans up to $45,000, it is 50% of the loan amount; for loans exceeding $144,000, it is the lesser of 25% of the loan amount or $60,000.

VA imposes no loan-to-value limits, and loans for 100% of value or nearly so are common. There is no legal ceiling on the loan amount, except that the loan may not exceed the appraised value of the house plus the "funding fee" described below. However, most lenders will not loan amounts in excess of about four times the maximum guaranteed amount, which is $60,000. Thus, VA loans above $240,000 are uncommon.

A one-time "funding fee" is charged for the VA guarantee, but it is insufficient to make VA's program actuarially sound, and losses are paid primarily out of appropriated funds. The "funding fee" varies with the loan-to-value ratio. If the ratio is 100% (no down payment), the fee is 2% of the loan amount; if the down payment is 5% or more, but less than 10%, the fee is 1.5% of the loan amount; and if the down payment is 10% or more, the fee is 1.25% of the loan amount. As with FHA, the VA fee may be added to the mortgage balance and financed.

c. Private Mortgage Insurers (PMIs)

Private mortgage insurers (PMIs) are corporations which insure mortgages in much the same manner as FHA and VA. Eight such companies are currently writing new mortgage insurance policies in the United States. Their claims payment approach is analogous to VA's, except that their "guaranteed amount" is generally between 20% and 30% of the loan balance at the time the claim is made. Again, a loss to the lender is possible but not likely. PMIs charge premiums, which are normally paid by the borrower. The usual premium is paid partly in cash at the time of closing and partly by monthly payments over the term the insurance is in effect. The maximum loan-to-value ratio is ordinarily 95%, but some of the PMIs have recently adopted "affordable housing" programs under which they may insure a loan as high as 97% of value.

B. Acts of Congress Preempting State Mortgage Law

Three important federal statutes preempt state mortgage law; they relate to due-on-sale clauses, alternative mortgage instruments, and usury.

1. Due–On–Sale Clauses

Section 341 of the Depository Institutions Act of 1982 expressly preempts state law which limits the enforceability of due-on-sale clauses in mortgages, and makes such clauses enforceable except in certain special cases. This provision is discussed in connection with due-on-sale clauses in Chapter VI, supra.

2. Alternative Mortgage Instruments

The federal agencies which regulate financial institutions have authorized, in recent years, the use of numerous new types of mortgage instruments which involve such features as adjustable interest rates, graduated payments, and the like. These new instruments are discussed in detail in Chapter XII, infra. However, this authority has extended only to federally-chartered institutions, while state-chartered banks, savings and loan associations, and credit unions, even if they have federal deposit insurance, derive their lending authority from state law and regulations. State regulators commonly attempted to issue regulations similar to those of the federal agencies in order to give their institutions parity in lending authority, but frequently their efforts were comparatively slow, were inhibited by state statutes, and contained limitations not found in the analogous federal regulations. The result was a lack of parity between federally-chartered and state-chartered lenders.

Congress addressed this problem in Title VIII of the Depository Institutions Amendments of 1982, known as the "Alternative Mortgage Transaction Parity Act of 1982" ("Act"). *It authorized all types of state-chartered financial institutions to make mortgage loans of the kinds approved by federal agencies for the equivalent types of federally-chartered lenders.* Thus, state law limitations on alternative mortgage loans became irrelevant except to the extent that they were broader than the analogous federal regulations. See Samlin, AMTPA– The Federal Alternative Mortgage Transaction Parity Act (Parity or Parody?), 54 Consumer Fin. L.Q. Rep. 129 (2000); Nelson & Whitman, Real Estate Finance Law § (4th ed. 2001).

a. Property Types Covered

To be covered by the Act, the loan must be secured by residential real estate, co-op stock, or a manufactured home. Thus, loans on commercial or other nonresidential property are not included.

b. Mortgage Types Covered

The Act covers all forms of adjustable-interest loans, whether the adjustment is explicit or is in the form of a renegotiation or roll-over provision. It covers loans with variations in term, repayment, or other features, and hence probably applies to GPM's. Shared equity and shared appreciation mortgages are explicitly covered. See *First Gibraltar Bank v. Morales*, 19 F.3d 1032 (5th Cir.1994) (Texas prohibition on reverse annuity mortgages was preempted).

c. Mortgage Clauses Covered

It is not clear whether Congress intend to preempt only the aspects of alternative mortgage loans that have some direct relevance to their "alternative" nature, or are all aspects and features of alternative mortgage loans preempted? For example, assume a state-chartered lender makes an adjustable rate loan that includes in its documents a prepayment fee clause. The applicable federal regulations permit prepayment fees, but state law prohibits them. Obviously prepayment fees have little to do with the adjustable rate feature of the loan. Is the Parity Act's preemption available to protect the lender in charging the fee? Several cases have held that the Parity Act applies, notwithstanding that prepayment fees are hardly an essential feature of adjustable rate loans and are unrelated to their adjustable character. *National Home Equity Mortg. Ass'n v. Face*, 239 F.3d 633 (4th Cir.2001); *Illinois Ass'n of Mortg. Brokers v. Office of Banks and Real Estate*, 308 F.3d 762 (7th Cir.2002); *Shinn v. Encore Mortg. Services, Inc.*, 96 F.Supp.2d 419 (D.N.J.2000). Contra, see *Black v. Financial Freedom Senior Funding Corp.*, 112 Cal.Rptr.2d 445 (Cal. App.2001), cert. denied 122 S. Ct. 2662 (2002); *Glukowsky v. Equity One, Inc.*, 821 A.2d 485 (N.J.Super.A.D.2003).

In 2002 OTS reversed the effect of these cases for independent (non-bank, non-thrift) lenders, such as mortgage bankers and state-chartered loan companies. It declared by regulation (12 C.F.R. § 560.222, effective Jan. 1, 2003) that Parity Act preemption would not apply to the use of late fees and prepayment fees by such lenders. (The preemption was left in effect for thrift institutions directly regulated by OTS.) The OTS action was apparently motivated by the desire to allow state and local "predatory lending" laws to govern independent lenders' use of late fees and prepayment fees. The court upheld the OTS decision in *National Home Equity Mortg. Ass'n v. Office of Thrift Supervision*, 271 F.Supp.2d 264 (D.D.C.2003), finding that OTS acted within its statutory authority and not arbitrarily or capriciously.

d. Lenders Covered

All depository institutions, HUD–approved lenders, and persons regularly in the business of extending credit on the security of property of the types mentioned in (a) above, are covered. Note that this includes mortgage bankers and similar businesses which are typically unregulated by either state or federal law. Transferees on the secondary mortgage market from these lenders are also covered.

e. Federal Regulations Applicable

State-chartered banks must conform to the regulations of the OCC; state credit unions must conform to the regulations of the NCUA. All other lenders (including both savings associations and unregulated lenders such as mortgage bankers) must conform to the OTS's regulations.

f. Reimposition of State Law

The federal statute permitted any state to reimpose state law and avoid the federal preemption, provided it acted prior to October 15, 1985. Several state legislatures took this action; they include Maine, Massachusetts, New York, South Carolina, and Wisconsin.

3. State Usury Laws

Congress preempted state usury laws for first lien loans secured by residential property by § 501 of the Depository Institutions Deregulation and Monetary Control Act of 1980, as amended by § 324 of the Housing and Community Development Amendments of 1980; see 12 U.S.C.A. § 1735f–7. The Office of Thrift Supervision (OTS) regulations interpreting this Act are found at 12 C.F.R. Part 590. Under the preemption, there is no interest rate ceiling. The principal features of the preemption are as follows:

a. Lender Types

Covered institutions include those which are federally regulated or which have federal deposit insurance, HUD–approved lenders, members of the Federal Reserve or FHLB system, and creditors under the Truth-in-Lending Act which make residential real estate loans exceeding $1 million per year. Loans by other lenders are covered if they are eligible for purchase by Fannie Mae, Freddie Mac, or GNMA. See *Pacific Mortg. & Invest. Group, Ltd. v. Horn*, 641 A.2d 913 (Md.Ct.Spec.App.1994).

Individuals who sell or exchange their own principal residences, and who extend financing for such transactions, are also covered.

b. Property Types

The loan must be secured by a residential house or apartment building, a condominium unit or a share of cooperative stock, a blanket loan on a co-op building, a manufactured home, or land which is improved or is to be improved with structures of the foregoing types. A loan to finance conversion of a rental apartment building to a condominium is covered, even though the borrower is a developer who does not reside or plan to reside in the building; see *FirstSouth, F.A. v. Lawson Square, Inc.*, 816 F.2d 1236 (8th Cir.1987). It is less clear whether a loan to a developer to construct a new residential subdivision on raw land is covered by the statute; compare *FirstSouth*, supra, with *Bank of New York v. Hoyt*, 617 F.Supp. 1304 (D.R.I.1985) (statute applies to construction loans on property to be developed for residential use).

c. Loan Types

The loan must be secured by a first lien on the property, effected by a mortgage, deed of trust, or installment contract. For co-op apartments, it must be secured by a first security interest in the stock and proprietary lease. For manufactured homes, it must be secured by an interest having first priority. The proceeds of the loan need not be used as purchase money.

d. Charges Covered

The Act frees from state law limitations the following: interest, discount points, and finance charges. It does not apply to state statutes governing prepayment penalties, attorneys' fees, late charges, or other state law provisions designed to protect borrowers. See *Grunbeck v. Dime Savings Bank*, 74 F.3d 331 (1st Cir.1996), noted 30 Suffolk U.L.Rev. 917 (1997) (federal statute does not preempt the application of New Hampshire statute prohibiting the charging of "interest on interest.")

e. Reimposition of State Law

The Act's preemption was ended in any state which adopted a law, between April 1, 1980 and April 1, 1983, stating that it did not want the preemption to apply to loans made in that state. Even if such a law was enacted, any loan or loan commitment made during the Act's effective period in that state continued to be binding at the higher rate. Any rollover loan made during the effective period may be rolled over later at a rate in excess of state law if its terms provide for an interest rate increase at the time of rollover. Even after April 1, 1983, a state may enact a law limiting discount points or other non-interest loan charges, and may thereby reimpose state law to that extent.

States which enacted statutes reimposing state usury law, thus overriding the federal preemption in whole or in part, include Colorado, Georgia, Hawaii, Idaho, Kansas, Maine, Massachusetts, Minnesota, Nebraska, North Carolina, South Carolina, South Dakota, and Wisconsin.

4. Mortgage Foreclosure Procedures

The concept of a general federal preemption of state mortgage foreclosure procedures has been discussed for many years, but has never been adopted by Congress. However, there are two statutes providing for foreclosure of mortgages held by the Department of Housing and Urban Development. The Multifamily Mortgage Foreclosure Act, enacted in 1981, created a federally-prescribed nonjudicial foreclosure process for HUD-held loans on multifamily housing projects. See 12 U.S.C.A. §§ 3701–17. In 1994 a similar act applicable to HUD-held single-family mortgages was enacted. 12 U.S.C.A. §§ 3751–68. These two acts both provide for appointment of a federal foreclosure trustee, a procedure that is available even in states normally permitting only judicial foreclosure. They give the borrower only a 21–day notice prior to foreclosure. Single-family home mortgagors are given a right one time each year to cure a default. The acts preempt any state antideficiency statutes, giving the government an absolute right to a deficiency judgment.

C. Preemption of State Law by Federal Agency Regulations

When mortgage loans are made by institutions which are chartered or regulated by federal agencies, those institutions may be free of state law, either because (1) there are specific contrary federal regulations, or (2) there is a general federal preemption as a result of pervasive federal control. There are many examples of such preemption; a few of them are identified below. See Duncan, The Course of Federal Pre-emption of State Banking Law, 18 Ann. Rev. Banking L. 221 (1999).

1. Redlining and Mortgage Disclosure

Federal law includes the Home Mortgage Disclosure Act (HMDA), the Equal Credit Opportunity Act (ECOA), and the Community Reinvestment Act

(CRA). The Office of Thrift Supervision (OTS) has adopted detailed regulations governing record-keeping, reporting, and examination for all federally-insured savings associations. See 12 C.F.R. Part 528.

a. OTS

OTS regulations preempt any state law with respect to procedure, record-keeping, and reporting; *Conference of Federal Savings & Loan Ass'ns v. Stein*, 604 F.2d 1256 (9th Cir.1979), aff'd 445 U.S. 921 (1980) (mem. opinion). See generally Note, State Regulation of Federally Chartered Financial Institutions: Washington's Anti–Redlining Act, 54 Wash.L.Rev. 339 (1979).

b. National Banks

For national banks, which are not subject to the OTS detailed record-keeping regulations, the HMDA nevertheless preempts state law with respect to record-keeping and disclosure. *National State Bank of Elizabeth v. Long*, 630 F.2d 981 (3d Cir.1980).

c. Substantive State Law

These cases do not hold the substantive state prohibitions against redlining or lending discrimination to be preempted; the *Long* case, supra, expressly holds state substantive law can be enforced by federal officials.

2. Cradle–to–Grave Preemption

Numerous cases hold that the Office of Thrift Supervision (OTS) regulations "occupy the field" of federal savings and loan operations and regulate them "from cradle to grave," leaving no room for the operation of state law. See California v. Coast Federal Savings & Loan Ass'n, 98 F.Supp. 311 (S.D.Cal.1951); Kupiec v. Republic Federal Savings & Loan Ass'n, 512 F.2d 147 (7th Cir.1975). There is no doubt that internal governance of federally-chartered institutions is indeed fully preempted by federal law; see Ideal Fed. Sav. Bank v. Murphy, 663 A.2d 1272 (Md.App.1995) (manner of election of board of directors); Federal Home Loan Bank Board v. Empie, 628 F.Supp. 223 (W.D.Okl.1983) (right of institution to advertise as a "bank" in violation of state law).

These cases, however, deal with internal corporate operations, relations with members and employees, etc., and should not be taken to preempt state law dealing with mortgage contracts or other matters. See Nelson & Whitman Real Estate Finance Law § 11.6 (4th ed.2001); *Fenning v. Glenfed, Inc.*, 47 Cal.Rptr.2d 715 (Cal.App.1995) (claim of violation of state securities law by S

& L service corporation was not preempted by federal law); *Departamento de Asuntos del Consumidor v. Oriental Fed. Sav.*, 648 F.Supp. 1194 (D.Puerto Rico 1986) (federal regulation of S & L's did not preempt Puerto Rico's usury ceilings on consumer loans made by S & L's); *Derenco, Inc. v. Benj. Franklin Fed. Sav. and Loan Ass'n*, 577 P.2d 477 (Or.1978) (federal law did not preempt state law requiring federally-chartered S & Ls to account for profits realized on tax and insurance escrow accounts). The strongest case to the contrary is *Kaski v. First Federal Savings & Loan Ass'n*, 240 N.W.2d 367 (Wis.1976), holding that variable rate mortgages "directly affect[ed] internal management and operation of Federal associations and therefore require[d] uniform control" despite the fact that there was no federal regulation on such mortgages at the time the loans in question were made. This decision is of dubious validity.

3. Express Preemption by Federal Regulation

In 1975 the Federal Home Loan Bank Board adopted a regulation preempting state due-on-sale law with respect to loans made by federally-chartered savings and loan associations, and permitting them to enforce such clauses. The validity of this regulation was upheld by the United States Supreme Court in *Fidelity Federal Sav. & Loan Ass'n v. de la Cuesta*, 458 U.S. 141 (1982). While the specific regulation involved has now become obsolete because of the much broader federal preemption of state due-on-sale law adopted by Congress in 1982 (see chapter VI of this Black Letter), the Court's opinion in *de la Cuesta* is a broad endorsement of the principle that the regulations of a federal agency, when acting within its statutory powers, may preempt contrary state law.

The difficulty, of course, arises when the agency has *some* regulations governing a field (such as mortgage lending), but none that expressly conflict with or purport to override certain specific state laws. After years of controversy, represented by the "cradle-to-grave" cases cited above, the Office of Thrift Supervision (OTS) determined to clarify the preemptive effect of its regulation of federal S & Ls in 1994. Its 1994 regulation states that, "to enhance safety and soundness and to enable federal savings associations to conduct their operations in accordance with the best practices . . . *OTS hereby occupies the entire field of lending regulation for federal savings associations.*" 12 C.F.R. § 560.2(a).

This statement seems broad and absolute, but the regulation, after giving numerous examples of preempted activities, provides that state rules of contract and commercial law, real property law, homestead, tort law, and criminal law are not preempted if they affect the lending operations of federal

S & Ls only incidentally, or if they are consistent with the standards of safety and soundness quoted above. Of course, these are debatable standards. Presumably the usual rules of mortgage law are encompassed within the list just given. However, there is considerable ambiguity in this "clarifying" regulation, and it is likely to generate continued litigation. See , e.g., *Washington Mut. Bank v. Superior Court*, 115 Cal.Rptr.2d 765 (Cal.App.2002), holding that 12 C.F.R. § 560.2's reference to preemption of "terms of credit" preempted a California statute prohibiting the charging of pre-closing interest on a home mortgage loan; *Konynenbelt v. Flagstar Bank*, 617 N.W.2d 706 (Mich.App.2000), holding that 12 C.F.R. § 560.2 did not preempt a state law that prohibited lenders from passing along to borrowers the fee for recording a mortgage discharge; *Chaires v. Chevy Chase Bank*, 748 A.2d 34 (Md.2000), holding that 12 C.F.R. § 560.2 preempted a Maryland statute limiting loan fees on small loans; *Turner v. First Union Nat. Bank*, 740 A.2d 1081 (N.J.1999), holding that 12.C.F.R. 560.2's reference to "loan-related fees" and other OTS regulations preempted New Jersey statutory limitations on the charging of attorneys' fees to borrowers in connection with loan originations.

Note that one effect of the OTS preemption regulation is to render federally-chartered thrift institutions outside the reach of state and local "predatory lending" statutes. See, e.g., *Opinion P–2003–5, OTS General Counsel*, July 22, 2003 (New Jersey predatory lending law preempted). Since OTS has virtually nothing in its regulations that impedes predatory lending, the agency is likely to come under increasing pressure either to adjust the scope of its preemption or to adopt substantive measures designed to curb predatory lending activities by thrifts. In 2003 the OCC proposed to preempt state predatory lending laws for national banks. The proposal generated a storm of criticism from groups representing borrowers and consumers.

D. Loans Held by Federal Instrumentalities

When a federal agency or instrumentality holds a mortgage loan which is in default, is that agency's range of remedies restricted by state law (such as antideficiency legislation, periods of redemption before or after sale, requirements for confirmation of sale, etc.)? *The applicable law is clearly federal law. Clearfield Trust Co. v. United States*, 318 U.S. 363 (1943). *However, the content of the federal law may (or may not) be determined by adoption of the state rule.* See Nelson and Whitman, Real Estate Finance Law § 11.6 (2d Ed.1985); Alexander, Federal Intervention in Real Estate Finance: Preemption and Federal Common Law, 71 N.C.L.Rev. 293 (1993). From 1959 to 1970 and in a few later cases, the courts adopted a court-made federal rule (generally favorable to the federal government) in nearly all cases. See *United States v. Victory Highway Village,* 662 F.2d 488 (8th Cir.1981) (under federal common law, there is no statutory redemption). However, since 1975, several cases have opted for adoption of state law. See e.g., *United States v. MacKenzie,* 510 F.2d 39 (9th Cir.1975) (no clause in mortgage purporting to preempt state law; court found no need for uniform federal rule). Moreover, several decisions apply state law because the agency's regulations or the relevant documents signed by the parties appear to adopt state law; see, e.g., *United States v. Whitney,* 602 F.Supp. 722 (W.D.N.Y.1985); *United States v. Johansson,* 467 F.Supp. 84 (D.Me.1979).

1. The *Kimbell* Test

In *United States v. Kimbell Foods, Inc.,* 440 U.S. 715 (1979), involving competing priorities in personal property liens, with government agencies (FmHA and SBA) as claimants against private lien-holders, the Supreme Court adopted the following tests to be applied in determining whether the federal courts should adopt state law as the rule of decision:

a. Is the nature of the federal program such that uniform federal law is required? (Here, no, since the programs involve transactions individually tailored to specific borrowers, collateral, etc., and already taking account of variations in state law.)

b. Would adoption of state law frustrate specific objectives of the federal program? (Here, no, since the agencies can draft the agreements in question to protect themselves; they are individually drafted anyway.)

Note that the opinion is unclear as to whether this "protection by drafting" would include the ability to draft and enforce provisions contradicting normally unwaivable state law, or provisions which specifically adopt federal law.

c. Would a uniform federal rule disrupt local commercial relationships predicated on state law? (Here, yes, since normal expectations about lien priorities would suddenly be frustrated if the federal government became involved.)

Hence, the Court concluded that the federal rule of decision in these cases should be state law. Note that most or all of these same considerations appear to apply to federal programs which involve real estate mortgages.

2. Post–*Kimbell* Cases

A number of lower federal courts have considered foreclosure questions involving federally-held mortgages after the *Kimbell* case. The results have varied. Several have applied *Kimbell* and developed a federal common-law rule more favorable to the government than state law; see *United States v. Landmark Park & Assoc.*, 795 F.2d 683 (8th Cir.1986) (perfection of assignment of rents). A good summary of cases involving preemption of state antideficiency statutes is found in *U.S. v. Rezzonico*, 32 F.Supp.2d 1112 (D.Ariz.1998). Perhaps the most extreme case is *Rust v. Johnson*, 597 F.2d 174 (9th Cir.1979), in which a Fannie Mae mortgage was held to be protected against extinction by the foreclosure of a (normally prior) city special assessment lien for street paving. *Kimbell* was distinguished on the ground that Fannie Mae does not operate local offices and does not individually negotiate the mortgages it buys, unlike SBA and FmHA.

Other cases have applied the *Kimbell* analysis and have adopted state law as the rule of decision on the ground that no important federal interest would be frustrated by doing so. See, e.g., *United States v. Irby*, 618 F.2d 352 (5th Cir.1980) (state rule as to conduct of foreclosure sale of leasehold interest); *United States v. Pastos*, 781 F.2d 747 (9th Cir.1986); (state redemption statute adopted); *Small Business Administration v. Bubert*, 61 B.R. 362 (W.D.Tex.1986) (state homestead exemption adopted). Note that all of the cases adopting state law seem to involve federal agencies with local offices, such as FHA, VA, SBA, and FmHA. None involve the secondary market agencies, Fannie Mae and Freddie Mac, which operate only on a nationwide, mass-purchase basis.

3. Ability of Secondary Market Agencies to Preempt State Law

A few cases treat Fannie Mae in foreclosure as having the same sort of federal interests as those of the government itself, despite the fact that Fannie Mae is really a federally-chartered private corporation. See *Rust v. Johnson,* supra. This position is highly debatable. Moreover, these agencies have thus far avoided enactment of specific regulations designed to preempt state law. Perhaps the agencies have been reluctant to test their own authority. While this area is extremely speculative, one case suggests some preemptive power may exist. In *Consolidated Farmers Mutual Insurance Co. v. Anchor Savings Ass'n*, No. 78–1871 (10th Cir., June 10, 1980, unpublished), the plaintiffs sued Freddie Mac for violations of state antitrust laws in its procedures for approving hazard insurance companies. The court held for Freddie Mac on the ground that its charter act provides: "The corporation shall be entitled to all immunities and priorities to which it would be entitled if it were the United States. . . . " Arguably this grant of "immunities and priorities" could include the power to regulate contrary to state law.

An opposing view is suggested by the decision in *Federal Home Loan Mortgage Corp. v. Dutch Lane Assoc.*, 810 F. Supp. 86 (S.D.N.Y.1992), holding that Freddie

Mac, when foreclosing judicially in federal court, was still required to comply with the notice provisions of New York state foreclosure law.

REVIEW QUESTIONS

1. T or F   The Federal Home Mortgage Banks make a substantial number of residential mortgage loans to consumers.

2. T or F   The Government National Mortgage Association (GNMA) is a substantial originator of federally subsidized mortgage loans to low and moderate income residential purchasers.

3. T or F   A mortgagee under a loan guaranteed by the Veteran's Administration (VA) is subject to greater financial risk than it would be under a Federal Housing Administration (FHA) insured loan.

4.   Where do Fannie Mae and Freddie Mac raise the capital that allows them to purchase mortgages on the secondary market?

5.   In State X, Friendly Savings and Loan Association, a state-chartered entity, wishes to make graduated payment adjustable rate mortgages (GPARMs) on residential real estate, but thus far, its state regulatory agency has not authorized such mortgages. The Office of Thrift Supervision (OTS) has approved such mortgages by federally chartered savings and loan associations. What are Friendly's rights? Explain.

6.   The law of State X invalidates any mortgage that secures a usurious debt. Friendly Savings and Loan Association (Friendly), a state-chartered but federally insured institution, has just commenced a judicial foreclosure action on a residential first mortgage executed in January, 1981. Mortgagor defended that the mortgage was invalid because the mortgage debt was usurious. Assuming that the mortgage interest rate did, in fact, violate the state usury law, how should the court rule on a motion to dismiss the counterclaim?

XII

Alternative Mortgage Loan Instruments

■ ANALYSIS

A. **Mortgage Forms and "Affordability"**
1. Graduated Payment Mortgage (GPM)
2. Mortgage Buy–Downs and Pledged Accounts
3. The Growing–Equity Mortgage (GEM)
4. The Shared–Equity Mortgage (SEM)
5. The Reverse Annuity Mortgage (RAM)

B. **Mortgage Forms and the "Portfolio Lag" Problem**
1. The Adjustable Rate Mortgage (ARM)
2. The Shared Appreciation Mortgage (SAM)
3. The Price–Level Adjusted Mortgage (PLAM)

Beginning in about 1980, both federal and state legislatures and regulators have authorized lenders to make a number of new types of mortgages which differ from the classic model of the level-payment fully-amortized loan. *These new mortgage forms are aimed mainly at home loans and generally have either (or both) of two principal objectives:*

- *To increase the affordability of housing by reducing monthly payments required by home buyers during the early years of the loan.*

- *To alleviate the financial squeeze which financial institutions experience when rising interest rates cause their cost of funds (essentially short-term interest rates) to exceed the return they are able to earn on their long-term mortgage portfolios.*

This "term intermediation" or "portfolio lag" problem caused major losses to most thrift institutions (S & L's and mutual savings banks) during the 1979–82 period. The new mortgage forms attempt to resolve this problem by giving the mortgage a shorter effective term, so that its interest rate will not be "locked in" over a long period.

This Chapter will examine the types of alternative loans authorized by the Office of Thrift Supervision (OTS) for federal savings and loan associations; the Office of the Comptroller of the Currency (OCC) for banks; the Federal Housing Administration (FHA); and the Veterans Administration (VA).

A. Mortgage Forms and "Affordability"

1. Graduated Payment Mortgage (GPM)

This type of loan carries monthly payments which increase annually by some specified percentage during the early years of the loan, and then remain constant thereafter. The increases are agreed upon when the loan is made and do not depend on future family income, interest rates, or market conditions. Payments in the early years under some plans are not sufficient to pay the entire accruing interest; hence, unpaid interest is added to principal, resulting in an increasing balance during the first few years.

Payments in the early years of a GPM are significantly lower than they would be under a standard mortgage of the same amount. Families of lower income can therefore qualify to buy houses. Of course, payments in the later years are higher than would be the case with a standard mortgage.

GPM home loan plans are available in a wide variety of formats. They may be made by banks, S & Ls, and most other lenders, and may be conventional (non-insured) loans or may carry FHA insurance or a VA guarantee.

Example: A borrows $60,000 for 30 years at 8.5% interest. A level-payment loan would require payments of $461.35 per month. If A instead gets a GPM loan insured by the FHA under § 245(a) of the National Housing Act, her payments will be as follows:

Year 1 $347.46

Year 2 $373.52

Year 3 $401.53

Year 4 $431.65

Year 5 $464.02

Year 6 & later $498.82

Thus, the borrower's initial monthly payment under the GPM loan will be $113.89 lower than under a level-payment loan. Of course, monthly payments in later years must be accordingly higher than under a level-payment loan, in order to fully amortize the loan over its 30–year term.

2. Mortgage Buy–Downs and Pledged Accounts

If a mortgage lender or investor is given a substantial front-end payment, it will be willing to reduce the interest rate which it considers acceptable. One manifestation of this phenomenon is the payment of "discount points" by borrowers to lender. The mortgage buy-down is another illustration of the same principle. *If a builder or seller is sufficiently eager to market a property, he or she may be willing to make a substantial front-end payment to the lender to induce the lender to offer the loan at a lower-than-market interest rate.*

In most buy-down programs, the interest rate reduction is on the order of 1% to 3%, and is scheduled to phase out (i.e., to rise to the market rate) over a period of 1 to 3 years. This sort of buy-down requires a smaller front-end fee than would be required if the interest rate were to be reduced for the entire life of the loan.

A pledged account is similar to a buy-down, except that the funds for the front-end payment usually come from a savings account owned by the borrower/buyer rather than cash paid by the seller of the property. The borrower may pay the amount in the account at the time of closing, or may "pledge" or assign the account to the lender under an agreement by which the lender can draw down the funds in the account over a period of time—generally the same period as the time during which the interest rate reduction is in effect.

3. The Growing–Equity Mortgage (GEM)

If a mortgage loan is made for a shorter term than the traditional 30–year maturity, the monthly payments are significantly increased. However, the average life of that loan will also be shorter than that of a 30–year loan. The average life takes into account not only the normal monthly payments, but also prepayments due to home sales, foreclosures, and other causes. The average life of a 30–year loan is probably on the order of 9 years, while that of a 15–year loan is perhaps closer to 6 years.

If a loan is originated at a discount (i.e., a front-end payment of the type described in 2. above), the impact of that discount in reducing the required interest rate depends on the expected life of the loan; the shorter the life, the greater the impact of the discount. Hence, a lender might be willing to make a 15–year loan (with a significant discount) at a considerably lower contract interest rate than a 30–year loan with the same discount. There has been a noticeable trend for lenders and borrowers to see this approach as mutually advantageous.

The concept can be carried one step further; the original payments can be based on a 30–year term, but the loan documents can provide for *regular annual increases in monthly payments.* Typical agreements call for increases of 4% to 7% of the monthly payment each year. The interest rate is fixed for the loan's life, so these additional monthly payment amounts are credited entirely to principal. Hence, the loan may be paid off in, say, 12 years even without considering prepayments or foreclosures. In effect, it is a 30–year loan with built-in gradual prepayments. Again, the interest rate can be significantly lower—typically on the order of 1% to 2% below the market rate for standard 30–year loans. The rate reduction is, in part, a result of the impact of discounting, discussed above, and in part a result of the normal term structure of interest rates, under which the market demands higher rates for longer maturities.

The GEM represents an attempt to increase affordability and also to mitigate the negative market impact of high interest rates, both by reducing interest levels and by reducing the period that a borrower is exposed to high interest. However, the GEM requires higher monthly payments than a 30–year level-payment loan.

a. The Biweekly Payment Loan

The concept of the GEM is carried out in a modest way by the biweekly payment loan, which has gained considerable market share in recent years. The borrower makes payments every two weeks, rather than each month. If the amount of the biweekly payment is one-half of the amount which would normally be paid on a monthly-payment loan, the result is that, in effect, 13 months' worth of payments rather than 12 are made each year. (There are actually 26 payments per year, each half of a standard monthly payment.) This additional payment results in a rather remarkable reduction in the term of the loan.

Example: Assume a loan of $100,000 at 12% interest, with monthly payments for 30 years. The monthly payment required is $1029. Now assume, instead, that the borrower makes biweekly payments of half of this amount, or $515. These payments will amortize the loan in 492 biweekly periods, or approximately 19 years. Thus, the loan term is reduced by 11 years.

The biweekly loan is of interest primarily to borrowers who receive their pay checks on a weekly or biweekly basis.

4.   The Shared–Equity Mortgage (SEM)

In a SEM, there are two owners of the property. One is the occupant and the other is commonly (but not necessarily) a relative who is willing to assist the occupant with the purchase. This co-mortgagor is entitled by agreement with the occupant to share in the appreciation which is realized when the property is later sold. In return, the co-mortgagor agrees to make some specific fraction of the monthly mortgage payments.

SEM's can take a wide variety of forms. When FHA first approved SEMs for its insurance program, it imposed the following requirements, which continue to be issues worth considering in any SEM arrangement:

(a) The co-mortgagor's proportion of monthly payments and of equity ownership must be the same. (The down payment can be allocated differently, however.)

(b) The occupant must pay at least 55% of the monthly payment.

(c) The occupant must have the right to buy out the co-mortgagor on 30 days' notice, with the price to be determined by an FHA-approved appraiser.

(d) Either party may sell his interest after giving the other a 30–day option to purchase it.

(e) The co-mortgagor may not force the sale or refinancing of the property except in the event of default by the occupant.

5. The Reverse Annuity Mortgage (RAM)

This mortgage form, intended mainly for elderly retired borrowers, involves the disbursement of the loan proceeds by the lender by periodic installments over a long time period. The borrower's home (presumably otherwise unencumbered) stands as security for the loan, but no repayments on a regular basis are expected. Instead, the loan will be repaid in a lump sum, including accrued interest, when the property is sold or upon the borrower's death. Thus the RAM is a method for elderly persons to receive a monthly income stream for living expenses by "using up" the equity in their homes, while at the same time continuing to occupy them. This sort of loan is also known as a Home Equity Conversion Mortgage (HECM). See Nauts & Bridewell, Reverse Mortgages–A Lawyer's Guide to Housing and Income Alternatives (1997); Hammond, Reverse Mortgages: A Financial Planning Device for the Elderly, 1 Elder L.J. 75 (1993).

The Texas homestead law had been construed to prevent homeowners from waiving their homestead protection in connection with RAM and home equity loans. As a practical matter, lenders would not make such loans in that environment. However, in *First Gibraltar Bank v. Morales*, 19 F.3d 1032 (5th Cir.1994), the court held that the homestead law's effect was preempted by the Alternative Mortgage Transaction Parity Act of 1982, discussed in Chapter 11 supra, thus making such lending feasible in Texas.

B. Mortgage Forms and the "Portfolio Lag" Problem

1. The Adjustable Rate Mortgage (ARM)

The ARM's objective is to shift some interest rate risk to the borrower, and thus to assist lenders in keeping their mortgage portfolio earnings up to market levels as rates change. *Under an ARM, the interest rate is adjusted periodically in accordance with fluctuations in some external index of rates on financial instruments.* Because of these regular rate adjustments, the lender views the ARM as the approximate economic equivalent of a series of short-term mortgages, each made at a current market rate.

Because they shift much of the risk of future rate fluctuations to borrowers, ARMs carry lower interest rates than corresponding fixed-interest mortgage loans. The spread between the two is commonly on the order of 1.5% to 2%, but will vary depending on economic conditions and on the terms of the particular ARM. See generally Browne, Development and Practical Application of the Adjustable Rate Mortgage Loan, 47 Mo.L.Rev. 179 (1982); Nelson & Whitman, Real Estate Finance Law, § 11.4 (4th ed.2001). Some of the matters which must be covered in the drafting of an ARM are as follows:

a. Frequency of Rate Change

While this point is entirely negotiable, many ARMs are written on the basis of an annual adjustment, and 6–month adjustment periods are not unusual. In many ARM loans, there will be an initial period of three, five, seven, or even as long a ten years during which the rate is fixed.

b. How Will Rate Increases Be Paid?

Three methods are commonly used to accommodate rate changes:

1) Increased monthly payments.

This may be unacceptable to some borrowers, since their incomes may not be high enough to accommodate the added obligation.

2) Lengthened term.

If the initial term is 25 or 30 years, as is usually the case, small rate increases can be handled by further term increases.

3) Negative amortization.

This means that unpaid interest is added to the principal; thus, the principal balance on the loan may rise rather than fall over time. This obviously increases the risk of potential default and loss to the lender, and mortgagees generally impose limits on the amount of negative amortization they will permit. There is good evidence that ARM loans with high loan-to-value ratios are riskier than fixed-rate loans with similar loan-to-value ratios. See Department of Research & Analysis, Office of Thrift Supervision, Mortgage Delinquency Rates for Portfolio Lenders: Some Factors to Consider (1997).

c. Index

The index provides a reference point for determining whether a rate increase will occur. Commonly used indexes include the following:

• U.S. Treasury paper, most commonly 1–year Treasury bills.

• The Office of Thrift Supervision's published average contract interest rate on purchase of previously occupied homes.

• The average cost of funds in the savings and loan industry, as published by the Office of Thrift Supervision, or the cost of funds in a particular Federal Home Loan Bank district, or of the particular institution making the loan.

Under the Comptroller of the Currency's regulations for national banks, the index must be readily available to and verifiable by the borrower and beyond the control of the lender. 12 C.F.R. § 34.22. OTS imposes similar requirements on federally-chartered thrift institutions; it provides that "any index used must be readily available and independently verifiable" and "must be a national or regional index," or some other index subject to OTS approval. 12 C.F.R. § 560.35.

In some cases, the loan documents may provide for use of an index that subsequently ceases to exist. In *Central Bank v. Colonial Romanelli Assoc.*, 662 A.2d 157 (Conn.App.1995), the index was specified as the prime lending rate of a bank that subsequently became insolvent. The court held that "When a variable interest rate is based on the rate of a failed institution, the trial court must determine whether the substitute rate is reasonable by examining the documents and testimony offered by the plaintiff."

d. Relationship of Index to Mortgage Rate

Most commonly the documents provide that the mortgage will follow the index rate on a "point-for-point" basis. That is, if the index rises (or falls) by one percent, the mortgage rate will also rise (or fall) by one percent.

Example: Assume the mortgage is made at 11.5%, and the index is the one-year Treasury bill rate, initially 9.0%. One year later, at the first adjustment date, the Treasury bill rate has risen to 9.25%. The mortgage rate will then be adjusted to 11.75%.

However, it is common for the *first year* rate (or sometimes the rate for the first two years) to be substantially lower than the rate which would be computed by using the stated "spread" between the index and the mortgage rates. Such an initial rate is sometimes termed a "teaser rate." Under this approach, there will be an increase in the mortgage rate as the second year, and perhaps the third year, begin, even if no change has occurred in the index. Thereafter, the mortgage rate will follow the index rate as explained above.

The purpose of "teaser rates" is to make the loan attractive to consumers, and to qualify them more readily in terms of household income. However, secondary market investors consider teaser rates risky, are extremely wary of them, and often place strict limits on the extent of "built-in" upward rate adjustment on loans they are willing to purchase.

e. Caps and Accumulation of Increases

The ARM documents may provide:

- A cap on the size of the regular rate increases (caps of 1% or 2% per year are common).

- A cap on total rate increases over the life of the loan (5% to 7% is common). A lifetime rate cap *must* be included in ARM loans on 1–to–4 family dwellings; § 1204, Competitive Equality Banking Act of 1987, 12 U.S.C. § 3806.

- That the lender may accumulate index increases which cannot be implemented because of such "caps", and apply them in later adjustment periods. (Note that some forms may be vague on this point. Ambiguities may arise, particularly if there are sharp fluctuations in the index rate over a short period.)

- A cap on the size of any increase in *payments* which results from rate increases. (7.5% per year is a common payment cap);

- Mandatory downward adjustments in rate if the index falls.

f. Prepayment

In many ARM documents, there is provision for partial or complete prepayment without penalty. This seems a fair arrangement, since it will permit the borrower to "escape" the loan if he or she feels that a proposed rate increase will exceed levels available through other lenders. However, there is no regulatory requirement that prepayment be "free," and some forms impose a penalty or permit free prepayment only within a fixed period (e.g., 30 days) after notice of a rate change is given.

g. Due-on-Sale Clause

The principal rationale of the due-on-sale clause in a fixed-rate loan is to give the lender leverage to compel an upward adjustment of the interest rate when the property is sold. This rationale is greatly attenuated in an ARM, since the rate will fluctuate with the market whether a sale of the property occurs or not. Hence, many ARMs (including the Fannie Mae–Freddie Mac single-family residential ARM forms) employ a much different due-on-sale clause than do fixed-rate documents. They typically permit acceleration by the lender only if the new owner fails to submit the usual credit information to the lender, or if the lender determines that the credit-worthiness of the new owner is unsatisfactory.

However, an ARM's rate will not necessarily track market rates perfectly, both because of lag time between a market change and the adjustment of the loan rate, and because of the rate caps which are found in many ARM's. Thus, some forms continue to employ a more traditional due-on-sale clause which will allow the lender to "call" the loan irrespective of the proposed new owner's credit-worthiness.

h. GPM Feature

An ARM may include a GPM feature; that is, a provision that the payments will rise annually based on a prearranged schedule, even if there are no interest rate increases. Typically, these payments are not subject to any greater increase if the index rate rises; instead, interest rates in excess of those covered by the scheduled payments are accommodated by means of negative amortization.

i. Conversion Feature

Some ARMs are written with a provision giving the mortgagor the right to convert to a fixed-rate loan during a specific window of time—say, the second through fourth years of the loan. A fee must generally be paid at the time of conversion, and the resulting interest on the fixed-rate loan is the rate in effect on the ARM at the time of conversion.

j. Disclosure Requirements

The Federal Reserve Board's "Regulation Z," which implements the Truth in Lending Act, requires essentially all institutional lenders to provide a standard set of disclosures when an ARM loan is made to an owner-occupant of a house. See 12 C.F.R. § 226.19(b). At or before the time an individual is given a loan application or charged a nonrefundable fee, he or she must be given a copy of the "Consumer Handbook on Adjustable Rate Mortgages," published by the Board and the OTS.

The applicant must also be informed that the interest rate, payment, and term of the loan may change; what index or formula used in making adjustments; an explanation of how the rate and payment will be determined, and how they relate to the index; and a variety of other information about the lender's ARM programs. The lender must give the applicant an historical example, based on a $10,000 loan amount, showing how a similar loan made 15 years earlier would have been affected by rate changes.

k. Risk of Error

Because the adjustment of rates and resultant adjustment of payments and balances on ARM loans is complex, lenders have a significant propensity to commit errors. The legal risks to which such errors lead are discussed in King, Night & Tate, Risks of Errors by Adjustable Rate Mortgage Creditors, 111 Banking L.J. 55 (1995).

2. The Shared Appreciation Mortgage (SAM)

This form of mortgage gives the lender the right to recover, as "contingent interest," some agreed percentage of the property's appreciation in value, as measured when it is sold or at some fixed date (e.g., 10 years) in the future. In return, the lender is willing to charge a lower fixed interest rate than the market would dictate on a standard mortgage. For example, the lender might agree to a 6% fixed interest rate when market rates are 9%, and in return be entitled to 30% of the appreciated value of the property 10 years from the date the loan is made. If the property is not sold by the end of the agreed period, the increment in value is typically determined by an appraisal, and the borrower must pay it in full. Since there are no sale proceeds out of which the contingent interest can be paid in this situation, the loan agreement usually provides that the lender will refinance the property in an amount which covers the existing loan's balance plus the contingent interest.

In a shared-appreciation mortgage on an existing property, it is necessary to establish the property's value with a base-line appraisal at the time the loan is made. In *Johnson v. American Homestead Mortgage Corp.*, 703 A.2d 984 (N.J.Super.A.D.1997), the borrower successfully established that the based-line appraisal was performed negligently and erroneously; she was permitted to recover damages from the appraisal company in the amount that the appraisal was less than the property's actual market value.

3. The Price–Level Adjusted Mortgage (PLAM)

In a PLAM the loan balance, rather than the interest rate, is adjusted. The PLAM also differs from the ARM in that the index is a measure of inflation (e.g., the Consumer Price Index) rather than a measure of interest rates. Typically the loan balance would be adjusted annually, and would always move upward if any inflation had occurred during the previous year.

The contract interest rate under a PLAM would be very low—probably about 4% to 5%. Interest rates under standard mortgages today include a factor which represents the lender's expectations about future inflation. During periods of very low or nominal inflation (e.g., the late 1950's), rates were stable at 4% to 5%, since lenders did not build any substantial expectation of inflation into their rate structures. The PLAM takes account of actual inflation as (and if) it occurs, thus making it unnecessary to build inflationary expectations into the rate.

A PLAM will probably require that payments be adjusted annually to the amount which will fully amortize the new remaining balance over the remaining loan term. Payments in the early years would be very low, and would rise annually if inflation occurred. Thus the PLAM is useful both in terms of affordability to borrowers and of protecting lenders against inflation.

While the PLAM is an intriguing concept, it has not proven very popular in the United States. Little reference to PLAMs is found in the regulations of the federal banking agencies or in the case law. Perhaps the reason is that if high inflation persists for a number of years, the balance on a PLAM loan can rise to seemingly stratospheric levels. Perhaps most borrowers are quite averse to such a risk.

REVIEW QUESTIONS

1. T or F   The Shared Appreciation Mortgage (SAM) is advantageous to lending institutions in any type of economic climate.

2. T or F   The Graduated Payment Mortgage (GPM) is designed to protect a lender in periods of rising long-term mortgage interest rates.

3. How does a "buy-down" enable some home purchasers to qualify for mortgage financing? Explain.

4. T or F   The early payments on a Price–Level Adjusted Mortgage (PLAM) will tend to be lower than a GPM of the same original amount.

5. What is meant by "negative amortization"? Under what types of home purchase mortgage formats will it occur? Explain.

XIII

Common Interest Ownership: Condominiums, Cooperatives and Planned Communities

■ ANALYSIS

This Chapter focuses on three nontraditional types of real estate developments which are generally characterized as forms of "common interest ownership." Each, in many respects, is similar to a detached-house single-family subdivision. There are important differences, however. First, density is greater than in the usual subdivision because greater numbers of people are permitted in smaller physical spaces. Second, the owners in such developments are engaged in management and self-government to a much greater degree than in the traditional subdivision. Homeowners' Associations not only enact rules and regulations for the common areas, they also levy and collect the functional equivalent of public property taxes and assessments.

A. Condominiums—Basic Concepts

For owner-occupants, the condominium is the most popular and pervasive alternative to the detached single-family dwelling. Unlike the cooperative member, the condominium owner clearly owns real estate. Each condominium purchaser acquires a fee simple ownership in the unit, together with an undivided tenancy in common interest with other unit owners in the common areas. While condominiums, in theory, might be created without statutory authorization, today every state has legislation governing their creation, operation and termination. Most "first generation" legislation was patterned after the FHA Model Condominium Act, promulgated in 1961. Today many states operate under "second generation" and some under "third generation" statutes. However, because the FHA Model Act was and continues to be pervasive in its impact, our first examination of basic condominium concepts will utilize the Model Act as backdrop. Later in this section we will focus in greater detail on second generation legislation.

1. Creating the Condominium

a. The Declaration

The condominium is created by the recording of a Declaration. The Declaration will contain, among other things, a legal description of the underlying land, a description of the building or buildings that will comprise the project, a legal description for each unit, and a description of the common areas.

A very important function of the Declaration is to assign to each unit a fraction or percentage. This fraction can be utilized for three purposes: (1) to determine the unit owner's percentage interest in the common areas; (2) to calculate each owner's liability for maintenance of the

COMMON INTEREST OWNERSHIP | 549

common area and its improvements; and (3) to determine the weight of each unit owner's vote for such purposes as amending the declaration, creating by-laws, and determining assessments and voting for directors of the homeowners' association. Under most first generation condominium statutes, the fraction or percentage is the same for all three of these purposes, and is determined by dividing the initial value of the unit by the value of the whole project.

It is helpful to view the declaration as the *constitution* for the condominium, if for no other reason than that it is difficult to amend. Many first generation statutes require either absolute unanimity or an extraordinary majority for amendment.

b. The By–Laws

If the declaration is the condominium constitution, the by-laws are the legislation that govern the day to day operation of the condominium. *This document will, for example, provide for internal administration, building maintenance, budgeting, assessment, capital improvements, occupant control, and the makeup and governance of the owner's association. It normally is less cumbersome to amend than the declaration.*

2. The Common Areas

The common areas consist of all of the condominium project except the inside of each unit. Such areas include the land on which the condominium building or buildings are situated, hallways, stairways, elevators, heating and air conditioning equipment, parking areas, gardens, and "all other parts of the property necessary or convenient to its existence, maintenance and safety, or in common use." Model Act § 2.

a. Ownership and Management

While a board of directors of the owner's association will manage the common areas, ownership of those areas is held by all unit owners as tenants in common.

b. Restrictions on Partition or Sale

Each purchaser owns a specific condominium unit in fee simple and an undivided tenancy in common interest in the common areas. Normally a cotenant has the right to force a partition of tenancy in common property. This is usually accomplished by a court-ordered sale of the property with the proceeds being divided among the cotenants according to their percentage interests. Statutes governing condominiums prohibit partition of the common areas, as well as the separation of unit ownership from common area ownership.

Note that if partition were permitted, title to the common areas could wind up in a non-unit owner, who theoretically could prevent usage of those areas by the unit owners or extract a high price for the privilege of using them. Think of what life in the condominium project would be like if the only access to one's unit were by helicopter. Similar problems could arise if the unit owner was permitted to sell his or her common area ownership and retain the unit itself.

3. The Owners' Association

Each unit owner is a member of the owners' association. While this association can be unincorporated, it often is organized as a non-profit corporation. The unit owners elect a board of directors to manage the condominium. In large projects the board, in turn, usually hires a management company to handle actual day-to-day management.

Incorporation of the owners' association may be helpful in limiting a unit owner's personal liability for contractual obligations incurred by the board of directors. However, incorporation will not necessarily shield such owners from tort liability arising from injuries to third parties using the common areas. This is because those areas are owned by the unit owners, not by the owners' association.

4. Financing the Condominium

a. New Construction

The financing of a new condominium project is similar to the financing of most other real estate developments. For example, a developer of a rental apartment building will first secure a construction loan to build the building and, in addition, obtain a commitment by a long-term lender to "take out" the construction mortgage after the building has been completed. In the condominium context, the developer will utilize a construction lender in much the same manner and, in addition, will seek a commitment from a long-term lender. However, both the take-out and the role of the long-term lender differ substantially from the apartment construction setting. First, unlike in the latter setting, the long-term borrowers will be numerous third party purchasers of the condominium units and not the developer. Second, as each condominium unit is sold, the construction lender will release its lien from that unit so that the long-term lender will be assured of getting a first purchase money mortgage on the purchaser-mortgagor's unit. The take-out, in effect, is piecemeal.

Two important by-products result from this financing arrangement. First, because the takeout is piecemeal, the construction lender will be insistent that the developer "pre-sell" some of the units before construction funds will be advanced. Second, the long-term lender who provides the purchase money to numerous purchasers will take special pains to ensure that the documentation for the condominium will enhance rather than weaken the value of the numerous first mortgage loans it ultimately will hold.

b. Resale of Condominium Units

Resales of condominium units are financed in much the same manner as the resale of detached single family dwellings. A purchaser, for example, may (1) pay off the seller completely in cash; (2) assume an existing first mortgage loan already on the unit; (3) obtain third party purchase money financing; (4) obtain purchase money financing from the seller or (5) utilize a combination of the above methods.

Note that initially institutional lenders were somewhat reluctant to lend to individual resale purchasers because of the significant "front-end" commitment of legal time to master the complexities of the project's documentation. Consequently, the best opportunity for obtaining such financing would be from the lender who made the initial loans to the purchasers from the developer. More recently condominium documentation has become much more uniform because of requirements mandated by Consequently, institutional lenders are less reluctant to make isolated resale condominium loans, since they can be reasonably assured that the documentation is uniform and not detrimental to mortgage lender interests.

5. The Unit as an Independently Mortgageable Entity

When a unit owner defaults on his or her mortgage, a foreclosure sale purchaser will obtain title to the foreclosed unit and to the percentage interest in the common areas attributable to that unit.

Unlike the situation within cooperative ownership, no blanket mortgage threatens the title of those unit owners who are prompt in making their individual obligations. The mortgage delinquency of one unit owner is thus not of such direct concern to his or her neighbor.

6. The Unit for Real Estate Tax Purposes

In all states, statutes establish the condominium unit as a separate entity for real estate tax purposes. Consequently, the failure of one unit owner to pay real estate taxes will result only in the foreclosure of the tax lien on that unit and its percentage interest in the common areas and will not affect title to other units in the condominium.

7.   Delinquency in Payment of Assessments

Two consequences flow from failure to promptly pay assessments levied by the owners' association. First, the delinquent owner becomes personally liable for the arrearages and, second and more important, the owners' association has a lien on the defaulting owner's unit and accompanying interest in the common areas. The lien normally is senior to all other liens on the unit except real estate tax liens and any first mortgage of record.

Example: R acquired Condominium Unit 10 in 2002 and gave E a first mortgage to finance part of the purchase price. In 2003, R borrowed $10,000 from F, a finance company and gave F a mortgage on Unit 10. In 2004, R became financially hard pressed and did not pay several monthly assessment payments. The owners' association commenced a foreclosure procedure and at the foreclosure sale, the unit was purchased by the owners' association. (*Result:* the owners' association owns Unit 10 subject to the mortgage in favor of E, but free of F's mortgage. The latter lien is wiped out even though it was perfected before the lien for unpaid assessments).

8.   Mechanics' Liens

Mechanics' liens may arise against an individual unit as a consequence of labor performed for or materials furnished to that unit or the common areas. When labor or materials are supplied for one unit, any mechanics' lien that may arise attaches only to that unit and its accompanying percentage interest in the common areas. If labor or materials are supplied to the common areas, any mechanics' lien will attach to each of the units and its accompanying percentage interest in the common areas. An individual unit owner may release the lien as to her unit by payment of a percentage of the lien amount that is the same as the unit's percentage ownership of the common area.

Example: Owners' Association directed M to install a new swimming pool in the common areas. M installed the pool but was not paid. M filed a $100,000 mechanics' lien against each of the units in the project. R, the owner of Unit 10, desired to have the mechanics' lien released from her unit. Her unit's percentage interest in the common area is 2%. She then tendered to M $2,000 in cash.

(*Result:* M must release Unit 10 and its interest in the common areas from the mechanics' lien. If M actually later forecloses on the lien, the purchaser at the sale will acquire title to those units (and their percentage interests in the common areas) whose owners who did not proceed in the same manner as R.)

Note that an individual unit owner theoretically could wind up paying her share of a common area improvement twice. Suppose, in the prior hypothetical that R had previously paid to the owners' association her share of a special assessment levied to pay for the pool. Suppose further that the treasurer of the association absconded with the association's money. As a result M was not paid and filed a mechanics' lien. R, in order to prevent her unit from being sold at lien foreclosure sale, would be required to fork over her proportional share of the pool cost for a second time.

9. Liability for Common Area Torts

Injuries arising out of the maintenance and use of the common areas present complex liability and procedural questions. Potential victims include the unit owners, their family members, invitees, and strangers. Negligent acts which cause injury may be committed not only by the foregoing categories of persons, but also by the association, its officers, directors and employees. It may be tempting to place great emphasis on whether the association is incorporated, since traditionally the shareholders are not personally liable for a corporation's torts. However, in the condominium context, this conclusion is probably quite misleading because the title to the common areas is, as we have noted earlier, in the individual unit owners, who arguably have a legal duty to maintain "their" property in a reasonably safe condition—a duty they cannot escape merely by employing an association (whether incorporated or not) to manage the property.

a. Association Liability

Courts often impose on the condominium association the same duty of care that is applicable to a landlord in a traditional landlord-tenant relationship. Thus, the association, like a landlord, will probably be required to exercise reasonable care for the safety of the residents in those areas under its control. See *Martinez v. Woodmar IV Condominiums Homeowners Assoc.*, 189 Ariz. 206, 941 P.2d 218 (1997); *Frances T. v. Village Green Owners Association*, 723 P.2d 573 (Cal.1986).

b. Director's Liability

The trend of the case law appears to impose on individual condominium association directors the same standard of care normally required of other corporate directors. According to the California Supreme Court, "to maintain a tort claim against a director in his or her personal capacity, a plaintiff must first show that the director specifically authorized, directed or participated in the allegedly tortious conduct; or that although they specifically knew or reasonably should have known that some hazardous condition or activity under their control could injure plaintiff, they negligently failed to take or order appropriate action to avoid the harm. The plaintiff must also allege and prove that an ordinarily prudent person, knowing what the director knew at that time, would not have acted similarly under the circumstances. . . . Even if their conduct leads directly to the tortious injury of a third party, directors are not personally liable in tort unless their action, including any claimed reliance on expert advice, was clearly unreasonable under the circumstances known to them at that time." *Frances T. v. Village Green Owners Association*, supra.

Some states, such as California, have enacted statutes that prescribe minimum liability insurance coverage to be carried by the condominium association for the benefit of both the association and its officers and directors. When that coverage is in effect, officers and directors generally may not be personally liable for normal negligence in excess of that coverage. See, e.g., West's Cal.Civ.Code § 1365.7.

c. Unit Owner Liability

In theory, because unit owners own the common areas as tenants in common, they are jointly and severally liable for damage claims arising out of use of the common areas. However, this common law liability has frequently been ameliorated by legislation and judicial decision. For example, a few states by statute broadly immunize unit owners from personal liability for any damages in connection with the use of the common areas. More commonly, states, either by statute or case law, limit each unit owner's liability to a percentage of total damages equal to his undivided ownership percentage in the common areas. See e.g., *Dutcher v. Owens*, 647 S.W.2d 948 (Tex.1983); Note, 35 Baylor L.Rev. 189 (1983). For an excellent analysis of the foregoing problems, see Freyfogle, A Comprehensive Theory of Condominium Tort Liability, 39 U.Fla.L.Rev. 877 (1987).

10. The Condominium Governing Body as Legislator

The governing body of the condominium owners' association operates much like a "city council" for the condominium. Indeed, the combination of high density and the rule making power of the governing board may make the board significantly more intrusive vis a vis the unit owners than a city council is with respect to the typical homeowner. According to the most frequently quoted statement of this governing board regulatory function,

> inherent in the condominium concept is the principle that to promote the health, happiness, and peace of mind of the majority of the unit owners since they are living in such close proximity and using facilities in common, each unit owner must give up a certain degree of freedom of choice which he might otherwise enjoy in separate, privately owned property. Condominium unit owners comprise a little democratic sub-society of necessity more restrictive as it pertains to use of condominium property than may be existent outside the condominium organization.

Hidden Harbour Estates, Inc. v. Norman, 309 So.2d 180, 181–182 (Fla.App.1975).

In assessing the validity of a regulation or by-law enacted by the governing board or the association, one must focus on several issues:

a.   Were Applicable Procedural Requirements Followed?

For example, the failure to comply with notice and hearing requirements mandated by state legislation, the declaration or bylaws may invalidate regulations promulgated by the governing board. Alternatively, a regulation may fail because approval by the requisite supermajority of unit owners was not obtained. See e.g., *Ridgely Condominium Association, Inc. v. Smyrnioudis,* 681 A.2d 494 (Md.1996) (bylaw amendment revoking right of commercial unit owners to have customers and clients use lobby was not merely a "use" restriction requiring a 2/3 vote of unit owners, but rather a restriction on an "interest in property" requiring consent of all unit owners).

b.   Do the Governing Documents Provide Substantive Authority for the Regulation?

Unless the governing statutes, declaration or bylaws authorize the regulation substantively, it may be *ultra vires.* For example, a condominium governing board may lack authority to authorize unit balcony extensions into common area. See *Carney v. Donley,* 633 N.E.2d 1015 (Ill.App.1994). Nor may an association deprive an owner of his or her interest in the common areas absent authorization by statute, the declaration or bylaws. See *Makeever v. Lyle,* 609 P.2d 1084 (Ariz.App.1980).

c.   Does the Regulation Satisfy a "Reasonableness" Test?

Assuming the governing board's regulation satisfies the first two requirements, it does not automatically ensure validity. Many courts then impose a "rule of reason" under which the governing board must demonstrate that its decision was reasonable. See *Board of Directors of 175 East Delaware Place Homeowners Assoc. v. Hinojosa*, 679 N.E.2d 407 (Ill. App.1997) (prohibition on dogs in highrise condominium deemed "reasonable"); *Neuman v. Grandview At Emerald Hills, Inc.*, 861 So.2d 494 (Fla.App.2003) (rule banning use of common areas for religious services not "unreasonable"). While "in practice a certain amount of deference appears to be accorded to board decisions, reasonableness review permits—indeed, in theory requires—the court itself to evaluate the merits or wisdom of the board's decision." *Levandusky v. One Fifth Avenue Apartment Corp.*, 553 N.E.2d 1317 (N.Y.1990). In the cooperative context, New York applies a "business judgment" rule. Consequently, "so long as the board acts for the purposes of the cooperative, within the scope of its authority and in good faith, courts will not substitute their judgment for the board's. * * * [U]nless a resident challenging the board's action is able to demonstrate a breach of this duty, judicial review is not available." Id. Arguably, this latter approach may also find acceptance in the condominium context. See *Lamden v. La Jolla Shores Clubdominium Homeowners Ass'n*, 21 Cal.4th 249, 87 Cal.Rptr.2d 237, 980 P.2d 940 (1999) ("we adopt today * * * a rule of judicial deference to community association board decision-making that applies, regardless of an association's corporate status, when owners in common interest developments seek to litigate ordinary maintenance decisions entrusted to the discretion of their associations' board of directors").

d. Does the Regulation Violate the U.S. or State Constitutions?

When a city council enacts an ordinance, it must pass constitutional muster because it constitutes "state action" for purposes of the 14th Amendment. Does state action therefore exist when a condominium board promulgates a regulation? For example, suppose a condominium board prohibits a unit owner from displaying an American flag from the balcony of his unit. According to one court, such an action violated the First Amendment because "was sufficiently attributable to the state to constitute action by the state." *Gerber v. Longboat Harbour North Condominium, Inc.*, 724 F.Supp. 884 (M.D.Fla.1989). Nevertheless, there is relatively little authority on the state action question. As the condominium form of ownership continues to expand, this issue will inevitably become more compelling. According to one commentator, resolving the state action issue requires asking the following questions:

(1) Has the state, through direct aid or active participation, substan-

tially involved itself with the operation of the condominium? (2) Has the condominium association exceeded the powers granted to it under state law in such a way as to usurp traditional governmental functions? (3) Has the condominium association, acting within the powers granted by state law, taken on a governmental role which is not primarily directed to, and justified by, the protection or enhancement of the unit owner's investment interests?

Weakland, Condominium Associations: Living Under the Due Process Shadow, 13 Pepperdine L.Rev. 297, 330 (1986).

B. Housing Cooperatives

The members of a housing cooperative are shareholders in a non-profit corporation, and the corporation owns the fee simple title to an apartment building or group of buildings. Each shareholder is also a lessee of a particular apartment and the corporation is the landlord. The purchaser of such an apartment is thus an owner in the sense that he or she owns corporate shares and a "proprietary lease." Cooperatives are found primarily in New York City and a few other urban areas. They represent a minor percentage of existing housing projects and an even smaller percentage of new housing construction. Since the 1960s their importance has largely been eclipsed by the substantial growth of condominium development.

1. Financing the Cooperative

New cooperatives are financed with construction mortgages. When construction is completed, the construction mortgage on the project is either converted to a long-term loan or another long-term lender pays off or "takes out" the construction loan and takes a new permanent first mortgage on the cooperative property. In either case, the result is a long-term blanket mortgage on the cooperative property. The individual purchaser's down payment for each unit is the difference between the sales price of the unit and that unit's pro-rata share of the blanket mortgage.

2. The Unit Purchaser's Payment Obligations

Each month the unit owner will make a payment to the cooperative corporation consisting of his or her unit's proportional share of debt service on the blanket mortgage, real estate taxes, insurance and common area maintenance. The owner usually is entitled to deduct for federal income tax purposes the portion of his or her monthly payment that is attributable to interest on the blanket mortgage and real estate taxes on the building.

3. Default by the Unit Purchaser

If a cooperative member defaults in making the required monthly payment (rent), he or she may be dispossessed and the cooperative corporation may foreclose its lien on the member's shares in the cooperative.

In theory, it would seem much easier to deal with the delinquent cooperative member than the condominium unit owner. Failure to make the monthly assessment payment is, in part, a failure to pay rent and thus a ground for eviction under typical unlawful detainer proceedings. However, because cooperators often have substantial equity investments in their units, courts are hesitant to allow summary termination of those interests. Courts thus have refused to terminate cooperative interests without a generous grace period for payment of arrearages. See *Moss v. Elofsson,* 194 Ill.App.3d 256, 550 N.E.2d 1228 (1990); *520 East 86th St., Inc. v. Leventritt,* 486 N.Y.S.2d 854 (N.Y.C.Civ.Ct.1985).

4. Disadvantages of Cooperative Ownership

The members of a cooperative are highly interdependent. Unlike the owner of a condominium or a detached single family dwelling, the cooperative owner might suffer a complete loss of investment even though she has never defaulted in her cooperative obligations. This is so because if either the blanket mortgage goes into default and is foreclosed or the cooperative building is sold for failure to pay real estate taxes, the individual unit owner's interest will be completely wiped out.

> *Example:* A cooperative consisted of 30 units of equal value. There was a $2,000,000 balance on the blanket mortgage on the building. X owned Unit 5 and had never defaulted in making over five years of monthly payments. Because of bad management and embezzlement of funds by the manager hired by the cooperative members, the blanket mortgage went into default, the debt was accelerated and the mortgage foreclosed. (*Result:* X's interest has been destroyed. The building is now owned by the foreclosure sale purchaser.)

Note that each cooperative unit is not a separate entity for purposes of real estate taxation. Because the tax assessment will be on the building, and not on the individual unit, owners may face the prospect of being required to pay their defaulting cooperator's share of real estate taxes, as well as their own, in order to prevent loss of the entire property at a real estate tax lien foreclosure sale.

5. Resale of Cooperative Units

The longer a cooperative project is occupied, the more the blanket mortgage debt decreases and, absent a decrease in the unit's market value, the larger the unit owner's equity becomes. When the unit is placed on the market for resale, a purchaser who is affluent or is a retired person who realized a substantial amount of cash from the sale of a home, may be able to pay cash. Other prospective purchasers, however, must obtain financing either from the seller or from third parties. Institutional lenders have sometimes been reluctant to provide long term purchase money financing at least for two reasons. First, it is doubtful that the owner's cooperative shares and proprietary lease together constitute real estate for mortgage lending purposes. Second, even if this "package" did so qualify, or a lender would not mind having only chattel security, it would be in a much more vulnerable position than a junior mortgagee in a more traditional setting. In the usual senior-junior lien situation, the junior lienor will sometimes opt to protect its interest by paying off a senior lien in default. In the cooperative setting, however, the lender on an individual unit faces the prospect not of paying off a senior lien on the unit, but rather of being required to satisfy or at least make the monthly payments on the blanket mortgage on the building.

Moreover, note that after a cooperative has "matured", the majority of its members may sometimes be persuaded to replace the blanket mortgage on the project with new first mortgage financing. Because such an action would increase the amount of the blanket debt that is attributable to each unit, it would thus decrease the amount of cash a prospective purchaser would need to raise.

Several states, including New York, Illinois, New Jersey, California, Massachusetts, and Minnesota expressly authorize state-chartered financial institutions to make loans on the security of individual cooperative units. In addition, the FHA is authorized to insure unit loans in buildings that are subject to a blanket mortgage that is FHA-insured. The Office of Thrift Supervision authorizes federally chartered savings and loan associations to make cooperative share loans on the same basis as loans on detached housing. In addition, the Department of Veterans Affairs (formerly the Veterans Administration) authorizes share loans under its guaranty program. Finally, Fannie Mae will purchase cooperative share loans originated by local lending institutions.

However, the proper method of foreclosing on individual cooperative units is uncertain. There is authority that a secured lender may foreclose by private sale under § 9–504 of the UCC. On the other hand, there is also case law that holds that the proprietary lease is real estate, so that a collateral assignment of it is not within the scope of Article 9 and will have to be foreclosed as a real estate mortgage. See *In re McNair*, 90 B.R. 912 (Bankr.N.D.Ill.1988). See also 2 Nelson & Whitman, Real Estate Finance Law (Practitioner Treatise) § 13.6 (4th ed.2002)

In a few states legislation has solved the foregoing problem. In New York, a statute adopts the view of prior case law that cooperative apartments are personal property, but also mandates that security interests in them must be perfected by filing an Article 9 financing statement in the local office in which mortgages on real estate are recorded. Under the New Jersey statute, cooperative units are treated as a special type of real estate, with transfers of title and perfection of security interests accomplished through recordation in the county recorder's office. The latter documents are recorded in the same way as real estate deeds and mortgages and are indexed in a master register maintained for each cooperative development.

C.   The Planned Community

The Planned Community (PC) typically is a subdivision in which an individual owns a fee simple absolute in a specific parcel of real estate and a membership or shareholder's interest in a corporation or association that, in turn, owns and manages the common areas.

Pennsylvania, for example, defines a planned community as:

> Real estate with respect to which a person, by virtue of ownership of an interest in any portion of the real estate, is or may become obligated by covenant, easement or agreement imposed on the owner's interest to pay any amount for real property taxes, insurance, maintenance, repair, improvement, management, administration or regulation of any part of the real estate other than the portion or interest owned solely by the person.

68 Pa.Cons,Stat. § 5103. The planned community is frequently confused with the planned unit development. "The PUD contemplates an independent community within a particular zone that allows the developer to vary overall density; the proportion of multiple unit dwellings to single unit structures; and the proportion of industrial, commercial, and residential units with fixed ratios established in the zoning ordinance." Utz, *Common Interest Ownership in Pennsylvania: An Explanation of Statutory Reform and Implications for Practitioners*, 37 Duquesne L.Rev. 465, 470 (1999). In other words, the PUD concept is a form of zoning that could be used in virtually any type of common interest ownership, including the planned community and the condominium.

1. Cooperatives and Condominiums Distinguished

Both cooperatives and condominiums entail the ownership of one's unit. However, in neither form of development does the individual typically own outright the land on which the unit sits. Rather ownership, in the case of the cooperative, will be in a corporation of which the unit owner is a shareholder. In a condominium, the land is considered part of the common area in which all of the unit owners have an undivided ownership. In the PC on the other hand, each owner actually owns in fee simple absolute the land beneath his or her unit. Where the individual units share common walls with neighbors, they are governed by party wall agreements or easements for support.

2. Ownership of the Common Areas

The common areas and recreational facilities in a PC usually are owned by a not-for-profit corporation or associations, the shareholders or members of which are the unit owners. Access to such areas is insured by conferring on each unit owner easements of ingress, egress and use.

3. Government of the Common Areas

The basic governing document for a PC is referred to variously as the "Declaration of Covenants" or the "Covenants, Conditions and Restrictions." This document governs land use, spells out how assessments are levied , and describes how the PC is to be governed. The homeowners' association (the not-for-profit corporation described above) is responsible for managing the common areas. Usually this task is delegated to a small committee of owners or a board of directors who, in larger PCs, may hire a management company to carry out the actual day-to-day management chores. Where voting is called for by unit owners, one vote usually is assigned to each unit. The board makes and enforces rules and regulations concerning occupant behavior, architectural changes, and related matters.

4. Levying Assessments

The homeowners' association and, in some instances, the board of directors have the authority to levy assessments to raise funds for management, repairs and improvements to the common properties. An unpaid assessment constitutes a lien on the unit of the delinquent owner. Normally, this lien will be subordinate to any first mortgages on units. Thus, a purchaser at the foreclosure sale of an assessment lien will purchase the unit subject to the first mortgage. However, when the first mortgage is foreclosed, the sale purchaser, whether the mortgagee or a third party, will have no obligation with respect to assessments arising prior to the foreclosure sale, but there will be liability for assessments that arise after the date of foreclosure purchase.

Example: R owned Blackacre, a house in a PC. E, a savings and loan association, provided part of the purchase money to R and took back a first mortgage on Blackacre. R then failed to pay $1,500 in assessments. Then E's mortgage went into default and E foreclosed. E purchased at the sale. (*Result:* E owns Blackacre free and clear of the $1,500 assessment lien, but E will be liable for assessments arising after the sale and such unpaid assessments will be a lien on Blackacre.)

The priority of the association's assessment lien as against mortgages (particularly non-first mortgages) can be a complex and controversial issue, and has been litigated frequently. The precise language of the Covenants will usually be the determinative factor, although in some states statutory provisions dealing with assessment lien priority have been enacted.

Note that some courts hold the view that the covenants must provide an "ascertainable standard" for determining assessments. See *Beech Mt. Property Owners' Ass'n v. Seifart,* 269 S.E.2d 178 (N.C.App.1980). Such a requirement is imposed to protect owners against uncertain future liability. Commonly, the covenants will specify a maximum assessment amount, but will also include a provision making increases automatic if there is a rise in the Consumer Price Index or some other similar measure.

D.   Condominiums—Second Generation Legislation

A majority of states have adopted "second generation" legislation to deal with numerous problems that arose under the earlier statutes patterned after the FHA Model Act. The most significant example of second generation legislation is the Uniform Condominium Act, which was originally promulgated by the National Conference of Commissioners on Uniform State Laws in 1977 (1977 UCA) and, in a slightly revised version, in 1980 (1980 UCA). States that have adopted one of the above versions include Alabama, Arizona, Maine, Minnesota, Missouri, New Mexico, North Carolina, Pennsylvania, Rhode Island, Texas, Virginia, West Virginia and Washington. Several other states have enacted substantially similar legislation. The following material in this section will focus on how both versions of the UCA and other second generation statutes deal with selected significant problems that arose under earlier legislation. Certain other changes brought about by second generation enactments will be covered in the context of specific problems considered later in this chapter.

1.   Condominiums on Leaseholds

The literal language of certain first generation statutes specified that the declarants must be "owners in fee simple". Most second generation statutes, including both versions of the UCA, authorize leasehold condominiums. In fact, both versions of the UCA prohibit the ground lessor from terminating a lease because the rent has not been paid as to any unit owner who pays his or her proportional share of the rent. See 1980 UCA § 2–106; 1977 UCA § 2–107.

2. The "Flexible" Condominium

First generation legislation for the most part envisaged the condominium as one multiunit building. Today, condominium developments commonly are multibuilding projects consisting of duplexes, townhouses and numerous other multifamily housing arrangements.

a. Problems Under First Generation Statutes

First generation legislation made it extremely difficult to amend a declaration once it was recorded. Often unanimity or extraordinary majorities were required for amendment. For example, a developer who has filed a declaration that identifies nine buildings, but who winds up building only five, may face liability to the owners' association for assessments on "phantom" units in the four unbuilt buildings. See e.g., *Fairway Villas Venture v. Fairway Villas Condominium Ass'n*, 815 S.W.2d 912 (Tex.App.1991). This situation can create difficulties for foreclosing construction mortgagees as well.

Example: D, a developer, recorded a declaration for a condominium that specified a three building condominium project, with five identical units in each building. After building and selling the five units in the first building, the developer experienced severe economic difficulties and the construction mortgage was foreclosed. E, the construction lender purchased at the sale. (*Result:* E now owns ten units (not yet built) and those units' percentage interests in the common areas. Consequently, under some first generation statutes, E faces the unpleasant choice of either finishing the two remaining buildings and selling those ten units or doing nothing and, as owner of the ten "phantom" units, being liable for two-thirds of the common area expenses indefinitely. Certainly the owners of the five existing units will be hesitant to agree to an amendment reducing the size of the condominium when to do so would mean that collectively they would be responsible for 100% of the common area expenses rather than one-third.)

b. Second Generation Approach

Second generation legislation often specifically permits the developer or his successor to provide in the declaration that the condominium may be contracted or expanded within a time certain (usually seven years) after the filing of the declaration. Thus our foreclosure purchaser, in the above example, could avoid its costly dilemma by electing to reduce the condominium to five units. Moreover, under both versions of the UCA, because of "special declarant rights," a purchaser at a construction mortgage foreclosure sale can elect to hold title "solely for transferring to another person" and, during that period, avoid the original developer's liabilities. See UCA § 3–104 (both versions).

3. Allocation of Common Area Interests, Votes and Common Expense Liability

As pointed out earlier, most first generation legislation requires a single common basis, usually (as in the FHA Model Act) tied to the initial "value" assigned to a unit, to govern the unit owner's percentage ownership interest in the common areas, voting, and assessments for common area expenses. Second generation legislation, in general, seems more flexible. For example, the 1980 UCA permits each of the above allocations to be made on a different basis. "[A]ll three allocations might be made equally among all units, or in proportion to the relative size of each unit, or on the basis of any other formula the declarant may select, regardless of the values of those units. Moreover, 'size' might be used, for example, in allocating common expenses and common element interests, while equality is used in allocating votes in the association. This section does not require that the formulas used by the declarant be justified, but it does require that the formulas be explained. The sole restriction on the formulas to be used in these allocations is that they not discriminate in favor of the units owned by the declarant." 1980 UCA § 2–107, Comment 1.

Some second generation jurisdictions have, however, chosen to confer less discretion on the developer. For example, Minnesota, in adopting the 1977 UCA, prohibited value from being used as a basis for allocation. Rather, the percentage or fraction allocated to each unit for each of the three items (common area ownership, voting, and common area expenses) shall be in "such manner that each of the items is equally allocated or is allocated according to the proportion of the area or volume of each unit to the area or volume of all units, and the items need not be allocated the same for all purposes. The declaration may provide that a portion of each common expense assessment may be allocated on the basis of equality and the remainder on the basis of area or volume of each unit." Minn.Stat.Ann. § 515A.2–108(a).

4. Lien for Unpaid Assessments

Under most first generation legislation, first mortgages take priority over the lien for unpaid assessments. Both versions of the UCA reverse that priority to the extent of unpaid assessments due during the six months immediately preceding a lien enforcement proceeding. See 1977 UCA § 3–115; 1980 UCA § 3–116. On the other hand, some second generation states that have adopted the UCA have retained full first mortgage priority. See Minn.Stat.Ann. § 515A.3–115.

E. Conflicts Between Condominium Developer and Purchaser

Many of the conflicts that arise between the developer and the purchaser are not unique to condominium ownership. Construction failures, delays and defects are common to all types of new construction. However, because of the complexity of condominium legislation and the fact that the developer retains substantial control over the development even after a majority of the units are sold, the opportunity for disagreement and discord is enhanced.

1. Quality of Construction

Condominium, cooperative, and PUD purchasers are generally afforded the same sort of protection by way of implied warranty against defects in design and construction that is given to purchasers of detached dwellings.

Note that both versions of the UCA contain express and implied warranty provisions that are markedly pro-purchaser. See 1977 UCA §§ 4–111, 4–112; 1980 UCA §§ 4–112, 4–113. For example, a declarant impliedly warrants that the condominium will be "(1) free from defective materials; and (2) constructed in accordance with applicable law, according to sound engineering and construction standards, and in a workmanlike manner." 1980 UCA § 4–114(b). The UCA provisions are patterned after the warranty provision contained in the Uniform Land Transaction Act (ULTA). Courts have generally been protective of condominium purchasers in these matters. See e.g. *Jablonsky v. Klemm*, 377 N.W.2d 560 (N.D.1985); Diamond and Raines, Consumer Warranty Issues in the Sale of Residential Condominiums, 20 Real Prop.Prob. & Trust J. 933 (1985).

2. Rescission Based on Material Change or Failure to Meet Completion Date

Courts have held that the purchaser has a right to rescind a condominium earnest money contract based on material changes in the condominium project or the fact that the unit was not completed according to contract specifications within a reasonable time after the agreed closing date. See e.g., Barber v. Chalfonte Development Corp., 369 So.2d 983 (Fla.App.1979) (elimination of recreation facilities and imposition of further restrictions on unit decoration); Reider v. P–48, Inc., 362 So.2d 105 (Fla.App.1978) (failure to remedy defective doors and other construction defects within a reasonable time after contract closing date).

Note that the condominium purchaser's contract remedies in the above situations are virtually identical to other housing purchasers. See I supra. Moreover, both versions of the UCA afford the purchaser 15 days after the receipt of certain disclosure documents to rescind for any reason. See section E(6) of this Chapter infra.

3. Developer Liability for Assessments on Unsold Units

When a condominium development does not sell out rapidly developers sometimes seek to avoid or limit their payment of assessments with respect to unsold units. Generally courts, in interpreting first generation legislation, have been unwilling to permit the developer to do so. See e.g., FHA Model Act § 23; Brooks v. Palm Bay Towers Condominium Ass'n, Inc., 375 So.2d 348 (Fla.App.1979). 1980 UCA § 3–115(b) provides that "common expenses must be assessed against all the units in accordance with the common expense liability allocated to each unit." Comment 1 indicates that the developer's unsold units must bear their full share of common expense liability.

4. Developer Self–Dealing While in Control of Owners' Association

Condominium purchasers are frequently shocked to learn that the developer, while in control of the association, entered into "sweetheart" contracts with developer-owned or related corporations or other entities committing the association to unreasonable long-term liabilities. Such agreements, for example, may commit the association to long term use of developer-owned or controlled recreational facilities. Sometimes long-term management contracts are at issue.

a. Judicial Approach

While earlier decisions were unsympathetic to purchaser attacks on developer self-dealing, recent results suggest an increasing willingness to allow owners' associations either to rescind sweetheart contracts or to recover from the developer, for the benefit of the association, unreasonable profits gained from such agreements.

Example: D developed Avila Condominium in the state of Florida. While D was an officer and in control of the owners'

COMMON INTEREST OWNERSHIP

association, he caused the association to enter into a 20 year lease to use recreational facilities owned by D's spouse. After unit purchasers took control of the association, the latter filed suit against D to recover for the association's benefit the difference between the rent reserved in the lease and the fair rental value of the facilities. The association claimed that D had a fiduciary obligation to it and that such duty had been violated. D moved to dismiss for failure to state a cause of action. (*Result:* the association's complaint stated a cause of action. "[A]ny officer or director of a condominium association who has contracted on behalf of the association with himself, or with another corporation in which he is, or becomes substantially interested, or with another for his personal benefit may be liable to the association for that amount by which he was unjustly enriched as a result of the contract. However, no director or officer shall be required to return any portion of money paid by the association where it is shown that he received the funds with the consent of the association or with the consent of a substantial number of individuals comprising the association.") See *Avila South Condominium Ass'n, Inc. v. Kappa Corp.*, 347 So.2d 599 (Fla.1977).

b. Legislative Regulation

While first generation legislation generally did not deal with developer self-dealing, there is now legislation in many states aimed at such activity. Virginia legislation, for example, provides that no lease or contract is binding after the developer loses control of the association unless it is ratified by a majority of the unit owners. Va.Code § 55–79.74(b). Florida grants broad authority to the association to terminate leases and contracts entered into by the association while developer-controlled. West's Fla.Stat.Ann. §§ 718.302, 718.3025. Both versions of the UCA deal with such problems in two ways. First, all executive board members appointed by the developer have fiduciary liability for all of their acts or omissions as board members. UCA § 3–103(a) (both versions). Second, the association has the power to avoid management contracts, recreational leases and certain other contracts entered into prior to the time the unit purchasers take control of the association. UCA 3–105 (both versions). Finally, Congress has conferred broad authority on unit owners to terminate self-dealing and unconscionable contracts and leases consummated prior to assumption of unit owner control. See The

Condominium and Cooperative Abuse Relief Act of 1980, 15 U.S.C.A. § 3601 et seq; *2 Tudor City Place Associates v. 2 Tudor City Tenants Corp.*, 924 F.2d 1247 (2d Cir.1991)(cooperative association had power to terminate garage lease with developer's affiliate entered into prior to time when developer sold control of cooperative to unit purchasers).

5. Control of the Owners' Association

Developers are understandably reluctant to relinquish control of the owners' association when a significant number of unsold units remain. They may fear that a purchaser-controlled association will levy assessments that would reduce significantly their margin of profit in the unsold units. Or they may simply fear that association-enacted rules may make it more difficult to sell the remaining units. On the other hand, purchaser-owners obviously have a strong interest in being able to control the operation of the condominium as soon as possible.

While most first generation legislation is silent on the control issue, institutional lenders and secondary market purchasers generally insist that the condominium documents provide for purchaser control of the owners' association after 75% of the units have been sold. The 1980 UCA § 3–103(d) states that "regardless of the period provided in the declaration, a period of declarant control terminates not later than the earlier of: (i) [60] days after conveyance of [75] percent of the units which may be created to unit owners other than a declarant; (ii) [2] years after all declarants have ceased to offer units for sale in the ordinary course of business; or (iii) [2] years after any development right to add new units was last exercised."

6. Disclosure as Purchaser Protection

An increasing number of states, either as part of second generation legislation or by other statute, impose substantial disclosure requirements on condominium developers. Florida, for example, imposes an extremely detailed disclosure requirement. A prospective purchaser will be given at least five and perhaps as many as 20 documents, many of which will be lengthy and quite technical. See West's Fla.Stat.Ann. § 711.69. Both versions of the UCA require substantial developer disclosure. It takes the form of a public offering statement, which must include not only the declaration, by-laws and other condominium documents, but about 20 other documents or items of information as well. See 1977 UCA § 4–102; 1980 UCA § 4–103. Each purchaser is given 15 days from the receipt of the disclosure statement to cancel a purchase agreement without cause. See UCA § 4–106 (both versions). In addition, if the developer fails to comply with the above requirements, the purchaser is afforded the right to sue for damages and to recover a penalty equal to 10% of the unit sales price as well. UCA § 406(c) (both versions).

It may be argued that the average condominium purchaser (and some lawyers as well) will not be able adequately to understand the significance of such voluminous and complex disclosure material. Indeed, it is possible that such disclosure requirements protect developers more than purchasers by affording them a defense against later purchaser suits based on developer fraud, misrepresentation or failure to disclose. One alternative to the disclosure method of purchaser protection is to a utilize a governmental agency to examine each proposed condominium project and make a public report of its findings. Hawaii has taken this approach; see Hawaii Rev.Stat. § 514–34 et seq.

7. **Other UCA Purchaser Protections**

Both versions of the UCA contain numerous other protections for the condominium purchaser. These are briefly summarized as follows:

    a.   The developer's promotional material must specify what "need not be built."

    b.   Structural and mechanical components of buildings must be "substantially completed" prior to the recording of the declaration.

    c.   Before a unit may be conveyed, a certificate of substantial completion of that unit must be recorded.

    d.   Casualty insurance with a minimum coverage of 80% of cash value of the insured property must be carried and, if there is a failure to do so, notice must be provided to unit owners.

    e.   Class actions for violation of the statute, the declaration, and the bylaws, including punitive damages and reasonable attorneys' fees, are specifically authorized.

8. **Priority as Between the Construction Lender and the Unit Purchasers**

Priority problems arise when a developer collects earnest money or down payments from unit purchasers prior to and during the construction period, and the construction mortgage is subsequently foreclosed due to the developer's default or abandonment of the project. If the purchasers' rights to buy units and their rights to recover these deposits (their common-law "vendees' liens") are junior to the construction mortgage, the purchaser at the foreclosure sale (usually the construction lender) will take the project free of any obligations to the unit purchasers. The purchasers may be left with valueless personal actions against an insolvent developer.

a. The Deposit as an Equitable Lien

In most jurisdictions the condominium purchaser, as a contract vendee, has an equitable "vendee's lien" on the realty to secure the return of earnest money in the event the vendor-developer defaults. See 2 Nelson & Whitman, Real Estate Finance Law (Practitioner Treatise) § 13.3 (4th ed.2002).

b. Construction Mortgage vs. Equitable Lien

The equitable lien will be junior to the construction mortgage if it arises after the mortgage has been recorded or, even if the construction mortgage is subsequent in time to the execution of the purchase agreement, if the purchaser's contract is unrecorded and the construction mortgagee has no notice of it.

In the latter situation described above, the purchaser's equitable lien should normally prevail because the construction lender seldom grants a loan without specifically inquiring about how many of the proposed units are "presold." Thus, the lender will probably be deemed to have actual knowledge of those contracts.

> *Example:* P, a purchaser, executed a purchase agreement with D, a developer, to purchase unit 10 in a condominium project to be built. P paid $2,000 in cash to D at the time of contract execution. Several other similar contracts were executed. D delivered the contracts to E, a construction lender who had agreed to make a construction loan if a sufficient number of the units were presold. E then made construction loan and took and recorded its mortgage. The construction loan went into default before completion of the project, E's mortgage was foreclosed and E purchased at the foreclosure sale. (*Result:* E purchased the partially completed condominiums subject to P's equitable lien claim of $2,000.) See *State Savings and Loan Ass'n v. Kauaian Development Co.*, 445 P.2d 109 (Hawaii 1968).

c. Subordination of Purchaser's Equitable Lien

Construction lenders may attempt to avoid the result in the above example by insisting that preconstruction purchase agreements contain language subordinating the purchaser's interest to the construction mortgage. Sometimes such subordination agreements are effective. See *Glenview State Bank v. Shyman*, 496 N.E.2d 1078 (Ill.App.1986). It is arguable, however, that such agreements are of doubtful value. The purchaser will usually possess little understanding of the significance of the subordination language, and it will seldom contain sufficient details of the proposed loan to which the purchaser is being requested to subordinate. By analogy to the cases we examined earlier involving subordination of purchase-money land vendors to construction lenders, there is a good argument that such subordination language will be deemed too vague or unfair to enforce. See Chapter X supra; 2 Nelson & Whitman, Real Estate Finance Law § 13.3 (4th ed.2002).

d. Purchase Agreement Subsequent to Construction Mortgage: Argument for Purchaser Priority

Even where the purchase agreement is executed after the construction mortgage has been recorded, the purchaser may sometimes prevail by utilizing one of two theories. First, if the construction loan default is caused in part by the construction lender's failure to supervise the disbursement of loan funds and the general progress of the project, the purchaser might argue that she is a third party beneficiary of the construction loan agreement. Consequently, one remedy for the lender's breach of that agreement is to subordinate the construction mortgage to the purchaser's claim to the earnest money.

Second, the purchaser may be able by analogy to rely on the cases we examined earlier that permit subcontractors and suppliers to assert an equitable lien on any undisbursed construction loan proceeds when a mechanics' lien claim is unavailable to them. The purchaser, it would be argued, has at least as strong a claim to those funds as do material or labor suppliers, especially where the purchaser's earnest money has been used in the project, but construction has been completed without utilizing all of the construction loan funds. See 2 Nelson & Whitman, Real Estate Finance Law (Practitioner Treatise) § 13.3 (4th ed.2002).

e. Statutory Escrow Requirements

Many second generation statutes require the developer to hold earnest money deposits in escrow until construction is completed and the units have been conveyed to their purchasers. Both versions of the UCA mandate escrowing; the requirement applies even to money paid to the developer under a non-binding "reservation agreement." In order to give the purchaser easier access to the earnest money after developer default, the UCA specifies that such funds must be held by a financial institution in the state where the condominium is located. See 1977 UCA § 4–108; 1980 UCA § 4–110.

9. **Third Generation Approach to Common Interest Ownership**

Planned communities and cooperatives have traditionally been subject to relatively little specific legislation of the type that governs condominiums. This is especially true with respect to the nature of the owners' association and protections for the unit purchaser. There has been substantial concern that the pervasive adoption of second generation condominium legislation, with its attendant purchaser protections, will encourage developers to utilize the PUD and the cooperative in large measure to avoid the application of those protections. The National Conference of Commissioners on Uniform State Laws took note of "an economic decision by developers to avoid, when possible, additional costs imposed by condominium legislation in the form of disclosure, escrow requirements, or restricted practices." Uniform Planned Community Act, Prefatory Note. The Commissioners also noted that while similar to condominiums, PUD's and co-ops "have operated for years under the corporate law without the benefit of specific statutory enablement, and in virtually all states, without the regulatory burdens and consumer benefits available to condominiums." Model Real Estate Cooperative Act, Prefatory Note.

Because of the above and related considerations, the Commissioners in 1980 adopted the Uniform Planned Community Act (UPCA) and in 1981 the Model Real Estate Cooperative Act (MRECA). Both acts attempt to apply to the PUD and the Cooperative the same general regulatory format and public policies that are reflected in both versions of the UCA. This is especially the case with respect to the role of the owners' association and purchaser protections.

In 1982, the Commissioners adopted the Uniform Common Interest owner-ship Act (UCOIA) which consolidates the UCA, UPCA and MRECA. While UCOIA did not change substantively any of the foregoing three acts, it created "a newly defined term—the 'common-interest community'—to describe collectively the condominium, cooperative and PUD regimes governed by the three separate Acts. This new definition has eliminated the need for repetition in UCOIA of the numerous provisions of UCA, UPCA and MRECA that are identical in the three acts, with the remarkable result that the length of UCOIA is only slightly greater than the length of UCA alone." Geis, Beyond Condominium: The Uniform Common Interest Ownership Act, 17 Real Prop.Prob. & Trust J. 757, 758 (1982).

In 1994, the Commissioners substantially amended UCOIA. Among other things, the amended version expands the concept of disclosure to purchasers, provides for greater developer flexibility as to future expansion or modification of the development, and gives greater power to associations in dealing with unruly and disruptive owners and their tenants. Thus far, UCOIA or substantially similar statutes have been adopted in five states.

The foregoing four acts are designed to afford states maximum flexibility in dealing with common interest ownership. For those states that desire comprehensive and consistent legislation governing all three types of common ownership, UCOIA is an inviting solution. On the other hand, for those states that want simply a modern condominium statute to replace existing first generation legislation, the adoption of UCA alone probably is sensible. "Finally, in states where existing 'second' or 'third' generation condominium statutes are seen as satisfactory, but a need for additional certainty and structure is desirable for planned communities or cooperatives, the two Acts governing those forms of ownership are available. Following adoption of one of the three constituent Acts, it would be very feasible, by carefully considered amendments, to adopt UCOIA and thereby extend coverage to include all forms of ownership in the field." Uniform Common Interest Ownership Act, Prefatory Note, 7 U.L.A. 474 (1997).

F. Restrictions on Unit Owner Transfer

The documentation for most cooperative and condominium projects places limits on the ability of the unit owner freely to transfer her or his interest to another. Implicit in such restrictions is the assumption that unit owners have a legitimate interest in having financially responsible fellow owners and in being able to exercise some degree of selectivity in choosing their neighbors.

1. Cooperatives

In many cooperatives, control over membership takes the form of an express prohibition on the alienation of a member's corporate shares without the consent of the corporate landlord. While such a direct restraint would probably be deemed an unreasonable restraint on alienation in the context of limiting a fee simple transfer of real estate, it has been assumed that the cooperative member's proprietary leasehold is governed in this context by the law of landlord-tenant. Since courts generally uphold tenant covenants not to assign or sublease without the landlord's consent (see Hill, Landlord and Tenant Law 210–211, 217 (4th ed. 2004)), the tendency has been to uphold such covenants in the context of the housing cooperative. See Browder, Restraints on Alienation of Condominium Units, 1970 U.Ill.L.F. 231, 231–232 (1970). Nevertheless, while courts may enjoin or rescind transfers that violate such covenants, they will be extremely reluctant to allow enforcement to work a forfeiture of the member's ownership interest to the cooperative association. See *In re Bentley,* 26 B.R. 69 (Bankr.S.D.N.Y.1982).

Moreover, the power to refuse consent is usually limited by fair housing legislation and ordinances. New York legislation, for example, prohibits a cooperative corporation from withholding "its consent to the sale or proposed sale of certificates of stock or other evidence of ownership of an interest in such corporation because of the race, creed, national origin, or sex of the purchaser." N.Y.–McKinney's Civil Rights Law § 19–a . .

2. Condominiums

Because a flat prohibition on condominium transfer without the consent of the owners' association would be deemed an unreasonable restraint on alienation, (see e.g., Aquarian Foundation, Inc. v. Sholom House, Inc., 448 So.2d 1166 (Fla.App.1984)) control over transfer is usually exercised through a right of first refusal conferred on the owners' association or its board of directors. This right, also known as a preemptive option, gives the association the right to purchase the unit should the owner decide to sell it. Typically, the language of the right will give the association a fixed period of time (usually 15 to 60 days) to either meet the terms of an offer that the unit seller is otherwise willing to accept or to allow the proposed transfer. Such rights can be a serious inconvenience to owners who place their units on the market for resale.

a. Right of First Refusal as an Unreasonable Restraint on Alienation

The right of first refusal will be deemed reasonable and thus not to violate the rule against unreasonable restraints on alienation so long as the association does not utilize it to exclude prospective purchasers because of race, creed, sex, or national origin. See Browder, supra at 257–259; Comment, 44 Miss.L.J. 261, 270 (1973); *Chianese v. Culley,* 397 F.Supp. 1344 (S.D.Fla.1975). The use of such a right to exclude for racial, religious, sex, or national origin grounds almost surely would run afoul of federal and state statutes or local ordinances prohibiting discrimination in the sale of housing.

b. The Right of First Refusal as a Violation of the Rule Against Perpetuities

The common law rule against perpetuities invalidates contingent future interests in property which may vest more than 21 years after any life in being at the time of its creation. A right of first refusal, if unlimited as to time, literally violates the rule because the owner of the burdened property could decide to sell and the holder of the right decide to purchase after lives in being at the time the right was created and 21 years. There is substantial case authority invalidating such rights. *However, some states have by statute, either generally or with particular reference to condominiums, exempted rights of first refusal from the rule. Moreover, most commentators agree that the rule should not be applicable to such rights in the condominium context.*

Professor Browder, for example, suggests several possible bases for upholding a condominium right of first refusal or the type described above against a rule against perpetuities attack. Among these are arguments that such a right: (1) is only a contractual one until exercised and is thus not a contingent future interest in property; (2) is fully justified by the social values inherent in condominium type of housing and (3) is subject to the exception to the rule against perpetuities applicable to possibilities of reverter and rights of entry. See Browder, Restraints on Alienation of Condominium Units, 1970 U.Ill.L.F. 231, 255–56 (1970). See also Comment, 44 Miss.L.J. 261, 272–73 (1973).

c. **Prohibition on Leasing as an Unreasonable Restraint on Alienation**

Condominium documents sometimes prohibit owners from leasing their units. Such restrictions reflect the understandable view that owners in possession tend to be more directly interested in and committed to the project than tenants and absentee owner-landlords. An owner for whom the condominium is her primary place of residence and only real estate investment is more likely to take an active role in project's management and operation than her absentee-landlord counterpart.

There is growing support for the view that such restrictions are not unreasonable restraints on alienation. See, e.g., *Shorewood West Condominium Ass'n v. Sadri*, 992 P.2d 1008 (Wash.2000) (rental restriction permissible, but must be implemented by amendment to declaration, not bylaws); *Woodside Village Condominium Ass'n, Inc. v. Jahren*, 806 So.2d 452 (Fla.2002); *Seagate Condominium Ass'n v. Duffy*, 330 So.2d 484 (Fla.App.1976); *Apple II Condominium Ass'n v. Worth Bank & Trust Co.,* 659 N.E.2d 93 (Ill.App.1995). This result is even more likely where the prohibition on leasing is for a fixed time period and where owner occupancy is viewed as a major purpose of the project. See *City of Oceanside v. McKenna*, 264 Cal.Rptr. 275 (Cal.App.1989) (ten year restriction on leasing condominium in a publicly financed project deemed reasonable and enforceable by injunctive relief). See also *Worthinglen Condominium Unit Owners' Association v. Brown*, 566 N.E.2d 1275 (Ohio App.1989) (amendment to condominium declaration prohibiting leasing by unit owners is not *per se* unenforceable against unit owners who purchased their units prior to the amendment; restrictions must be judged by whether they are reasonable in light of the surrounding circumstances). See Grassmick, Minding the Neighbor's Business: Just How Far Can Condominium Owners' Associations Go in Deciding Who Can Move Into the Building?, 2002 U.Ill.L.Rev. 185; Randolph, Changing the Rules, 38 Santa Clara Law Rev. 1081 (1998).

G. Conversion of Rental Housing to Condominiums and Cooperatives

Owners of existing rental housing sometimes seek to convert it to condominium or cooperative status. The reasons for this are varied. Some, for example, argue that it is more likely to occur where, from a landlord's perspective, there is a weak housing market. Others point to rent control or the threat of its enactment, as the culprit. Finally, and probably most important, apartment building owners believe that they can obtain a higher price for a rental building sold piecemeal through the conversion process than through a single sale. In other words, for such owners, the value of the sum of the parts is greater than the value of the whole.

1. The Conversion Controversy

Opponents of conversion argue that the conversion process results in displacement of low and middle income groups to provide homes for those who can "afford to pay the higher prices which the converted apartments command. Indeed, studies indicate that the burden of conversion falls most frequently on low and moderate-income and elderly persons. At the same time, the conversion of a building . . . can lead to a substantial increase in property value, a result which proponents believe can be an important factor in curtailing the problem of declining urban tax bases. Proponents also point out that conversion . . . in inner-city areas . . . frequently results in the stabilization of the building concerned, thus providing an important technique for use in neighborhood preservation and revitalization." 1980 UCA § 4–112, Comment 1.

2. Statutory and Ordinance Regulation of the Conversion Process

Numerous legislatures and city councils have responded to the conversion process by enacting a wide variety of regulatory measures. In Silver and Shreve, Condominium Conversion Controls (An Information Bulletin of the

Community and Economic Development Task Force of the Urban Consortium, 1979) the authors identify legislative control of the conversion process under the three headings we summarize below:

a. Consumer Protection

1. Disclosure requirements.

2. Property reports, prepared by independent engineers, on the buildings and systems.

3. Compliance with building and/or housing codes.

4. Estimates of projected operating costs and other cost factors.

5. Minimum standards with respect to laundry, storage, sound transmission, and other qualities.

6. Limitations on the converter's control of the owners association.

7. Warranties and associated escrow accounts.

8. A cooling-off period following signing of a contract of purchase.

9. Penalties for the converter's failure to comply with the foregoing.

b. Tenants' Rights

1. Notification to tenants of intent to convert, and possibly a right to a hearing or even a requirement that a specified percentage of tenants consent to the conversion or agree to purchase their units.

2. Lengthy periods of notice to vacate (from 90 days to 3 years.)

3. A right of first refusal to purchase one's present unit.

4. A requirement that existing fixed-term leases be honored by the converter, although the tenants may be given an option to terminate them after notification of the conversion.

5. Relocation assistance, either by cash payment or by finding alternate rental accommodations.

6. Prohibition on coercion and harassment.

c. Protection Against Displacement

1. Conversion moratoria.

2. Requirements that vacancy rates or surpluses exceed specified levels before conversion may proceed.

3. Protection for low-income housing, either by requiring that the converter price a given percentage of the units for low-income buyers or by prohibiting conversions which will adversely affect the overall supply of low-income housing.

3. The Uniform Condominium Act and the Model Real Estate Cooperative Act

Both versions of the UCA deal with conversion in two ways—one to protect a unit purchaser and another to aid the existing tenant. First, the converter is required to provide additional information in the public offering statement, including an engineering report on the structural, mechanical, and electrical systems of the building, the converter's estimate on their useful life (or an express disclaimer of such a representation) and a list of outstanding code violations and the estimated cost of their correction. See 1977 UCA § 4–104; 1980 UCA § 4–106. Second, 120 days written notice of intent to convert must be afforded existing tenants, and for a 60 day period from the date of that notice the tenants have a preemptive right to purchase their units at the public price. If a tenant fails to exercise the option within 60 days, the converter cannot sell to another in more generous terms for a 180–day period. See 1977 UCA § 4–110; 1980 UCA § 4–112. Similar provisions are contained in the MRECA. See §§ 4–106, 112.

4. Legal Attacks on Condominium Conversion Regulation

The legislation and ordinances described above have been subjected to a wide variety of constitutional and related attacks, albeit without much success. Some of the more significant of these theories are described below.

a. The Uncompensated Taking Argument

Some have argued that conversion control legislation and especially those statutes or ordinances that place a freeze or moratorium on conversion constitute a taking under federal or state constitutions for which compensation is required. Most cases have relied on the theory that a property owner does not have a constitutional right to the most beneficial use of her property and that therefore, such restrictions are not so onerous as to constitute an invalid taking. See *Griffin Development Company v. Oxnard*, 703 P.2d 339 (Cal.1985); Silver and Shreve, supra. A similar analysis has been used to sustain regulations that require a specific percentage of existing tenants to consent to the conversion. See *Hornstein v. Barry*, 560 A.2d 530 (D.C.App.1989).

b. Equal Protection

It is sometimes argued that conversion regulation violates the 14th Amendment Equal Protection Clause or similar state provisions because it discriminates against certain classes of owners—namely, those who wish to dispose of their property by piecemeal sale. Normally, this type of regulation is not subject to "strict scrutiny" equal protection analysis, but rather is upheld if there is any rational connection between the classification used and a valid state purpose. Most courts will probably find that a conversion moratorium, for example, has some rational connection to the valid governmental purpose of ensuring adequate and affordable housing to its citizenry.

c. The State Law Preemption Argument

Some have been successful in attacking city ordinances regulating conversions on the ground that they conflict with or are preempted by state legislation. For example, a city ordinance that puts a moratorium on conversion may be found to conflict with state legislation that seems to authorize conversion, but merely requires notice to tenants as a condition precedent to conversion. Or, where the state has enacted a comprehensive set of protections for tenants in a conversion building, a court may simply find that the state legislature has "filled the field" or preempted the entire area so as to prohibit municipal ordinances dealing with conversion in any way. See *Claridge House One, Inc. v. Borough of Verona*, 490 F.Supp. 706 (D.N.J.1980) (one year local moratorium preempted by comprehensive state regulatory scheme). But see *Griffin Development Company*, supra.

H. The Time Sharing Concept

The past several decades have witnessed the significant growth of "time-sharing", a concept that permits a person to purchase an interval of a week or more in a condominium building in a recreation or vacation area. For the purchaser, interval ownership affords the opportunity to "own" one's own piece of a recreation area without the high cost associated with the purchase of a year-round condominium or vacation home. The purchaser presumably also avoids ever-escalating hotel or lodging costs. For the developer, the advantage is simple. The profit margin on interval sale is usually substantially higher than on the selling price of a non-time-share condominium unit. As in the conversion process, the developer takes advantage of the logic that in certain settings the sum of the parts will be greater than the whole.

1. Nature of the Ownership

Because time-sharing developed largely without the benefit of accompanying legislation, numerous methods of interval ownership have evolved. Some of the more common methods are described below.

a. Interval Estate

This form of ownership consists of "(i) an estate for years in a unit, during the term of which title to a unit rotates among the time share owners thereof, vesting in each of them in turn for periods established by a fixed recorded schedule, with the series thus established recurring regularly until the term expires, coupled with (ii) a vested undivided fee simple interest as a tenant in common in the remainder of that unit." 1977 UCA § 4–103.

Note that this form of ownership is also known as "interval ownership". The purchaser receives two distinct interests. First she acquires an estate for years for a time period in each year during which she is entitled to occupancy. This estate will vest annually for a fixed number of years, usually equal to the reasonable life of the building. Second, she obtains a vested remainder in the unit as a tenant in common with other interval owners.

Example: D grants, bargains, sells and conveys to P unit week No. 29, in Condominium Unit No. 311, Fairview Condominium, Boone County, Colorado, during the period from 12:00 noon on the first day included in Unit Week 29 as defined in the Declaration until 12:00 noon on the Saturday immediately following the day on which ownership commenced and commencing again during each succeeding calendar year until and including the year 2033, together with a remainder over in fee simple absolute, as tenant in common with other interval owners (as defined in the Declaration) of Unit Weeks in the above described condominium, in a percentage interest determined in the Declaration.

b. The Time Span Estate

The time span estate involves the conveyance to each purchaser of a percentage undivided tenancy in common interest in fee simple, coupled with a right to occupy the unit during specified times. This concept is also known as "time sharing ownership" (TSO).

Example: "D grants, bargains and sells and conveys to P in fee simple absolute an undivided .02% interest in Unit 311, Fairview Condominium together with the exclusive right to occupy said unit during week 29 as defined by the Declaration."

c. The Fee Simple Estate

The purchaser receives a fee simple absolute estate which is described as conferring the right to possession during a specified period each year. This type of ownership is explicitly recognized in some states by statute. See Utah Code Ann. § 57–8–6.

Example: D grants, bargains, sells and conveys to P, her heirs, successors and assigns forever Week 29, Unit 311, Fairview Condominium, said conveyance conferring on P the right to occupy said unit during Week 29, which period is described more fully in the Declaration.

d. Other Ownership Approaches

The past decade has witnessed the creation of a variety of methods of interval ownership. Some developments may combine ownership of an interval in a particular development with the right to transfer occupancy rights each year to other developments managed by the developer. Others may involve ownership of shares in a corporation that, in turn, owns the vacation project. The "owner" does not receive rights in a particular week or a particular unit. Rather, he or she acquires shares or a membership in that corporation together with a specified number of points. These points may be used to purchase the right to occupy a unit at a wide variety of resorts. Computer formulas that monitor supply and demand are used to determine how many points are required for any particular week or type of unit. Points may also be used in some cases to purchase occupancy for daily, rather than weekly periods.

e. The License or Contract Right Approach

Under this form of "ownership", the purchaser does not receive an interest in real estate, but merely a license or contract right to use a specific unit during a certain week or weeks for a predetermined number of years.

2. Some Problem Areas

Certain problems are unique to time-share ownership. Some of the more significant issues are considered below.

a. Limitations on the Right to Partition

Where the time span estate is utilized, each owner possesses a percentage undivided tenancy in common interest in the unit and thus each owner in theory has the right to force a partition sale of the whole unit. Consequently when this form of ownership is used, restrictions on the right to partition are contained in the declaration. Usually, the right is suspended for a period that approximates the reasonable life of the building.

While such a limitation on the right to partition is arguably a restraint on alienation, courts will probably determine that it is valid, so long as the exercise of the right is suspended for a reasonable period of time. Periods that approximate the reasonable life of the building are probably reasonable. See Comment, Legal Challenges to Time Sharing Ownership, 45 Mo.L.Rev. 423, 432 (1980).

State statutes also frequently impose limitations on the partition right. Consider the language of the North Carolina statute:

> When a time share is owned by two or more persons as tenants in common or as joint tenants either may seek a partition by sale of that interest, but no purchaser of a time share may maintain an action for partition by sale or in kind of the unit in which such time share is held

N.C.Gen.Stat. § 93A–43 (1999).

b. Bankruptcy of the Developer

Under the first three timeshare ownership methods described above, the purchaser receives some type of fee interest in real estate. Consequently, her ownership is not jeopardized by subsequent developer bankruptcy. However, where the ownership falls into the fourth category, developer bankruptcy in the past has sometimes proved to be fatal to the timeshare owner. To the extent that the purchaser's ownership right was characterized as merely contractual and executory, it was capable of being terminated by a bankruptcy trustee who asserted the power to avoid executory contracts under § 365 of the Bankruptcy Code. In response to this problem, Congress in 1984 amended § 365 to give the fourth category timeshare purchaser essentially the same protection in developer bankruptcy as is afforded an installment land contract vendee when her vendor goes into bankruptcy. In other words, the trustee's right to reject the contract of such a timeshare purchaser is subject to the latter's right to obtain his or her rights under the contract by completing payments under it. See 11 U.S.C.A. § 365(i).

c. Liability for Common Area Injury

To the extent that the first three methods of time-sharing ownership are utilized, the owner will have the same liability for injuries occurring on the common areas as that borne by traditional condominium owners.

d. Liability of Co-owners for Injury to Third Parties Occurring in Unit

To the extent that the time share involves, as in the interval ownership and fee simple absolute situation, the ownership of separate real property interests, the negligence of the owner of one time period in a particular unit probably cannot be imputed to owners of other time periods in that unit.

However, the time span method entails undivided tenancy in common ownership in the unit itself. Hence there is some danger that the negligence of the owner of one time period will be imputed to other time period owners. The individual owner, however, may be aided by the argument that where the injury is attributable solely to the independent act of a single person, that the latter alone is liable. See Comment, supra at 438.

3. Legislative Regulation of Time Sharing

Almost half of the states have enacted timesharing legislation. A significant number of the statutes are comprehensive in scope. See e.g., West's Fla.Stat.Ann. §§ 721.01–.28; Va.Code 1950, §§ 55–360 to 55–400.

Two model timeshare acts have served as the impetus and guide for much of the foregoing legislation. In 1980 the National Conference of Commissioners on Uniform State Laws issued the Model Real Estate Timeshare Act (MRETSA). This act is detailed and comprehensive and includes within the concept of "time share estate" any right to occupy a unit "during [5] or more separated time periods over a period of at least [5] years." MRETSA § 1–102(18). The drafters intended to include within the foregoing definition each of the four ownership methods described earlier. The Act's organization parallels the Uniform Condominium Act and extends much of the latter's consumer protection provisions to timeshare purchasers. In addition, the National TimeSharing Council of the American Land Development Association and the National Association of Real Estate License Law Officials (NTC/NARELLO) jointly drafted the Model Timeshare Act. The latter act is less complex and detailed than MRETSA and affords developers greater flexibility.

4. **Management, the Owners' Association and the Time–share Owner**

In theory time-share owners, as in the traditional condominium, collectively control the management of the project through an owners' association. The reality, however, is significantly different. First, because the economic stake of each undivided owner is usually relatively small, most owners seldom take the time to become active in project management. Second, owners of a particular unit may be scattered over several states and countries and only a small fraction of them will be in residence at a time. Thus, their ability to organize, oversee management and exchange information is limited. Consequently, professional management (almost always by the developer or its affiliates) exercises significantly more power than in a traditional condominium context.

MRETSA attempts to encourage owner participation by providing for initiative, referendum and recall so that owners more readily can change management or institute significant policy changes. See MRETSA §§ 3–115–117.

REVIEW QUESTIONS

1. T or F   The common area of a planned community is normally owned by the unit owners as tenants in common.

2. T or F   Resale financing is equally difficult for both condominium and cooperative units.

3. T or F   A unit owner in a particular condominium project is assigned a percentage of 5%, which percentage is to govern her voting rights, common expense liability and common area ownership. In all probability, she owns a condominium unit governed by first generation legislation.

4. T or F   A unit owner in a condominium wishes to sell his interest in the project swimming pool to a relative who does not live in the project. He will not be permitted to do so.

5. T or F   Because the owners' association governs the common area of a condominium, unit owners have no liability for torts committed thereon.

6.   A contractor who installed a new elevator in a condominium building and who was not paid, filed a mechanics' lien on the condominium property for $50,000. Our client, Mary, is an owner of a unit in the building. How can she make sure that she will not lose title to her unit in the event the mechanics lien is foreclosed?

7. T or F   Condominium legislation uniformly prohibits the creation of a condominium on a leasehold.

8.   What is meant by the term "sweetheart contract" in the condominium context?

9. T or F   Preconstruction condominium purchase agreements often contain language subordinating the purchaser's interest to the construction mortgage. Such language will be effective.

10.   How can preemption be utilized to attack local ordinances regulating condominium conversions?

11.   To what extent is management likely to exert greater control in a time share building than in a traditional condominium setting? Explain.

12.   In what particular significant way do both versions of the Uniform Condominium Act protect a condominium purchaser who decides after executing a purchase agreement that purchasing a condominium was not such a good idea after all?

13.   When will a condominium developer typically lose control of the owners' association? Explain.

*

APPENDIX A

Answers to Review Questions

■ I. CONTRACTS FOR THE SALE OF LAND

1. *True.* The check will probably be a sufficient writing to comply with the statute of frauds. It is signed by B, the party to be charged; it identifies the land; it stipulates a cash sale, so that no further financing terms are needed; and it identifies both parties. Thus, all essential terms are present in the writing, and S can enforce the contract.

2. *False.* The statement is correct as to an oral modification, at least if the contract as modified still involves the sale of land. However, an oral agreement to rescind the contract is effective; since no contract of sale results, no writing is needed.

3. In general, the acts mentioned (part payment, possession, and substantial improvements) are sufficient to constitute "part performance," and to permit enforcement despite the oral nature of the contract. However, here it is the seller who is attempting to rely on part performance. Courts which use the "evidentiary" theory would probably permit the seller to do so, since the acts of the buyer are strong evidence of a contract. Courts which use the "fraud" or "estoppel" theory would probably reject the seller's claim, reasoning that the acts of part performance were not those of the seller and that he has engaged in no detrimental reliance.

4. *True.* In general, a vendor can enforce a real estate contract against a purchaser by specific performance, despite the fact that the vendor is getting only money, which is not unique. The presence of the liquidated damages clause does not usually act as a bar to specific performance unless it clearly makes retention of the deposit the only remedy; this one does not do so. Unless there is some other inequity in doing so, V can enforce the contract.

5. The contract does not make time of the essence, and there are no circumstances mentioned (such as a rapidly fluctuating market) which would cause a court to consider time essential. Hence, P is entitled to a reasonable extension of time. Most courts would agree that one week is reasonable. V is still bound by the contract, and P can enforce it against him. However, V is entitled to any damages resulting from the week's delay, such as additional interest, taxes, and utility costs on the property, but reduced by the week's fair rental value if V occupies it during that week.

6. *True.* The condition was obviously inserted in the contract for P's benefit, to enable him to cancel the contract if he did not get the desired financing. Since the condition benefits only P, P is entitled to waive it and go forward with the contract. V is not harmed by this approach, and gets all that he bargained for.

7. *False.* Unless the contrary is provided, every contract is deemed to contain a covenant that title will be "marketable." Any significant lien or encumbrance is sufficient to make title unmarketable unless the contract stipulates that title will be subject to it. The restrictive covenant is an encumbrance, the title is unmarketable, and Sellers is in total breach. Hence, Sellers cannot enforce the contract. It does not matter whether Barnes is being reasonable in refusing to take the property. (Note that in some states, Sellers is liable to Barnes for loss-of-bargain damages, while in others if Sellers acted in good faith he is liable only for restitution of Barnes' earnest money and out-of-pocket expenses.)

■ II. CONVEYANCES AND TITLES

1. *True.* If a deed is obtained by fraud in the execution, it is absolutely void and can be set aside by court decree even if the land has passed to a BFP. Fraud in the execution exists when the grantor does not know that the document being signed is a deed, as here. Contrast this with fraud in the inducement, in which the grantor realizes that a deed is being signed but does so because of false representations; in the latter case, the deed is considered only voidable and will not be set aside in the hands of a BFP.

2. The call will probably extend to the road itself, rather than to the boundary of the adjacent land. In the usual priority of interpretation of deeds, calls to artificial monuments (such as roads) prevail over calls to adjacent tracts of land (such as the Thompson farm). This conclusion could be reversed if there were extrinsic evidence suggesting a contrary intent. If the conclusion stands, it may mean that the grantor has attempted to convey some land he does not own; he may therefore be liable on one or more covenants of title in the deed.

3. *False.* By the majority view, a deed which is delivered to the grantee with an oral condition is considered to have been unconditionally delivered. Thus, Daughter would have title. A minority view would enforce the condition, and in this case would consider the deed undelivered and ineffective since the condition was never fulfilled.

4. *False.* The statute of limitations on the present covenants (seisin, right to convey, and against encumbrances) begins to run when the deed is delivered. Hence, an action on these covenants is now barred, even though the easement would clearly have breached the covenant against encumbrances. With regard to the future covenants (warranty, quiet enjoyment, and further assurances), no action can be brought until there is an eviction—some threat of or actual interference with Evelyn's possession. Here there has been no eviction, so Evelyn cannot yet bring an action on the future covenants. However, the statute of limitations does not commence running until eviction, so if an eviction occurs in the future she may be able to bring such an action.

5. The Bank has a valid mortgage under all three types of recording acts. Under a race-type act, the Bank need merely record first, which it did. Under a notice-type act, the Bank must pay value and take the mortgage without notice. Giving a contemporaneous loan is considered value, and the Bank had no notice, so it qualifies. Under a notice-race-type act, the Bank must qualify in both of the ways mentioned above; it did so. Note that it is irrelevant that A paid value or was a BFP; only the BFP status of Bank, the subsequent purchaser (mortgagee), is significant.

6. Vendor has an action for damages against Escrowee for breach of his fiduciary duty to follow his instructions. Vendor also has an action in damages against Purchaser, probably on the basis of fraud. If Vendor prefers instead to seek an order setting aside the deed for lack of delivery, he can probably obtain it. By the majority view this is true despite the BFP status of B; a deed which is undelivered is void, even if the land has passed into the hands of a BFP. This rule has been strongly criticized, and there is some contrary authority.

■ III. INTRODUCTION TO THE LAW OF REAL ESTATE FINANCE

1. *False.* The early English common law mortgage transaction took the form of a conveyance of a fee simple absolute subject to a condition subsequent. If the mortgagor paid the debt on law day, he had a right to reenter and terminate the lender's estate. Otherwise, the lender already had title to the mortgaged land and no further action by the lender was necessary.

2. *False.* Even after the foreclosure remedy was created, English equity courts continued to take the position that mortgagees had title to the mortgaged premises so long as the mortgage remained unsatisfied. With title went the right to possession. Mortgagee, however, nevertheless had the duty to account for such rents and profits on the mortgage debt.

3. In foreclosure by sale, the mortgaged real estate is sold at public auction to the highest bidder, with any sale surplus going to junior lienholders, if any, and then to the mortgagor. Under strict foreclosure, if the mortgagor does not pay off the debt by the date set by the court, complete title to the real estate vests in the mortgagee.

4. *False.* The deed of trust is essentially a power of sale mortgage with the power residing in a trustee rather than in the sheriff. With few exceptions, such instruments are governed by traditional substantive mortgage law with its attendant mortgagor protections. Thus, it is more appropriate to refer to the deed of trust as a mortgage variant.

5. *False.* Under the lien theory, the mortgagor retains both the legal and equitable title until a valid foreclosure takes place.

6. *True.* The balloon mortgage typically covers a two to ten year period. Payments made during this period do not fully amortize or "pay off" the mortgage debt. Rather, a rather large unpaid balance or "balloon" becomes due at the end of the term.

■ IV. THE USE OF MORTGAGE SUBSTITUTES

1. *False.* The agreement by the mortgagor to convey is an unenforceable clog on mortgagor's equity of redemption. Unless the mortgagor is willing to give

mortgagee a deed in lieu of foreclosure, foreclosure is the mortgagee's only remedy for realizing on the mortgage security.

2. *False.* Mortgage intent must be established by "clear and convincing evidence."

3. *True.* The statement is true in the sense that, in a conditional sale transaction, the grantee-mortgagee, by giving the option or similar interest back to the grantor-mortgagor, has already conceded that no absolute conveyance was intended.

4. *False.* While avoidance of mortgage law is an important motivation for the conditional sale transaction, the grantee may also be attempting to avoid the impact of usury law. Moreover, the transaction is also sometimes used for federal income tax reasons.

5. *False.* In most jurisdictions such a "negative covenant" at most creates an *in personam* contract right in the lender's favor and not a lien on the borrower's real estate.

6. An installment land contract is a substitute for a mortgage. It is a form of seller purchase money financing. An earnest money contract, on the other hand, governs the buyer and seller for a short period of time until the closing date, at which time, if financing is involved, permanent financing instruments such as mortgages or installment land contracts are executed.

7. Some courts that enforce forfeiture clauses will do so only if the forfeiture is mitigated by restitution principles. Thus, title to the contract land will be permitted to vest in the vendor only if the vendor returns to the vendee payments made under the contract to the extent that they exceed vendor's actual damages. The restitution amount, for example, could be the difference between the installments paid and the fair rental value of the premises for the payment period.

8. When the contract land is worth less than the contract price, forfeiture would be an unwise remedial choice because, once the vendor chooses forfeiture, the election of remedies doctrine prohibits the vendor from obtaining the equivalent of a deficiency judgment. On the other hand, a suit for specific performance, if successful, would give the vendor the full contract price for the land. Such a remedy, of course, normally is only available if the contract contains an acceleration clause and, as a practical matter, is valuable only if the vendee is able to satisfy a judgment for the price.

9. *True.* Generally true. It is true that such legislation aids the vendee in the sense that the vendor must comply with certain notice and grace period requirements. On the other hand, where the vendor complies with those requirements, courts are much more hesitant to relieve a vendee from a forfeiture than where such legislation is non-existent. Thus, the vendor ultimately is the primary beneficiary of such legislation because it tends to institutionalize or legitimatize forfeiture as a remedy.

10. In a majority jurisdiction the answer is true because recording by the vendee's mortgagee provides the vendor with constructive notice of the existence of the mortgage on the vendee's interest. Consequently, the vendor would have a duty to notify the mortgagee of any action to invoke forfeiture. In a minority jurisdiction, recording does not suffice to establish such constructive notice. Rather, vendee's mortgagee must provide the vendor with actual knowledge of the mortgagee's existence in order to impose on the vendor a duty to notify the mortgagee of an intent to invoke forfeiture. Thus, in a minority jurisdiction the answer is false.

11. Some jurisdictions characterize a vendor's interest as personalty as well as realty. This result is reached either by applying equitable conversion or on the ground that the right to the payments is personalty. Thus, in order to protect themselves against subsequent lien creditors or the vendor's trustee in bankruptcy, careful lenders to the vendor utilize both recording methods.

■ V. RIGHTS AND DUTIES PRIOR TO FORECLOSURE

1. Under the title theory, the mortgagee has the right to possession and thus the rents and profits from the mortgaged premises from the date of mortgage execution until its foreclosure or satisfaction. Lien theory mortgages, however, have no such right to take possession.

2. In most lien theory states, if the mortgagee is "let" into possession by the mortgagor or if possession is acquired by virtue of purchasing at a void foreclosure sale, he will be permitted to remain in possession until the mortgage debt is satisfied. This is also the case if mortgagee takes possession after mortgagor abandons the premises.

3. *True.* A mortgagee in possession has the duty of a prudent owner—to manage the property in a reasonably prudent and careful manner. After deducting the costs of such management all remaining rents must be applied to the mortgage debt.

4. *False.* The enforcement of such a clause pending foreclosure or earlier does defeat the spirit of the lien theory because the mortgagee is getting the fruits of possession (rents) prior to foreclosure. However, enforcement does not destroy the equity of redemption because mortgagor still retains the right to redeem in equity by paying off the mortgage debt at any time until a valid foreclosure has occurred. Indeed, under the assignment of rents clause, the rents will be going to pay off the debt and thus, indirectly, to enhance the mortgagor's equity of redemption.

5. *False.* One would think that because the title theory mortgagee has title and the right to possession from the inception of the mortgage, a receiver should be easy to obtain. However, it can also be argued that such a mortgagee has an adequate remedy at law—ejectment. In practice, there is relatively little difference in the standards for appointment as between title and lien states.

6. *True.* Partially true. In many jurisdictions, if the mortgagee cannot otherwise satisfy the judicial conditions precedent for a receivership, the presence of such clauses will not enhance the prospect of appointment. However, in some jurisdictions they create a rebuttable evidentiary presumption that appointment is proper.

7. *False.* Prior to the 1992 Regulation and the 1996 Statute, there were decisions holding that a mortgagee who acquires title to the mortgaged real estate by purchasing at the foreclosure sale becomes an "owner and operator" for purposes of CERCLA and thus loses protection of that statute's "security interest" exemption. However, the 1996 Statute makes it clear that the latter protection from liability applies to a mortgagee-purchaser and continues so long as it "seeks to sell * * * the facility at the earliest practicable, commercially reasonable time, on commercially reasonable terms."

8. *False.* Probably false. While the common law in many states affords the mortgagee that option, the Fannie Mae–Freddie Mac form, which is in pervasive use, specifies that "insurance proceeds shall be applied to restoration or repair . .. [where such restoration or repair] is economically feasible" and will not lessen mortgagee's security.

9. *False.* Generally false. While mortgagees do reap profits from escrow or reserve accounts and this has generated litigation and legislation, the predominant purpose for the requirement is to protect the mortgagee's security interest. Because unpaid real estate taxes have priority over all mortgages, no matter when they are executed or recorded, mortgagees understandably want to ensure that such taxes get paid.

■ VI. TRANSFER BY THE MORTGAGOR

1.   False in most jurisdictions. In the vast majority of jurisdictions, merely taking "subject to" an existing mortgage does not make the grantee personally liable on the mortgage debt. In a very few states, such language may in certain situations create a presumption of assumption.

2.   *True.*   Extrinsic evidence in the form of other writings or oral statements is admissible to show that an assumption was intended.

3.   *False.*   While in many jurisdictions such an assuming grantee is not personally liable because the immediately preceding grantee, the promisee, was not liable, the Restatement Second would reverse this result. If so, mortgagee will qualify as a third party beneficiary if it was an "intended" and not merely an "incidental" beneficiary.

4.   Under the traditional common law rule, mortgagor will prevail. This rule provides that if a mortgagee gives an extension of time to an assuming grantee by a binding agreement with him or her, the mortgagor is discharged. This result is based on the suretyship principle that a binding extension of time given by a creditor mortgagee to a principal debtor completely discharges a surety (mortgagor). Moreover, because G agreed to an increase in interest rates, there clearly is consideration for the extension. If, however, the mortgagee reserved in the mortgage the right to extend or modify the mortgage terms, no release generally takes place. Such a reservation, however, in the extension agreement is ineffective. If the note is negotiable, the UCC is applicable and the mortgagor will be released if there is an express reservation of rights in the extension agreement, rather than in the mortgage itself.

5.   *True.*   Most courts recognize that such clauses are restraints on alienation. While some courts have held that such restraints are unreasonable unless utilized to protect the mortgagee's security, a growing majority view them as reasonable even when utilized for the purpose of raising the interest rate. At least one court, interestingly, has held that such clauses do not even constitute restraints on alienation.

6.   Installment land contracts usually contain a provision prohibiting assignment by the vendee without the vendor's consent.

7.   *True.*   Generally true. If a violation of the no-transfer clause is a default that would be a ground for termination of the contract, the vendee's transferee would automatically lose the contract land. On the other hand, a mortgage due-on-sale violation, at worst, triggers acceleration of the mortgage debt. The transferee in such a situation could avoid losing the land at a foreclosure sale by paying off the accelerated debt. This difference between installment land contract no-transfer provisions and mortgage due-on-sale clauses in part explains why courts are more willing to enforce the latter clause than the former.

8. Yes. Generally a due-on-sale clause is enforceable unless the transfer falls within one of the exceptions to enforceability contained in the Garn Act. While one of these exceptions prohibits due-on enforcement incident "to a decree of a dissolution of a marriage . . . or from an incidental property settlement," this language (as well as that of the other exceptions) applies only where the mortgaged real estate consists of less than five dwelling units. Since this problem involves a 10 unit apartment building, the above exception is inapplicable and the due-on clause is therefore enforceable.

9. No. As emphasized in the previous problem, a due-on clause is enforceable unless it falls within one of the Act's exceptions. One of those exceptions prohibits enforcement where the transfer consists of "the granting of a leasehold interest of three years or less *not* containing an option to purchase." While the lease in our problem is for less than three years, it does contain a purchase option and therefore the due-on clause is enforceable upon execution of the lease.

■ VII. TRANSFER BY THE MORTGAGEE

1. *False.* The terminology describes the process by which originating mortgagees sell some of their mortgage loans to both private and governmental institutional purchasers.

2. *False.* While such a promissory note may incorporate the terms of the mortgage by reference, it may state that it is secured by a mortgage on real estate and refer to the mortgage for purposes of prepayment and acceleration rights.

3. *True.* While a holder in due course takes free of personal defenses that the maker could have utilized against the original payee-mortgagee, he is subject to "real defenses," one of which is "such misrepresentation as has induced the [maker] to sign the [promissory note] with neither knowledge nor reasonable opportunity to obtain knowledge of its character or its essential terms." UCC § 3–305(2)(c). In our fact situation, A did misrepresent the nature of the documents. Moreover, in view of M's limited education and commercial or legal knowledge, and the fact that A and M were in an attorney-client relationship, it is probable that M possessed "neither knowledge nor reasonable opportunity to obtain knowledge" of its nature and terms. Thus the misrepresentation constituted a "real defense" to which H, even though a holder in due course, will be subject.

4. A transferee of a promissory note often obtains an estoppel certificate (a written statement from the maker-mortgagor that the note is valid and subject to no defenses by the maker-mortgagor) because he is fearful that holder in due course status will be unavailable. The certificate will protect the transferee against maker-mortgagor assertion of both personal and most real defenses.

5. *False.* Courts that recognize the "close-connection" concept utilize it to deny holder in due course status to those holders of negotiable notes who are too closely connected to the original holder. A variety of statutes and rules employ the same or a similar concept.

6. *False.* After a negotiable note has been assigned to a holder in due course, payment to the original mortgagee or to anyone other than the assignee or its agent generally does not constitute a valid payment of the mortgage debt.

7. Yes. Because the assignee of a non-negotiable note takes subject to all of a maker-mortgagor's defenses, maker-mortgagor's payments to the original mortgagee made before the maker-mortgagor received notice of the assignment, must be credited against the mortgage debt. A few states hold, however, that where a final payment is being made on a non-negotiable note, since it would constitute negligence for maker-mortgagor to fail to demand production of the promissory note, the final payment to the mortgagee will not, as against the assignee, be credited against the mortgage debt.

8. *True.* This is because the recording of the assignment constitutes constructive notice of it to the grantee. Indeed, if the note is negotiable, payment to anyone other than the assignee is ineffective whether or not the assignment was recorded.

9. *False.* Normally the grantee will take the land free and clear of the mortgage debt. This result represents the victory of recording act policy over the UCC philosophy of protecting holders in due course. The innocent land buyer who relies on the public record prevails over the HDC.

10. *True.* While this point was disputed under old Article 9, Revised Article 9 makes it clear that "The security interest in the promissory note is covered by this Article even though the note is secured by a real-property mortgage." The security interest attaches to the mortgage lien as well as the note.

11. *False.* In the absence of contrary language in the participation agreement, most courts today hold that the participants should share in the foreclosure proceeds on a pro-rata basis and not based on the order in which each participant received its participation interest. Thus, the foreclosure proceeds should be divided according to each participant's percentage interest. Thus each should receive 25% of $500,000, which is $125,000.

■ VIII. DISCHARGE OF THE DEBT AND MORTGAGE: BY PAYMENT OR OTHERWISE

1. *False.* Generally false. At common law there was no right to prepay a mortgage debt. Today mortgage notes commonly permit prepayment, but some lenders exact a prepayment charge. Prepayment charges are often limited by state statute.

2. *False.* Prepayment penalties are charges *for returning money* and not interest for the *right to use* money.

3. *False.* While lenders seldom exact more than a 6 months' interest penalty, there has been at least one occasion when a charge equal to 50% of the debt has been upheld. In that case the charge was deemed reasonable because it represented a fair approximation of the additional federal income tax obligation the vendor would incur because of the prepayment.

4. *True.* There is case authority that invalidated a late payment fee of 2% of the unpaid mortgage balance. Indeed, state statutes and federal regulations often limit such charges to the lesser of a relatively small fixed charge or a percentage of the late payment.

5. Probably no. A court would probably determine that niece's promise cannot be reduced to a money equivalent and thus is incapable of being secured by a valid mortgage on real estate. Some states, such as Maine, have enforced mortgages securing obligations of support.

6. If a mortgagee takes a deed in lieu of foreclosure and there is a junior mortgage on the real estate, the junior mortgagee may argue that not only is his mortgage still valid, but the senior mortgage no longer exists because of the merger of the mortgage and the debt in the same person. While most courts would reject the application of the merger doctrine in such a situation, the holder of the deed in lieu will still have to foreclose in order to wipe out the junior lien. Before taking a deed in lieu, a mortgagee should examine the title to determine whether subsequent liens exist. If they do, foreclosure, not the deed in lieu, should be the remedy.

■ IX. FORECLOSURE

1. It is a clause contained in a mortgage that gives the mortgagee the option, in the event of mortgagor default, to declare the entire mortgage debt due and owing.

2. Because the mortgage contains no acceleration clause, mortgagee will not normally be able to foreclose for the full amount of the mortgage debt. If the property is capable of physical division, a court could order a portion of the mortgaged land foreclosed to satisfy the unpaid installments. If the property cannot be so divided, a court in rare instances may order a sale of all of the land free and clear of the mortgage. If a surplus occurs the court could, in effect, supply the acceleration clause and utilize the surplus to prepay the entire debt. More probably, the court would simply order all of the land sold subject to the remaining mortgage debt.

3. *False.* Only those junior to the mortgage being foreclosed are necessary parties.

4. The senior lienholder can be made a party where the foreclosing mortgagee is seeking to ascertain the amount and terms of the senior lien or where the actual priority status of the "senior" lien is in doubt.

5. *False.* Under the majority rule, Lessee, even though an intentionally omitted necessary party, is unaffected by the foreclosure and is still bound by the lease. In order to discourage such mortgagee manipulation of the foreclosure process, a few courts give the omitted lessee the option of being bound by the lease or treating it as terminated.

6. The omitted owner has the right to redeem *the land* by paying the foreclosure sale purchaser the mortgage debt. Such a redemption will take the purchaser out of the picture. On the other hand, while the omitted junior lienor can redeem by paying the purchaser the amount of the senior mortgage debt, she only purchases a mortgage and not the *title to the land*. Moreover, the foreclosure purchaser, standing in the foreclosed mortgagor's shoes, can always preemptively redeem by paying off the mortgage debt of the omitted junior lienor.

7. The omitted junior lienholder normally would choose statutory redemption because it affords him the right to redeem title to the land, whereas exercise of equitable redemption rights would simply make him an assignee of a revived first mortgage. The problem, however, is that the omitted junior normally will not have such a choice. Most jurisdictions hold that statutory redemption is available only to those previously validly foreclosed. Since the junior lienholder was an omitted party he was not validly foreclosed and thus is left with equitable redemption rights only.

8. *True.* Judicial supervision at the various stages of the foreclosure process probably reduces significantly the number of errors that would otherwise arise in an unsupervised foreclosure setting. In addition, because judicial foreclosure is an adversary proceeding, the chances are good that procedural and substantive defects will be called to the court's attention. Finally, because judicial foreclosure is a civil action, once the time for appeal has expired, it will become final and subject only to extremely limited collateral attack.

9. If a defect renders a foreclosure sale void, no title, legal or equitable, passes to the sale purchaser. Mortgagor will be able to regain the land at any time unless the sale purchaser or her successors obtain title by adverse possession. If, however, the defect renders the sale merely voidable, legal title passes to the sale purchaser although the equitable title does not. Consequently, if the land gets into the hands of a BFP, the mortgagor will lose the ability to regain the land.

10. *True.* At least if the mortgagee or trustee under a power of sale did not intentionally engage in conduct to accomplish that result. There is some authority, however, that "intentional chilled bidding" renders the sale void.

11. *True.* The majority of courts permit the mortgagor either to set aside the sale and regain the land or, in effect, to say to the purchaser, "Keep the land; I want damages." A minority holds that the damage remedy is unavailable unless the land is in the hands of a BFP.

12. *False.* Probably false. To the extent that procedural due process requires a hearing prior to power of sale foreclosure, many courts would hold that the mortgagor's hearing right must be specifically provided for by legislation. Moreover, there is a strong argument that the mortgagor should not have to take affirmative action to guarantee a hearing. Under this view, a statute must provide that a hearing is automatically triggered whenever a mortgagee initiates a foreclosure proceeding.

13. *True.* Most power of sale legislation is probably unconstitutional if the requisite state or federal action is present. Even though there is some authority that GNMA, as a foreclosing entity, is not the government for purposes of the 5th Amendment's federal action requirement, the Veteran's Administration is more likely to be treated, for foreclosure purposes, as a direct instrumentality of the United States.

14.   *True.*   The surplus represents what is left of the mortgage security or res. From this principle flow two rules: (1) the liens and other interests terminated by the foreclosure attach to the surplus in the order of priority they enjoyed prior to foreclosure and thus, (2) the foreclosed mortgagor's claim to the surplus is subordinate to all valid liens terminated by the foreclosure.

15.   Because the mortgagor and, in some instances, foreclosed junior lienholders, have the right to redeem from the sale purchaser, the latter, for the redemption period, has a defeasible title. Moreover, during this period the mortgagor often retains the right to possession. Further, there is currently in many states a very tangible economic disincentive to third party bidding. It is true that if redemption occurs, the sale purchaser is assured of being repaid the amount of the foreclosing sale price together with interest thereon at a statutorily mandated rate. However, because such statutory interest rates have not kept pace with market rates, the rate of return to the sale purchaser will usually be significantly lower than that available from other comparable investments.

16.   *False.*   The rule does not immunize the mortgagor from personal liability but rather makes foreclosure a condition precedent to any attempt to obtain a deficiency judgment against her. If the mortgagee first sues on the note, the mortgagor may have that action dismissed.

17.   *False.*   Under § 533 of the Servicemembers Civil Relief Act, a mortgagee cannot foreclose on a mortgage executed prior to the mortgagor's entrance into the military service during the period of that service unless authorized to do so by court order. In our fact situation, such an order was not obtained. Consequently, P's title is not only unmarketable, but because a foreclosure in violation of § 533 is probably void, P in all likelihood has no title at all to Blackacre.

18.   First, the holder of the real estate mortgage will be stayed from commencing any type of foreclosure proceeding or from pursuing any such previously commenced proceeding. Second, to the extent that the trustee in bankruptcy determines that the mortgagor has equity in the real estate, the property may be sold by the trustee either subject to the mortgage or free and clear of it. If the latter course is pursued, the mortgagee's lien claim will be transferred to the sale proceeds. If the former option is carried out, the mortgagee will then be free to foreclose its mortgage against the real estate now owned by the purchaser from the trustee. Third, should the trustee determine that the mortgagor has no equity in the mortgaged real estate, the mortgagee will be permitted to foreclose under state law. Finally, in any event, to the extent that the mortgage security proves insufficient to satisfy the mortgage debt, the mortgagee will be treated as a general unsecured creditor as to such a deficiency.

19. In the Bankruptcy Reform Act of 1994 ("1994 Act"), Congress seems to make the foreclosure sale the cut-off point for asserting the right to deaccelerate. However, according language in the legislative history, "if the state provides the debtor more extensive 'cure' rights (through, for example, some later redemption period), the debtor would continue to enjoy such rights in bankruptcy." Thus, where states have long post-sale statutory redemption periods, the foregoing legislative history raises the possibility that Chapter 13 deacceleration will be permitted during those periods. Thus, *Taddeo* may arguably continue to be used to set aside sales during an applicable statutory redemption period.

■ X. SOME PRIORITY PROBLEMS

1. It is a mortgage on real estate taken by a third party, often an institutional lender, whose funds were utilized in the acquisition by the mortgagor of that real estate.

2. *False.* The purchase money doctrine affords the purchase money lender priority over *prior* liens arising through the mortgagor-buyer. Subsequent lienors who have paid value and who take their mortgages without knowledge of the prior unrecorded purchase money mortgage (and, in some jurisdictions, who record prior to the recording of the latter mortgage) will have priority over the purchase money mortgage.

3. Under the accession concept, to the extent that a mortgagor makes improvements on Blackacre, they are subjected to any pre-existing mortgage on Blackacre. An after-acquired property clause in a mortgage on Blackacre is utilized to ensure that the mortgagee acquires a lien on Whiteacre and other separate tracts acquired subsequently by the mortgagor.

4. True to some extent. Normally the holder of a junior lien is treated as taking subject to a possible time extension of the debt secured by a senior mortgage. However, E–1 stands a good chance of being subordinated to E–2 at least as to any increase in the E–1 debt attributable to the increased interest rate. The junior lienor arguably is likely to be prejudiced by the interest change modification. If E–2 were ever forced to redeem the E–1 mortgage in order to protect its interest, the amount required to do so will be more than could have been contemplated at the time the E–2 mortgage was created.

5. *False.* Under Article 9 of the UCC, once building materials such as bricks, lumber, beams, etc. are incorporated into a building, any pre-existing chattel mortgage on them is no longer valid. However, Acme, as an unpaid supplier, may be able to perfect a mechanics' lien on Blackacre.

6. *False.* Under the 1972 Code, the chattel mortgage will lose priority to the real estate mortgage unless a fixture filing is made before the chattel is affixed to the real estate or within 10 days thereafter.

7. The Pennsylvania system confers on the subcontractor or supplier a direct lien right of his own even though the general contractor has been fully paid. Under the New York system the aggregate amount of liens that may be collected out of the improved real estate is the contract price in the main contract between the general contractor and the owner less payments properly made to the general contractor. Under the Pennsylvania system, the owner could wind up paying significantly more than the main contract price to free the real estate of mechanics' lien claims, whereas under the New York system, payment of the main contract price to the general contractor will normally insulate the real estate from further lien claims.

8. In states that follow the Pennsylvania system, such waiver language is usually enforceable against both subcontractors and suppliers as well as the general contractor. In New York system states, such a general lien waiver is generally unenforceable.

9. The answer depends upon where the transaction took place and whether the subsequent advance by E–1 was obligatory or optional. In almost all states, if the advance was obligatory in the sense that the mortgage or a collateral agreement imposed a contractual obligation to make future advances, it relates back to the date of the original mortgage and takes priority over liens that arise between that date and the time of the advance. Thus if E–1's subsequent advance was obligatory, it has priority over the E–2 mortgage. If, however, the future advance was optional or discretionary on E–1's part, it will usually be junior to any intervening lien as to which the future advances mortgagee had notice. In a majority of states, E–1's advance, if optional, would lose priority to E–2 only if E–1 had actual knowledge of the E–2 mortgage. Under the minority view, E–1 will be charged with constructive notice because E–2 recorded its mortgage before the E–1's subsequent advance.

10. The dragnet clause in a mortgage purports to make the mortgaged real estate security for other, unspecified, debts that the mortgagor may already or in the future owe to the mortgagee. Such a clause creates a species of optional future advances mortgage. Unlike in the case of more traditional future advances mortgages, such as construction loans, the lender and borrower rarely contemplate future advances. Most often the dragnet clause is simply "thrown in" by the mortgagee on the theory that it could come in handy later.

11. Some have argued that the stop notice remedy is too likely to be used by dishonest claimants to blackmail the owner and construction lender into paying inflated claims. This can occur because the filing of a significant claim often forces the construction lender to withhold a substantial amount of the loan proceeds and consequently construction may be significantly delayed.

12. The primary judicial theories have been based on unjust enrichment and third party beneficiary concepts.

13. *False.* Litigation over an executory subordination agreement is most likely to arise after a seller refuses to go through with the whole purchase agreement or simply balks at its subordination provisions. Once the purchase agreement is carried out, the subordination has already taken place and it is thus no longer executory. Disputes over executory subordination agreements will most likely be litigated in the context of an action by the purchaser for specific performance of the earnest money contract.

14. *False.* At this stage a court is normally dealing with a second subordination agreement that refers specifically to the terms of the construction loan. Consequently, problems of indefiniteness or vagueness have usually already been obviated.

■ XI. GOVERNMENT INVOLVEMENT IN THE MORTGAGE MARKET

1. *False.* The Federal Home Loan Banks make no loans to individuals at all. Their function is to provide credit to their member thrift institutions.

2. *False.* GNMA's major role today is to guarantee mortgage-backed securities issued by private lenders.

3. *True.* The VA guarantee is based on a sliding scale. For example, for loans up to $45,000, it is 50% of the loan amount and for loans greater than $144,000, it is the lesser of 25% of the loan amount or $60,000. If the mortgaged real estate were to decline in value so much that the foreclosure price plus the guaranteed amount is less than the loan balance, the difference will represent loss to the lender. Under an FHA insured loan, however, the mortgagee may either assign a loan in default to the FHA and receive 99% of its balance or may foreclose and acquire title to the property, and then transfer it to FHA for 100% of the loan balance. The financial risk to a VA lender is thus somewhat greater than to the FHA lender.

4. Both entities historically raised much of their capital by selling notes and debentures in the capital markets. They still do so to some extent, but today the great majority of their capital is raised by selling securities collateralized by pools of mortgages they hold.

5. The Alternative Mortgage Transaction Parity Act of 1982 (the "Act") authorizes all types of state-chartered financial institutions to make residential real estate mortgage loans of the same types approved by federal agencies for federally chartered institutions. Since GPARM's are authorized by OTS, Friendly is permitted to utilize GPARM's even though they are unauthorized or prohibited by state regulation or legislation. This result would not follow if Friendly's state legislature had opted out of the federal preemption prior to October 15, 1985.

6. In section 501 of the Depository Institutions and Monetary Control Act of 1980 (the "Act"), as amended, Congress preempted state usury laws for loans secured by residential real estate. First mortgage loans and institutions whose deposits are federally insured are covered by the Act. While the states were authorized to opt out of the federal preemption, they needed to do so by April 1, 1983. In our problem we are dealing with a first mortgage loan executed after the effective date of the Act and a federally-insured savings and loan association. Assuming that State X did not opt out of the federal preemption, state usury law is inapplicable and the counterclaim should be dismissed.

■ XII. ALTERNATIVE MORTGAGE LOAN INSTRUMENTS

1. *False.* Because the SAM lender is willing to accept a lower than market mortgage interest rate in exchange for a percentage of any appreciation in the value of mortgaged property, this type of mortgage can only be profitable during a period of rising real estate prices. To the extent that a lender foresees relatively stable real estate prices, it will either avoid the SAM entirely or at least will demand a relatively high mortgage interest rate or a higher share of any future appreciation.

2. *False.* The primary purpose of the GPM is to enable home purchasers who possess adequate future income potential to obtain mortgage financing when their current income is insufficient to qualify them for a standard evenly-amortized long-term mortgage loan. Under the GPM, the payments during the first several years are lower and during the later years are higher than in the case of the standard mortgage. Some lenders protect themselves against future market interest rate increases by using a Graduated Payment Adjustable Rate Mortgage (GPARM). This format allows the borrower the advantage of the GPM but the mortgage interest rate would be adjusted in accordance with changes in an interest rate index.

3. In a "buy-down," a mortgage lender agrees to make a loan to a purchaser at a below market interest rate in exchange for the payment to it by the home seller or other third party of a substantial front end sum. As a consequence, the purchaser who does not satisfy the income requirements for a market interest rate loan may be able to qualify for one written at a below market rate.

4. *True.* In a PLAM, the lender is protected against inflation because the loan balance is adjusted from time to time (typically annually) to reflect changes in an index of actual inflation. Because of this protection afforded to the lender's investment, it will be willing to accept only a "real" rate of return—that interest rate that it would demand in a non-inflationary economy. Consequently, the contract interest rate under a PLAM would be very low—probably about 4% to 5%. On the other hand, the interest rate on a GPM, as well as on most other mortgages today, reflects not only a "real" rate of return, but also the lender's expectations about future inflation. Thus, even though GPM payments are reduced somewhat during the early years of the loan, they will probably be significantly higher than the payments during the first year under a PLAM.

5. Where monthly loan payments are insufficient to satisfy the interest that accrues each month, the principal balance of the loan increases, rather than decreases, each month as the unpaid interest is added to the loan balance. This situation is referred to as "negative amortization." It will occur in some types of GPM's where payments in the early years are not sufficient to satisfy the entire accruing interest. It can also be present in those ARM's where an increased interest rate is implemented by capitalization (addition to principal) of interest rather than by increasing monthly payments or extending loan maturities. Perhaps the ultimate example of negative amortization is the Reverse Annuity Mortgage (RAM), where the mortgage debt increases monthly not only by any unpaid interest that accrues but also by the amount of the monthly disbursements of the loan proceeds to the mortgagor.

■ XIII. PLANNED UNIT DEVELOPMENTS, CONDOMINIUMS AND COOPERATIVES

1. *False.* Typically ownership resides in a not-for-profit corporation, the shareholders of which are the unit owners.

2. *False.* While some lenders in the past hesitated to provide condominium resale financing, most are now willing to do so. This is because the condominium unit is a separate entity for mortgageability and real estate tax purposes. Because the cooperative unit is usually subject to a large blanket mortgage on the entire building and units are not subject to separate real estate taxation, potential resale lenders fear that their liens will be placed in jeopardy by a default in the blanket mortgage or in real estate tax payments. Moreover, many institutional lenders traditionally have been either required or inclined to take real estate mortgages only. Consequently, doubt as to what type of security the cooperator's corporate shares and proprietary lease would provide is another deterrent to lender willingness to finance such resales.

3. *True.* Many first generation statutes patterned after the FHA Model Act provided for one percentage figure to govern each of the three situations. Under most first generation statutes the percentage or fraction is arrived at by dividing the initial value of the unit by the value of the entire property. Second generation legislation, on the other hand, often permits each of the three allocations to be made on a different basis.

4. *True.* All condominium legislation prohibits a unit owner from separating his ownership in a unit from that in the common areas.

5. *False.* Because the common area is owned by the unit owners as tenants in common, they have joint and several liability as landowners for claims resulting from use of the common area.

6. Under most condominium legislation she can protect herself, if necessary, by paying that fraction of the lien claim that is the same as her percentage ownership of the common areas. By so doing, she releases her unit and common area ownership from the lien.

7. *False.* While much of the first generation legislation required that the declarant have fee title to the underlying ground, second generation statutes authorize such leasehold condominiums. Such ground leases, however, cannot be terminated as to any unit owner who pays his or her proportionate share of the ground rent.

8. The term refers to a contract entered into by a developer-controlled owners' association and developer-owned or related corporations or other entities committing the association to unreasonable long-term obligations, such as management arrangements or leases of developer owned or controlled land.

9. *False.* Probably false. Not only will the purchaser possess little understanding of the subordination language, it will probably contain insufficient detail concerning the construction loan to which the purchaser is being asked to subordinate. Thus a court may very well determine that the language is too vague or unfair to enforce.

10. Some local ordinances have been deemed to conflict with state condominium legislation that regulates conversion, but not as restrictively as the local ordinance. For example, an ordinance that places a moratorium on conversion may be found to conflict with state legislation that imposes notice requirements on conversion, but otherwise seems to authorize it. In addition, it could be argued that where pervasive conversion regulation has been enacted at the state level, the state has "filled the field" and left no room for local regulation.

11. Time-share owner influence in management is limited for several reasons. First, most owners are on-site for only a limited period each year. Second, they are likely to be dispersed over a wide geographical area. Consequently, the ability to organize owners and exchange information is limited. Finally, since most such owners have a relatively small financial stake in the project, the intensity of their interest in management performance will likely be relatively low.

12. Both versions of the Uniform Condominium Act afford the purchaser 15 days from the receipt of the condominium disclosure statement to rescind the purchase agreement without cause. See UCA § 4–106 (both versions).

13. While most first generation legislation is silent on this point, most institutional lenders and secondary market purchasers of mortgages on condominium units insist that the condominium documents provide for loss of developer control after 75% of the units have been sold. Second generation legislation contains similar restrictions on developer control. See 1980 UCA § 3–103(d).

*

APPENDIX B

Practice Examination

This examination consists of four questions, all of which should be completed in three hours.

QUESTION I *(Suggested time: 50 minutes)*

In 1965 Owens purported to sell Greenacre to Able for $1,000 cash. Greenacre is a parcel of unimproved mountain land which is inaccessible by road during six months of each year due to snow. Owens gave Able a deed which granted Greenacre to Able in fee simple and contained all covenants of title. Able did not have a title examination made. Able immediately recorded his deed, obtained an unsecured loan from Bank, and used the funds to build a vacation cabin on the land. Unknown to Able, Owens' grandfather was the true and sole owner of Greenacre.

From 1965 to the present, Able has paid taxes on Greenacre and lived in the cabin for one month each summer. The cabin and land have otherwise been unoccupied. Able's possession was not sufficiently continuous to give him title by adverse possession. Bank placed a sign on the land at the time of construction which read: "Built with financing from Bank." The sign has remained in place, readily observable, ever since.

In 1988 Owens borrowed $5,000 from Charlie. In 1992 Owens' grandfather died, leaving Greenacre to Owens by will. In the winter of 1993 Charlie induced Owens to deed Greenacre to Charlie in full satisfaction of the $5,000 debt, which was then past due. Charlie had no actual knowledge of Able's claim to Greenacre. The deed contained all covenants of title.

Title searches in the state are customarily made in the grantor-grantee indexes of the official records. The recording statute reads:

> "Any unrecorded conveyance is deemed void as against a subsequent taker for value without notice."

Who owns Greenacre? Discuss.

QUESTION II *(Suggested time: 50 minutes)*

Bill Burrows is a small-time subdivider and homebuilder. On January 1 he approached Major Mortgage Company and explained that he had three houses under construction on land that he owned in fee simple. The houses were partially completed, and Burrows, who had been financing their construction out of his own cash, had run out of money. Major agreed to make funds available to Burrows in the amount of $45,000 to complete the project, with $15,000 to be advanced when the roofs were on the houses, another $15,000 when the rough plumbing, heating, and electrical work was completed, and the final $15,000 when the houses were finished.

Burrows executed a promissory note, negotiable and payable on demand, for $45,000 with interest at 12% per annum to Major. At Major's insistence, he also executed a deed to the three lots to Major, which orally promised him that he could buy back all of the lots by paying $15,000 for each lot, plus 1% of $15,000 for each month from the date of the deed, at any time after the completion of construction. It was assumed that Burrows would do so from the proceeds of the sales of the houses to customers.

Burrows continued the project on schedule, and Major advanced the first two draws as agreed. Meanwhile, in March, Major began running into financial trouble. To raise cash, it borrowed a large sum from First National Bank, giving as security for the loan (among other assets) an assignment of the Burrows note and a deed of the Burrows land. Major and the bank had had no prior dealings. Burrows was not informed of this transaction. When Burrows finished the houses in June, he demanded the final $15,000 draw from Major, but by this time Major had declared bankruptcy and all of its officers were under indictment for embezzlement; it had no net worth and did not advance the final $15,000 to Burrows.

Burrows now has found buyers for his houses, and has approached the Bank, demanding a reconveyance of all of his land and offering the Bank to repay the $30,000 he received plus interest. Assume you have been retained by the Bank, which has asked you the following questions:

a. If Burrows refuses to satisfy the full $45,000 debt, can the Bank retain title to the land? In order to do so, is it necessary or appropriate for the Bank to bring some judicial action similar to a foreclosure, or to hold a "power-of-sale" type of foreclosure? Discuss fully.

b. Can the Bank recover the full amount of the note, $45,000 plus interest, from Burrows by a personal suit? What defenses can Burrows be expected to raise in such a suit, and how can the Bank meet them? Discuss fully.

You may assume that the jurisdiction has no one-action, anti-deficiency, or other relevant statute, but has enacted the Uniform Commercial Code. You need not consider the effect of federal law, if any.

QUESTION III *(Suggested time: 50 minutes)*

Owens was the owner of a tract of land in the State of Euphoria. When he bought the land he gave a mortgage on it to the seller, Mann, as partial payment. This mortgage had, at all relevant times, a balance owing of $20,000. Subsequently Owens needed money for his children's college education. He borrowed money from Mutter, giving him a mortgage on the same land. At all relevant times this mortgage had a balance owing of $5,000. Both mortgages were recorded immediately upon their delivery. Mutter had full knowledge of Mann's mortgage, but Mann did not know about Mutter's.

In January of 1996 both mortgages came due and Owens defaulted on them. Both mortgagees accelerated. Owens pled for additional time to pay. Mutter was sympathetic, but Mann was not. Mann proceeded to foreclosure on the property by judicial action. However, Mann did not have a title examination made before filing his foreclosure action, and he did not name Mutter as a defendant or otherwise notify Mutter of the foreclosure.

Bain was the successful bidder at Mann's foreclosure sale, which occurred in July, 1996. He bid $23,000. Of this money Mann retained $20,000, and the remaining $3,000 was turned over by the court to Owens, who placed it in his savings account, where it still remains. Owens did not mention Mutter to anyone, and Mutter did not know the foreclosure was taking place.

In September, 1996, Mutter finally lost patience with Owens and commenced a statutory procedure to foreclose his mortgage under its power of sale (a permissible action under Euphoria law for mortgagees). He searched the title, and for the first time discovered the July 1996 foreclosure sale. He sent appropriate notices under Euphoria law to Owens, Mann, and Bain. Before Mutter's foreclosure sale, he was visited by Bain, who offered Mutter a certified check for $5,000 in return for a quitclaim deed to the property. Mutter refused this offer. At Mutter's foreclosure sale on December 1, 1996, the only bidder was Mutter himself (a permissible procedure under Euphoria law). He bid the amount of his debt ($5,000), executed an appropriate deed to himself, and took possession of the land.

The land is worth $30,000, and both Mutter and Bain would like to have title to it. Discuss fully their rights as against one another and any other relevant persons. There is no statutory post-foreclosure redemption in Euphoria. Please ignore costs and expenses of foreclosure, attorneys' fees, and other miscellaneous costs.

QUESTION IV *(Suggested time: 50 minutes)*

Evans obtains a loan of $50,000 from a local bank to finance his acquisition of a gasoline service station in the state of Anomaly. The loan is guaranteed by the Small Business Administration (SBA), an agency of the U.S. Government. He gives the bank a mortgage on the station real property, executed on a form supplied by the local office of the SBA. The form contains a clause which provides "In the event of a foreclosure, mortgagor shall be personally liable for any deficiency notwithstanding any contrary law of the state of Anomaly."

Evans defaults on his payments and the bank assigns the mortgage and note to the SBA. SBA forecloses by power of sale, but the sale brings only $40,000. The outstanding balance, including expenses and accrued interest on the loan, is $50,000. SBA brings an action in federal court for the $10,000 deficiency. A statute in Anomaly prohibits all deficiency judgments on purchase-money mortgages, and provides that this protection for mortgagors is non-waivable. What should the court's decision be? Discuss.

■ ANSWERS

■ QUESTION I

When Owens purported to sell the land to Able in 1965, Owens had no title and thus could convey none. When he subsequently obtained title from his grandfather's will in 1992, the usual operation of the doctrine of estoppel by deed would be to pass title instantly and automatically to Able. The deed Owens had given Able contained all warranties of title, and hence would undoubtedly be held to make the doctrine operate.

However, the rights of Charlie, a third party who may be a bona fide purchaser, have intervened. The "notice" type recording act in effect here may be construed to treat Able's deed as unrecorded, and thus to protect Charlie. Since searches of titles are made in the name-type indexes in the jurisdiction, a deed which a grantor (here, Owens) executed and recorded before he got title may be considered to be outside the chain of title. This may follow from the fact that it is a great deal of additional effort for title searchers to check the grantor index for adverse conveyances by each owner for the period prior to the time each of them got title. The majority of cases have adopted this view, and would treat the deed from Owens to Able as unrecorded.

Even if this result follows, it will do Charlie no good under the recording act unless Charlie is a BFP. There are two aspects of BFP status—lacking notice and paying value. Charlie had no actual knowledge of the Owens–Able deed or of Able's claim. However, Able was in possession for one month of each year. It is unclear whether Charlie visited the land before taking his deed, but if a visit would have disclosed Able's possession, then Charlie has constructive notice of it. This point may turn on the factual question whether Able was in possession during the time just before Charlie took his deed, or whether the property was accessible during that time. Arguably no visit to the land would be required, and no notice would be imputed, if the land could not be physically reached.

The bank's sign was present on the property at all times, but it is doubtful that the sign would give any notice of Able's claim, since it makes no mention of Able's name and is equally consistent with Owens' ownership of the land. Of course, any other signs or obvious personal property present on the land which would identify Able as its possessor might be sufficient to put Charlie on constructive notice and deprive him of BFP status.

To prevail, Charlie must also pay value. Here he took the deed in satisfaction of a preexisting $5,000 debt. Logically, this should be considered value, since Charlie gave up his claim on the debt itself in return for the deed, and thus incurred a substantial legal detriment. However, a number of cases have treated this situation as analogous to the taking of a mere mortgage to secure an antecedent debt, and thus as not involving the payment of value. This situation is analytically distinguishable, and Charlie should be considered as having paid value.

Thus, if Charlie can show that he had no constructive notice of Able's claim, he will probably prevail over Able. Able, incidentally, will then have an action on the covenants of title in the deed he received from Owens. However, the "present" covenants will probably be barred by the statute of limitations, and only an action on the "future" covenants (specifically, warranty and quiet enjoyment) can be maintained. Moreover, Able will be limited to recovery of the $1000 he paid for the land plus interest, and probably the expenses of defending the suit by Charlie, if any. This total recovery may be considerably less than the land's present value.

■ QUESTION II

(a) Even though the conveyance by Burrows to Major took the form of an absolute deed, there is a very strong likelihood that a court would consider it a mortgage. There are several factors which point to this conclusion. The "price" which Burrows received was only $45,000—apparently much less than the properties were worth—and he also signed a note promising to repay that price. The repurchase price was computed on the basis of a fixed principal plus a monthly percentage factor, making it analogous to interest. Burrows was allowed to retain possession of the property. Economically, he had a strong incentive to repay the note in order to preserve his very large "equity" in the property. For all of these reasons, the deed will almost surely be regarded as a mortgage.

If the deed is a disguised mortgage, the Bank cannot simply retain title, but must foreclose. Since there is no power of sale in the deed, the foreclosure will have to be judicial in nature. Moreover Burrows has, as does every mortgagor, the right to redeem at any time prior to foreclosure. It does not matter whether the promissory note is delinquent or not. Assuming he can raise the cash needed, he can exercise this right against the Bank and have title free of the Bank's claim. If the Bank refuses to accept his tender, he can bring a suit to redeem the mortgage.

However, if Burrows fails to redeem, the Bank can foreclose and can also get a personal judgment against Burrows, either in lieu of foreclosure (since there is no one-action rule) or for a deficiency, if any, after foreclosure (since there is no anti-deficiency statute.)

(b) Burrows received only $30,000 from Major, yet he signed a note for $45,000 plus interest. The question thus arises as to how much he must pay to redeem his land. In substance, he is raising a defense of partial failure of consideration on the note—i.e., that he did not get all of the loan proceeds, and so should not have to repay the full stated balance of the note. This defense is a "personal" defense under Article 3 of the Uniform Commercial Code, and hence is not assertable against a Holder in Due Course (HDC).

This raises the question whether the Bank is a HDC of the note. To qualify, the Bank must pay value and take without notice of the maker's defenses. It is fairly clear that the Bank paid value by advancing substantial funds to Major in return for the note and deed. However, it is unclear whether the Bank had knowledge that the final $15,000 was not advanced. Even general knowledge by the Bank that Major was in serious financial difficulty and about to become insolvent might well be enough to deprive the Bank of HDC status. However, Major and the Bank had not had prior dealings, so there is no direct evidence of such knowledge by the Bank.

The note itself was negotiable in form and appears to have been properly negotiated to the Bank. Hence, in the absence of other facts, it appears that the Bank was a HDC and has immunity from Burrows' defense of partial failure of consideration.

■ QUESTION III

When Mann foreclosed his mortgage judicially without naming and serving Mutter, Mutter became an "omitted junior lienor." Hence, Mann's foreclosure was not binding on Mutter. Bain, the successful bidder at Mann's foreclosure sale, acquired two interests at that sale: Owens' fee title or "equity of redemption" and Mann's mortgagee interest. Since there was still an outstanding second lien interest in Mutter, these interests which Bain acquired could not merge together to form an unencumbered fee simple.

When Mutter subsequently decided to foreclose his junior mortgage, he was acting fully within his legal rights. Since his mortgage had not been affected by Mann's previous foreclosure, Mutter was entitled to foreclose. However, he was also obligated, like any other mortgagee before foreclosure, to accept a tender of redemption from the person who owned the equity of redemption. In the present case that person was Bain, who had acquired Owens' equity of redemption in the Mann foreclosure sale. Mutter should have accepted the $5,000 tendered by Bain and released the mortgage. Since Mutter refused to do so, Bain could have brought an action in equity to redeem the mortgage, in effect compelling Mutter to accept the $5,000.

Bain did not bring such an action at that time, and Mutter proceeded to foreclose the junior mortgage. Since Mutter bought at his own sale, there would seem to be no bar to Bain's now bringing an action to redeem, even though he did not do so immediately after his offer to redeem was rejected. No rights of third party BFP's have intervened. It is very unlikely that any statute of limitations or notion of laches would bar Bain's action.

If Bain's action to redeem were successful, the court would set aside the Mutter foreclosure sale. Mutter would get the $5,000 which Bain tendered, and Bain would then have the fee simple title to the land. Thus, Bain would have invested $23,000 at the first foreclosure sale and an additional $5,000 in the redemption, and would have property worth $30,000—not a bad situation, although not as advantageous as he expected when he bid at the first foreclosure sale.

If the court declined to set aside the sale and let Bain redeem, perhaps because of Bain's laches in not suing to redeem more promptly, then Mutter would have the fee title. However, since he was foreclosing a second mortgage, his foreclosure sale could not cut off the "revived" first mortgage, which is now held by Bain as mentioned above. Thus, Mutter would have acquired for $5,000 a parcel of land worth $30,000 with a mortgage on it for $20,000—something of a windfall to Mutter. Since he bid the amount of his debt, he is not entitled to any deficiency judgment against Owens. In effect, his bid has established that he is fully paid off.

If Bain is not allowed to redeem, he will have lost the land which he believed he was acquiring for $23,000, and would have a mortgage of $20,000 on the land instead. This leaves Bain with a net loss of $3,000. At the same time, Owens still has the $3,000 surplus in his savings account. A court might find some theory for awarding this $3,000 to Bain, although we are aware of no authority for doing so.

■ QUESTION IV

In general, the courts apply federal common law when a mortgage is foreclosed or a note enforced by an agency of the federal government. However, the courts sometimes adopt state law as the federal rule of decision. A U.S. Supreme Court opinion (*United States v. Kimbell Foods*) suggests three criteria for determining whether the state rule should be adopted.

First, is a uniform national rule required for the operation of the federal program? Here, it is doubtful that uniformity is needed; the SBA operates on a local level, and obviously expects to cope with state law variations, as shown by the fact that the SBA form refers specifically to Anomaly law.

Second, would any specific objectives of the SBA program be frustrated by adoption of state law here? Apparently the only frustration would be in the inability to collect the deficiency; this is costly to the government in some individual cases, but it is doubtful that many deficiencies can be collected anyway, and the frustration is only financial and not operational in nature.

Third, would adoption of a federal rule disrupt local commercial relationships or expectations? Here there are no third parties, such as junior lienors who expect to have some specific priority (as was the case in *Kimbell Foods*); the only rights at issue are those of the mortgagor himself. He may have expected to be free of deficiency liability, but was warned by the language of the mortgage that the government believed it could collect. Thus, a federal common law rule allowing the deficiency judgment seems neither harsh nor disruptive.

The arguments for and against use of a national common law rule seem about equally balanced. No severe problems would be generated by employing either approach. In such cases, it is probably better policy to defer to local law.

The language in the mortgage itself is arguably sufficient ground for allowing the deficiency judgment. However, state law would normally treat such language as nugatory, since the bar on deficiencies is nonwaivable. Hence, the mortgage language can be efficacious only if the court decides that some federal common law rule should preempt state law on the issue of waivability. While this is technically a different issue than that discussed above, the policy arguments are similar. Again, there is no strong ground for overriding state law with federal law, and the court would probably adopt state law, holding the mortgage language ineffective and barring the deficiency judgment. See *United States v. Dismuke*, 616 F.2d 755 (5th Cir.1980), finding the SBA barred from collecting a deficiency judgment where it failed to obtain a judicial confirmation of the sale. Such a confirmation is a precondition to a deficiency judgment under Georgia law.

*

APPENDIX C

Text Correlation Chart

Black Letter Land Transactions and Finance	Nelson & Whitman, Real Estate Transfer, Finance & Development (6th ed. 2003)	Madison, Zinman & Binder, Modern Real Estate Financing and Land Transfer (2d ed. 1999)	Korngold & Goldstein, Real Estate Transactions (4th ed. 2002)	Lefcoe, Real Estate Transactions (4th ed. 2003)	Hill, Basic Mortgage Law (2001)	Malloy & Smith, Real Estate Transactions (2d ed. 2002)
Chapter I Contracts for the Sale of Land	2-94, 111-120	19-64	72-154	75-156	1-11, 75-81	106-107, 129-167, 237-269, 275
Chapter II Conveyances & Titles	121-258	64-121	154-336, 14	235-368	117-118, 11-19, 5-8	301-502, 628
Chapter III Introduction to the Law of Real Estate Finance	95-111	123-147	346-354, 459-467, 485, 492, 357, 452	157-196	17-27, 199-205	565-572, 741-751
Chapter IV The Use of Mortgage Substitutes	260-342	147-158, 295-296	355-357, 506-512	487-489	20-26, 81-87, 92-106	811-813, 820-845
Chapter V Rights and Duties Prior to Foreclosure	343-424	127-128, 441-460, 631-649, 326-337	357, 494, 503, 913	369-403	25-26, 52-63	569-596
Chapter VI Transfer by the Mortgagor	425-461	344-353	419-431	211-224	157-179	—
Chapter VII Transfer by the Mortgagee	461-506		431-444	224-233	179-198	701-732
Chapter VIII Discharge of the Debt and Mortgage	506-548	317-326, 351, 433-437, 439-440	427, 659, 193, 198, 483, 813, 818, 821	197-210	142-157	672-700, 218-225, 793-795

Black Letter **Land Transactions and Finance**	Nelson & Whitman, Real Estate Transfer, Finance & Development (6th ed. 2003)	Madison, Zinman & Binder, Modern Real Estate Financing and Land Transfer (2d ed. 1999)	Korngold & Goldstein, Real Estate Transactions (4th ed. 2002)	Lefcoe, Real Estate Transactions (4th ed. 2003)	Hill, Basic Mortgage Law (2001)	Malloy & Smith, Real Estate Transactions (2d ed. 2002)
Chapter IX Foreclosure	549-826	461-587	457-506, 805, 825-859	405-460, 466-479	199-289	763-810
Chapter X Priority Problems	827-864, 972-1012	158-166, 1046, 134-148, 369-400, 1034-1043	418, 388, 723-749, 402-411, 417, 682, 387	521-530, 109-111, 563-584	117-142, 304-319, 300-305	655-658, 859-875, 911-923, 937-938
Chapter XI Government Involvement in the Mortgage Market	892-941		358-369, 397-402		320-324, 173-179	
Chapter XII Alternative Mortgage Instruments	941-954	301-302	370-385	481-486, 489-501	27-35	626-659
Chapter XIII Planned Unit Developments, Condominiums, and Cooperatives	1013-1155		536-563		510-562	

APPENDIX D

Glossary

A

Abatement In the context of specific performance of contracts for the sale of land, the term refers to the right of a purchaser to obtain enforcement of the contract together with a reduction in the contract price against a seller whose title is partially defective, or who has less land than the contract calls for.

Absolute Deed An instrument that on its face evidences all of the characteristics of an actual transfer of title to real estate. A court may find that it was intended to be security for a debt; if so, it will be treated as a mortgage. Security intent can be established by extrinsic written or oral evidence.

Acceleration The process by which a mortgagee, after mortgagor default, is able to make the entire mortgage debt due and payable.

Accession A real property rule that makes subsequent improvements on land subject to a pre-existing mortgage on the land.

Accretion A process by which a river or stream may shift its location gradually so as to cause a buildup of soil on one bank.

Action at Law for a Writ of Entry A judicial equivalent of Entry without Process. After a judicial determination of default, the amount owing and a judgment for possession, the mortgagee may enter the foreclosed real estate. The result is strict foreclosure.

Adjustable Rate Mortgage A mortgage format under which the lender is permitted to adjust the mortgage interest rate from time to time in accordance with fluctuations in some external index.

After-Acquired Property Clause A mortgage provision that makes subject to the mortgage not only the specifically described real estate, but also any real estate that the mortgagor subsequently acquires.

Amortization The application of part or all of payments by a borrower to reduce the outstanding principal balance of the loan. If the loan is "fully amortized," the last regular payment fully discharges the principal balance of the loan.

Arrearages In a mortgage loan context, delinquent installment payments.

Arrearages Legislation Statutes in effect in many states that permit the mortgagor to defeat acceleration by tendering the amount that would have been due (late installments plus interest) in the absence of default and acceleration.

Assignment of Rents Clause A provision in a mortgage or a separate agreement that gives the mortgagee a security interest in rents from real estate. Rents are real estate and security interests in them are governed by real estate mortgage law.

Assumption An agreement by which a grantee of mortgaged real estate becomes personally liable on the mortgage debt.

B

Balloon A final loan payment which is typically much larger than the preceding regular payments and which fully discharges the principal balance of the loan.

Bargain and Sale Deed An early English deed which took the form of a contract of sale, but with no further consideration to be paid. Under the Statute of Uses, the courts treated it as transferring legal as well as equitable title.

Binder Another term used to describe an earnest money contract. See Earnest Money Contract.

Blanket Mortgage A long-term mortgage on the real estate owned by a cooperative; a mortgage on a group of lots or parcels.

Boundaries by Acquiescence The relatively lengthy process by which a boundary is established by long recognition and acceptance of it.

Boundaries by Agreement The process by which owners of adjacent parcels fix their boundary by explicit oral agreement if they are uncertain or unaware of the correct location or there is a dispute about it.

Boundaries by Estoppel The fixing of a boundary between parcels because one owner erroneously represents to the other the location of the boundary and the second relies on that representation to his detriment. The party who misrepresented the boundary is then precluded from denying its accuracy.

Boundary by a Common Grantor When a grantor who sells parcels by lot number erroneously marks a boundary line on the ground, purchasers must regard the line as binding notwithstanding its incorrect location.

C

Chapter 11 A bankruptcy proceeding to provide for reorganization, not liquidation of the debtor. Reorganization plans often provide for extension of debts and broad judicial control over both secured and unsecured creditors. It is used largely by corporate or other business entities.

Chapter 12 A bankruptcy proceeding designed for the family farmer. It was enacted to extend to the family farmer the reorganization protections afforded the salary and wage earner under Chapter 13.

Chapter 13 A bankruptcy proceeding that is to some extent the Chapter 11 equivalent for individuals. It provides for the rehabilitation of personal debtors and the restructuring and extension of their debts.

Chilled Bidding Conduct by a mortgagee, or by a beneficiary or trustee under a deed of trust, that suppresses or discourages bidding at a foreclosure sale.

Clogging the Equity of Redemption Any agreement in the mortgage or contemporaneous therewith by which the mortgagor agrees to waive, cut short, or otherwise limit her right to pay off a mortgage in default but not yet foreclosed.

Close-Connectedness Doctrine A doctrine used by some courts to deny holder in due course status to an assignee of a negotiable note who is too closely connected commercially to the original holder-mortgagee.

Commercial Mortgage-backed Securities (CMBS) Securities that are collateralized by a pool of mortgage loans on commercial properties. The securities may be issued in a series of "tranches" having varying maturities, interest characteristics, and priorities vis-á-vis one another.

Common Areas Those physical areas in a condominium or a planned unit development to which all unit owners have access. To the extent that certain areas not physically a part of individual units may be used by less than all the unit owners, such areas are referred to as "limited common areas."

Concurrent Condition A contract condition which is expected to occur simultaneously with a party's performance. See Condition.

Condition A provision in a contract specifying that some event or fact must occur or exist in order for a party to be under a duty of performance.

Condition Precedent A condition that must occur before a party has a duty of performance.

Conditional Subordination An agreement that conditions the subordination of a land vendor's purchase-money mortgage to a construction mortgage on some event, such as the application of the construction loan proceeds to actual construction costs.

Conditional Sale An absolute deed transaction where there is a second written document that does not contain language of defeasance, but rather imposes on the grantee a duty by way of a contract or option to resell to the grantor-mortgagee the real estate described in the absolute deed.

Condominium A method of owning a living unit or commercial space in a multi-unit project under which the owner holds fee title to the unit itself and an undivided tenancy in common interest in the common areas of the project.

Condominium By–Laws To the extent that the declaration is the constitution of a condominium, the by-laws represent the legislation that governs the day-to-day operation of the condominium.

Construction Mortgage A type of mortgage loan in which the proceeds are paid out as the construction of the building progresses. It is a type of future advances mortgage.

Contract for Deed Another term to describe an installment land contract. See Installment Land Contract.

Conversion In the real estate development context, the term refers to the process by which rental buildings are transformed into condominiums or cooperatives.

Cooperative A term used to describe a method of apartment or unit ownership under which the cooperator is both a shareholder of a corporate landlord that holds fee title to the apartment building and a lessee under a proprietary lease on the "owned" unit.

Covenant Against Encumbrances A present covenant contained in a warranty deed that warrants that the title being conveyed is free of mortgages, liens, easements, leases or other interests that would impair the title being conveyed.

Covenant of Seisin A present covenant contained in a warranty deed that is, in substance, a promise that the grantor owns the estate being conveyed.

D

Death Escrows An escrow under which the delivery of the deed out of escrow is made conditional on the grantor's death.

Declaration The basic governing document or "constitution" for a condominium. It is relatively difficult to amend.

Dedication A mode of conveyance of land from a private owner to the public generally or to a specific public body.

Deed in Lieu of Foreclosure The common practice by which a mortgagee takes a conveyance of the mortgagor's fee title in satisfaction of the mortgage debt and as a substitute for foreclosure.

Deed of Trust A power of sale mortgage variant under which the trustor (mortgagor) conveys Blackacre in trust to a trustee to be held as security for the payment of a debt owing by the trustor to the beneficiary (mortgagee).

Defeasance Language in a mortgage that makes it clear that the "conveyance" to the mortgagee will be ineffective if the mortgagor pays the debt in a timely fashion. Alternatively, a provision in a commercial mortgage that permits the borrower to substitute other security, such as United States government debt instruments, in place of the real estate. The purpose of such a defeasance clause is to permit the real estate to be freed of the mortgage lien without prepaying the mortgage loan.

Deficiency Judgment If a foreclosure sale yields less than the mortgage debt, most states permit the mortgagee to obtain a judgment for the difference. Such deficiency judgments are subject, however, to a substantial amount of statutory regulation.

Delivery of Deed Any act by which grantor evidences an intent to make a deed presently operative.

Direct State Action A term utilized to describe a type of state action or federal action for purposes of the 14th and 5th Amendments respectively where private parties utilize statutory foreclosure procedures with the help of state officials.

Dragnet Clause A type of mortgage provision that purports to make the mortgaged real estate security for other, usually unspecified, debts that the mortgagor may already have incurred or may in the future incur to the mortgagee. While the dragnet clause makes the mortgage a species of future advances mortgage, the mortgagor and mortgagee rarely have in mind any specific future advances.

Due-on-Encumbrance Clause Mortgage language that gives the mortgagee the option to accelerate the mortgage debt in the event the mortgagor further encumbers or mortgages the real estate without mortgagee's consent.

Due-on-Sale Clause Mortgage language that gives the mortgagee the option to accelerate the mortgage debt in the event the mortgagor, without mortgagee consent, transfers or conveys all or any part of his or her interest in the mortgaged real estate.

E

Earnest Money Contract An executory contract for the sale of land. It is also known as a "binder," "purchase agreement," "deposit receipt, offer and acceptance," or "marketing agreement." This type of contract governs the buyer and seller from the time of its execution until the date of closing, when title normally is conveyed to buyer and financing instruments, if any, are executed.

Encouragement Theory A theory for finding state or federal action under the 14th and 5th Amendments based on governmental encouragement of private action that, if carried out by the government, would be unconstitutional.

Encumbrances Another term to describe mortgages, liens, leases, easements, or other interests affecting the title to real estate.

Entry Without Process A minor nonjudicial foreclosure method in effect in two or three states by which a mortgagee, after default, may take possession of the mortgaged real estate without legal intervention. Then, after the expiration of a time period that varies from one to three years, the mortgagor's equity of redemption is barred. The result is a non-judicial strict foreclosure.

Equitable Conversion A judicial concept that treats the vendor's interest in a contract for the sale of land as personalty and the purchaser's interest as realty during the contract's executory period. The concept is associated with both earnest money contracts and installment land contracts.

Equity of Redemption The right of a tardy mortgagor to satisfy the mortgage debt at any time until there has been a valid foreclosure. The concept was developed in English Chancery and applies in every American jurisdiction. Alternatively, the term is used to refer to the ownership position of the mortgagor that gives rise to the right of redemption.

Equitable Redemption The mortgagor's exercise of her right, as the holder of the equity of redemption, to pay off a mortgage in default at any time until a valid foreclosure has occurred.

Escrow An escrow is the process by which an instrument, such as a deed, is deposited with some custodian with instructions that it should be delivered to another party on the occurrence of some future condition.

Escrow for Taxes Most mortgagees acquire the payment each month of ¹⁄₁₂ of the estimated annual real estate taxes and casualty insurance premiums attributable to the mortgaged real estate. The funds in this "escrow" or "reserve" account are usually commingled with the mortgagee's general assets.

Estoppel A judicial fairness concept that is used to deny relief to a party whose action or failure to act causes another party to act in reasonable, detrimental reliance thereon.

Estoppel by Deed A doctrine that holds that a grantor who obtains a valid title to land after having purported to convey that title to a grantee will not be permitted to deny that the title he has obtained belongs to the grantee.

Estoppel Certificates A document executed by a maker-mortgagor certifying that the note is valid and that it is not subject to defenses by the maker-mortgagor. It is commonly requested by a transferee of the note and mortgage when there is reason to believe that the transferee will not have holder-in-due-course status.

Ex-parte Receivership The appointment of a receiver, usually pending foreclosure, without affording notice or the right to a hearing to the mortgagor or other interested parties prior to such appointment.

Exception Language in a deed by which the grantor withholds conveyance of some pre-existing interest, such as a certain physical part of the land.

Exoneration A legal requirement that, when real estate passes to a devisee or heir under a decedent's estate, any outstanding indebtedness encumbering the real estate is to be discharged out of the personal assets of a decedent-purchaser's estate. The encumbrance may be, for example, a mortgage or the obligation to pay the purchase price of the real estate under a contract of purchase entered into by the decedent before death.

Extrinsic Evidence Evidence which does not appear on the face of a document, but which is available from other sources such as statements by the parties and other circumstances surrounding the transaction.

F

Fair Value Legislation A type of antideficiency legislation in some states that requires a deficiency judgment to be measured by the difference between the mortgage debt and the "fair value" of the foreclosed real estate.

Fannie Mae (formerly the Federal National Mortgage Association (FNMA)) A privately owned and managed corporation chartered by the federal government that is engaged in purchasing residential mortgages on the secondary market.

Farmers Home Administration (FmHA) A division of the Department of Agriculture engaged in making direct mortgage loans to farmers and in home mortgage insurance and guarantee programs in rural areas and small towns.

Federal Housing Administration (FHA) A component of the U.S. Department of Housing and Urban Development (HUD) which insures mortgage loans made by private lenders on residential real estate.

Fee Simple Estate In the context of a time-sharing condominium, an ownership method that gives a grantee a fee simple absolute estate in a unit that confers the right to possession during a specified period each year.

Feoffment With Livery of Seisin An early English method of conveyance by which the transferor met the transferee at or near the land to be transferred and handed over a twig or clod while reciting to witnesses that the transfer was being made.

First Generation Condominium Legislation Terminology used to refer to the initial condominium legislation enacted in the early 1960's. Much of this legislation was patterned after the FHA Model Condominium Act and is still in effect in many states. See Second Generation Condominium Legislation.

Fixture A term used to describe a former chattel which, while retaining its separate physical identity, becomes so attached to real estate as to become a part of it.

Foreclosure The process, whether judicial or otherwise, by which the equity of redemption of the mortgagor and the interests of all others junior to the mortgage being foreclosed are terminated.

Foreclosure by Sale The foreclosure process, whether judicial or power of sale, by which the mortgaged real estate is sold at a public sale.

Forfeiture A remedy sought by an installment land contract vendor after a vendee defaults. If forfeiture is allowed the vendor terminates the contract, retakes possession of the real estate, and retains all payments made by the vendee.

Freddie Mac (formerly the Federal Home Loan Mortgage Corporation (FHLMC)) A congressionally-chartered, privately-owned corporation that purchases mortgages on the secondary market.

Further Assurances A future covenant contained in a warranty deed that is a promise to execute any document that might be needed in the future to perfect the title which the original deed purported to transfer.

Future Advances Mortgage A mortgage transaction in which part of the loan proceeds will not be paid out to the borrower until a future date.

G

Government National Mortgage Association (GNMA or "Ginnie Mae") A component of the U.S. Department of Housing and Urban Development that is primarily engaged in purchasing on the secondary market federally subsidized residential mortgages originated by local lenders, and also in guaranteeing payment of securities backed by FHA and VA mortgages.

Governmental Function Theory A theory used to characterize private action as state or federal action for 14th and 5th Amendment purposes when a private party is carrying out uniquely governmental activities.

Graduated Payment Adjustable Rate Mortgage (GPARM) A mortgage format that combines the features of the graduated payment mortgage (GPM) and the adjustable rate mortgage (ARM).

Graduated Payment Mortgage (GPM) A mortgage loan that carries monthly payments which increase annually by a specified percentage during the early years of the loan and then remain constant thereafter.

Grant Method by which, in very early English history, non-possessory and non-free-hold interests, such as leaseholds, easements and future interests, were transferred by a written instrument under seal.

Growing Equity Mortgage (GEM) A mortgage loan that is fully amortized over a significantly shorter term than the traditional 25 or 30 year mortgage, and which may have payments which increase each year.

H

Holder in Due Course A status conferred on certain promissory note holders that insulates them from defenses to collection or foreclosure that are "personal," as opposed to "real." Such status is achieved if: (1) the promissory note is negotiable, (2) the process by which the note is transferred constitutes a proper negotiation, and (3) the holder is in "due course" by virtue of acquiring the note in good faith and without notice of defenses or defect and paying value.

I

Implied Assumption A very few states hold that where, in addition to conveyance "subject to" the mortgage, the full value of the land is the agreed-upon purchase price and the purchaser deducts the mortgage amount from it, the purchaser becomes personally liable on the debt. Hence such a transaction is treated as an assumption transfer even though there is no explicit assumption agreement.

Installment Land Contract A contract for the sale of real estate under which the vendor provides financing for the purchaser by agreeing to accept part or all of the purchase price in installments to be paid over a period of time. The vendor-lender retains legal title until the contract price is fully paid. The installment contract is a substitute for a purchase-money mortgage, and is utilized to avoid the "pro-mortgagor" aspects of traditional mortgage law. It is also known as a "contract for deed" or "long term land contract."

Intermediate Theory Under this mortgage theory, the mortgagor has both legal and equitable title (and thus the right to possession) to the mortgaged premises until default. After default, legal title and the right to possession shift to the mortgage.

Interval Estate A form of time-sharing ownership that consists of an estate for years in a unit, during the term of which title rotates among time share owners, together with a vested undivided tenancy in common fee simple interest in the remainder of that unit.

Inverse Order of Alienation Under this marshaling principle, where a mortgagee has a lien on several parcels, some of which have been sold by the mortgagor after the mortgage was executed, and others of which are retained by the mortgagor, the mortgagee is required to foreclose first on the land retained by the mortgagor, and then (if necessary to satisfy the debt) to foreclose on the other parcels in the inverse order of their transfer by the mortgagor.

Involuntary Prepayments Those prepayments of the mortgage debt that occur because of factors beyond the mortgagor's control. These would include prepayments caused by a condemnation or the payment of insurance proceeds on account of a casualty loss to the mortgaged premises.

J

Judicial Enforcement Theory A theory for purposes of the 14th and 5th Amendment that would find governmental action where a court enforces a private agreement that would be constitutionally unenforceable if the party suing were the government.

Judicial Foreclosure A civil judicial proceeding to foreclose a mortgage. It entails service of process on all persons who are necessary parties, formal pleadings and a judicial trial.

Junior Lienholder One whose mortgage or other lien is subordinate to or subject to a senior lien or liens.

L

Late Payment Charges Charges exacted by mortgagees when installment payments are tardy. Such amounts are usually calculated as a percentage of the late installment, but, in a few situations, are calculated as a percentage of the unpaid principal balance of the loan.

Latent Equity Language used to describe a defense to the enforcement of a promissory note or to foreclosure that is capable of being raised by a third party, and which therefore will not be disclosed in an estoppel certificate given by the mortgagor-maker. See Patent Equity.

Lease and Release A common law method by which a possessory fee simple was transferred without using feoffment with livery of seisin. The conveyor would first grant a written lease to the conveyee with a short duration and then immediately thereafter, by a second writing, would transfer the reversion to the conveyee (a release).

License or Contract Approach When used in the context of a time-share condominium, refers to "ownership" that confers on the purchaser only a right or license to use and not a real estate interest in a certain unit during a certain week or weeks for a predetermined number of years.

Lien for Unpaid Assessments A lien that arises on a condominium unit and its undivided ownership in the common area when a unit owner fails to pay regular or special assessments levied by the owners' association or its board of directors.

Lien Theory A mortgage law theory, in effect in a majority of states, which holds that until a valid foreclosure has taken place, the mortgagor has both legal and equitable title to the mortgaged real estate. The mortgagee's interest is that of a lienholder only.

Liquidated Damages Clause In the context of a contract for the sale of real estate, a contract provision defining the amount of damages that will be owed as a result of a breach of the contract by one of the parties.

Lis Pendens Doctrine This doctrine concerns persons who acquire an interest in real estate which is subject to litigation. If the real estate is specifically described, it is taken subject to the final outcome of the litigation. In the mortgage context, the doctrine operates to bind a necessary party who acquires an interest in the mortgaged real estate *after* the commencement of a foreclosure proceeding. Because of this doctrine, it is unnecessary for a foreclosing mortgagee to serve such parties with process in the foreclosure action.

Long Term Land Contract Alternative terminology to describe an installment land contract. See Installment Land Contract.

Loss Payable Policy A rarely used casualty loss insurance policy under which the mortgagee is a mere appointee of the mortgagor to receive payment. Mortgagee's right to recover on the policy is completely dependent upon mortgagor's right to do so.

M

Marketable Title Acts Legislation in effect in about 18 states that attempts to limit the time period which must be covered by a title search.

Marketing Contract Another term used to describe an earnest money contract. See Earnest Money Contract.

Marketable Title A title to land which is free of all reasonable risks of attack, and which a reasonable purchaser would find acceptable.

Marshaling The power of a foreclosing court to determine in what order two or more parcels of mortgaged land will be sold, in order to minimize the harsh impact of the foreclosure on grantees or junior lienholders.

Mechanics' Lien A lien conferred upon unpaid contractors, workers and suppliers of materials, whose labor or supplies are used in connection with real estate which they have improved.

Merger A mortgage law concept that holds that when a mortgagee's interest and the fee title coincide and meet in the same person, the lesser estate, the mortgage, merges into the fee title and is extinguished. Sometimes the merger doctrine is also used to destroy the mortgage debt. In the context of an earnest money contract, the term describes a situation where, at the time of closing, the contract's covenants of title are "merged into the deed" and thus destroyed.

Metes and Bounds A legal description of real estate in which every line which is part of the parcel's boundaries is described.

Monuments Physical objects or entities that are used as references for land descriptions.

Mortgagee A lender who employs a mortgage to take real property as security for a debt.

Mortgage-backed Securities See Commercial Mortgage-backed Securities; Securitization.

Mortgage Buy–Down A process by which a real estate seller or developer pays a substantial front-end amount to a mortgage lender to induce the lender to make the purchaser a loan at a lower-than-market interest rate.

Mortgagee in Possession The status conferred on a mortgagee who takes possession pursuant to title theory rights or who is "let" into possession by a lien state mortgagor. The mortgagee is permitted to collect rents and profits, but is under a strict duty to account for them on the mortgage debt.

Mortgage Warehousing An informal practice whereby holders of notes and mortgages use them as security for short-term borrowing. Often the holder-mortgagee is a mortgage banker who delivers the notes and mortgages to a short term lender as security for a line of credit advanced to the mortgage banker by a commercial bank. When the mortgage broker finds secondary market purchasers or securitizes the mortgages, the proceeds from the sales or securitizations are used to pay off the short term lender and the notes and mortgages are returned to the mortgage broker for delivery to those purchasers or the securitization pool.

Mortgagor A person who subjects real estate to a mortgage as security for a debt.

N

Name Indexes Two sets of index books maintained in a recorder's office, one of them alphabetically by the last names of grantors and the other alphabetically by the last names of grantees.

Necessary Party A person whose joinder in judicial foreclosure is required in order to accomplish the purposes of foreclosure—i.e., to put the sale purchaser into the shoes of the mortgagor as of the date the foreclosed mortgage was executed.

Negative Amortization A term used to describe a mortgage payment setting in which monthly payments are insufficient to pay accruing interest. While this occurs, the principal balance of the mortgage increases.

Negative Covenant as Mortgage A promise by a borrower to a lender that so long as the debt to the lender remains outstanding, certain specified property owned by borrower will not be encumbered or transferred.

Negotiable A term used to describe a promissory note that is payable to "order" or "bearer" and that does not, subject to certain exceptions, incorporate by reference the terms of any mortgage that secures it.

Negotiation A term used to describe the transfer of a promissory note by endorsement where the transferee takes it for value, in good faith, and without notice that it is overdue, has been dishonored, or is subject to any defense or claim to it on the part of any person.

New York Mechanics' Lien System A type of mechanics' lien system under which the maximum aggregate amount of liens that may be collected out of the property is the contract price contained in the main contract between the general contractor and owner less payments properly made to the general contractor.

"Notice" Type Statutes A type of real estate recording act which allows a subsequent taker to prevail against a prior unrecorded claimant if the former took without notice of the latter's claim and paid value.

"Notice–Race" Type Statutes A type of real estate recording act under which a subsequent taker prevails against a prior unrecorded claimant if the former takes without notice, pays value and records first.

O

Obligatory Advance A term used to describe a disbursement under a future advances mortgage that the mortgagee is legally required to make.

Office of Thrift Supervision (OTS) A federal agency, part of the U.S. Department of the Treasury, that regulates federally-chartered thrift institutions.

One-Action Rule A rule in effect in a few states that requires a mortgagee to foreclose on the real estate prior to seeking relief against the mortgagor personally on the debt.

Optional Advance A term used to describe a disbursement under a future advances mortgage that is discretionary on the mortgagee's part.

Owners' Association The basic governing entity for condominiums or planned unit developments. In the condominium context, it usually is either an unincorporated association or a nonprofit corporation.

P

Part Performance A judicially-created exception to the Statute of Frauds that permits an equity court to utilize certain tangible acts of the purchaser, such as payment, taking possession, or making substantial improvements as the basis for enforcing a contract that otherwise does not satisfy the writing requirement of the statute.

Participation A term used to describe a practice by which an originating or "lead" mortgage lender sells fractional interests in one large mortgage loan or in portfolios of individual loans.

Partition An action brought by a joint owner of real estate to have the jointly owned land physically divided between or among the joint owners or to have the whole property sold and the proceeds of the sale distributed to such owners based on their undivided fractional interests in the property.

Patent Equity Language used to describe a defense to the enforcement of a promissory note or to foreclosure that can be asserted by the maker-mortgagor. Such a defense can be brought to light by requiring the maker-mortgagor to execute an estoppel certificate. See Latent Equity.

Pennsylvania Type Mechanics' Lien System A type of mechanics' lien system that confers on the subcontractor, suppliers or workers a direct lien right even though the general contractor has been paid.

Personal Defenses Defenses to collection of a negotiable promissory note to which a holder in due course is immune. They include failure or lack of consideration, breach of warranty, unconscionability and fraud in the inducement.

Pervasiveness Theory An argument that significant and wide-ranging statutory or regulatory governance of private conduct is a proper basis for finding governmental action for 14th and 5th Amendment purposes.

Planned Community Usually a subdivision in which an individual owns a fee simple absolute in a specific parcel and a membership or shareholder interest in an entity that owns and manages the common areas.

Planned Unit Development A type of residential community that is the product of zoning or related governmental authorization that permits land subdivision and development with greater flexibility in lot size, front and side yard requirements, street width, and related matters than is normally associated with traditional subdivision methods.

Plat A map approved by some local government agency which meets certain standards of format and accuracy and which identifies lots and their legal descriptions.

Pledged Accounts A process by which a buyer-mortgagor pledges to the lender a savings account which the buyer has built up, and in turn the buyer obtains a below-market-interest loan. See Mortgage Buy–Down.

Portfolio Lag See "Term Intermediation."

Power of Sale Foreclosure A nonjudicial foreclosure process utilized in about half the states. The foreclosure sale is conducted by the person holding the power of sale. That person is most often a trustee under a deed of trust, but may be a sheriff or a public trustee in some states.

Prepayment Charges or Penalties A fee exacted by a mortgagee from a borrower who chooses to prepay a mortgage debt.

Price-Level Adjusted Mortgage (PLAM) A mortgage format under which the loan balance is adjusted periodically to reflect inflation in price levels. The interest rate on that balance remains fixed for the life of the loan.

Private Mortgage Insurers (PMI's) Non-governmental entities that insure mortgage loans. They represent private counterparts to the Federal Housing Administration (FHA) insurance program.

Proper Party A person whose interest is not junior to the mortgage being foreclosed, but whose joinder nevertheless may be important to a successful foreclosure.

Purchase-Money Mortgage A mortgage taken by a lender, who may be either a vendor or a third party, to finance the mortgagor's acquisition of the mortgaged real estate.

Q

Quitclaim Deed A deed which contains no covenants concerning the quality of title. The term "quitclaim" is construed by courts to negate any such covenants.

R

"Race" Type Statutes A type of real estate recording act which allows a subsequent taker to prevail against a prior unrecorded claimant if the former records before the latter.

Rate Cap In an adjustable rate mortgage (ARM), a clause which limits interest rate increases, on either an annual or a lifetime basis.

Real Defenses Defenses to the collection of a promissory note to which even a holder in due course is subject.

Receiver In the mortgage law context, a person appointed by the court prior to foreclosure to take possession of the mortgaged real estate for the purpose of preserving it and collecting rents.

Rents collected less the expenses of the receivership must be applied to the mortgage debt.

Redeeming The process which permits a person holding an interest which is junior to a mortgage in default to pay off that mortgage and either have it discharged or take an assignment of it.

Reformation An equitable remedy by which a court under certain circumstances will modify or recast language in a document to reflect the actual intention of the parties.

Reliction A process by which a river or stream may shift its location so as to cause a recession of water from its bank.

REMIC A Real Estate Mortgage Investment Conduit, an entity which issues mortgage-backed securities and which qualifies for favorable tax treatment under the 1986 Tax Reform Act.

Reservation Language in a deed which creates in the grantor a new interest in the land which did not exist independently before the deed.

Restitution In the installment land contract setting, a vendor may sometimes be granted the forfeiture remedy, but be required to return to the vendee a portion of the payments the vendor has received, to the extent that they exceed vendor's actual damages. In an earnest money contract context, the term refers to the right of one party to recover the value of the benefits conferred on the other party at some prior stage of the contract's life.

Reverse Annuity Mortgage (RAM) A mortgage format under which the mortgage loan proceeds are disbursed periodically over a long time period to provide regular income for the borrower-mortgagor. The loan will usually be repaid in a lump sum when the mortgagor dies or the property is sold.

Right of First Refusal The holder of such a right has the option to purchase the grantor's real estate on the terms and conditions of sale contained in a bona fide offer by a third party to purchase such real estate, provided it is an offer that the grantor is otherwise willing to accept.

Right to Convey A present covenant in a warranty deed that, for the most part, is the same as the Covenant of Seisin. See Covenant of Seisin.

Root of Title For purposes of marketable acts, the term refers to a deed in the chain of title recorded earlier than some fixed number of years before the search being made.

S

Scire Facias A legal, as opposed to equitable, form of judicial foreclosure. After mortgagor default, the mortgagee obtains a writ of Scire Facias, which is an order to show cause why the mortgaged property should not be sold to satisfy the mortgage debt. If mortgagee prevails, the court will issue a writ of levari facias directing an execution sale of the mortgaged real estate.

Second Generation Condominium Legislation Terminology used to describe state condominium statutes enacted within the past few decades to deal with a variety of problems not covered by early or "first generation" legislation.

The Uniform Condominium Act is an example of such legislation.

Secondary Mortgage Market The market in which mortgage loan originators sell the loans they have created to other investors. The two largest such investors in the United States are Fannie Mae and Freddie Mac.

Securitization The process of issuing debt securities in the capital markets that are based on, and will be paid from, the payments received by the issuer on a pool of mortgages held by the issuer. At least three models of securitization are commonly used: (1) participation certificates, in which each security represents a fractional share of direct ownership in the underlying pool of mortgages; (2) pass-through securities, in which the securities are collateralized by the pool of mortgages but payments on the mortgages are passed-through pro-rata to the holders of the securities; and (3) mortgage-backed securities which are, in the aggregate, paid from the payments made on the underlying mortgages, but with numerous classes or "tranches" of securities having varying characteristics in terms of maturity, interest structure, and priority vis-á-vis one another. See Commercial Mortgage-backed Securities.

Security First Rule The requirement imposed in a few states that a mortgagee foreclose prior to seeking relief against the mortgagor personally on the debt. See One–Action Rule.

Shared Appreciation Mortgage (SAM) A mortgage format that gives the lender the right to recover, as "contingent interest," some agreed-upon percentage of the property's appreciation in value measured when it is sold or at some other future fixed date.

Shared-Equity Mortgage (SEM) A mortgage format under which a purchaser-occupant and another person (often a relative) become co-owners and co-mortgagors of real estate. Usually the non-occupant owner pays all or a substantial part of the monthly payments and is entitled to share in any appreciation when the real estate is sold.

Servicemembers' Civil Relief Act (formerly Soldiers' and Sailors' Civil Relief Act) World War II federal legislation, still in effect, that affords a variety of protections to servicepersons against both secured and unsecured creditors.

Standard Mortgage Policy A widely used type of casualty insurance policy that not only insures the mortgagee individually but specifies that the mortgage coverage "shall not be invalidated by any act or neglect of the mortgagor."

State Housing Finance Agencies Entities created by state government that utilize funds obtained from issuing tax-exempt bonds to make below market interest rate mortgage loans on housing for low and moderate income residents.

Statute of Uses A 1536 English enactment that converted many equitable interests in land to legal interests.

Statutory Redemption A statutory process in existence in about half the states that permits the mortgagor and certain other persons whose interests were cut off by foreclosure to redeem the fee title to the land from the person who purchased at the foreclosure sale. Usually the redemption amount is the foreclosure sale price (plus interest and certain expenditures that the foreclosure purchaser has made on the real estate). The period for redemption varies from a few months to a year.

Stop Notice Statute An alternative to the mechanics' lien remedy that allows contractors, suppliers and workers to make and enforce a claim against the construction lender, and in some instances, the owner, for a portion of the undisbursed construction loan proceeds.

Straight Bankruptcy A term used to describe the most common type of bankruptcy (Chapter 7) where the debtor's assets are liquidated for the benefit of creditors and the debtor obtains a discharge from her obligations.

Strict Foreclosure A rarely used method of mortgage foreclosure by which a court orders the mortgagor to pay the mortgage debt within a judicially determined reasonable time. If the mortgagor fails so to pay, the title vests in the mortgagee without a public sale. Strict foreclosure is sometimes employed by a court to terminate a junior lien whose holder was improperly omitted from a foreclosure of a senior mortgage, if the court concludes that the junior lien has little or no value.

"Subject–to" Transfer A transfer of mortgaged real estate to a grantee who agrees that the real estate will continue to be security for the mortgage debt, but who does not assume personal liability for that debt. Such a transfer is sometimes referred to as a "non-assumption" transfer.

Subordination Agreement An agreement by which one holding an otherwise senior lien or other real estate interest consents to a reduction in priority vis-á-vis another person holding an interest in the same real estate.

Subrogation When a person pays in full a mortgage debt which, in fairness, should have been paid by another person, the payor is "subrogated" to the rights of the creditor who was paid. This means that the payor receives an assignment by operation of law of the creditor's right to collect the debt and the creditor's security and priority. The payor may then assert these rights against the person who, in fairness, should have paid the debt initially.

Surplus The amount of the proceeds from a mortgage foreclosure sale that exceeds the amount owing on the mortgage being foreclosed.

T

Title Insurance A promise by a title insurance company to indemnify the insured party if the title to land is not in the condition stated on the face of the policy and the insured suffers a loss as a result.

Term Intermediation The activity of a financial institution, such as a savings and loan association, in borrowing short-term funds from depositors and lending them for longer terms to borrowers (e.g., on mortgages). The institutions may suffer financial distress when their cost of funds (essentially short term interest rates) rises to a level that exceeds the rate of return on their mortgage portfolios. This situation is also referred to as "portfolio lag."

Third Generation Common Interest Legislation Terminology used to describe state legislation that provides comprehensive and consistent coverage in one statute of the condominium, cooperative and planned unit development. The most prominent example of such legislation is the Uniform Common Interest Ownership Act (UCOIA).

Third Party Beneficiary Theory A contract law doctrine utilized in many states as the doctrinal basis for allowing a mortgagee to recover on the mortgage debt against an assuming grantee. It is also a theory that supports the right of a subcontractor or supplier to an equitable lien on undisbursed construction loan proceeds.

Time-Sharing A term used to describe a concept that permits a person to purchase an interval of a specified period of time each year, typically in a condominium unit in a recreation or vacation area.

Time of the Essence To the extent that a contract makes "time of the essence," a late tender of performance by one party is a material breach and fully excuses the other from performing.

Time Span Estate A type of time-sharing ownership whereby the grantee receives a percentage undivided tenancy-in-common interest in fee simple in a unit, coupled with a right to occupy the unit during specified times. This type of ownership is also known as "time sharing ownership" (TSO).

Title Theory A mortgage law theory that holds that from the date of the mortgage execution until the mortgage is satisfied or foreclosed, legal title and the right to possession belongs to the mortgagee. Mortgagees seldom exercise (and probably would not be permitted by the courts to exercise) rights under this theory until a mortgage default occurs.

Torrens Title Registration An alternative to the conventional recording system that involves the issuance of a certificate of title by the government, similar to those used for motor vehicles.

Two Funds Theory A theory of marshaling which holds that, where a senior mortgagee has the right to foreclose on two parcels of real estate, while another mortgagee has junior mortgage rights in only one of the parcels, the senior mortgagee should be compelled to foreclose first against the parcel which is otherwise unencumbered.

Tract Index A page or set of pages in an index book in the recorder's office devoted to listing all documents which affect a particular tract of land.

Tranch One of a set of mortgage-backed securities, all of which are collateralized by the same pool of mortgages, but which vary from one another in terms of maturity, interest structure, and priority vis-á-vis one another. See Securitization.

V

Vendee's Lien An implied lien, similar to a mortgage, to aid a purchaser of real estate in obtaining restitutionary damages from a defaulting seller.

Vendor's Lien An implied lien, similar to a mortgage, recognized by equity courts in favor of a seller of real estate for the unpaid portion of the purchase price on land.

Veteran's Administration (VA) An independent federal agency that, among other things, operates a mortgage loan guarantee program for eligible veterans.

W

Wage Earner Plan A popular term used to describe a Chapter 13 bankruptcy proceeding.

Warranty and Quiet Enjoyment Two separate future covenants contained in a warranty deed each of which is held to promise that the title will be as described in the deed and will not be subject to any encumbrances.

Warranty Deed A deed which explicitly contains covenants concerning the quality of title it conveys. A "full warranty" or "general warranty" deed contains all three present covenants (seisin, right to convey, and against encumbrances) and all three future covenants (warranty, quiet enjoyment, and further assurances). In some states statutes impute some or all of these covenants of title from the use of specific words, such as "grant."

APPENDIX E

Table of Cases